Preface

Twelve years have passed since the first edition of this book appeared. As succeeding editions have shown these have been twelve highly eventful years for public administration. Fortunately for the author, however, most of the storm clouds now gathering over the public sector did not begin to appear until after the third edition had been completed. Consequently, that edition did not seem to require any drastic or dramatic overhaul to accommodate them.

Nevertheless, the last three years have brought further changes to the public administration scene, and this new fourth edition has sought to take note of them. Thus, there is some discussion of policy analysis, contingency theory, and professional ethics. Also noted are additional developments in the Senior Executive Service (SES), public unionism, the Freedom of Information Act, and a host of other issues. Some topics, such as zero-based budgeting (ZBB), have received more attention; other topics, such as planned program budgeting system (PPBS), have received less. And nearly half the chapters have been outfitted with new case studies.

Prodding me along have been the perceptive comments of professors Sylvan H. Cohen, Slippery Rock State College; Burnet V. Davis, Alma College; J. P. Heim, University of Wisconsin; John Rouse, Ball State University; Robert H. Stoudemire, University of South Carolina; and A. B. Villanueva, Western Illinois University. In some cases the advice of one conflicted with the advice of another; in other instances I simply lacked the time and talent to integrate their suggestions into the text (it's a much more difficult task, at least for me, than many might suppose). Accordingly, none of them will find all their ideas adopted. Still I have been conscious of their remarks at all times and have tried to make use of them when I could.

In conclusion I would like to thank the political science editor at Allyn and Bacon, Al Levitt, for having once again effectively midwifed a new offspring of the original text.

Contents

For
PATRICIA,
Tender Comrade

Library of Congress Cataloging in Publication Data

Berkley, George E.
    The craft of public administration.

    Includes index.
    1. Public administration.   I. Title.
JF1351.B47 1984   350   83-21505
ISBN 0-205-08127-4

Printed in the United States of America

10 9 8 7 6 5 4 3 2 1   89 88 87 86 85 84

THE CRAFT OF
Public
Administration

FOURTH EDITION

George E. Berkley
University of Massachusetts

ALLYN and BACON, INC.

BOSTON   LONDON   SYDNEY   TORONTO

The Craft of Public
Administration

The Craft of Public Administration

1

The Administrative Craft

Not so very long ago, an author wrote a book dealing with the changes that organizations are undergoing in a technological society. He proudly entitled his work *The Administrative Revolution*. His publishers liked the book but hated the title. Why? The answer is simple. In their opinion, any book with the word *administrative* in its title simply would not sell.[1]

Although they finally published the book under its original title, there is no gainsaying the fears and doubts that prompted their attempt to rechristen it. The word *administration* does conjure up connotations of colorlessness, and it does cause most readers to turn away or, to use a more current phrase, turn off. While administration, particularly public administration, is America's fastest-growing industry, it arouses more apathy than ardor and inspires more distaste than devotion.

Without stopping to probe the roots of the antiadministration syndrome, let us take a look at the subject itself to see if such an attitude is justified. Is administration best depicted as a leafless tree growing sadly in a bleak landscape, or can it be thought of as a lush and luxuriant plant busily sprouting all kinds of interesting blossoms?

The Heart of the Matter

A classic textbook defines administration simply but graphically in this opening sentence: "When two men cooperate to roll a stone that neither could have moved alone, the rudiments of administration have appeared."[2] Such a concrete if elementary illustration has much to tell us about just what administration is and what it is not.

Administration, first of all, is *people*. A stone sitting by itself on the side of a hill is certainly not administration. Nor does a stone that, through some act of nature, rolls down a hill constitute administration. People have to be present before administration can take place.

Second, administration is *action*. Two men watching or admiring or leaning on a stone does not, in itself, constitute administration. They have to be doing something before administration can enter the picture. There is no such thing as inactive administration (although many who have to deal with administrative agencies sometimes believe otherwise).

Third, administration is *interaction*. One man moving a stone or two men each independently moving stones in separate fields are not examples of administration in action. (And remember, there is no other kind.) In order for their activity to become administration, their efforts must in some way be related. This does not mean that they have to be aware of each other's activity. But somewhere in the background there must be some coordination between what each of them is doing. Administration, by its very nature, involves *people relating to other people*.

People interacting with other people to accomplish tasks—this, indeed, is what administration is about. Yet that is not all that administration is about. A further ingredient is required, for not all work activity involving human interaction can bear the administrative label. The prisoner and his guard, for example, may have an intense relationship involving the moving of stones or, more likely in this case, the making of little stones out of big ones. Yet we would not define this relationship as administrative in nature. Rather, the prisoner is the recipient of a network of administrative relationships involving the guard with his co-workers and his superiors. Strange as it may sound, the prisoner is a beneficiary, albeit in this instance usually an unwilling one, of administration. He is the client of an administrative service, not a participant in the creation of such a service. Put in other words, he is closer to the administrative product than he is to the administrative process.

The line that separates administration from other types of human interaction often becomes blurred and fuzzy. Take the relationship between a professor and her students. In this case, the students are the clients and, hopefully, somewhat more willing ones than the prisoner we just cited. They are the beneficiaries, although some of them might dispute the use of such a term, of an administrative process involving the professor, her colleagues, her dean, the department secretary, and even the building custodian.

But now let us assume that the class is one in biology and the professor and students decide to undertake a joint project, such as investigating the pollution of a nearby river in order to write a report for the state legislature. At this point, the relationship starts to change. Now, they are *mutually* involved in a joint endeavor. In their former relationship, they both might have had a convergent interest, in that the students may have wanted to learn as much as possible about biology (you will note that this example is purely theoretical) and the instructor may have wanted to teach them as much as possible about biology. But the situation was nevertheless different. The students were there to obtain a product; the professor was there to dispense it. Consequently, the students were no more engaged in an administrative relationship with their teacher than are the customers of a department store administratively engaged with the store's salesclerks, buyers, and so on.

This introduces a new element in our definition. Joint activity is an essential part of all administration. This does not mean that such activity must always be spontaneous or voluntary. A young man may be drafted against his will into the army. He may be sent even more against his will to a foreign base. Yet in performing whatever role may be assigned to him at that base, he will be participating in administration. Like it or not, unless he wishes to brook disciplinary action, he will be involved with others in a common effort, namely that of maintaining what at least his superiors will claim to be the nation's security.

To sum up, administration is a process involving human beings jointly engaged in working toward common goals. Administration thus covers much, if not most, of the more exciting things that go on in human society. Why, then, should anyone feel justified in wanting to color it gray?

Art, Science, or Craft?

The very title of this book indicates that it classifies administration as a craft. Why this classification instead of another? Why should we not consider administration an art or a science?

Science is characterized by precision and predictability. A scientific rule is one that works all the time. As a matter of fact, rules in science are considered to be so rigid and final that they are not called rules at all but laws. Two parts of hydrogen combined with one part of oxygen will *always* give us water—or steam, or ice, depending on the temperature—regardless of where and when the amalgamation of the two elements takes place. Of course, if the apparatus combining them is dusty or if someone switches it off at the wrong time or if any of countless thousands of other things happen, the formation of H_2O may not occur. But this does not invalidate the formula. With other factors kept out of the process—and in pure science it is often fairly easy to keep out intrusive factors—we can combine hydrogen and oxygen on a 2:1 basis with the certainty that we will derive some form of water.

Some sciences, or some aspects of science, do not, it is true, achieve such a 100-percent level of predictability. Quantum theory, for example, is predicated on the predicted behavior of only some, not necessarily all, of the particles involved. Many of the more scientific aspects of the social sciences similarly deal with expectations that govern only a portion of the elements being scrutinized, not all of them. For example, many social scientists feel that they have established pretty much as a scientific law the theory that political participation correlates with education and affluence. Put more explicitly, they feel that their research has proved that the more educated and/or the more affluent people are, the more they will tend to participate in democratic politics. To justify such an adamant stand, they point out that this theory has been tested under a variety of conditions both in this country and abroad and generally has been substantiated. Voting and other forms of political participation will almost invariably be greater in those communities or neighborhoods where education and/or affluence is greater. However, one cannot automatically assume that any person who has a Ph.D. and a fifty-thousand-dollar-a-year salary—the two do not always go together—will be a feverish participant in the political process. Indeed, one cannot even be sure that he or she will be a voter. In similar fashion, one cannot single out an individual at the bottom rung of the education-affluence ladder and automatically assume that he or she is estranged from, or antagonistic to, politics. Obviously, *some* low-income and less-educated people participate quite intensively in politics, while *some* of the well-educated rich have never even bothered to register to vote. Yet, with it all, the latter are much more likely to take a more active role in politics than are the former. Science here reigns, although somewhat imperfectly, by establishing degrees of probability.

What does all this tell us about administration? Actually, quite a bit, although it may not add up to a completely clear picture. Few things involving administration ever do. Administration makes or should make great use of scientific data, laws, and theories. The use of mathematics and computer sciences in some aspects of budgeting is a fairly obvious example. The utilization in personnel work of somewhat less definitive but nevertheless statistically valid material developed by psychologists is another. Thus, administration uses these types of scientific data, but is it a science itself?

In attempting to answer this question we should note that the utilization of science is not confined to the sciences themselves. Music, for one, bases itself on laws of harmony that are quite mathematical. Painting depends on laws dealing with the colors of the spectrum. Yet, both music and painting are arts, not sciences. In a sense, the same holds true for administration. Administrators make use of scientific laws, techniques, and data. But they do so in ways that allow a great deal of free rein to the individual imagination and temperament. Usually a variety of successful ways exist for dealing with any particular problem, and any administrator can devise yet another one. Furthermore, problems are rarely, if ever, identical, and it would be difficult to evolve any equations that would cover all cases. In algebra we know that if $2x = 4$, then x will *always* equal 2. We are almost never that certain about any "law" in administration. The equations change depending not only on the circumstances but also on the personality of those dealing with them. And this should not be viewed as an erasable imperfection. It is, rather, an integral part of the administrative process. Like the painter and composer, the administrator uses science, but, also like them, he uses it in ways that tend to reflect his own mood and personality.

Does this make administration an art? Here, again, the picture is far from crystal clear. As we have noted, administrators, like artists, do tend to work in individual and often highly imaginative ways, employing a varied mix of materials, including intuition, in their labors. One person's administrative product is never quite the same as another's, just as one composer's symphony differs from another's. Individual style tends to show through in both cases, although it is certainly more pronounced in the latter field.

But administration is not an art, for there is a difference that, while often illusive, is nevertheless vital. Artists create works of aesthetics; administrators solve problems or at least attempt to do so. Therefore their respective end products and the criteria used for evaluating them tend to differ. Although we can state with some certainty that Beethoven was a great composer, no one can state with the same certainty that he was greater than Bach. Nor can one say that Mozart was greater than Brahms or that Mendelssohn wrote better music than Liszt. Each was doing his own thing, so to speak, and our judgments of their accomplishments depend heavily on our tastes and inclinations.

To some extent, our personal tastes and inclinations enter into our judgment of administrators—but only to some extent. For in administration there are usually some objective standards that can be applied in evaluating the work that administrators do. Each administrator may have his or her own way of proceeding, and each administrator's problems may be unique, but in most cases there is an objectively desirable and determinable goal to be met. In his classic work *Administrative Behavior*, Herbert Simon ably addresses himself to this point. "The criterion which the administrator applies to the factual problems is one of efficiency. The resources, the input, at the disposal of the administrator are strictly limited. . . . It is his function to maximize the attainment of governmental objectives (assuming they have been agreed upon) by the efficient employment of the limited resources that are available to him. . . ."[3]

Admittedly, making judgments on administrative efficiency, particularly when it comes to weighing the efficiency of one administrator against that of another, is not always an easy task. But to some degree at least, it can be, and is, done. No such criterion would ever be utilized in evaluating a work of art. There is good music and bad music, good painting and bad painting. But who has ever heard an efficient symphony or viewed an efficient picture?

Consequently, if we turn to the last category, that of craft, we find a more suitable, or at least a more comfortable, classification. The woman who paints a picture that hangs in a museum is an artist. The man who brings his easel and palette into the museum to copy this picture is a craftsman. The latter has an objective standard for the goal he is trying to meet and against which he can be judged. He may use a variety of techniques and materials in his effort to achieve this goal. But the goal remains the same. Another painter-craftsman with the same aim may mix paints differently, shade light differently, or do a host of other things that the former craftsman did not do. But he or she is striving for the same end, and an outside observer can usually determine who was the more successful.

A more persistent hypothetical problem will further point up the fact that administration can be viewed as neither a science nor an art but only as a craft. Let us assume that a city is divided for the purpose of garbage collection into two distinct and equal sections. One team of sanitation workers under an assistant sanitation commissioner is assigned to each section, with the objective of keeping the streets clean. One of the assistant commissioners may choose to have his people work straight eight-hour shifts five days a week; the other may choose to bunch the efforts of his crew at key times in the week and work them for longer periods of time on fewer days. One may try to improve the conditions of work by conducting a promotional campaign designed to persuade the residents of his section to switch from garbage cans to cellulose bags. The other may deem it more fruitful to ask the police to crack down under the street litter law. One may offer his men extra inducements if they do their job successfully, while the other may hold out to his crew the prospect of more time off. The ways in which each team goes about its work may differ depending on the personalities of their administrative leaders, the personalities of the workers, and a variety of other factors. But an objective standard exists for comparing the relative efficiency of each: which produces cleaner streets?

Most administrative activity does not lend itself to such an easy evalu-ation as the example just given. When it comes to assessing the efficiency of a foreign policy operation, to take just one example, assessments and judgments can become very tricky. The administration of a policy often becomes hard to separate from the policy itself. (This is an important is-sue in public administration, which we will explore in greater detail later.) Furthermore, there is not always agreement on the criteria or the objective against which success or failure is to be measured. And, in many cases, varying conditions will complicate our comparison. In the street-cleaning case, for instance, one team may excel over another team only because its streets are in a lower-density section of the city, which has less garbage. Or it may outperform the other team because its district is closer to the incinerator, thereby cutting down the travel time needed to send its dump trucks back and forth.

Nevertheless, despite all these complicating factors, in most administra-tive situations there is an objective standard lurking somewhere, shadowy and illusive and hard to apply though it may be. At the same time, there is almost never a precise formula that will invariably work best in all sit-uations. Not only do the situations change, but the ideas that may be ap-plied to handling them are almost as infinite as the human mind.

Another example, this one from history, will provide further support for our contention that administration may be more easily categorized as a craft than as an art or a science. As the New Deal reached its height, Harry Hopkins and Harold Ickes emerged as Franklin Roosevelt's most valued and trusted aides. Each man was given a substantial chunk of the federal public works and relief programs to administer. However, as they acquired power they became increasingly suspicious and jealous of each other. Word of their growing rivalry and animosity soon leaked out. This caused their respective partisans or opponents in the government, in the press, and in the public at large to leap to the attack or to the defense, as the case may have been. Washington was abuzz with rumors of the feud, and the fact that so many others were choosing sides was producing dis-ruption throughout the governmental network.

The situation placed Roosevelt in a quandary. If he fired or encouraged the resignation of either of these men, he would lose not only a tried-and-tested aide but would alienate and antagonize the man's admirers and supporters. On the other hand, if Roosevelt issued a statement denying the feud, he would only succeed in acknowledging and giving credence to the rumors. Here was an administrator with a problem.

Roosevelt decided to solve his problem by embarking on one of his fa-mous conservation tours and taking Ickes and Hopkins with him. For nine days and nights the trio wound their way by train and automobile through the American countryside, inspecting dam sites, forestry projects, and other New Deal undertakings. At every opportunity, Roosevelt lavished public praise on his two associates and played up their importance in his administration. And every night he sat down with both of them for a poker game.

By the time the presidential party had arrived back in Washington, the rumors of the feud had begun to dissolve. The steady stream of news and pictures of the men standing shoulder to shoulder had had their effect. And, in fact, it appeared that the two men ended the junket on much better terms. One administrator had solved a pressing problem.

Roosevelt used a great deal of artistry and imagination in dealing with this situation. Yet he was not creating a work of art but resolving a difficult problem. At the same time, however, Roosevelt was certainly not acting as a scientist, for what he did does not lend itself to easy formularization. His solution, although it might provide some ideas for other administrators faced with similar dilemmas, certainly does not lend itself to an all-embracing equation. Such a solution, for instance, would not have proved of much use to George Washington when he confronted the somewhat similar challenge of dealing with the bitter fight between his two top aides, Alexander Hamilton and Thomas Jefferson. For one thing, there were no conservation projects to inspect, no trains to transport the visiting party, and no photographers to take and send back pictures of their amicable visitations. Furthermore, Hamilton and Jefferson were probably not the type of men who would be amenable to such treatment, and certainly it would be hard to imagine the somewhat austere Father of Our Country sitting them down to nightly poker sessions.

In summary, administration uses artistry but is not an art. It uses science but is not a science. It is more properly thought of as a craft, seeking to achieve goals and to meet standards, and in so doing, often managing to utilize all the creativity and capacity that its harried practitioners can muster.

Public and Private: Is There a Difference?

Since we now have a better idea of what administration is, let us proceed to describe and designate the different forms it may take. In some respects these forms are as numerous as the various fields that apply it. There is health administration, welfare administration, university administration. Within these fields each institution often has its own type of administration, which can differ considerably from that of a counterpart institution. But in another sense, there are virtually no essential differences, since administration deals with the working relationships of human beings, and this common denominator is often a stronger unifying bond than the disparateness of the numerators. It is sometimes said that administration is everywhere the same, and to some degree this is true. Running a hospital or a factory, a small field unit or a large bureaucracy presents the essentially similar problems that tend to crop up when human beings seek to work cooperatively.

Be this as it may, it is helpful in furthering our understanding of administration to distinguish the two broad areas where it is utilized—the public and private sectors. Since this book will focus on the public sector, it might be useful to spell out those ways in which public administration differs from private business administration.

The first distinguishing characteristic is public administration's much greater reliance on, and vulnerability to, the law. Legalism in general and laws in particular tend to circumscribe and influence the operation of a public institution much more than they do a private one. "This pervasive legal context is among the principal distinctions between public and private enterprise," note John M. Pfiffner and Robert Presthus. "In private management one is assured that he can do anything not specifically forbidden. In public administration, on the other hand, discretion is limited by a great number of laws, rules and regulations."[4] To put it more succinctly, in private administration the law generally tells the administrator only what he *cannot do;* in public administration, the law tells him what he *can* do.

The much greater preoccupation of public administration with the law is manifested in various ways. For example, a young campaign aide to a politician seeking high office in a New England state was horrified when he learned that the campaign committee had decided to make cash payments to reporters of a local newspaper in return for favorable publicity for the candidate. To the aide, this was rank corruption. However, there was nothing criminal in what was being done. The newspaper reporters were not working for a public institution but for a private one. It was up to the newspaper itself to determine whether or not it would allow its employees to accept fees from political candidates for "public relations services." What the reporters were doing may not have been very ethical in terms of their profession, but neither they nor those who were paying them were committing an illegal act. However, similar behavior by public employees would, in most jurisdictions, violate a conflict-of-interest law, and disclosure could result in the employees not only being dismissed from their jobs but even prosecuted.[5]

Most newspaper reporters, of course, do not accept payoffs, but even so, their conduct often varies greatly from what we expect from public employees. News concerning socially prominent people receives much greater space than the comings and goings of the less-well-off, and while this to some extent can be justified in terms of reader interest, the discrepancy often far exceeds justifiable limits. More significantly, the marriage of the daughter of the friend of an editor or the opening of a new store by an advertiser is likely to receive exaggerated attention. Even the newspaper's book review editor is likely to be heavily influenced by personal contacts and approaches in determining which few of the thirty thousand books published annually he or she will choose for review. Thus, even a newspaper that is vigorous and sincere in ferreting out and denouncing corruption in government can be committing numerous acts every day that, if done by a public agency, would bring the wrath of the community down on its head and land its officials and employees in jail.

This discussion of the discrepancy between the way newspapers behave and the way public agencies are expected to behave is not intended to show the venality of the former but the vulnerability of the latter. A much more ethical and impartial pattern of behavior is expected and demanded from public organizations than from private ones. If the laws that govern the acts of public institutions were applied to private institutions, most of the management and staff of the latter would end up behind bars.

The legal limitations placed on public agencies contribute to, when they do not actually create, many of the other differences that demarcate them from private enterprise. Government organizations must usually operate in something of a goldfish bowl, subject to continual scrutiny from politicians, the public, and the press. They must generally be ready to open their doors and their books to virtually any outsider, even though the outsider's interest in the agency may be prompted by no more than idle curiosity.

There are, of course, exceptions to this rule. The Central Intelligence Agency (CIA) has not been known to maintain an open-door policy to all and sundry who may wish to examine its records and find out just what it is up to around the world. The Defense Department rarely reveals the details on its deployment of troops and resources, particularly during the conduct of a war. On the local scene, a police department may not choose to open up its files on a current investigation, and a welfare agency may refuse to make public the names and circumstances of particular clients. Nevertheless, while many exceptions and qualifications exist, public agencies are expected to be much more open to public inspection and public investigation than are private ones.

The legal context within which the public sector functions also helps explain why its employees usually enjoy greater rights as well as greater obligations. Public employees benefit in many ways from the legal restrictions and restraints that are customarily imposed upon government operations. Their jobs are more secure, their pensions and perquisites are more certain, and their paths to promotion are more stabilized. Like most of the benefits in public administration, this one is a mixed blessing. If their risks are less, then so are their rewards. Public employees often experience fewer opportunities for rapid advancement, rotation, and displays of individual initiative than do their counterparts in the private sector.

What is true for the employees is likely to be true for the organization. Public agencies frequently possess less flexibility than private ones. They find it much harder to shift direction, change procedures, and revamp operations. Firmly enmeshed in a tight web of legality, the public organization typically must follow prescribed procedures and aim at traditional targets.

Underlying this state of affairs is the greater need of the public organization to hold itself accountable. Its obligations extend not just to a particular group of shareholders or sponsors but to the public at large. It is not supposed to do simply what it wants, how it wants. Rather it is supposed to do what the public wants in ways that the public, or its elected representatives, have decreed. Responsiveness and responsibility—these are held forth and hailed as the hallmarks of public administration in a democratic society.

The private organization also suffers restrictions, of course, but these usually hinge on its need to make a profit. As long as it is advancing to this goal, it enjoys considerable latitude in the way it operates and in the specific targets it may set for itself. This profit motive accounts for another feature that many feel distinguishes the two types of administration, namely differences in their efficiency. There is a widely held opinion that because private organizations work under the whiplash of profitability, and because they are freer to initiate and innovate, they are more efficient than public ones. The fact that an opinion is widely held does not in itself make it valid, and this opinion has encountered heavy opposition. While comparisons between private and public operations are not always easy to make, given the divergent nature of their activities and ends, a case can be made for the potentially equal, if not greater, efficiency of the public sector.

This case was perhaps best expounded by Paul Appleby in his landmark work *Big Democracy*. Appleby put forth the claims of public administration in the area of efficiency by posing a series of questions. Which types of operations, public or private, he asked, are more subject to the pressures of pull and privilege? Which more readily puts the boss's relatives on its payrolls, and which does more of its purchasing from favored friends rather than from the cheapest possible suppliers? Which has executives who are more apt to act on the basis of personal whim and caprice and who are more likely to hire, fire, and assign employees for subjective reasons and in an irrational manner?

As for charges of wasteful duplication, which are so often flung at the public sector, Appleby responded by asking about the duplication involved in retailers selling the same goods, gas stations working all four corners of the same intersection, and milk- and oil-delivery people plying the same routes. Furthermore, in noting the existence of budget bureaus, legislative bodies, the press, and other overseers of public spending, Appleby questioned which had the most oversight and control against waste. In a somewhat deeper vein, he posed these questions: Which produces the most wasteful products? Which engages in the most fundamental and most productive research?[6]

Moving from the theoretical to the practical, we can obtain some glimpse of the claims and counterclaims of the two contending sides by examining the efficiency of the public sector when it engages in private-sector activities. There have been and are a host of public enterprises, in this country and even more in other countries, that produce goods in competition with private firms. What does the record show?

To a large extent, the answer depends on which part of the record one examines. In this country, U.S. government shipyards have often found few defenders when accused of inefficiency, and this is one reason why their activities have suffered drastic curtailments in recent years. On the local level, John Lindsay found on assuming the mayoralty of New York in 1966 that the city was making its own batteries and asphalt at costs far exceeding what these commodities could be purchased for on the private market. Overseas, the Nora Commission, appointed by the French parliament in the 1960s, discovered that the productivity of enterprises owned by the French government fell significantly below those in private hands. In Britain many idealistic socialists in the early 1960s began expressing doubts and even despair over the questionable results chalked up by those industries that the Labour government had nationalized in the late 1940s.

There is, however, another side of the balance sheet. In this country, the Tennessee Valley Authority, as well as many municipal power plants, have operated with results ranging from merely satisfactory to superb. In Europe, many Swedish public enterprises have competed successfully with private companies. Similarly, government ownership of the controlling interest in Germany's Volkswagen plant and Holland's KLM Airline has not prevented these firms from registering impressive earnings records. And the entirely government-owned-and-operated British Overseas

Airlines Corporation has made a profit almost every year since 1964. This is an earnings record that many private airlines can only envy.[7]

We may conclude by noting that public administration does differ in certain significant ways from private administration. These largely hinge on the greater legal accountability of the former as compared to the greater flexibility of the latter. Determining which is the most efficient remains a complex question, subject not only to variances in products and procedures but also to differences in conditions and criteria. Both public administration and private administration are and have been changing in ways that are stimulating to see and exciting to experience. And after completing our journey along the highways and byways of the administrative process, we will take another look at the fence separating the private and public domains. We may then determine if the fence these days is all that high, and we may wonder if, in the future, there will or should be any fence at all.

The American Political System

Many of those who first thought and wrote about public administration regretted and resented the widespread tendency to view their subject as a branch of politics. They insisted on calling attention to public administration's essentially pristine nature. To the extent politics conditioned administration, so, they claimed, it contaminated it.

Typical of these theorists was Woodrow Wilson. As a young professor in 1887, Wilson authored an article in which he asserted that "the field of administration is a field of business. It is removed from the hurry and strife of politics. . . . It is a part of political life only as the methods of the counting house are a part of the life of society, only as machinery is part of the manufactured product."[8] To Wilson, as well as to many others of his time, administration should concern itself with means, not ends, with simply doing things well and not with deciding what things to do well.

Today we know better, or believe we do. Modern theorists, to say nothing of modern practitioners, acknowledge and accept a much wider role for their discipline. Public administrators today do not, and to some degree cannot, limit themselves merely to executing the policy of their political masters. The complexity and challenges of their craft force them to create policy as well. Nor can they ignore the political system within which they operate. This system imposes itself on and influences nearly everything they do. He or she who would function effectively as a public administrator would do well to learn the main features of the political system within which his or her administrative activities will be carried on.

WHERE THERE'S A WILL . . .

Clever and determined public managers can often create and implement policies that their ostensible political masters have publicly repudiated. For example, soon after he was appointed to chair the Securities and Exchange Commission, William Lucius Carey decided that floor traders on the stock exchanges served no useful purpose and should be outlawed. When Congress refused to pass the bill that he filed to accomplish this aim, he simply used his existing authority to promulgate new rules for floor traders. Under these rules, they would have to pass a stiff qualifying exam and fill out a lengthy form at the end of each day itemizing their transactions. Under these new rules the number of floor traders declined from three hundred to thirty. Chairman Carey had, to all intents and purposes, accomplished his goal.

Majority Rule, Minority Rights

The first feature almost everyone thinks of when it comes to describing the U.S. political system is democracy. Although meanings of this much-misunderstood and misapplied word vary, most will agree with the dictionary's definition of it as "a form of government in which the supreme power is vested in the people and exercised by them or their freely elected agents."

What happens when the people disagree? Then the answer customarily given is "majority rule." It is here one has to exercise some caution. If 51 percent of the people voted to put the other 49 percent into concentration camps, we could hardly call this an exercise in democracy; and the example is not as farfetched as it sounds. Hitler put a lot of people into concentration camps, and there is little question that he would have won a free election in Germany by a sweeping majority during the late 1930s and early 1940s. Yet not even Hitler would have called his regime a democracy.

Thus, when we think of democracy we must not only think of majority rule, but also of minority rights. This complicates the problem enormously, and especially for public managers who must carry out the majority's mandate while simultaneously safeguarding basic minority interests. Public administration in a democratic society is a delicate and difficult task, requiring of its practitioners generous amounts of tolerance and tact. Those lacking such capacities may well do better in other fields.

Democracy Divided

Of course, democracy scarcely makes the United States unique. Many countries can claim similar status. However, some characteristics of U.S. democracy differentiate it from that of other nations.

The most distinctive difference, the one foreign visitors seem to notice first, is our formidable degree of fragmentation. In 1830, France's Count Alexis de Tocqueville, after a tour of the new nation, pronounced it the most decentralized country in the world. More than half a century later, Britain's Lord Bryce, after a similar tour, expressed amazement at the amount of government carried on at the grass roots. More recent visitors have shared their views.

The United states has some eighty thousand governments. Thanks to our federal Constitution, fifty-one of these—the states plus the national government—possess sovereign power. The cities, towns, counties, educational districts, and special districts that make up the rest may lack such sovereignty yet still show a surprisingly strong degree of political development. As a result, power is widely dispersed throughout the political system.

At each level of government still more fragmentation can be found. The federal government and all the states operate under a separation-of-powers principle, which divides power between independent legislative, executive, and judicial branches. At the local level, the situation varies, sometimes power is more consolidated, sometimes it is less.

Thus we find political power strewn in bits and pieces over a vast and variegated landscape. To be sure, efforts to bring some cohesion to this piecemeal political apparatus continually go on. The federal government has evolved an elaborate grant-in-aid system to induce (some would say bribe) state and local governments to do what Washington wants them to do. These governments were receiving some $82 billion for such purposes in 1980. President Reagan's frantic budget-cutting efforts arrested the growth rate of these grant-in-aid programs but not the growth itself, for during the early 1980s the amount of dollars flowing from Washington to grass-roots governments continued to increase.

As for horizontal fragmentation, the search for coordination and coherence here has gradually shifted power away from the legislative and into the executive branches. This has occurred at both the national and state levels despite the fact that their respective constitutions continue to enshrine the separation-of-power principle. Developments have been even more dramatic at the local level. The growth of strong mayor and city-manager governments, the emergence of county executives and, in a few instances, the advent of metropolitan governments combining county with municipalities, attest to this stepped-up search for cohesion.

Both the fragmentation and the attempts to alleviate it produce consequences that the public manager may ignore only at his or her peril. By
far the most crucial one for administrators is the division in authority and
responsibility. Few indeed are those U.S. agencies and their administrators who can lay claim to an exclusive and well-demarcated area of competence and control. Instead, nearly all the action areas in modern administration constitute divided, and in most cases disputed, territory where
several agencies often jostle and even joust with each other in their relentless quest for influence and impact. One study of human-services directors in North Carolina showed them spending 13 percent of their work
day dealing with officials of other governments. They actually spent more
time on such intergovernmental matters than they did in supervising their
staffs.[9] An earlier and more elaborate study of the federal government's
welfare programs concluded that "federal enforcement is a diplomatic
process. It is as if the terms of a treaty, an agreement of mutual interest to
government parties, were more or less continuously negotiated . . . negotiations over a single issue may go on steadily for several years and intermittently for a decade."[10]

Pollution control offers another example of how the patchwork distribution of power in our system bedevils and often baffles the public servant. The federal government now operates approximately twenty-five programs to curb pollution; at the same time, virtually all states and many
communities have programs of their own. Getting all these endeavors to
mesh often makes for a tiresome, time-consuming task. To cite just one
instance, it took the town of Junior, West Virginia, over five years to satisfy the demands of six federal agencies whose approval it needed to
build a sewage treatment plant.

The Reagan administration has sought to simplify the federal government's grant-in-aid program and to ease up on its standards as a way of
inducing the states and their communities to accept less money. But such
efforts, even if successful, may not lighten the public manager's task. Less
federal control may only leave him or her more vulnerable to the constraints that other governments and special interest groups may seek to
impose. While all democratic governments require of their public managers tolerance and tact and patience and persistence, our own brand of
fragmented democracy will continue to demand that those who hope to
accomplish anything worthwhile possess these and even more desirable
qualities.

Personalism

The oft-used term *bureaucracy* really has two meanings. In its most
popular sense it merely refers to any substantial public organization or

group of organizations, as in "federal bureaucracy" or the "welfare bureaucracy."

The other meaning is more specialized: it refers to a particular method or manner of administration. A bureaucracy in this sense of the word is an organization or group of organizations that operate in a particular way.

What constitutes the bureaucratic way of doing things? The German sociologist Max Weber was the first to define it. He saw it as an impersonal system operating on the basis of "calculable rules" and staffed by full-time and professional (as opposed to political) employees. It presupposes a hierarchy, but this hierarchy is based strictly on organizational rank, not on social status or other considerations.

The chief characteristics of a bureaucracy in Weber's sense of the word was its uniform, nonarbitrary and nonpersonal method of administering the public's affairs. "Bureaucracy," wrote Weber, "is like a modern judge who is a vending machine into which the pleadings are inserted along with the fee. The machine then disgorges the judgment based on reasons mechanically derived from the code."[11]

In Weber's view, bureaucracy becomes a bloodless mechanism, devoid of all the capriciousness and color we associate with human activity. Yet the positive features of such an administrative approach must not be overlooked. Impersonality also implies impartiality; professionalization opens the possibility for an employee-selection system based less on social status than on personal skill.

The bureaucratic way of doing things has made great headway in Europe, especially in Germany. As such, it has brought more uniformity, predictability, and equality to public administration. Bureaucratic systems, to be sure, often show great resistance to change, since they rest upon a highly systematized administrative arrangement. Their devotion to "calculable rules" often makes true bureaucrats slavishly "go by the book" regardless of the situation, but even this can sometimes prove advantageous. France, with its long history of unrest and upheaval, has often been held together by its plodding but persistent bureaucracy.

If the bureaucratic style has pretty well conquered the public sector of Western Europe, it has scored somewhat less success in this country. The political system of the United States is highly personalized, and this necessarily affects our administrative system as well. Just as personalities so often count for more than parties or principles in policy making, so do personalities often outweigh "calculable rules" in policy execution. This is not always true, but it is true enough to differentiate U.S. administration from that of many other democratic countries.

Our lessened respect for the rules provides many rewards. Though U.S. administration has often, and rightly, been accused of stodginess, it is perhaps less guilty of such offenses than its continental counterparts. In general it is much easier to bend, if not break, the rules in the United States than elsewhere in the democratic world.

Our administrative setup can usually accommodate more easily individual idiosyncrasies, as well as individual initiative. Before breaking out into cheers, the antibureaucratic enthusiast would do well to note some of the benefits that we thereby tend to forego. A system more open to the influence of individual personality will be more open to caprices and whims as well. It will also be more vulnerable to corruption, as the calculable rules become more easily manipulated; and if change can sometimes come earlier, then such change may spring not just from public demand but from personal desire.

The distinctiveness of U.S. administration in this respect should not be overstated. The bureaucratic way of doing things is scarcely any stranger to our shores. Nor, for that matter, are the systems of other countries incapable of capriciousness or change. Yet, bureaucracy in the sense in which Max Weber defined it has characterized, for both good and ill, our public sector less than that of many other modern countries, and the U.S. administrator would do well to appreciate this fact and adjust to it accordingly.

Legalism

The intense decentralization of the United States was not the only feature of polity that struck the young Count de Tocqueville when he visited the country a century and a half ago. He was also startled by the prominence of lawyers and the predominance of legal processes in the system's operations. He noted with amazement how in the United States nearly every political issue of importance ends up in a courtroom.

This tendency has not abated but has accelerated in the century and a half since de Tocqueville's visit. Today the country harbors two-thirds of all the world's lawyers, while its courts have extended their reach into virtually all areas of political life. Judges now decide not only major policy disputes but minor details of policy execution. The 1970s, for example, saw a federal judge in Boston determine how many basketballs a local high school should have, and another federal judge in Alabama determined the right degree of heat for hot water in a state mental health hospital. In no other land do the bench and bar figure so formidably in the workings of everyday life.

The consequences of this trend for public managers are both many and great. As noted earlier, public administration by its very nature enjoys, or suffers, depending on one's point of view, a close relationship with the law. It is the law, or rather laws, which set up public agencies, prescribe and proscribe their activities, and supply them with resources. Today,

the relationship has become much closer, notes David Bazelon, the articulate and perceptive federal appeals judge in Washington, D.C., "as the
constitutional right to due process of law expands, more and more administrators will find themselves locked into an involuntary partnership with
the courts."[12]

For most administrators that time has already arrived. And for most of
them the partnership is not only involuntary but unpleasant. Although at
times they look to and lean on the courts to help them dispose of a disruptive issue or to back them up on a controversial matter, in most instances they view the court's role in their affairs from a quite different
perspective. To the average administrator the increasing legalization of
the U.S. polity has meant harassment and hindrance in the fulfillment of
his or her functions.

One need not range very far or wide to find reasons for such sentiments.
The hiring and firing of employees, the purchase of equipment, the adoption or even adjustment of a simple operational guideline have all produced costly and frustrating litigation. To the activist administrator, the
law and its practitioners often seem to exist merely to tie their hands.

Aggravating the problem for many public administrators is the fact that
their craft is becoming increasingly results oriented. This contrasts
sharply with the legalistic approach, which stresses the correctness of procedure. To the legal mind, for example, justice is not a product but a
process.[13]

One must not, of course, overlook the benefits that may, at least occasionally, result from the increasing legalization of the administrative process. Explosive issues often become defused when shifted to the legal
system. Citizens are protected from abuses of authority. Politicians and
administrators are constrained from acting rashly and without due regard
for the rights of others. Still, those who would toil in the vineyards of the
public sector must bear in mind that they labor under the scrutiny of more
than their superiors. What they do and, more importantly perhaps, how
they do it can ever more easily get them ensnarled within the coils of the
law.

Antigovernmentalism

In many industrial countries, government generally is viewed as a positive good that exists to protect and preserve its citizens. The powers that
it is given are not given reluctantly but expectantly. The citizen expects
the government to act, and to act forcefully if need be, to resolve problems and to improve the conditions of life. Furthermore, those who work
for the government are also viewed in a somewhat favorable light. Government service is not looked upon at all as being demeaning. On the

contrary, it is sometimes considered to be a mark of prestige, even at its lower levels.

Unfortunately for the U.S. administrator, such is not the case here. We Americans have decidedly mixed views about government activity, and although we want to see public services delivered in an efficient manner and are increasingly outraged by the failure to do so, we are sometimes loath to invest our governmental structure with the scope and power to take the forceful action that the achievement of such a goal may require. "I own, I am not a friend to very energetic government," said Thomas Jefferson, and large sectors of the American populace have echoed his sentiments ever since. Deeply implanted in our political culture is the attitude that that government governs best which governs least.

This belief weakened during the 1930s, when so many became so heavily dependent on the government for actual survival. During the 1960s a substantial number of Americans again began looking to the government to solve such social ills as poverty, illiteracy, ill health, and crime. However, the failure of many government programs to measure up to expectations helped revive the long-standing opposition toward governmental activity. Other factors and forces also enter into this negativism. We will examine these in greater detail shortly, but first let us look at an example of some of these characteristics of the American political system in action.

CASE STUDY

The Delaware Runs Dry[14]

The state of Delaware has little control over the river that bears its name. The 330-mile waterway originates in southern New York State, wends its way along the borders of Pennsylvania and New Jersey, and then passes through Delaware before emptying into the Atlantic. In its daily course, it manages to provide substantial amounts of water for all four states and some of their largest cities. Since the region the Delaware serves holds almost one-tenth of the nation's population and employs almost one-seventh of its work force, the river has sometimes been considered the most important of America's waterways.

Until the spring of 1961, the Delaware had generally fulfilled the demands that its host states had placed upon it, and water experts confidently expected that it would continue to furnish sufficient water for the growing region until 2010. This, however, was the last time they expressed such a hope, for the following August a drought descended on the entire middle Atlantic region. The dry spell continued for four years, and by the spring of 1965, New York City's water resources were down to about one-fourth of their capacity. Northern New Jersey's reservoirs were similarly afflicted, while the situation in much of the rest of the region was as bad, if not worse. The crisis precipitated a series of events, which have been summarized and assessed by Richard A. Hogarty in an illuminating case study, "The Delaware River Drought Emergency." The problems that the drought dramatized and the ways in which they were resolved shed valuable light on the political system within which the U.S. administrator must ply his trade.

It should be noted that although the Delaware up to the time of the 1961 drought had managed to supply the water needs of all those who depended upon it, this had not prevented its beneficiaries from wrangling among themselves as to who was to get how much of its valuable resources. In 1928, New York City obtained state approval for a new reservoir system that would divert substantially increased waters from the Delaware. New Jersey and Pennsylvania became incensed at the proposed diversion and filed suit to halt it. Their case gradually climbed up the judicial ladder, reaching the Supreme Court in 1931. The Supreme Court ruled that the proposed diversion was subject to the doctrine of equitable apportionment and that New Jersey and Pennsylvania had "real and substantial rights in the river that might be reconciled as best they may." The Court did grant New York City about two-thirds of the additional water it was seeking, but it indicated that this might not prove to be a permanent solution. In the prophetic words of Justice Oliver Wendell Holmes, who wrote the majority decision, "the possible experience of the future may make modifications of the plan as it now stands necessary in unforeseen circumstances."

In 1936, the four basin states formed the Interstate Commission on the Delaware River Basin (INCODEL), but they gave it little regulatory or operational power. The commission prepared a comprehensive plan for the physical development of the river in the early 1950s, but the plan fell by the wayside when it failed to secure the needed approval from one of the four states, Pennsylvania. With the failure of the plan, the commission ceased to play any significant role.

In 1952, New York City, once again eager to proceed with some reservoir construction, petitioned the Supreme Court to modify its 1931 decree and allow the metropolis to tap more water from the Delaware. The Court moderately increased the city's water allowance and agreed to a substantially greater allowance of water once its projected new reservoir system was completed. (The plans for the reservoir had still not been fully worked out by 1965. Consequently, New York was still operating under the modest increase permitted by the Supreme Court's earlier decree when the drought problem reached its climax.)

In 1953, the governors of New York, New Jersey, and Pennsylvania decided to explore again the possibilities of developing a single governmental unit to handle the basin's water resources. The hurricanes of that year added impetus to their efforts, for they exposed and intensified the difficulties that the lack of a coordinated and cohesive mechanism had engendered. As Hogarty notes, "the region's water planning and policy machinery was balkanized, complex, and cumbersome. Approximately 849 local governments, 42 counties, 4 states and an estimated 252 water supply enterprises had some sort of policy-making responsibility in water management. Superimposed upon this jurisdictional maze were about 18 federal agencies, 14 interstate agencies and countless private firms including giants like United States Steel."

By 1959 the governors had worked out a plan for a permanent basin agency to be established by an interstate-federal compact. By 1961 all the states and the federal government had approved it, and the Delaware River Basin Compact (DRBC) came into existence. The compact was unique in many respects. For one thing, it was the first such arrangement to include the federal government as a voting member. Second, the interstate agency envisioned by the compact would have "strong regulatory powers and extensive authority over allocation, diversions and releases of water in the basin." It was given an office and a staff and was believed to be functioning well when the full impact of the drought began to be felt in the fateful spring of 1965.

It was on June 14 of 1965 that New York City suddenly shattered the uneasy peace, which had for some years prevailed along the Delaware River basin. With no prior announcement, the city on that day began diverting substantially more water for its own use. Its action quickly triggered expressions of anger and alarm in the other three states, which were already being deeply troubled by the developing drought. The city of Philadelphia was particularly worried, for with less and less fresh water coming in from the Delaware, the "salt line" in the city's existing water supply would rise to dangerous levels. Moreover, the situation in most of the rest of the region was nearly as threatening.

Representatives of the four governors and the federal government hurriedly met on June 23 to discuss and, so they hoped, decide the issue. Their meeting, however, only produced a decision to call a public hearing to determine the full extent of a problem that was now as much political as it was physical. While such a hearing was required as a prerequisite to taking action under the interstate compact's emergency powers, it by no means guaranteed that such powers would be or could be invoked. All five signatories would have to consent to such action, and with New York State quite sensitive to the problems of its major city, such unanimity might prove hard to muster.

Following hard on the heels of the June 23 conclave, Governor Richard Hughes of New Jersey summoned a meeting of the governors, along with federal representatives, for July 1. Hughes acted in his capacity as chairman of the compact, but goading him on was the desperate turn of events in his own state. Some of New Jersey's cities were faced with the alternative of importing water in tank cars at enormous cost if the drought continued and if New York City's increased diversion was allowed.

The governors of New York and Pennsylvania, Nelson Rockefeller and William Scranton, declined Hughes's call to attend the meeting, although they did send representatives. Secretary of Interior Stewart Udall and Delaware Governor George Terry, however, did show up. New York

City, although it had no official status at the conclave, sent a delegation of its own. The meeting failed to produce a mutually acceptable solution, although one compromise plan did seem to have possibilities and was targeted for further study.

In the meantime, the public hearing authorized by the earlier meeting was held on July 7. It produced convincing evidence as to the severity of the crisis. It also produced much testimony blaming New York City not just for diverting more than its share of water from the Delaware, but for failing to undertake what others thought were necessary conservation measures. New York City spokesmen, as might be expected, vigorously denied such charges. After the hearing, the compact's commissioners and staff members gathered in executive session for five hours. (New York City was excluded, since it was not a member of the commission.) They managed to agree to some limitation on the amount of water that New York state could keep for itself and its communities. New York State's representatives, ever mindful of the political importance of New York City and not wishing to push it too far, gave only limited and grudging acceptance. This was the first of several difficult and hard-fought agreements reached by the DRBC on its tedious and troublesome way to a solution. And, although such bargaining and negotiation did produce progress, it took a new development to move the issue toward a real resolution.

The governors had been asking for federal aid almost since the crisis began. Particularly active in this regard was Governor Hughes, who had aggressively supported President Lyndon Johnson's election the previous year. The president himself, meanwhile, had been showing increasing interest in water problems, particularly in desalinization, which he considered to be the most effective long-term method for "drought-proofing" major metropolitan areas as well as farm regions. (He was also well aware of the importance of some of these areas to the future of the Democratic party, particularly in the congressional elections that would occur the following year.) On July 14 Johnson expressed concern over the drought and said he had asked federal officials to study the situation and suggest ways in which the federal government could help. On August 7, Interior Secretary Udall sent him a memorandum urging the initiation of coordinated intergovernmental planning and suggesting, as a first step, inviting the four governors, along with the mayors of the affected major cities, to a Washington meeting.

The meeting was held on August 11, after which Johnson moved swiftly. He launched a series of steps that, while they brought no short-range solution in themselves, produced prospects of long-term financial aid to the distressed states and localities. By using such prospective aid as an inducement, the federal government succeeded in prodding them to work out a "water bank" and take other immediate steps both to conserve water and to apportion it more equitably among themselves. The state governments came under particular pressure to exercise greater con-

trol in coordination of their own water resources and to show more leadership vis-à-vis their own communities lest they lose out on the federal
government's generosity.

The case is, indeed, a complicated and a complex one, and this short
summary does little justice to its many components and phases. However,
even such an abridged version as this affords a glimpse of the American
political system at work.

The most apparent feature is that of fragmentation. Not only were four
quite sovereign states involved in the dispute, but their largest cities
played important and somewhat independent roles. New York City, Philadelphia, and other cities sent their own representatives to the various
meetings that finally produced some solutions. Furthermore, the tensions
that hampered the achievement of a resolution existed not just between
the states themselves but, at least in some cases, between the state governments and their own communities. Governor Scranton's attempt to assert state government authority in Pennsylvania was opposed by the
Greater Philadelphia Movement and other local organizations and leaders. As for Governor Rockefeller, he and his state water commissioner, in
their dealings with New York City, "often found themselves," says Hogarty, "in the role of protectors rather than deciders." From the standpoint of the state water commissioner, "there was never any question
about his backing up New York City. State officials could not concede
that the city was violating the 1954 Supreme Court decree."

The case also illuminates the extensive role that legalistic techniques
and devices tend to play in our political system. Although the courts were
not dragged into the drought crisis, they had been utilized in two previous disputes concerning how much water New York City was to obtain.
Actually, some of those involved in the drought decisions wanted to take
New York City again to court, but others felt that such a step would take
too long. They also pointed out that a functioning agency existed to handle such matters and that the Supreme Court always required litigating
parties to exhaust all administrative remedies before seeking its help.

Finally, the impact of personality presents itself throughout the case.
Governor Scranton not only had trouble from local organizations in Philadelphia but had deep trouble from a leading member of his own party,
who opposed him at every step. The personality of the mayor of New
York City played a major role in the proceedings. He had shrugged off all
the initial warning signs of the crisis, and his rather lackadaisical attitude
certainly precipitated some of the dramatic action the city found itself
constrained to take at a later date. And had the water commissioner of
New York City been more amiable and also amenable to outside suggestions, the problems might have been resolved at a much earlier phase.

But perhaps the most startling and the most significant way in which
the accident of personality intruded itself into the course of events occurred much earlier, during the fight for the plan that the previous interstate commission (INCODEL) had devised during the 1950s. It will be
recalled that this plan failed to be adopted because one state, Pennsyl-

vania, had said no. However, Pennsylvania's rejection resulted from the fact that a subcommittee of its state senate failed to approve the plan by one vote. Thus, solely because one obscure state legislator in one of the affected states refused to give his approval, a physical development plan that might well have averted the entire crisis never saw the light of day.

The Bureaucracy at Bay

Like so many new political and social trends, it started, or at least surfaced, in California. And like so many of the innovations that bubble up in that trendy state, it emerged through the referendum process. It bore the title Proposition 13, and to many, the number in its name soon took on an added hue of misfortune, as its effects began to reverberate across the land.

For Proposition 13 called for a sharp reduction in local property taxes even if it required a scaling-back of services to accomplish it. It signaled a revolt of the U.S. public against its public sector. It spelled the end of what some of the proposition's supporters had termed the nation's "bureaucratic binge."

The movement to curtail government expenditures and activities soon spread to other states. Not all attempts to duplicate what happened in California succeeded, but nearly every state, along with most local governments, felt some effects, and nearly all found themselves forced to respond. And in 1980 this surge of antitax, antigovernment sentiment helped elect a president and a Congress committed to carrying out its basic mandate.

Predictably many public managers reacted, at least initially, with resentment or regret. They, along with numerous public-spirited citizens, saw in this movement an indication of the new narcissism, a manifestation of a more selfish society. As RIF, Reduction in Force, became a well-known and much-feared acronym, and as symposia and seminars in "cutback management" proliferated, many public managers felt and feared that they were presiding over the withering away of the welfare state.

Yet many were willing to concede the validity of some of the reasons behind the public's reaction. From 1950 to 1980 government bureaucracies had grown 159 percent. This was almost four times the growth that occurred in the "productive" sector of the economy (manufacturing, mining, construction, transportation, and utilities) during the same period. Government spending had, of course, kept pace. By 1980 it was absorbing 42 percent of the nation's personal income, while increased government borrowing was threatening to push this figure still higher. In 1979, for example, governments of all kinds in the United States borrowed *ten times* as much as private industry. These huge accumulations of debt, so critics contended, were not only saddling the taxpayers with future costs of principal and interest but were driving up interest rates and depriving private industry of the credit it needed for modernization and expansion.

NEVER SAY NO

A conscientious attempt at cutting the federal government's costs proved costly to Andrew Bavas. When the HEW intergovernmental affairs expert received an automatic thirteen-hundred-dollar raise in 1979, he decided to turn it down. Said the forty-nine-year-old Bavas, "I really didn't need the money. I had no debts, and my mortgage ends in two years." The government, he reasoned, needed the money more than he did.

His superiors, however, reacted with rancor. They informed him that his unorthodox act would not be tolerated since it might encourage cost-conscious officials to pressure their subordinates to follow his example. So, he received the unwanted raise. He also received an even more unwanted transfer to Philadelphia. This latter move caused him to resign, with the observation, "I guess I've got no future as a government bureaucrat."

To be sure, the impact of this upsurge in government spending was often exaggerated. If the public sector was growing faster than the private sector, then was this not merely reflective of a broader trend, a trend away from the production of goods and toward the production of services? And if high rates of interest caused by government borrowing were preventing the private sector from getting the funds it needed for capital investment, then why was it that the lowering of interest rates in 1982 brought no immediate spurt in capital spending? Nevertheless many citizens apparently did not see it quite this way, and their complaints and cavils did not lack foundation. In 1950 the federal income tax, for example, was taking 11 percent of the average worker's paycheck. In 1980 it was absorbing over 22 percent, and since pay increases themselves had barely kept pace with inflation during the previous decade, it is no wonder that the public was starting to lash out at the most obvious and convenient source of its distress.

These sentiments might have remained more muted if the taxpayers believed that their public officials were at least spending their money wisely, but they did not feel this to be the case. One Gallup poll in the early 1980s indicated that the average citizen believed that 48 percent of all federal expenditures were swallowed up by waste and fraud. Lending a sliver of substance to this rather startling belief were the frequent headlines pointing to examples, real and alleged, of governmental misdoings. Although the most sensational exposures dealt with abuses of a criminal or near-criminal nature, many less sensational instances of misfeasance or nonfeasance had also come to light. When a new chairman of the Federal Communications Commission tried to change the commission's office hours from 8:30–4:30 to 9:30–5:30, so that people calling from the West Coast could find someone in if they telephoned after 1:30 PM their time, the FCC's employees rebelled. As a result, the hours had to be left as they were. When a journalist wandered through the Department of Agriculture, he found large numbers of people milling about the corridors or lingering in the cafeterias at all hours of the day. Riding in the elevator he heard one employee tell another, "I'd like to be sick tomorrow, but I can't; the woman I work with plans to be."

Conditions seemed scarcely any better in most state houses and city halls. In many jurisdictions constant dollar increases in such services as police, fire, education, and street cleaning had been accompanied by rising crime, increased fires, lower educational scores, and dirtier streets. More significantly, many municipalities were finding that they could contract out a growing number of their functions to private industry at only a fraction of what it had cost to perform them themselves.

The public sector thus found itself on the defensive. Even many of its hitherto loyal friends appeared to have turned against it. For example, *Harper's,* a liberal magazine long known for supporting well-intentioned government action, carried three articles in its October 1979 issue blasting the federal bureaucracy. One accused it of increasing inflation, another for aggravating the oil problem, while the third blamed it for mishandling a recent accident at a nuclear power plant. As if this wasn't enough, the same issue of the magazine contained a short story satirically depicting what happened when the San Francisco Giants were taken over by the city government and thereby put under civil service. The team's manager found that he couldn't take a pitcher off the mound during a game without giving him a hearing and that he had to accept a left-handed second baseman and a two-fingered catcher, since they stood at the top of the civil service list, the catcher having received bonus points for his handicap.

More surprising and much more significant was the discontent over public-sector performance that was being voiced within the public sector itself. An exhaustive study of civilian managers in the U.S. Navy, for example, showed that their principle source of job stress was frustration over the slowness of accomplishing anything.[15] And if a pro-public-sector magazine like *Harper's* could criticize and condemn the bureaucracy, then a magazine written largely by and for bureaucrats was doing much the same. In its January/February issue of 1982, *Public Administration Review* carried one article flaying municipal administrators for driving up

---

BUREAUCRATIC BANKERS

While business executives like to boast of their superiority over bureaucrats when it comes to efficiency, some studies indicate they should temper their tongues. A 1982 study of forty-eight thousand managers and
other employees at eleven major banks showed an alarming degree of
"overmanagement." Said the study's author, Charles K. Rourke, the president of a Massachusetts management-consulting firm, "while many
bankers blame their financial problems on the current recession, the productivity problems facing U.S. banks today are directly related to bloated
and overstaffed management structures."

---

the cost of housing by piling up and zealously enforcing their master
plans; another article took public managers to task for trying to meet the
needs of the handicapped in the most wasteful way; and a third article
blasted the federal bureaucracy for spending too much on public
relations.

Their own growing awareness of their sector's shortcomings was
prompting many public managers to view the new "crisis in confidence"
as a possible blessing. When *Public Administration Times* conducted a
survey of public managers in California in the wake of Proposition 13, it
found them surprisingly hopeful.[16] One fairly typical respondent said the
new fiscal constraints "may force us to do the things we have always
thought we needed to do anyway." Others even went further. As one of
them put it, "the post–proposition 13 era, the 'era of limits' . . . is a time
of opportunity for public managers. There will be a premium placed on
innovation. Managers will have a chance to accomplish organizational reforms that have been only thought of and talked about in the past."[17]

Furthermore, despite all the understandable fear and trembling over
job security, the situation might well be creating expanded career opportunities for some public-sector employees. These are the well-trained and
highly talented, who find their abilities increasingly in demand. In Massachusetts, for example, only nine towns established some form of town-
administrator position from 1976 to 1980. But from 1980, when the state
had begun to put its own version of Proposition 13 into effect, until 1982,
some thirty towns took such a step. The era of cutback management could
well mark the time when professional public administration fully came of
age.

Ralph Waldo Emerson once noted that for every wall there was a door.
For the truly competent and committed public administrator the "bureaucrat as boogyman" syndrome now sweeping the country may not only be
erecting a wall, but also opening a door to a career of superior challenge
and fulfillment.

Notes

1. The book in question is the author's own prior work, *The Administrative Revolution: Notes on the Passing of Organization Man* (Englewood Cliffs, N.J.: Prentice-Hall, 1971).

2. Herbert A. Simon, Donald W. Smithburg, and Victor A. Thompson, *Public Administration* (New York: Alfred A. Knopf, 1950), 3.

3. Herbert A. Simon, *Administrative Behavior* (New York: Free Press, 1947), 186.

4. John M. Pfiffner and Robert Presthus, *Public Administration*, 5th ed. (New York: Ronald Press, 1967), 427. In regard to the subsequent sentence in the text, Donald S. Vaughn, Chairman of the political science department of the University of Mississippi, points out that the law also tells the public administrator what he cannot do. In a letter to the author, Professor Vaughn cites the first eight amendments of the U.S. Constitution as a case in point.

5. The reader will no doubt understand the writer's reluctance to give further details of this episode. However, the writer does vouch for its veracity.

6. Paul H. Appleby, *Big Democracy* (New York: Alfred A. Knopf, 1949), chap. 5.

7. Professor D. Durasoff of the University of Oklahoma claims that "private" companies also receive large, nonbudgeted subsidies in the form of guaranteed loans, publicly built highways, etc.

8. W. Woodrow Wilson, "The Study of Administration," *Political Science Quarterly* (June 1887). This landmark piece has been frequently reprinted in anthologies on public administration.

9. Laurel A. Files, "The Human Services Management Task: A Time Allocation Study," *Public Administration Review* (November–December 1982).

10. Martha Derthic, *The Influence of Federal Grants: Public Assistance in Massachusetts* (Cambridge, Mass.: Harvard University Press, 1970).

11. H. H. Gerth and C. Wright Mills, eds., *From Max Weber: Essays in Sociology* (New York: Oxford University Press, 1946), 197.

12. David Bazelon, "The Impact of the Courts on Public Administrations," *Indiana Law Journal* (Fall 1976).

13. This view has been articulated by Alan M. Dershowitz in *The Best Defense* (New York: Random House, 1982). However, the same theme runs like a leitmotif through many other statements and writings by legal authorities. Oliver Wendell Holmes, for example, once said that his job as justice of the U.S. Supreme Court did not require him to "do" justice but merely to see that the rules of the game were followed.

14. Richard A. Hogarty, *The Delaware River Drought Emergency*, Inter-University Case Program no. 107 (Indianapolis, Ind.: Bobbs-Merrill, 1970). All material, including quotes in this section, is taken from this case.

15. Alan W. Lau et al., "The Nature of Managerial Work in the Public Sector," *Public Administration Review* (September–October, 1980).

16. *Public Administration Times*, vol. 1, no. 8 (1978).

17. John J. McTighe, "Management Strategies to Deal with Shrinking Resources," *Public Administration Review* (January–February, 1979).

2

The Anatomy of
Organization

Stripped to its essentials, an organization consists of two or more people engaged in a cooperative effort, working toward a common goal. Thus, the two men engaged in stone moving, which we depicted in the previous chapter, constitute, whether they know it or not, an organization or at least the rudiments of one. All administration requires an organization of some shape, size, or kind, and all organizations carry on some measure of administrative activity.

The Basis of Organization

The structure of most public organizations is a good deal more complex than that of the two imaginary stone-movers. In launching our foray into this rather formidable field, we may find it useful at the outset to examine what is called the basis of organization. We owe this concept to Luther Gulick, one of the trailblazers in U.S. administrative theory. Gulick classified organizations into four different types, depending on their basis or fundamental orientation.[1] Many dispute the utility of his classification scheme, and nearly all will concede that his categories overlap. Yet examining them can deepen our understanding of modern organizational life.

The first category consists of organizations established on the basis of

30

purpose. These organizations are oriented essentially toward accomplishing some specific, although often broad, task. Examples of such organizations abound. A school system is structured to teach children; a fire department is arranged and operated to put out fires; an army is designed to fight wars; and so on. All of these organizations tend to include all the functions necessary to accomplish their essential purposes.

As the reader may quickly surmise, purpose has long been the most prevalent basis of public organization, at least in this country. Yet there are three other categories of organizational basis, and all of them seem to be growing in importance. One of these categories is that of *process.* A process organization is oriented not so much toward accomplishing a specific goal but toward performing certain types of functions. A good example of such an agency is a city law department. Typically, at least in a large city, this department will consist of a group of lawyers who service other departments. One lawyer may represent the city's urban renewal authority in the use of eminent domain. Another may defend the city's Public Works Department in lawsuits. A third may prosecute errant police officers in disciplinary hearings. All of them thus may be engaged in helping to accomplish a wide variety of specific purposes, but all of them are united through the means they utilize—the law.

The third basis of organization is that of *place.* Organizations put under this heading are structured primarily toward serving a particular locale. So far, only a few public agencies strictly meet the classification standards for this category. One example is the neighborhood city halls that Boston and a few other cities have established. These are centers designed to provide a variety of services to all the people who live in a particular neighborhood. In performing this task, they may utilize a variety of processes and strive to accomplish a variety of purposes. What underlies everything the neighborhood city hall does is the providing of services to those who live in a particular place.

If we wish to make our classification criteria less strict, we can lump a host of organizations in this category, since nearly every field unit of every public agency is, in a sense, place oriented. The local firehouse, the local police station, the local elementary school are all designed to perform services for particular areas. Yet they are all part of purpose organizations oriented toward, respectively, putting out fires, and preserving public order. Consequently, they properly cannot be labeled place organizations.

The fourth and last basis of organization that Gulick identifies is that of *clientele.* Like place organizations, to which they are often closely linked, clientele organizations have not been a common feature of our administrative landscape. These agencies are built around the need to serve a particular group of people. One notable example is the federal government's Bureau of Indian Affairs. This agency is designed to provide a variety of services to all Native Americans regardless of the region in which they live. Although its efforts may not have been all that successful, judging from the discontent now being voiced on the reservations, this at least has been its primary aim. Another example was the federal government's Children's Bureau, which, from the time of its creation in 1912 to its dismemberment and virtual abolition in 1969, sought to furnish a variety of services to children. It proudly claimed that it serviced the *whole* child.[2]

As we have already noted, purpose organizations have traditionally dominated American public administration in theory as well as in practice. The Presidential Commission on Organization of the Executive Branch of the Government, better known as the Hoover Commission, warmly endorsed and embraced this organizational basis when it issued its report in 1950. Although most federal agencies already had adopted a purpose orientation, the commission felt that even more of them should do so. Recommendation 12 of its report addressed itself forcefully to this point: "The numerous agencies of the executive branch must be grouped in departments as nearly as possible by major purposes in order to give a coherent mission to each department." The commission's rationale was contained in a terse sentence that followed its recommendation: "By placing related functions cheek-by-jowl overlaps can be eliminated and, of even greater importance, coordinated policies can be developed."[3]

The commission, in throwing its weight so solidly behind the purpose concept, did not offer critiques of the other bases of organization. Others, however, have pointed out that place or clientele organizations offer too few opportunities for utilizing specialized services or even for establishing a satisfactory division of labor. Furthermore, both place and clientele organizations tend to become highly vulnerable to improper influences from the areas or the groups that they serve. Process organizations, on the other hand, while they provide the best opportunities for making use of specialization and for allowing specialists to practice and develop their skills, tend to lose sight of the main aim of public administration, which, of course, is the delivery of basic services. In a process organization, professionally interesting activities tend to take precedence over vitally needed ones. Means tend to predominate over ends. Finally, these three other bases of organization tend to encourage a proliferation of departments and a disunity of action in solving public problems.

Despite long-term popularity of the purpose concept and despite the reservations that were long voiced regarding the other three bases of organization, signs began to appear during the 1960s that the pendulum was starting to swing in other directions. For instance, more and more administrative activity began focusing on clientele or place or a combination of the two. Some of these activities were brand-new endeavors, such as pov-

---

SINGULAR PURPOSE

In the very nature of things, an agency employed for two purposes must fulfill both imperfectly, partly because while fulfilling the one it cannot be fulfilling the other, and partly because its adaptation to both ends implies incomplete fitness for either.

—Herbert Spencer (1892)

---

erty programs, which, in their overall concept, were and are designed to provide a package of services to a distinct group of people. Another example is that of agencies dealing with the elderly. From the Department of Health and Human Services Bureau of the Aging down to local Golden Age Centers, these organizations aim at aiding a particular group of citizens in a variety of ways.

The formation of the Department of Housing and Urban Development was something of a triumph for the clientele approach, since HUD's essential reason for being is to service a particular clientele, primarily the nation's city dwellers, and to give them a voice in the cabinet. The same trend has manifested itself at the state level. Even the battle cry of the old Children's Bureau to care for the whole child began to reemerge early in 1971 when the New York City Board of Education approved a $43 million appropriation to finance a new breakfast program in the city's schools. According to a report in the *New York Times,* the program was placed in the budget by the school system's Chancellor Harvey B. Scribner "probably as much to establish a philosophy as to meet a need." Said the *Times,* "Dr. Scribner appears to be insisting that unless the schools take care of the children's physical as well as intellectual welfare, those who need attention most are least likely to get it." The report, which was written by the newspaper's education editor, concluded with these words: "The question of how to deal with the whole child—including his family, if any, and including even such problems as disease and drug abuse—is real and must be faced."[4]

Clientele is not the only alternative basis of organization that is gaining in popularity. As we will see when we discuss staff services later in this chapter, process organizations are also growing in number. Place, too, as we will notice when we examine centralization later in this book, is also acquiring increased acceptance as at least a partial basis for organizational structure. The point to keep in mind is that a single-minded emphasis on purpose, as typified in the Hoover Commission proposals, can no longer, if it ever did, meet the needs of modern administration. Delivering public services in today's technological society is a complex, delicate, and ever-changing task. As such, it is forcing administrators to review all the options they have available for organizational basis, and to modify their approach or even to adopt a totally new one as they strive to fulfill their goals in a rapidly changing society.

Points about Pyramids

The pyramidal form tends to dominate the structure of most work organizations of any size. The reasons for this are fairly easy to discern. The organization must delegate its work to a vast number of individuals. In order to make sure that they do the work delegated to them and to see to it that their efforts in doing it are coordinated, the organization typically establishes supervisors. These supervisors may themselves become so numerous that they in turn require supervisors. As a result, one or more levels of hierarchy tend to emerge in any sizable work organization with each level dwindling in numerical size until the top is reached.

So pervasive is the pyramidal concept that it even characterizes the operations of organized crime. In his book *Theft of the Nation*, sociologist Donald Cressey points out that each of the twenty-four or more Mafia "families" in the United States is under the command of a boss, or *capo*. The *capo* and his immediate aides oversee a group of *caporegime*, or field managers, who act as chiefs of the families' operating units. These field managers, all of whom are supposed to be of equal status, supervise a varied number of subordinates. Frequently, these subunits spawn further subunits, comprising five or so "button men" under a section head.[5] In many respects the Mafia family is organized along lines not dissimilar to those of say, a municipal welfare department.

Perhaps the smoothest and most orderly pyramidal pattern found in the public sector is the infantry division of the army. The soldiers are grouped into squads under the control of sergeants. The squads are formed into platoons under the leadership of lieutenants. The platoons are collected into companies under the command of captains. The progression continues up to the apex of the divisional triangle, which is headed by the division's commanding general.

However, and this is a point that bears continued emphasis, nearly every organization is part of an even bigger organization, and so the infantry division and its general are answerable to still others above. The pyramidal process continues into the higher levels of the Pentagon, where the secretary of the army joins the secretaries of the navy and the air force in being accountable to the secretary of defense. The latter, meanwhile, occupies one of twelve seats in the cabinet, a body presided over by the president of the United States.

Even much less authoritarian organizations than infantry divisions or Mafia families tend to assume, to a greater or lesser degree, this pyramidal form. A large university, for example, will often contain many diverse types of subunits and many varying and shifting levels of authority. Yet we will generally find that the professors are under the leadership of their department chairman, the chairmen are responsible to their deans, the deans are answerable to their chancellors or whatever the heads of their respective colleges may be called, while the chancellors are accountable to the president of the entire university.

From the tendency of large and particularly bureaucratic organizations to shape themselves into a triangle, we draw certain important concepts. Among them are unity of command, chain of command, and span of control. The meaning and importance of *unity of command* is fairly obvious. It bases itself on the old proverb that no one can serve two masters. This maxim generally has been deemed true for a work organization, particularly one that is operating under the bureaucratic norms of delegation, specialization, and accountability. Requiring an individual or a group to respond to the orders of two or more superiors will, it has been held, produce conflict, confusion, and often chaos. If unity of command does not exist, such deficiencies, it is contended, will not only characterize those being commanded but those doing the commanding. In other words, multiple superiors will not only confuse their subordinates but also each other.

One of the most ardent admirers of the unity-of-command principle was Alexander Hamilton. "That unity is conducive to energy will not be disputed," he wrote in his famous *Federalist Paper 70.* "Decision, activity, secrecy and dispatch will generally characterize the proceedings of one man in a much more eminent degree than the proceedings of any great number, and in proportion as the number is increased, these qualities will be diminished."[6] An old-world contemporary of Hamilton, Napoleon Bonaparte, shared this view. The great French conquerer once said that when it came to fighting a war, he would rather have one bad general than two good generals.

The unity-of-command principle, it should be evident, frowns on the use of boards and commissions. Such multiple-headed bodies have been considered suitable only for organizations of a semijudicial nature, such as regulatory commissions, or for certain policy-making or advisory functions. If an organization is administering a program, if it is *doing* things, then the reins of its authority should converge eventually into one pair of hands. Only in so doing will responsibility be pinpointed and conflicting orders, internecine warfare, and a host of other organizational ills be avoided.

Unity of command usually requires a chain of command, for in any large organization the person at the top cannot oversee all that is going on below. He or she needs others to help do this. Frequently, these helpers themselves cannot supervise all those beneath them. As a result, several echelons of command may emerge through which authority is supposed to pour or seep downward in a neat, orderly flow. With unity of command, the captain of A company does not give orders to the soldiers of B company. With chain of command, the battalion major does not give orders directly to soldiers from either company but works through their commanding officers. Even less structured organizations observe, at least to some degree, the same principle. The college dean, if he or she has reason to be disturbed by the behavior of a particular professor, will usually first contact the professor's department chairman before taking any direct action against the troublesome faculty member.

A third concept that the pyramidal structure spawns is span of control. Unlike the first two, this does not in itself constitute a principle but rather serves as a frame of reference. In other words, span of control is not something that the organization *ought* to have but something it *does* have. Span of control refers to the number of units, be they individuals or groups, that any supervising unit, be it an individual or a group, must oversee. The problem consists in making sure that the number of these subunits is neither too many nor too few—or, to put it differently, to make sure that the supervisor's span of control is neither too great nor too small.

How much is too great and how much is too small? Unfortunately, the slippery and shifty world of administration provides no hard-and-fast criteria for automatically determining such things. As with so many other questions concerning this capricious craft, the only intelligent answer is the highly unsatisfactory one "it all depends." The proper span of control hinges on the type of work being done, the type of employees doing it, the degree of geographical dispersion of the employees, and a multitude of other factors. And these factors often can be deceptive.

To take a hypothetical example, it would appear that a foreman who is overseeing a group of laborers performing routine chores in a compact work area would be able to supervise a greater number of people than can a senior scientist who is heading up a team of colleagues, each of whom is engaged separately in a unique and intricate task in various parts of a dispersed laboratory complex. But the situation can be reversed. The scientists can work on their own and may insist on doing so. The assembly-line workers, on the other hand, may dislike their work and even each other. Thus, the harried foreman's effective span of control may be less than that of the chief scientist.

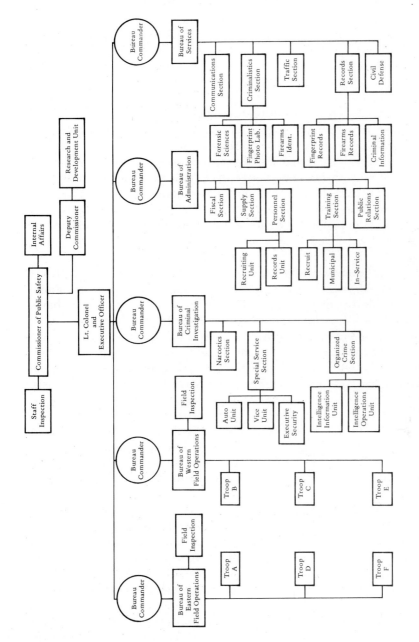

This is an organization chart of the Massachusetts State Police, a public agency that has 1,433 employees, of whom approximately 868 are troopers. The five bureau commanders hold the rank of major while captains head up six field troops as well as many of the other subunits. Each of the six troops consists of 33 men and women, including lieutenants and sergeants. Do the spans of control seem too broad or too narrow? Does the chain of command seem too short or too long? (*Source: Massachusetts Department of Public Safety.*)

Public administration in America has generally functioned with relatively narrow spans of control. It is rare to find a manager overseeing more than twelve subordinates or subunits, while it is not rare to find managers overseeing as few as three. In some cases union contracts limit spans of control by requiring a fixed ratio of supervisors to supervised. Police unions, for example, often insist on a sergeant for every eight and sometimes every seven police officers.

This situation has led to a proliferation of supervisors. It has been estimated that the ratio of supervisory to rank-and-file personnel in most government agencies is at least 50 percent greater than in private industry. At one time people joked that the Spanish army supposedly contained one officer for every three men. Today over half the men and women in the United States Army hold some kind of advanced rank.

For many years, however, the highest level of many governments often offered an exception to this tendency. Governors and big-city mayors frequently found themselves with an amazing array of agencies reporting and answering to them alone. But during the 1960s and 1970s several of these states and municipalities carried out far-ranging reorganizations, combining and consolidating agencies with the aim of making their governmental machinery more manageable. New York City, for instance, amalgamated over a hundred independent departments, bureaus, and offices into ten "superagencies" under the mayor's direct control.

That such consolidations can create problems as well as cure them came to light in 1970 when New York City's highly regarded commissioner of hospitals suddenly resigned. The real reason behind his resignation, so it was felt, lay in the new and diminished status that the reorganization had brought to him and his department. Previously he had reported directly to the mayor. But, since his department had now become a subunit of a "superagency," the city's new Department of Health Services, he reported to the health commissioner. This had curtailed the hospital head's access to the mayor and weakened his influence, hence his departure.

In reporting on the resignation, the *New York Times* raised some questions. "Have these superagencies, designed to encourage rational planning in city government, merely added to the red tape and imposed another bureaucratic layer between the city officials and the mayor? Have they discouraged able men from taking commissionerships? Is Mayor Lindsay, in fact, less accessible to his commissioners than was Mayor Robert F. Wagner?"[7]

Some of the questions that the critics and experts were raising regarding New York City's reorganization accomplishment had already been suggested by Herbert Simon nearly twenty-five years before. In a widely heralded article published in 1946, Simon challenged much of the con-

ventional wisdom regarding span of control. He noted that one of the
"proverbs of administration" calls for limiting the number of subordinates
and subordinate agencies that report directly to any one administrator.
But, he pointed out, this contradicted another proverb of administration,
that administrative efficiency will be increased "by keeping at a minimum the number of organizational levels through which a matter must
pass before it is acted upon."[8]

The tighter the span of control, the more numerous are the intervening
levels between top and bottom. This tends to increase both paperwork
and procrastination. It also leads to decisions being made and policies
being formulated too far from the scene of the action itself. And it leads,
as the New York City example brings out, to difficulties in acquiring and
retaining the services of top-notch people in vitally important but no
longer top-rated positions.

Simon's caveats and the New York City example may point up the difficulty of using span of control as a frame of reference, but they do not
render it useless. As with so much in public administration, it becomes a
question of finding a proper balance for each particular situation. In finding this balance, we must assess all the specific circumstances involved
and we must keep in mind that a gain achieved by moving in one direction will always be offset by *some* losses. These losses do not, however,
have to cancel out the gain completely. If an executive has one hundred
agencies under his or her tutelage, then some consolidation is nearly always called for, even at the expense of creating more administrative levels. However, every consolidation carries a price tag that we must be willing to pay if we wish to reap the benefits.

The span of control concept, it should be noted, is not the only point
about pyramids that has come under attack. The unity of command and
chain of command principles also present some problems. We will be in
a better position to evaluate these after we examine the meaning and import of the terms *line* and *staff*.

Line and Staff

The paradigm pyramids that we erected above in discussing Mafia families, infantry divisions, and large universities consist of what are called
line personnel. Unfortunately from the standpoint of neatness and order-
liness in model building, there is another group of people to be considered. These are the staff personnel. Again, as in the term *bureaucracy,* a
confusion in the use and meaning of words may arise. In ordinary discourse, we are accustomed to using the term *staff* to describe all the
working members of an organization. But in administration, *staff* has a

more specialized meaning, covering certain types of organizational personnel and not others.

Let us begin by first defining the line employees. They are the ones *directly* concerned with furthering the organization's goals. They catch the crooks, heal the sick, pave the roads. The staff people are supposed to help them accomplish such ends. Staff personnel draw up the job classifications, program the computers, provide the legal services, coordinate and check (if they do not actually set up) the budgets. The personnel, finance, legal, and other such units of an organization constitute its staff service, and it is their employees who are most accurately referred to as the "staff."

Viewed as organizations themselves, the staff units are usually formed on the basis of process. For example, the organization's computer center typically comprises a group of people engaged in the same process while serving, within the context of the larger organization in which they operate, a variety of purposes, places, and clienteles. In a school system, the center may be simultaneously preparing figures on attendance records for the superintendent and principals, correlating statistics on retarded children for the director of special education, and trying to pinpoint certain cost trends for the budgeting department. This last-named chore points up the fact that staff agencies may not only serve line departments but also other staff units.

The bureaucratic pyramid, in its most pure and pristine form, makes no provision for staff units and their personnel. And traditionally, they have played only a small and shadowy role in the functioning of work organizations. What place they occupied was usually at the hands or feet of the organization's leader, providing him with advice and assistance of various kinds. The boss of a Mafia family, to cite one traditionally structured organization, usually has a *consiglieri* or counselor. The *consiglieri* is most often a partially retired, older line official who now advises the boss but who gives no orders to anyone.

In modern times, staff services have increased tremendously and staff personnel have swollen in number. They are now occupying an ever-greater place in the organization's structure, playing an ever-greater role in its activities, and consuming an ever-greater chunk of its budget. In so doing, they are providing the organization with new strengths and also new problems.

The problems stem basically from what we noted at the outset—that the model pyramid makes no provision for staff units. It is hard, at times almost impossible, to establish their correct niche within the organization's hierarchy. Staff people tend to be specialists whose expertise does not lend itself to a scaled ranking except, possibly, within their own ranks. To phrase the problem in another way, the authority of a line unit is fairly definite. It knows which units are above it and which ones are below it. The authority of staff units is much more nebulous and elusive. Such authority will be determined by whatever need the line units have for the staff group at a particular time; the proficiency it can exercise in meeting this need; the administrative and, if you will, political skill with which it handles its relationships with other units within the organization; and a variety of other factors.

Underlying the uncertainties of this situation is the basic principle that specialization tends to destroy hierarchy. The more the members of an organization are differentiated from each other in terms of specific and separate skills, the harder it becomes to array them on a ladder like scale. For, as management expert Peter Drucker has pointed out, knowledge, in and of itself, knows no hierarchy. There are no higher or lower knowledges. Thus, the ever-increasing presence of staff people is disturbing and disrupting bureaucracy and bureaucratic organizations. More specifically, they are undermining the cherished bureaucratic principles of unity of command, chain of command, and span of control.

Once again, it was Herbert Simon who first called attention to this fact. In his article "The Proverbs of Administration" cited earlier, he pointed out that to the extent that specialization comes in through the organizational door, unity of command goes out the window. Unity of command requires one channel of authority but specialization creates several channels of authority. The specialists, in one form or another, start giving orders. The fact that these orders are not labeled as such and stem not from rank but from expertise does not fundamentally alter the situation. If the organization intends to use their energies and abilities, it must respond to what the specialists say. And to the extent that their capabilities are utilized, the authority of line personnel, particularly those in a supervisory capacity, is weakened and diminished.

Needless to add, this situation tends to generate a good deal of conflict. The staff are there to serve line personnel, and sometimes their activities are accepted as such. Indeed, at times, line people will complain or get annoyed at the staff people for not sharing enough responsibility. They will pressure the personnel department to handle some of their more ticklish employee-relations problems such as getting rid of an undesirable employee. More often, however, the line personnel resent and repel the intrusions of the staff people. To the liners, the activities of the staffers frequently seem more subversive than supportive.

It is easy to see how this works. The head of a hospital's radiology department wants to buy some new equipment, and she has in mind one particular make that she deems the most suitable for her purposes. But

the hospital's purchasing agent informs her that he must put his equipment order to bid and accept the lowest quotation submitted. Then the
radiology chief wants to hire a foreign-born radiologist who she feels
could be a valuable addition to her department. The hospital's personnel
department tells her that the person does not meet certain residency requirements. While worrying about these problems, the radiology chief
has to interrupt her work in order to supply certain data that the hospital's
computer center has asked for. (One of the lesser complaints of line people is that the staff personnel take up too much of their time.) At this
point, the chief radiologist wonders if things would be better if the hospital could do away with all these "outsiders" and let those whose task it
is to heal the sick get on with the job of doing so.

Other less overt problems also color and cloud line-staff relations. Felix
A. Nigro and Lloyd G. Nigro point out that staff employees are often
younger and better educated than line officials.[9] Both differences provide
a fertile terrain for the development of discord. When the line employees,
who are often old-timers, see the new "whiz kids" moving into high-pay-
ing jobs and starting to exercise authority over their activities, tensions
rise. What aggravates the situation still more is that the line personnel
fear, often with some justification, that the staff people will discover and
point up deficiencies in their work and behavior.

The Nigros point out, however, that staff personnel also have their
problems. The services they provide are indirect and often intangible.
Their work is not only hard to evaluate but hard to credit. They erect no
playgrounds, build no buildings, pave no roads. They do not even hand
out driver's licenses or public assistance checks. In short, they produce
no palpable products that the public can utilize, let alone admire. This, in
turn, often gives them another disadvantage vis-à-vis their confreres of the
line. The latter can and frequently do build a base of political support
among elected officials or among the organization's clientele. The staff
person largely remains excluded from such sources of organizational
strength.

Line officials themselves often are skilled in the ways of politics and in
some cases owe their positions to the use of such skills. They frequently
possess, or at least acquire, more dexterity in the handling of people
within the organization as well as without. In many cases, their ability at
organizational gamesmanship more than compensates, in terms of power
and position, for what they lose in lack of specialized expertise. They may
also be tougher and more ruthless than their staff peers. "You can always
tell a staff man," sneers line business executive Robert Townsend, "by
the number of people he has fired."[10]

To reduce the rivalry and rancor that may creep into line-staff relationships, organizations try to integrate the two as much as possible. They may make the staff people spend time familiarizing themselves with line functions and line personnel, sometimes to the point of requiring them to perform some line functions for specified periods of time. Or they may recruit their staff people from the ranks of the line personnel, giving them special training for their new positions. This is a practice that the Forest Service has used with some success. Unfortunately, however, this practice does not always provide the best trained or best qualified staff specialists. It also tends to make the organization too inbred, a problem we will examine in chapter 3.

As for handling the line personnel, organizations are supplying them with increasing doses of in-service training or encouraging them to take courses in outside educational institutions. One of the benefits of such educational programs is that the line people acquire more awareness and appreciation for the competencies of the staffers and the complexities of their work. The liners frequently find that their teachers and many of their fellow students will be staff personnel, and this helps build a base of understanding between the two groups.

The education of line personnel and the honing of their capacities illustrates a more fundamental trend leading to the gradual diminution of the gap between line and staff in modern administration. Both groups are actually becoming more alike. Staff employees are taking on quasi-line functions, while line employees are acquiring specializations associated with the staff. In many a large metropolitan high school, for example, the social worker and the guidance counselor are participating, to some degree, in the instructional process. The teachers, meanwhile, through becoming more specialized, are developing some of the attitudes and ambivalences of the staff. The teacher of retarded children may technically be a line employee. But he or she may feel, act, and relate to the organization in much the same way as a member of the staff.

Current organizational trends are, as Simon somewhat foresaw, making such concepts as unity of command, chain of command, and span of control less and less useful. Modern organizations are paying diminishing deference to such bureaucratic and hierarchical rules all the time. But though less useful than they have been, they are by no means obsolete. While all organization members must become more attuned to responding to diverse and occasionally divergent lines of authority as the various specialists make their weight felt, the need for at least a coordinating nexus will remain. And while span of control and chain of command may become more frequently disrupted, these concepts still cannot be completely ignored. There remains the need for some orderly flow of communication and authority within an organization. The modern administra-

tor confronts the challenge of retaining the basic benefits that these pyramidal points were designed to produce, while adapting to the requirements that an age of increasing specialization and innovation imposes. It
is no easy task. But, then, little that is worth doing in administration, or
anything else for that matter, ever is.

Centralization

One issue that has bothered and bewildered public managers since the
beginning of public organization is centralization. In early times their
concern focused largely on how to achieve it, for in those days even the
simplest communication between headquarters and field often took
weeks, months, or, in a few instances, years. Thus Egyptian pharaohs, Roman emperors, and Chinese mandarins spent a good deal of time wonder-
ing and worrying about how to get a handle on their distant subunits and
subordinates.

In more recent times the emphasis has shifted. Now the number-one
concern often centers on how much centralization should be achieved.
For centralization is no longer viewed as an unmixed blessing. In fact its
opposite, decentralization, has become the watchword, if not the battle
cry, of many theorists and practitioners involved in the administrative
craft.

In the previous chapter we saw how decentralization has characterized
our country's *political* system since its very inception. But while such political decentralization may facilitate and foster *administrative* decentralization, it does not necessarily insure it, at least not in all instances. Political decentralization calls for policies to be developed as much as
possible at the lower levels (the "grassroots"). Administrative decentralization requires that those organizations charged with carrying out these
policies allow their subunits a large area of autonomy in interpreting and
applying them. When a city institutes, say, its own health program, we
can call this an example of political decentralization at work. But if its
health department refuses to set up neighborhood centers or, if it does,
insists that even their most minor decisions must be made at headquarters, then we cannot say the program is administratively decentralized.

As should be evident, centralization and decentralization are relative
terms. Virtually every organization of any size and scope must to some extent decentralize, for once it sets up subunits of any kind it must grant
them some degree of discretion in carrying out their functions. The question therefore becomes one of deciding how far this discretion should go.
Many argue that it should be pushed to the maximum limits, and they can
muster some good arguments to support their case.

Decentralization

Decentralization and Its Delights

Decentralization tends to encourage flexibility. The closer decisions are made to the scene, the more likely that such decisions will be characterized by suppleness and speed. The decision makers can take into account those factors affecting their particular situation and act accordingly. Decentralization provides for the fact that conditions, problems, and people are not everywhere the same.

In stimulating quicker and more flexible decision making, decentralization may improve the decision-making process. "We have learned," wrote Douglas McGregor, "that if we push decision-making in an organization as far down as we possibly can, we tend to get better decisions." McGregor, an enthusiastic advocate of decentralization, did not stop there, however. He also claimed that decentralization improved not only the quality of the decisions but the quality of the decision makers. "People tend to grow and develop more rapidly and they are motivated more effectively" when decision making becomes decentralized, he maintained.[11]

There is undoubtedly some truth in McGregor's assertion. Allocating more authority to those farther down the line or out in the field makes their jobs more challenging and interesting. In this manner, the decentralized organization may find it not only easier to hone the capacities of its employees, but also to recruit and retain high-caliber personnel. Topnotch people do not like to work for organizations that curtail the scope of their initiative and enterprise. Consequently, they are not likely to be attracted to organizations that are close-fisted when it comes to conferring discretion.

While decentralization seems to benefit subordinates and subunits, it can improve conditions at the center as well. It reduces the burden of decision making and control at headquarters, giving its personnel more time to concentrate on formulating policy and shaping programs. We have already seen the importance of free time in fulfilling the functions of leadership. Decentralization can confer increased amounts of this valuable commodity on those who need it most.

Many of the advocates of decentralization go further and point out ways in which it can alleviate the work load throughout the organization. A decision that must be referred from field office to headquarters leads to more work all the way along the line. The field office must communicate to headquarters, and headquarters must communicate back to the field. The work of both has thus been increased. If the field office can make the decision on its own, then the matter stops right there. There is less paperwork for both units, and the problem of communication overload is alleviated.

A remarkable example of this principle at work is provided by Sir Ian Hamilton in his memoirs of British army life in India at the turn of the century. His experience involves only two people, but it illustrates the same principle that so often rules relations between headquarters and subunit operations.

> In 1896 I was Deputy Quartermaster-General at Simla; then, perhaps still, one of the hardest worked billets in Asia. After a long office day I used to get back home to dinner pursued by a pile of files three to four feet high. The Quartermaster-General, my boss, was a clever, delightful work-glutton. So we sweated and ran together for a while a neck and neck race with our piles of files, but I was the younger and he was the first to be ordered off by the doctors to Europe. Then I, at the age of forty-three, stepped into the shoes and became officiating Quartermaster-General in India. Unluckily, the Government at that moment was in a very stingy mood. They refused to provide pay to fill the post I was vacating and Sir George White, the Commander-in-Chief, asked me to duplicate myself and do the double work. My heart sank, but there was nothing for it but to have a try. The day came; the Quartermaster-General went home and with him went the whole of his share of the work. As for my own share, the hard twelve hours' task melted by some magic into the Socialist's dream of a six hours' day. How was that? Because, when a question came up from one of the Departments I had formerly been forced to compose a long minute [memorandum] upon it, explaining the case, putting my own views, and endeavoring to persuade the Quartermaster-General to accept them. He was a highly conscientious man and if he differed from me he liked to put on record his reasons—several pages of reasons. Or, if he agreed with me, still he liked to agree in his own words and to "put them on record." Now, when I became Quartermaster-General and Deputy-Quartermaster General rolled into one I studied the case as formerly, but there my work ended: I had not to persuade my own subordinates: I had no superior except the Commander-in-Chief, who was delighted to be left alone: I just gave an order—quite a simple matter unless a man's afraid: "Yes," I said, or "No!"[12]

Finally, decentralization may facilitate and foster more rapport with the organization's clientele. Subunits such as field offices are obviously in a better position most of the time to know what the special needs of their own clientele may be. With more authority in their hands, they can respond to these needs more effectively. The clientele, on its part, will frequently find it easier to communicate its desires and demands to a branch office in its own area than to a central office far away.

Decentralization and Its Disappointments

While the case for decentralization seems quite compelling, there remains some less appealing aspects to be considered. For one thing, decentralization curbs specialization. The large unit can develop and retain a much greater variety and depth of expertise than can the subunit. A simple and hypothetical, though essentially realistic, example will illustrate this problem.

A city may have a choice between maintaining a central health center with ten doctors or operating ten smaller neighborhood health centers with one doctor each. If the latter option is chosen, then obviously each doctor must to a great extent be a general practitioner, able to deal with a variety of health problems. If the centralized center is chosen, then it becomes possible to employ a pediatrician, gerontologist, et cetera. The centralized health unit can offer a variety of services that the neighborhood units cannot hope to provide without substantial increases in the overall health services budget.

This brings us to another aspect of the question. Operating the ten neighborhood centers is likely to be more expensive. It may require ten different custodians to take care of the physical plant of these centers, while one large facility, though it might need more than one such custodian, would probably require fewer than ten. The combined heating bills for these neighborhood centers will likewise be much greater than the heating cost of one larger unit. Perhaps more important is the expense of sophisticated medical equipment that may be required but that would not be in constant use at a local health center. Thus, for these and many other reasons, it should be possible to provide greatly increased health services for the same amount of money if the service remains centralized.

The potential economies from centralization should not be exaggerated. Centralization itself has its costs, and these tend to become greater the more extensive it becomes. Any function can be centralized only just so far, and then any economies produced start to diminish and finally turn negative. Still, centralization does permit a grouping of activities, bulk purchases of supplies, the use of heavy equipment such as large computers, and other practices that can lower overall costs.

Centralization can also open up as well as seal off opportunities for the organization's personnel. As we have already seen, it allows more chances for a person to develop specialized skills and to work with others in his or her specialty. It may also simplify and expedite transfers from one subunit to another. A caseworker employed in a municipal welfare system may find it hard and almost impossible to move if she discovers, for example, that she has few opportunities for promotion at her present job or that she cannot get along with her boss. In a statewide system, she can more easily relocate to another office in another locality.

The United States correctional system offers an illustrative example of some of the drawbacks that decentralization may present. In writing about prisons, former Attorney General Ramsey Clark notes "some 125,000 employees are scattered through an impossible maze of jurisdictions throughout the country. Jails across the street from each other—one run by the county, the other by the city—are still commonplace. The time spent moving prisoners from one facility to another and the risk involved each time are reasons enough to abolish one. . . ." Clark then goes on to say, "Local prisons do not, and in the nature of things cannot, have the staff, the range of skills or the number of prisoners necessary to provide the services required. They are less able to provide the special services needed by female and juvenile offenders.[13] It is for reasons such as these that Clark advocates statewide prison systems.

Lacking centralization, an organization may experience a lot of expensive and injurious duplication. A study of a Michigan high school that allowed its teachers considerable leeway in picking their books found that the seniors had read George Orwell's *Animal Farm* three times, once in an English course, once in a government course, and once in a social relations course. Some of the seniors had also read Hawthorne's *The Scarlet Letter* three times. John Lindsay, on becoming mayor of New York City, found that three city departments maintained street paving programs and that eight departments ran youth programs. Not one of them knew what the others were doing.[14]

Those who distrust decentralization even find its presumed virtues a cause for concern. A subunit in a decentralized organizational setting may achieve more closeness to its clientele, but, they ask, is this always a good thing? The clientele may have ideas of its own that run contrary to the interest of the broader public, which the organization is supposed to serve.

The Forest Service has been sensitive for a long time to the decentralization issue, and it is an additional reason why the service rotates its rangers as a regular policy. The Forest Service is afraid that they will become "captured," as it were, by their immediate constituencies, thus doing damage to its proclaimed ideal of providing the greatest good to the greatest number. Herbert Kaufman, in his study of the rangers, found that this fear was no idle concern.[15]

Kaufman reports that one ranger who was an active member of the local chamber of commerce in his district mentioned how he "looked the other way" when he thought the business group was operating a resort area without the rather expensive liability insurance required under the terms of its special-use permit. Another ranger sought to dispose of timber through many small sales. This allowed many local people to bid for the wood, but it involved more paper work for the service and brought lower prices to the government. At least one ranger allowed grazing permits for small herds to help local farmers, another permitted a dump to continue, and so forth. If the Forest Service, with its high degree of cohesion, is still vulnerable to constituency capture, one can imagine what can happen to other organizations whose members have not been so heavily imbued with an organization's ideals and codes and who are not subject to regular rotation.

What makes the problem of constituency capture still more serious is that in many cases it is not the entire constituency that does the capturing. Usually, a subunit becomes most susceptible to influence from only the more articulate and aggressive elements among its clientele. And these elements may have interests that not only diverge from the general public, which is paying the bills, but may even contradict the interests of the majority of the other clients. For example, an organization of nursing home operators will usually exert much more pressure on a local administrator than will their patients. And the interests of the operators often conflict with the interests of those entrusted to their care.

Of course, client groups sometimes do exercise undue pressure at headquarters as well as on the field office, but it is usually much more difficult for them to do so. This is true for a variety of reasons. For one thing, people removed from the scene are likely to be more neutral and impartial. Familiarity may confer knowledge; it also engenders entanglements. In one of Voltaire's short stories, entitled "La Vision de Babouc," there is the following dialogue between the protagonist and an angel who wishes to send him to Persia:

> But, seigneur, said Babouc humbly, I have never been in Persia; I don't know anyone there.
>
> So much the better, said the angel, you will not be partial.

It is for this reason that when the Italian police recruit a young man from, say, Naples, they will, after his training, send him to serve in Genoa. A Genoan, on the other hand, may find himself policing Naples. The lack of intimate knowledge and associations with the area he polices enables the Italian police officer to enforce the law, so it is felt, without fear or favor.

Another factor that contributes to the vulnerability of subunits to clientele capture is that such subunits are often less visible and less easily held to account by the public, politicians, and the press. Let us go back to our hypothetical health centers. If the city decides to maintain one central health facility, then it becomes much easier for everyone concerned to determine just what the city's health department is doing and how well it is doing it. If it decentralizes into ten centers, then the local newspaper, the city councillor, and the interested citizen must try to keep tabs on ten times as many operations. Furthermore, since none of these neighborhood centers would be nearly as important as one central health center, none will arouse much outside interest generally.

This lack of visibility permits and even encourages abuses. With the press, the public, and others giving less attention to the individual, decentralized facility, other interest groups will usually find it easier to exercise influence. And since the local administrator will lack the support as well as the control, which a higher-visibility operation tends to evoke, the administrator may become more and more disposed to yield to neighborhood pressures. If the entire neighborhood becomes concerned with the center, this is one thing. However, it is unlikely that it will. Indeed, the neighborhood residents will probably not know too much about it, since each center, as we have seen, will not be receiving much attention from the news media, city councillors, and others, because it is only a neighborhood institution. As a result, those with the most direct interest in the center, such as those seeking certain forms of patronage, may become the center's "public."

An example of the kind of disaster that decentralization can create is offered by an experiment that New York City launched in the late 1960s. Confronted with a crisis-ridden school system, the city decided to break it up into over thirty fairly separate districts. The scheme won the enthusiastic endorsement of the Ford Foundation, the local press, civil rights groups, and other reform-minded people.

The plan was to allow the new local districts as much autonomy as possible, with each to have its own superintendent hired by its own elected school committee. "If it works in Scarsdale," said one of the slogans used by its sponsors, "then it can work for Ocean Hill"—the latter being one of the city's low-income sections that would be "liberated" through decentralization.

Difficulties developed from the very beginning. Despite a plethora of publicity, only 15 percent of the eligible voters turned out for the first local school board elections. Each election after that brought a further dropoff in participation, so that by the 1979 election, less than 9 percent of the city's electorate were casting ballots. Small and often selfish cliques came to dominate many of the school districts, and all kinds of irregularities in budgeting and personnel practices developed. Resistance to integration grew stronger, while reading and other academic scores went down.

There was a marked increase in conflict within the school system. Local groups of residents fought each other for control of school budgets. Black groups battled with the teacher's union over personnel policies. Superintendents struggled against school boards seeking to strip them of their powers.

Costs mounted apace. By 1977 New York City was spending about five hundred dollars per pupil per year more than most other big-city school systems. Yet its net spending per pupil for instruction, guidance and career planning came to substantially less than the national average. The discrepancy lay in administrative costs created by decentralization. New York City had one school administrator for every 208 students while the average for eighteen other major cities was one for every 632.

Despite such calamitous consequences, the system stays in existence with no serious efforts being made to change it. Those who supported its creation, while they have long stopped singing its praises, understandably dislike admitting their error. And, of course, the bureaucratic pathologies of conservation and survival will, in the absence of determined pressure to the contrary, keep it in operation. And so the system continues to function today, a superb example not only of the dilemmas inherent in decentralization, but, more generally, of how the hopes of the best and the brightest can so often light the way to disillusionment of despair.[16]

CASE STUDY

HUD Goes to the Grass Roots[17]

In 1969 George Romney took over the reins of the U.S. Department of Housing and Urban Development. He did so with a burst of enthusiasm and elan. Not only was HUD one of the newest federal agencies—it had been formally created only four years before—but it was one with a most challenging and timely mission. He was eager to see what it, and he, could do.

Right away, however, he found himself faced with formidable problems. Though comparatively recent in origin, HUD had already become bogged down in paperwork and procrastination. It was administering a potpourri of programs and, apparently, not administering most of them very well.

Romney looked to decentralization to supply part of the solution. As president of American Motors, he had used this device to help bring the beleaguered automaker back to profitability. And his subsequent experience as a quite successful governor of Michigan had persuaded him that the grass roots could and should play a greater role in governmental activity.

His first move was to get control of his department's far-flung operations by centralizing all power in his own office. This may seem a strange way to decentralize, but actually it is generally recognized as a necessary first step in undertaking such a process. A person or an office must possess authority before it can be given away. Romney's first initiative therefore was to make sure his office possessed authority by curtailing some of the discretion exercised by the agency's ten regional offices and its functional units in Washington.

Romney then gave away a goodly amount of this authority to some seventy-seven HUD local field offices. "HUD employees at the area offices," he told researcher John Rouse, "are more familiar with local conditions and are in better positions to make judgements on HUD's programs and to be most effective with these programs. The local employees work closely with the local government leadership and are able to involve local officials in the decision-making process. The local HUD employees are more informed with respect to local conditions."

About half of these field offices would handle only the department's mortgage-insurance program. The other half would operate all the agency's other programs, such as model cities, urban renewal, public housing, etc. Since these offices would of necessity be more thinly staffed than the ten large regional offices that had previously discharged such functions, they would not have the in-depth specialization that the latter had enjoyed. Area office employees would therefore have to be generalists, with both the right and the responsibility to carry out or to oversee, as the case may be, a large and rather diverse number of activities in their locales.

The decentralization scheme went into effect, and soon a network of local offices were handling most of HUD's ordinary business. In the process, these offices and their employees were making numerous decisions affecting the shape and fate of the department's programs in their respective areas.

How did it work out? Rouse's study, carried out five years later, attempts to supply some answers. In the process it also sheds some light on the dilemmas of decentralization.

In polling HUD employees Rouse found mixed reactions to the experiment. As might be expected, area office employees responded more positively than did regional office employees, for much of the authority gained by the former was at the expense of the latter. But even the area office employees gave decentralizaton a rather spotty scorecard. For example, only a bare plurality said that their contacts with state and local officials had increased, and while 37 percent said such contacts had become more cooperative, 44 percent said they had not.

Did decentralization benefit their own careers? Some 46 percent of area office employees said yes, but almost as many, 40 percent, said no. Almost two-thirds expressed a wish for still more decentralization, but many also indicated reservations. "The wisdom of decentralization was often met with skepticism in the field," reports Rouse. "The necessity of decentralization was always in question."

It should come as no surprise that employees at the regional offices showed still less enthusiasm for the new arrangement. Only one out of five felt it helped their careers, and a full three-quarters did not wish to see it carried any further. Rouse speculates, on the basis of his study, that tensions between field and region may have increased under decentralization.

These mixed feelings were also voiced by many state and local officials who dealt with the federal agency. "The best feature of the area office concept," said a midwestern official, "is the interface, the direct, one-to-one contact where problems are administrative in nature. The Area Office concept facilitates the ease of administration." But, he went on to point out, "the majority of HUD's thrust has been lost in developing program objectives since the area offices were established. The interpretation of programs is vastly different among states and area offices."

Another official, this one from a southern state, was unqualifiedly negative in his assessment. "Bureaucratic layering has resulted from decentralization," he claimed. "The clarity of decision-making was better when the regional office was in charge. The regional office decision-making is probably more cost-effective, provides better economies of scale and there existed clearer responsibility for decision-making. . . . Sometimes you never know who is making decisions."

Since even under decentralization HUD could not afford to operate an office in every community using its services, some communities felt terribly shortchanged. For example, Knoxville, in eastern Tennessee, was made the site of the state area office, while Memphis, in western Tennessee, had to be content with a program representative. Memphis officials found they now had to work through four levels of HUD—the local program representative, the Knoxville office, the regional office in Atlanta, and Washington—rather than the three levels that previously existed. What's more, the Atlanta regional office, with which they had previously done business, was closer and more convenient than Knoxville. "Memphis has not been helped by decentralization," complained one official. "It is easier to fly to the regional office in Atlanta." Moreover, "the quality of employees at the area office is not as good as that of the Atlanta regional office. The difference is that the area office people are not as well acquainted with the programs."

This last point touches on a sore spot alluding to many others. As "generalists," area office personnel lacked the necessary knowledge to deal with all the complexities contained in HUD's various programs. As one employee put it, "HUD is now operating like the post office. If you want a ten cent stamp, you go to one window. If you want a 50 cent stamp, you go to the same window. General Motors does not operate in this manner. Different programs appeal to different user groups."

Some local officials also expressed dismay over the additional costs that, in their view, decentralization must have entailed. More local offices meant that a greater share of HUD's budget had to go to paying the administrative expense involved in staffing and maintaining them. This, so they reasoned, made less money available for the programs themselves. One maintained that HUD's clients were "getting the shaft," while another labeled the scheme the "Romney Follies."

But not all those who did business with HUD deplored the new decentralization. "HUD employees are well aware of what our problems are and know our city's needs," remarked a director of human resources for a moderate-size midwestern city. "The closer to the action that you can get, the better response and personal contact one enjoys. Previously we had to go to Dallas for everything. Calling the shots from Dallas for several states is ridiculous. It's comparable to coaching a football team from Dallas."

Another local administrator echoed these sentiments. "The area office is in touch immediately with community problems. The area office director understands local problems and the local governments have the director's attention." This official felt that HUD's headquarters people were making scapegoats of the area offices to hide their own deficiencies.

Rouse's polls of HUD employees can also be interpreted as showing some measure of success for the decentralization effort. To be sure, no absolute majority believed that the agency's contacts and cooperation with local public managers increased appreciably. Still, substantial numbers did express such an opinion. They vastly outnumbered those few who felt that the agency's relationships with its local clientele had actually declined. (The rest felt that it merely had remained much the same.)

Finally, one should note that decentralization could not, in a sense, have come at a worse time. Just a year before it began, Congress had passed the ambitious Housing and Urban Development Act of 1968, which had given the department many new and nettlesome responsibilities. Furthermore, the department was called upon to discharge these responsibilities under difficult conditions, including inadequate funding and rising interest rates.

In summing up his study of the agency's adventurous attempt to decentralize, Rouse poses the crucial question: "Is HUD, as a federal department, better off because of decentralization?" He then answers it in these somewhat equivocal words "Well, yes and no." The yes comes from the fact that the handling of many routine, though often irksome, administrative matters, such as minor budget alterations, interpretation of grant-in-aid contracts, and the overseeing of basic procedures, may have improved; No comes from the fact that problems touching on fundamental program issues may have increased. Certainly administrative decentralization can be a feasible as well as desirable goal. In fact, as some of the material to be covered later will make clear, it may even be a necessary one. But it must be approached with caution and care. As Rouse puts it, "Centralization and decentralization require a good balance between the two concepts; and they demand no letup in administrative skill to achieve the proper bureaucratic balance."

Notes

1. Luther Gulick and L. Urwick, *Papers on the Science of Administration* (New York: Institute of Public Administration, 1937), 15.

2. For a more detailed critique of the various bases of organization, see Schuyler C. Wallace, *Federal Decentralization* (New York: Columbia University Press, n.d.), 91–146.

3. *Hoover Commission Report* (New York: McGraw-Hill, 1948), 24.

4. "Role of the Schools: Should They Be Totally Involved in a Child's Life?" *New York Times*, 24 January 1971, News in Review section.

5. Donald R. Cressey, *Theft of the Nation* (New York: Harper & Row, 1969), chap. 6.

6. Alexander Hamilton, John Jay, and James Madison, *The Federalist* (New York: Modern Library, n.d.), 455.

7. *New York Times*, 5 March 1970.

8. Herbert A. Simon, "The Proverbs of Administration," *Public Administration Review* (Winter 1946).

9. Felix A. Nigro and Lloyd G. Nigro, *Modern Public Administration*, 3rd ed. (New York: Harper & Row, 1973), 122.

10. Robert Townsend, "Up the Organization," *Harper's Magazine,* (March 1970).

11. Douglas McGregor, *Leadership and Motivation* (Cambridge, Mass.: MIT Press, 1966), 121.

12. Sir Ian Hamilton, *The Soul and Body of An Army* (London: E. Arnold, 1921), pp. 235–236, quoted in Herbert A. Simon, *Administrative Behavior* (New York: Free Press, 1947).

13. Ramsey Clark, *Crime in America* (New York: Simon and Schuster, 1970), 234.

14. Nat Hentoff, *A Political Life: The Education of John V. Lindsay* (New York: Alfred A. Knopf, 1969), 91.

15. Herbert Kaufman, *The Forest Ranger* (Baltimore, Md.: Johns Hopkins Press, 1960), 76–80.

16. For a report on the system's administrative costs, see *New York Times,* 20 June 1977. Other accounts of the system's problems will be found in numerous other editions of the *Times* during the 1970s. See, for example, the issues of 2 May, 3 May, and 5 May 1973, 24 December 1974, 10 December 1978, among others. Also see Diane Ravitch, "Community Control Revisited," in *Commentary,* February, 1972.

17. Material for following case study is drawn from John E. Rouse, Jr., "Administrative Decentralization as a Complement to Revenue Sharing: A Case Study of the HUD Programs" (Paper presented to the annual meeting of the American Political Science Association, Chicago, 1975).

3

The Physiology
of Organization

Early writers on organization were largely concerned with questions of structure. They tended to believe that any organization would function well if only it were well designed. One of the earliest and most influential of such thinkers was Frederick W. Taylor, a steel mill laborer who worked his way up to the rank of chief engineer. In his climb to the top, Taylor felt he had learned the basic secrets of good organization, and he incorporated his ideas into a book that he published in 1911. His short work, *The Principles of Scientific Management*, became extraordinarily influential.

Taylor claimed that there was "one best way" for doing every job and that it could be determined through scientific and systematic study. He believed ardently in task specialization and maintained that each job should be broken down to its smallest component before being assigned to one or more men. The assembly line may be viewed as a triumph of Taylorism. While he did not completely neglect the behavioral side of administration, he felt that high wages would generally suffice to elicit employee cooperation and compliance. And since any organization that structured itself along the lines he suggested would automatically be in a better position to pay such higher wages, scientific management, in Taylor's view, would eliminate nearly all causes of dispute and disagreement between employees and employers.

Taylor's ideas acquired their greatest popularity in the business world, but the same basic approach, that is, viewing administration as a matter of constructing scientifically thought-out organizational arrangements, permeated public administration theory as well. As early as 1887, a brilliant young professor of government named Woodrow Wilson wrote that public administration, like any field of business, could be organized strictly on a technical basis.[1] Such extraneous factors as politics need not intrude, for, said Wilson, public administration was a part of politics only as the methods of the countinghouse were a part of society or as machinery was part of the product it manufactured. By the early 1900s, Max Weber seemed to see such a development emerging in public administration. His bureaucratic model, with its emphasis on such things as hierarchy, systematized procedures, and formalized rules, seemed to embody many of the basic approaches, or at least attitudes, of Taylor's scientific management.

In 1926 L. D. White published the first American textbook on public administration.[2] Basing himself on the premise that administration was destined to remain the central problem of modern government, White claimed that it was essentially a single process that was applicable everywhere. Its objective was efficiency, and in striving to achieve this objective, it could at least aspire to becoming a science. Although his book did not slight the role of theory and values in the administrative process, he felt that these would be obtained from political science. Social and emotional factors played small roles in White's administrative world.

But while White, following in the path of Wilson and Weber, was attempting to construct a field of public administration along systematic and somewhat mechanical lines, a social worker and educator named Mary Parker Follett was marching to the beat of a different drummer. Follett had become impressed with the psychological factors that she had seen at work in her active life as an organizer of evening schools, recreation agencies, and employment bureaus, and as a member of statutory wage boards. Already the author of two books on political science, *The New State* and *Creative Experience,* she embarked on a series of speculations in the 1920s that were to signal the advent of a new era in administrative theory.

In various papers and articles, Follett depicted administration as being essentially involved with reconciling individuals as well as social groups. An organization's principal problems, in her view, consisted not only in determining what it wanted its employees to do, but in guiding and controlling their conduct in such a way as to get them to do it. And this, she indicated, was a much more complex task than previous writers had suggested. Follett not only anticipated what was to become the human relations school of administration, she also foreshadowed the humanistic school that was to grow out of it. She urged organizations to stop trying to suppress the differences that may arise within their boundaries. Instead, they should seek to integrate these differences and thereby allow them to contribute to the organization's growth and development. She advocated replacing the "law of authority" with the "law of the situation," and she admonished organizations to exercise "power *with*" rather than "power *over*" their members.[3]

While Follett's writings did not go unnoticed, they failed to score the impact that similar ideas would later achieve. This was perhaps due partly to the fact that she was a woman writing in a society that was not yet attuned to taking women thinkers too seriously. A more severe and serious obstacle, however, may have been the fact that she was an iconoclast, challenging the sacred credos of her time. However, in 1932, one year after her death, the hallowed principles of scientific management received a more shaking jolt. A team of researchers headed by Harvard Business School Professor Elton Mayo completed five years of study at the Hawthorne plant of the Western Electric Company.[4] Their research showed that many problems of worker-management relations resulted not from insufficient task specialization or inadequate wages, but from social and psychological forces that were often quite complex. The "Hawthorne experiments," as they were subsequently to be known, constituted the first systematic research to expose the "human factor" in work situations. The study marked a major turning point in the history of administrative theory and practice.

The role of the human factor in administrative thought gained further emphasis and importance when Chester Barnard published his landmark work *The Functions of the Executive* in 1938. Barnard was a former president of the New Jersey Bell Telephone Company who had also served as state director of the New Jersey Relief Administration. Basing himself on his rich background in the practical world, supplemented by some wide-ranging reading and some serious thinking, Barnard attempted to set forth an all-embracing theory of organization. He defined organizations as co-operative and essentially dynamic systems that are engaged in a process of continual readjustment to their physical, biological, and social environments. The theoretical framework he set up was quite complex and not completely successful, but his work contained many new mind-opening insights, some of which we will be drawing upon later in this chapter.

Follett, Mayo, and Barnard were followed in the 1940s by numerous other thinkers and researchers, including Dwight Waldo, William H. Whyte, and, perhaps most notable of all, Herbert A. Simon.[5] The latter's brilliant 1947 book *Administrative Behavior* rigorously challenged the sacred tenets of scientific management and opened additional vistas in this new area of human endeavor. From then on the writers and researchers become too numerous to mention, but some notice must be given to the humanistic school of administration, which began to emerge in the 1950s and which has been receiving increased attention in recent years. Pioneered by such people as Chris Argyris, Douglas McGregor, and Rensis Likert, humanistic theory accepted wholly the human relations component in administration but carried it still further, arguing for a more humanitarian approach to the whole administrative problem.[6] The humanistic school bases itself on the following assumptions:

• People are not naturally passive, lazy, and dumb; on the contrary, they are generally eager for opportunities to show initiative and to bear responsibility.
• Work is a natural activity, and people by nature want to perform it.
• People work best in an environment that treats them with regard and respect and encourages them to develop and utilize their abilities.
• There is no inherent and intrinsic conflict between the goals of the organization and the goals of the individual member. Meeting the goals of the individual will only make the organization itself more productive.

A still newer approach to administration appeared on the scene in the 1960s with the development of systems analysis. Systems analysis, with its elaborate diagrams, mathematical symbols, and somewhat obscure and obtuse jargon, tends to frighten off some students. Yet its essentials are fairly easy to grasp. In terms of administration, it views organizations as systems that absorb "inputs" and disgorge "outputs." The inputs largely take the form of demands and resources. To these are added "within-puts," which are new resources and/or demands generated inside the organization as it processes its initial inputs. The outputs can also take many forms, including some that were not intended. Furthermore, the outputs affect future inputs, thus providing a "feedback loop."

Within the organizational system, several subsystems or structures are at work. These include the production or technical system, which carries out the organization's main mission; its maintenance and support systems, which keep the organization itself functioning; and the adaptive system, which helps it adjust to new factors and forces. Every organization strives to achieve a balance among its subsystems as well as among all the other conflicting influences that continually threaten to disturb and disrupt its equilibrium. Its basic goal is to maintain itself in a steady state called homeostasis. Its survival hinges on its ability to achieve equilibrium as well as on its ability to ward off disorganization and disintegration (entropy). This it seeks to do by importing more resources than it expends.[7]

It is important to underscore the fact that the systems-analysis school and the humanistic school are extensions of rather than deviations from the human relations movement. Not only are they not in conflict with the human relations approach, but they are also not necessarily in conflict with one another. One of the most valuable books to emerge in administrative behavior in more recent years has been *The Social Psychology of Organizations,* by Daniel Katz and Robert L. Kahn. A model of the human relations approach, their work utilizes systems analysis to present much research and data that support the humanistic viewpoint. (It will be referred to frequently throughout the following pages.)

A more important and much more obvious point to bear in mind is that the field of organizational behavior is extraordinarily rich and complex, and new developments are occurring in it all the time. In this chapter we will be concerned with only three aspects of the subjects—motivation, the role of the informal organization, and organizational pathologies—and even these will be treated in rather summary fashion. Subsequent chapters will also draw on materials in this field, but no introductory text can substitute for some well-rounded reading. This would include reading the authors previously mentioned as well as regular perusal of such magazines as *Public Administration Review,* published by the American Society of Public Administration, and *Personnel,* published by the American Management Association. The student may find the field of organization physiology not only highly important but highly intriguing as well.

Motivating People

When, at the beginning of the book, we analyzed our two men moving a stone, we failed to answer a very vital question: What induced them to lift the stone in the first place? This question brings us to the very core of the organizational problem. In order for an organization to function, indeed in order for it to exist, people must be willing and able to do the things it wants them to do. Thus, a primary task for any organization is to develop ways to motivate its members to fulfill the organization's purpose and pursuits.

It is no easy task. By the mid-1930s, Chester Barnard was able to note that "if all those who may be considered potential contributors to an organization are arranged in order of willingness to serve it, the scale gradually descends from possibly intense willingness through neutral or zero willingness to opposition or hatred." Barnard then went on to add (and the emphasis is his) *"The preponderance of persons in a modern society always lies on the negative side* with reference to any particular existing or potential organization. Thus of the possible contributors only a small minority actually have a positive willingness."[8]

Barnard further pointed out that while some would always feel more organizational loyalty than others, not only would they amount to less than a majority, but their positive feelings would also suffer lapses. Their loyalty would fluctuate depending on time, circumstance, etc. Consequently, any work organization confronts a basic dilemma. Its processes and pursuits usually require a stable and uniform degree of commitment, but those who are supposed to render this commitment often have quite different ideas.

MILES LAW

Rufus E. Miles, Jr. proudly claims to have parented Miles Law. The law states simply that "where you stand depends on where you sit."

Miles says he discovered the law while serving as a division director of the former Bureau of the Budget. He noted that a budget examiner might be a constant critic of an agency whose budget he oversaw, yet if the examiner were to be later hired away by the agency, he or she would promptly do a 180-degree turn and become one of the agency's most adamant advocates. Thus, what position a bureaucrat takes depends on what position he or she is in, or "where you stand depends on where you sit."

Miles also likes to point out how John Gardner, as chairman of President Johnson's Task Force on Education, authored a report strongly favoring the removal of education from the Department of Health, Education and Welfare. Shortly thereafter Gardner was appointed secretary of HEW. When asked whether he now planned to push for education's removal from HEW, he firmly and flatly rejected any such nonsensical idea.

Some writers have approached the question and its potential answers from the standpoint of what might be called needs fulfillment. In their view, formal organizations motivate their members by trying to meet certain of the members' needs. These needs are classified in varying ways, but perhaps four basic categories can be distinguished: material needs, social and emotional needs, ego needs, and a fourth category, which one writer, Chris Argyris, calls "self-actualization" needs.

Before going on to discuss these various needs and the ways organizations seek to accommodate them, we should take note of a further aspect to this subject. The late psychologist Abraham M. Maslow maintained that one's needs formed an ascending scale, with each need more basic than the next. In this manner, a person first wishes to gratify physical needs; that is, he or she wants the physical means to survive. Once that need has been met, he or she wants to have safety or security needs accommodated, and so on up the ladder. Thus, fulfilling certain primary needs only brings other needs to the fore. Or, looked at in another way, certain "higher" needs are not even perceived by an employee until his or her various "lower" needs have been met.[9]

Many writers on administration, most notably Douglas McGregor, became attracted to Maslow's "hierarchy of needs" theory and swallowed it whole. Others, however, have remained skeptical that man's needs could be grouped or scaled in such a fashion. There is research to support both sides. This book will try to sidestep the entire controversy. For our purposes, the examination of human needs and their meaning for organizational motivation will be put into the four basic areas already mentioned, with no attempt made to claim that any one need is "higher" or "lower" than another, although the material itself may suggest such a hypothesis.

Material Needs

Meeting its members' material needs must perforce be for the average work organization its most basic means of motivating these members to work. Certainly, few employees are in a position to devote their full-time efforts to any work organization without receiving a paycheck in return. They will, however, give the organization that employs them a certain minimum of effort in order to obtain the wherewithal to support themselves and their families. In this sense, material needs can claim top priority in motivating people to help carry out organizational purposes.

There is little dispute over this rather elementary fact. The question that does arise is just how much will employees give of themselves for such material-needs fulfillment alone? The answer supplied by those who have studied the subject is fairly unanimous: not very much.

Although he wrote in the midst of the Great Depression, that is, at a time when material-needs satisfaction was in fairly short supply and hence could be a prime motivator, Barnard voiced the belief that pay or monetary rewards as such were among the weakest inducements an organization could offer to gain the support and allegiance of its members. Subsequent research was to bear him out. In the 1960s, a group of researchers at the University of Michigan took a survey of 1,533 working people, asking them, among other things, to rank various aspects of their work in order of importance. The respondents placed "good pay" in fifth position, after "interesting work," "enough help and equipment to get the job done," "enough information to do the job," and "enough authority to do the job."

Industrial sociologist Frederick Herzberg, who has devoted a good deal of attention to this problem, has attempted to put material needs and their satisfaction into perspective. In a book entitled *The Motivation to Work,* written in cooperation with two of his associates, Herzberg claims that money, fringe benefits, and even working conditions only motivate people if they are *not* satisfied. In other words, the influence of such factors can only be negative, not positive. Or, to put it more explicitly, poor financial conditions can cause people to give less than the minimum to their organization, but good financial conditions will not usually make them give any more than the minimum. As Herzberg puts it, "It would seem that as an affector of job attitudes, salary has more potency as a job dissatisfier than as a job satisfier."[10]

One question immediately arises. What about bonuses and pay promotions? Do not these tend to propel people toward increased productivity? Here, the subject becomes intertwined with ego-need satisfaction, which we will be looking at shortly. However, when it is divorced from ego needs, then the answer remains the same. They do not motivate, at least not very much. When, for example, the organization gives its entire work force a pay increase, it usually does not receive back any appreciably greater output *unless* the salaries that they had been paying had been causing dissatisfaction. By removing, or at least alleviating, such dissatisfaction, the organization may reduce turnover and curb malignancy as well as employee sabotage. It may also bring overall employee performance up to a basic minimum, but that usually is about all it can expect.

At this stage a further question arises. If material-needs satisfaction is such a poor motivator of employee performance, then why all the constant fuss about it? Why do employees grumble so frequently over pay and benefits?

The answer is twofold. For one thing, pay and benefits that workers view as inadequate are, as we have noted, prime *dissatisfiers*, and this alone can cause grievances galore. More important, perhaps, is that frequently an organization's members carp and complain about pay when they are really dissatisfied over lack of employer regard, boredom, or something else. This can be seen in the frequency of employee strikes, which, while they often cite increased pay boosts as their prime demand, often end up costing the employees more than they can ever hope to exact from the organization they are striking against. Wages may appear to be the issue even to the strikers themselves, but the real causes may lie elsewhere.

Douglas McGregor pointed to a fatal flaw in the use of material-needs satisfaction as an organizational motivator. Fulfilling such needs, he pointed out, gives the employee only the means to satisfy ends outside the work environment. The satisfaction is not found through the job itself, and therefore while necessary, this will never in itself move employees to do much more than they have to do while on the job.

There are two other aspects to the limitation of material-needs satisfaction as a motivator of people, which should be taken into account. The first is that while meeting material needs does not motivate very much, refusing to meet material needs, that is, trying to motivate people by threatening to deprive them of their material needs, often renders even less satisfactory results. As Katz and Kahn point out, "The man who complies for fear of punishment plans and longs for the day when he can escape or overpower the person whom he obeys."[11] The same can be said of an employee's attitude toward the organization that puts him or her into such a position. Here deep-seated desires for getting back may take the form of employee sabotage, a persistent problem for many organizations.

Another limitation on the use of material-needs satisfaction as a motivator is found in the current trends in modern society. As society becomes more affluent, and as this affluence trickles down to its workers in the form of increased possibilities for saving money, increased job opportunities, unemployment compensation, and so on, material needs fulfillment, at least at a minimum level, becomes less and less of a problem. As McGregor noted, man tends to live for bread alone only when there is little bread.[12] The welfare state, even in its still-imperfect form, tends to undermine the ability of an organization to use the manipulation of material needs as a motivator of employee performance.

Another trend of the technological society that is also shrinking the boundaries of this motivation technique is the growth of professionalism. Productivity for the professional means creativity, and creativity probably responds less to material inducements than any other form of employee output. Threats of material deprivation, on the other hand, can even prove counterproductive. A professor may be a poor teacher, and it is possible that a gentle prod, such as a poor evaluation by his or her students, may cause improvement. But a threatening exhortation from the dean to start teaching better within two weeks or face immediate dismissal would probably be either so anger provoking or alarming that his or her teaching would fall to new lows.

As if all these limitations were not enough, there is a final one that a public administrator must reckon with. Given the nature of most public-employee personnel systems, the public administrator usually has a good deal less discretion in using monetary incentives than does an administrator in the private sector. Promotions often come only through examination or, in some instances, through political influence. Organizational discretion in terms of dismissal may be even more sharply curtailed. Therefore, the public organization in particular, while it certainly cannot discard the use of material motivators, must usually seek out and make use of additional ways and means of persuading its people to assist it in achieving its purposes and fulfilling its mission.

Social and Emotional Needs

It has long been known that work organizations usually provide their members with more than just a livelihood. Over a half century ago, Max Weber pointed out that in seeking to control the actions and elicit the loyalty of their employees, organizations will often provide them with an identity and socialize them into a culture. People need a sense of social solidarity, a sense of belonging to a group. The "boys at the plant" or the "girls at the office" frequently develop ties not unlike those of members of a family or at least a clan. The pattern of relationships that evolves may not always be amicable, but it almost always becomes important in the lives of those involved.

If the work group becomes a sort of extended family, the workplace may become a subcommunity. The organization members may come to think of themselves as its citizens or, if they are deeply disgruntled, its subjects. In any event, they often perceive the organization as playing a major role in their social and emotional lives.

Organizations frequently seek to capitalize on this situation to build organizational loyalty and thereby motivate members to serve organizational goals. Symbols, codes, rituals, and other devices may be brought into play to enhance the employee's sense of oneness with the organization. Special dress, such as uniforms, also tends to foster such feelings. And if the employee can believe that he or she is part of a group that has a special and noble mission to perform, so much the better.

The organizations that most frequently come to mind when we think of such techniques are the armed services, particularly the marines, and the police, particularly, perhaps, the FBI. Members of such organizations tend to develop such a heightened sense of organizational identity that they start to develop the trappings of a distinct culture. Religious organizations may go even further in this respect. Take, for example, the Catholic priesthood with its codes of dress, codes of living, and its special sense of pursuing a noble purpose. The rather awe-inspiring induction ceremony, whereby the priest-to-be prostrates himself on the floor, cannot help but instill in him a feeling that he is now becoming part of something that is much larger than himself and that will henceforth govern and guide his life.

Probably the most important element in shaping organizational identification is shared experience. This is particularly true if such experience involves struggle and sacrifice. "After almost twenty years of working with and observing firefighters in every conceivable emergency," writes a battalion chief of the New York City Fire Department, "I've concluded that the glue which holds this great department together is a combination of brotherhood and love. The misery, suffering and pain which we firefighters share creates a bond which those outside the fire service cannot comprehend. Wives, mothers, sweethearts—none can intrude into this unique fraternity that comes from being truly brothers."[13]

Of course, most organizations cannot hope to elicit the obedience of the Roman Catholic priesthood or develop the bonds of brotherhood that may characterize a fire department. But nearly all of them benefit to some degree from the fact that most of their members manage to feel some sense of identity with their fellow workers, and thereby with the organization itself. At a minimum, this will help induce people to show up for work more often than might otherwise be the case. At a maximum, it can enable the organization to call upon its members for a degree of dedication and devotion far beyond the level that material inducements alone could ever achieve.

The meeting of social and emotional needs thus constitutes a valuable tool in the public administrator's kit, and wise administrators will know how to make use of it. They may not only allow but encourage employee groups, such as bowling teams or credit unions. They may hold office Christmas parties and sponsor annual picnics. Through public relations and other devices they may try to build the image of the organization in the community, thereby giving their employees a sense of pride in being part of an agency that is playing a vital and positive role in community betterment.

However, in public administration as in most other things in life, everything has its cost, and sometimes the cost of trying to meet social and emotional needs becomes exorbitant. This does not simply include the financial outlays that may be involved but rather the side effects that such efforts, when successful, often engender. Strange as it may seem, an organization can inspire too much allegiance for its own good.

When an organization builds feelings of solidarity and a heightened sense of morale among its employees, it also tends to build walls around itself. The more self-sustaining and cohesive it becomes, the more self-contained and more self-involved it becomes. And self-involvement, of course, may make the organization increasingly isolated from its environment. This isolation can produce two negative effects.

The first of these effects has received little systematic study and remains somewhat speculative. However, there are indications that too much organizational isolation can actually backfire in terms of creating cooperative bonds between members and subunits within the organization. To gain an appreciation of this first problem in isolation, let us turn back and examine the ancient city-states of Greece. In speaking of these city-states, political theorist George H. Sabine points out how "the very intimacy and pervasiveness of its life, which was responsible for much of the moral greatness of its ideals, led to defects which were the reverse of its virtues. In general, the city-states were likely to be prey to factional quarrels and party rivalries *whose bitterness was as intense as only rivalry between intimates can be.*"[14] (Emphasis added.)

What Sabine noted in Sparta and Athens, others have noticed in certain modern-day organizations, such as the police, the armed services, and others. Those organizations known for their solidarity and cohesiveness tend to develop intense intragroup tensions, rivalries, and hostilities. To an outsider, the police seem to display a remarkable degree of solidarity and mutual protectiveness. This to a great extent is true. Yet when sociologist William Westley began studying U.S. police forces in the 1950s, he was struck by the high degree of distrust that seemed to pervade relationships between police officers even when they belonged to the same unit.[15] Studies of the German gestapo, an even more isolated organization, show that feuds flared up so frequently and so flagrantly within that grim organization that its policies met frequent defeat from within.[16] Studies of organized crime indicate a similar phenomenon. Sociologist Donald Cressey claims that members of crime syndicates engage in an intense amount of wrangling and rivalry.[17] Petty disputes easily become inflamed into major ones, and attempts at adjudication frequently only add fuel to the fire.

It may be argued that police officers and criminals are not typical and their behavior in response to organizational separation may not be reflective of other groups. Nevertheless, there are indications that this same response to isolation occurs elsewhere as well. Memoirs of those who have served in the armed forces, religious orders, underground movements, and other organizations that tend to create a strong sense of organizational distinctiveness and demarcation from society reveal somewhat similar responses.

Poets and novelists have sometimes called attention to this pattern. In Dante's *Inferno,* the punishment for lovers is to be chained together so that they may never be separated. As a result they must endure the greatest of all punishments, that of seeing their love degenerate into hostility and hatred through perpetual propinquity. Charles Dickens in his novel *Hard Times* offers this trenchant observation: "All closely imprisoned forces rend and destroy. The air that could be healthful to the earth, the water that would enrich it, the heat that would ripen it, tear it when caged up."

The perceptive Mr. Dickens, in another of his novels, *Bleak House,* also called attention to a second and a more significant setback that organizational self-involvement can produce. In speaking of the Court of Chancery of his day, he said, "The evil of it is that it is a world wrapped up in too much jeweler's cotton and fine wool, and cannot hear the rushing of the larger world outside. . . . it is a deadened world, and its growth is sometimes unhealthy for want of air."

Here Dickens put his finger on a phenomenon that has been noted by many modern and more systematic researchers. The more an organization and its members acquire a sense of separate identity, the less receptive they become to change and innovation. In his near-classic study of the U.S. Forest Service, Herbert Kaufman emphasizes the strong sense of identification that the organization manages to develop in most of its rangers. This spirit of cohesiveness and unity enables the service to gain many operational objectives. But, Kaufman also notes that "an individual imbued with the spirit of an organization, indoctrinated with its values, committed to its established goals and customary ways, and dedicated to its traditions, is not likely to experiment a great deal, nor even to see the possibilities suggested by unplanned developments."[18]

Kaufman's study *The Forest Ranger* was published in 1960. As the conservation movement gathered steam during the latter part of that decade, some of the problems he alluded to began to be seen. The Forest Service came under increasing attack from conservation groups for going about its tasks in an overly methodical and unimaginative manner. To many outsiders, its operational manner and methods seemed to suggest an avoidance of, and even an aversion to, new scientific developments and new social concerns. For example, when some research indicated that fires were, in certain cases and under certain conditions, actually good for forests, the service reacted with horror. The rangers had become too steeped in the tradition of firefighting ever to look on fire as anything but an enemy and a scourge.

The same problem has been noted by a private industry. In 1972, Distiller's Corporation–Seagram Limited began deliberating on whether to move its headquarters from New York City to the city's suburbs. It finally decided to stay in Manhattan. Its decision was based on a study it had made, which stated, among other things, that "if employees dealt almost exclusively with others from the company, there would be a tendency to reinforce existing patterns of behavior; there would be a danger of mental lethargy. In the long run this would have a deleterious effect on productivity."[19]

One interesting illustration that points up both the possibilities as well as the problems that organizational solidarity can produce occurred in the 1972 presidential election. The campaign organization put together by Senator George McGovern was infused with a remarkable esprit de corps. It inspired a sense of mission, and it developed into a remarkably compact and cohesive unit for an organization of this type. This development played a great role in producing the string of primary victories that brought McGovern the Democratic party's presidential nomination. But afterward, this same development helped set the stage for his crushing defeat in November. His campaign organization had become too isolated and self-involved to cooperate operationally or compromise ideologically with other elements of the Democratic party, such as precinct chairmen and labor leaders. The inability and even reluctance on the part of many McGovernites to build a broad coalition behind their candidate helped pave the way for the Nixon landslide in November.

Thus, we see that meeting social and emotional needs has its limits as far as achieving organizational purposes is concerned. The more the members are "at home" in the organization, the more they make it an integral part of their lives, the more they will tend to be put off from their environment. Carried too far, this can prove counterproductive for all concerned.

Another factor also casts doubt on the desirability of seeking to elicit large amounts of organizational loyalty. For illustration of this factor, we once again look to a British novelist, this time the contemporary writer Graham Greene. Writing in late 1972, Greene recalls overhearing many years previous a farmer describing some laborers he was using. "They are admirable workers and they are so loyal," said the farmer. The workers he was describing were inmates of a neighboring insane asylum.[20]

Greene's recollection has some special significance for the modern administrator. Organizational loyalty does not correlate well with intelligence and discernment. Those who have the ability as well as the emotional stability to serve the organization well also are apt to be the most reluctant to render any exaggerated allegiance to it. For the modern organization, confronted with a growing complexity of tasks and a growing need for proficient people, this can prove a serious dilemma. High-level professionals in particular tend to identify with their profession and not with their workplace. They can be quite critical of an organization that does not meet their professional goals. The modern administrator thus must deal with the ironical fact that the less fully a member identifies with his or her organization, the more likely such a member is to be valuable to the organization.

Current trends in our society tend to compound the problems that meeting social and emotional needs often produce. "The risks of concentrating attention and energies inward are directly proportional to the magnitude and rate of change in the world outside the organization," write Katz and Kahn.[21] The world, as we all know, is changing rapidly, and those who have studied our contemporary technological society feel that this trend will continue and even accelerate. This makes it increasingly dysfunctional for organizations to try to meet their members' social and emotional needs too fully, for the more they do so, the more they enmesh the members within the organization and cut them off from outside influences. Organizations will find themselves less and less able to endure the risks of stagnation that separation from the outer society can produce.

All of this does not mean that meeting social and emotional needs no longer has any role to play in motivating organizational members. Even the most creative and critical professionals still have social and emotional needs, which an organization can help to fulfill. And in so doing, the organization can evoke a modicum of loyalty, which can prove helpful in achieving organizational goals. But the days when an organization can call

upon its employees to take an oath of all-out allegiance are rapidly drawing to a close. The trend of the time makes such occurrences increasingly
less likely and increasingly less useful.

Ego Needs

One of the experiments that Elton Mayo and his colleagues undertook at
Western Electric's Hawthorne plant was to place a group of young women
who were assembling telephone relays in a test room and observe their
responses to changing work conditions. For two years the researchers
studied the response of the women as the lighting was increased and then
decreased, as rest pauses were introduced and then abolished, and so
forth. The one fact that stood out and that somewhat startled the researchers was this: No matter whether the changes they introduced were pleasant or unpleasant, the response of the women in terms of production
moved in only one direction—up![22]

The conclusion eventually drawn from this important experiment was
that attention and recognition *in and of* themselves tend to generate a positive response. The women were thus seen as reacting to the fact that they
had become objects of attention and, as a result, were responding positively no matter what particular form the attention took. Of course, had
unpleasant changes been introduced as a real and permanent policy, the
response would undoubtedly have been quite different. But, as a laboratory test, such changes only signaled continued interest in their behavior,
and so their responses were uniformly favorable.

Another interesting bit of research, which bears some relationship to
the Hawthorne experiment, involved the case of the weeping waitresses.
In the late 1940s, William H. Whyte wanted to find out why waitresses so
frequently broke into tears. He discovered that they often became caught
in a cruel vise. The customers would clamor insistently for their orders,
but the more urgently the waitresses relayed this to the counter hands,
the more the latter would make them wait. To meet their own ego needs,
the counter hands felt they had to show the waitresses and their customers that they were not to be bossed. Caught between these two ob-
durate forces, the waitresses often ended up weeping.[23]

Fortunately, a device existed to eliminate the problem. This was the
prong. When the waitresses put their orders on a prong, the ordering process became systematic and arbitrary, the counter hands no longer felt
any threats to their egos, and much of the tension evaporated.

The lessons, or at least one of the lessons, of both of these research
studies is clear: employees want to be recognized. They have ego needs
that require fulfillment, and the organization, by fulfilling these needs, can

help achieve its own purposes. The recognition of such ego needs and their potential as motivators of men was not in itself a new and sensational discovery. Organizations and their leaders from earliest times have been aware of the existence of such needs and had often sought to utilize them. However, the Hawthorne experiment and Whyte's research showed how widely and deeply such needs extended and how varied were the ways that existed for responding to them.

Administrators seek to accommodate ego needs in a variety of ways. Promotions, bonuses, medals, a bit of praise, or even a pat on the shoulder have all been pressed into play. Sometimes it is a matter of assigning a desk by the window or changing a title from assistant director to deputy director. (The latter device was used frequently during the 1960s as the term *assistant* fell into disfavor.) A new and more challenging assignment can also help fulfill ego needs. These devices deal with the ego-needs problem on an individual basis.

There are also ways of meeting such needs on an organization-wide basis. For example, an organization may set its recruitment standards high, or at least claim that it is doing so, in order to make its members feel that they are among "the Chosen." Similarly, the organization may boast of how small a percentage of its recruits make it through the training or probationary stage. The organization may seek to boost its own image in the community so that its members will take more pride in belonging to it. As Robert Presthus has noted, "The status of one's occupation can be augmented by the status of the organization in which one works."[24]

However, the assuaging of ego needs, like all the motivators we have been examining, poses problems as well as potentialities. Utilized on an individual basis, it can breed an excess of rivalry and competition. One person's reward is another one's deprivation. It can induce the individual to act in ways that can prove inimical to organizational purposes. "The man who competes for external rewards," say Katz and Kahn, "is likely to ponder how he can obtain the reward without the circuitous and strenuous business of compliance."[25] The pursuit of recognition can become an end in itself, and its consequences may not always dovetail with the goals of the employing agency.

Trying to meet ego needs on an organization-wide basis is often difficult and sometimes almost impossible. A sanitation department may find it quite difficult to make the chests of its employees swell with pride by instilling them with the idea that they belong to an elite organization engaged in a glamorous enterprise. Yet ego needs continue to count, and in a mass society where people frequently feel left out, the fulfillment of these needs acquires increased importance. The adept administrator will strive to meet such needs while avoiding some of the pitfalls they present.

The "Highest" Needs

Earlier, when speaking of material needs, attention was called to McGregor's statement that such needs were satisfied only off the job. An organization trying to use material-needs satisfaction to motivate its employees was utilizing a motivator that was not directly job connected. And as we noted, this may account for the weaknesses of such satisfiers in inducing workers to do more than a bare minimum toward fulfilling organizational purposes.

In a more limited sense to be sure, something of the same problem may confront the organization when it tries to boost employee performance through meeting social, emotional, and ego needs. While such satisfactions are more directly linked to the job, they are still somewhat extrinsic to the actual work process. They relate more directly to the workplace and the worker than to the work itself.

The humanistic school, which arose during the 1950s, sought to add a new and penultimate motivator to the list. This was the satisfaction that an employee obtained from simply working, regardless of ego, social, material, or any other satisfactions.

One of the first writers to call attention to this new bundle of motivators was Argyris. In his 1957 book *Personality and Organization*, this psychologist claimed that the employee has a thrust toward "self-actualization," which the usual organizational setup continually tends to thwart. The traditional methods of running an organization, said Argyris, are really more suitable for handling children than adults. But, he argued, this does not have to be the case. It is possible to design and operate organizations that enhance rather than inhibit the individual's development and hence satisfy his basic needs to realize himself in his work.[26]

Three years later Douglas McGregor published *The Human Side of Enterprise*. In this and in subsequent writings until his death a few years later, McGregor hammered away at the theme that work could be and should be a source of self-fulfillment in and of itself, and that organizations should reshape themselves so that this can occur. McGregor saw no inherent conflict between organizational goals and individual goals. "People are not by nature passive or resistant to organizational needs," he emphasized. "They want to take on responsibility and express themselves through creative and productive work. The essential task of management," he insisted, "is to arrange organizational conditions and methods of operation so that people can achieve their own goals best by directing their own efforts toward organizational objectives."[27]

What are these conditions? McGregor and others who took up this theme call generally for less hierarchy and more humanity in organizational life. They stressed expanded scope and encouragement for individual initiative and enterprise through allowing employees to make many of their own decisions on the job and to participate in the making of others. Work should be designed not only to be challenging and changing, but it should also provide pervasive possibilities for the employees to experience what is called *closure,* or the sense of completion that is obtained from finishing a measurable unit of work.

Subsequent research has, at least in part, validated much of McGregor's argument. Katz and Kahn report that "if there is one confirmed finding in all these studies of worker morale and satisfaction, it is the correlation between the variety and challenge of the job and the gratifications which accrue to workers." Although exceptions exist, still "by and large, people seek more skill-demanding jobs than they hold, and as they are able to attain these more demanding jobs, they become happier, better adjusted and suffer fewer health complaints."[28]

What about job performance and productivity?

The early research on this question reported only a weak though positive correlation between self-actualization principles and organizational output. But in recent years more and more studies have emerged pointing to a stronger connection.

One rather interesting study that bears a distinct relationship to this issue, though it does not address it directly, came to light in 1976. Psychologist Jay Hall surveyed five thousand managers in various business firms. He separated them out into three categories—good, average, and poor, on the basis of their performance. He then found that the good managers were driven mainly by the desire for self-actualization, the average managers were concerned with ego status, and the poor managers were preoccupied by both security-safety needs and ego status. This last group, said Hall, "wavered back and forth trying to satisfy both needs and failed to accomplish either very well.[29]

A more definitive study appeared five years later when Rensis Likert published the findings of an exhaustive investigation undertaken by the Institute of Social Research. The institute surveyed twenty thousand business managers plus ten times that number of nonsupervisory employees. The results, reported Likert, were remarkably clear-cut. Those managers achieving the highest productivity exhibited almost uniformly the following characteristics:

• They were supportive, approachable, and interested in the well-being of their subordinates.

• They formed their subordinates into cooperative, problem-solving teams, with many of them not only holding membership in more than one group but serving in different roles. For example, a person might be a leader of one group but only a member of another.

• They kept their subordinates well informed of plans and well supplied with the resources necessary for their jobs.

• They set forth high, no-nonsense goals and expected high-quality performance not only from their subordinates but also from themselves.

Likert called this management method *participative,* or *System 4,* to distinguish it from three other supervisory strategies, which he called *punitive authoritative* (System 1), *benevolent authoritative* (System 2), and *consultative* (System 3). The study's outcome, he stressed, left no doubt that System 4 works best.

However, this research almost exclusively involved business firms. Would its results also prove true for government agencies?

Likert answered with an emphatic yes. He claimed that navy ships and installations that came closest to using System 4 boasted a reenlistment rate that averaged *thirty times* the rate of those using System 1 or 2. In addition he cited an air-force study showing a dramatic drop-off in plane failure attributable to faulty maintenance once the maintenance crews adopted the participative, or System 4, approach.

Impressive as such research results may be, they cannot be accepted uncritically. For one thing, those doing the research usually believe in participative administration, and despite their commitment to and competence at the maintenance of high scholarly standards, such a belief could conceivably influence their conclusions. For another thing, the focus on "higher needs" does impose limits and liabilities of its own. The increased participation it requires can retard an organization's responsiveness, for participatory decision making usually means delayed decision making. Small problems may become bigger ones while opportunities may become lost as everyone involved insists on having his or her say. Also, such System 4 approaches may generate a lot of organizational "noise." This comes not only from the debates and disputes within subunits but from an intensifying rivalry between subunits as their increased independence stimulates them to go their own way.

Nevertheless, the trend toward self-actualization seems likely to continue and even accelerate. The complex and constantly configurating tasks that increasingly beset public organizations make it more and more valuable, if not actually necessary, for them to develop and draw upon the best that every employee has to offer. This is especially true of the more educated and professional employees, whose proportion in the public work force is rapidly rising. Such employees not only desire but demand organizational arrangements that fulfill their highest needs.

It is not only the professionals who are asking the organizations they serve to fulfill such needs. In recent years workers at all levels and in all fields have started to insist on having more respect and regard given to them as individuals. They also want to share in the decisions that govern their work and to enjoy the satisfaction of seeing their talents fully developed and productively utilized. For the organization of the future and, indeed, for the organization *with* a future, the upward path to the highest rung of the needs ladder may well be the only way to go.

CASE STUDY

Adding Minds to Muscle at NNSY.[30]

In recent years U.S. administrators have become more aware of and alert to what their counterparts in other countries are doing. Japanese administration in particular has drawn their attention, thanks to the remarkable productivity organizations in that nation often exhibit. Much of this productivity seems related to the participatory methods Japanese firms and agencies employ. One of these methods, which has come under particular scrutiny, is a device called the Quality Circle.

A Quality Circle, or QC, usually consists of anywhere from three to fifteen employees engaged in a common operation. The group gathers at regular intervals to discuss and develop ways of improving their operation's output, both in terms of quantity and quality. The QC, in effect, makes workers into "in-house consultants" and in so doing it not only develops and draws upon their abilities but also strengthens their commitment to their jobs. Membership in the group is always voluntary, but in Japan almost no one refuses to participate.

Would the QC work in the United States? Suspecting that it would, Lockheed in 1974 began establishing such groups in its Missile Systems Division. Soon thereafter the firm reported that the QC's were returning six dollars in savings and output for every dollar they cost to operate. Lockheed's success has since stimulated many other business firms, such as Westinghouse, Polaroid, Honeywell, and even stodgy General Motors, to embark on similar experiments.

By 1979 the QC was starting to ignite some interest among public managers. One of these was Navy Captain Alfred Kurzenhauser. Sparking his interest was the fact that the Norfolk Naval Shipyard, which he commanded, did not operate with the immunity from competition that most other governmental facilities enjoy. As an "industrial funded" activity of the U.S. Navy, the Virginia shipyard received work based on the quality, scheduling, and cost of its output. Although NNSY, as it was called, was the navy's oldest and largest shipbuilding facility, it had to compete with other naval shipyards, including some that were privately owned.

As a first step Captain Kurzenhauser set up an eight-member "management breakthrough" committee. This group pored through and exhaustively discussed the available literature on the subject. It also traveled to Jackson, Mississippi, to view the operation of such circles at a Sperry Vickers plant.

The committee recommended a one-year pilot program with the following structure:

- A steering committee, to set policy and goals and also to select "facilitators"
- A coordinator, to oversee QC operations and train those involved
- Facilitators, who would be drawn from the ranks and would be used to encourage the formation of QCs, to educate their members, and to guide their progress
- An outside consultant familiar with the QC concept to advise and assist in its general implementations
- Finally, the QCs themselves, composed of volunteers willing to serve one hour a week
- A QC leader, chosen by the group and who might or might not hold a supervisory position in the work unit.

In seeking to enlist middle management and rank-and-file support, the committee took care not to oversee or even overpublicize the program. The members did not want to attract volunteers who were primarily interested in getting "brownie points" for themselves by signing up for a program to which they would otherwise have remained indifferent.

Initially six circles came into being. Two of them almost immediately collapsed, but five others soon emerged to replace and add to them. In July 1979 the nine circles began operating.

The consultant trained the facilitators for three days and the circle leaders for two days. The circle leaders then imparted half of their training to circle members using the first eight weekly one-hour sessions to do so. The training included brainstorming techniques; cause-and-effect analysis; Pareto analysis, focusing on the "vital few" areas of work that cause most of the problems; the use of checksheets, sampling, and other tools of data collection; and the use of charts, graphs, and other means of presentation. All of this was intended to help circle members carry out their basic mission, which was to identify problems, seek out solutions, and, then, with management approval, implement them. The facilitators would help members gather the information and elicit the cooperation they might need from outside units in doing so.

The units were allowed to pick their own names, and the ones they chose reflected the zest with which their members approached their new assignment. "Sparkers, "Rectifiers, "Dry Dock Club, Solution Seekers, and "Red Eye Express" were some of the labels that emerged.

Brainstorming proved the most popular problem-solving device. Each member was encouraged to present the problem or problems that he or she viewed as the best for the group to tackle. The circle would then try to pinpoint their possible causes, breaking down each problem into separate components with the use of diagrams and data.

There were many successes the first year. The most spectacular one, in terms of savings, was also one of the simplest. The Solution Seekers were bothered about the waiting time for tools. They took a survey and found the delay averaged twelve minutes. There were, at the time, three separate windows, each dispensing different types of tools and each with its own computer to track them. A worker frequently had to go to two or three windows to obtain the tools needed.

The circle developed a system allowing each window to distribute all the various kinds of tools with all three using a common computer to track them. The new system cut the average waiting time to five minutes, saving the shipyard an estimated $200,000 a year. (The savings were calculated by converting the minutes saved to hours and then multiplying the number obtained by the yard's average-hourly-wage costs.) Meanwhile the cost of implementing the new scheme amounted to only $225, which represented the expense of having new signs painted for three windows.

Other groups, it must be said, produced far less savings, and four of the nine actually ran at a loss. Whatever savings they managed to generate failed to cover the expense of their operation. (There expenses included the cost of one hour a week per member in pay, their facilitator's time, their share of the program's overall costs, and the cost of implementing their suggestion.) One circle, calling itself Wild Bunch, met for 310 hours at a computed cost of $3,649. It also expended another $1600 in manpower and material cost to implement its suggestions. The result was a change that saved $211.

On balance, however, the QCs produced over a $.25 million in savings at a total cost of less than $40,000 the first year. Moreover, most of the costs were one-time expenditures, while the savings could be expected to continue indefinitely, thereby making the return on investment still more remarkable. And, of course, as the QCs become more familiar with and expert at their problem-seeking and problem-solving task, they may well become more productive in the future. The self-actualization approach, or at least one of its techniques, seems to have worked and worked well at NNSY.

The "Other" Organization

In our examination of ego needs we saw how a group of young female employees at Western Electric reacted positively to every change made in their working conditions while they were working in the test room. However, another experiment conducted along the same lines produced quite different results.

Mayo and his colleagues persuaded the management of the company to put a group of men engaged in making parts of telephone switches on a piece-rate system. Since this new system would allow the men to increase their earnings without undue physical strain, and since these were depression times, when most workers seemed desperate to earn more money, both the researchers and the company expected a great jump in productivity. Their expectations came to naught. The output of the men remained the same.

The research group then began to investigate why the workers responded, or rather failed to respond, in the way they did. Unlike the young female relay assemblers, most of whom had expected to get married and leave their jobs before too long, the male workers had developed a work culture of their own. They had become a cohesive and compact group with their own codes, rules, and norms. Among these rules were prohibitions against doing too much or too little work. So solidly entrenched were these understandings among the male employees that they remained impervious to any blandishments from management. The men rationalized that the incentive plan was an attempt to eventually cut out some jobs or to reduce wage rates. The company assured them that such was not the case and pointed to its record, which indicated no instance of its ever having acted in such a manner. But this failed to move the employees. They remained adamant, and productivity went on at the same level as before.[31]

What Mayo and his associates had come up against was what is sometimes called the *informal organization*. This phenomenon has interested and intrigued organizational theorists ever since, and a good deal of research activity has been devoted to probing its ramifications. These ramifications have been found to be large indeed.

Organizational charts and manuals of procedure, it seems, rarely provide us with an accurate picture of an organization. There is a good deal more lying under the surface, and what is not official or even readily visible is often the most important. Even the most formal organizations, which pride themselves on going strictly "by the book, rarely do so. For example, an informal system of authority, which supersedes, at least to some extent, the formal one, may and often does arise. In the army, the lieutenant clearly outranks the sergeant. But when the sergeant has had twenty years of army service while the lieutenant is fresh from a college ROTC program, it may well be the sergeant, rather than the lieutenant, who actually ends up running the platoon.

Communication is another thing that often flows through informal channels. The office grapevine is usually faster and more complete than the office memo. Aboard a ship, for example, the real communications center is often not the captain's office but the kitchen or galley, and the navy cooks are usually better sources of news than commanding officers. This is how the term *scuttlebutt* came to have its current meaning.

The informal organization may give rise to a network of relationships for which the organization chart and the manual of procedure provide few clues. All employees in the office may be of the same grade, but Jones, the oldest, gets the seat nearest the window, while Smith, the youngest, fetches the coffee for the 10:30 A.M. break. All the employees are to do the same work, but since Black does better at processing form A while Brown performs better in processing form B, the As end up on Black's desk and the Bs on Brown's.

A case study frequently used in public administration courses offers a vivid example of how completely the informal organization can diverge from the formal one. Entitled *The NLRB Examiner,* it deals with a series of events that occurred in the Los Angeles office of the National Labor Relations Board during the mid-1930s, when the NLRB was in the early stages of its existence. The head of the office showed signs of being highly partial to employers and to the union organization that was closest to employers, the old AFL. The examiners themselves tended to favor the more militant CIO and became incensed over what they regarded as their boss's favoritism. So they formed an organization of their own, hiding reports and information from the head of the office, leaking material, and otherwise providing aid to the CIO unions and seeking to establish their own connections to headquarters in Washington. Anyone looking at the office's organizational chart and examining its promulgated rules and procedures would have obtained a wholly erroneous idea of just how the NLRB's Los Angeles office was operating in those hectic days.[32]

One of the most extreme examples of how the informal organization can overwhelm the formal organization is the U.S. prison. Ostensibly, prisons are run by wardens and correction officers according to prescribed rules and regulations. In practice, this has rarely been the case. Sociologists and criminologists who have studied prisons have found out that traditionally most prisons have been run by the prisoners themselves. This does not mean that prisons are democratic institutions; they are indeed far from it. Rather, the supervisory personnel, faced with the enormous difficulties involved in everyday prison operation, eventually give up and surrender basic control to what are often the toughest inmates in the institution.[33]

There is much brutality and ugliness in the typical prison, but those who have studied prisons feel that more of it results from too little, rather than too much, application of official authority. There are some exceptions to this, particularly at smaller institutions, and it should be said that in recent years prison officials generally have been asserting more control over penal facilities. But traditionally prisons have evolved a whole subculture including beatings, homosexual gang rapes, and other grim and gruesome rituals, while the prison officials avert their eyes and try to get through the day with a minimum of trouble.

Of course, in most cases the informal organization does not loom quite so large on the administrative scene, and its role should not be over-stressed. It modifies and colors the formal organization but does not radi-cally alter it. No matter how expert and experienced a sergeant may be, and no matter how naïve and nervous the lieutenant may be, it is the lieu-tenant and not the sergeant who bears the final responsibility for the pla-toon. Consequently, there is a limit as to how much authority the sergeant can acquire and how much the lieutenant may abdicate. Nevertheless, some informal elements influence the operation of nearly all organiza-tions, and the administrator must be alert as to what they are and what they do.

There are two aspects of informal organization that merit some special attention. One concerns the role of informal rules; the other concerns the role of small groups.

Whose Rules?

Nearly all organizations seek to prescribe a set of rules and have their members follow them. But what they seek they do not always find. If we take the entire country as an organization, we find that from 1919 to 1933 it prohibited the sale of liquor only to discover that during this period more liquor was sold than ever before. Today, the laws of many states re-garding gambling, marijuana, and prostitution are flouted with almost equal impunity.

Employees of organizations are like citizens of nations in that they tend to obey only those rules they believe in. As sociologist Alvin Gouldner has pointed out, workers will accept a rule only if it is legitimate in terms of their values. They will not accept it just because those who issued it had a legal right to do so.

Employees also become quite adept at evading rules or bending them to suit their needs and desires, and the more rules the organization tends to set down, the more dexterous its members may become in this respect. "Any complex, maze of rules," write Katz and Kahn, "will be utilized by the guardhouse lawyers in the system to their own advantage."[34] In this fashion when the rules run into employee resistance, the employees may use them to defeat rather than serve the organization's purposes.

Sometimes employees do this by simply enforcing the organization's rules to the letter, thereby creating all kinds of pandemonium. Traffic po-lice have driven their departments to despair by merely giving out a ticket to every motorist that deserved one. Such action floods the police department with a sharply increased workload and a sharply increased number of complaints from the community's more substantial citizens. In 1970, French customs inspectors, incensed over the failure of the govern-ment to meet their demands, staged a "strike" by simply inspecting thoroughly every piece of baggage that visitors brought into France. In doing what they were supposed to do, they virtually paralyzed operations at France's international airports and disrupted travel in Europe generally.

The informal organization not only achieves frequent and sometimes spectacular success in sabotaging the formal organization's rules, but it also manages to establish and enforce rules of its own. Many of these rules have to do with work output. Those who exceed the informal quota may be branded as "ratebusters," while those who fail to carry their fair share of the load may earn the title of "chiseler." Seniority is another rule that governs many procedures of many informal organizations. Those who have seniority on the job are to get the better assignments and the more congenial conditions. The most junior members may not only be given the short end of the stick but may also be subjected to various kinds of petty harassments, such as being sent to fetch the "left-handed monkey wrench." Sometimes the harassment is not so petty. Hazing rituals of college fraternities at one time resulted in frequent injury and occasional death to initiates of those organizations.

Probably no informal rule is more widespread than the ban on "squealing." This prohibition is instilled in most Americans during their school years and tends to stay with them through the rest of their lives. The taboo against "tattling" is so widely and deeply ingrained that even those who would stand to benefit from it tend to dislike it. The "informer" or "spotter," no matter how useful he or she may be, rarely wins esteem in the eyes of management, and though the informer may increase his or her earnings, seldom enhances chances for promotion.

While the organization often encounters difficulty in enforcing its own rules, the informal organization usually succeeds quite well in securing support and adherence to its own codes of behavior. Sanctions against offenders can take many forms, not excluding violence. Prisoners who depart from the informal rules can meet injury and even death at the hands of their fellow inmates, and when a New York City policeman named Frank Serpico decided to inform on corruption within the police force, he received several death threats from some of his irate colleagues.[35] However, the sanction most frequently invoked is that of the "silent treatment." The erring member is cut off from all social intercourse and all unnecessary conversation. When West Point cadet James J. Pelosi refused to resign from the academy on being accused by his fellow cadets of cheating in 1971, he was forced to room alone and to eat alone at a ten-man table at the cadet mess hall. Protesting his innocence, Pelosi stuck out the "silence" until he graduated eighteen months later.[36] He was the only cadet in the academy's history ever to survive such a protracted ordeal. (The next year the cadets abolished the practice.)

Many informal rules, it should be noted, are quite benign. Alvin Gouldner indicates that while the Golden Rule remains an unattainable goal, it has become a nearly universal norm and as such governs a good deal of organization behavior. If people do not naturally love their neighbors as themselves, they do tend to help others who have helped them or at least refrain from injuring them. Gouldner claims that this norm is as ubiquitous and as important as the incest taboo in modern society.[37] As such it counteracts the harshness that other rules, both formal and informal, may produce in organizational operations.

The Small Group

The basic unit for the formal organization may be the division, the department, the section, or all three plus others as well. The primary basis for the informal organization is generally the small group. Although many informal norms and rules are organizationwide, many others are promulgated and enforced by small work groups. The small group consists of no set number of individuals. Rather, it designates any group whose members are in continual face-to-face contact with each other. Such groups often follow the structural lines of the formal organization. The small group in the army infantry is typically the squad. In the university it is usually the department. But whether or not it conforms to any formally recognized structure, forces from within itself customarily dictate a good deal of its behavior.

The importance of the small group springs chiefly from the importance of primary relationships over secondary relationships in human behavior. Those we work with every day on a person-to-person basis invariably become more important to us than those whom we see infrequently or with whom we conduct relations at a distance. Out of such primary relationships come norms, codes, procedures, and the means for their enforcement. The famed "silent treatment" is most powerfully exercised on those with whom we are in daily contact.

An interesting example of how the small group develops and enforces its own rules is found in Peter Blau's *The Dynamics of Bureaucracy*. Blau reports on an office of a federal agency that had certain law-enforcement powers over business. Many times businessmen caught violating the law by agents would make implicit if not explicit offers of a bribe. The agents uniformly rejected such offers, for it was not only against organizational policy but against their own code to accept them. However, the agents also had learned to make use of these attempts to suborn them. Such bribe offers became a valuable lever in prodding the businessmen into settling the case on their, the agents', own terms.

"Being offered a bribe constituted a special tactical advantage for an agent," writes Blau. "An employer who had violated one law was caught in the act of compounding his guilt by violating another one. Agents exploited this situation to strengthen their position in negotiations."[38]

In refusing to accept bribe offers the agents were abiding by the organization rules. However, these rules also called for agents to report such attempted bribes to their superiors. Here the agents departed from the formal rules, for to them reporting bribe offers constituted "squealing," and "squealing" constituted one of the most cardinal of sins. Blau could find only two cases in the recollection of all the agents present in the office where one of their number had ever reported the offer of a bribe. The agent in one of the cases had left the office. In the second, the agent concerned remained at work but was still undergoing the punishment of ostracism. This agent stoutly maintained his "innocence," claiming he had only turned in the businessman after the latter had pressed his bribe offer vigorously and in the presence of other parties. However, the agent's protestations were to no avail. None of his colleagues would have any dealings with him that were not absolutely necessary for the conduct of office affairs. Such are the workings of small groups and informal organizations.

The Informal Balance Sheet

The informal organization and the small groups that make it up can obviously do a great deal of damage. They may and often do subvert the very purposes of the organization, because they show a persistent tendency to do what is most congenial to their members and reject organizational endeavors that may conflict with their own basic goals. The British sociologist Michael Banton was told, in studying a U.S. police organization, that "first the front office decides and then the locker room decides."[39] He was left with the distinct impression that it was the locker room's decision that was truly decisive.

The informal organization cannot only make things difficult for the formal organization, but it can also make things hard for its own members. Not only are the ratebusters or the chiselers usually punished, but sanctions may also be invoked against the member who dresses differently, who espouses radical views, or who in any way speaks or acts in a manner that marks him or her as "different."

Sometimes the informal organization acts in an entirely opposite way, but this can prove even more counterproductive to organizational goals. It may cover up for one or more of its members who fail to do what is expected of them. The alcoholic who arrives back from lunch in a stupefied state may be allowed to sleep it off in an unobtrusive place while the rest of the group tells the supervisor that he is gone on an official errand. Such practices not only harm the organization but also the individual, because he is allowed to continue without confronting his problem or making attempts to resolve it.

Finally, the sense of team loyalty with which the informal organization imbues its members can generate a variety of evils. This could be widely seen during the U.S. Senate Watergate hearings in 1973. Queried as to why he did not speak up at meetings where "dirty tricks" were planned, Herbert Porter, the youthful scheduling director for the Committee to Reelect the President, replied, "I was not one to stand up in a meeting and say this should be stopped. I kind of drifted along." Pressed further by Senator Howard Baker as to why he remained silent, Porter added, "In all honesty, probably because of the fear of group pressure that would ensue, of not being a team player."[40]

Yet, the informal organization also has a positive role to play, and organizational theorists are coming more and more to accept and avow this fact. Note the following quotations:[41]

> The incompleteness of the formal plan provides a vacuum which like other vacuums, proves abhorrent to nature. (Simon, Smithburg, and Thompson)

> No organization chart and no book of policies and procedures can specify every act and prescribe for every contingency encountered in a complex organization. To attempt such specification merely produces an array of instructions so ponderous that they are ignored for the sake of transacting the business of the organization. Moreover, even if such specifications could be provided, they would soon be out of date. . . . (Katz and Kahn)

> It would not, in any sense, be an exaggeration to assert that any large organization would come to a grinding halt within a month if all its members began behaving strictly in accordance with the structure of responsibility and authority defined by the formal organization chart, the position description and formal controls. (McGregor)

> Reduced to its formal power, to the theoretical pact which constitutes it, every organization, every human enterprise is incapable of adapting itself to its environment. (Michel Crozier)

What these writers are saying is obvious: *The formal organization cannot exist without its informal counterpart.* All organization design is inevitably incomplete and imperfect, for there is simply too much complexity and variability in the interaction of human beings ever to be compressed into a formal system. As employees come and go, as new technologies develop and new problems arise, the formal plans and procedures, no matter how well designed originally, become increasingly outmoded. Periodic revamping can help but can never hope to keep pace with the rate and sweep of the changes taking place that affect organizational operations. Consequently, the all-important facts of organizational life frequently become the unofficial ones.

If Ms. Green tends to wield the authority that belongs to Ms. White, then more often than not, Green possesses some competence that White lacks. If the seasoned sergeant exercises more authority than does the neophyte lieutenant, then undoubtedly many a soldier's life has been saved because of it. As a matter of fact, young ROTC lieutenants used to be told, "Be good to your sergeant lest he carry out every order you give." And if small groups tend to call the shots as they see them, then often they see them much better than does top management.

This brings us to the question of how the informal organization affects organizational productivity. We have already noted several ways in which it can sabotage and subvert organizational goals. However, it can also do the reverse. Elton Mayo and his colleagues found in their Western Electric studies that informal work-group norms could affect productivity in a positive way. More recently, Katz and Kahn have stated that the correlation between the informal group norms and productivity is likely to go in the way the organization would like to go. "Though the relationship of cohesion with productivity can go in either a positive or a negative direction," they write, "the relationship is more often positive than negative in the studies done to date."[42]

This brings us finally to the role of the small group. Research indicates that the larger the size of the work unit, the greater the rate of absenteeism and accidents. Small groups meet social and emotional needs, and whether or not they are the "highest" needs, such needs remain important for organizational purposes. In another of his books, *Bureaucracy in Modern Society,* Peter Blau writes that "the effective enforcement of unofficial standards of conduct in cohesive work groups has important implications for official operations. Many studies," he adds, "have found that the existence of cohesive bonds between co-workers is a prerequisite for high morale and optimum performance of duty. . . ."[43]

This does not mean that the organization should remain oblivious to the harm that small groups can do, not only to the organization but also to their own members. By facilitating and even fostering rotation, organizations can alleviate many of these problems. Promoting organization-wide activities and stimulating employees to take training outside their subunit, even outside the organization itself, are other devices that may help prevent small groups from becoming too ingrown and hence too injurious to all concerned. But in general, administrators have shown an increasing disposition to accept the small group and to work with it. To quote Katz and Kahn again, "The effective supervisor . . . regards the value of the group to each individual as a potential asset rather than as a bureaucratic irrelevancy or a threat to authority. As a result, he devotes a good deal of effort to creating a cohesive work group, a group in which each member finds the fact of membership rewarding."[44]

The ultimate aim is to make the formal and the informal organization converge. Can this be achieved? According to Argyris, informal organization results from the desires of organization members to satisfy various needs that the formal organization neglects or even thwarts. He reports on studies he has done of two departments of a business corporation. One department did not attempt to meet such needs, and consequently its members developed informal ways of satisfying them. The other department made ample provision to meet these needs, through job security, personal recognition, variety, and challenge in work assignment. As a result, says Argyris, morale was high, personal relationships were warm, and the need for informal organization was hardly felt.[45]

Organizational Pathology

Organizations, like individuals, often act in strange, irrational, and, at times even self-destructive ways. But, as with individuals, such organizational behavior usually has a logic of its own, albeit one that is frequently perverse and sometimes pathological. This aspect of administration is often classified as organizational pathology. The term is somewhat misleading, for pathology implies an abnormal condition, and this is not the case with the pathologies of organization. They are widespread and deep rooted and few organizations manage to escape their pernicious influences completely. Consequently, the subject warrants a good deal of scrutiny and study.

The Pathology of Persistence

At one time tuberculosis was a disease widespread in the United States as well as elsewhere, and many sanatoria were erected to treat its numerous sufferers. Then in the early 1950s, a new drug came on the market that could effect, at least in most cases, a prompt and complete cure. Soon the new medicine had reduced this hitherto scourge to minimal proportions. But it had no comparable impact on the institutions that TB had brought into existence. While the drug soon depopulated most TB sanatoria, it did not eliminate them. Many states—Maine is just one example— continued to operate TB sanatoria with as few as five or six patients until an increasingly exasperated U.S. Public Health Service finally forced some consolidations. However, as late as 1973, many states, probably the majority, were still operating some sanatoria that were being used only to about 25 percent of capacity. In TB, the physical pathology proved much easier to treat than the institutional one.

The first pathology of organization is, thus, persistence. Self-preservation is as much a law of organizational life as it is of biological life, and the institutional organism, unlike the biological one, usually achieves a much greater success rate. The ability of organizations to survive in the face of adversity has often amazed and even astounded administrative observers.

Persistence is probably the most widespread of all organizational pathologies. While the federal government did exert pressure on states in its partially successful attempt to close down or consolidate unneeded TB sanatoria, the federal establishment still retains a great many examples of the persistence pathology within its own house. To take one example, the National Screw Commission was set up during World War I to standardize parts for military equipment. It has not held a weekly meeting or issued a report in decades, but when last heard from it was still maintaining a suite of offices and a bureaucratic payroll. Another agency of dubious utility to the country's weal is the National Teatasters Commission. Like the Screw Commission, it has not become known for the vigor of its efforts in carrying out any needed public purpose, and early in his first term, President Nixon issued an order abolishing it. But midway through his second term the order had still not been carried out.[46]

Then there is the Subversive Activities Control Board, which was set up under the Internal Security Act of 1950 to register Communists as foreign agents. The Supreme Court soon stepped in and stripped the agency of its powers. But in so doing, the Court did not thereby end the board's existence. The SACB continued on largely unnoticed until President Johnson named the husband of one of his favorite secretaries to a twenty-seven-thousand-dollar-a-year position as a member of its board. President Nixon expressed his support for the outmoded agency and said that he would try to find something for it to do. But by the end of his first term, there were no indications that he had succeeded in giving the SACB anything of any usefulness to perform.

The problem is certainly not a new one. In 1937, the Commission on Administrative Management in the Government of the United States, the Brownlow Commission, could say in tones of rather despairing humor, "there is among government agencies great need of a coroner to pronounce them dead, and for an undertaker to dispose of the remains."[47] The problem, it should be added, is not in any way peculiarly a part of

U.S. bureaucracy. A survey by the University of Rome's Department of Government Studies in 1972 showed that Italy had fifty-eight thousand government agencies.[48] They included

• an office to grant loans to persons who had suffered damage in eruptions of Mt. Vesuvius. (The last eruption had occurred in 1906.)
• an agency to take care of the orphans of World War II. (The youngest such an orphan could have been by that time was twenty-eight years old.)
• a bureau to license carrier pigeons.
• an agency to administer pensions for veterans of a battle that was fought in 1896. (The agency would not tell the researchers just how many veterans of this encounter were still alive.)

The Pathology of Conservatism

Organizations not only show a remarkable ability to prolong their existence, but they also display a noticeable facility for prolonging their traditional ways of doing things. Their means and methods of operation frequently exhibit a persistent penchant for the tried and true. "Organizational logic is essentially conservative," writes Robert Presthus, "for it honors consistency, tradition, the minimization of individual ends in favor of collective ends, and the wisdom of history rather than the wisdom of men."[49] A British writer, R. G. S. Brown, in noting the same tendency, adds an additional perspective as to its causes. "A really creative idea is likely to disrupt the smooth flow of business and therefore leads to faction." Since organizations want to avoid disruption, they "will usually find it easier to turn down an unorthodox idea than approve it."[50]

Change, it should be kept in mind, always poses threats. It can alter career opportunities, favoring new skills and training and thus new leadership abilities. It implies new priorities along with a reallocation of resources. Even those who would seem to benefit from the change may find it fearful. For example, the decision to equip submarines with nuclear power meant a dramatic upgrading in the submarine's role in national defense. Yet, submarine commanders opposed the plan when it was first conceived in the 1950s. A nuclear submarine, among other things, would require two crews and two commanding officers, who would alternate in operating it. This meant that no officer or crewman could claim the submarine as "my ship." Submarine commanders would not accept this, and so they fought against its development.[51]

As organizations grow older, this problem of routinization becomes greater. Like individuals, organizations tend to become increasingly inflexible with age. Values and procedures become not only established but entrenched. And, again like an individual and even like a society, an organization develops a heritage and seeks to pass it on to its new generation.

William A. Wayson, Director of Urban Education at Ohio State University, sees these factors as explaining why school systems have often failed to respond to the pressures for change. In his analysis, which could also be applied to most other organizational settings, he notes that "ways of doing things gain validity with longevity. The length of their utilization is cited as proof of their effectiveness. . . . Newcomers enter as novices and are taught by tribal elders 'how it is done around here.' . . . By the time they are eligible for promotion, they have incorporated these priorities and taboos into most of their thinking. . . . When new and creative responses are demanded, the bureaucrat looks inept, feels paranoid and becomes defensive."[52]

Examples of rigid routinization abound. From 1937 to the fall of 1972, the Boston Fire Department did not reassign a single fire company. Yet during this thirty-five-year period the city's population drastically changed and shifted. As a result, some sections now had more than double the proportion of firefighters on a per-capita basis than other sections, although frequently the former sections were the areas that were now having the least fires. Similar situations can be found in many other U.S. cities. Indeed, some older cities still maintain a string of small and now decrepit firehouses dating back to the time when fire wagons were drawn by horses, which had to be changed frequently while en route to the blaze.

The reader again should be wary of believing that such patterns of persistence are endemic only to local governments. The federal government is itself a frequent offender. In 1970, for instance, the Department of Agriculture was still subsidizing the production of pitch pine. However, pitch pine had become totally obsolete when the navy had decided to abandon sailing ships over a hundred years before.

When confronted with pressures to change, organizations can react quite rigorously if not ruthlessly. "If you must sin, then sin against God and not against the bureaucracy," Admiral Hyman Rickover once said, "for God may forgive you but the bureaucracy never will."[53]

Rickover's statement probably reflects the trials and tribulations he experienced in developing, against considerable internal resistance, the navy's nuclear submarine. However, bitter as his experiences may have been, at least one other navy innovator had an even tougher time. This was William Sims, who, as a naval lieutenant at the turn of the century, sought to institute a new and vastly improved method of naval-gun sighting. When stoutly rebuffed by the navy's top brass for his outlandish ideas, he appealed over their heads to President Theodore Roosevelt. The naval-minded president liked Sims's proposals and saw that they were implemented. Although the innovation is credited with transforming naval gunnery from a haphazard art to a rather precise science, and, in so doing, vastly increasing the navy's efficiency, the admirals were not appeased. Toward the end of Roosevelt's second term they started making plans to court-martial Sims once his benefactor had left the White House. Fortunately, Sims got wind of the scheme and communicated news of it to Roosevelt, who managed to squelch the plot before he left office.

Another pioneer in the armed services did not fare so well. This was army General William "Billy" Mitchell, who became impressed with the potential of air power during World War I and began to push for a strong air force after the hostilities ended. As part of his campaign, he offered to sink some captured German vessels to demonstrate just what bomb-carrying planes could do. Congress and the press liked the idea and finally forced a reluctant military establishment into staging such an exercise. Despite numerous handicaps and restrictions designed to hamper his operations, Mitchell and a small group of pilots inflicted such heavy damage on the target vessels that some naval officers present actually broke into tears. They thought that they were witnessing the impending demise of everything they believed in and had devoted their lives to.

When the military authorities still refused to respond, Mitchell began taking his case more and more to the public, calling explicitly for a separate air force. He was demoted and transferred and eventually court-martialed. He died in 1936, only a few years before his outlandish ideas were all too grimly validated in World War II.[54]

The Pathology of Growth

Having devoted considerable attention to the seemingly innate and inherent tendency of organizations to conserve their existence as well as their existing ways of doing things, it is now time to consider one aspect of change that organizations actually welcome and often strive for. This concerns changes in size. Organizations do all they can to ward off threats to their stability except in the area of growth. Most of them tend to welcome and embrace opportunities to grow larger, as long as the growth involves only a change of magnitude or at least does not substantially disturb their established processes and procedures.

This growth syndrome was first spotted by that amusing and all-too-accurate British commentator C. Northcote Parkinson. In his 1957 work, *Parkinson's Law and Other Studies of Administration*, Parkinson identified growth as the first and foremost law of administrative behavior. Although he furnished figures to back up his contention, Parkinson elicited more chuckles than concern. In 1970, he returned to the fray, and with even more complete figures. To cite just one of them, he noted that in

1935 Great Britain employed only 1,023 officials in London to administer a swollen empire upon which, so its proud boast went, the sun never set. In 1960 this once vast array of colonies which had included India, Ceylon, and a good deal of Southeast Asia and Africa had dwindled away to a few outposts such as Bermuda and St. Kitts. However, the number of employees needed to run this now shrunken and quite miniature empire had grown to 2,827, an almost threefold increase.[55]

This deeply rooted drive on the part of organizations toward expansion can be seen almost everywhere in the public sector. The very fact that public employees now constitute nearly 20 percent of the nation's work force is at least partly attributable to this particular pathology. To take a more specific example, hospitals expanded their facilities tremendously during the 1960s as government aid to do so became available. By 1971, the American Hospital Association reported that on an average day over 186,000 hospital beds were empty.[56] In some areas, such as greater Boston and Los Angeles, the number of surplus hospital beds had reached the one-fourth mark.[57] Yet there were hospitals even in these cities that were eagerly and busily planning still further expansion.

This growth dynamic may appear to contradict the stagnation syndrome noted previously, but actually it more often reinforces it. One clue to this may be found in a statement by the noted eighteenth-century British conservative Edmund Burke. "A state without the means of some change," wrote Burke, "is a state without the means of its preservation."[58] As with a state, so with an organization. An organization often wishes to grow in order to continue in existence and to continue operating in its existing ways.

PLUS ÇA CHANGE . . .

". . . then we went out and saw the manner and trouble of dockeing such a ship; which yet they could not do, but only brought her head into the docke and so shored her up till next tide. But, good God, what a deal of company was there from both yards to help to do it, when half the company would have done it as well; but I see it is impossible for the King to have things done as cheap as other men."

—*Samuel Pepys,* 1667

To see just how this works in terms of organizations, we refer once again to Katz and Kahn. Growth, note these two writers, creates new opportunities for promotion, transfer, prestige, and power, and it can alleviate a good deal of internal conflict. "Because each subsystem will mobilize all its forces for self-preservation, it is easier for management to meet internal problems by adding rather than subtracting."[59] Almost all organizations are subject to some pressures for change from time to time, and adding new structures and functions is one way to avoid changing existing structures and functions. Thus, it is the forces that make for stability in the organization that help generate the forces for its expansion.

There are, of course, other forces at work. Parkinson cites two factors that foster the expansion urge. "An official wants to multiply subordinates not rivals," he claims, for subordinates increase his prestige and power while rivals obviously endanger it. Also, "officials make work for each other" since the more employees there are, the more memos they exchange, the more conferences they hold, and so on.[60] Finally, there is the organization's own hunger for the prestige and potency that only size can confer.

We will have more to say about some of these other growth forces shortly. At this point it would be useful to point out that some parts of the organization tend to grow much more rapidly than others. The two most favored growth areas seem to be the upper levels and the administrative and auxiliary spheres.

Let us return to Parkinson. From 1938 to 1967, he tells us, the number of vessels in the British navy declined from 308 to 114, a diminution of almost two-thirds. The reduction in tonnage was probably even more severe, since it was the larger ships that were the most heavily phased out. Battleships and aircraft carriers, for example, were eliminated completely. During this period, however, the number of admiralty officials and clerical staff increased from 11,270 to 33,574. Thus, a two-thirds cutback in the fleet was accompanied by a threefold expansion of headquarters personnel.[61]

Again we should not regard such phenomenons as peculiar to any one country. At the end of World War II, the United States had 12 million men and women under arms. They were directed by 139 three and four-star generals and admirals. In 1972, as Senator William Proxmire has pointed out, we had only 2.5 million men and women in our armed forces, but the number of our three- and four-star generals and admirals had burgeoned to 190.[62] Unfortunately Proxmire's protest went essentially unheeded for ten years. Later another member of Congress, Representative Les Aspin found the Navy employing 3,867 captains to operate 464 vessels. Such are the workings of organizational "logic," if logic is the right term to use.

This phenomenon does not stop short with military organizations. The rule of what might be called "inflation at the top" can be found at work almost everywhere. From 1970 to 1973, the U.S. Postal Service determinedly embarked on a cost-reduction program, and in so doing eliminated over sixty-three thousand employees. At the same time, the number of assistant postmasters general more than doubled, going from eight to seventeen. After three years of reducing costs, the Postal Service had twenty officials earning forty-two thousand dollars or more a year.[63]

Both United States and the British citizens can take some solace, however, from the fact that Italian taxpayers undoubtedly have it worse. A 1972 survey in Italy showed that the country's national government had nearly sixty-thousand individuals bearing the official title of "president," and all of them were collecting full-time salaries. The Italian army, meanwhile, had more generals than the United States Army, although the Italian military force is less than one-third as large as ours. As for the Italian navy, it actually had more admirals than it had vessels.[64]

Inflation at the top meshes with the other characteristic of organizational growth—its tendency to take place in the administrative or nonline branches. Most of the additional generals, admirals, and assistant postmasters general tend to be assigned to matters other than fighting battles or delivering mail. Students of public administration need look no further for examples of this trend than their own institution. If they are seeking a good subject for a term paper in public administration, they should examine the proportion of administrators to faculty members in their own college or university and see how the ratio has changed over the years. Almost certainly they will find that the number of administrators has grown at a much faster rate than the number of employees directly engaged in the educational process. Although teaching is supposed to be the primary purpose of the university, the number of those actually performing this mission is rapidly being surpassed by the number of those handling the auxiliary functions.

Not all of this trend can be ascribed to organizational pathology. There are some perfectly valid reasons for organizational growth to occur disproportionately in the upper levels and in nonline functions. We noted that staff units were growing faster than line units and why this was so. The increase in specialization and specialized services spurs on staff growth. And this increase in professionalization accounts for much of the tendency for such growth to occur at the top. Professionals and specialists usually cannot be brought in at the lower levels.

However, there are other and less healthy forces at work in stimulating this type of growth. Much of the swelling that takes place in the higher levels may reflect the workings of the "Peter Principle." As developed by Laurence J. Peter, the principle states that people are promoted to their level of incompetence. This means that a person who does a job well is advanced until reaching a position that he or she no longer can handle. The organization tends to be cluttered with such people, claims Peter, and tends to deal with them in ways that aggravate the problems we have

been examining. Two of the methods he cites are the "Percussive Subli-
mation," in which the incompetent is kicked further upstairs to an innocuous position, and the "Lateral Arabesque," in which the incompetent is
sidelined to another innocuous position at the same level.[65]

Although Peter exaggerates his "principle," both in terms of amuse-
ment and analysis, it does contain a germ of truth. It has become quite
difficult to get rid of people who can no longer (if they ever could) handle
their jobs, and organizations have frequently attempted to solve this problem by creating new positions for them. There is, however, a still-more-
basic reason for the organizational trend to top-heaviness. It relates very
directly to the basic reason why organizations tend to grow in the first
place.

Growth, as we saw earlier, allows an organization to smooth and settle
conflicts by appeasing various forces and factions both within and without
its boundaries. Growth at the upper levels only aids and abets this process of conflict resolution. By expanding promotional possibilities organizations give more people more prestige and power. They therefore
meet their ego needs and keep them from becoming too dispirited. It is
becoming quite common, for example, for a soldier, when his enlistment
period is up, to bargain for a higher rating as a price for reenlisting. One
result is that the simple stripeless private, the supposed backbone of the
landed military, now constitutes a minority in the army.

The Territorial Imperative

According to biologist Robert Ardrey, all animals, human beings definitely included, are slaves to the territorial imperative.[66] They seek to
carve out a space for themselves and to repel all those who would intrude
upon it. Whether or not this is biologically true—the claim has been bitterly disputed by many biologists—it does seem to apply to organizations.
Organizations are continuously accused of not only overzealously protecting their own boundaries, but also of constantly seeking to enlarge them.
According to theorist Anthony Downs, "Every social agent is essentially
a territorial imperialist. He seeks to expand the borders of his various
zones and policy space or at least to increase his degree of influence
within each zone." And, adds Downs, "even pure conservatives are im-
perialists in policy space."[67]

Administrative history is dotted with numerous examples of this bit of
bureaucratic pathology. There were the aggressive attempts by the Department of the Interior to take over the Forest Service from the Department of Agriculture; the more successful attempt of the Federal Security
Agency, later changed to the Department of Health, Education and Welfare, to appropriate the Children's Bureau from the Department of Labor

in the 1940s; and the serious struggle waged by the air force to keep the navy from developing its own missile program. It can safely be said that most organizations have engaged in territorial disputes during some part of their existence, and some have been involved continuously in such battles.

Sometimes such altercations flare up on grounds that would baffle and bemuse outsiders. In the spring of 1973, a truly divisive dispute broke out in New York City between the Central Park Zoo and the Bronx Zoo over the custody of a ten-pound baby gorilla named Patty-Cake. The tiny simian had been born in the Central Park Zoo, but early in her infancy she had been sent to a hospital with a broken arm. After setting the arm, the hospital sent her to the Bronx Zoo for recuperation. However, once the arm was mended, the Bronx facility refused to give her back to the Central Park Zoo, saying that Patty-Cake was also suffering from malnourishment and other ills as a result of her previous poor treatment at Central Park.

Needless to say, the Central Park Zoo became incensed at such allegations and countercharged, claiming that Patty-Cake was being overcoddled at the Bronx Zoo, where her attendant was feeding her with a bottle and dressing her in diapers and, occasionally, in tiny skirts. Central Park insisted that she be returned so that she could be raised by her natural mother, who could best train her to cope with the exigencies of gorilla life in captivity.

The battle between the zoos escalated to such a point that the city's parks, recreation and cultural affairs commissioner had to hire an animal psychologist as a hundred-dollar-a-day consultant to adjudicate the matter. (He eventually issued a two-thousand-word report, recommending that Patty-Cake be returned to her natural mother at the Central Park Zoo.)

The territorial imperative is an important bureaucratic pathology, but administration is replete with contradictions, and here we confront one of them. Although agency aggrandizement is a common feature of administrative life, an opposite trend can also be discerned. While agencies may often show a pronounced penchant for empire building, they may almost as frequently display an annoying aversion to taking on new functions and activities as well as the desire to shed some of those they already have. Police departments generally dislike having to enforce traffic laws and have fought, successfully in most instances, attempts to have meter maids put under their control. School systems have exasperated more people by refusing to undertake additional activities than by aggressively seeking them. Many school departments had to be pushed into taking on many of the programs they operate today, such as school lunches and vocational guidance. Herbert Kaufman and Wallace S. Sayre, in their study of New

York City, found that both the Departments of Hospitals and Corrections had tried to avoid taking on treatment programs for narcotics while the Department of Health was trying to have the inspection of buildings put entirely under the aegis of the Department of Buildings.[68]

At the federal level, the Department of Agriculture resisted taking on many of Franklin D. Roosevelt's new farm programs, forcing him to set up independent agencies to operate them. When these new agencies developed their own clientele and expertise, they became more bothersome to Agriculture outside its organization than within it, and so the department agreed to house them. In like manner, when Roosevelt set up new and special agencies during World War II, the established federal departments offered no resistance. As Chester Bowles pointed out, "It relieved them [the existing agencies] of new reponsibilities in uncharted areas of government which could inevitably bring them into conflict with Congress and subject them to criticism from the press."[69] In 1953, the State Department actually took the initiative in having its information activities transferred into the hands of a new and independent United States Information Service.

To note two completely divergent pathological trends may seem somewhat illogical, but actually there may be some method in this madness. A possible guideline does exist for determining when agencies are most likely to practice the territorial imperative and when they are most likely not to do so.

From a lifetime of studying as well as working in bureaucratic organizations, David W. Barkley has observed that the fiercest and most frequent jurisdictional disputes seem to be *intraagency* in character.[70] Barkley's observation may provide a clue to understanding why agencies can behave in such contradictory ways. It may well be that public organizations aggressively seek activities that fit or complement their existing functions. This may be particularly true when these activities might otherwise go to their rivals. On the other hand, they may, thanks to their innate conservatism, shun activities that would take them into new, unknown, and possibly disturbed waters. Similarly, when they have no fear that an activity will be lodged in the hands of their competitors, they may even welcome an opportunity to get rid of some functions they already have.

An example of Barkley's rule could be the dispute raised within the military during the 1950s over who was to control missile development and funds.[71] The air force, as we have previously noted, sought to keep the navy from obtaining authorization to proceed with a missile program of its own. This in itself can be seen as an intraagency dispute, since both services are branches of the Department of Defense. More significant is the fact that when the navy finally won out and secured such authorization, it then found itself with an even more vigorous dispute on its hands. Two of its own subunits, the Bureau of Aeronautics and the Bureau of Ordinance, began contesting so vigorously and even vehemently for jurisdiction over the program that the navy felt constrained to set up a new unit, the Special Projects Office, to handle the task. Such are the workings of the territorial imperative.

The Pathology of Status

That human beings in nearly all cultures tend toward status seeking is well known. That organizations also tend toward status seeking is becoming equally well known, at least by those who have observed them in operation. Organizations, as we have perhaps tiresomely noted, are simply collections of human beings, and so it is scarcely any cause for wonder that they reflect the foibles and failings of those who compose them.

The pathologies of growth and imperialism that we have already examined bear witness to such status strivings. But status seeking may take many other forms as well. A subunit may seek to free itself from the organization of which it is a part in order to enjoy the greater status of being an independent agency. Next it may strive to secure recognition as a full-fledged cabinet department. Another subunit may seek to attach itself to the office of the chief executive, or, if it is already there, it may resist transfer to another agency since that might bring about a loss of prestige.

We see examples of this all the time. One reason the Children's Bureau resisted transfer from the Department of Labor to the Federal Security Agency in the late 1940s was that the FSA was not a cabinet department, and therefore the Children's Bureau, in becoming one of the FSA's subunits, would suffer a loss of status. Meanwhile, the upward-oriented FSA managed to evolve itself into a cabinet department in the 1950s, as did the Housing and Home Financing Agency in the 1960s. (The latter is now the Department of Housing and Urban Development.) In 1978, the Office of Education finally won its independence from the Department of Health, Education and Welfare and became a separate cabinet department.

Sometimes status struggles concern the use of physical space. An agency may seek a site that is closer to the seat of power or simply one that offers a prestigious address. Or it may do battle for a bigger and/or more beautiful building at its existing site. Or, if it shares a building with others, it may compete vigorously for more commodious floor space or for a top-floor location with a better view.

Other physical resources also easily become transformed into status symbols. The admirals of most navies eagerly sought the building of more battleships long after it became apparent that airplanes could easily blast them out of the water. Today the U.S. navy continues to press for the construction of mammoth and costly aircraft carriers despite the fact that many defense experts, including some ex-navy men, claim that such vessels are far too vulnerable to be worth the billion-dollar price tags they entail. Similarly, the advent of the missile age brought little diminution in the ardor of the air force for heavy bombers. As for civilian agencies, they can rarely boast of a more prudent approach. Hospitals, for instance, dearly love to acquire new and shiny apparatus even though such apparatus may not be needed to accommodate the health needs of the community. Pennsylvania's outspoken former Insurance Commissioner Herbert Denenberg used to claim that while New York City had seventeen hospitals and could perform open-heart surgery, only five such facilities were needed.

Open-heart surgery is not only a matter of equipment but also of activity, and this brings us to another and often crucial area where status struggles occur. Agencies and their subunits search for status by seeking to expand their role. If open-heart surgery provides on example of this, heart transplants offer an even better one. When such an operation was performed with some success in a South African hospital in the mid-1960s, other hospitals, particularly U.S. ones, eagerly embarked on this new and prestigious pursuit. Considerable resources were consumed in the enterprise, resources that could have more profitably been used elsewhere.

Status-seeking or status-sustaining motives often reinforce an organization's natural resistance to change. One factor behind the navy's refusal to abandon its outmoded battleships in World War II, and one reason why it so avidly wishes to build large and vulnerable aircraft carriers today, lies in the prestige that large vessels seem to confer. Similarly, in the early 1980s the U.S. Army was eagerly developing a huge supertank even though some experts were pointing out how new, advanced antitank weapons were already making such lumbering leviathans obsolete.

The Pathology of Self-Service

Many of the bureaucratic pathologies that we have been examining are obviously interrelated. In like manner, many of them relate to a final pathology, which serves as a partial basis for most of the others. This is the tendency of organizations to serve their own interests rather than the interests of their public or their clients.

One of the most complete examples of such a pathology has been found in mental hospitals. In his book *Asylums,* sociologist Erving Goffman points out that though such institutions are designed to treat and care for the mentally ill, they are also designed to provide a livelihood and an agreeable workplace for their staffs. According to Goffman, the latter goal easily and customarily supersedes the former one. Institutions for the mentally ill are run primarily, he says, for the benefit of their employees, not their clients.

Goffman's judgment may have been too harsh. Certainly efforts have been made in recent years to open up these institutions, and the press, the public, and political leaders have devoted increasing attention to their problems. Furthermore, we should note that mental institutions may have a particular ability to indulge in such goal displacement thanks to the fact that their clientele are not in a position to exercise any effective countervailing power. Therefore, we should not suppose all organizations can or do act in the same manner. Yet, a good many public bureaucracies do display the same tendency.

We have already seen instances of this in our examination of other types of organizational pathology. When hospitals insist on purchasing redundant equipment, performing expensive operations of dubious worth, and increasing their already surplus number of beds, they are serving basic needs of their staff, particularly their physicians. The doctors like the new equipment and enjoy the opportunity to make a name for themselves by engaging in various medical experiments that often do not provide a proportionate payoff in *overall* patient care. And almost all the staff benefits from the opportunities that an enlarged capacity can provide.

Hospitals should not bear the brunt of this diagnosis. Libraries, for example, in deciding when they will stay open will usually choose daytime hours over evening hours and weekdays over weekends. The public would obviously benefit from a reversed set of priorities. A library that is open on Sunday and closed on Monday would most likely accommodate the citizens of the community in a much better way than one that is open on Monday but closed on Sunday. Yet anyone who has used libraries knows what the priority is most likely to be. Other institutions tend to behave in the same way. Few public agencies, as a matter of fact, hold any evening or weekend hours because the convenience of the staff must take precedence over the convenience of the public.

In our earlier discussion of informal organization, we noted how prisons have often been run more by their inmates than by their staffs. This too reflects, at least in part, the tendency toward institutional self-accommodation. Maintaining control in a prison is no easy job, and so it becomes more convenient to let the inmates, or rather a small group of inmates, take on the task. In recent years, with the continued growth of prison unrest, prison officials have resorted to another self-serving strategem. According to former U.S. Attorney General Ramsey Clark, wardens have started "to release the most violent criminals before they cause trouble inside and are so relieved to see the dangerous ones go that they disregard the public safety—and the fact that most will be back before long."[72]

Perhaps no organization has developed self-accommodation into such a fine art as the art museum. A hypothetical example will best illustrate what is an everyday reality. Suppose a museum has twenty masterpieces, which are viewed by 1 million people a year. Suddenly the museum obtains a bequest of $1 million, which it can use either to acquire another masterpiece or to take steps, such as lowering its admission fees, that would bolster its number of visitors to 1.5 million a year. If it buys the masterpiece it will increase the total amount of art absorbed by the public by 5 percent. If it spends the money in the alternative manner, it will increase the amount of art viewed by the public by some 50 percent. Thus, if the museum's goal is to maximize its aesthetic service to the community, it should adopt the second choice in spending its new bequest.

Unfortunately, the typical art museum would not dream of doing so. Rather, it will hungrily go after the additional masterpiece. After all, a new and valuable painting adds to the aesthetic enjoyment of the staff and gives them something to boast about in talking with workers from other museums. "The American art museum," writes art critic Robert Hughes, "still tends to be an institutional parody of the robber baron's castle, staking its prestige more on acquisitions than functions." And Hughes points out that though New York City's famed Metropolitan Museum speaks in lofty tones of "bringing art to the people," it reinstituted its admission fees during the same year it spent over $5.5 million to acquire one new painting.[73]

What is particularly pernicious in this bit of museum madness is that it has driven up the cost of masterpieces horrendously, so that all museums now have fewer prized works than they would otherwise have been able to acquire. In recent decades, the prices of prized artworks have soared to stratospheric levels, and Hughes claims that "the chief perpetrators" of this phenomenon are the museums who bid feverishly against each other in a massive and mounting ego race. The situation has enriched many art dealers and private collectors while it has resulted in fewer people seeing fewer works of art than would otherwise have been the case.

Pathology and Its Price

The portrait of museums forcing up the prices of paintings by desperately trying to outbid each other is only one of the more egregious examples of the cost of organizational pathology. Agencies without clients, hospitals with rows of empty beds, and armies equipped to fight the last war impose obviously unnecessary burdens on the public purse. However, organizational disease bears still other price tags that are less readily seen.

The inherent conservation of organizations frequently forces presidents, governors, mayors, and other chief executives to set up new agencies and subagencies when they wish to do something new. The "New Frontier" and "Great Society" programs of presidents Kennedy and Johnson in the 1960s brought a host of new agencies onto the Washington landscape. Similar, if more limited, efforts at state and local levels did the same. Pollution control, energy, and other emerging issues of the 1970s resulted in a rash of new organizations at all levels of government.

One consequence of this constant trend is an increasingly unmanageable administrative apparatus. This in turn often leads to remedies that are worse than the disease. At state and local levels it has sparked and spurred the trend to create "superagencies," which, as we saw in the previous chapter, can cause troublesome problems of their own. In Washington it has encouraged presidents to centralize more control in the White House. In some instances this has amounted to setting up whole new bureaucracies to run key governmental functions, such as foreign affairs and poverty programs.

Another and possibly more costly consequence of adding on agencies are the problems created in terms of coordination. Squeezing an ever-increasing number of agencies into a relatively fixed amount of bureaucratic territory puts these agencies on a collision course with each other. This can cause not just confusion but calamity, for sometimes an agency will expend more energy and effort in curbing and even curtailing a competitor than in trying to achieve its own purported goals.

The pathology of growth presents similar problems. As an agency grows in size, not only does its output usually fail to grow proportionately, it may actually fall. In other words, an organization may increase its number of employees by 20 percent only to see its productivity *decrease* by, say, 10 percent. Here, too, the problem is one of coordination. As Peter Drucker has noted, "The more people have to work together, the more time will be spent on 'inter-acting' rather than on work and accomplishment."[74] Another management consultant, Martin R. Smith, claims that "contrary to popular belief, the overstaffed organization does not get out more work than the leaner organization. People devote their time to the wrong tasks in the fat department and they are constantly tripping over each other."[75] Herbert Simon puts it in a more pithy manner: "It is not very easy to thread a needle if one person holds the thread and another the needle."[76]

As an organization becomes bloated, the costs of this interactional process climb. Former Deputy Secretary of Defense David Packard found this to be true in the Pentagon's defense-procurement activity, his special area of attention during his term of service. Once noting that "we have a real mess on our hands," Packard went on to say, "We don't need more people in the act—we need fewer people. We overorganize, overman, overspend and under accomplish.''[77] Military history supplies substantial confirmation of Packard's observation regarding the dangers of over-abundance. The Germans used only 150,000 men to defeat, in six weeks, a French army that was actually ten times as large. Genghis Khan conquered half the world with an army that was only one-half the size of the present New York City bureaucracy. And the Israeli army, which is considered even by our own military establishment to be, person for person, a more effective fighting force than our own, has one general for every 21,000 enlisted men, while the U.S. Army has one general for every 1,600 enlisted men.

The price of pathology, we should remember, cannot be assessed in only monetary terms. There is also the cost in human suffering from services wrongly rendered or not rendered at all. George Teeling Smith, who directs the Office of Health Economics in Great Britain, has pointed out that a hospital will exert every effort to obtain funds for a new kidney machine. The same amount of money would alleviate much more human misery if it were spent on such simple but nonprestigious tasks as widening the front doors of the rooms and apartments of paraplegics who have to use wheelchairs.

A final point remains to be considered. To what extent are the organizational pathologies we have been examining limited to public and semi-public institutions? Does the private sector manage to avoid them?

There is certainly evidence to indicate that such has been the case. While the U.S. Army was still maintaining horse cavalry during the 1930s, the blacksmiths in the private sector were rapidly going out of business. Profit does provide a direct and decisive feedback to the private sector, and a business can and usually does go bankrupt if it is not providing in a reasonably efficient manner those goods and services that the public actually wants. While business can to some extent manipulate its markets by advertising, the annals of business are strewn with highly advertised products, such as Edsel cars, Champale beer, chemise dresses, and midi skirts, which the public rejected. Even supposedly monopolistic industries are limited in the extent they can ignore the needs of efficient production without suffering losses. The steel and auto industries have achieved much lower earnings growth than business as a whole during the past decade, while such giants as Dupont, Alcoa, and even IBM have seen their share of the markets in their respective industries steadily fade. The winds of change cut through the private sector with a much greater force and greater impact than they do through the bastions of public bureaucracy.

On the other hand, however, profit seeking may generate its own pathologies, such as an excessive and even counterproductive competitive atmosphere. Furthermore, business is becoming more bureaucratized all the time. Those who manage the typical large firm are no longer those who own. Thus, many of the pathologies of the public sector are pushing their way into the private sector as well. Martin R. Smith tells of a firm that used to allow the manufacturer of its packaging machinery to provide all the engineering services needed to keep the machinery operating properly. This the machinery maker was willing to do at no additional cost. In time, however, the firm began to wonder if it could do a better job of servicing the equipment by itself.

It first hired a specialist for this purpose. The specialist soon decided he needed some specialized equipment for his work. Then, he persuaded the company to engage a technician to operate the testing equipment and a machinist to implement the machine design changes that the specialist was drawing up. By this time paperwork was becoming a problem, and so a secretary was added.

"Within two years after the company had hired an engineer to perform a very specific task," writes Smith, "it had established an Engineering Machinery Department with a payroll of six people and an expensive testing laboratory to maintain. This, mind you, supplanted the free services provided by the packaging machinery manufacturer!"[78]

Notes

1. Woodrow Wilson, "The Study of Administration," *Political Science Quarterly* (June 1887). Reprinted, in part in Donald C. Rowat, ed., *Basic Issues in Public Administration* (New York: Macmillan, 1961).

2. Leonard D. White, *Introduction to the Study of Public Administration* (New York: Macmillan, 1926).

3. Some of Follett's papers may be found in Henry C. Metcalfe and L. Urwick, eds., *Dynamic Administration* (New York: Harper & Row, 1940).

4. Elton Mayo, *The Human Problems of an Industrial Civilization* (New York: Macmillan, 1933). Also see F. J. Roethlisberger and William J. Dickson, *Management and the Worker* (Cambridge, Mass.: Harvard University Press, 1946).

5. Dwight Waldo, *The Administrative State* (New York: Ronald Press, 1948); William H. Whyte, *Human Relations in the Restaurant Industry* (New York: McGraw-Hill, 1948); Herbert A. Simon, *Administrative Behavior* (New York: Free Press, 1947); J. G. March and H. A. Simon, *Organizations* (New York: John Wiley, 1958).

6. The best-known works of these authors are Chris Argyris, *Personality and Organization* (New York: Harper & Row, 1957); Douglas McGregor, *The Theory of Human Enterprise* (New York: McGraw-Hill, 1960); and Rensis Likert, *New Patterns of Management* (New York: McGraw-Hill, 1961).

7. This brief summary of some of the elements of systems analysis as applied to organizational behavior is taken from Daniel Katz and Robert L. Kahn, *The Social Psychology of Organizations* (New York: John Wiley, 1966) and from David Eastman, *The Political System* (New York: Alfred A. Knopf, 1966).

8. Chester Barnard, *Functions of the Executive* (Cambridge, Mass.: Harvard University Press, 1968), 84.

9. Abraham M. Maslow, *Motivation and Personality*, 2nd ed. (New York: Harper & Row, 1970). See in particular pp, 35–38.

10. Frederick Herzberg, Bernard Mausner, and Barbara Block Snyderman, *The Motivation to Work* (New York: John Wiley, 1959), 83.

11. Katz and Kahn, *Social Psychology of Organizations*, 303.

12. McGregor, *Human Enterprise*, 41.

13. Joseph E. Galvin, "Now Listen to a Firefighter's Plea," *New York Times*, 20 January 1972, Op-Ed page.

14. George H. Sabine, *A History of Political Theory*, 3rd ed. (New York: Holt, Rinehart and Winston, 1961), 15–16.

15. William A. Westley, "Secrecy and the Police," *Social Forces* (March 1956).

16. See, for example, Heinz Hohne, *The Order of the Death's Head: The Story of Hitler's S.S.* (New York: Coward-McCann, 1970).

17. Donald R. Cressey, *Theft of the Nation* (New York: Harper & Row, 1969), 209–210.

18. Herbert Kaufman, *The Forest Ranger* (Baltimore, Md.: Johns Hopkins Press, 1960), 235.

19. *New York Times*, 9 June 1972.

20. Graham Greene, "The Virtues of Disloyalty," *The Observer*, 24 December 1972.

21. Katz and Kahn, *Social Psychology of Organizations*, 42.

22. Roethlisberger and Dickson, *Management and Worker*.

23. Whyte, *Restaurant Industry*.

24. Robert Presthus, *The Organizational Society* (New York: Random House, 1962), 291.

25. Katz and Kahn, *Social Psychology of Organizations*, 303.

26. Chris Argyris, "The CEO's Behavior: Key to Organizational Behavior," *Harvard Business Review* (March–April 1973).

27. Douglas McGregor, *Leadership and Motivation* (Cambridge, Mass.: MIT Press, 1966), 15.

28. Katz and Kahn, *Social Psychology of Organizations*, 364.

29. Jay Hall, "What Makes a Manager Good, Bad or Average?" *Psychology Today* (August 1976).

30. This case study is based on the following article: Stephen Bryant and Joseph Kearns, "Workers Brains as Well as Their Bodies: Quality Circle in a Federal Facility," *Public Administration Review* (March–April 1982). The authors are both employees of the U.S. Office of Personnel Management.

31. Roethlisberger and Dickson, *Management and Worker*, 552.

32. William H. Riker, *The NLRB Examiner*, Inter-University Case Program no. 15 (Indianapolis, Ind.: Bobbs-Merrill, 1951).

33. Vincent O'Leary and David Duffy, "Managerial Behavior and Correctional Policy," *Public Administration Review* (November–December, 1971).

34. Katz and Kahn, *Social Psychology of Organizations*, 350.

35. Peter Maas, *Serpico* (New York: Viking Press, 1973).

36. *New York Times*, 7 June 1973.

37. Alvin W. Gouldner, *Patterns of Industrial Democracy* (Glencoe, Ill.: Free Press, 1954).

38. Peter Blau, *The Dynamics of Bureaucracy* (Chicago: University of Chicago Press, 1955), 152.

39. Michael Banton, *The Policeman in the Community* (London: Tavistock Publications, 1964), 117.

40. *Time*, 18 June 1973, 19.

41. Herbert A. Simon, Donald W. Smithburg, and Victor A. Thompson, *Public Administration* (New York: Alfred A. Knopf, 1950); and Katz and Kahn, *Social Psychology of Organizations*. Douglas McGregor's statement is from his posthumously published book *The Professional Manager* (New York: McGraw-Hill, 1967). The quote from Crozier is from *La Société Bloquée* (Paris: Editions du Seuil, 1970).

42. Katz and Kahn, *Social Psychology of Organizations*, 379.

43. Peter M. Blau, *Bureaucracy in Modern Society* (New York: Random House, 1956), 56.

44. Katz and Kahn, *Social Psychology of Organizations*, 327.

45. Argyris, *Personality and Organization*.

46. Editorial, "Do We Need All This Advice?" *Boston Herald-American*, 4 May 1973.

47. *Administrative Management in the Government of the United States.* (Washington, D.C.: Government Printing Office, 1937, 34.

48. *New York Times*, 1 July 1972.

49. Presthus, *Organizational Society*, 291.

50. R. G. S. Brown, *The Administrative Process in Britain* (London: Methuen, 1970), 248.

51. Harvey M. Sapolsky, *The Polaris System Development: Bureaucratic and Programmatic Success in Government* (Cambridge, Mass.: Harvard University Press, 1972), chap. 2.

52. Quoted by Fred M. Hechinger in "Principals: Call for New Breed of School Leader," *New York Times*, 21 March 1971, News in Review section.

53. Quoted by a speaker from the floor during a panel session at the annual convention of the American Society for Public Administration, Los Angeles, 1973. Although I was unable to find out the context in which Rickover made the statement, it sounds so typical of him that I have little doubt of its authenticity.

54. For an account of both Sims's and Mitchell's ordeals, see Clark R. Mollenhoff, *The Pentagon* (New York: Pinnacle Books, 1972), chaps. 3 and 5.

55. C. Northcote Parkinson, *The Law of Delay* (New York: Ballantine Books, 1970), 4–5.

56. *Christian Science Monitor*, 1 August 1971.

57. *Los Angeles Times*, 2 April 1973.

58. Michael Curtis, ed., *The Great Political Theories* (New York: Avon Books, 1962), 49.

59. Katz and Kahn, *Social Psychology of Organizations,* 24.

60. C. Northcote Parkinson, *Parkinson's Law and Other Studies of Administration* (New York: Ballantine Books, 1964), 17.

61. Parkinson, *Law of Delay,* 2–3.

62. William Proxmire, *Uncle Sam: The Last of the Bigtime Spenders* (New York: Simon & Schuster, 1972), 66–67.

63. *Los Angeles Herald-Examiner,* 2 April 1973.

64. "A Plethora of Presidents," *Time,* 29 January 1973.

65. Laurence J. Peter and Raymond Hull, *The Peter Principle* (New York: William Morrow, 1968).

66. Robert Ardrey, *African Genesis* (New York: Dell Publishing, 1963).

67. Anthony Downs, *Inside Bureaucracy* (Boston: Little, Brown, 1966), 216.

68. Herbert Kaufman and Wallace S. Sayre, *Governing New York City* (New York: Russell Sage Foundation, 1960), 262.

69. Chester Bowles, *Promises to Keep* (New York: Harper & Row, 1971), 155.

70. David W. Barkley, in observations made to the author.

71. Sapolsky, *Polaris System,* 78.

72. Ramsey Clark, *Crime in America* (New York: Simon & Schuster, 1970), 214.

73. Robert Hughes, "Who Needs Masterpieces at Those Prices?" *Time,* 19 July 1971, 52–53.

74. Peter F. Drucker, *The Effective Executive* (New York: Harper & Row, 1967), 31.

75. Martin R. Smith, *I Hate to See a Manager Cry* (Reading, Mass.: Addison-Wesley, 1973), 9.

76. Simon, *Administrative Behavior,* 238.

77. David Packard quoted in Proxmire, *Uncle Sam,* 68.

78. Smith, *Manager Cry,* 7.

4

People and Personnel

Since organizations are primarily clusters of people, it logically follows that personnel policies and practices play a primary role in organizational life. "Let me control personnel," George Kennan has said, "and I will ultimately control policy. For the part of the machine that recruits and hires and fires and promotes people can soon control the entire shape of the institution."[1]

Few administrative theorists or practitioners would dispute this statement, and in the course of history, few able administrators have thought or acted otherwise. However, their attitudes and approaches to the subject have often differed. Thomas Jefferson, for example, believed that civil servants should be provided with "drudgery and subsistence only" so that they would not want to stay too long in office.[2] This would enable the country to escape the establishment and growth of an administrative class, a development that Jefferson greatly feared. His fears were echoed by a U.S. business journal in the 1920s, which published an editorial stressing "the urgency of keeping this country's civil service inffective lest it become dangerous."[3]

Most writers on and practitioners of administration have, however, taken a different tack, and through the years increasing effort has gone toward improving the capabilities and enhancing the stature of those who toil in the public sector. Today, the stress almost everywhere is placed upon strengthening the competency of civil servants, and it is with this goal in mind that the subject of personnel will be pursued here.

Procedures and Policies

Public organizations in this country essentially use one of two different methods of establishing and operating personnel systems. One method stresses political appointment and election, the other emphasizes an objective determination of merit.

Political appointment and election has a long, proud history in the United States. Units of the Revolutionary army frequently elected their own officers, and once the hostilities ended, states and their communities undertook to elect most of the administrators they would need. This practice has persisted in many places up to the present day, and no other major country in the world elects so many of its administrators as does the United States. Most state governments elect at least some officials whose tasks would be regarded in Europe or Canada as purely administrative. Many cities and towns, particularly older ones, follow the same practice. Some New England communities elect as many as fifty officials. Newer areas of the country, such as the Far West, disdain such practices, but even they maintain county organizations with a high number of elective posts.

Political scientists have tended to frown on this practice, and with good reason. Although election is supposed to give the people a deciding voice in determining who will administer their government, it tends to lead to all sorts of abuses, such as confusing and misleading promises and campaign funding from special interests. Underlying all such problems is the fact that most of the electorate finds it impossible to know all the candidates for whom they must vote. A study done some years ago in Michigan showed that 73 percent of those polled could not identify the state's secretary of state, 75 percent could not name the state highway commissioner, 77 percent had no idea who the superintendent of public instruction was, 80 percent did not know the state attorney general, and a full 96 percent were at a loss to name the state treasurer. This survey was carried out shortly after a state election in which most of the respondents presumably had cast ballots for those whose names they now did not know.

Politically appointing administrators is a practice that also dates back to colonial times. Even John Adams, who considered himself something of a paragon of political propriety, felt constrained to provide his ne'er-do-well son-in-law with a government job. Such practices gained increased favor with the arrival of Andrew Jackson at the White House. Jackson strongly adhered to Jefferson's belief in rotating public servants in office. At the same time he did not believe that this would entail any loss of public confidence. As he put it, "The duties of all public servants are, or at least admit of being made, so plain and simple that men of intelligence may readily qualify themselves for their performance."[4] Of course, Old Hickory's espousal of this philosophy was fortified by the fact that he had a virtual army of job seekers at his back who were clamoring loudly for the plums of patronage.

From Jackson's time on U.S. presidents found themselves frequently besieged by persons seeking positions on the public payroll. One aggressive appointment seeker jumped into Abraham Lincoln's carriage to press his case while the president was riding through Washington. Lincoln started to listen to him but then drove him away, saying, more in despair than in anger, "No, I will not do business in the street."

When a disappointed job seeker assassinated President James Garfield in 1881, the nation's appetite for such administrative practices began to change. However, political appointment continues to play a prominent role in U.S. administrative life. Our presidents have nearly one hundred times as many appointments to fill as do British prime ministers. At the lower levels, political appointment still prevails in many states. While the governor of Wisconsin has only twenty jobs to fill and the governor of Oregon has fewer than a dozen, New York State's chief executive has nearly twenty-one thousand positions at his disposal, and Pennsylvania's governor can name fifty thousand to state posts.[5]

But the assassination of President Garfield did have its effect. It gave rise to an alternative method of recruitment, namely the merit system. Two years after the president's violent death, Congress passed the Pendleton Act, setting up a systematized procedure for hiring and employing vast categories of federal civil servants. The merit-system principle has continued to grow ever since. Today it not only embraces over 90 percent of all positions in the federal government but includes increasing numbers of employees in state and local governments as well. About two-thirds of our states now have what are called comprehensive merit systems, which cover the vast majority of their jobholders. And even the remaining states make some provisions for merit-system appointments. The federal government has helped prod states and municipalities to move in this direction, for federal grants-in-aid frequently require the recipient agency to operate a merit system of some sort. Thus, HEW will not hand out any funds to a local welfare department that uses political appointment to recruit its caseworkers.

Although the merit principle has consistently climbed in public favor, the more traditional method of political appointment continues to have its supporters. Its backers claim that such a system provides government with more flexibility and responsiveness. Elected officials, or at least officials appointed directly by elected officeholders, are in a better position to control administrative activities and translate program proposals into action. Admiral Lord Fisher rebuilt and strengthened the British navy by "promoting *his* men," claiming that "the secret of effectiveness is favoritism."

According to its detractors, a merit system leads eventually to a triumph of mediocrity, with initiative and enterprise sacrificed to the pressures of security and the forces of stagnation. Finally, even when a merit system encourages merit, it may lead only to a "meritocracy," which shuts out otherwise capable people who cannot pass its tests or meet its formal and sometimes fatuous requirements.

Some who voice this view compare Chicago to New York City. The merit principle was always less firmly ensconced in the midwestern metropolis than in the eastern one, and in 1975 it was abolished in Chicago altogether. But the claim has continually been made that "Chicago works," while New York City seems to have generally floundered and failed. It took the combined efforts of New York State and the federal government to rescue the nation's largest city from bankruptcy in 1975.

But though the merit system may have lost some of its luster through the years, it retains a good deal of support from both theorists and practitioners. If it leads to a "meritocracy" then, they say, this is still likely to be more egalitarian and more in conformity with democratic ideals than a system built on political contacts and allegiances. When operated properly, it recruits the better people and encourages them to stay and develop their capabilities.

Its supporters also deny that merit-system employees will automatically block the implementation of new policies by elected officials. They point to Great Britain, where the top officials of the bureaucracy, despite the fact that they themselves were largely members of the upper classes, cheerfully implemented the rather sweeping socialist policies of the Labour government that took office in 1945. (A less appealing example of this same flexibility is the German civil service, which displayed few qualms in carrying out Hitler's policies in the 1930s.[6]) If Chicago seems to "work" better than New York City, then a somewhat greater acceptance of the merit system in the latter city is probably not responsible. California cities seem to have fewer problems than New York City or even Chicago, but their bureaucracies are almost completely covered by well-enforced merit systems. An editorial in the *Los Angeles Times* of April 5, 1973, credited "the momentum of a strong and professional civil service" for the fact that the United States's third largest city did not suffer "some of the malignancies that infect other major American cities."

Recruitment

If the merit principle has become the most widely accepted basis for personnel operation in U.S. administration, it nevertheless continues to catalyze controversies and pose problems. In terms of recruitment, there is first the task of making sure that the system is truly merit rewarding. Most civil-service systems make extensive use of comparative examinations to bring this about. While such exams may more impartially weigh the merits of the various candidates than would a system built on favoritism or capriciousness, they still offer difficulties of their own.

For one thing, the exams must be predictive. In other words, high scores on the examinations should correlate with high performance on the job and vice versa. Unfortunately, in the majority of cases little attempt has been made until recently to ensure that such correlations exist. A joint survey by the Office of Economic Opportunity, the Department of Labor, and the National Civil Service League in 1970 found that only 54 percent of all state and local governments conducted any test validation, and most of these governments limited such validation efforts to only a few agencies. Other recruitment standards were also found to have gone unvalidated, often with damaging results to all concerned. The survey team came upon one city that desperately needed thirty-eight dogcatchers but could not hire a single one. The criteria for the job called for all recruits to have high school diplomas plus two years experience in handling animals. None of the few people who could meet these qualifications wanted the job.[7]

The issue of the validity of tests and other recruitment criteria has come to the fore in recent years, thanks to the stepped-up efforts to recruit members of minority groups into government service. Civil rights supporters claim that many of these criteria serve to exclude blacks, Puerto Ricans, Chicanos, and others. In so doing, they thus fail to determine the true capability of a job applicant. A study in Chicago found that a black police recruit would perform as well as a white recruit who scored 10 percent higher on the entrance exam.[8] In other words, the entrance test failed to measure the true ability of black applicants for police work in comparison with white applicants.

The federal government has been moving to require test validation as a means of ensuring and expanding equal opportunity. In January 1973 the Department of Justice filed suits against the fire departments of Boston, Los Angeles, and Montgomery, Alabama, charging that their recruitment tests, qualifications, and selection standards generally "have not been shown to be required by the needs of the fire department or predictive of successful job performance."[9]

The move to include more members of minority groups in public administration is part of a larger movement aimed at making government agencies more representative of the public they serve. This brings us to another issue in administration. Government agencies have at times become "captured" by one or more particular sectors of society. The "captive" agency—the term is Brian Chapman's—tends to recruit heavily from one particular ethnic, religious, social, or geographical group. Many U.S. police forces, for example, have long been dominated by men of Irish descent. The army at one time drew a disproportionate number of its members, particularly at the officer level, from white southerners. And the Foreign Service long leaned toward upper-class Anglo-Saxons with preparatory school and Ivy League backgrounds to fill its ranks.

Such tendencies, it should be noted, do not necessarily spring from any intentional policy on the part of the agency concerned. Often it may arise by chance and then continue as members of the particular group involved are drawn toward the agency where so many of their fellow members are employed. Whatever the reason, capture by a particular group does bestow some benefits on an agency. Having personnel from a similar background eases communication problems and creates more harmonious operations. However, there are also costs to be paid.

The spy scandals that blew up in Great Britain during the 1950s illustrate just what these costs can be. These spies, who were agents of the Soviet Union, were also, like most of their associates, members of the British upper classes and graduates of prestigious universities. As a result, their fellow members of the establishment could never believe that they could be traitors, although the behavior of some of them should have led their superiors and co-workers to wonder. Referring to two of these Soviet agents, Guy Burgess and Donald Maclean, Robin Maugham writes, "These two outrageous characters would never have lasted two months if they'd been working for some reputable business company. They would have been sacked. Why were they kept on by our intelligence service? Why? Because in those days our intelligence service was run by an 'Old Boy' network and backed up by an Establishment of cryptoqueer ambassadors."[10]

Another example of the costs of capture was the domination of the German Foreign Office by members of the Junker class during World War I. According to historian Barbara Tuchman, the Junkers reinforced each other's provincial tendencies. Not only did they fail to win friends for Germany but they succeeded in losing many of the friends the country already had.[11]

An agency that draws its recruits from all sectors of the population will stand a better chance of escaping these problems. More importantly, such an agency will more likely become infused with new ideas and new energies. It is more apt to be responsive to other organizations as well as to the diverse publics it is supposed to serve. Katz and Kahn cite research showing that homogeneous groups "produced fewer high-quality solutions than did heterogeneous groups" and, so these authors claim, an organization that continues to recruit one type of employee comes to resemble itself more and more closely as time passes until it turns into a virtual caricature of itself.[12]

Public organizations should not only broaden their recruitment base but should make sure that they draw from this broader base the maximum number of A-1 applicants. Government agencies, at least in this country, have often been quite lax in this regard. Many have made little use of advertising and other publicity techniques. Furthermore, their competitive examinations, irrespective of their validity or lack of same, have often been cumbersome and costly to prospective employee and employer alike. Processing the tests, meanwhile, usually entails a waiting period during which time many of the better recruits receive and accept job offers elsewhere.

Here again, fortunately, change is slowly coming. Many agencies have begun to recruit more aggressively, and some are abridging and even eliminating the examination process. The latter tendency has been particularly pronounced in certain professional fields. Thus, doctors, nurses, and teachers who possess requisite certification are seldom subjected to examinations when they choose to work for a public hospital or school system. This trend seems likely to grow as professionalism increases in society and as the need for flexibility and responsiveness grows in public personnel policy.

PREPARING FOR PUBLIC SERVICE

The rule of the present day is, that every place shall be open to public competition, and that it shall be given to the best among the comers. I object to this, that at present there exists no known way of learning who is best, and that the method employed has no tendency to elicit the best. That method pretends only to decide who among a certain number of lads will best answer a string of questions, for the answering of which they are prepared by tutors, who have sprung up for the purpose since this fashion of election has been adopted. When it is decided in a family that a boy shall "try the Civil Service," he is made to undergo a certain amount of cramming. But such treatment has, I maintain, no connection whatever with education. The lad is no better fitted after it than he was before for the future work of his life.

Anthony Trollope (1815–1882)
in "An Autobiography"

Trollope wrote nearly forty novels, in addition to essays, reviews, and other articles, while serving successfully in the British Postal Service.

Although it is desirable for public agencies to recruit aggressively, it is also important for them to do what is in effect the opposite. They should discourage the unsuitable as much as they encourage the suitable. A shy introvert or a violence-prone individual should not be induced to take a police exam, while the person who cannot stand routine should not be encouraged to seek a file-clerk position. The personnel administrator should try to dissuade the overqualified as much as the underqualified. A Ph.D. is likely to turn into as poor a sorter of mail as would the semiliterate who has difficulty reading simple addresses.

One government agency that takes great care to discourage the unsuitable from seeking to join its ranks is the Forest Service. Being a forest ranger means long hours of rigorous, responsible, and often lonely work usually performed in rather isolated outposts. It also means constant rotation. In its recruitment effort, the service tries to make it very clear that those who would find such a life distasteful should seek their careers elsewhere.[13]

In 1968, the British army began trying a new device designed both to encourage those equipped for military life to join up and to discourage the unsuitable from doing so. Prospective enlistees were offered a chance to try out the army on approval. Any young man contemplating an army career could enlist for a four-day trial period. If he found it to his liking, he could then sign up for a full term. If, on the other hand, he found it was not his cup of tea, he could leave with no hard feelings and with $11.80 in his pocket, his pay for an abbreviated term of military service.[14]

The Postrecruitment Phase

The personnel agency, once it has cleared a group of recruits, will then usually place their names on a list. Such a list is rarely alphabetical. Rather, it runs in order of eligibility with the top scorers on the exam placing first and continuing down the line. However, many other factors may also figure into the standings. One of these is veterans' preference. The federal and most state and local civil-service systems award some bonus points to those who have served in the armed forces. The federal government bestows five points for such service alone and five additional points if the applicant qualifies as a disabled veteran.

Agencies customarily take their recruits from the top of the list, but here again there are some exceptions. In some cases, particularly for higher-level positions, the rule of three may apply. This permits the appointing authority to skip the top scorer or even the second scorer on the list of qualified applicants. They can choose any of the top three. The advantages of permitting such discretion for certain positions are obvious. An applicant may score highest in a well-thought-out exam for public relations officer, but if he exudes unpleasant breath and changes his shirt once every two weeks, he is not likely to perform the agency's public relations duties in the most effective manner.

In addition to these perfectly proper ways of relaxing their requirement to take recruits from the top of the list, agencies sometimes resort to more surreptitious strategies. They may hold off taking any recruits at all until they can be sure that enough people at the top of the list will have found other jobs or moved away so that some favored person or persons farther down the list can be reached. The lists themselves usually expire after one or two years, and an agency may wait until such a list expires in order to gain someone who will be on the new list. Or the appointing authority may let the list expire and discourage attempts to set up a new one, choosing instead to fill positions on a temporary basis.

There is nothing inherently suspect about temporary appointments, and virtually all merit systems make some provisions for them. Usually such appointments can be made only for prescribed periods, such as thirty working days. Abuses have come when such appointments are indefinitely extended. The federal government and some state and local jurisdictions have taken steps to counteract this by prohibiting any temporary appointee from serving successive terms in any particular position. However, many other jurisdictions are more lenient—hence, the ability of Chicago mayors to name precinct captains to temporary positions lasting several years and even decades.

Assuming that the recruit has qualified for and received an appointment, he or she still has some hurdles to surmount before claiming full-fledged membership in the organization. One of these is the probationary period. During this time the recruit can be dismissed without the safeguards that protect those who have successfully passed such a phase. Probationary periods vary in length from six months to six years. The six-month term is common in some state and local governments, while the federal government and some other subnational jurisdictions require one year of service. However, it is common to vary the time somewhat, depending upon the nature of the position. While a fledgling sanitation man may acquire permanent status in six months, his colleague on the police force may have to wait a full year. At the same time, the local schoolteacher may not be given tenure for three years. The largest waiting periods are usually found at colleges and universities, where new faculty members may have to serve six years before becoming tenured. Some positions, such as political appointments to high-level posts, confer no privileges or permanency at all.

Another aspect of the postrecruitment phase concerns training. Some agencies do nearly all their own recruit training. These include police departments, fire departments, and the like. Other public bodies, such as school systems and public health agencies, expect the newcomer to have acquired the needed basic skills beforehand. Generally, the higher the professional level of the position, the more likely it is that the recruit for that position will have obtained the essential training prior to his or her appointment.

Training of all kinds is receiving increasing attention in public administration today. It has become an accepted fact that a fast-moving and fast-changing society exhibits a high need for, and must place increasing emphasis on, wide-ranging and high-level skills. It was not so long ago that a typical police officer's training consisted of some on-the-job supervision. Now he or she is likely to receive many weeks' and even several months' schooling at a police academy. The same holds true for many other public positions. Street cleaners are now more apt to operate fairly complicated equipment rather than merely push brooms, and so they, too, must receive a minimum of instruction to cope with their once-simple tasks.

The fastest growing area of attention in regard to training lies in what is called in-service training. The upsurge of interest in this subject arises from the growing realization that in a modern society such as ours, scarcely anyone is ever fully trained for the rest of his or her career. Not only must skills be continually upgraded, but new skills must frequently be acquired if the employee and the organization are to meet the shifting demands and the changing work patterns that are so characteristic of our present time. More and more administrators are accepting the notion that education is a lifelong process and that the organizations they manage must plan to provide training on a nearly nonstop basis throughout an employee's career.

This brings us to the question of whether an organization should seek to do its own in-service training or whether it should require or encourage the employee to obtain such training from an outside source. Distinct advantages accrue to the organization that does its own in-service training. It should know best just what skills it wishes to develop and what general abilities it wishes to foster. As a result, it can target its training accordingly. Also, the organization may achieve some financial savings in using its own training personnel and facilities. Finally, employees may accept such training more readily and absorb it more rigorously, for they can see a direct connection between the training and their organizational life.

But calling in outsiders or sending employees to outside educational institutions may also afford advantages. First, it allows the organization to tap a much wider variety of training talent and training facilities than it is likely to have within its own boundaries. Then, while outside training can sometimes be more costly, it can also on occasion be cheaper. This is particularly true when doing its own training would require the organization to hire people and buy equipment that it cannot fully utilize. Most important of all, perhaps, is the fact that in-house training deprives the employee of the expanded range of educational experience and contacts that can come when the education is obtained at an outside institution. Attending classes where the instructor and fellow students represent different intellectual and organizational backgrounds may enable the employee to absorb new ideas and perspectives that will invigorate not only the work performance but the entire approach to work problems. The late philosopher Alfred North Whitehead once said that no mind that has been stretched by a new idea will ever shrink back to its original dimensions, and an organization interested in improving the intellectual capabilities of its employees will probably find that outside education often does this stretching process better than in-house training classes.

In fiscal year 1971, the U.S. government spent over $200 million in training programs of more than eight hours' duration for its employees. (Programs that ran less than eight hours were not reported.) The average length of these training programs was forty-eight hours. And although 74 percent of this training was administered by government agencies themselves for their own employees, these figures represent a modest decline from the 80 percent in-house figure for 1967.[15]

Promotion

Once an employee has cleared all the hurdles and achieved full status as a member of the organization, he or she then normally starts to think about the possibilities for promotion. Such advancement may come in the form of a simple pay increase, an increase in grade at the present level, or a move up to a new level, usually involving at least some new duties and responsibilities.

Merit systems customarily provide two basic criteria for promotion: seniority and merit. In the majority of instances, both factors enter into consideration. The question to be answered is Which is the most conducive to effective administration?

The answer at first seems obvious. Merit is normally deemed the best and most beneficial method for determining who shall rise and who shall not. Seniority presents obvious drawbacks. It rewards the incompetent along with the competent. It offers little inducement for the employee to upgrade skills or exert his or her best efforts. A seniority system may make it harder for an organization to attract the best and the brightest and may make it even more difficult for it to retain them once they find that moving upward merely is a matter of biding one's time. When those who occupy the upper positions are still enjoying good health, this wait can seem nearly endless.

For these reasons, seniority has often served as a whipping boy of civil service, and the dominant role it has played in many merit systems has made them seem far from meritorious. Yet, seniority does have benefits of its own to bestow. First, it is the most truly impartial system possible for conferring promotion. No merit measures can ever achieve the complete objectivity of the seniority principle, for though a dispute may arise as to whether employee A is better than employee B, no dispute is every likely to spring up over the question of which of them joined the organization first.

As a completely neutral system for promotion, seniority may also put a damper on disruption and discord. There is little incentive to backbite or backstab when such activities are doomed to go unrewarded. Strange as it may seem, the fact that employees have little motivation to seek short-cuts to the top *can*, at least in some instances, induce them to concentrate better on their existing work.

Seniority also can, and the emphasis again is on *can*, stimulate productivity in another way. An employee who knows that her promotion is assured by the gradual piling up of seniority may have far fewer fears when it comes to speaking out as to what she thinks is wrong and what she thinks will make things better. Since her advancement does not depend on the benign approval of those above her, she may be more inclined to offer suggestions and criticisms when they seem warranted. This will be seen more fully when the problem of employee evaluation is examined.

A seniority system also tends to encourage employee identification with the organization and to reduce turnover. Employees' investment in the job grows every day, for each day's work brings them closer to promotion.

Seniority thus has its blessings, and the wise administrator would do well to keep them in mind. It is particularly useful in deciding who gets first choice in such things as vacation time, desk location, and the like. And it probably does not deserve the blame that it so often is made to bear for the poor efficiency of many public organizations. As we have seen, seniority has advantages of its own in terms of productivity, and some organizations, such as Japanese industrial firms and government agencies, have not found their rather rigid seniority systems any major deterrent to achieving an extraordinarily high output.

However, the trend everywhere is for decreasing the emphasis on seniority in promotion. Civil-service systems in this country are gradually whittling down the prominent position that they had previously accorded this method of promotion. The federal government today makes little use of it as such, and many other jurisdictions are reducing its role. Most administrators favor genuine merit systems, at least for major promotions, and most writers on administration agree with them.

Promotion by merit requires some way of determining merit and this opens up another set of problems. Two basic means exist for making such determinations—examinations and performance. Competitive examinations are the most impartial, and as such may confer some of the benefits associated with the seniority system. They reduce the role of internal politics and ensure all employees something of an equal opportunity to move upward.

Be this as it may, using competitive examinations as a basis for determining promotion is going out of favor. Again, the federal government now makes little use of such devices in deciding who is to be promoted and who is not, and many state and local civil service commissions are slowly starting to follow suit. There are many reasons for this trend. For one thing, exams are bothersome for administrators to give and for employees to take. Also, the exams cannot be given every day, and once given they must be corrected and tabulated. This procedure usually entails a waiting period, which can be exasperating to the employee and disruptive to the organization, which may need someone to fill the vacant post right away.

A much more important consideration is the fact that examinations do not, and in many cases probably cannot, determine just how well the applicant will fare in the new role. Supervisory positions, for example, require leadership qualities, and these are difficult to determine by answers to written questions. Two examples illustrate some of the problems that may occur. The joint OEO, Labor Department, and National Civil Service League survey cited earlier found a case where a mechanic had received seven provisional promotions to shop foreman. Each time he performed outstandingly in his position, but each time he lost it when he flunked the written test. The other example concerns the case of a New York City patrolman who was found by the *New York Times* on February 20, 1973, to possess a Ph.D. in psychology. Why was he only a patrolman? It seems that Officer Harvey Schlossberg had been spending so much time doing his graduate work that he failed to study enough for the sergeant's exam and so had failed it. Consequently, despite all his education and his useful skills as a psychologist, Dr. Schlossberg was still pounding a beat.

But whether an organization relies on seniority or merit, and whether it measures merit by examination or performance, a further question arises: To what extent should an organization promote its own members at all?

This brings us to the issue of *lateral entry*. Organizations may fill upper-level positions from within or without. When they accept outsiders for posts other than those at the bottom level, they are using what is called lateral entry. It is an almost universal practice in the private sector, but is far less common in the public one. Many public organizations, such as most police departments, fire departments, and sanitation departments, make no provision at all for lateral entry except for occasional highly specialized positions. Other organizations, such as school departments, may allow lateral entry only at the uppermost level. Thus, the school superintendent may come in from outside the school department, but the assistant superintendents and the principals will all have to come up from the ranks.

Lateral entry is distinctly a two-edged sword. Its flagrant use can easily undermine an organization, for it seals off promotional opportunities from those who are already serving it. Organizational employees who see the positions they prize go to those who, in their opinion, have not worked for them become disheartened and discouraged. The more able and aggressive employees will tend to leave the organization. At the same time, the caliber of those applying for its rank-and-file positions will tend to fall, since these entry positions will hold out little chance for advancement. Carried to an extreme, lateral entry can lead to a caste system such as the one that characterized many European armies in bygone years, when no soldier could ever hope to advance to officer level.

Lateral entry can also present other problems. The organization has obviously had far less chance to study the outsider than it has its own people, and so it runs a greater risk in giving him or her a position of responsibility. Furthermore, no matter how capable a person may be, there is no telling how long it will take the new employee to adjust to the way things work in that particular organization. In some instances, this adjustment may never take place.

Lateral entry thus seems like a dangerous device. Yet an administrator may find that lack of lateral entry can pose even greater perils. Only through a lateral entry system can an organization take advantage of the vast range of talent and techniques that society has to offer. This involves not just specialized positions, although they are becoming more numerous and important all the time, but also more generalist posts. In an age when increasing numbers of young people are starting their careers after having acquired one or more college degrees, an organization must be able to offer them posts commensurate with their abilities if it hopes to stave off stagnation. Finally, the outsider brings fresh ideas and different perspectives. He or she often sees things that are wrong that insiders do not see, and may suggest and make changes that they never would have considered.

With such factors as these in mind, public organizations are beginning to look more favorably on lateral entry. State governments are starting to follow the federal government in instituting management intern programs. Police departments are beginning at last to give extra pay and credit toward promotion for education achieved beforehand. As O. Glenn Stahl, the author of the country's leading text on personnel administration, has written, "Policies which accept and encourage entry at all levels . . . are the order of the day."[16] It is not a question of abandoning entirely promotion from within. Such a step, for reasons that we have already seen, would in many cases prove disastrous. Rather, it is a question of striking a balance. And striking balances is what administration in general is all about.

Problems and Paradoxes

The foregoing constitutes something of a quick tour through the sprawling fields of personnel administration. As such, it suffices only to develop a nodding acquaintance with what some believe to be administration's most basic aspect. In this section we will center our attention on some particular personnel problems of the 1970s. They yield no easy answers, but as has been persistently stressed throughout this text, little in modern-day administration ever does.

Equal Opportunity

With the exception of trade unionism, which we shall examine in a subsequent chapter, probably no issue of recent years has so engulfed personnel administration in controversy and confronted administrators with problems as the quest for equal opportunity. Public administration is obviously a very integral part of modern society, and as such it cannot remain oblivious to society's pressures and concerns. As the drive for minority-group rights has gathered momentum, it has shaken and buffeted public personnel administration along with many other aspects of American life. There is no question that personnel administration stood in need of a shake-up. Even the federal government cannot boast of a glorious history in this area.

Take the issue of women's rights. There is no disputing the fact that women consistently suffered from discriminatory practices in the federal government during most of its history. In 1864, Congress passed a law setting the maximum salary for women in the federal service at six hundred dollars a year. For performing the same work, men could receive up to eighteen hundred dollars. The passage of the Civil Service Act in 1883 did not appreciably change matters. The top scorer in the first civil service exam to be held following the law's enactment was a young Vassar graduate named Mary Frances Hoyt. But despite Ms. Hoyt's proud performance, she, along with her contemporaries and successors, had to put up with deep-seated prejudice. As late as 1911, a civil service commissioner stated that the government should try not to hire women stenographers because blonds were "too frivolous" and brunets were "too chatty."[17]

Needless to say, blacks often fared even worse. Woodrow Wilson, according to historian John Morton Blum, "permitted several of his cabinet members to segregate, for the first time since the Civil War, whites and Negroes within existing executive departments. Throughout the South the discharge or demotion of Negro employees attended the New Freedom."[18] In response to liberal protest these policies were eventually checked, but discriminatory treatment still held sway over vast stretches of the federal bureaucracy. At the beginning of World War II, the army confined black soldiers largely to engineering and quartermaster corps, the navy only permitted blacks to serve as mess attendants, and the marines simply refused to accept black recruits at all.

Yet, despite this record of intolerance and even ill will, the federal government during most of its history has been light years ahead of the private sector as well as many state and local governments in offering opportunities to minority groups and women. Blacks frequently found federal employment something of a haven in the whirling tide of prejudice that encompassed so much of American life in previous eras. Women, from 1923 on, benefited somewhat from the Classification Act, which stipulated that "the principle of equal compensation for equal work irrespective of sex shall be followed."

The outbreak of World War II saw a good many discriminatory barriers burst asunder. All the armed services began establishing black units in branches hitherto reserved for whites, and all of them eventually opened up their officer ranks to black candidates. They also set up women's auxiliary corps. Furthermore, President Roosevelt issued an executive order outlawing discrimination in defense industries as well as in government. The policies adopted and the results obtained appear rather slight by today's standards, but by the standards of those times they seem momentous.

Affirmative Action

Since World War II, progress toward equal opportunity has been persistent, if often painful. Each president has nudged the federal governrent further along the way to this goal, although some have shown much more zeal than others. State and local governments, sometimes responding to court insistence, sometimes to federal government prodding, and sometimes to pressures from within their own constituencies, have by and large followed suit.

By the 1970s the goal of equal opportunity had, in some areas, given way to a greater goal—that of equal or near-equal representation. This aim proved much more difficult to achieve, but governmental efforts to attain it produced some important consequences, not only in terms of increasing the numbers of minority members and women in governmental ranks, but in bolstering the caliber of certain civil service operations.

The courts were in the vanguard in spurring efforts to expand and enhance the equal-representation goal. For one thing, the courts held that if a government agency had discriminated against any racial, religious, or sexual group in the past, it would now be required to discriminate in favor of them until the past injustices had been remedied. Thus, many police, school, and other governmental departments throughout the country were ordered to allocate a sizable proportion of their future vacancies for minority group members. To take just one example, the once lily-white Alabama State Police were ordered to appoint blacks to half of all future job openings until the proportion of blacks in the force roughly equalled their proportion in the state's population.

The courts also moved to make government agencies with few minority employees prove that their entrance exams were not discriminatory. In order to satisfy the court's standards, they would have to show that such exams did properly measure potential work performance and that those recruits doing well on the tests tended to do well on the job. Many agencies found that their tests failed to meet such standards, and so had to redesign them.

A third and much more controversial move aimed at amplifying minority employment in government originated with the Civil Service Commission. In 1971 the commission directed federal agencies to set specific "goals" for minority-group employment and to establish timetables for their achievement. This step soon sparked a spate of charges and countercharges, during which the term *reverse discrimination* became commonplace.

Affirmative Action, as the commission named its program, called on both public and private employers to exert greater efforts toward finding and training minority and women employees, and toward placing them in more challenging positions. It did not explicitly require or suggest that they be given preferential treatment. This, though, was the claim that irate members of the white male majority began to assert, and evidence came to light to lend some substance to this complaint. For example, Samuel Solomon, a special assistant in HEW's Office of Civil Rights, investigated twelve cases of alleged reverse discrimination in colleges and universities and found all of them justified. Said Solomon, "I'm getting the impression that most institutions are engaged in some form of discrimination against white males."[19]

Nevertheless, female and minority progress toward the higher echelons of the public sector continued to be slow. From 1976 to 1979, women holding top-level federal jobs rose from 5.1 percent to 6.7. While this represents a better than 25 percent increase, it still left them with a sharply disproportionate disadvantage because they comprised one-half of the federal work force.[20]

The 1980s saw a more conservative Supreme Court still willing to wield its gavel in behalf of minority and female rights. In 1981 the Court broadened the terms under which women may sue employers who pay them less than men doing similar work. The five-to-four decision settled a suit brought by women guards at an Oregon county jail who were being paid only 70 percent of what male guards were earning. The county had claimed that the female guards oversaw only one-tenth as many prisoners and, moreover, performed certain clerical duties that the male guards did not do. But the court ruled for the plaintiffs.[21]

In rendering its decision, however, the Court sidestepped the real issue of the case; namely the question of *comparable worth*. This principle requires a job to be paid the same as any other job judged to be equally demanding. Since many jobs typically held by women, such as those of librarian, frequently earn less than many jobs typically held by men, such as those of engineer, the comparable-worth principle would primarily benefit women. However, although the Court refrained from ruling on this principle, Senator Edward Kennedy took the cudgel in behalf of the concept of comparable worth. The following year he introduced legislation aimed at establishing and enforcing guidelines that would institute what would be the most sweeping step yet in the drive for women and minority rights.

In 1982, however, the Supreme Court struck again, this time voiding a Connecticut promotion test, even though the test had not prevented minority members from obtaining promotion. While a substantially smaller proportion of minority applicants had passed the test, this had not prevented Connecticut from promoting them, because the test constituted only one element among several used to determine promotions. Nevertheless, the Court ruled that any part of a promotion procedure having a "disparate effect" on minority members cannot be utilized unless it has been thoroughly validated, i.e., found predictive of the applicant's later performance in the job for which it is being used.[22]

The majority once again numbered only five, and the four dissenters protested sharply, claiming that the decision would impose a great burden on state and local governments without producing a competent work force. "Moreover, the Court's decision," they said, "may result in employers employing *fewer* minority members." (Emphasis is in the original.)

At about the same time the court was cracking down on Connecticut, the federal government was, in effect, cracking down on itself. In a move with potentially far-reaching implications, the Office of Personnel Management abolished its Professional and Administrative Career Examination. Known as PACE, the exam had served as the main avenue for college graduates to enter federal government service. The OPM said it was doing away with the test because too few minority members were passing it and because devising a different test to correct this problem had proven too difficult. (The federal government was under a consent decree worked out by the Carter administration, with the courts requiring the use of a selection method that would insure that the number of blacks and Hispanics hired be proportional to the number seeking jobs.) Henceforth, said the OPM, college-entry positions at the GS-5 and GS-7 levels would be filled by internal mobility and displaced-employee programs.

NO A FOR FEDERAL AA

When it comes to instituting Affirmative Action programs the federal government may not always practice what it preaches. From 1972 to 1977 the percentage of women in the blue-collar work force at private shipyards rose from .5 to 5.4 percent, a nearly eleven-fold increase. In shipyards owned and operated by the federal government, however, the number of such employees rose from .7 percent to a mere 1.4 percent. According to researchers Edward Clynch and Carol Gaudin, the much greater increase in the private facilities stemmed from the fact that the Maritime Commission, which controlled contracts to the private yards, was able to exercise more influence over them than the Civil Service Commission was able to exert over the federal bureaucracy.

Meanwhile, the cutbacks in personnel that most federal, state, and city governments were confronting under the financial pressures of the early 1980s were threatening to undo much if not most of whatever progress women and minority members had made. Since a disproportionate percentage of such jobholders had only recently acquired their positions, the seniority standards governing most governmental layoffs were threatening to fall heaviest on them. However, those agencies under court orders to increase the proportion of minority members in their work force soon found this requirement taking precedence over seniority procedures when it came to laying off employees. District courts told them to cut back more white and/or male employees instead, and appeals courts in Tennessee, Ohio, Michigan, and Massachusetts upheld these rulings. In the fall of 1982, the U.S. Supreme Court refused to hear appeals from teachers' unions in Boston and Kalamazoo, Michigan, against such lower-court decisions, thus establishing the supremacy of Affirmative Action guidelines over the heretofore near-sacred principle of seniority in determining who shall stay and who shall go.

Affirmative Action has caused headaches for many a public manager and heartaches for some employees, but we should not overlook the benefits it has bestowed. It has forced public agencies to broaden and intensify their recruiting efforts, to examine the validity of their exams, and to question the value of many of their recruitment and promotion criteria. It has opened up governmental organizations and stimulated innovation. It has made the administrative branch more representative of the populace it serves. In coping with the stress it tends to generate, these benefits should not be forgotten.

Performance Ratings

If an organization is going to use merit rather than sheer seniority as a basis for promotion (or demotion), and if job performance rather than test performance is to provide the basis for determining merit, then just how does one determine job performance? The most common device used is a performance rating system. Such a system essentially calls for superiors to rate their subordinates. The system seems simple, but in practice it generates all kinds of complications and controversies.

The nub of the performance rating problem lies in the lack of objective data and procedures for making it work effectively. Even when a supervisor desperately wants to be fair and impartial, there is often little in the way of neutral criteria that can be applied and that will be immune to personal whims and caprices. And when a superior does not feel such impartiality to be imperative, he or she can be very whimsical and capricious indeed.

The most common result of a performance rating system is ratings that are too high. "In any bureaucracy," writes management consultant Chester Burger "the general attitude is to give the underdog the benefit of the doubt. Because after all, I have nothing to lose by it, if he gets promoted, it isn't interfering with me in any way, it's not costing me anything."[23] So superiors, wanting to be popular with their personnel, tend to give most of them and sometimes all of them ratings of at least satisfactory, whether they deserve it or not. If an employee demonstrates weaknesses, the superior may find excuses. In this manner, mediocrity manages to score another of its many triumphs in organizational life.

Less widespread but much more injurious, perhaps, is the reverse reaction. Supervisors may and sometimes do use performance ratings to arbitrarily damage and even destroy a person's career. This can sometimes take the form of a seemingly innocuous statement, such as "The individual is well placed at her present level of management." Or it can take a more virulent tone and produce a much more vicious effect.

Vietnam produced many such efficiency-rating casualties. In his book

The Best and the Brightest, David Halberstam cites one high-ranking State Department official and several military officers whose realistically pessimistic reports from the conflict area incensed their superiors and earned them disastrous performance ratings. In one case that was reminiscent of the story of Admiral Sims (see chapter 3), the army actually gave serious thought to court-martialing a lieutenant-colonel named John Vann, ostensibly for talking to newsmen, but actually, according to Halberstam, for his annoying appraisals and pessimistic predictions on the course of events.[24]

Since adverse performance ratings, even if not widely used, constitute a potential threat to any employee, the whole performance rating system may engender behavior that is far from consistent with organization goals. Fear of a poor rating frequently will cause subordinates to become too subordinate (i.e., to conform too much to their superior's whims and wishes). Such fear stifles innovation, constructive criticism, and even communication. In a study of a federal law-enforcement agency, Peter Blau found that agents "were reluctant to reveal to their superiors their inability to solve a problem for fear that their ratings would be adversely affected."[25]

Some organizations, such as the Foreign Service and the navy, operate under a "selection-out" rule, whereby a person who has a consistently poor rating or who has not earned a promotion in a stipulated period of time is subject to dismissal. This personnel procedure makes performance ratings even more important, for now they not only determine advancement but employment itself. As such, selection-out only intensifies the problems that performance ratings present. Arthur Schlesinger describes the Foreign Service system as "in effect a conspiracy of the conventional against the unconventional,"[26] and apparently many Foreign Service officers view it even more harshly. According to former FSO William Bell, members of the service speak of their promotional system as resembling a "high-rise outhouse, constructed so that each person—except for those at the very bottom—is subject to deposits from those above but can deposit in kind upon those below." Adds Bell, "Whether it is accurate or not, *belief* in its validity creates a formidable operating reality."[27]

One of the most caustic critics of performance ratings was Douglas McGregor, who filed a lengthy bill of particulars against such devices. According to McGregor, performance ratings are as bothersome and unsettling to superiors as they are to subordinates. They consume too much time in preparation, review, and frequent argumentation. What is more, they can rarely claim much validity, for usually it is impossible for the superior to make with precision the fine distinctions they often demand. Subordinates often say they want such ratings, claiming that they like "to know where they stand," but McGregor disputed this. Usually, the em-

PERSONNEL EVALUATION FOR MANAGERS   FORM DPA 57

The Commonwealth of Massachusetts

NAME OF PERSON EVALUATED	POSITION TITLE AND GRADE	ORGANIZATIONAL UNIT	Period covered by this evaluation
NAME OF EVALUATOR	POSITION TITLE AND GRADE	ORGANIZATIONAL UNIT	MONTH DAY YEAR FROM TO

INSTRUCTIONS: At the beginning of each evaluation period, the manager to be rated should review this form and be informed of the factors on which his or her performance will be evaluated. All ratings must be done by persons who have supervised the manager for at least 90 days. This rating will represent your evaluation of the manager's actual performance on his or her present job.

SUGGESTIONS: Consider only one factor at a time. Don't let your rating in one influence your rating of another. Base your judgement on the requirements of the job and the manager's performance in it as compared with others doing similar work. Carefully read the description of each factor before making each entry, and assign the rating which most nearly describes your opinion.

GRADING: Performance will be evaluated by the immediate supervisor (*) and, when necessary, the reviewing supervisor (**) by placing a check mark (✓) in the appropriate box in the numerical scale from 1 to 10, based on the following standards:

If the manager's performance demonstrates ability that is —
— outstanding and far exceeds job standards, check the box numbered 10.
— above average, exceeds job standards, check box 7, 8 or 9.
— average, meets job standards, check box 4, 5 or 6.
— below average, does not meet job standards, check box 1, 2 or 3.

FACTOR	EVALUATION BELOW AVERAGE 1 * 2 ** 3, **	AVERAGE 4 * 5 ** 6 **	ABOVE AVERAGE 7 * 8 ** 9 **	OUTSTANDING 10 *
JOB KNOWLEDGE Adequacy of professional skills, experience and knowledge to do the job.	Lacks the understanding, skill and experience to perform the job. Requires constant supervision.	Has sufficient knowledge, skills and experience to perform tasks with a minimum of guidance.	Has a good knowledge of the work to be performed. Above average understanding of procedures.	Has a thorough understanding of the job and all related procedures, laws regulations and technical tasks. Extensive professional skill and experience.
PRODUCTIVITY Meeting established standards of quality and quantity of work production.	Fails to meet established deadlines. Production does not meet established standards. Requires a high degree of assistance.	Work is generally accurate and complete. Meets established standards and deadlines.	Completes assignments on time with above average results. Accepts additional tasks when requested.	Consistently completes complex assignments quickly and accurately. Regularly does more than required with exceptional competence.
COMMUNICATION: ORAL Oral facility with language which expedites results while maintaining relationships; maintain channels.	Frequently fails to achieve understanding from listeners. Speaks in poorly organized fashion. Has difficulty articulating thoughts.	Has adequate ability in making an oral presentation. Occasionally is required to repeat or amend position to achieve desired response.	Presents ideas and material in an effective manner. Has above average ability to obtain agreement and support for desired goals.	Outstanding ability to present ideas and articulate thoughts to diverse audiences and organizations. Expedites results through ability to command positive responses.
COMMUNICATION: WRITTEN Presenting and explaining ideas clearly and effectively in writing; developing written work in a logical and comprehensive manner.	Lacks the ability to provide written communications in a logical, understandable and timely manner. Requires constant re-write and editing.	Written communications are readable and understandable with only occasional need for editing and rewriting. Usually completes written assignments within prescribed time limits.	Effectively presents thoughts in writing in a very understandable style with very little need for interpretation or repetition.	Consistently writes complex directives, letters, reports, etc. in a clear, concise, highly understandable style. Writing is convincing and timely, and achieves desired results.
LEADERSHIP Inspiring teamwork and productivity; maintenance of discipline; stimulating suggestions; checking the work of subordinates.	Is unable to motivate staff to meet organization goals in an efficient and effective manner.	Maintains effective work output by utilization of available personnel resources.	Effectively utilizes the skill of available staff to obtain a high degree of productivity. Maintains good level of morale; promotes teamwork.	Obtains outstanding productivity and quality of work while maintaining excellent morale. Maintains positive relationships with other agencies.
MANAGEMENT SKILLS Efficient use of staff and budget to achieve agency goals; establishing and shifting priorities as necessary; effective delegation of authority; implementing policies and procedures.	Has difficulty utilizing staff and resources efficiently. Overlooks priorities of goals and objectives. Lacks understanding of management skills required.	Accepts established priorities and utilizes resources to meet them. Plans activities and directs subordinates while achieving average results.	Uses staff and budgetary resources efficiently. Implements policies and procedures and has above average ability to adjust priorities to meet goals and objectives.	Achieves agency goals and objectives through superior management skills. Outstanding use of human and budgetary resources to meet priorities. Delegates authority effectively.

(over)

FACTOR	BELOW AVERAGE 1 • •• 2 • ••• 3 • ••	AVERAGE 4 • •• 5 • •• 6 • ••	ABOVE AVERAGE 7 • •• 8 • •• 9 • ••	OUTSTANDING 10 •| ••
PROBLEM SOLVING AND DECISION MAKING Logical and practical thinking; objectivity and deliberation in decision making; application of knowledge and skills to new situations; foreseeing consequences or recommendations.	Is unable to adapt to problems of above average difficulty. Does not analyze all facts of problem. Will not make decisions, or makes them hastily or too slowly.	Recognizes problems as they occur and contributes to their resolution. Makes suggestions for improvement. Usually coordinates decisions to achieve desired objectives.	Applies a highly logical approach to problems presented. Makes suggestions for improvement and carries them through promptly. Suggest conclusions that are accepted. Provides alternate approaches when necessary.	Anticipates and analyzes difficult situations before they become problems. Logically and quickly applies corrective action with superior results. Generates new and innovative ideas.
AFFIRMATIVE ACTION Demonstrating active support of AA goals; knowledge and communication of AA information; monitoring and evaluating activities and progress.	Fails to implement AA goals, activities monitoring and evaluation.	Accepts responsibility for achieving goals. Informs staff. Works to resolve problems and implement policy.	Analyzes situations and provides solutions to achieve goals with above average results.	Outstanding ability to achieve agency goals. Initiate action, expedite results.
INITIATIVE & RESPONSIBILITY Self-starting action; willingness to take the lead and be responsible for decisions, enthusiasm for improvement; working independently with success; open-mindedness toward opposing views.	Is reluctant to accept more than what is perceived to be the required job. Displays little or no initiative. Objects to suggestions for improvement.	Will accept responsibility for work assigned. Displays initiative on selected projects. Seldom seeks out additional work.	Works independently with success. Obtains above average results with self-initiated projects. Is open minded to opposing views.	Develops new and original programs with constant success. Takes responsibility for all actions and results. Exceptional ability to adapt to relevant objections or suggested improvements.
STAFF DEVELOPMENT AND TRAINING Development and training of new employees through instruction and by example. Setting and measuring standards of performance; conducting instructive performance appraisal discussions.	Does not set standards for agency tasks nor evaluate employees' performance. Fails to train or develop staff for job improvement and upward mobility.	Periodically measures workers performance against set standards. Routinely instructs staff and assists in improvement of work habits.	Sets standards and measures degree of achievement with individual workers in a cooperative manner. Implements training to improve performance. Sets above average example.	Exceptional ability to develop staff through participative management and regular performance review. Supports upward mobility through the efficient utilization of training programs.

Evaluator's comments (to include recommended areas and methods for improvements):

_____

Reviewing Supervisor's comments (Reviewing supervisor must evaluate the employee when the evaluator's rating totals more than 95 or less than 40):

_____

Comment of person evaluated:

q

Total numerical rating _____

Signature _____

Total numerical rating _____

Signature and Title _____

I have reviewed this rating and it has been discussed with me.

Signature _____   Date _____

Here is an evaluation sheet used to appraise the performance of managers in the Massachusetts state government. Note that it includes provisions for comments by both the reviewing supervisor and the person being evaluated.

ployee just wants reassurance, he said, and if the rating is a bad one, it only makes him more anxious, more defensive, and more unrealistic in his behavior.[28] The more the subordinate is likely to merit criticism, the less likely he is to respond effectively to it. (It might be interesting to compare the problems of performance ratings with those posed by the grading systems used in U.S. higher education.)

McGregor suggested as an alternative that an employee be allowed to rate him- or herself with the rating being based on progress toward certain goals that the employee will have previously determined in cooperation with the superior. This proposal seemed outlandishly naive when McGregor first articulated it in the late 1950s. Today, however, a few private firms, such as the Gillette Company and Stone and Webster Engineering, Inc., have adopted such a plan. The employees fill in the rating sheet, and the superior adds comments if he or she in any way disagrees.

Few if any public agencies have gone so far, but many now allow employees to look over their own ratings and append their own comments. This undoubtedly prevents much inaccuracy and injustice. However, it may do so only at the cost of reinforcing the more common tendency of giving some employees higher ratings than they might deserve. Superiors, especially when confronted with civil service systems that virtually lock in poorly performing subordinates, may wish to spare themselves the added unpleasantness of arousing their ire.

Far more threatening to many superiors is another innovation, which as yet remains little used in either government or private industry. But its time may be coming. This is the two-way rating system, which gives subordinates the chance to rate their superiors. "Perceptions by subordinates of their supervisors," says Donald C. Stone, "are far more reliable than those that supervisors make of subordinates." Numerous studies, he claims, have authenticated this. Such a dual system also appears to have quite an effect on supervisors. "When a superior sees a printout composite evaluation by his subordinates," says Stone, "the shock is high on the Richter scale."[29]

Job Classifications

Nearly all public personnel organizations have some system of job classification. The federal government, for example, divides its positions into eighteen basic grade levels, ranging from grade 1 to grade 18. Each level pays more and, ostensibly, requires more in terms of ability and output than the level below it. Within each grade level there are twelve steps, each paying more than the preceding one. The upper steps of any grade actually pay more than the lower steps of the grade just above it. Consequently, an employee who is working at the eleventh step of grade 12 will be earning more than an employee who is at the first step of grade 13. Of course the latter will eventually outdistance the former, since he or she is working in a higher-level classification. Advancement from one step to another takes place chiefly on the basis of time served. Advancement from one grade to another is based more on merit, although in practice seniority often plays a larger role.

The premise underlying classification schemes is that different jobs require varying degrees of ability and impose varying amounts of responsibility. The adoption of a classification plan has long been considered essential for the effective operation of a merit system, for it is designed to place the emphasis on *what* a person knows rather than *who* the person knows. It provides a basis for, although it does not guarantee, a neutral and workable personnel operation which, without fear or favor, can reward good performance and penalize its opposite. Furthermore, it can do this in open and objective ways.

One crucial question among the many that job classification poses is how many classifications should there be? Should the various jobs be strung out into a large number of separate grades and levels, or should they be compressed into a comparatively few broad categories. If the federal government's personnel system features eighteen grades with twelve steps each, is this too many or too few or just about right?

The problem is obviously a relative one to which there can be no precise answer, since there are no precise criteria defining narrow and broad classifications. To some the federal government's eighteen grade levels may seem too many; to others they may seem too few. However, we do know that moving in either direction will yield various advantages and disadvantages.

A personnel system employing many and hence relatively narrow classifications will be able to tailor its jobs more precisely to a particular level. If there are two classifications for typists rather than one, better typists can be placed in the upper class and less-capable typists can be put in the lower one. Thus, if typist A does better work than typist B, then A can be given a higher rating than B. It is further assumed that A will not only be given more money and more status but will also be given more difficult and more responsible assignments. In this sense, using many relatively narrow categories can be fairer to all concerned.

Narrow categories also permit more extensive use of promotion as an incentive. More levels mean more possibilities for moving up. At the same time, such promotional opportunities can be used as a sanction against those who fail to perform adequately. If typist B makes many errors in her copy or is unduly slow in getting out her assignments, she may find herself forgoing the better pay and prestige that advancement to a higher level would bring.

Many public organizations have relatively few classification levels, particularly in the lower range of jobs. Postal workers, police officers, fire fighters, and others can usually move up only to a position of command. Since there are relatively few such positions in most organizations, opportunities for promotion remain limited. Some 60 percent of all Postal Service employees retire at the same job level they had when they started work. The majority of police officers face the same fate, despite the additional possibility they have of moving up to detective as well as to the command position of sergeant. This contrasts with, say, the German system, whereby a police officer can advance several notches in rank before assuming any substantial supervisory responsibility. The Germans find their system enables them more easily to reward a policeman for good work. Conversely, they can more easily discipline him or her for poor performance by simply delaying his upward advancement.[30]

Despite these merits, however, narrow and therefore numerous job classifications present distinct difficulties. The more classifications there are, the more personnel work the organization must do. Each classification must be carefully described and demarcated, and then each job must be carefully plugged into the right classification. This results in a system that is not only costly but also cumbersome and complicated.

Although utilization of numerous and narrow classifications can alleviate discord, since those performing somewhat more demanding tasks can then more easily receive recognition for doing so, it can for the same reasons create tensions of its own. "Why should he or she be classified higher than I am when my job requires as much or more responsibility as his or hers?" is a constant complaint. Arguments frequently flare up over whether a position should be put in one class or another. For example, in a regional office of one federal agency, a personnel officer balked at classifying a job at grade-14 level despite pleas and exhortations from the agency's other top officials that he do so. It seems the personnel officer himself held only a grade-13 position, and it was felt that he could not bring himself to categorize the new post at a higher level than his own. Problems such as these run rampant when classifications are numerous.

Generally, the more classification levels there are, the more personnel games may be played. One of these is called *job evolution.* An employee finds herself stuck at her present level and unable to move up due to the lack of openings above her, so she strives earnestly to get her existing job reclassified upward. A sympathetic supervisor may assist by adding to her job some new duties, thereby strengthening her case. If the employee is finally successful, then others seek to follow suit, and so the game begins all over again. This is the basis of some of the "inflation at the top," which we noted in a previous chapter. Jobs have a tendency to keep evolving upward.

Probably the most important impediment that a highly scaled classification scheme imposes on effective administration is inflexibility. The
more numerous and narrow the classifications, the harder it is to rotate
people from one job to another. In similar fashion, it becomes more difficult to change the nature of the work assigned to any individual, for the
new assignments may mandate a change in grade level. An employee may
protest vigorously that the task he or she is being given is above or below
the assigned grade level.

To gain a better awareness of how this operates, let us take a somewhat
extreme hypothetical case. Imagine two identical agencies doing the
same work and having the same number and types of personnel. The first
arranges its employees into five categories; the second groups its people
into twenty-five categories. In the first agency, anyone holding a job
equivalent to, say, grade 3 in the second can be easily moved to what
would be a grade-1 or grade-5 job in the second agency. Or the work can
be altered in the same manner. Thus, the first agency is in a much better
position to innovate and change.

McGregor was a constant critic of tight and constricting classification
schemes. He pointed out that no two people will ever perform in the
same position in the same way, and even one person does not do the same
work in the same position over a period of time. Conditions change, as do
skills, abilities, and perceptions of priorities. Consequently, the position
is actually changing continually. Hard-and-fast position descriptions, he
contended, not only promote inflexibility but signify a lack of realism.[31]

One final aspect of the issue is also worthy of note. The broader the
classification scheme it uses, the more egalitarian the organization is
likely to be. Numerous, narrow classifications can result in a complex
pecking order, which creates many social as well as economic distinctions
between employees. To take what might be called the limiting case, assume that an organization had only one job classification. It would then
be completely egalitarian as far as its personnel system went. The more
an organization approaches this situation, the more "democratic" it is
likely to become.

What are the trends for the future? Contemporary society is generating
considerable pressures on public organizations to hold down administrative costs, to encourage innovation and flexibility, and to increase democ-
ratization. For these reasons it seems likely that the direction of personnel
administration will be toward broader rather than narrower classification
schemes as we will see later. At this point it is useful to keep in mind that
such a trend may increase administrative effectiveness in many ways. Research indicates that the fewer the differences in prestige and status
within a group, the more stable the group tends to become and the more
likely its members are to accept internal leadership. In addition, commu-

nication most probably will improve. It is possible that some organizations will need to retain relatively narrow classifications, and some might benefit from even more classifications than they now have. But the overall tendency seems to lie in the opposite direction.

Rank-in-Job, Rank-in-Man

There are two basic ways of classifying personnel. One arranges them on the basis of the work they do; the second on the basis of their personal qualities, such as seniority and skill. The first is called *rank-in-job,* the latter is titled *rank-in-man.*

The U.S. military operates under the rank-in-man arrangement. A lieutenant, for example, becomes a captain when he or she has achieved the requisite seniority, performance ratings, and so on. He or she is then, usually (although not always) posted to a new job in keeping with the new grade. Most of the civilian sector of the federal government, however, holds fast to the rank-in-job system. A person holding the grade of GS-12, for example, would not normally become a GS-13 until a job carrying that grade opens up or until his or her present job is upgraded and reclassified.

The division between the two systems is obviously not hard and fast. A sudden spurt in the number of vacancies in upper-echelon grades, as may occur in wartime, would normally result in more lower-grade military officers being promoted to fill them. Conversely, a GS-12 may not win promotion to a vacant GS-13 position unless he or she has demonstrated the qualities believed necessary to handle it. Yet, a difference does exist. One system bases itself primarily on the individual, the other on the functions he fulfills.

Which system works best? For O. Glenn Stahl, whose text *Public Personnel Administration* reigned through four decades and six editions as *the* book in the field, there was little to dispute. Rank-in-job, said Stahl, was the "logical corollary of the systematic subdivision of responsibilities and the specialization of labor." Such a system, said Stahl, "fits in nicely with managerial efforts to clarify lines of responsibility, to establish clear-cut modes of procedure, and to facilitate coordination among all parts of a far-flung administrative machine. The very knowledge of actual duties being performed under all assignments contributes to this end."[32]

To many, rank-in-job seems much more compatible with democratic values than does rank-in-man. When people are ranked and paid according to the job they do, then the principle of "equal pay for equal work" enjoys a better chance of become realized. To Stahl, this is perhaps the system's greatest virtue.

Rank-in-job would seem less conducive to corruption and abuse. No one gets recruited or promoted until there is a specific set of duties for him or her to perform. It may also slow down, although not eliminate, the natural tendency for organizations to expand their upper echelons. Certainly, it would seem to be somewhat easier for rank-in-man organizations to promote more people upward than it would be for those operating under rank-in-job to do so. After all, the latter must at least have or create specific high-level jobs before it can move people up the organizational ladder.

However, the rank-in-man system is not without advantages and assets. And its virtues in modern-day administration seem to be acquiring more attractiveness and appeal.

The primary virtue of this system is its flexibility. People may be rotated or assigned to different jobs much more easily because whatever they do, they do not lose their rank. Similarly it becomes much easier to enlarge or enrich their present jobs because no rigidly written job descriptions exist to define their duties. No one usually minds very much "working out of grade" in a rank-in-man system, for no one really loses his or her grade in doing so. There is even less resistance to abolishing jobs, because the employee knows that he or she will still retain rank.

Rank-in-man systems can be expected to produce less paper work, less grievance negotiation, and less pushing of problems upward. Although the U.S. military can offer excellent examples of all these problems, still, if it operated under a rank-in-job scheme, the problems would probably be worse. (Think of what it would be like if a sergeant, during a battle in which his lieutenant was killed or disabled, refused to take over the platoon because he would be working out of grade!) Finally, rank-in-man is also considered conducive to the building of organizational loyalty.

However, it is in its potential for increased flexibility that the greatest attraction of rank-in-man currently lies. Our fast-moving and constantly changing technological society is putting a premium on this attribute, and this may lead many civilian personnel systems to view the rank-in-man scheme with more favor than they have done in the past.

Centralization of the Personnel Function

The growth of civil-service merit systems brought the development of centralized personnel agencies. Such centralization was deemed necessary to provide the resources for drawing up and administering a comprehensive merit system. In performing such a task, most personnel agencies also take on a significant control function vis-à-vis the various line agencies. To the extent that such centralized personnel agencies recruit and train personnel; set up classification and pay schemes; and establish the standards for promotion, demotion, and dismissal, they exercise a good deal of influence over line administrators.

There are many advantages in having centralized personnel agencies—usually called civil-service commissions or boards—undertake such functions. It impedes, when it does not block, the pressures of patronage and the forces of favoritism. It also produces more professionalism in personnel practices, because a central personnel agency can obviously assemble more data, expertise, and knowledge in this field than can an individual line agency.

Centralization of the personnel function also provides distinct advantages in recruiting and rotation. The prospective government employee who is willing to work for more than one particular agency does not need to file separate applications. Instead, he or she can file with the centralized personnel agency. Sometimes, a person can take one test to qualify for several different jobs. For example, the New York City Civil Service Commission gives the same examination to applicants for the Housing Police, the Transit Authority Police, and the City Correction Department, and the successful examinee can move into any one of these agencies on the basis of available openings and one's own preferences. There are obvious savings here in expenditure of time by all concerned. In like fashion, if an employee wishes to rotate to another agency, he or she may find the way smoothed by a centralized personnel unit that not only knows which agencies need which people at which time, but that also, through its recruiting and staffing functions can more easily arrange the transfer.

But, a strong centralized personnel agency also has its negative aspects. The line agency often feels it knows better just what kind of people it needs and resents having to let the personnel people have the last word. Furthermore, it is time-consuming to have to wait for the central personnel agency to draw up and administer examinations or to approve promotions or new job classifications or changes in existing ones. A centralized personnel agency may also drain administrative energies and consume administrators' time in yet other ways, because negotiations, sometimes protracted ones, are frequently required before the line department can move in many areas. Finally, such a system robs a line agency of authority and discretion, and in so doing it can make the achievement of its goals more difficult.

When civil-service merit systems were starting to become established, the trend was definitely toward centralizing personnel functions. Today, however, the currents of change may be blowing in the opposite direction. The mounting need for flexibility and expediency is prompting a tendency in some areas to strengthen the authority of the line agency and its administrators in regard to personnel matters. The fact that a technological society makes technical competence more important and political contacts less useful in administrative performance reinforces this trend. It therefore reduces the need to have a central personnel agency to prevent abuses. Central personnel services will still be needed, for they offer the advantages cited earlier, but their role may change to one of providing advice and assistance rather than constraint and control.

Residency Requirements and Moonlighting

Questions involving residency requirements and moonlighting are often slighted by writers on administration, yet they are sources of a good deal of conflict in many state and local governments. Years ago, when government jobs were regarded as prized plums, it was customary to restrict them to residents of the constituency being served. Outsiders, it was felt, had no right to enjoy the fruits of other people's taxes. The emergence of the welfare state and the (generally) full-employment society has somewhat changed this attitude. Public positions are no longer quite so prized. Yet, residency requirements continue to exist in many jurisdictions. The U.S. Civil Rights Commission found in its 1970 survey that 28 percent of local governments still use residency requirements for some jobs. And in many cases where they are not formally written into the law, tacit rules or informal pressures exist to force certain public employees to live in the jurisdictions in which they work.

A case can be made on behalf of such restrictions. The resident employee is closer to the scene of work and can therefore be called to duty more expeditiously. This can prove advantageous to the local government, particularly when it comes to such employees as police and fire personnel, whose services may be required in emergencies. Residency requirements also are believed to give the employee more knowledge of, and more of a stake in, the constituency he or she serves. Finally, many still consider it only fair that the employee make purchases and pay taxes in the locality that supplies him or her with the wherewithal to do so.

But residency requirements are, first of all, hard to enforce. They are frequently honored more in the breach than in the observance. Then, their constricting effort adds to employee dissatisfaction and may make recruitment more difficult. The question of proximity to the workplace in case of emergency may not be moot, since bordering communities may lie closer to the employee's scene of work than some sections of the municipality that employs him or her. A fire fighter who is employed in, say, the Queens borough of New York City will be able to respond to an emergency call much faster if he lives in Long Island than if he resides in any of the other four boroughs of New York City. Finally, requiring municipal employees to live within the city limits may make them too formidable a force in city politics. In many cities and towns, municipal employees have become the most influential pressure group in local politics.

The equal opportunity problem weighs in on both sides of this issue. One Civil Rights Commission Chairman once called for the abolition of such requirements, because they may be used to deter minorities from obtaining and maintaining government jobs. However, the issue could cut the other way. As Spanish-speaking and black citizens come into control of more municipal governments, they may find that residency requirements can be used either to make sure the work force of such cities provides increased opportunities for minority-group members, or, conversely, to keep members of the white majority from fleeing the city altogether. Newark, for example, turned down a white out-of-state applicant for a high financial post when the prospective job taker refused to agree that he would live in the city proper.

During the mid-1970s the pressure for residency requirements began to grow. City officials became increasingly alarmed over the steady loss of middle-class whites to the suburbs. And city dwellers became increasingly annoyed at the steady rise in city-employee salaries and benefits. The two forces were buttressed by an additional factor: city jobs had become increasingly desirable thanks not only to their improved wages and benefits but also because of the shortage of many white-collar jobs in the private sector. As a result, no city needed have any fears about a dearth of suitable applicants if it were to require city residency for those who sought or held city jobs.

The issue reached a boiling point in 1976 when a dismissed Philadelphia fire lieutenant took his case to the U.S. Supreme Court. Lieutenant Francis McCarthy had been discharged four years before for failing to maintain a "bona fide" residence in the city. He had claimed to be living in Philadelphia with his mother while his wife and ten children resided in a suburb. In an unsigned opinion, the court ruled in *McCarthy* v. *Philadelphia Civil Service Commission* that the residency requirements used to fire McCarthy did not constitute a violation of his constitutional rights.

The Court's decision triggered a new trend to expand and enforce such restrictions. Chicago, New York City, New Haven, Boston, and a host of other cities began creating new residency requirements or began clamping down under those already on the books.

Moonlighting is another issue often neglected in discussions of personnel administration. Yet it, too, has become a matter of abiding concern to many administrators. Like residency requirements, moonlighting, or the practice of holding one or more additional jobs outside one's regular public employment, is a phenomenon that chiefly plagues local governments. However, many state governments and even some federal agencies have not gone unaffected. Prison and jailhouse guards, police officers, sanitation workers, building inspectors, and others are frequent moonlighters. Fire fighters are possibly the biggest moonlighters of all, because their professional employment not only provides them with the opportunity but even with the accommodations to sleep during their normal working hours.

Moonlighting poses problems, some obvious and some not so obvious. In the first category is the dissipation of the employee's energies away from what should be his or her main focus of attention. A former commander of the Chicago police once noted that moonlighting reached such a level within his department that for many of his officers police work had actually become their second job.[33] The situation in many other government agencies in Chicago and elsewhere is almost the same. In a time when public organizations are being pressed to produce more and better results, many find their efforts to do so being sapped by widespread employee moonlighting.

In the not-so-obvious category are the problems involving conflict of interest. Public employees will naturally tend to look for and accept off-duty work in areas in which they have some expertise. This will often bring them into conflict with their governmental responsibilities. The police officer who serves off duty as a bouncer in a cabaret and the building inspector who does off-duty maintenance work for a real-estate firm may find themselves placed in a position where they cannot always serve the public interest and at the same time the interest of their employers.

Despite these concerns, many state and local governments have found that barring moonlighting, as many of them do, proves ineffective. The moonlighting still goes on, only now it is practiced in a secretive and *sub rosa* manner. Furthermore, employees grow resentful, because they feel that what they do on their own time is and should be their own concern.

It should also be noted that employee moonlighting can in some instances prove useful to a public organization. It may alleviate organizational in-groupism and may provide the employee with useful experience and contacts with the larger society. Sometimes, the off-duty job supplements rather than conflicts with the public one. For example, when New York City Police officers were officially allowed to moonlight, many took outside jobs as taxi drivers. Soon, a wave of arrests occurred, as would-be robbers of taxi drivers found themselves confronted by seasoned and armed police officers.

The best solution may lie in allowing but controlling moonlighting. Employees can be required to report the name or names of their outside employers, the nature of the employment itself, and the hours involved. Certain restrictions may also be imposed. British fire departments, for example, allow their personnel to moonlight even though fire fighters in Britain are required to be on the job fifty-four hours a week, in comparison to the forty- or forty-eight-hour week worked by their U.S. counterparts. However, no British fire fighter is permitted to work in outside employment for eight hours prior to a tour of duty.[34] Public employers should also move to make their employees' regular jobs more challenging and rewarding. In the long run, this is probably the best if not the only true solution to the moonlighting dilemma.

The Public Employee and Politics

The Civil Service Act of 1883, often referred to as the Pendleton Act, after the name of its congressional sponsor, stipulated that no civil-service employee could be punished or threatened with punishment for refusing to make a political contribution. In 1907, President Theodore Roosevelt expanded these safeguards by means of an executive order that prohibits any classified employee from taking an active part in a partisan political campaign. In 1939 Congress formalized and strengthened these provisions by enacting the Hatch Act. A year later it passed what was known as the second Hatch Act, which extended these restrictions to numerous state and local employees whose work was financed to any extent by federal funds. States, meanwhile, began enacting legislation to place similar constraints on their own employees. Today about four-fifths of the states have laws curtailing the political involvement of state and even local government workers, although in many cases these state laws lack the rigor and inclusiveness of the federal legislation.

The Hatch Act does permit federal employees considerable freedom in nonpartisan politics. They may not only participate but also run in campaigns for school committee and city council when these elections are nonpartisan. They can also sign a nomination paper, vote in a primary, and contribute up to five thousand dollars in a partisan contest. Active campaigning in such elections, however, is taboo.

Although the effort to depoliticize public employment was originally designed to protect employees, it has in recent years started to produce the reverse. In 1972, the National Association of Letter Carriers along with six individual employees and six local Democratic- and Republican-committee chairmen filed a suit claiming the Hatch Act was unconstitutional. The postal union won an initial victory in the Federal District Court of Washington, D.C. The judges held the act unconstitutional on grounds of an "overbreadth in the sensitive area of free expression," and also on grounds that it was too vague. The court stressed the latter point particularly. In its words, the act "talks in riddles, prohibiting in one breath what it may be argued to have allowed in another, leaving the citizen unguided but at hazard for his job."[35]

On June 25, 1973, however, the Supreme Court, in a six-to-three decision, overturned the lower court's finding and upheld the Hatch Act's constitutionality. The restrictions that the law imposes, said the Court, are necessary "if the government is to operate effectively and fairly." The similar state laws also received the Supreme Court's blessing.[36] Hence the legal aspect of the issue has been, at least for the time being, resolved. But other aspects of the issue continue to pester and plague present-day administrators. The Hatch Act may be accepted as lawful, but that does not mean it is universally accepted as just.

Critics of the act claim that it turns public employees into second-class citizens. They further note that with the growth in public employment, the act is depriving nearly 20 percent of the nation's work force from full participation in the democratic process. What is more, it is disfranchising a group that is on the whole more knowledgeable about government than is the public generally. As a result, valuable inputs into government decision making are being lost.

PATRONAGE BEFORE THE BENCH

In recent years, the Supreme Court has handed down two decisions reducing the role of political patronage in governmental personnel policies. In *Elrod* v. *Burns* (1976), the Court forbade the Democratic sheriff of Cook County, Illinois, from dismissing Republican deputy sheriffs unless he could show such dismissals as serving a "vital governmental end." Four years later in *Branti* v. *Finkel*, the justices called the firing of a Republican assistant public defender by his newly elected Democratic superior a violation of First Amendment rights. In both decisions the dissenting justices, who numbered four in the first case and three in the second, claimed the majority's ruling to be too vague and too broad.

Supporters of the act maintain that it is needed now more than ever. With the proportion of government employees rising, and with more and more of them joining militant unions, the danger, in their view, has arisen that the public employees will wrest full control of the government from the rest of the population. Some claim that this has already happened in some cities where public employees have become the dominant force in municipal elections. Another danger cited by the Hatch Act supporters is that individual public employees running for elections or supporting others who do will grant or withhold services on the basis of whether the client is backing them or their opponents. Finally, there is the danger that federal employees may be more easily cajoled or coerced into helping incumbent officers win reelection if the restrictions of the Hatch Act are removed.

Some sentiment for liberalizing the Hatch Act surfaced in 1968. At that time a presidential commission appointed to examine the question made its report. It recommended allowing a federal employee to run for any local office, not just a nonpartisan one, as long as the post was not full-time and did not provide more than a nominal compensation. The commission split evenly on whether to allow federal employees to become party, ward, or precinct committee members. And it released a poll showing that half of the federal work force favored some easing of the Hatch Act's restraints, although a sizable minority wished to maintain the status quo.

Congress took no decisive action on the commission's proposals until 1975. At that time, under the urging of federal and postal worker's unions, the House and Senate passed a bill allowing employees covered by the Hatch Act to run for partisan office. However, President Ford vetoed the measure and the bill's supporters failed to muster the necessary two-thirds majority to overcome the president's rejection. President Carter submitted legislation in March 1977 to reduce the restrictions of the Hatch Act for those holding "nonsensitive" jobs. Given the fact that most federal employees are Democrats, the legislation was given a fairly good chance of winning enactment in the Democratic-controlled Congress. Yet somewhere along the line the bill dropped out of sight. Apparently even congressional Democrats harbor fears about the consequences of granting greater political freedom and power to federal employees.

CASE STUDY

Automation Comes to California[37]

Change seems to come easier and faster in California. Whether it concerns protecting the environment, promoting new administrative mechanisms, or permitting new forms of sexual expression, California has often led the way. Therefore, it should come as no surprise to learn that it was in California that electronic data processing first ignited the interest of the public sector.

More specifically, it ignited the interest of Walter S. Bashline, who was then serving as chief of the tabulating section of the state's Department of Employment. Bashline had just read the new IBM manual and had become convinced that he could save the state some two hundred thousand (1954) dollars by replacing his conventional tabulating machines with electronic data-processing machinery (EDPM).

Bashline knew that if he was to accomplish this he would have to act fast. The department was planning to construct a new building, and it would have to alter the design plans to accommodate the EDPM system. Should the plans be approved and the construction started without such alterations, the opportunity to take advantage of this new technology would be lost for the foreseeable future. Thus, speed was of the essence.

One fortuitous factor working in Bashline's behalf was the department's new director, William A. Burkett. A "political" appointee of the state's new governor, Burkett was anxious to prove himself. He was eager to make constructive changes, especially if they could be shown to save money.

But this advantage seemed more than offset by a deterrent. Changing over to EDPM would eliminate from 166 to 184 jobs. Such a reduction could not be achieved through simple attrition over the two-year change-over period. What's more, the people who would become redundant would nevertheless be needed to keep the present system working until the final moment. If they started to leave ahead of time, the department's whole operation could collapse. Compounding the problem still more was the fact that the whole work force had become "gun shy" as a result of other layoffs brought on by previous economy moves. Indeed, the department's personnel officer, Lynwood Steedman, fearing that another layoff would shatter employee morale, had persuaded the department's management to support a well-publicized program for a "stabilized work force."

After securing a go-ahead from the department director, Burkett, Bashline's first move was to talk with Steedman. Both men soon realized that they would somehow have to effect the change while retaining the services and loyalty of the employees to be displaced. They also realized that the conventional machine operators could easily find jobs elsewhere, since such skills were in strong demand. Consequently, they could leave as soon as they heard the news. At the same time, the department would find it almost impossible to locate trained operators to run the machines on a temporary basis should the machine operators leave ahead of time. Furthermore, those not scheduled for discharge would have to be trained to operate the new EDP machines.

California's civil-service system did not make their task any easier. The system consisted of a multiplicity of relatively narrow classifications. Furthermore, employees could not usually move from one class to another without passing an exam.

Steedman and Bashline began developing a strategy to deal with these difficult obstacles. Their first decision was to "level" with the employees and tell them right away what was coming. On one afternoon in late March 1954, the tabulating section's workers were summoned to a meeting where they were informed of what the department was planning to do. Steedman expressed the hope of finding suitable positions elsewhere for all the permanent employees to be displaced, but he admitted that he could not guarantee that no layoffs would occur.

The employees seemed somewhat stunned by the announcement and soon began subjecting the two managers to a drum-fire of questions. However, Steedman and Bashline were both surprised and gratified to find that most of the questions dealt with the impact of the change on the section and the department rather than on the individuals who asked them.

As a next step, Steedman and Bashline set up an advisory committee. It consisted of various staff officers and line managers of the department together with a member of the state's civil-service agency. This committee soon became more than just an advisory body. Under Bashline's and Steedman's leadership, it ended up making most of the decisions regarding the changeover. Moreover, its members, by participating in its decisions, bound themselves and the employees in their sections to these decisions. And by acting as a communications conduit—keeping all affected sections informed and responding to whatever ideas and fears these sections might express—the committee maintained employee morale and loyalty.

Bashline soon realized that transferring surplus employees to other jobs, as they became vacant, within his own section would not suffice to absorb them all. He then hit upon the plan of transferring clerical employees to other sections of the department, even though in most cases their jobs would remain unaffected by EDPM. He would then use their now-vacant positions to absorb his machine operators. These machine operators would thus be available to run the conventional tabulating machines while the conversion was taking place.

Taking such a step, however, would mean breaching civil-service regulations, for the machine operators would then be working "out of class." Fortunately, the civil-service representative on the advisory committee agreed to the idea and persuaded his agency to go along with it. Some of the section heads on the committee at first objected, for they wanted to be able to pick their own replacements for vacancies in their sections. They did not like the idea of having their sections serve as dumping grounds for Bashline's surplus workers. But Steedman, although only a staff and not a line officer, made the decision favoring Bashline's plan, and he warned the section heads that Director Burkett's standing would be hurt if the conversion was delayed.

Eventually, most of the section heads accepted the idea, and some even volunteered to build up a supply of vacant jobs to accommodate Bashline's transferees. As vacancies within their units arose, they filled them with temporary employees until Bashline needed these slots.

Now came the delicate and potentially divisive problems of implementation. What mechanism should be used to determine who was to go and who was to stay?

The advisory committee decided to let the employees themselves determine how this should be done. The tabulating section employees were asked to form a committee to make recommendations. Once formed, this committee decided in turn to poll all the section's employees who were likely to be affected. The polls showed that they wished such transfers made on the basis of seniority. The employee committee forwarded this recommendation to the advisory committee, which promptly adopted it.

The conversion then proceeded to take place with reasonable smoothness. Problems did develop, although not all of them were the department's doing. (A key piece of equipment dropped from a fork lift while being unloaded at San Francisco's airport, and this delayed things for a month.) Bashline subsequently said that he would never again attempt a conversion "of this magnitude" within the same time limits.

But by 1958 the new machines were saving the state nearly five hundred thousand dollars a year in wage costs and were processing claims much more smoothly and speedily than the old system. And guides were taking visitors through the department's new building, pointing out the "million dollar's worth" of new and shiny equipment, noting its near-miraculous efficiency (237,000 additions a minute), and ending their spiel with the proud claim that "no permanent employees were laid off because of the installation of this equipment. Permanent employees affected were transferred to other jobs in the department or elsewhere in state service where they are needed."

Gamesmanship

Almost any system involving human beings will create complications and complexities that its inaugurators will have failed to foresee. Civil service is no exception. As it has gradually expanded throughout the country's public sector, ways to get around it have grown apace. Skillful and shrewd administrators have developed numerous devices to bend and even break its constricting regulations and rules.

Starting with selection, we find agencies sometimes tailoring the specifications for a particular position or group of positions so that only one individual or group can qualify. For example, a state Department of Public Utilities was once ordered to put its position of general counsel under civil service. The agency did so but stipulated that anyone applying for the post must have at least fifteen years' experience working as an attorney for a public-utilities regulatory commission. As it happened, the only person available who could meet that criterion was the man already holding the position.

When a truly competitive list of applicants is made up and those whom the agency wishes to choose fail to place near the top, other strategies may come into play. The agency head may simply delay filling the vacancies until he or she becomes reasonably sure that the front runners have become discouraged and located other jobs. He or she then can reach farther and farther down the list to fill the slots. This obviously can help those individuals favored but who ended up lower down on the list. Sometimes agencies may let the list expire altogether in the hope that when a new exam is given, and a new list is made up, those whom they wish to select will have placed in a higher position. (This hope has a good chance of being realized, since it will usually be those who did well on the exam before who most likely will have gone on to take jobs elsewhere. Those who fared less well may have failed to find something suitable and will be more disposed to take the exam again, especially if they feel that the agency really wants to hire them.)

Another method used to circumvent the civil-service selection system is to again let the list of eligible recruits expire and then hire the people the agency wants as "temporaries." Temporaries are usually supposed to work only for a fixed time period. Thirty working days or six weeks is a frequent limit. However, some civil-service systems allow agencies to rehire temporaries almost indefinitely. This not only permits the agency to evade the civil-service selection procedure but its tenure rules as well. A temporary knows that if he or she does not do what the agency wants, he or she may not get rehired when the six-week appointment runs out.

Prior to its abolition of civil service in 1975, Chicago had made wide use of this scheme. Of the city's forty-four thousand employees, some eight thousand were classified as temporaries. Some of these "temporaries" had held their jobs for twenty-five years or more, and many of them were earning over twenty thousand dollars a year. Needless to add, perhaps, is the fact that most of these provisional employees were members of the mayor's political organization, with several of the better-paid ones serving as precinct captains.

Once he or she has a favored applicant on board, there are many ways for the superior to protect and promote the interest of the favored subordinate or for the subordinate to protect and promote him- or herself. If there is no classified position that seems worthy of the recruit's talents or connections, he or she may be put into a classification that does not exist, pending a review that never comes. Or, the agency may place the pet subordinate in an existing classified position and then add a function or two to it so that it can then ask for the position to be upgraded. Subordinates themselves often show considerable ingenuity in advancing their interests in this way. A clever or ambitious employee, seeing no prospects for early advancement to a higher position, may ask for more responsibilities at her present grade. When and if she obtains them she will then ask that her present position be reclassified upward. This technique is known in the civil service as *job evolution*. Sometimes it occurs without any new duties being added to the position but rather arises out of a supposedly new "awareness" of the duties that the position already entails.

Some "grade creep" would certainly seem necessary given the increasing sophistication of society and hence the increasing skills needed by those who seek to manage it. More and more government jobs have become more and more complex, thereby requiring more and more qualified people to handle them. Nevertheless, administrators and their agencies have through the years shown an ability to manipulate and even mangle the apparently not-so-sacred tenets of civil-service systems. And one of the results of such stratagems has been more grade creep than would otherwise be the case.

Some of the more overt and offensive instances of grade creep were uncovered by the Civil Service Commission in a two-year study, the results of which were announced in late 1978. The study showed that virtually 20 percent of the entire federal work force was classified incorrectly, and, as might be expected, most of these errors lay in grades that were too high, rather than in those that were too low. According to the commission, these errors were costing the taxpayers nearly a half billion dollars a year.[38]

Evidence indicates that such over-grading errors may exist in state and local levels of government as well. Even publicly owned universities do not appear exempt. An audit of the City University of New York in 1979 found several administrative-staff employees holding high faculty rank. The supervisor of custodians, for example, held the rank of full professor. An assistant librarian was on the payroll as an associate professor. All told, eighty-seven, or over half of 166 nonteaching employees at three of the university's schools, were overclassified, at a cost of more than half a million dollars a year to the financially hard-pressed facility.[39]

A still more remarkable revelation regarding civil-service gamesmanship has surfaced in recent years. This concerns the federal government's supposed "shadow work force." In seeking to evade the manpower ceiling set by the White House, many federal agencies have taken to hiring what are called full-time part-timers. The employees work virtually full time, except for the time when the annual audit of federal employees is made. They are then conveniently removed from the public payroll. They are sometimes called "twenty-five-and-ones" since they stay on the payroll for twenty-five out of the federal government's twenty-six pay periods.

The exact number of these very real yet phantom workers is unknown, but the Office of Management and Budget estimates that the Forest Service alone employs between seven and eight thousand such workers (a number that amounts to approximately one-third of the Forest Service's official payroll). Many other agencies also use them. "The real problem," according to one veteran bureaucrat, "is that a lot of agencies have more money than personnel slots; and if they are really ingenious, they'll find some way to use it to get more bodies."[40] The pressures of or-ganizational pathology—in this case the relentless drive to expand—fre-quently finds ways of overcoming any obstacle.

There are other, more legitimate, ways of working around manpower ceilings. They include hiring people as consultants, contracting with the private sector for various goods and services, and, of course, turning over programs to other levels of government to run. The device of the public corporation can also be brought into use. Thus, the more than several thousand employees of the Legal Services Corporation, who provide free legal services to the poor, do not show up on any government payroll. The same holds true for the Consolidated Rail Corporation (Conrail), the U.S. Post Office, and others.

A persuasive argument can be made that such efforts at evading hiring limits are in many cases caused by the unrealistic attempt to give federal agencies more to do while trying to claim that federal employment is holding steady. Nevertheless, the fact that such subterfuges have come into common use reflects badly on the administrative sector and makes the task of its defenders increasingly more difficult.

Reform: The Second Wave

A century after the inauguration of civil service, a new wave of reform was on the rise. Mounting furor over the weaknesses and woes, real and imagined, of governmenal personnel systems were stimulating a variety of corrective endeavors. Some wanted to throw out the merit-system prin-ciple altogether, arguing that political leaders were coming under so much pressure to perform that they most likely would employ the most capable, even if they possessed unshackled power to appoint whom they pleased. Others did not wish to go so far. They were seeking merely to modify existing civil service systems in order to give government man-agers a freer hand to reward good work and penalize the bad.

By far the most important of the efforts was the federal government's Civil Service Reform Act of 1978 (CSRA). The most sweeping piece of civil-service legislation since the system was founded, the act replaced the long-standing Civil Service Commission with two new agencies: The Office of Personnel Management and The Merit Systems Protection Board. Previously the now-defunct Civil Service Commission had not only administered the system but had adjudicated complaints against it. This often made the commission its own police officer. Henceforth, the two functions would be carried out by separate agencies.

Of much greater import, however, was the greater discretion and flexibility it brought to federal managers. Previously, in order to discipline or dismiss an employee, the superior had to show that the "preponderance" of the evidence supported the superior's case. Now only "substantial" evidence would be needed. Although such disciplinary moves would still be difficult, they should be somewhat easier to put into effect than had previously been the case. For example, a supervisor would be able to fire an employee who had received four valid complaints in one year for discourtesy or rudeness to a member of the public. Prior to the act's passage, such evidence of poor performance would not have sufficed.

The greatest interest centered on the more positive part of the reform. This called for the creation of a Senior Executive Service, which all the federal government's managerial elite could join. If an eligible public manager opted for the SES, he or she gave up tenure in his or her present post and risked transfer to new duties, as well as being bounced back to his or her original rank. The incentive was the chance to increase his or her salary by up to 20 percent, and to win additional bonuses for exceptional effort.

Compared to the rewards and punishments used in private industry, these may seem quite limited. Nevertheless, their adoption marked a new departure for the federal government, and as the deadline for enrollment came around in July 1979, observers wondered just how many of the eight thousand top public managers eligible would apply. Many felt that few members of this bureaucratic elite would be tempted, but when the program was officially launched on July 13, over 95 percent of them joined.[41]

Unfortunately, the euphoria that enveloped the launching of CSRA soon ended. A survey of high-level federal executives a year later showed that while over half judged the performance standards being used to evaluate them to be fair, less than a quarter felt that the appraisals based on these standards had helped improve their performances or had even aided them in assessing their strengths and weaknesses.[42]

Another poll the same year spotlighted a greater source of discontent. This concerned the distribution of bonuses. Congress, to be sure, had reduced the amount of money for such awards, and this no doubt contributed to the complaints. But many of the majority who failed to receive bonuses protested bitterly that whatever money was available was not distributed fairly. In their view the flexibility written into the act had only opened the door to favoritism.

Meanwhile, some agencies appeared to have acted with undue generosity in rewarding "merit." The National Aeronautics and Space Administration, for example, gave cash awards to nearly half of its 520 senior employees. Among those receiving them was the manager of the space shuttle, whose program was not only two years behind schedule but had been plagued with cost overruns. This executive received ten thousand dollars in extra pay for meritorious performance. Among others receiving bonuses at NASA were three members of the Bonus Review Board itself.[43]

Further polls the following year brought more problems to light. One found 80 percent of all responding executives believing that the system lacked sufficient incentives to retain competent managers. Another showed that not only did nearly two-thirds of all SES executives believe the bonus awards to have been made in an unfair manner, but that nearly a quarter thought the whole SES system should be abandoned.[44]

There were, however, some positive sides to the CSRA picture. For example, although the number of employees appealing disciplinary actions had gone up markedly, the new Merit Systems Protection Board had cut the time necessary to process these appeals almost in half. What's more, only 3 percent of all agency decisions were being reversed by the board on grounds of procedural error.

At the beginning of 1982 the National Academy of Public Administration issued a report giving CSRA a mixed scorecard. The academy deplored the uneven distribution of bonuses, the lack of progress in developing SES candidates, the lack of experimentation, and the generally poor morale resulting in part from such problems. At the same time it welcomed the increasing placement of minority members and women in top-level jobs, the installation of performance-appraisal systems, and the indications that the SES had not led to any politicalization of the civil service. The reform, reported the academy, was, after three years, a mixture of "fair successes and painful disappointments."[45]

Meanwhile, the federal initiative, plus continued financial pressure, is spurring on reform efforts at the grass roots. At the beginning of the 1980s five states had either recently undertaken or were currently engaged in wholesale reorganizations of their public personnel systems. Many other jurisdictions were feeling great pressure to follow suit. Public-interest groups of one kind or another were vigorously and often vociferously urging drastic civil-service reform in Colorado, Massachusetts, Philadelphia, and elsewhere. The criticisms underlying these calls to action often parallel each other. In Philadelphia, the city's civil service was charged with being control oriented rather than service oriented and therefore more concerned with procedures than accomplishment. In Massachusetts, a task force bewailed the fact that a position in state government was too often regarded as a place to be rather than as a place to do something.

"Let the public service be a proud and lively career," said John F. Kennedy in his first inaugural address. Now, more than twenty years later, the public sector of the United States is alive with attempts to bring that hope closer to reality.

TRADING TITLES FOR TYPEWRITERS

Thanks to Ronald Reagan's attempt to reduce federal expenditures the federal government now employs typists earning up to $45,000 a year. One of them is James McHugh, who formerly oversaw a $27-million budget at the National Institute on Alcohol Abuse. Another is Delores Finister, who supervised public health programs. They are among the many furloughed federal executives who decided to stay on at a lower position. Says McHugh, "when they came back with an offer of a [position as a] secretary, I said I was not the world's greatest secretary but I can type." And he added, "If it is something or nothing, I'll take something." (UPI dispatch, May 24, 1982)

Notes

1. Quoted in John Franklin Campbell, *The Foreign Affairs Fudge Factory* (New York: Basic Books, 1971), 139–140.

2. Ibid., 47.

3. Quoted in George E. Berkley, *The Administrative Revolution: Notes on the Passing of Organization Man* (Englewood Cliffs, N.J.: Prentice-Hall, 1971), 141.

4. Quoted in Paul Van Riper, *History of the United States Civil Service* (New York: Harper & Row, 1958), 36.

5. Martin Tolchin and Susan Tolchin, *To the Victor* . . . (New York: Random House, 1971), 96.

6. See Richard Greenberger, *The 12-Year Reich* (New York: Holt, Rinehart and Winston, 1971), chap. 9, for an illuminating picture of Hitler's impact on the German civil service.

7. Herschel Cribb, "Public Jobs and the Disadvantaged," *Opportunity* (October 1972).

8. Cited in Patrick V. Murphy, *The Criminal Justice System in Crisis* (Syracuse, N.Y.: Maxwell School of Citizenship and Affairs, 1972).

9. *Boston Sunday Globe*, 28 January 1973.

10. Robin Maugham, *Escape from the Shadows* (New York: McGraw-Hill, 1973), 175.

11. Barbara W. Tuchman, *The Zimmerman Telegram* (New York: Bantam Books, 1971), 113.

12. Daniel Katz and Robert L. Kahn, *The Social Psychology of Organizations* (New York: John Wiley, 1966), 404.

13. Herbert Kaufman, *The Forest Ranger* (Baltimore, Md.: Johns Hopkins Press, 1960), 161–165.

14. *New York Times,* 15 December 1968.

15. U.S. Civil Service Commission, "Employee Training in the Federal Service FY 1967" (Washington, D.C., Government Printing Office, 1968).

16. O. Glenn Stahl, *Public Personnel Administration,* 6th ed. (New York: Harper & Row, 1971), 20.

17. For an informative article covering these and other developments in the federal government's policies toward women employees, see Jayne B. Spain, "The Best Is Yet to Come," *Civil Service Journal* (January–March 1973). Ms. Spain was vice-chairman of the U.S. Civil Service Commission.

18. John Morton Blum, *Woodrow Wilson and the Politics of Morality* (Boston: Little, Brown, 1956), 115–116.

19. Samuel Solomon, *Parade,* 3 June 1973, 18. For an interesting and informed, albeit one-sided, view of this whole problem see Nathan Glazer, *Affirmative Discrimination* (New York: Basic Books, 1975).

20. *New York Times,* 28 September 1980.

21. *Public Administration Times,* 15 June 1981.

22. State of Connecticut v. Teal, (1982).

23. Chester Burger, *Executive Under Fire* (New York: Macmillan, 1966), 223.

24. David Halberstam, *The Best and the Brightest* (New York: Random House, 1969), 202–205, 248–249.

25. Peter Blau, *Bureaucracy in Modern Society* (New York: Random House, 1956), 50.

26. Arthur M. Schlesinger, Jr., *A Thousand Days* (Boston: Houghton Mifflin, 1965), 386.

27. William A. Bell, "The Cost of Cowardice: Silence in the Foreign Service," in Charles Peters and Timothy J. Adams, eds., *Inside the System* (New York: Praeger Publishers, 1970), 223.

28. Douglas McGregor, *The Theory of Human Enterprise* (New York: McGraw-Hill, 1960), 85.

29. Donald C. Stone, "Innovative Organizations Require Innovative Managers," *Public Administration Review* (September–October, 1981).

30. George E. Berkley, *The Democratic Policeman* (Boston: Beacon Press, 1969).

31. McGregor, *The Theory of Human Enterprise,* chap. 7.

32. Stahl, *Public Personnel Administration,* 51–52.

33. In a statement to the author. The former official wishes to remain anonymous.

34. This information was obtained by the author through interviews conducted in London, December 1972.

35. *New York Times,* 1 August 1972.

36. *New York Times,* 26 June 1973.

37. Material for this case was taken from James R. Bell and Lynwood B. Steedman, *Personnel Problems in Converting to Automation,* Inter-University Case Program no. 44 (Indianapolis, Ind.: Bobbs-Merrill, 1959).

38. *Government Manager,* 4 December 1978.

39. *New York Times,* 12 July 1979.

40. *Washington Post,* 26 August 1979.

41. Several accounts of SES and its development have appeared in *Public Administration Times*. See in particular the issues of November, 1978 and August 1979. There have also been some useful accounts in the popular press. An example of the latter is a story by David Broder in the *Washington Post*, 30 June 1979.

42. Lloyd G. Nigro, "Attitudes of Federal Employees Toward Performance Appraisal and Merit Pay: Implications for CSRA Implementation," *Public Administration Review* (January–February 1981).

43. Bernard Rosen, "Uncertainty in the Senior Executive Service," *Public Administration Review* (March–April 1981). Also see an interesting exchange of letters between Krishna K. Tummala and Rosen in the November–December 1981 issue of the same journal.

44. *Public Administration Times*, 1 July 1981.

45. *Public Administration Times*, 1 January 1982.

5

The Rise of
Public Unionism

Public Unionism: Pro and Con

At the beginning of the 1960s not a single written contract existed between a teacher's union and a U.S. school system. In the beginning of the 1980s thousands of such contracts were in effect covering more than two million teachers. The principal teachers' union, the National Education Association, had become the second largest union in the nation. It had also become the most powerful single lobbying group in many state houses, and one of the most powerful lobbies in Washington.[1]

As with the teachers, so with other groups of government workers. The 1960s and 1970s were times of unprecedented growth. Formerly an insignificant subunit within the AFL-CIO, the American Federation of State, County and Municipal Employees (AFSCME) had become the AFL-CIO's largest constituent group. By the start of the 1980s approximately 40 percent of all public employees belonged to unions, compared to only a little over 20 percent of their private-sector colleagues.

It all started in Wisconsin. In 1959 that state enacted the nation's first compulsory collective-bargaining law for public employers. But the real impetus occurred three years later when President John Kennedy signed Executive Order 10988 giving federal workers the right to organize and bargain collectively. This step not only opened up the federal bureaucracy to unionization but spurred on the states to do the same. By 1975 over two-thirds of the states and most of their major cities were employing heavily unionized work forces.

This sharp and relatively sudden spurt in trade unionism among public workers provoked much comment and concern. While some hailed the development, others deplored it. Examining the arguments of both may provide a useful perspective for assessing its implications for public administration.

Unions as Problems

On a philosophical basis opponents of public-employee unionism claim that such unionism is unjustified and unwarranted. The public employee does not labor to provide a profit to his employers. Thus, no basic divergence of interest exists between management and labor, since the former do not benefit by depriving the latter. All are public servants, charged with executing the people's wishes as expressed through their elected representatives, votes on referenda, and other means. Trade unionism in general and collective bargaining in particular, say the opponents, erode the whole concept of government work as a public service.

Unions are also accused of perpetuating and even expanding some of the worst features of public personnel systems. These include promotion by seniority and rigid tenure rules, which make it difficult to fire or demote a delinquent or deficient employee. They also make public managers ever more careful about having employees work out of grade. Public employee unions, say the critics, encourage public organizations to meet challenges and solve problems by simply adding more people. Writes a former New York City budget director, "If you have five men on the back of a fire engine, the union wants seven, and if you've got seven, they want nine."[2] All these practices increase costs, reduce flexibility, and impede innovation.

The impairment of innovation can take a variety of forms. When New York City announced the consolidation of eight of the city's seventy-two police precincts, the first step toward implementing a long existing and carefully drawn out plan, the Patrolmen's Benevolent Association organized mass meetings of one thousand or more citizens in every affected area. After two precinct houses were closed, the consolidation efforts came to an abrupt halt. The city's police department also launched an experiment involving the use of patrol cars in a residential middle-class section. The demonstration project resulted in a 35-percent reduction in response time, a lower accident and injury rate, and good visibility of, and citizen support for, the police. But the PBA has managed to keep the experiment confined to the small district in which it originated.[3]

Unions can undermine management in still other ways. They diffuse responsibility and make accountability more difficult to pinpoint. The problem becomes still worse when public managers themselves form unions or associations that take on a unionist coloration. In order to bargain collectively they sometimes even resist efforts to classify themselves as managerial employees. In February 1973, New York City school principals, contesting a Board of Education ruling that they held managerial positions, appealed to the state's Public Employment Relations Board to reclassify them in a nonmanagerial category.[4]

Unionization has greatly increased the political involvement of public employees. These unions provide forums, publicity, poll workers, and, most important of all perhaps, generous financial contributions to public officials who think, or at least vote, their way. When the postal unions finance a testimonial dinner for the chairman of the House Post Office and Civil Service Committee, as they have done, they do so obviously with the hope of obtaining sympathetic treatment from his committee. Some unions, especially the National Education Association, have proven remarkably adept in getting their members named or elected delegates to both state and national Democratic party conventions.

Public employee unions probably exert the most influence in those large cities with partisan elections. Members of municipal unions and their families can sometimes cast almost half the votes in a local Democratic primary. And since the Democratic party candidate almost invariably wins in most of these cities, these unions can determine who will be the city's next mayor. In 1975 Philadelphia Mayor Frank Rizzo gave the city's work force a 13-percent pay boost a few months before the election. Though Rizzo had been under heavy fire for mismanagement, he handily won reelection. "There's no question about it," New York City's municipal union chief Victor Gotbaum once boasted, "we have the ability to elect our own boss."[5]

Finally, and perhaps most seriously, public unionism's critics condemn it for encouraging and embittering labor disputes. This, they contend, has caused the number of public employee strikes to escalate from a mere 15 in 1958 to 478 in 1975. In the latter year, nearly 2.25 million man-days of labor were lost through such largely illegal walkouts.

Public employee strikes have prompted even staunch labor loyalists to fret and frown. Franklin Roosevelt, though a strong supporter of the then-weak U.S. labor movement, once castigated such strikes as "unthinkable and unsupportable."[6] More recently some government officials have pointed out that certain natural restraints on union demands exist in the private sector but not in the public sector. A union that seeks too much from a business firm may only put the firm, and therefore itself, out of business. Governments, however, rarely go out of business. Instead they simply seek to exact the additional costs from their constituents. The absence of an automatic lid on employee demands, say the critics, has led to excessive demands and, when not met, to excessive strikes. And given government's role as a provider of welfare and protector of the public safety, virtually any strike at all can seem excessive.

Unions as Possibilities

The lengthy list of accusations that can be and has been made against public employee unionism does not shake the faith and determination of the movement's supporters. They continue to stand firm, not only in discounting the negative but in affirming the positive. And a rationale does exist for viewing the growth of unionism as a beneficial factor in the development of public administration.

Let us start with the issue of strikes. David Ziskind, a one-time official of the U.S. Department of Labor, wrote a book entitled *One Thousand Strikes of Government Employees*. The book was published by the Columbia University Press in 1940, a time when there were few public employee unions of any significance. The incident is illustrative of a point that trade union proponents zealously propound: unions in themselves do not cause strikes. On the contrary, they more often prevent strikes from occurring and shorten those that do occur.

In many, if not most, public employee strikes of recent years, the union's membership has spoken and acted more militantly than its leadership. Often, the union officials have called strike actions only in response to intense membership pressure. And, when they have not responded promptly enough, the union leaders have often found themselves with a wildcat walkout on their hands. A famous sixteen-hour Montreal Police strike that broke out in October 1969 was a wildcat operation that union officials actually helped bring to a speedy end. A New York City Police strike the following winter saw some enraged strikers actually storm their own union offices because they felt the union leadership had not been sufficiently aggressive in fighting for their rights. The big post office strike of 1970 began with disgusted postal employees calling in sick. Said *Newsweek* magazine, "Union officials have been warning Congressional Postal Committee members, the administration and the Post Office that they were rapidly losing control of an increasingly unruly membership."[7] When it came to getting the strikers back to work, AFL-CIO President George Meany helped postal union leaders in urging employees to accept the government's proffered terms.

Economist Thomas C. Schelling has pointed out how "in war one may hope that the enemy government remains intact, thus assuring that there is an authority to negotiate with and to discipline the enemy troops themselves."[8] In a sense, the same holds true for warfare between labor and management. The existence of an organized union with a reasonably strong leadership provides an authority to negotiate with and to "discipline the enemy troops."

But if unions can help to end strikes, they can help even more in preventing them. At the outset it should be noted that union leaders tend to fear strikes, for such actions drain union treasuries and, when unsuccessful, can turn the membership against the union. Thus, union leaders much prefer to resolve disputes by negotiation. In so doing they offer management many opportunities for alleviating and avoiding disruption and discord in its labor relations. The union can bring problems to management's attention in time for management to act on them before they explode. It will provide employee representatives to whom management can talk and, if they see some validity in management's case, they can transmit it to the employees with more credibility than management can ever hope to achieve.

The closing of the Community Services Administration by the Reagan administration offers an example of the positive role unions can play even when their interests have been injured. The agency's employees' union lobbied vigorously to keep the agency alive. But, in the words of one official who helped shut it down, "once Congress acted, their [the union's] leadership was very forthcoming in advancing numerous constructive suggestions which we found most useful."[9]

Unions will, it is true, usually insist on making an input into administrative policy, but such an input need not constitute a roadblock to administrative improvement. Unions naturally tend to favor at least some generally approved administrative practices. For example, they will usually fight against favoritism, for favoritism benefits a few over the many, and the many always have more potential votes at union meetings. Unions may, therefore, resist any policies that permit discriminatory or arbitrary treatment. Then, in order to improve the prestige of their membership, union leaders will often seek to raise recruiting requirements and promote professionalism. Some unions even run career development programs. Union publications usually carry some material concerning new developments in the vocational fields of their membership.

When it comes to innovation and change, unions can also play a constructive role. This is the conclusion of Anthony F. Ingrassia, the director of labor-management relations for the U.S. Civil Service Commission. According to Ingrassia, employee resistance to change is usually a defensive reaction that arises when the employees feel that something is being imposed upon them. If they or their representatives are included in the planning process, they may not only go along with the plans but can even contribute to their formulation. He recommends the establishment of "meaningful cooperative committees" which will solicit and listen to employee ideas and reactions.[10]

To cite just one example of what Ingrassia may have had in mind, the Federal Bureau of Prisons in 1971 decided to set up a pilot project for training federal correctional personnel. Union leaders were included from the very beginning of the project, and the president of the Council of Prison Locals was made a member of the "Board of Visitors." The result was a successful program that has improved the operation of the federal prison system. (The bitter prison unrest that swept over the United States in the early 1970s, it should be noted, was almost exclusively confined to state and local institutions.)[11]

One final feature that can be credited to public employee unions is the ability to bring public-sector problems before the public. Teachers' unions have often done this, and the unionized teachers of Los Angeles even passed up a 5-percent pay raise in 1969 in order to secure improvements in the city's educational system. The union representing New York City's correction officers repeatedly called attention to the severe overcrowding in the city's jails. Unfortunately, their pleas in this instance went unheeded until rioting broke out in 1972.

That public employee unions can improve as well as impair public administration has not gone unrecognized by administrators themselves. Picot B. Floyd, the city manager of Savannah, Georgia, claims that unions offer municipal administrators such advantages as "clarification of the role of management in the urban setting; a decrease in labor problems; better employee performance; an increased *esprit de corps;* and a source of support for changes that may be needed in personnel administration." Floyd urges his colleagues to "take advantage of the opportunities that are presented to city governments by organized labor groups."[12]

The Bargaining Process

An administrator who is entering into negotiations with a recently established union will often feel like an early Christian entering a lion-filled arena. He or she should remember that a union usually arises as the culmination of a long and mounting series of disputes and disgruntlements. Consequently, the union's first negotiations are often the most militant. Added to these problems is the fact that the union representatives are inexperienced and untested. They know that their members are waiting to see what they can do, and so they feel they must prove themselves.

As a result of these conditions, the initial phases of union-management relations are likely to prove much more trying than later ones. If admin-

istrators fail to keep this in mind, they may let themselves in for more turmoil and trouble than necessary. Later, when collective bargaining becomes an established and even routine procedure in organizational life,
they may find the atmosphere starting to ease. Rarely will such negotiations become a simple cut-and-dry operation, however. Each round of
talks presents its own problems. Administrators who have weathered
many such bargaining sessions usually have developed a series of strategies and stratagems to deal with them. While each may have his or her
own special techniques, there are a few general rules that many have
found helpful.

First, to bargain effectively with unions, an administrator must believe
in such bargaining. This is essential for two reasons: (1) a negation of such
a process will most likely be communicated to the labor representatives
and will, in turn, make them hostile, and (2) no administrator can ever
learn how to make full use of collective bargaining, of how to turn it to
his or her agency's advantage, unless he or she believes that such a possibility exists.

Turning to another rule, it is important for administrators who are involved or who are about to get involved in contract negotiations to encourage the involvement and elicit the support of middle management
and even first-line management, such as foremen. This is not always easy
to do, since many low-ranking managers identify with the rank and file.
Indeed, the union may indirectly bargain for these people as well as for
its own members, because a pay increase for the rank and file will usually
bring a pay increase for middle management as well. In some agencies,
the pay of first-level supervisors is fixed at a certain percentage over that
of the people they supervise.

Nevertheless, despite these difficulties, it is worthwhile to seek their
support, since middle and first-line managers can often contribute to the
bargaining process. They usually know best what the rank and file really
want and what will satisfy them. Also, they will be the ones who will
have to implement the new contract. This means that the contract is likely
to prove more workable if their comments are obtained before it is
worked out. Finally, excluding middle managers or paying little heed to
what they have to say may only alienate them all the more from the administrative side and intensify their identification with those they
supervise.

The public manager should also take care to come to the bargaining table with proposals of his or her own. In other words, management should
not simply react to labor's demands but make some demands itself. Furthermore, a manager will be well advised not to negotiate all the union's
demands first. Instead, he or she should press forward with settling some
of management's claims before all the union's requests have been dealt

with, lest management lose all its leverage before its own concerns are thrashed out.

Administrators should be careful, however, to see that the union's negotiators do not leave the bargaining table empty-handed. They must be given some victories. Managers who seek to undermine the union representatives will only succeed in making these representatives and the membership more intractable. The management negotiator should remember that his or her union counterpart may have to contend not only with competition from within but also from without, for other unions may be eager to supplant the existing one. Finally, the union representatives will almost always be needed to enforce whatever settlement is arrived at. Weakening their position is not going to help management in accomplishing this enforcement task.

For some of the same reasons, administrators would do well not to let the negotiations drag on too long, for this too may make the membership more militant and hence more difficult for their representatives to control. Another factor that may create similar problems for management is negotiating during an election. And once issues have been negotiated, the settlements should be put in writing so that the union spokespeople cannot easily repudiate them if they later find the situation more propitious for making even stronger demands.

One final fact should be kept constantly in mind. In the public sector as in the private sector, trade unions are not primarily economic organizations, and their fundamental role is not merely to secure economic benefits. They are essentially a means whereby employees seek to avoid manipulation. Employees form unions to protest against their dependent position and to assert their right to self-determination. The economic issues that so often dominate the dialogue, while by no means unimportant, are still more often than not secondary. The more fundamental issues are those that involve human dignity and human rights.

When Collective Bargaining Fails

When the two sides become stalemated and the bargaining process breaks down, alternatives are available for avoiding a strike. The first of these is what is called *fact-finding*. Under this process, an individual or, as happens more frequently, a panel is set up to review the disputed issues and make recommendations. These recommendations are not binding, but if the fact-finding machinery has been properly constituted, and if its analysis of the facts is accurate, both sides will be under a good deal of pressure to accept its suggestions.

To be effective, the fact-finders must be acceptable to both sides. During the Philadelphia school strike of 1972–1973, the teachers' union asked for either fact-finding or arbitration. The Pennsylvania Labor Relations Board finally appointed a fact-finder, but it was one that the union found unacceptable. As a result, the fact-finder's subsequent recommendations were rejected and the strike became the second longest school strike in U.S. history.[13]

Another device that is sometimes used when labor-management negotiations founder is *mediation*. The mediator or, in some cases, mediators actually help carry on negotiations between the disputing parties. They may group both sides around a table and try to find ways to open up previously entrenched positions or to point out possibilities for conciliation. On occasion, when a dispute has gotten out of hand and tempers have reached a boiling point, the mediator may put the two sides in separate rooms and run from room to room in a continuing effort to break the deadlock. Some jurisdictions authorize fact-finders to mediate when their recommendations have failed to dissolve the differences separating the parties involved.

Needless to point out, mediation is quite an art. According to one experienced practitioner, a good mediator should

- have a good sense of timing, knowing when to advise each side on when to make each move;
- avoid relieving the parties themselves of responsibility to solve the dispute;
- be able to distinguish the power contest between the parties from internal power considerations (such as union leaders fearful of losing face with their own members);
- avoid passing on the merits of the respective positions.[14]

Neither mediation nor fact-finding assures a peaceful settlement to a labor dispute. For that type of guarantee we must turn to a third alternative, *arbitration*. This device differs from the other two in just one crucial respect: it produces a definite decision and usually one that is binding on both sides. When binding arbitration has been agreed upon, the arbitrator's word is final and there is no further appeal.

Of course, if arbitration is not accepted by either party at the outset, it does not guarantee a peaceful resolution. But it is rarely utilized without such prior concurrence. One typical way of going about the process is for each side to choose a representative and for the two representatives to choose a third member of what then becomes an arbitration panel.

Administrators tend to view third-party proceedings such as fact-finding, mediation, and arbitration with mixed feelings. While they recognize that such devices help considerably to avoid strikes, they often feel that they result in decisions that, from a management perspective, are more often than not injurious. Third parties have nothing at stake except their own future business in getting cases to mediate or arbitrate. Thus, they show a tendency, it is felt, to split the issue down the middle, with perhaps some leaning toward the labor side. Some administrators question not only the leaning toward labor but whether most disputes should automatically be split down the middle in any case. They feel many issues simply do not lend themselves to that type of decision. In any case, management loses control in such proceedings, and decisions are made by those who cannot be fully aware of all their implications, and who in any case do not have to live with them.

Unionists have tended to look more favorably on third-party intervention. They have particularly favored arbitration. As one fire fighters' union official once expressed it, without compulsory arbitration in the background, collective bargaining for employees becomes collective begging.[15] Beyond that, public employee unions continue to strive for the right to strike. They may not wish to make use of it very often for reasons stated previously, but possession of such a right gives them the most valuable weapon a union can usually possess when it starts to bargain collectively. "One cannot deprive 20 percent of the work force of the essentials of democracy without harming the basic freedom of all Americans," Jerry Wurf, the late president of the AFSCME, declared, while the late AFL-CIO President George Meany once stated that "a free collective bargaining system contemplates that at the end of the road there can be a strike. . . . If you don't like that then take out the word 'free.' "[16]

In behalf of this position, it is useful to point out that employees of privately owned hospitals, electric companies, water works, gas plants, and shipyards enjoy the right to strike. Why, it is sometimes asked, should employees of comparable government-owned institutions not possess similar privileges? Drivers on certain bus lines in Manhattan and the Bronx operated under a private contract in 1962 and thus had the right to strike. A few years later, when the lines had been taken over by the metropolitan transit agency, this right was lost. Yet the drivers were doing exactly the same work they were doing before.

The American Assembly, a nonpartisan institute affiliated with Columbia University, reached the conclusion at its fortieth gathering in the fall of 1971 that it was time to move in this direction. A panel of seventy top-level government, legal, academic, business, and labor leaders recommended that public employees be allowed a limited right to strike after "obligatory procedures" have been exhausted. In making this recommendation, they cited not only some of the considerations already noted, but pointed out that management itself may be better off, for such strikes "often result in lost wages [for public employees] and no real discomfort for public employers whose revenues continue unimpaired."[17] The issue of the right to strike will continue to provoke discussion and debate as the public employee union movement continues to grow.

The Seventies and Eighties: Surge and Setback

As the growth of unionism continued into the 1970s, its attendant problems seemed to be overshadowing its benefits. Public employee organizations were flexing their muscles in ways that had started to arouse increasing anxiety and alarm.

For one thing, their involvement in politics had deepened considerably. Public employee unions had begun making substantial campaign contributions, and were following up this support with other campaign help, such as distributing leaflets, doorbell ringing, and telephoning. Lobbyists for public employee labor groups had become pervasive and persuasive forces at city hall, the state house, and Capitol Hill. Commented William Walsh, who heads the ten-member Washington lobbying team of AFSCME, "A public employees union that doesn't recognize that political action is a corollary to collective bargaining is simply out of touch."[18]

The effects of this political effort were beginning to be widely felt. One relatively minor but quite illustrative example concerned the federal government's policy regarding vendors in public buildings. In 1936, Washington initiated a policy of letting blind people operate stands selling snacks and sundries in its buildings. In the 1960s federal employee organizations started squeezing out these blind vendors in order to replace them with vending machines, the profits of which would go to employee recreation associations. Spokesmen for the blind introduced a bill in 1970 to protect the blind vendors. However, public employee groups saw to it that the bill never got out of committee.

A much more significant example of public employee power occurred in the fall of 1974, when President Ford sought to delay for three months a scheduled pay increase for federal workers. Congress, in response to union pressure, promptly overrode the move, thus ending rather abruptly the short-lived "honeymoon" phase of the new administration.

But it was at the state and local level where the clout of public unionism seemed to have proven most powerful. By 1975 sanitation workers in San Francisco were earning seventeen thousand dollars a year, which was more than many engineers were making in the region's budding Silicon Valley. Generous fringe benefits added appreciably to the burden. Fire fighters with full seniority in New York City that year were earning more than thirty-five thousand dollars in salary and fringes combined. As the *New York Times* dolefully commented, "New York is working for its unionized civil service workers, not vice versa."[19]

The great and growing gains scored by the unions had not occurred simply through political pressures. Union leaders had become quite proficient in using more traditional tactics as well. One of these was the "whipsaw." This stratagem calls for the union to make a breakthrough by scoring a special success in negotiating with a particular community or with a particular agency. Having made the "breakthrough," it then often becomes easy to broaden the front by seeking comparable concessions from other agencies and/or communities.

The mounting militancy of the unions reflected the mounting militancy of their members, many of whom had become increasingly irritated by overtly political and generally poor management policies. But it was often fanned by jurisdictional fights between the unions themselves, with each trying to outbid each other for the public employee's affections. For example, when New York City found itself on the brink of bankruptcy in 1975, the American Federation of Teachers union, which covered the city's schools, showed great reluctance in modifying its hard-line position. Finally, in late 1976 the union's president, Albert Shanker, agreed to forego collective bargaining in favor of a labor board to determine wages and conditions for city teachers. No sooner had he made this concession than the NEA, which had been trying to take the teachers away from the federation, called a press conference to denounce Shanker's conciliatory gesture. Said NEA President John Ryor, "It is incomprehensible that Albert Shanker . . . has unilaterally and without consulting his own members, abrogated the right to collective bargaining."[20]

This example from New York City illustrates another aspect of the growth in union membership and militancy. Much of this had taken place in, and was directed at, the governments of the nation's larger cities. And it was precisely these governments that were being hit by the growth of other costly problems, such as crime and arson. Thus, union power was pushing hardest against the weakest links in the country's governmental chain.

The Turning of the Tide

Eventually and inevitably a reaction against growing union power arose. It was catalyzed, if not caused, by the increasing financial strain that governments of all kinds, but especially those of the larger cities, were undergoing. Even before California's Proposition 13 signaled the start of taxpayer rebellion, Cleveland, Baltimore, Detroit, and other major cities had started to pare down their work forces despite strong and strident resistance from their municipal unions.

Such efforts were not confined to the weaker metropolises of the northeast and midwest. In Seattle Mayor Wesley Uhlman fired a popular fire chief who had refused to comply with Uhlman's cost-cutting directives, and when the irate firemen's union launched a recall election, the mayor easily won it, receiving almost two-thirds of the vote. In San Francisco when city workers went out on strike over a canceled pay increase, city officials put the issue to the voters, who overwhelmingly endorsed their action. The following year, San Francisco's usually prolabor electorate approved by majorities of nearly seven to one two ordinances aimed at curtailing public union power. One required the mandatory firing of any city worker who goes on strike; the other required, in the event of an impasse in union-management negotiations, that the union's final offer be submitted to the voters in a referendum.

This did not mark the end of the matter. San Francisco also sued the six striking unions for damages. Eventually five of the labor organizations withdrew from the suit by pledging not to strike or honor a picket line against the city. But the plumbers union decided to fight. The case dragged on until the summer of 1982, when a local jury finally awarded the city $4 million in damages against its recalcitrant plumbers.[21]

State governments too had also toughened their stance considerably. With the exception of Tennessee, which granted collective-bargaining rights to teachers, no new state since 1975 has passed collective bargaining legislation, and some of those that had already enacted such laws began to tighten them.

As a result of such a shift in actions and attitudes, public employee strikes began to decline. Only 300 such strikes occurred in 1981, representing a near-50-percent drop from the 593 recorded just two years earlier. Taking note of such developments, as well as the budget crunches that often underlay them and a well-publicized victory by the Reagan administration in crushing a strike by airplane controllers, *Public Administration Times* reported at the end of 1981 that "a realignment in the balance of power between public sector unions and the governmental entities whose employees they represent is underway. . . ."[22]

Government's new get-tough policy toward its trade unionists had naturally given heart to those who have long warned of the damage such organizations have caused and the dangers they pose. It has given rise to a new term, the *give-back*, and to new slogans, such as "No is also an answer" and "A governmental job is not for life." But slogans are not solutions. As we have seen, public employee unions can play a positive and productive role in administering the public sector. Moreover, crude attempts to crush them can provoke a counterproductive hostility. Those who administer the apparatus of government must continue the search for other, and better, solutions.

Searching for Solutions

During the early years of public unionism, the solution most often advanced to avert clashes and to promote equity was binding arbitration.

However, as we saw earlier, this solution seemed to incur more favor from labor than from management. By the late 1970s, the antipathy of public managers to this device had grown and hardened.

Arguments against arbitration centered on the alleged failure of arbitrators to take into account the overall impact of their decisions. Such decisions, said its opponents, often had a "ripple effect," prompting other public employee groups to seek for themselves whatever favorable conditions resulted for the group whose case had been arbitrated. Arbitrators were also accused of being too narrow in their approach and, in general, of being too prolabor.

As a case in point, opponents could cite what happened in Oakland, California, after the city had instituted binding arbitration in 1973. Oakland subsequently sought to eliminate thirty-six jobs in its fire department. The fire fighters' union took the issue to arbitration. The arbitrators not only ordered the city to reinstate the dismissed fire fighters but to cut their work week by four hours and to hire sixteen additional employees to keep the department at full strength.

Although the Oakland incident was probably an extreme case, it was close enough to the general pattern of such settlements to increase the developing disenchantment of public managers for the whole process. As the mayor of St. Paul, Minnesota, put it, "The ability of the municipality to pay seems to be the last item to be considered in binding arbitration."[23]

However, by this time a new form of arbitration had arisen that offered the hope of eliminating or at least modifying some of the method's more objectionable features. Called *last best offer*, or LBO, it provided that each side, once collective bargaining had reached an impasse, submit its last best offer to an arbitrator. The arbitrator then should simply pick the offer that seems the best. It was felt that the desire to have their last best offer selected would move both sides to a more responsible position. At the same time, it would prohibit the arbitrator from devising his or her own settlement and imposing it on the disputing parties.

By 1977, Connecticut had instituted LBO for all municipal employees except teachers. Wisconsin was also using it for certain employee groups, while Michigan was making use of it on a case-by-case basis. Some other jurisdictions had also experimented with LBO.

How has it worked? The final results are not yet in, and no definitive judgment can yet be made. In Wisconsin it appears to have generally led to less generous awards. However, it is done without prior fact-finding, and, it has been pointed out, lower awards to unions usually occur when fact-finding has been omitted. In Arlington, Massachusetts, where it was used to resolve a pay dispute with the community's fire fighters, the results, as far as the town manager was concerned, were almost disastrous. The arbitrator had picked the union's last best offer, and this broke the parity then existing between the town's fire and police departments. This, in turn, caused the police as well as other town employees to seek new pay increases.[24]

In the view of critics, LBO tends to favor the unions as much if not more, than normal binding arbitration. Under LBO, the unions know by the time an impasse is reached what management is prepared to give. So they supposedly have nothing to lose by scaling their demands somewhat higher and taking a chance that the arbitrator will pick their offer instead. LBO also has been accused of delegating power to a third party and thereby thwarting democratic rule by representative government officials. (The same criticism, to the extent that it may be valid, could of course apply to normal binding arbitration as well.) Finally, LBO, like other forms of arbitration, detracts from the desire of the parties to resolve their disputes through the collective bargaining process itself. To borrow a sexual analogy, collective bargaining under LBO becomes a form of foreplay without consummation.

Another solution that has been suggested to improve labor-management negotiations, or at least their outcomes, is open bargaining. In other words, allow the press and the public to sit in on the negotiating sessions. Such a system, so it is said, would make both sides behave and bargain more responsibly. Unions, for example, might hesitate to make political threats, such as promising to work for the defeat of elected officials, if their basic demands are not met. The whole process would also better inform the public, who must, after all, foot the bill.

The unions have registered the strongest protests against such "goldfish bowl bargaining." AFSCME head Jerry Wurf claimed that it would make image-conscious public officials behave less, rather than more, responsibly. Bringing in newspeople and TV cameras, he said, is like "waving a naked girl at a guy who's been locked away for years—they (the politicians) just go crazy." Others claim that subjecting union negotiations to "sunshine" laws might, in effect, lead to two different types of bargaining sessions. One would be the formal, open one; the other would be the closed, informal one, where the real issues would be thrashed out.

So far the open bargaining approach has not made much headway. However, a new labor-relations law in Florida does provide for such "sunshine" bargaining. Milwaukee, while hesitating to go the whole way in this regard, has instituted some expanded and formalized arrangements to encourage and elicit more public awareness of, and participation in, the city's labor relations. When a union's proposals are submitted, the city holds public hearings where anyone who wishes may comment on them. Negotiations then go on in private, but once an agreement is reached, another public meeting is held to disclose it. The agreement then becomes binding unless three-fourths of the city council reject it.

A still-more-sweeping suggestion for invoking public involvement in the collective-bargaining process is to subject all agreements reached to a referendum. As has been seen, this was the course taken by San Francisco in 1976. Since then, some have suggested its widespread adoption. Predictably, the union leaders have balked at such an idea. They claim that such agreements are often quite complex and that it would be almost impossible to adequately inform the public so that they could intelligently vote on them. Others point out that the citizens are likely to be too parsimonious and too punitive and that such attitudes could work against the public as well as the union's interest, at least in the long run.

Still others, however, see some merit in the idea. One of these supporters is Sam Zagoria, former director of the Labor-Management Relations Service of the U.S. Conference of Mayors. Says Zagoria, "A public sector union is not entitled to more than the conscience of a community is willing to dictate. . . ." As for the charge that the public is likely to prove too close-fisted, Zagoria replies: "If the community doesn't want to pay for good teachers, for example, then it will have to live with the consequences."[25]

One instance where a union took the initiative in bringing such a referendum about occurred in Denver in August of 1981. The city's fire fighters' union decided to take its disagreements with the city over a new contract to the voters. And the fire fighters won. However, the victory came by way of a special election in which only 20 percent of Denver's voters turned out. Furthermore the city spent no money of its own to campaign for its position, while the fire fighters spent heavily. At that, the union won by only 118 votes out of some forty-five thousand cast. Such factors limit the victory's value in predicting the outcome of other such occurrences.[26]

One solution gaining increasing favor from government officials is the hitherto "nonsolution"; that is, a strike. Experience indicates that the effects of such strikes may not be as harrowing and as horrible as once thought. San Francisco, as we have seen, held up fairly well during a strike that lasted more than a month. Even police strikes may not be as disastrous as feared. As a last resort, the struck community can always call on the governor to send in the National Guard to relieve its distress.

As we have seen, more and more municipalities and states have shown a willingness to accept a strike rather than accept an expensive labor settlement. The Michigan Municipal League has recommended a limited right to strike as an alternative to compulsory arbitration. Seattle's Mayor Uhlman and his city successfully weathered a ninety-eight-day strike by the city's Light Department employees, the longest such walkout in the history of the state of Washington. Uhlman, anticipating the strike, had trained the department's supervisory workers for a year ahead of time so they could keep the lights on if the lighting crews walked out.

The secret to successfully sustaining a strike is, perhaps, the secret to handling all or most all of the labor troubles that occur in the public sec-

CASE STUDY

Turbulance at the Tower[28]

The Professional Air Traffic Controllers Organization came into existence after President Kennedy signed his famous executive order authorizing collective bargaining in the federal service. With only fifteen thousand members, PATCO, as it was called, comprised less than 1 percent of the federal civilian work force. But during the two decades of its existence, it would cause more trouble and create more turmoil than all the other thirty-five hundred federal employee organizations combined.

PATCO's seemingly chronic complaints centered not just on compensation but on working conditions. The controllers persistently protested that Federal Aviation Administration policies and management practices only exacerbated the stress that their sensitive jobs naturally subjected them to. And when their complaints failed to secure an adequate response, they frequently responded with a job action of some kind. In 1968, PATCO initiated a nationwide slowdown of air traffic with the irate controllers insisting they would work only "by the book." This was followed the next year by two days of "sick-outs" and a year later by a three-week "sick-out" involving 15 percent of PATCO's membership.

A more serious job action took place in March 1971 as the Easter weekend got underway. Some one thousand controllers failed to report for work, disrupting air traffic throughout the nation. This sick-out was sparked by the FAA's suspension of three Baton Rouge controllers who refused to accept reassignment to other cities. But other factors were also at work. The union leaders wanted restored certain rights that the union had lost as a result of earlier job actions. The membership wanted better equipment and less overtime work. This last point soon received some support from the National Transportation Safety Board, which, by pure coincidence, issued a report at the time of the sick-out saying that FAA management policies were endangering public safety. The board especially criticized the practice of rotating controllers from one shift to another.

The FAA took the union to court, and armed with the antistrike provisions of the U.S. code, it quickly procured an injunction against PATCO. Furthermore, since federal judges were appointed, and since PATCO's membership in any case was small and spread out, the federal judiciary was prepared to back up its rulings. Meanwhile FAA administrator John Shaffer conceded that his agency had used the injunctions as a "security blanket" to make up for the fact that it "had not worked hard enough on labor-management relations in the past." Once the controllers were back at work, the FAA initiated efforts to improve training for supervisors and to improve the flow of communication from the rank and file to the agency's higher echelons.

But the fall of the same year found PATCO's members again in a pee-vish mood. This time the airlines responded by agreeing to give control-lers eight free rides a year for "orientation." This appeased the control-lers for a while, but in the spring of 1975 PATCO filed suits against FAA claiming a shortage of manpower that was endangering the public safety. The union lost this suit and the following year it failed to get the U.S. Civil Service Commission to give controllers at Chicago's O'Hare Airport a pay boost.

In December 1977 PATCO was once again negotiating with the FAA and once again was threatening a slowdown if a new agreement was not reached. A contract was signed, but the following spring the union once more threatened a slowdown unless airlines added free overseas "orien-tation" flights to the domestic ones they had already given. This time the airline said no, and when the union responded as it promised, the FAA took it to court, where a federal judge fined the organization one hundred thousand dollars.

Two years later the controllers were once again unhappy. They an-nounced a "withdrawal of enthusiasm" in August 1980 which delayed flights until the FAA secured a restraining order against the union. But by now the controllers had decided, alone among federal unions, to back the candidacy of Ronald Reagan, and as soon as the elections were over they began readying a new list of demands.

Federal air controllers were then earning a base salary of about thirty thousand dollars which with overtime brought their average earnings up to about thirty-four thousand dollars. They could also retire at age fifty with a minimum of twenty years service. Their first demand was for a pay schedule that would give them seventy-three thousand dollars a year plus a thirty-two-hour week. They soon scaled back their wage demand to sixty thousand dollars, which still equaled the earnings of a cabinet secretary.

The Reagan administration counteroffered with a pay hike of 11.4 per-cent, a far more generous offer than the new Republican administration was prepared to offer any other federal union. PATCO's leaders approved the offer, but the members in a mail ballot rejected it. Not wishing to abandon their positions and their leadership role, the union's officers quickly sided with the members. And on August 3, 1980, the federal gov-ernment was hit with its first major strike, as more than two-thirds of the nation's 17,500 air controllers walked off and remained off their jobs.

The administration reacted by threatening to dismiss the strikers and gave them forty-eight hours to return to work. Only one thousand re-sponded, leaving another eleven thousand still on strike. The administra-tion then made good on its threat. FAA supervisors began sending out form letters saying "Dear _____this is notice that I intend to remove you from your position . . ." Reached at his California mountain retreat, Pres-ident Reagan issued a statement refusing even to call the controllers' ac-tion a strike. "There is a law that federal unions cannot strike against their employers, the people of the United States," said the president. "What they did was terminate their own employment by quitting."

The strike proved far less disruptive and damaging than the controllers had hoped and the public had feared. Over a year earlier the FAA, under a different administration, had drawn up a plan in the event of such an emergency, and the agency now put the plan into effect. The towers were manned by three thousand supervisors, five thousand nonstrikers and nearly one thousand military controllers assigned to help out. The number of flights were cut back by 20 to 25 percent. Most remaining flights were delayed but relatively few were canceled. A survey by *Time* magazine three weeks after the strike began found "evidence that the FAA's plan . . . was making flying in some ways even safer" than it was before. "The working controllers were going about their jobs with an *esprit de corps* that had been sadly lacking when the more militant unionists . . . were among them." And it quoted one Los Angeles controller as claiming that previously PATCO members had "filed grievances on every little thing and management retaliated," but that now "we can move three times the traffic because we're all working together."

Airline pilots apparently agreed with this assessment, for none of them balked at taking off and landing aircraft at airports staffed with only half the controllers they once had. And while the heads of the AFL-CIO and the United Auto Workers Union marched before the TV cameras in PATCO's picket lines, no union gave the embattled controllers financial or any other form of tangible support.

Confronted with the prospects of a disastrous defeat, PATCO began indicating a willingness to call off the strike. But the president indicated that he was standing firm. Part of his obduracy may have been based on the fear of what would happen when striking controllers would return to work alongside those who had remained at their jobs. But there was little doubt that President Reagan was savoring the prestige and influence that his victory was giving him.

In October, three months after the strike began, the Federal Labor Relations authority decertified PATCO for "willfully and intentionally" violating federal law. The following summer PATCO lost its appeal of the decision in court. The next month the union declared bankruptcy. A longtime thorn in the side of the federal bureaucracy had been removed.

The strike did bring certain things to light. It showed that a union could get too inflated with its own importance and too disdainful of the public interest. It also pointed up the tendency of all public organizations to overstaff. Airport authorities have found that their towers can give equal if not better service with far fewer controllers. Only thirteen thousand controller positions are authorized for the foreseeable future.

But the strike also underscored the role of mismanagement in fomenting such disputes. Shortly after it began, a study done three years earlier by two psychiatrists was revealed. This study found that controllers did work under conditions of severe stress, but that much of it came from tensions in their relationships with supervisors. The psychiatrists gave authoritarian managerial practices much of the blame for the fact that controllers tended to behave impulsively and also tended to develop high blood pressure much more frequently than other federal workers. Another study commissioned by the Department of Transportation after the strike had ended backed up these findings. It also cited "high-handed" and authoritarian supervisory practices as contributing greatly to the controllers' problems. So the air controllers strike of 1981, selfish and self-seeking as it may seem, nevertheless further supports the contention that faulty management greatly contributes to, when it does not actually cause, such extreme expressions of employee discontent.

tor—good management. Nearly all sides consider this the *sine qua non* of good labor relations. And mediocre management has probably caused more labor trouble than militant union leadership. Says E. B. Pealer, Assistant Director of Personnel for the city of Hartford, "More management people organize unions than union people do."[27]

Many management people agree with this argument. Union excesses, say some, spring often, and perhaps even most often, from managerial misdeeds and mistakes. The real key to achieving peace on the public labor front may lie in developing better administrative policies and better administrators.

Notes

1. For an interesting insight into the power of teacher groups, see John C. Wahlke et al., *The Legislative System* (New York: John Wiley, 1962).

2. *Creative Budgeting in New York City: An Interview with Former Budget Director Frederick O'R. Hayes* (Washington, D.C.: Urban Institute, 1971), 27.

3. Ibid., 26–27.

4. Editorial, "Schools Without Leaders," *New York Times,* 27 February 1973.

5. Kenneth Y. Tomlinson, "Can Public Employee Unions Be Controlled?" *Reader's Digest,* (April 1977).

6. *New York Times,* 22 March 1972, sec. 6. *New York Times,* 1 February 1973. George Bennet, "Tools to Resolve Labor Disputes in the Public Sector," *Personnel* 50, no. 2, (March–April 1973).

7. *Newsweek,* 30 March 1970.

8. Thomas C. Schelling, "Economic Analysis of Organized Crime," Appendix D, *Task Force Report: Organized Crime,* U.S. President's Commission on Law

Enforcement and Administration of Justice (Washington, D.C.: Government Printing Office, 1967), 122.

9. *Public Administration Times,* 15 December 1981.

10. Ingrassia's remarks were made during a panel session at the annual convention of the American Society for Public Administration in Los Angeles, 1973.

11. Norman A. Carlson, "Designing and Selling a Staff-Training Program: A Case Study," *Public Administration Review* (November–December 1971).

12. Picot B. Floyd, "Some Aspects of Staffing for the Urban Crisis," *Public Administration Review* (January–February 1971).

13. Albert Shanker, "The Philadelphia Story, 1973," *New York Times,* 25 February 1973 (paid advertisement).

14. Bennet, "Tools to Resolve Labor Disputes."

15. *Boston Herald-American,* 28 March 1973.

16. These and similar statements will be found in "Collective Bargaining in the Public Sector: A Symposium," *Public Administration Review* (March–April 1968) 131.

17. *New York Times,* 1 November 1971.

18. *New York Times,* 6 March 1975.

19. *New York Times,* 8 July 1975.

20. *MTA Today,* 8 December 1976.

21. *Public Administration Times,* 1 August 1982.

22. *Public Administration Times,* 15 December 1981.

23. "Bucking the Unions and Looking for Cash," *Time,* 21 July 1975.

24. *Boston Sunday Globe,* 26 January 1975.

25. Quoted in Neal R. Peirce, "Employment Report/Public Employee Unions Show Rise in Membership, Militancy," *National Journal,* 30 August 1975.

26. *Public Administration Times,* 1 November 1981.

27. Statement made at the Northeast Regional Conference of the American Society for Public Administration at Hartford, Connecticut, October 1975.

28. The following case study is based largely on news reports published at the relevant times. Of special interest are a story in *Time,* 24 August 1981, an editorial in the *New York Times,* 9 August 1981, and an Associated Press dispatch of March 17, 1982.

6

Leadership

During the late 1930s, J. Robert Oppenheimer seemed to have found happiness teaching theoretical physics at the University of California at Berkeley. A shy and nervous man, he was pleased with the fact that he seldom had to venture into the laboratory, let alone the workaday world outside the campus. Instead, he could spend much of his time working out equations on his blackboard and indulging in his favorite hobby, which was reading mystical Hindu poetry in the original Sanskrit. True, he contributed money to political causes that seemed to meet his ideals, and he did enjoy a reasonable amount of social life. But he was largely occupied with theoretical physics and esoteric poetry when World War II broke out.

The war wrought great changes in Oppenheimer's peaceful and sheltered existence. In a few years, he found himself assembling and directing a task force of over one thousand scientists and technicians in developing the atomic bomb. This involved, among other things, running an entire community, because the scientists, along with their wives and children, were forced to live in sealed-off seclusion in an isolated area in New Mexico. As everyone now knows, the Los Alamos community stayed together, the scientists accomplished their work, and the bomb was built. Afterward, many of the physicists involved agreed that no one but Oppenheimer could have done it.[1]

The rapid transformation of the shy and nervous professor into the forceful and effective administrator is but an extreme example of one of the most fascinating phenomena in administration—the mystery of leadership. For leadership and the qualities it demands have puzzled and perplexed many an administrative theorist over the course of time. Peter Drucker, a noted business writer and management consultant, reports that "among the effective executives I have known and worked with, there are extroverts and aloof, retiring men, some even morbidly shy. Some are eccentrics, others are painfully correct conformists. Some are fat and some are thin. Some are worriers and some are relaxed. Some drink quite heavily and others are total abstainers. Some are men of great charm and warmth, some have no more personality than a frozen mackerel."[2]

Thus, anyone who hopes to spell out the qualities of a leader is embarked on a perilous and problematic mission. One helpful and by now rather obvious observation, however, can be made at the outset. Leadership is to a great extent determined by the needs of the situation. "It is more fruitful to consider leadership as a relationship between the leader and the situation than as a universal pattern of characteristics possessed by certain people,"[3] Douglas McGregor once noted. In a similar vein, William J. Reddin, after surveying the research on management style, concluded that "no single style is naturally more effective than others. Effectiveness depends on a style's appropriateness to the situation in which it is used."[4] There is, in short, no ideal leadership style and most probably no ideal leader who can ably handle all situations.

Adolf Hitler provides an interesting illustration of this. His great if gruesome career as leader of Germany is certainly well known. Less well known is his army career during World War I, although he served over four years in combat and twice won medals for bravery, Hitler ended his military service holding the rank of corporal. Since promotion comes quickly in wartime to those who survive, anyone assessing Hitler's record in 1918 would have rated him a poor prospect to become even a shop foreman in civilian life, let alone the most powerful single individual in the world of his time.

Hitler's peculiar leadership abilities needed a particular situation in which to flourish. They required not only the conditions that existed in Germany during the postwar period but that Hitler have the leading role in any movement or government with which he should become connected. In a subordinate post, no matter how high it might have been, *der Führer* would most likely have been a washout. Some leaders simply cannot lead unless they occupy the pinnacle position. As Paul Appleby once noted, "there are men who would be poor as ordinary section heads in a bureau but who would be able and effective as Secretary of the Department."[5]

If some leaders can only lead when no one is above them, others can only lead successfully when the reverse is true. There are people who would do well in the second highest position of a very large organization but who would flounder if placed in overall command of even a quite small one. In other words, they are natural seconds-in-command. Arthur Schlesinger puts Dean Rusk, who served as secretary of state during the Kennedy and Johnson administrations, into this category. Writes Schlesinger of Rusk:

> He was a superb technician: this was his power and his problem. He had trained himself all his life to be the ideal chief of staff, the perfect number-two man. The inscrutability which made him a good aide and a gifted negotiator made him also a baffling leader. When assistant secretaries brought him problems, he listened courteously, thanked them and let them go; they would depart little wiser than they came. Since his subordinates did not know what he thought, they could not do what he wanted. In consequence, he failed to imbue the Department with positive direction and purpose. He had authority but not command.[6]

Situational differences requiring different leadership styles do not just concern matters of hierarchical level. Different types of organizations may also demand different types of leaders. Many a successful business executive has failed miserably after attempting to transfer his or her administrative prowess to the public sector. Few public-sector executives have had the opportunity to test their leadership skill in commanding a business firm, but probably they would produce a comparable failure rate. Furthermore, any particular organization may need different leaders at different stages of its existence. Revolutions, for example, often bring to the fore vastly different kinds of leaders, depending on the stage they are in. Thus, a fiery Trotsky may give way to a crafty Stalin, and a charismatic and flamboyant Marat may be replaced by a stolid and ruthless Robespierre.

The relationship of leadership ability to the particular situation requiring it makes the task of defining and detailing a list of general leadership qualities difficult and possibly even deceptive. Yet, certain qualities do seem to characterize at least many if not all leaders in many though not all situations. And although the list does not constitute a formula—one could possess all the qualities on the list and still be unable to lead—it does provide something of a basis for the student to gain a perspective on one of the most intriguing and enigmatic aspects of the administrative craft.

Qualities of Leadership

Probably no quality is more pertinent and pervasive among successful leaders than the quality of optimism. To lead successfully, one must believe that his or her leadership will make a difference. No matter how dark and dismal the journey, he must be able to see a light at the end of the tunnel.

Harlan Cleveland, who served successfully in many leadership roles, lays particular stress on his quality of leadership. "Prophecies of doom," he reminds us, "do not in fact move people in action."[7] Indeed, they are more likely to have the reverse effect. In order to be happy, a man must believe in the possibility of happiness, the great Russian writer Tolstoy once pointed out. The same holds true for leadership. In order to exercise leadership, one must believe in its possibilities.

That energy and enterprise must accompany such optimism should be fairly obvious. This does not mean that every luminary in the ranks of leadership must put him or herself forth as a whirlwind of activity. Yet, even if the leadership position has been thrust upon a person, one cannot hope to meet its obligations without some deliberate and diligent application of one's talents. Leaders often do not seem to be working hard at their jobs, but such appearances can be deceptive. A leader may be relaxed and easygoing but laziness and indolence will usually lead to failure.

What about intelligence? Certainly, it is rare to find a leader who is both dumb and successful, and some have been extraordinarily brilliant. Take Napoleon and William Pitt, those young titans who confronted each other across the English Channel at the beginning of the nineteenth century. Each was at home in a variety of disciplines, including mathematics, languages, and the law. In this country, meanwhile, a president had come to power who was accomplished in architecture, science, agriculture, law, political theory, and nearly every field of study of his time. Nevertheless, when it comes to correlating mental ability with leadership, some qualities seem much more crucial than others.

One vital intellectual skill is verbal ability. Skill in the use of communication generally accompanies leadership ability, no matter what the particular situation may be. A ditch digger who becomes the foreman of his work gang will most probably be able to communicate better than all or at least most of the other members of the gang.

An interesting study on this point was done many decades ago. Researchers tested people from various occupations as to their vocabularies. It was a multiple-choice test, which presented the testee with numerous words, ranging from the commonplace to the obscure. Each word was followed by four others, one of which was a synonym. The object was to pick the synonym. The group that placed highest on the test were business executives, who outscored all the professional groups, including college professors. The test was given at a time when relatively few business people had a college education. Yet, as a group, they demonstrated the greatest facility at word recognition.

An ability to communicate, at least when he wanted to, apparently played a key role in Dean Rusk's rise to administrative prominence. Although sharing Arthur Schlesinger's view that Rusk was more suited for a number-two than a number-one position, journalist David Halberstam points up this valuable Rusk quality in his book *The Best and the Brightest.* "A brilliant expositor, he had a genius for putting down brief, cogent and forceful prose on paper—a rare and much needed quality in government," reports Halberstam.[8] It was this ability, reflected in the cables that he sent back while serving with the army in India during World War II, that led to Rusk being "discovered" by his superiors and being slotted for the wider opportunities that came his way when the war ended.

A much more complex question when it comes to relating leadership with intellectual skills concerns the qualities of creativity and judgment. The problem is that these two qualities are not always compatible. Good idea people, as Katz and Kahn point out, tend to be enthusiastic and somewhat impulsive and may fail to subject their ideas to searching criticism. They frequently have a hard time translating ideas into action, and when they do succeed in doing so, they may fail to follow through because they soon sprout another idea that they want to work on.

Katz and Kahn maintain that leadership puts more of a priority on reasoned judgment than creativity, and if a leader can have only one of these qualities, he or she is better off with the former. One can always make up for lack of creativity by surrounding oneself with people who possess such a trait.[9] This to a great extent was true of Oppenheimer. Although a brilliant physicist, he was not considered a particularly creative one. His talents lay in being able to analyze the work of others and, in so doing, to spur them on to greater efforts.

The question of judgment leads us to another quality, which is still more difficult to define. Perhaps an illustration will serve as the best introduction to its discussion.

The story is told of the president of a major steel company who was inspecting one of his plants. He suddenly noticed two men puffing on cigarettes in an area where smoking was forbidden. He went over to the two men, handed each of them an expensive cigar, and said good-naturedly, "Smoke these outside, boys."

This simple incident conveys some of the flavor of successful leadership. Good leaders rarely lose their heads or give in to their emotions. Instead, they deal with situations and the people involved in a disinterested manner best designed to achieve the results they have in mind. This observation is confirmed by research. Burleigh Gardner cites one study of several hundred executives, which showed that they maintained a detached, objective view of their subordinates. Other studies, says Gardner, tend to corroborate this finding.[10]

This does not mean that a good leader should be a cool and clammy individual lacking all the human qualities of warmth and empathy. It rather indicates that he or she is able to keep his personal feelings in check and to appraise objectively the needs of the situation.

Of course, the chronicles of history overflow with accounts of petulant and peevish people who have scored successes as leaders. And certainly some situations seem to require such qualities as detachment and objectivity much less than do others. But many who appear to have disregarded these principles have not really done so. Adolf Hitler offers one example. While undoubtedly a neurotic if not a psychopath, he could nevertheless, at least at the earlier stages of his career, assess situations with a cool and shrewd eye and act accordingly. Hitler's chief architect and subsequent minister for war production, Albert Speer, tells in his memoirs of the first time he saw Hitler. The Nazi leader had come to address the students at Berlin University prior to his assumption of power.

> His appearance ... surprised me. On posters and in caricatures I had seen him in military tunic, with shoulder straps, swastika armband and hair flapping over his forehead. But here he was wearing a well-fitted blue suit and looking remarkably respectable. Everything about him bore out the note of reasonable modesty. Later I learned that he had a great gift for adjusting—consciously or intuitively—to his surroundings.[11]

His speech itself, notes Speer, also showed that Hitler knew his audience. Instead of an intellectually vapid harangue, the Nazi leader delivered to the students a rather carefully worded lecture on history that was mixed with a good deal of humor.

The Swiss psychologist Jean Piaget, well known for his pioneering work with children, offers an observation that may aid in summing up this rather illusive leadership quality. Piaget points out that when a child stands in front of another person, he will tend to identify the other person's left arm as his right and vice versa. This is because the arm of the person he is facing is on the same side as his own. The child is unable to put himself in the other person's shoes.

As people grow older, they usually manage to make this change, at least to the point of distinguishing between the right and left sides of a person they are facing. But everyone still retains some degree of difficulty in seeing situations from the other person's position, particularly when more than physical position is concerned. The good leader will be able to do this better than most. By being able to coolly assess situations from the various points of view of those concerned and to act accordingly, he or she exercises the influence that leadership betokens.

Qualities in Question

The preceding list of leadership qualities is admittedly a short one and may seem more notable for what it omits than for what it includes. Left out are at least three characteristics that are usually associated with leadership—technical proficiency, decisiveness, and charisma. Let us examine them in turn.

Government in the United States has traditionally placed a great emphasis on technical competency in selecting leaders for its various administrative agencies. Americans generally insist that school superintendents be educators, public health commissioners be doctors, and public works commissioners be engineers or at least persons with some engineering background. Appointing technically trained people to administrative positions is often equated with progressive government and is considered a repudiation of administration by political hacks. A city-manager-run city will more likely appoint a professional law enforcement specialist as its police commissioner than will a city dominated by political bosses, although the latter also seem to be bending to this trend. As for the federal service, a 1966 report by the Committee on Economic Development stated that nearly half of the top executives in the federal government were trained in mathematics, science, engineering, or medicine.[12]

Many European countries, however, view the matter quite differently. They stress administrative skills and background rather than demonstrated technical expertise. When France consolidated its two major police forces in 1968, the government appointed as its new police head a man who had previously been the chief of staff in the Ministry of Education. He was neither an educator nor a police officer but simply a professional administrator.

Which is the right approach? There are no hard-and-fast answers to this question. Certainly technical expertise has much to commend it. A person who understands the actual work of his subordinates will possess very definite assets when it comes to directing them. Katz and Kahn cite studies done on railroads, power plants, and heavy industry that showed that those foremen who were the most technically competent were generally the foremen whose work teams were the most productive.[13] At a minimum, a supervisor who is technically expert can gain the respect of his or her subordinates in a way that a nontechnician would be unable to do.

Yet, administrative theorists even in this country have long looked askance at the "specialist syndrome." The leader of an organization or an organizational unit must be able to relate the unit to its external environment. This, so the claim goes, is best done by a professional administrator. He or she is much more likely to possess the expanded frame of reference that the leader needs to manage his organization in a productive manner. Failure to assess the external environment can be and often has been disastrous to many organizations.

Furthermore, the technically trained and experienced leader has usually built up a network of prior associations and preferences. The leader's very background makes him or her more prone to favor some activities than others and to listen to some people more than others. He or she may lack the overall and objective perspective that the generalist administrator can provide.

These considerations acquire heightened importance the more one moves up the organizational ladder. As many writers have pointed out, the higher the administrative level, the more time the administrator spends on "external" in contrast to "internal" matters. Furthermore, as Katz and Kahn note, the larger and more complex an organization becomes, "the greater will be the commonality of their management substructures."[14] This indicates that since organizations are becoming larger and more complex all the time, their administrative positions are becoming more and more alike and thus demanding less and less specialist skills.

Other factors also lend support to the oft-heard administrative adage that "the technician should be on tap and not on top." As David E. Lilienthal has said, the technician's work usually has a terminal point. There is the bridge to be built, the vaccine to be discovered, the patient to be cured and discharged. The administrator has to think in different terms. His or her task is never done, because in administration there is never any real completion.[15]

One saw some of these problems at work in the Vietnam war. According to former Undersecretary of the Air Force Townsend Hoopes, the military leaders could only think in terms of winning the war. They avoided the question of whether some means of achieving victory might produce more problems than they solved or whether it would even be in the United States' interest to win the war in the first place. Theirs was a "can do" policy, which, while productive and useful in some situations, can prove disastrous in others.[16] Indeed, as specialists, the military in Vietnam even went further and failed to question the efficacy of the means they were using to achieve their own limited goals. Thus, instead of questioning the usefulness of airpower to begin with, they devoted their efforts to trying to make it more efficient.

One thing is certain, and that is that the abilities that make a person a proficient specialist in his or her field do not automatically equip him or her for administrative leadership in that field. The first-rate teacher all too often turns into the third-rate principal. In writing about scientists and administration, C. P. Snow observed that "to be any good, in his youth at least, a scientist has to think of one thing, deeply and obsessively, for a long time. An administrator has to think of a great many things widely, in their interconnections, for a short time."[17] Of course there are exceptions, such as Oppenheimer, or, for that matter, Snow himself. But more often than not, the qualities that make for excellence in a specialty do not co-incide and frequently conflict with the qualities that make for excellence in administering organizations devoted to that specialty.

In summary, then, we may say that technical competence in the field is an advantage to an administrator, presuming that everything else is equal. The problem is that everything else is usually not equal. Thus, while such competence may have its uses, particularly at the first level of su-pervision, it tends to pose increasing disadvantages as one moves to the higher reaches of organizational life. Thus, it is omitted here as a neces-sary quality for administrative success.

Another quality that is often imputed to successful administrators is the ability to make quick decisions. To be sure, decision making is what administration is basically all about. George C. Marshall maintained that the capacity to make decisions was the rarest gift that the gods could give a person.

However, when one scrutinizes the record of many notable government executives, one frequently finds not a chronicle of speedy decision mak-ing but almost its opposite. Historians have constantly commented on Franklin Roosevelt's persistent penchant for procrastination. Some claim it was his most characteristic trait. Winston Churchill was also not keen on making decisions that did not demand immediate action. Unless it was imperative to make a major decision at once, Churchill would approach it by calling a meeting, asking for various views. Then he would ask for memoranda on the subject and then hold another meeting. It is also inter-esting to note that while John F. Kennedy sought to present himself as a firm and decisive leader, his favorite book was a biography of a British prime minister named Melbourne. And Lord Melbourne was a leader who ardently espoused and acted on the belief that "when in doubt what should be done, do nothing."[18]

Business leaders sometimes show the same trait. Alfred P. Sloan, Jr., the man who is credited with building General Motors into the giant it is today, never made a decision involving personnel the first time it came up. He might make a tentative judgment and even doing that might take him several hours. Then, he would put the matter aside and tackle it again in a few days time. Only when the same name came up two or three times in a row would he proceed. It was this practice, says Peter Drucker, that helped give Sloan his wide reputation for picking winners.[19]

The Sloan example provides an insight into the reasons why successful leaders often seem loath to exercise the foremost prerogative of their po-sition—decision making. They realize the complexities and implications that may arise from any significant decision they may make. This is particularly true in government where there are so many different interests to contend with. A decision by a governmental administrator may cause reverberations throughout the staff, other governmental agencies, the legislative branches, clientele groups, the press, and the public. And all of them must be taken into account. Furthermore, a good decision maker must be like a good billiard player: everytime he goes to hit the ball, he must figure out just what will happen when that ball hits another ball, which in turn will hit another. Any decision of consequence is likely to set off a chain of events whose ultimate impact may prove difficult to discern.

For reasons such as these, speedy decision making does not always make for good decision making, and good decision makers have usually taken cognizance of this fact. While there is little disputing the fact that any administrator has to be able to make decisions before time runs out, many of the best executives have persistently preferred to stretch the time limit to the near maximum. As society and the apparatus that governs it become increasingly complicated, we may find that quick decision making, although it occasionally will be necessary, will become less and less characteristic of successful administration.

The final item on what might be called the "left-out list" of leadership qualities is charisma. The capacity to be colorful and heroic, to stir the emotions of people and capture their hearts and minds, has long been regarded as a powerful leadership tool. Many of those we regard as outstanding leaders have possessed this trait. They include not just political leaders such as Roosevelt and Churchill but also some more purely administrative leaders such as Robert Moses, New York City's famous builder of bridges, highways, and parks; and Harry Hopkins, FDR's dynamic aide.

But charismatic leadership can be not only disadvantageous but even dangerous. Charisma, say Katz and Kahn, "is a means by which people abdicate responsibility for any consistent, tough-minded evaluation of the outcome of specific policies. They put their trust in their leader who will somehow manage to take care of things." In so doing, charisma reduces democracy and equality in an organization, because "charisma requires some psychological distance between leader and follower."[20]

The dangers of such a state of affairs are readily apparent. A charismatic leader will usually fail to develop fully the capacities of his or her subordinates. Instead, they will become overly dependent upon him or her. When the leader is absent, the organization will tend to flounder, and when he or she departs for good, it may fall to pieces.

Charismatic leaders usually inhibit communications. Subordinates become too deferential to supply the leader with unpleasant information or advise against policies that may be unwise. Often, they lose the ability to discriminate between wise and unwise policies, for they have surrendered much of their capacity for independent judgment. This can be crucial, since a charismatic leader may not only be forceful but also foolish.

ELIZABETH THE EQUIVOCATER

When Elizabeth I took over the reins of the English government in 1586, she found herself, according to one of her biographers, Lytton Strachey, "a sane woman in a universe of violent maniacs." Europe was being torn apart by rival nationalisms and rival religions, and every faction was bidding for England's support.

Elizabeth responded with indecision and inertia. She dodged and ducked, vacillated and equivocated, while furious jousts for power swirled around her. "Such was her nature," said Strachey, "to float, when it was calm, in a sea of indecisions, and, when the wind rose, to tack hectically from side to side."[21]

Strachey maintains, however, that in doing so she had by far chosen the best course. In fact, her ostensible indecision may have saved both her and her country for "had it been otherwise, had she possessed, according to the approved pattern of the strong man of action, the capacity for taking a line and sticking to it—she would have been lost. She would have become inextricably entangled in the forces that surrounded her and, almost inevitably, swiftly destroyed."

History provides us with numerous examples of charismatic leaders who vigorously led their nations down the road to ruin. Hitler and Mussolini are two examples that come frequently to mind. But we do not have to reach so high to find instances of how charismatic leadership can malfunction. Robert Moses may have built more bridges, tunnels, and highways than any man in recent history, but many New Yorkers today are questioning the wisdom of all his activity. His final masterpiece, the New York City World's Fair of 1965, turned out to be a startling disaster.

The case of Ernest Lawrence offers another illustration of how charisma can lead to catastrophe. A University of California physicist like Oppenheimer, Lawrence possessed charismatic qualities. As a result he became head of an important laboratory at the university and persuaded many younger scientists to work with him in building two highly expensive devices, which turned out to be unworkable. Physicists elsewhere had branded both projects as silly and impractical from the start, but the charismatic Lawrence had wangled sufficient funds, and his star-struck sub-ordinates gave him enthusiastic support.

It is perhaps fortunate, then, that charisma seems to be dying out as a leadership quality. As columnist James Reston of the *New York Times* has remarked, we are becoming a nation of the bland leading the bland. Some have bemoaned this fact, since the charismatic leader often lends color and excitement to administrative activity. However, he or she also imbues it with other and less desirable elements as well. Furthermore, there are much more genuine ways of making administration exciting, and some of these may become apparent as we proceed to examine other aspects of the leadership question.

Techniques of Leadership

Can leadership be learned? Many writers on administration believe it can be, at least to some extent. Certainly, there are tools and techniques that administrators make use of in accomplishing their tasks. To cover them all would be impossible, for not only space but knowledge is lacking. Every successful administrator manages to create one or two new ways of oper-ating that are useful to him or her though they may not be utilizable by others. However, observers have noticed that some basic techniques seem to prove helpful to most administrators in seeking to accomplish their trying tasks.

Budgeting One's Time

A good manager must know how to manage time. More specifically, he or she must know how to keep events from crowding in and consuming too much of his or her working life. The manager must know how to reserve time for him- or herself and not be continually at the beck and call of the worried subordinate or the anxious client.

To Peter Drucker, this is a cardinal element in successful leadership. None of those he has ever known, he says, has managed to accomplish very much unless he could carve out of his working day fairly large slices of time for himself. He needs to do this in order to apply his energies to the broader and more long-range implications of the problems and deci-sions that constantly come before him. And unless he carefully budgets his time, he will expend his energies putting out brush fires and never treating the underlying causes. "The effective decision maker . . . always assumes that the event that clamors for his attention is in reality a symptom," writes Drucker. "He looks for the true problem. He is not content with doctoring the symptom alone."[22]

Unfortunately many administrators neglect this admonition. As Henry Mintzberg points out, "job pressures drive the manager to be superficial in his actions—to overload himself with work, encourage interruption, respond quickly to every stimulus, seek the tangible and avoid the abstract, make decisions in small increments and do everything abruptly."[23]

Administrative history abounds with instances and illustrations of such behavior. And as the size and scope of the administrative task has grown, such "crisis management" has become common. One study of a metropolitan school system found its top administrators spending about 80 percent of their day on matters requiring their immediate attention. Little thought was devoted to uncovering and resolving the more basic problems that had produced this constant flow of demands on their time.

American presidents have also fallen prey to such practices, and often to their regret, as the brief and bumpy career of Jimmy Carter indicates. Carter quickly became involved in a slew of issues, ranging from major overhauls of the country's energy, welfare, and health-care programs to setting up the schedule for staff use of the White House tennis courts. Spreading himself so thin, he failed to develop his policies in depth. As a result his policies and programs often seemed inconsistent and subject to abrupt changes depending on whatever crises had arisen or whatever shift had occurred in the public mood. In 1980 he became the first elected president—his predecessor Gerald Ford had been appointed—to fail to win reelection since Herbert Hoover.

Naturally, the process of reserving time for oneself can be overdone. President Nixon, in particular, may have overused this technique. According to one article that was published before the Watergate hearings, Nixon wanted "chunks of time that are not planned, partly to give himself an opportunity to react, partly to initiate on his own terms rather than on someone else's."[24] While a laudable goal, it eventually led him into conferring too much authority and responsibility on his chief aides, notably H. R. Haldeman, with rather unfortunate consequences for the president and the country. But Nixon's case, while perhaps not unique, is exceptional. Most administrators err too much in the opposite direction, and this tendency produces unfortunate consequences of its own.

Putting First Things First

This principle reads like a truism. Of course, an administrator must put first things first. Still it is often disregarded, largely because of the problems raised above. To establish proper priorities requires the chunks of

time that administrators too frequently fail to allocate to themelves. Time
in itself, of course, will not necessarily give the administrator all he or she
needs to order priorities. Some guidelines are also necessary. Peter
Drucker offers the following:

- Pick the future as against the past.
- Focus on opportunity rather than on problems.
- Choose your own direction rather than climb on the bandwagon.
- Aim high, aim for something that will make a difference, rather than
for something that is "safe" and easy to do.[25]

Franklin D. Roosevelt in many ways seems to have followed such a
course. He was almost entirely future-oriented, and his focus was definitely set on what could be done rather than what could not. In the words
of Frances Perkins, his first secretary of labor, Roosevelt "did not like to
make a recommendation *not* to do something. He liked to recommend
things to be done."[26] Although he kept himself open to advice and counsel, he certainly chose his own direction and, in war and peace, he kept
his aims high, sometimes, perhaps, too much so.

The Maintenance of Options

Anyone who manages to travel down the corridors of power will likely
receive more than once the admonition to "keep your options open." This
is a tactic used by leaders throughout government, whether their seat of
power is in a legislative body or an administrative agency. It is one reason, and probably the most important one, why so many shrewd leaders
are so slow in making decisions. Every decision that a leader makes tends
to commit him or her in some way; it therefore tends to narrow options.

The advantages of keeping one's options open are fairly obvious. It increases flexibility and maintains wider ground in which to maneuver. It
provides more leeway for shifting and changing if the situation itself calls
for it. Essentially, the more options a leader has, the more power he or
she has. Consequently, a leader will often be as reluctant to surrender options as he or she will be to sacrifice formal power.

Option maintenance, however, can be and often is carried too far.
Through postponing definitive action in order to maintain his or her options, a leader can acquire a reputation for temporizing and vacillating.
Also, the leader may end up losing all his or her options, for events will
have overtaken him or her.

President Lyndon Johnson may have been guilty of both types of errors
in his conduct of the Vietnam war. At the beginning of 1964, says David
Halberstam, Johnson decided to hold off making a decision on what to do

until after the fall elections. During that year, "opportunities were lost for possible political negotiation, of reevaluation of American attitudes, of perhaps convincing the American people that it wasn't worth it, that the Vietnamese themselves did not care that much about the war. Instead," says Halberstam, "they . . . decided not to deal with Vietnam, but to keep their options."[27] During this period the situation deteriorated while the United States became increasingly entrapped. Disengagement was still possible but was, at least politically, much more difficult. And so Johnson moved toward escalation.

Later in that war, Johnson and his administration foreclosed his options by making too many commitments. As Townsend Hoopes points out, by sponsoring supposedly "free" elections in South Vietnam, the administration committed itself to the government that these elections produced. This, in turn, restrained the United States from carrying on serious negotiations that might call for a coalition government. Indeed, we had gone so far in pledging support to the shaky Thieu regime that we could not risk anything that might topple it. Our own prestige was at stake. As Hoopes has put it, "in short, President Johnson and his close advisors had so defined our national purposes and so conducted the war that a compromise political settlement would be tantamount to a resounding defeat for United States policy and prestige. Accordingly, it could not be faced."[28]

Sunk Costs

President Johnson and his associates who brought us into Vietnam can also be judged guilty of committing another commonplace blunder in leadership: falling prey to *sunk costs*. We have already encountered this problem in our discussion of organizational pathology in chapter 3. It is one that haunts all administrations and all administrators. Indeed, it influences many different types of people in many different areas of life.

To gain a better appreciation of how pervasive this particular problem is, let us turn for a moment to the stock market. If a small investor with little knowledge of the market buys a stock and sees it go down in price, he or she will most likely hold on to it. To sell it would mean taking a loss, and this the investor is usually reluctant to do. Instead, he or she will hold on, hoping that it will eventually recover and enable him or her to "get out even." The seasoned speculator, so books on the stock market tell us, adopts a completely different approach. When a stock goes down, he or she usually disposes of it fairly promptly. In this manner losses are cut.

One of the reasons why so few people ever become successful in the stock market is their inability to cut losses. It is also a reason why there are so many unsuccessful administrators. For the same principle holds true for government and most any enterprise. Only the proficient practitioners know when to bail out of a losing proposition.

Peter Drucker calls this the practice of "sloughing off yesterday," and he enshrines it as a near-sacred precept for the effective executive. Such an executive, he says, periodically reviews his organization's programs, the good as well as the bad, and then poses the question: Would we go into this now if we weren't already doing it? "And unless the answer is an unconditional 'yes,' they drop the activity or curtail it sharply."[29]

The U.S. government obviously failed to do this in Vietnam. Halberstam quotes John McNaughton, an assistant secretary of defense, as saying early in the war, "I think it gets harder every day, each day we lose a little control, each decision that we make wrong, or don't make at all, makes the next decision a little harder because if we haven't stopped it today, then the reasons for not stopping it will still exist tomorrow, and we'll be in even deeper."[30]

The problem with sunk costs, as McNaughton's statement implies, is they tend to pile up. The more an administrator puts into an effort, the more he or she becomes wedded to it. The administrator has committeed not only such resources as time and money but also prestige. Each day spent upon the losing project increases his or her investment in the undertaking, and thus makes its abandonment still harder. The books written by Halberstam and Hoopes on Vietnam vividly illustrate how difficult "sloughing off yesterday" can become.

Vietnam was not the first war that was perpetuated and expanded because of an inability to cope with the problem of sunk costs. According to historian Barbara Tuchman, the contending powers in World War I had reached a virtual stalemate by 1916. Neither side could advance. Yet, neither side responded to President Wilson's constant pleas for peace. Their obduracy was dictated in part, says Tuchman, by the fact that they did not know how to explain to their respective citizens why so much bloodshed had been incurred with so little to show for it. So the war continued and intensified.[31]

Sometimes the issue of sunk costs is deliberately put forth to prolong a project. During the Vietnam war, the argument was frequently made that withdrawal from this seemingly senseless conflict would mean that all the American lives that it had taken would have been expended in vain. Consequently, according to the rather strange but effective logic that was sometimes used, we had to stay in the war and sacrifice more lives. Similarly, in 1971 when Congress was debating whether to end subsidies to the proposed supersonic transport plane, the plane's backers pointed to the near billion dollars that had already been spent as a reason for continuing the dubious project. Fortunately, Congress refused to buy the argument and the program ended.[32]

The average administrative leader does not deal in such grandiose proj-

ects as wars and supersonic aircraft. Nevertheless, he or she is likely to
spend too much of an agency's resources prolonging a policy or a program
that has been tried and found wanting. While he or she will take care not
to jettison every project as soon as it shows a few flaws, the leader will
also make sure his or her investments do not develop into a deepening
quagmire. He or she will know how to slough off yesterday.

Mobilizing Resources

A newly appointed school principal, in taking stock of the resources at her
command, may itemize such things as her staff, her equipment, and her
school building, together with the budget that she has been allotted to
keep the school operating. However, if she is a good administrator, she
will know how to muster many more resources than these alone.

She will first of all familiarize herself with all the staff services that may
be available at the school department's headquarters and try to make maximum use of them. Then, she will check other governmental institutions,
such as libraries and recreation centers, to see what possibilities they may
hold for assisting her in her mission of educating children. She will look
to the community for additional aid. She may ask mechanics, carpenters,
and the like to drop into the classrooms and demonstrate and explain their
skills to the youngsters. She may ask business people to donate certain
commodities that the school can use. She may call upon the parents for
all kinds of help. For example, if the father of one child works on the local
newspaper, she may ask for some help in publicizing a school project or
event.

As with the principal, so with most other administrators: the wise ones
will know how to mobilize resources. This technique of leadership is
much more important for a public administrator than for a private one, for
he or she is usually in a better position to ask for and obtain help without
having to pay for it. True, he or she may not be in as good a position as a
school principal, since schools enjoy a rather special place in the hearts
and minds of the community. But nearly every public manager can develop some outside sources of support. To take other examples, a police
chief can ask the local bar association to help in drawing up a legal manual for his police officers, or he can ask the schools to publicize a new
traffic safety program, or he may request a local university for research assistance in compiling and evaluating data. The possibilities are almost
endless.

Friends and Enemies

One resource that a good administrator is always trying to increase is his
or her number of friends. This does not mean that successful leadership

requires a charming, ingratiating personality. Friendships in government are usually constructed in other ways. The adept administrator will seek to build and expand a network of friendships based for the most part on what he or she does rather than on what he is.

He or she will rarely hesitate to do a favor as long as it does not involve a sacrifice of integrity or a disproportionate loss of another resource, such as time or influence. Doing favors is like putting money in the bank (i.e., building up an account that one may need to draw upon sometime in the future). The administrator also realizes that he or she cannot know in advance just whose support may sometime be needed, so he or she does not confine amicable responses merely to those who currently possess substantial degrees of influence. The politician who is out of office may someday be in office; the obstreperous and seemingly uninfluential client may turn to writing letters to the newspaper.

This may seem somewhat cynical and manipulative, but it need not be. Indeed, an administrator who naturally likes to provide help and assistance will probably perform this role not only more naturally but also more effectively.

One thing that the wise leader pays particular attention to is the keeping of promises. He or she realizes that nothing can cause more loss of support and respect than commitments made but not kept. Consequently, a wise leader does not make commitments rashly. As Robert Townsend says, "The world is divided into two classes of people: the few people who make good on their promises (even if they don't promise as much), and the many who don't. Get in Column A and stay there. You'll be very valuable wherever you are."[33]

While building up a base of friendship and support, a public administrator will simultaneously go out of his way to avoid making unnecessary enemies. Charles Frankel, after a stint as an assistant secretary of state, noted that a person "isn't seriously committed to the business of government if he is prepared to disagree with people just for the pleasure of speaking his mind. The art of politics consists in not making enemies unintentionally."[34] A nineteenth-century English writer, Henry Taylor, put it this way: "A statesman should be by nature and temper the most unquarrelsome of men, and when he finds it necessary to quarrel, should do it, though with a stout heart, with a cool head."[35]

Taylor's comment also provides some clues as to how a leader should conduct him- or herself during those times, and such times are inevitable in every administrative career, when he or she must confront enemies and not friends. Good administrators do not usually seek out fights, but they realize that they cannot always avoid them, and one of the cardinal rules in waging them successfully is to maintain a cool head. As one big-city mayor once remarked, never get angry unless it's intentional.

The cool-headed administrator will also observe some other rules when engaged in a bureaucratic battle. He or she will try to determine as much as possible the conditions of the fight, such as the time, the place, the issue. He or she will also seek to avoid fighting more than one battle or fighting on more than one front at the same time. As a New England town manager once noted, "I make sure that if I'm fighting with one of my selectmen, I'm on excellent terms with the other two."[36]

The battling bureaucrat eschews personalism as much as possible. He or she does not make personal attacks and seeks to sidestep personal issues. He or she also appreciates the fact that symbolic issues are often more incendiary than real issues and so will often attempt to defuse and deemotionalize the controversy by continuing to pay homage to the appropriate symbols. Thus, a welfare administrator who is seeking to liberalize a benefits program may still find it useful to reaffirm his or her belief that people who can work should work.

Like a good chess player, the good leader is prepared to lose some pawns and even an occasional knight or bishop in order to win the game. In other words, he or she is prepared to sacrifice the less important for the more important. Furthermore, he or she knows that total victories are rarely possible in a democratic government and may not even be desirable. The leader at all times leaves opponents with a face-saving retreat route and will usually stand ready to make some conciliatory gesture. If it is a question of phasing out a program that opponents want continued, he or she may offer a short reprieve and some further study. If it is a question of blocking a program that he or she believes is wrong, he may offer to go along with a demonstration project to test it out.

John F. Kennedy observed these rules during the Cuban missile crisis and thereby helped prevent this critical turn of events from igniting a war that no one really wanted. When he clamped a naval blockade around Cuba, he also gave Russia's Premier Khrushchev a promise not to invade the island nation. This promise enabled Khrushchev to back down without too great a loss of prestige.

When a leader manages to score a complete victory, he or she will, if truly wise, be magnanimous rather than vindictive to his vanquished opponents. Churchill spent most of the 1930s bitterly assailing the appeasement policies of his own party's prime ministers, Stanley Baldwin and Neville Chamberlain. But after being vindicated and installed in office himself, Churchill took great care to keep Chamberlain, then dying of cancer, personally informed of events. And when Churchill heard that angry Britons had stoned Baldwin's car, he invited his discredited opponent to a well-publicized two-hour lunch.

Of course, not even the best of leaders always win their battles, but when they lose, they know how to accept it with good grace. They do not nurse personal grudges, for they are well aware that such feelings will in the end hurt them more than those at whom they are directed. Dwight Eisenhower once said that when anyone had played him false, he would simply write the man's name down on a sheet of paper, throw it into the wastepaper basket, and forget it. Good administrators will learn how to take their defeats without embitterment and, realizing that government still goes on, will prepare themselves to do better next time.

Ruffling the Waters

If the smart administrator shows more discretion than valor in picking fights, this does not mean that he or she always tries to suppress conflict. To some extent one may even encourage it—within one's own organization. It may seem strange, but actually a certain amount of tension has its place in any effective organization. Conflict, provided that it does not get out of hand, may uncover the weak spots in the organization that need remedial action. It may also improve the flow of communication and increase the number of policy options.

Many observers have called attention to this fact. Herbert Simon pointed out how "jurisdictional disputes are an important means of bringing to the top administrator significant issues of policy, and of preventing these from being decided at lower levels without his knowledge. Similarly . . . they are a means of informing him about the characteristics and viewpoint of his subordinates."[37]

Other writers go even further in stressing the value of discord. For Peter Drucker, the right decision requires a certain amount of disagreement, for only such disagreement will bring out all the issues involved and thereby enable the decision maker (or makers) to arrive at a full understanding of just what is involved. Such disputes prevent administrators from becoming prisoners of their subordinates, stimulate everyone's imagination, and provide more alternative areas of action than would otherwise be the case. An effective decision, says Drucker, is not a consensus based on the facts but a judgment based on disagreeing opinions.[38]

Harlan Cleveland claims that organizations are actually too peaceful. Cooperation, he says, comes too easily and "people are, if anything, too conformist." He admonishes public managers to pay heed to the "fruitfulness of friction" and create within their organization an adequate "web of tension." The tension should be deemotionalized and depersonalized. No one should argue out of personal animosity for another or out of fear for his or her own personal security. But people should argue. "The muscles of an organization are like the muscles of a drunk: if they are too relaxed, he doesn't achieve much real coordination."[39]

The Management of People

The public manager primarily is concerned with managing people. It is on how he or she performs in this area that his effectiveness will largely be judged. Never an easy task, managing subordinates has become increasingly difficult during the past decade or so. But there are ways of making this job more agreeable and effective.

To begin with, the good administrator exerts every effort to obtain the best possible subordinates. She puts aside any fears that they might outclass her or show her up. She knows that the better they perform, the more her organization will achieve. And the more the organization achieves, the more successful she, as its leader, will be. Furthermore, top-notch people will stimulate and spur her on to performing more effectively.

Many administrators, to be sure, do not take this approach. In this way they signal their own shortcomings. Princeton mathematician Andrew Weil has promulgated what he calls Weil's Rule. According to Weil's Rule, a first-rate person will surround him- or herself with equals or betters; a second-rate person will surround him- or herself with third-rate people; and a third-rate person will only be able to tolerate fifth-rate subordinates and co-workers. C. Northcote Parkinson has said much the same thing. In his own inimitable style, he notes that "if the head of an organization is second-rate, he will see to it that his subordinates are all third-rate; and they will, in turn, see to it that their subordinates are fourth-rate. There will soon be an actual competition in stupidity. . . ."[40]

Top-notch subordinates do present problems. Aside from their propensity to outshine their chief and to insist on speaking up for what they believe, both of which are assets to an administrator, they will very likely not stay with him or her very long. They will tend to seek out other opportunities when they feel they have pretty much exhausted the possibilities of their present position. And since they are high-caliber people, they will usually experience little difficulty in finding something better or at least something different. But this is a situation that a wise administrator is prepared to live with. He will even boast the many subordinates he had who have gone on to make their mark.

In short, the capable administrator will appreciate the lines that steel magnate Andrew Carnegie chose for his tombstone: "Here lies a man who knew how to bring into his service men better than he was himself."

Delegation

When Moses assembled his people for the Exodus, he picked the ablest among them and put them in charge of groups of varying numbers. Those selected were given the authority to settle all lesser matters and make all lesser decisions themselves, passing up to the prophet only the most important issues. Delegation has played a crucial role in administration ever since. No administrator can hope to do everything him or herself. He or she must delegate. And if the administrator picks the best possible people for subordinates, he or she must delegate even more, for they will insist on substantial chunks of authority in order to exercise and hone their capabilities.

Administrative history abounds with examples of the success that can come when an administrator knows how to delegate authority to others. It was one of the reasons responsible for the success of George C. Marshall. As secretary of state, Marshall always divested himself of his authority when he had to leave on a mission. As Acheson puts it, "General Marshall was meticulous that when the door to his aircraft closed, the command passed. He even on occasion asked for instructions when a wholly novel and unexpected point arose."[41]

Another military man who showed an unusual capacity for delegation in handling a civilian position was General Ismay, Churchill's chief civilian aid during World War II. Ismay had two assistants whom he allowed almost as much authority as himself. Contrary to traditional military practice, for example, he did not require all matters to pass through his hands before going to Churchill. As a result, whenever any one of the three men was absent, the other two had no trouble filling in. The fact that his assistants could deal directly with anyone prevented bottlenecks from arising.

The value of delegation has also been substantiated by more systematic research. According to Katz and Kahn, "the extent of delegation has proved to be one of the predictors of productivity of many kinds."[42]

But delegation also has perils and pitfalls, which to be avoided require adherence to a few guidelines. First, the leader should not just delegate trivia. He or she should, rather, delegate substantial assignments along with the authority to carry them out. Sending a subordinate on a mere errand is delegation of a sort but it is not the sort that makes for wise administration. He or she should remember that when it comes to delegating an important assignment, the subordinate, although he or she may have less knowledge and experience than the delegator, will, at the same time, be able to devote more time, effort, and most likely, zeal to the task than will the superior.

Beware of delegating to too few people. The administrator who relies on just one or two subordinates to handle major assignments may end up as their captive. Moreover, as Seymour Berlin and his associates point out, "They can become screens and filters rather than eyes and ears, and they can get between you and the rest of your agency. To accomplish your mission, you need numerous ties into your agency."[43] President Eisenhower, who relied heavily on Sherman Adams, and President Nixon, who depended greatly on his aides John Ehrlichman and H. R. Haldeman, were both brought to grief partly as a result.

Finally, the administrator should bear in mind that some things cannot be delegated. These include responsibility for:

- creating the climate of the organization;
- representing the organization;
- establishing the basic policy of the organization;
- the overall performance of the organization.

Participation

In a sense, participation in decision making is merely delegation writ large. In another sense, delegation of authority is participation writ large. In any sense, both are interwoven strands of the same tapestry.

Participation, however, can take in many more people and many more aspects than can be accounted for by the term *delegation,* at least as it is commonly understood. Essentially, it means allowing as many people as possible to make as many decisions as possible and to share to the maximum extent possible in making other decisions. It means giving subordinates a "piece of the action."

How big a piece? The answer usually given to this question is "as big a piece as they can handle." However, this is an answer that tells everything and nothing, because how much they can handle is all too often wrapped up with the superior's estimate of their abilities in this respect.

Many modern-day theorists believe that the average subordinate can participate much more than he or she is now allowed to do, with positive results for all concerned. The real problem, they claim, is that managers are too reluctant to permit or too unable to stimulate such increased participation. A bureau or office head may call in subordinates, tell them of a decision he or she has reached, and then ask for their comments. This, the manager may feel, is participatory management. And so it is, after a fashion. Others, however, would say that the better approach would be to call in people before making any decision. He or she would then explain the problem and get their suggestions first. In the former instance, they may be too cowed to give frank reactions once they know what he or she has in mind. And even if this were not the case, their framework for thinking would be somewhat curtailed by the presence of a tentative decision already lying on the table.

Participation can take many forms. Employees can be allowed to determine many of their work conditions, such as hours. They can be asked to contribute their ideas to overall organization policy. They can even play a role in selecting their own superiors.

Its advantages are also many. It generally leads to more informed and better decisions, since more minds and more varieties of experience have gone into making them. It also leads to better executed decisions, for those who are to carry them out have had some say in their formulation. And it stimulates employee development. "One of the most important conditions of the subordinate's growth and development," wrote Mc-Gregor, "centers around his opportunities to express his ideas and to contribute his suggestions before his superiors take action in matters that involve him."[44]

Participatory decision making does have drawbacks. For one thing, it delays, sometimes extensively, the taking of action. It does not always lead to a better decision and occasionally may produce a worse one. It can be terribly time-consuming to all involved and can at times lead to increased bickering. Furthermore, as we noted in discussing delegation, the responsibility still remains in the hands of the person in charge, and he or she must bear the brunt of the burden when the decision turns out to have been wrong.

Sometimes participatory decision making is hampered by the reluctance or the inability of the employees themselves to make use of it. Many may react with fear and distrust at being offered such a new role. Others may rush in before they realize the responsibilities it entails. Public managers wishing to embark on the participation route are usually well advised to begin by taking small steps, letting their employees first share in the making of minor decisions and then gradually proceeding to more major ones.

Participatory management has chalked up its score of failures, but it has also achieved many notable successes. The California State Insurance Compensation Fund adopted wide-scale participation in a reorganization it undertook in 1967. It produced a dramatic reversal in the fund's hitherto declining fortunes. The United States Forest Service has allowed a certain amount of participation by taking surveys of how rangers feel about certain issues and then using the results of these surveys as a basis for action. Abroad, extensive use of participation has contributed to the dazzling growth rates recorded by Yugoslavia and Japan. The Israeli army allows its soldiers to help select candidates for officer training, while the Israeli communal settlements, or kibbutzes, decide almost every issue by member deliberation and vote. Certainly, both these Israeli institutions have given a good accounting of themselves in the development of that tiny but formidable nation.

Education and Rotation

If participation can improve the employee's knowledge and skills, then it is only one of many devices for doing so. The perceptive public manager will make use of a variety of techniques for encouraging employee growth. These may include formal education and training, discussed in chapter 3, and rotation.

By means of rotation, employees enlarge their work experience and increase their abilities and knowledge. They also acquire a broader and deeper understanding of the organization and how its various parts interrelate. Even if their main job is comparatively limited, they will be able to perform it better if they see how it fits in the overall scheme. Rotation also helps to keep people from becoming bored or growing stale. And it prepares the better ones for more responsible roles.

The Forest Service has made extensive use of rotation, and one reason why it does so is to develop the ranger's capabilities. As Herbert Kaufman writes, "The Service does not wait until vacancies occur; it shifts men to replace each other in what looks like a vast game of musical chairs but for the serious purpose of giving them a wide range of experience in preparation for advancement to positions that require a broader understanding of national forest administration than can possibly be gained in long assignments at a single duty station."[45]

Too much rotation, however, can produce adverse effects for both the organization and the employees. If employees feel that they are mere pawns being shuttled arbitrarily about at will, they can become quite dispirited. Even if they perceive the value and need for such rotation, they may, if it occurs too rapidly, fail to immerse themselves deeply in any one assignment, preferring merely to keep things running smoothly until they go on to something else.

The State Department, among all its other ills, suffers, so it is thought, from too much rotation. It is unusual for an assistant secretary of state to serve more than two or three years, which doesn't give them enough time to master the intricacies of their position. As for Foreign Service officers, they are regularly rotated from post to post as part of department policy. In his book *Anatomy of the State Department*, Sloan Simpson says this encourages them to spend too much time thinking about their future opportunities and to spend too little time confronting their existing challenges.[46]

But while it does have its limits and while it can be abused, rotation is still a valuable tool for increasing employee and organization performance. It can and should be applied on an interorganizational basis as well. Employees should be allowed and encouraged to move from one organization to another. Here, suitable retirement policies will help. Transferable pensions, for one thing, will facilitate interorganizational mobility and keep employees from "drying out" in an organization. Possibilities for early retirement are also advantageous. They make organizational change easier and create promotional opportunities. Good circulation can be almost as vital to a healthy human organization as it is to a healthy human organism.

Speaking Up for Subordinates

McGregor once told of a mechanical superintendent of a small manufacturing company who swore at, drove, and severely disciplined his men. Yet, somehow he managed to maintain a remarkably high morale and productivity in his shop. His behavior did not bother his employees as much as it did a staff group that was seeking to carry out a human-relations program in his shop. They could not understand how he managed to break all the "rules" of good management and still do as well as he did.

When they examined the situation further, they found other factors at work. First, the barking superintendent was considered a "square shooter," who, if he behaved rather roughly, also behaved with scrupulous fairness. He took a genuine interest in his subordinates and was always ready to advance them a few dollars until payday or to render some other form of aid without adopting a patronizing attitude.

However, the most important means by which he elicited his men's loyalty was his constant readiness to go down the line for them with his own superiors. During a ten-year period he had twice stormed into the "big boss's office," as his men fondly recalled, to protest a decision that he felt was unfair to "his boys." When in one of these instances the boss rejected his protest, the superintendent promptly resigned, clamped his hat on his head, and strode out of the yard. The "big boss" actually ran after him, caught him as he was going out the gate, and capitulated on the spot.

According to McGregor, the story illustrated a valuable principle of leadership: The leader must be willing, and must be able, to represent subordinates to his or her own superiors. He or she must have influence higher up and must use it to protect the rights of those beneath him.[47]

McGregor's observation and the anecdote he provides are supported by more systematic research. Katz and Kahn cite a study done at the Detroit Edison Company that found that supervisors who were following what are considered good human-relations practices were not developing any greater morale or productivity in their units than those engaging in less desirable supervisory practices. Further study indicated that the "good guy" supervisors were not effectively relating either themselves or their subordinates to those higher up.

"The conclusion urged on us," say Katz and Kahn, "is that the most effective leader in a pivotal organizational role is not the perfect bureaucrat (rational, role-actuated, heedless of primary bonds) but rather the successful integrator of primary and secondary relationships in the organizational situation."[48]

ADMIRABLE ADMIRAL

It was Horatio Nelson's skill in working with his subordinates almost more than his sense of seamanship that earned him his place as history's most famous admiral. From his very early experiences in command, Nelson displayed a remarkable dedication to his men's welfare. He would go to great lengths to provide them with proper food and supplies and would pay out of his own meager resources for the postage on their letters home. On one occasion he virtually camped outside the British admiralty office for three weeks to make sure they would be fully paid.

He was quick to give them credit and slow to censure them, at least directly. He usually refrained from asking of them what he would not do himself, and when injured in battle would insist on waiting in turn to get his wounds dressed.

When serving in the West Indies, he would always take one of his midshipmen along to receptions at the governor's house, believing that teenagers needed a change from shipboard society. Later, as commander of the Mediterranean fleet, he would hold councils of war with his captains, send out questionnaires to get their views, and invite them to his flagship for a meal over which they would discuss the fine points of naval strategy.

Nelson generally sought to lead not by exhortation but by example. His sense of concern and respect for his men proved so salubrious that he was able to write, "I had the happiness to command a Band of Brothers."

Praise, Censure, and Sanctions

As we saw in chapter 3, people have ego needs, and any organization would do well to acknowledge them. The same holds true for the organization's leaders. They should make adequate provision to recognize the ego needs of their subordinates.

The easiest and cheapest way of doing this is by praise. A few laudatory words cost the giver little while they may mean much to the recipient. Praise is a device that belongs in every administrator's tool kit.

But praise is not quite so cheap as many imagine. Like money, the more of it there is, the less it is worth. An abundance of praise depreciates its value. Consequently, an administrator will do well not to lavish it about. Only when used sparingly, though not necessarily stingily, does it achieve its greatest effect. If an employee needs continual praise, then something is usually wrong either with the employee or with the organization. The latter may have created conditions that require the employee to look for continual reassurance.

George C. Marshall was a leader who was far from prodigious in giving praise. This made his employees appreciate it all the more. Dean Rusk, who served under Marshall in the State Department after World War II, says he only once evoked a favorable comment from his chief. As Rusk was wearily getting ready to leave after having worked a fourteen-hour day, Marshall remarked, "You've earned your pay today, Mr. Rusk." Commented Rusk later, "So I took that lesson from the greatest man I've ever known. If you have very good people it isn't necessary to compliment them. They know how good they are."[49]

Not all public managers will want to be as parsimonious with praise as was George Marshall. However, they will find it useful not to overspend in this direction. They may also find some other guidelines helpful:

• Praise at the appropriate time. A compliment loses its value the longer it is delayed.
• Praise the deed, not the person. It is not who the person is but what he or she does that is important. Praising the person can lead to all sorts of problems, including, oddly enough, an increase in the individual's insecurity. He may become too fearful of falling from favor.
• Praise in descriptive terms, not qualitative terms. Do not say simply "That was a good report." Say, rather, "That report covered all the matters I needed to know about."

What holds true for praise also, to a great extent, holds true for censure. All employees will need criticism at one time or another, but here too it should be rendered at an appropriate time and on a somewhat impersonal basis. Martin R. Smith offers some helpful pointers in this regard:

• Stress the positive aspect, encouraging the employee to build up skills and proficiency in the area in which he or she has proven weak.
• Concentrate on performance and those aspects of personal behavior that are distinctly job-related.
• When possible, be indirect, but make sure that the employee gets the message. One device is for the manager to talk about his or her own past mistakes.

• Pick the right time. One good occasion for giving criticism is when the manager is also conferring praise. Calling attention to weaknesses while singling out strengths makes the former action more acceptable.[50]

Smith stresses that criticism to be effective must be directed toward a *correctable* fault that is substantially detracting from a person's *performance*. It does little good to criticize someone for something that does not bear on the job, and it may do harm to criticize the employee for something he or she cannot change. Peter Drucker goes a step further. He urges executives to focus on what a person can do rather than what he or she cannot do. Everyone has weaknesses, notes Drucker, but the effective executive, instead of becoming overly concerned with them, concentrates on the subordinate's strengths. These the supervisor seeks to build and utilize while, at the same time, looking for ways to minimize the impact of the employee's liabilities. Drucker claims this is what makes Japanese organizations function with such remarkable efficiency despite the fact that they almost never fire anyone. They accept a person for what he or she basically is and concentrate their attention on developing whatever assets the person may have.[51]

These are wise admonitions for an administrator to follow. Yet even the best of administrators will come across employees who seem unable or unwilling to make any positive contribution at all to organizational goals. Invoking sanctions, such as suspension or transfer, may help in some cases but not all. The manager will then be faced with the question of dismissal.

Firing an employee is often the hardest job an administrator has to do. It is always unpleasant not only to the subordinate and the superior but also to others in the organization. For the public manager, it poses particular problems, since he or she often has to deal with civil-service regulations, which make dismissal difficult. Usually, the superior can only take such action when he or she is prepared to go before an appeals board and offer solid grounds for the action, backed up by reasonably hard evidence.

Yet discharging the hopeless employee can confer benefits on all concerned. Not only does it make the manager's subsequent task easier but also, in most cases, it lightens the load of other employees as well. As Parkinson says, "All experience goes to prove that the effective leader must be pitiless toward the disloyal, the careless and the idle. If he is not, the work falls too heavily on the willing men. The sense of belonging to a picked team is soon lost in an organization where the useless are still included."[52] The head of a large chemical laboratory had similar sentiments in mind when he said he would like to automatically fire his lowest-producing employee every year. When asked "Why?" he replied, "Simply to keep up the morale of all the others."[53]

There are two additional people who are likely to benefit whenever the dismissal process is appropriately invoked. One is the person who could and wants to do the job that the malfunctioning employee is holding. The other is the dismissed employee. "Any person holding down a job that he is unable to do is tense, angry and frustrated," says Smith. "This situation is almost certain to affect his health and his family life."[54] Often a malfunctioning employee could do well at some other post. Retaining him at his present position only keeps him from realizing his own potentials. And if his problems are too severe for him to hold any job, and if he refuses to take any action on these problems while employed, then dismissal may help him finally to confront them.

Dismissal does not need to be unnecessarily difficult. In many cases the manager may wish to call in the employee for a talk about performance and in the midst of the conversation raise the suggestion that the employee might be happier working somewhere else. He or she may offer to ease up on the person's duties to let the employee shop around for a more congenial position.

Some leaders have resorted to other stratagems. When Franklin Roosevelt wanted to get rid of an official, he would gradually reduce the man's authority and responsibility while also consulting him less and less. Gradually, the official would get the hint and tender his resignation for "personal reasons." Roosevelt would accept the resignation "reluctantly," voicing great public praise for the departing official's "untiring efforts."

John F. Kennedy would proceed somewhat more harshly. He would plant newspaper reports that the official was planning to resign. After reading a sufficient number of these reports, the official would grasp what was happening and turn in his resignation.

Lower-level administrators have made use of both tactics. They will take away a person's assignments and fail to invite him or her to meetings, or they will circulate a rumor through the office that the individual in question is planning to leave. The first tactic is used more widely than the second and is certainly less offensive. Sometimes a variation of this method is used whereby the person is simply assigned to something he or she does not want to do. This can also hasten the employee's departure.

But no matter what strategies one may wish to use, any manager must be prepared to fire people on occasion. One of the most important traits a leader can possess, it has been said, is the willingness to give pain. This may be harsh but it is also humane. Almost anyone who has worked in or studied public organization in the present-day United States would agree that a more aggressive policy in dismissing people would diminish rather than increase overall employee frustration, to say nothing of the frustration experienced by clients and taxpayers. Thus, the good public manager must be prepared to fire people. He or she owes it to all concerned.

EXECUTIVE WELFARE CASES

One of the motivations for the Carter administration to modify the protection given government workers from dismissal was the discovery of several "high level welfare cases" on the federal payroll. These involved people in high paying jobs, sometimes being paid fifty thousand dollars a year, who never showed up for work. In many instances their presence was not even wanted, and they were, in effect, being paid to keep away. Some hadn't been seen in their offices for years.

Carter's aides tried to get rid of them under existing rules but found they were spending 30 percent of their time on dismissal procedures, only to have their discharge proceedings overruled for technical reasons. It was hoped that the rule changes in the Civil Service Act of 1978, though minor in themselves, might improve this situation.

Managing the Manager

Many of the precepts that managers should use in handling subordinates should also be applied to themselves. In particular, they should be as concerned with their own development as with the development of their employees. Otherwise, they may find that their administrative skills, instead of improving, may actually decline with accumulating experience.

One administrator who zealously followed this rule was Napoleon. "The art of government is not to let me go stale," he once said. He showed in the course of his life that he meant what he said. Napoleon read widely and deeply and made a point of picking the brains of the best men of his time. When he sailed on his ill-fated expedition to Egypt, he took along a group of France's greatest scientists and scholars for his own entertainment and enrichment. While exiled to Elba, he developed an enthusiasm for agriculture and soon invigorated the tiny island's agrarian economy. The fact that Napoleon not only conquered most of Europe but left France with legal and governmental institutions that exist up to the present day is in part a tribute to his almost constant self-development.

Administrators who toil in lesser vineyards can still take a page from Napoleon's book. And the fact that they work within a democratic setting only adds urgency to the task. They must continually reach out for new knowledge and experience from both within and without their organizations.

This can mean more than just reading books or attending executive seminars and conferences, although all these things are important. It can mean joining and participating in other organizations. For example, the Forest Service has found that its better executives usually participate, and often quite actively, in civic, fraternal, and religious organizations. They do so on their own time, but the outside expenditure of energies apparently does not detract from but enhances their work as foresters. Many other organizations have had the same experience, and some private organizations, though unfortunately very few public ones, encourage such activities.

In recent years some executives have found more dramatic ways of broadcasting their experience pattern. Trans-World Airlines, for example, actually requires its top officials to spend one day a month at a lower-level job, such as writing out tickets or handling baggage. Few executives may wish to go so far, but it may be a good practice for the head of the clinic to see a few patients and for the head of the welfare office to continue to carry a small caseload of clients. An administrator who never does anything but administer the activities of others may eventually lose perspective on just what those activities entail. At a minimum, he or she should on occasion get "out in the field" and talk with those whom he or she does not normally talk to in the course of daily activities.

One administrator who really went far afield to widen his range of experience was John R. Coleman, president of Haverford College. Coleman decided that his life had become too wound up with "words and politics and parties" and that he was forgetting certain elementary things about people. So, in 1972, he took an unusual sabbatical. Keeping his true identity secret, he wandered throughout the eastern seaboard, working at whatever jobs he could find. Before the fifty-one-year-old college head returned to the campus, he had been employed as a garbage man, ditch digger, farmhand, and kitchen helper. Not all of his experiences were pleasant, but they were all useful.[55]

But even such dramatic gestures as Coleman's may not suffice to keep administrators on their toes, and sooner or later they should start thinking of moving on. "Nobody should be chief executive of anything for more than five or six years," says Robert Townsend. "By then he's stale, bored and utterly dependent on his own clichés—though they may have been revolutionary when he first brought them to the office."[56] Five or six years may be too early, particularly if he takes advantage of some of the other devices we have discussed to keep himself fresh and invigorated, but, nevertheless, the time will usually come when he or she has ceased to grow in the job. When that time comes, the good manager will pass over the reins to someone else and move along. For that is the way good managers go on to become still better ones.

CASE STUDY

The Supreme Allied Commander[57]

When the *New York Times* polled a group of historians in 1961 as to how they ranked America's presidents, Dwight D. Eisenhower scored a rating of 22. This placed him in the low average category, rated even below Herbert Hoover. Eisenhower's place in history fortunately does not rest on his presidential record alone. Ten years prior to entering the White House, he assumed command of what has been called "the most extensive and cooperative military alliance in history." His conduct of this command provides an excellent example of administrative leadership and assures Eisenhower a notable niche in the history of democratic leadership.

When World War II first broke out, Eisenhower was only fifty years old and held only the rank of lieutenant colonel. Yet, he had already given signs of the promise that was soon to be fulfilled. As a cadet at West Point, he had always remained in the upper third of his class and would undoubtedly have finished near the top if he had not been something of a minor hell-raiser. (He rated in the bottom third of his class in conduct.) Later, he attended the Army War College at Fort Leavenworth and graduated from its one-year course as valedictorian of his class.

His military career itself had also supplied indications that he was no ordinary soldier. He early saw the value of the tanks, and while George Patton was writing articles boosting the tank in the *Cavalry Journal*, Eisenhower was doing the same in the *Infantry Journal*. Both men, of course, saw their pleas go largely disregarded. (In France at this time, an elongated colonel named Charles de Gaulle was making the rounds of Parisian publishers with a book urging a greater role for tanks. His superiors had already turned down his outlandish suggestions.) Eisenhower showed equal prescience and even more enterprise when it came to airplanes. Seeing in them another major weapon of the future, he took flying lessons at the age of forty-six and earned a pilot's license. He was not a man to let himself go stale.

Eisenhower had also showed that he understood something about the behavioral side of management. "Morale," he once wrote, "is at one and the same time the strongest and the most delicate of growths. It withstands shocks, even disasters, on the battlefield, but can be destroyed utterly by favoritism, neglect or injustice." He also had committed himself to the goals of maintaining a mature objectivity in his working life. Among the principles he had written down for himself were "Remember that belligerence is the hallmark of insecurity" and "Forget yourself and personal fortunes."

Finally, Eisenhower had also demonstrated a fairly good capacity at verbal communication. This will come as a surprise to those who are old enough to recall the stumbling syntax that so often characterized his press conferences as president. Yet, as an aide to General MacArthur in the 1930s, Eisenhower drafted most of the eloquent general's speeches. During his mission as commander of the Allied forces in World War II, he drafted delicate orders that were considered models of tact and understanding, wrote over one hundred letters to his own commander, George C. Marshall, and managed to carry on a fairly lively personal correspondence as well. In one letter to a former West Point classmate, he wrote, "I think sometimes that I am a cross between a onetime soldier, a pseudo statesman, a jack-legged politician and a crooked diplomat. I walk a soapy tightrope in a rainstorm with a blazing furnace on one side and a pack of ravenous tigers on the other. . . . In spite of this, I must admit that the whole thing is interesting and intriguing."

The above description not only indicates an ability to put ideas into words but also provides a fairly accurate description of just what his job entailed. For heading up the Allied forces turned out to be one of the most challenging administrative tasks in history.

Eisenhower was picked for this difficult assignment by George C. Marshall, who had spotted his abilities and had started grooming him for higher responsibilities once he, Marshall, had become chief of staff. When Marshall found that he could not take on the commander's role himself, since Roosevelt wanted him to stay in Washington, he sent Eisenhower in his place. It proved to be a fortunate choice.

The difficulties confronting Eisenhower stemmed not so much from the military as from the political situation. There were all kinds of people, parties, and pressures that had to be skillfully managed. They included the various British armed forces and their various leaders, British public opinion, British political leaders, many different and often conflicting French interests, other Allied forces and their governments (including the exile governments in London), and then, of course, his own troops, their commanders, his military and political superiors in Washington, and the American press and public opinion. All these, plus the persistent pressure to bring the European war to as speedy an end as soon as possible with a minimum of Allied bloodshed, required masterly managerial skills.

Eisenhower approached this trying task with modesty and geniality. He would share his thoughts with his subalterns as if they were his co-equals, and he framed his commands as if they were advice. In the view of one of his biographers, the British Brigadier General Sixsmith, he was a superb delegator of authority, and yet he was able "to keep his finger on all that was going on. His subordinates were able to see that they were expected to act, they were told what was in Eisenhower's mind, and they knew he would not shrink from his responsibility."

Regarding this latter point, Eisenhower issued a directive early in the campaign that newspaper stories criticizing him should not under any circumstances be censored. When it came time for the cross-channel invasion of France, he prepared a statement for use in the event that the invasion misfired. In this statement he accepted full blame for its failure. And during the actual campaign across Europe, he shrugged off persistent attempts in the British press to give all the credit for Allied successes to the British generals Montgomery and Alexander.

One good illustration of Eisenhower's managerial skill was his handling of General George C. Patton. Eisenhower recognized that Patton was in many ways an excellent combat commander, particularly when it came to tank warfare. He further realized that the Germans had a very high estimation of Patton and feared him as they feared no other Allied combat general. But Eisenhower also was painfully aware of Patton's many weaknesses, such as his egoism, his officiousness, and his reactionary cast of mind.

When Patton on two occasions slapped American soldiers who had been hospitalized with bad nerves or battle fatigue, thus setting off an uproar in the United States, Eisenhower refused to take the easy course and relieve him of command. Instead, he ordered Patton to make personal apologies to the slapped men, the medical personnel, and all others concerned. Patton, who was desperate to continue in command, complied. Two years later when the savage Nazi counterattack almost upset the Allies in the historic Battle of the Bulge, Patton's adept rescue of the besieged U.S. forces vindicated Eisenhower's action.

He tolerated Patton as long as he could, but after the war ended and Patton insisted on employing ex-Nazis in his zone of occupation, Eisenhower moved to replace him. However, even at this point he tried to ease the aging general's humiliation. He asked Patton whom he would like as a replacement, and when Patton named someone who was acceptable to Eisenhower, the American commander appointed him.

His tact and concern were in evidence not only in handling his commanders. He also regularly toured the ranks, talking with the soldiers, and looking after their well-being. He sharply reproved any base commander who utilized his best facilities for administrative quarters instead of giving them up for the rest and relaxation of the men who were doing the fighting.

Behind his modest geniality lay a great singleness of purpose. He realized that the alliance would falter and flounder unless there was a single overall commander, and he made sure that this was accepted and acknowledged. He also took steps to see that throughout the Allied forces all issues would be discussed and decided on considerations other than national pride. His creation of an integrated command—integrated not only in combining the forces of several nations but also in combining both the army and navy of these nations—is considered his greatest accomplishment.

He also knew how to put first things first. Thus, in North Africa he deferred his integration scheme, important though it was, in order to capture Tunis before the bad weather set in. And when Roosevelt urged him to lead the troops into Rome, thus glorifying his own and the U.S. role in the city's liberation, he refused in order to get to England more quickly and thus have more time to work on the coming invasion of France.

Regarding the French invasion, Eisenhower had originally wanted to have an invasion of southern France accompany the cross-Channel attack. Owing to a shortage of landing craft and other factors, he continually had to scale down his plan, but he did not scuttle the idea until the very end. In Sixsmith's view, this decision "was typical of the man," for "he liked to keep his options open."

As a military strategist, Eisenhower did make his share of mistakes. He allowed the German military divisions in Sicily to escape, he balked at sending his airborne division to capture Rome, and he opened up a hole in his front that permitted Hitler to launch the perilous and costly Battle of the Bulge. It took the Allied forces, despite their complete domination of the air and their vast superiority on the ground, nearly a year after the time they crossed the channel to bring Germany to defeat.

But, according to Sixsmith, he was by no means a poor strategist either. And he was constantly beset by conflicting pressures. In the north, Montgomery was insisting that the full Allied thrust be put into his own hands. He was supported by a feverish public opinion in England, not simply because he was their general but also because they feared the German rockets that were being launched from the area that Montgomery was trying to capture. Farther south, there was Patton, champing at the bit, demanding more gasoline and other scarce supplies as well as men. Since American public opinion needed a hero of its own, Patton could not be completely restricted. Meanwhile, the French were clamoring for the liberation of Paris, a move that would not only detract from the route of advance but could hinder further advances, since supplies and the trucks to carry them would have to be siphoned off to maintain the city afterward.

On balance, Eisenhower handled his strategist role adequately and his administrative and political role superbly. This is Sixsmith's view, and it seems to reflect the consensus of others who were in a position to know. When Germany finally surrendered, General Marshall, who was not, as we have seen, overly given to effusive praise, sent him a long and truly effusive letter of congratulations: "You have commanded with outstanding success . . . you have met and successfully disposed of every conceivable difficulty . . . you have triumphed over inconceivable logistical problems and military obstacles . . . you have made history, great history for the good of mankind. . . ."

Churchill shared much the same view. Shortly before Roosevelt died, the British prime minister wrote him expressing "admiration of the great and shining qualities of character and personality which he [Eisenhower] has proved himself to possess. . . ." But most important of all was the judgment of British Field Marshal Montgomery, the petulant prima donna who chafed and complained at the way Eisenhower had restricted him all during the war. Said Montgomery afterward, in words reminiscent of those used by the Los Alamos physicists to describe Oppenheimer, "No one but Ike could have done it."

But if Eisenhower performed so well in the highly sensitive and highly political role of supreme Allied commander, why was he such an undistinguished president?

There are many possible answers to this question and all of them may contain some element of truth. For one thing, he may not have been such a poor president as historians have believed. Eisenhower himself thought that his greatest contribution was to keep the United States out of war, and in view of the actions of his successors, that accomplishment may not have received its due. Eisenhower, like Kennedy and Johnson, also came under pressure to invade Vietnam, but when such a course was urged on him by his secretary of state and his military chief of staff in 1954, he asked that Congress and other nations be sounded out first. When reaction from both quarters was negative, he scuttled the idea.

Another answer may be found in his age. He was ten years older when he entered the White House than when he took over the supreme Allied command, and while sixty-two is not an unusually advanced age for high political office—Churchill was in his late sixties during World War II and Clemenceau was in his late seventies when he headed France during World War I—the years take their toll on some people more than others. The fact that for over three years during the war he worked day and night, smoking four full packs of cigarettes a day and getting no exercise, certainly did not contribute toward his later vigor.

But most of all, the answer lies in the point raised at the start of this chapter, and that is the situational nature of leadership. Leaders create their situations, to be sure, but situations also create their leaders. Such was the case with Dwight D. Eisenhower.

Leadership and Its Limits

A new textile-mill manager once decided, on assuming his new responsibilities, that things would go best if he indicated to one and all that things were going to be run his way. On his first day in the job, he strode into the weave room, walked up to the union business agent, and, after making sure the man was the person he was seeking, announced, "I am the new manager here. When I manage a mill, I run it. Do you understand?"

The business agent nodded and then waved his hand. The workers who had been closely watching the encounter promptly shut down every loom in the room. The union official then turned to the manager and said, "All right, go ahead and run it."

This story illustrates one very real yet often-overlooked or at least underestimated aspect of leadership: it is very much a two-way street.

"In a bureaucracy that contains people with brains and consciences," wrote Charles Frankel following his tour of duty in Washington, "an unspoken bargain binds the man at the top to his subordinates. If they are to be the instruments of his will, he must, to some extent, be an instrument of theirs."[58] Most writers on administration would agree. "A manager is often described as someone who gets things done through other people," notes the British organizational theorist Rosemary Stewart. "We tend to forget that this means he is dependent upon them."[59]

In a complex bureaucracy the problem intensifies. Tsar Nicholas II was one of the few truly autocratic rulers of his time. Yet he experienced constant frustration in getting his smallest orders carried out. "I do not rule Russia," the weary monarch once sighed. "Ten thousand clerks do."[60]

American presidents have consistently discovered their office to provide far less power than they had thought. Franklin Roosevelt depicted Lincoln as a "sad man because he couldn't get it all at once, and nobody can." Roosevelt's own battles with his bureaucracy are almost legendary. He once wearily described his efforts to handle government agencies as akin to boxing a featherbed.

Roosevelt's successors, Truman and Eisenhower, suffered from the same problem. John F. Kennedy took office with the idea of changing Washington bureaucracy. But he found that when he wanted a simple sign taken down, it did not come down, even after he had given the order for its removal three times.

President Nixon, at the time that the Watergate scandals were breaking, was widely said to have amassed a frightening amount of power. Yet Watergate in many respects proved the opposite. He tried to get the Internal Revenue Service to crack down on his enemies, but all he could manage to achieve was a few simple audits, something that almost any citizen could engineer with a well-worded letter to his or her regional IRS representative.

Nixon, or at least his administration, was also thwarted in attempts to halt an antitrust prosecution of ITT, to obtain funds from the Central Intelligence Agency for the incarcerated Watergate burglars, to prevent disclosure of the break-in by his "plumbers" of the office of Dr. Ellsberg's psychiatrist, to limit certain investigations by the Securities and Exchange Commission, et cetera. The fact that the Nixon administration approved plans for breaking and entering and other felonies is certainly frightening. Yet the fact that it felt constrained to do so may indicate a lack rather than a plentitude of power. And in any event, Nixon's master plan for such incidents was stymied by a bureau chief, J. Edgar Hoover, who was supposedly serving at the president's pleasure.

The limitations of lesser executives are even greater. To many students, the president of their university may seem like an omnipotent figure, at least as far as their immediate needs are concerned. Yet, college presidents usually find themselves walking a very narrow tightrope, having to balance carefully the needs and wishes of trustees, faculty and administrative staff, students, and community officials. As for deans, their plight is still worse. The relationship of a dean to his or her faculty and students, so one dean has said, is that of a fire hydrant to a dog.

Even when he or she seems to possess sufficient power to command obedience, the leader still may find the going rough. Stewart relates how "one unpopular manager worked himself almost into the grave as his subordinates always did what he asked them to do and never did anything else." And she adds, "The more a manager needs the cooperation of his staff—and the more skilled and interrelated the work, the more he will need it—the less he can rely on formal authority to obtain it."[61]

It would seem from all this that the leader's lot is scarcely a happy one. Many who view it with awe and wonder from the outside would find it sheer torture to experience from the inside. Yet it does have its challenges and its charms.

David Lilienthal, who held such posts as the chairmanships of the Tennessee Valley Authority and the Atomic Energy Commission, once defined leadership as a humanistic art. It requires, he said, "a humanistic outlook on life rather than mere mastery of technique. It is based on the capacity for understanding of individuals and their motivations, their

---

LEADERSHIP QUALITIES

. . . as a Secretary conducting political correspondence, I could not issue an order or express an opinion, without satisfying various persons very unlike myself, that the thing was fit to be done. I was thus in a good position for finding out by practice the mode of putting a thought which gives it easiest admittance into minds not prepared for it by habit; while I became practically conversant with the difficulties of moving bodies of men, the necessities of compromise, the art of sacrificing the non-essential to preserve the essential. I learnt how to obtain the best I could, when I could not obtain everything; instead of being indignant or dispirited because I could not have entirely my own way, to be pleased and encouraged when I could have the smallest part of it; and when even that could not be, to bear with complete equanimity the being overruled altogether. I have found, through life, these acquisitions to be of the greatest possible importance for personal happiness, and they are also a very necessary condition for enabling anyone, either as theorist or as practical man, to effect the greatest amount of good compatible with his opportunities.

—*John Stuart Mill* (1806–1873) in *Autobiography*

fears, their hopes, what they love and what they hate, the ugly and the good side of human nature. It is an ability to move these individuals, to help them define their wants, to help them discover, step by step, how to achieve them."[62]

The challenge of leadership is thus the challenge of humanism itself. Its successful exercise lies less and less in giving orders and more and more in developing the innate capacities of human beings. But to this must be joined something else, a sense of mission bolstered and buttressed by some degree of vision. The story is sometimes told of three stonecutters who were asked what they were doing. The first replied, "I am making a living." The second, busily at work, answered, "I am doing the best job of stonecutting in the whole country." The third, looking up with a gleam in his eye, said "I am building a cathedral."[63]

The conclusion is obvious. Only the third can become an effective manager.

Notes

1. The material on Oppenheimer in this chapter is drawn mainly from Nuel Pharr Davis, *Lawrence and Oppenheimer* (New York: Simon & Schuster, 1968).

2. Peter F. Drucker, *The Effective Executive* (New York: Harper & Row, 1967), 22.

3. Douglas McGregor, *Leadership and Motivation* (Cambridge, Mass.: MIT Press, 1966), 73

4. William J. Reddin, *Managerial Effectiveness* (New York: McGraw-Hill, 1970), 35.

5. Paul H. Appleby, *Big Democracy* (New York: Alfred A. Knopf, 1949), 41.

6. Arthur M. Schlesinger, Jr., *A Thousand Days* (New York: Fawcett World Library, 1967), 403.

7. Harlan Cleveland, "A Philosophy for the Public Executive," in *Perspectives on Public Management* ed. Robert T. Golembiewski (Itasca, Ill.: F. E. Peacock, 1968).

8. David Halberstam, *The Best and the Brightest* (New York: Random House, 1969), 318–319.

9. Donald Katz and Robert L. Kahn, *The Social Psychology of Organizations* (New York: John Wiley, 1966), 293–294.

10. Burleigh Gardner, "Successful and Unsuccessful Executives," *Advanced Management* (September 1948).

11. Albert Speer, *Inside the Third Reich* (New York: Macmillan, 1970), 18–19.

12. John J. Corson and R. Shale Paul, *Men Near the Top*, Supplementary Paper no. 20 issued by the Committee for Economic Development (Baltimore, Md.: Johns Hopkins Press, 1966).

13. Katz and Kahn, *Social Psychology of Organizations* 328.

14. Ibid., 115.

15. David E. Lilienthal, *Management: A Humanist Art* (New York: Columbia University Press, 1967), 17.

16. Townsend Hoopes, *The Limits of Intervention* (New York: David McKay, 1969), 79–80.

17. C. P. Snow, *Science and Government* (New York: New American Library, 1962), 73.

18. Anyone who believes that dynamic dictators are immune to such a tendency may find the following quotation from Adolph Hitler of interest. "Unless I have the incorruptible conviction: *This is the Solution,* I do nothing—not even if the whole party tried to drive me to action. I will not act. I will wait, no matter what happens." Quoted in Walter C. Langer, *The Mind of Adolf Hitler* (New York: Basic Books, 1972), 81.

19. Drucker, *Effective Executive*, 32.

20. Katz and Kahn, *Social Psychology of Organizations*, 318.

21. Lytton Strachey, *Elizabeth and Essex* (New York: Harcourt, Brace & World, 1969).

22. Drucker, *Effective Executive*, chap. 6.

23. Henry Mintzberg, "The Manager's Job: Folklore and Fact," *Harvard Business Review* 53 (1974).

24. R. W. Apple, Jr., "Haldeman the Fierce, Haldeman the Faithful, Haldeman the Fallen," *New York Times Magazine*, 6 April 1973.

25. Drucker, *Effective Executive*, 111.

26. Frances Perkins, *The Roosevelt I Knew* (New York: Harper & Row, 1964).

27. Halberstam, *Best and Brightest*, 303.

28. Hoopes, *Limits of Intervention*, 125. Also see p. 68.

29. Drucker, *Effective Executive*, 104–108.

30. Halberstam, *Best and Brightest*, 368.

31. Barbara W. Tuchman, *The Zimmerman Telegram* (New York: Bantam Books, 1971), 123.

32. See *New York Times*, 7 March 1971, sec. E, p. 4, for an account of how this factor was finally overcome.

33. Robert Townsend, "Up the Organization," *Harper's Magazine* (March 1970).

34. Charles Frankel, *High on Foggy Bottom* (New York: Harper & Row, 1968), 98.

35. Henry Taylor, *The Statesman* (New York: New American Library, 1958), 77. This fascinating little book was originally published in 1836.

36. In a statement to the author. Anonymity was requested.

37. Herbert A. Simon, *Administrative Behavior* (New York: Free Press, 1957), 145.

38. Drucker, *Effective Executive*, 148.

39. Cleveland, "Philosophy for Public Executive."

40. C. Northcote Parkinson, *Parkinson's Law and Other Studies of Administration* (New York: Ballantine Books, 1964), 103.

41. Dean Acheson, *Present at the Creation* (New York: W. W. Norton, 1969), 193.

42. Katz and Kahn, *Social Psychology of Organizations*, 332.

43. Seymour S. Berlin et al., "A Guide for Political Appointees: Entering the System," *Good Government* (Winter 1972).

44. McGregor, *Leadership and Motivation*, 60–61.

45. Herbert Kaufman, *The Forest Ranger* (Baltimore, Md.: Johns Hopkins Press, 1960), 176.

46. Sloan Simpson, *Anatomy of the State Department* (Boston: Houghton Mifflin, 1967), 36–37, 39–40.

47. Douglas McGregor, *The Theory of Human Enterprise* (New York: McGraw-Hill, 1960).

48. Katz and Kahn, *Social Psychology of Organizations*, 321.

49. Halberstam, *Best and Brightest*, 321.

50. Martin R. Smith, *I Hate to See a Manager Cry* (Reading, Mass.: Addison-Wesley, 1973), 108.

51. Drucker, *Effective Executive*, chap. 3.

52. Parkinson, *Parkinson's Law*.

53. William English, retired director of chemical research at Polaroid Corp., in an interview with the writer.

54. Smith, *Hate to See Manager Cry*, 186.

55. *New York Times*, 10 June 1973.

56. Townsend, "Up the Organization."

57. The principal source of material for this case study is E. K. G. Sixsmith, *Eisenhower as Military Commander* (New York: Stein & Day, 1973). Another source is Ladislas Farago, *Patton: Ordeal and Triumph* (New York: Dell Publishing, 1970).

58. Frankel, *Foggy Bottom*, 56.

59. Rosemary Stewart, *The Reality of Organizations* (New York: Anchor Books, 1972), 48.

60. For an interesting and informative view of some of the Tsar's leadership problems, see the earlier chapters of Robert K. Massie, *Nicholas and Alexandra* (New York: Atheneum, 1969).

61. Stewart, *Reality of Organizations*, 82.

62. Lilienthal, *Management*, 16–17.

63. Peter F. Drucker, *The Practice of Management* (New York: Harper & Row, 1954), 122.

7

Communication

Through the years, administrators and administrative theorists have placed increasing emphasis on communication. In the 1930s, Chester Barnard called attention to the fact that "a common purpose must be commonly known, and to be known must in some way be communicated. With some exceptions, verbal communication between men is the method by which this is accomplished."[1] Writing in the 1950s, Herbert Simon put even greater stress on the role of communication. "It is obvious," he noted, "that without communication there can be no organization, for there is no possibility then of the group influencing the behavior of the individual. Not only is communication absolutely essential to organization, but the availability of particular techniques of communication will in large part determine the way in which decision-making functions can and should be distributed through the organization. . . ." Simon went on to conclude that "only in the case where the man who is to carry out a decision is also the best man fitted to make the decision is there no problem of communication—and in this exceptional case there is of course no reason for organization."[2]

More recent writers have assigned communication an equal if not more important role. They consider such organizational ingredients as solidarity and support, along with command and control, to be closely tied in with organizational communication. Some even view organizations as essentially systems of communication and regard all or nearly all organizational problems as communication problems. Such an approach may well go too far, but it can sometimes prove helpful. For example, Charles Redfield tells of one successful consultant who, when he embarks on an organizational study, stations himself in the mailroom and "by plotting the lines of actual communication, he can sometimes build a more accurate organizational chart than the one that hangs on the wall in the president's office."[3]

Communication presents as many problems as any other aspect of administration, if not more. There are, first of all, the technical problems. When the Germans invaded France in 1940, they utilized Teletypes, advanced field telephones, and other devices to maintain a rapid flow of communication among all the parts of their fast-moving military organization. The French, however, relied heavily on the old dispatch system, whereby orders issued from Paris would be carried by dispatch runners on motorcycles. This not only seriously slowed down communication but often eliminated it altogether, for the runners sometimes never reached their destinations. They would either become the victims of accidents or of strafings and bombings from the ubiquitous German aircraft.

The French had other communication problems besides merely technical ones. Prior to the German onslaught, they had received from Vatican sources the proposed route that the Germans were planning to use through Belgium. But Paris refused to believe the report, since the proposed route did not seem to them militarily sound.[4] This illustrates a further communication problem: sometimes the information is properly sent and received but then is simply disregarded.

Many countries have experienced this problem. During the same war, the Germans paid handsomely for some British battle plans that had been carefully photographed by a valet of the British ambassador in Turkey.[5] However, once they obtained possession of the documents, the Nazis failed to act on them. Similarly, the Soviet Union was repeatedly warned of an impending German attack in 1941. One source was the famous double agent Richard Sorge, who supplied them with the exact dates of the scheduled invasion. But Stalin shrugged them off. In the postwar period, the United States received numerous reports from our embassy in China forecasting the impending collapse of the Chiang Kai-shek regime and the Communist assumption of power. But when the predicted event occurred, it caught everybody in Washington by surprise.

Experience alone does not necessarily solve such problems. When World War I broke out, the French general staff fell into possession of authentic German documents clearly indicating that the Germans would march through Belgium. This would normally call for the French to shore up their left flank to counter and turn back the thrust. But the French had based their strategy on a strong center and clung to this position despite their new information. Thus, their later experience in 1940 was a dupli-cate of their 1914 errors.

A more common problem is simply failing to request information from the right parties. Khrushchev in his memoirs blamed Russia's abortive in-vasion of Finland in World War II on such a failure. The Soviet intelli-gence services had known about the powerful Finnish defense system all along, but no one in the high Soviet command bothered to ask them about it. The disaster cost the Russians nearly one million lives.[6]

Not all manifestations of this problem are so sweeping and dramatic. But they occur all the time. A detective investigating a case may fail to consult the police officer who first handled the case and did the initial investigation. This failure, which happens in police forces all the time, scarcely contributes to efficiency in fighting crime. The detective may spend days and weeks tracking down a suspect when the police officer who first dealt with the matter knows all along where the suspect is living.[7]

However, it is not only a failure to consult that makes the work of de-tectives more difficult than it needs to be. Often, the patrolman will not tell the detective what he knows even when the detective asks him, for he may be angry at not being allowed to pursue the matter on his own or he may have a grudge toward that particular detective. Thus, information can be impeded as much, if not more, by intention as by error.

Parties involved in a communications network of any kind may not only withhold information but may also intentionally distort it. But the distor-tions that come about through maliciousness are far and away exceeded by those that occur through mischance.

To obtain an idea of how widespread a problem this is, we have only to examine the most simple and most intimate organization in current soci-ety—the married couple. In their highly respected book, *The Mirages of Marriage*, William J. Lederer, M.D., and Don D. Jackson estimate that husbands and wives miscommunicate about 20 percent of the time. To offer an example, they cite a case where the wife has a habit of rubbing her nose when she is angry. An occasion arises, however, when, in talking to her husband, she rubs her nose simply because it is itching. The hus-band, who is well aware of what this usually means, assumes that she is angry. Since he cannot imagine any reason why she should be, he starts to get irritated at her for allegedly becoming so. His defensive tone then starts to make her annoyed, which in turn confirms him in his initial re-action. And so their marriage has to ride over another bump on the road to bliss.[8]

Communications problems arise not just from information that is too slow, too incomplete, or too distorted but from information that is simply too abundant. This is the problem of communication overload. Harold

Nicolson claimed that this was one of the greatest problems at the Paris Conference that followed World War I.[9] The conference's forty-eight committees generated so much information that it was impossible for anyone, including the conference's major decision makers, to know what was going on. James MacGregor Burns blames too much communication for the failure of the United States to take advantage of concessions from the Japanese in 1941, concessions that might have averted the Pacific war. "The problem was too much information, not too little—and too much that was irrelevant, confusing and badly analyzed."[10]

Occasionally, this communication problem also arises by intent. For example, school superintendents sometimes purposely flood their school-board members with reports and other documents, which, although complete accurate, are so voluminous as to make it impossible for the board members to know what is happening. As the board members struggle in vain to keep abreast of the swelling tide of information, the superintendent calmly proceeds to do pretty much what he or she wants to do.

Most overload problems, however, arise from sheer force of circumstances. And the circumstances that make for too much communication are increasing all the time. The growth of complexity, specialization, interdependence, and some of the other features of today's organizational world is constantly leading to the generation of more and more information. This process is being aided and abetted by the growth of communications technology. Consequently, an organization may take great care and achieve great success in developing excellent lines and flows of communication only to sink under the profusion of information that may develop as a result.

To sum up, in tackling the problem of communication, the administrator would do well to keep in mind a statement attributed to the nineteenth-century British novelist Samuel Butler. "Communication of all kinds is like painting—a compromise with impossibilities."

Formal and Informal

Communication falls into two basic categories—formal and informal. They are easily defined. Formal communication is written communication; informal is oral. Of course, not all communication is verbal. Attitudes and even ideas can be transmitted by means of inflection, gesture, and "body language." But though nonverbal communication definitely has a place in organizational life, its role is usually not very great and in any case is hard to analyze and define. Consequently, our attention will be directed to verbal communication.

What factors govern the use of one form of verbal communication over the other? Under what conditions does formal communication take precedence over informal and vice versa?

Generally, two facts foster the use of formal communication. One of these is size. As organizations grow, they tend to make increasing use of formal communication and, correspondingly, diminishing use of its opposite. The other factor is public character. Public organizations tend to rely more heavily on formal communication than do private ones. A brief examination of the merits of formal communication will show why this is true.

Formal Communication: The Advantages

Formal communication fosters accountability. This factor alone makes it indispensable for governmental affairs, particularly in a democracy. Unless the public and those who serve its information needs, such as the press and legislators, can find out what orders were given and who gave them, it cannot make the judgments needed to ensure truly democratic government.

By facilitating accountability, formal communication puts a restraining hand on arbitrariness, capriciousness, favoritism, and discrimination of all kinds. By proceeding on formal instructions and keeping records of their transactions, public officials find it much more difficult, although certainly not always impossible, to depart from acceptable standards of impartiality and fairness. Of course, the rules and standards themselves may be unfair, but if so, this is at least a matter of public record and can be easily determined.

Many of the scandals and other sensational events of recent years that have shed valuable light on governmental operations point up this advantage of formal communication. Take, for example, the case of the Pentagon Papers. These disclosed a great deal of valuable information on the country's conduct of the Vietnam war. Had Defense Secretary Robert McNamara not directed that such reports be written, much of this information would have escaped public view.

The Watergate affair also provides a good illustration of the relationship that formal communication has with pinpointing responsibility in government. Had there not been a certain amount of documentation regarding these events, then exposure and prosecution of the misdeeds it involved would have been greatly impeded and possibly nullified. Had there been still more extensive use of formal communication, then many more elements of this nefarious affair might have been more deeply and successfully explored. Without formal communication, the work of the journalist, to say nothing of the work of the historian, would frequently become implausible and even impossible.

Watergate and the Pentagon Papers are only two of the more dramatic incidents that spotlight the utility of formal communication, at least when it comes to serving the interest of the public. Other illustrations occur on an everyday basis. Early in 1973, a special commission set up by New York State to investigate New York City's property-tax situation found there were no written procedures or manuals to guide the city's assessors in their work. The absence of such formal materials resulted in the "frivolous application of discretionary standards," which in turn had opened the door to favoritism and other forms of political abuse.[11]

To pursue the matter further, let us suppose that all the city's assessors were deeply committed to performing their tasks accurately and fairly, and let us further suppose that the city administration was determined to let them do so. Could New York City's property tax payers then be assured that they were being treated rationally and impartially?

The answer is no. Without a uniform and written set of standards and criteria, the chances are that assessments would still be unevenly imposed and administered. What one assessor is likely to emphasize in making an assessment, another assessor is likely to make light of. To one assessor, high ceilings in a building give it added charm and space and hence add to its value. To another assessor, high ceilings may mean additional heating and cleaning costs and hence detract f om a building's value.

Formal communication thus tends to curb the disparities and discrepancies, which can occur even without express design. With all the best will in the world, distortions can and usually will creep in when formal communication is totally absent. Written communication allows everyone concerned to receive the same message and to check back on it if he or she is at any time uncertain as to what it says.

This brings us to still another asset of formal communication. It saves time. In any large organization, it would be difficult indeed to issue all instructions orally. Not only would distortions occur as the message was relayed from person to person or group to group, but time would be needlessly consumed. Written communication allows an almost infinite number of people to receive the same message at the same time, and if they forget any portions of it, they do not have to check back to the sender of the message, for they now have it in front of them.

Written communication can also save time when it travels in the other direction. It would be virtually impossible for any large and complex organization to receive orally all the information that it may need to obtain from its far-flung operations. Its phones would be constantly tied up and its offices would be continually filled with people relaying what they think headquarters needs and wants to know. In the same way, putting things in writing can save a superior's time in handling information from subordinates. He or she can usually read memoranda from several different people in the time it takes to talk to just one of them. This also allows the supervisor to schedule time better, for he or she can allocate periods of the day or week for reviewing such messages.

For reasons such as these, busy executives have often encouraged their aides to put things in writing even though such aides may work in close physical proximity to them. Robert McNamara was especially emphatic on this point. He always discouraged oral briefings from anyone because, as he put it, "I can read faster than they can talk."[12]

Written communication also allows information to be more fully developed with all of its ramifications discussed. Issues of any importance usually require such treatment. The document that results can then be circulated to others for still further analysis, until all possible points of view have been solicited and all aspects have been explored.

Finally, written communication not only helps inform the recipient but may also do the same for the sender. Francis Bacon once said than an index is chiefly useful for the person who makes it and the same can be said for many of the memoranda, reports, et cetera that flow through the corridors of bureaucracy. By putting down data and ideas in writing, the administrator or an aide frequently sees things that were missed before. Expressing ideas in written form usually assists the person doing it to seek details previously disregarded and to see relationships and implications that were previously missed. Many a bureaucrat will frequently testify that he or she did not fully understand an issue until after writing a memo about it.

There are thus good reasons why the written word looms so large in the operations of government. We should bear them in mind when we discuss some of the less attractive aspects of this phenomenon.

Formal Communication: The Disadvantages

Shortly after he was appointed secretary of Housing and Urban Development in 1969, George Romney held a press conference and displayed a stack of paper that stood two and a half feet high and weighed fifty-six pounds. This, he said, represented all the paper generated by an application for a single urban-renewal project.[13]

Although the problem, as Romney explained it, was caused more by faulty organization than by a sheer obsession with formal documents, it does illustrate that one of the ways in which organizational pathologies work is by a profusion of paper. The very use of the written word tends to encourage its further use, and many a governmental organization, and not a few private ones, have found themselves swamped in a sea of documentation.

Romney's display is only one of many incidents that have from time to time cast a chilling light on this problem. During World War II, for example, there was a celebrated Office of Price Administration price order on fruitcake that consumed six pages of fine print. It was one of the most famous orders that the red-faced OPA ever turned out.

But though the paper problem is as old as bureaucracy itself, it seems to show great resistance to correction. A congressional report in 1966 estimated that there were three hundred sixty thousand forms in use by the federal government. By 1972, the number of such forms was thought to have grown to more than eight hundred thousand. Harold Koenig, the head of a National Archives team that was trying to reduce the paper explosion, estimated that at least thirty billion copies of these forms were circulating every year. A Senate subcommittee put the total cost of printing, shuffling, and storing the forms at close to $18 billion.[14]

Few organizations have managed to escape the ravages of the paper revolution. Former FBI Director J. Edgar Hoover consistently boasted that the FBI was not a bureaucratic agency, and when one considered the highly personalized manner in which he ran the agency, he was to some extent right. Yet the FBI did not manage to avoid the maze and craze of documentation. Its agent's manual encompassed thirty-two thousand rules and regulations, and its files would have filled an area equal in space to twelve football fields. When an agent in Philadelphia was scheduled to speak at a dinner, his office sent out a report on the event to headquarters and thirty-seven other field bureaus and then filed the report under eleven different categories in its own files.[15]

PAPER CHASE ENDS

On Janury 1, 1980, a long disputed change finally occurred in the federal government: the bureaucracy switched from using $8\frac{1}{2} \times 10\frac{1}{2}$-inch paper to $8\frac{1}{2} \times 11$-inch paper.

The half-inch expansion in length was the result of nearly ten years of study groups, committee meetings, and memo interchanges. It was estimated that the larger-sized paper would save the government over $8 million a year since it would allow an additional five or six lines per page. More importantly, it would put the government in step with private industry, which uses eleven-inch-long paper almost exclusively. In some federal departments letters from private firms had to be photocopied on smaller size paper in order to fit federal files. Canada had made a similar changeover three years before.

In a desperate effort to stem the ever-swelling flow, Congress enacted the Paperwork Reduction Act of 1980. This legislation gives the Office of Management and Budget near absolute authority to approve all activities, such as requests for information, that would generate more paper. Sponsors of the act claimed that a mere 1 percent reduction in bureaucratic paperwork would save the nation a billion dollars. The act also established the Federal Information Locator System to provide an index to information sources within the federal government. Such a system would, it was hoped, encourage federal agencies to share information and keep them from collecting data that other agencies had already compiled.[16]

The states too have been moving ahead to abort or at least abridge the rising tide. Minnesota, Ohio, Washington, Kentucky—these are only a few of those states that have launched paperwork-reform measures. When an inventory in Indiana showed that the state had 68,300 different forms, officials managed to eliminate 20,000 of them within the following two years.

Praiseworthy and productive as such steps may be, one must not lose sight of the fact that the growing crush of paper is in many respects a symptom of other organizational problems, not just a problem itself. One frequent cause is an insufficiency of delegation. A superior who insists on making all decisions personally and who needs to know everything that is going on, down to the smallest detail, will find his or her desk piled high with memoranda, reports, requests. In like manner, an agency that has split duties among several subunits when they could be handled by one will also add to its paper problems. This, according to Romney, was the problem at HUD. An urban-renewal application had to travel through the hands of too many assistant secretaries.

Some of the very advantages of written communication lead to its abuse. If it promotes accountability, then it also fosters self-protection. People may put something in writing so that they cannot be accused of having done something improperly or so that they can point to the record later on and show where they were right. "A civil servant's job is precarious," a French police official once remarked in the American television program "McCloud." "We stand on a mountain of paper. The higher the mountain, the more secure the civil servant." Although the speaker was fictional, the tendency he called attention to was very real. Harold Macmillan, who served as a British aide to General Eisenhower in World War II, and as such was the recipient of a constant stream of written communication, once claimed that "directives are more useful in protecting the writer than in instructing the recipient."[17]

Sometimes people write more than they need to simply to show how industrious they are. And often superiors are quite impressed with such industry. Joseph Califano was a prodigious writer of memoranda when he served on Lyndon Johnson's staff. Although in Califano's case the motivation was probably a genuine desire to reach the president on many issues, his diligence did not go unnoticed. Once when Johnson heard another aide speak somewhat disparagingly of Califano, the president retorted, "Don't criticize Califano. There's never been a man around me who wrote so many memos."[18]

Whatever the causes of paper profusion, its cost can be immense. We have already seen some estimates of the cost involved in printing, storing, and circulating forms. Other costs may also be included. A memo may save the superior's time but may consume inordinate amounts of the subordinate's time that also bears a price tag. It is not uncommon for a public employee to spend a day or more drafting a memorandum on an issue that could have been settled in a ten-minute conversation with the superior. When this occurs, the time factor involved in formal communication is usually working against the organization instead of for it.

Each piece of paper, we should remember, tends to spawn offspring of its own. One person's contribution evokes a similar or even greater contribution from others. If A sends a memo to B, then B must often send a memo back. B may at the same time send a memo to C asking him or her for comments. C even may not have waited for B to act. If C has heard about B's memo, then he or she may feel inclined to do some memo writing on personal initiative. In order to make the memo better, C may send a memo to D seeking some additional information, which, in return, produces a memo from D. And so it goes.

Meanwhile, the ever-bulging files start to produce problems other than just the costs of storage. J. C. Masterman, in describing Great Britain's remarkably successful effort to convert German agents to double agents during World War II, says the files on some of these double agents grew to over thirty-five volumes. This, he said, made it "difficult and wearying and time consuming to master the essentials of each case in a reasonable space of time and with some degree of certainty that no essential feature has been overlooked."[19] Thus, completeness of information, carried too far, can lead to less information, or at least less information that can be used easily.

Needless to say, all these problems have an impact on the organization's employees. Formal communication by virtue of being formal is less humane. It may have a dispiriting and even deadening effect on human relations. Indeed, people actually start to turn off when too many formal communications pour in on them, and the messages themselves end up in wastepaper baskets unread.

Finally, we should note that while formal communication usually is clearer and less liable to be misunderstood than its opposite, this is not always the case. The story is told of how J. Edgar Hoover became irked at the sender of a memo because the sender had not left wide-enough margins for the FBI chief to scribble his comments. Since wide margins were a bureau policy, he wrote on it "watch the borders" and sent it back. For the next week FBI agents fanned out on the Mexican and Canadian borders in the bewildering belief that their boss wanted them to keep a vigil.

Informal Communication

Oral communication offers a solution to many of these problems. It does not flood the person or clog the files. It can evoke immediate feedback, which in turn can lead to a resolution of any issues and clarification of any points that may be involved. In so doing, the one who is doing the communicating can be assured that his or her information has been received. It permits the use of shading and emphasis and gesture. And it certainly is more human and often more humane. People are now dealing together directly.

Informal communication is heavily used in Japanese industry and government. The Japanese prefer face-to-face contact and rarely send inter-office memoranda. Superiors spend considerable time "walking the floor" and talking with their employees. Conferences are common at all levels and are often conducted in an informal and relaxed atmosphere. Judging from Japan's growth rates and productivity levels, it does not seem to have hurt their administrative processes.

Efforts are also under way in this country to substitute oral for written communication. President Johnson's task force on cutting red tape, for example, urged federal officials to make more extensive use of the telephone and less use of "time-consuming written communications."[20] It is quite possible that the use of oral communication will grow apace in governmental agencies, though it will most likely never replace formal communication altogether. For reasons that we noted earlier, the written word and the printed document will probably continue to serve as the mainstay of the communications process in any developed democracy.

A Note on Grapevines

Any agency that has an informal organization will also have an informal communications system, which is often referred to as the "grapevine." And since informal organizations are found in almost all organizations, grapevines tend to be ever-present.

Grapevines can also be terribly efficient. "With the rapidity of a burning powder train," says Keith Davis, a professor of management who has studied grapevines for over twenty years, "information flows out of the

woodwork, past the manager's door and the janitor's mop closet, through
steel walls or construction-glass partitions."[21] What is more, Davis claims
that well over three-fourths of all this information is accurate.

Even when it is not accurate, says Davis, it may convey a psychological
truth, for many rumors that run rampant through an organization are
"symbolic expressions of feelings." If the rumor has it that a certain employee is planning to quit, it may reflect the wish on the part of fellow
employees that he or she would quit. Or it may simply reflect the employee's own desire to leave.

Davis advises managers to pay careful attention to the grapevine's information, for it may tell them more than they know about what is going
on within their organization. He also urges them to disseminate whatever
information they have in order to counter whatever errors the grapevine
may be spreading. Beyond that there is little that the administrator can
do, because the grapevine, he says, "cannot be abolished, rubbed out,
hidden under a basket, chopped down, tied up or stopped." Managers
might just as well accept it, for it "is as hard to kill as the mythical glass
snake which, when struck, broke into fragments and grew a new snake
out of each piece."

Means and Methods

Modern-day administration can avail itself of an ever-growing number of
devices as it seeks to cope with its communication needs. Some might argue that the current plethora of communication tools and techniques is
aggravating rather than alleviating communication problems because the
more such means are available, the more they may be used. Others would
argue the contrary, claiming that organizations are not making enough use
of the vast variety of current techniques. It is possible that in this case
both sides are correct.

In this section we will examine a few of the basic components of organizational communications systems, leaving some others for the following
section, where communication flow will be discussed.

Memoranda

The memo has come to symbolize the communications process of present-
day bureaucracy, and well it does. It is easily the most used, and probably
overused, communications device in many public organizations. Administrative personnel not only send memos to each other but even to
themselves.

Self-directed memos are actually some of the most useful. They not only help an administrator organize his or her thoughts but provide a record of important events. This can be particularly valuable when it comes to matters that are crucial or controversial. For example, when a client or a politician has tried to exert unwarranted and unacceptable pressure on an administrator, he or she may dictate a memo for the file covering all the details of what happened. He or she may need to refer to this if the disgruntled favor seeker tries to take action against the administrator.

Memos will also be needed for other matters, but the good administrator will utilize them with care. He or she will, first of all, make memos brief and encourage others to do the same. Some executives have laid down a rule requiring all memos sent to them to be only one page in length. As an unvarying rule, this is probably a bad one. Many matters simply require more explication than can be handled in one page, and an arbitrary cutoff may lead to arbitrary action on the matter being covered. If the memo is to be the basis for decision making, then the recipient should want to know all the possible decisions that can be taken along with their respective pros and cons.

ACRONYMS ANONYMOUS

Ernest L. Boyer says that during his short term as U.S. commissioner of education, he was asked to sign a letter containing the following paragraph:

This workshop is part of an RFP issued by 10C aimed at helping SEAs better serve LEAs with reference to the LEA/Prime Sponsor agreements called for under the YETP portion of YEDPA. Starting with this workshop, SEA participants will be asked to form SEA data collection teams in each State to collect data regarding current LEA/Prime Sponsor agreements now in force. Given these data, 10C will then host a series of seminars aimed at collecting specific 'best practices' in existence. The project will culminate in a series of 10 regional conferences aimed at sharing what has been learned with SEAs, LEAs, and DOL personnel.

The difficulties and potential embarrassment that may result from trying to promulgate and enforce a "one-page rule" are illustrated by what happened to one city manager when he issued a memo to his department heads instructing them on the art of writing brief, one-page memos. His own memo attracted nationwide attention, for it took him several pages to get his one-page idea across to his subordinates.[22]

But if it is unwise for public managers to uniformly decree one-page memos, they should encourage them or at least encourage brevity, and not only in memoranda but in all forms of communication. Good students usually learn in writing their academic papers that they cannot and should not use all the material they may have compiled, no matter how fond and proud of this material they may have become. Good bureaucrats should learn the same lesson.

Communications professor Marvin H. Swift provides a pungent example of the long and the short of memo writing.[23] Sam Edwards, a mythical manager, finds that everybody in the company is taking advantage of the company copying machines for their personal use. It is costing the company a pretty penny. So he fires off the following memo:

To: All Employees
From: Samuel Edwards, General Manager
Subject: Abuse of Copiers

It has recently been brought to my attention that many of the people who are employed by this company have taken advantage of their positions by availing themselves of the copiers. More specifically, these machines are being used for other than company business.

Obviously, such practice is contrary to company policy and must cease and desist immediately. I wish therefore to inform all concerned—those who have abused policy or will be abusing it—that their behavior cannot and will not be tolerated. Accordingly, anyone in the future who is unable to control himself will have his employment terminated.

If there are any questions about company policy, please feel free to contact this office.

Such a memo, says Swift, is not only discourteous to the employees but is also unnecessarily verbose. The message could be better conveyed in the following way:

To: All Employees
From: Samuel Edwards, General Manager
Subject: Use of Copiers

Copiers are not to be used for personal matters. If there are any questions, please contact this office.

A comparison of the two memos will further show that not only is the second one shorter but it is also clearer. Brevity and clarity often go hand in hand, and the latter is as important as the former in effecting good communication. The wise administrator will encourage simple, straightforward sentences that get directly to the point. Sometimes, of course, sensitive matters will require more indirect treatment, but even in those instances there is little need for the prolix prose that characterizes so much organizational writing.

A memo once sent by the State Department to its division chiefs offers some helpful hints along this line. It read in part:

It has become increasingly apparent that the sophisticated, legalistic and prolix prose sometimes employed in intragovernmental communications is predictably inappropriate in replying to relatively simple questions from the general public, which has little experience with or tolerance for such language.

A useful check on the readability of prose is [the] Fog Index. It is based on the length of words and sentences. The Fog Index of the first paragraph, above, is 23, well above the graduate student level, 17. The Fog Index of this paragraph is 9, slightly over that of *Time* magazine. Our goal will be to replace the former with the latter.[24]

FOREIGN LANGUAGE STUDY

Some employees of the Food and Drug Administration once decided to compile a dictionary to help people learn "bureaucratese." Here are some sample definitions from the new dictionary:

Infrastructure—(a) the structure within an infra; (b) the structure outside an infra; (c) a building with built-in infras.

Meaningful—(a) opposite of meaningless; (b) the same as full of meaning; (c) when used as "meaningful relationship," it is what used to be called being in love (archaic).

In depth—(a) opposite of shallow; (b) opposite of out of depth; (c) should always be used before words such as *study, research, analysis,* and *review* so that readers will think that you didn't do a quick and dirty job. . . .

Humor, as the above suggests, is a valuable ingredient in many memoranda. As we noted earlier, one of the big problems in formal communication is that recipients tend to throw it away unread. Attempts to overcome this by requiring them to initial it do not really solve the problem, for almost anyone who has worked in a large public organization will have initialed many a memo to which he or she has given only the most cursory attention. Humor, along with brevity, clarity, and a minimization of memoranda generally, can help any administrator in getting memos read. However, "humor" that obviously ignores the feelings and sensitivites of co-workers or the public can produce grave problems for the administrator and should be avoided. Witness the case of New York City's former school principal Maurice Shapiro.

In 1968, the New York City Board of Education temporarily suspended Shapiro, giving as one of its reasons a memorandum in the form of a letter that the sixty-year-old educator had sent to each of his teachers on January 4, 1966. The communication reads as follows:

I wish to welcome back all of you and I am sure we will have a wonderful year for 1966.

I would like to call the following to your attention:

1. Be attractive at all times. Shave face and chin before coming to school. This applies to men also. We are inviting talent scouts and Hollywood producers to P.S. 96, Manhattan, so we wish you to be at your best at all times.

2. You wear high heels at your own risk. They are especially dangerous if you are doing Folk Dancing.

3. Dress attractively, not as if you were pushed out of bed by an exuberant lover. If you wear a low-cut dress, we do not approve of falsies.

4. Unless you are bald, please have your hair combed suitably.

5. If you wear a dress above the knees, be careful how you sit, unless you are in the teacher's lunchroom, or in my office.[25]

Forms

Few communication devices cause as much aggravation and annoyance as forms. And our preceding discussion showed how extensive and expensive their use can become. Yet, they are, if properly used, savers of time, energy, and money. Police officers, for example, often find report writing the hardest part of their jobs. Few, however, would argue the need for providing some written information covering their activities. Court cases alone make such information necessary. However, some police forces have begun developing forms to cover accidents and many of the other matters that demand police involvement. If such a form is clear and complete, it can be a boon to all concerned.

Clarity and completeness in forms are not qualities that can be taken for granted. Although some forms are too long, many are too short. This leads to faulty action or to further efforts to provide the necessary information. Clarity is another important ingredient that is often lacking. Robert Townsend urges any executive to fill out every form him or herself before permitting it to be used by the organization. This will give an idea as to how effective—and how necessary—it is.[26]

Reports

A somewhat less symbolic but perhaps still more controversial communications tool is the report. That ebullient Englishman C. Northcote Parkinson flays this device with all the verbal vigor—and it is considerable—at his command. One of his famous laws contends that reports will be written regardless of whether the writer has anything to say.[27] Many who have worked in bureaucracies that stress them will share Parkinson's belief. It is truly amazing how sometimes the most unproductive person can turn out impressive reports filled with information attesting to his or her productivity.

Writing and reading reports also consume the valuable time of more productive people. As such, reports can be quite costly. When John P. Fishwick took over the presidency of the Norfolk and Western Railroad in 1970, he cut the number of reports that his executives had to write by almost one-third. The railroad's accountants estimated that this simple step saved the company over five hundred thousand dollars a year, enough to purchase two new locomotives.[28]

Nevertheless, reports do have their place in administration. Martin R. Smith offers two guidelines for their intelligent use. First, they should be limited to one page; second, they should be written and filed only when the project discussed is completed. "Periodic progress reports," he claims, "inevitably waste time. Besides the author who sweats out filling empty space with empty words, there are the frustrated readers who are impatiently attempting to glean the information they need from ten pages of rubbish."[29] Unless limited to concise summaries of completed action, people will end up spending their time writing about progress rather than accomplishing it.

Copies of Correspondence

One truly excellent way of disseminating information is through circulating carbons or photocopies of correspondence. Such documents can often be substituted for memoranda with much better effect. The material that a memo would cover is often available in a letter that the would-be memo writer has either received or sent. By simply having copies of this correspondence sent to all those who might have an interest in, or a need for, the information, one not only saves the time of doing some additional writing but also ensures more likelihood that the information one is seeking to convey will be absorbed. People will read such messages with much more alacrity than they will read memos. In some cases, they will be pleased and flattered to have received it. This is particularly true when the superior is circulating his or her own correspondence to subordinates.

Manuals

Most organizations of any size prepare handbooks for their employees to guide them in their work as well as their general organizational life. The

Forest Service at one time used to issue a manual that ran to seven volumes of about three thousand pages each. It was designed to cover almost any possible aspect or potential problem of a forest ranger's job. The physical format consisted of looseleaf binders so that new material could continually be added to or substituted for existing material in the appropriate categories.

This manual, which served as the agency's Bible or Baedeker, was slated for three additional volumes when complaints over its unwieldiness began to mount. The agency then canceled the scheduled new volumes and began to scale down the existing opus. This illustrates anew one of the problems with such communication devices. They are not only expensive to prepare and revise but are also time-consuming and tedious to read. Furthermore, if an employee always has to check the manual for every decision, he or she will fail to develop much decision-making ability. And since no manual, no matter how complete, can hope to cover every conceivable contingency, the pre-formed decisions that it prescribes will in many instances be less satisfactory than the ones that can be made by those at the scene.

Nevertheless, such manuals can have their uses. One personnel specialist, Don E. Jones, recommends that such handbooks provide the employee with the general policies and philosophy of the organization, including a statement as to what the organization is trying to accomplish. At the same time, they should cease and desist from trying to spell out details for handling every potential problem that may arise. Policies that are clearly stated will allow employees to make more decisions on their own—and usually better ones than the organization can make for them.[30]

Staff Mettings

Prior to the battle of Mechanicsville early in the Civil War, General Robert E. Lee summoned all his general officers to a joint meeting. The gathering, unprecedented in the annals of U.S. military history, aroused some alarms. Many feared the risks that it would present in terms of secrecy and security. Yet it went off smoothly and secretly, as some forty men with star-spangled epaulets on their gray uniforms sat around their new commander on the lawn of a country home in Virginia exchanging information. Lee skillfully solicited their ideas and discussed his own, taking care, however, not to divulge anything that could prove harmful if leaks did, in fact, develop.

The meeting yielded many benefits. It helped the generals to know and understand each other and gave them an overall grasp of the situation that confronted the Confederacy at what seemed a rather dark hour. As for Lee himself, it not only provided him with much useful information on the condition of his troops but also on the temperaments and talents of those who commanded them. And it established his authority as their commander. It thus set the stage for the rather spectacular series of victories that were to ensue.[31]

The staff meeting, so rare in Lee's day, has become a fixture of modern-day organizational life. Its development has, in certain respects, paralleled the development of democracy itself, for the staff meeting is, at least to some extent, a manifestation of the democratic impulse. However, its successful utilization can be furthered by the observance of a few simple guidelines.

A good staff meeting should have some structure. A brief agenda should be prepared and, if possible, circulated beforehand. And an effort should be made to finish the agenda before the meeting breaks up. This means that the chairperson of the meeting must exercise some care to stick to the agenda while the meeting is in progress.

But this rule is often breached, and sometimes rightly so. A meeting that sticks too closely to a printed document will not generate the ideas and information that make such meetings most successful. Furthermore, an approach that is too businesslike may annoy and alienate its participants, particularly if they are people who possess humanistic orientations, such as many social workers, or artistic temperaments, such as many architects. A former executive vice-president of one of the country's largest breweries once related that when anyone said something that was not absolutely relevant to the issue being discussed at his company's board of director's meeting, there would be a slight and chilling pause, after which the meeting would proceed as if the person had not spoken. Such techniques usually will not work in the public sector.

The adroit meeting chairperson must thus engage in a careful balancing act, trying to keep the meeting from wandering too far afield while at the same time taking care not to keep it under too tight a rein. Setting a reasonable but fairly firm time limit and announcing this at the outset can help.

Throughout his conduct of the meeting, the chairperson should try to encourage the interchange of all information and ideas that can be useful for those attending to know. He or she should at the same time discourage detailed discussion of matters that concern only a few of the participants. They should be encouraged to get together by themselves later on. It is imperative to provide an atmosphere where anyone who has something to contribute will feel free to do so. It is equally imperative to make sure that no one feels obligated to speak when he or she has nothing to say.

Seating arrangements can also play a role in making these meetings successful. Grouping the members down the sides of an elongated table with the chairperson at the head may help in getting through the agenda quickly but may also inhibit communication, particularly between the members themselves. Attention naturally focuses on the person sitting at the head. Consequently, many administrators find that a circle arrangement works much better. A creative brainstorming session may require an even more open and relaxed atmosphere.

At the end of every meeting, the chairperson should sum up the ground that has been covered and the decisions, if any, that have been made. He or she should also point out what further activity will have to be taken pursuant to the matters raised in the meeting. It may be useful to back up the oral wrap-up with a subsequent written summation, which could be circulated to those who may not have attended the meeting as well as to those who did.

How often should staff meetings be held? There is no hard and fast answer to this question. Some mutual funds have staff meetings twice a day, once in the morning before the securities exchanges open up, and again in the afternoon when they close. A team of detectives working on a tough case may also meet at the start and at the end of each working day. In most cases, however, fewer meetings are desirable. Lenin once warned his comrades on the dangers of "meeting sickness," and Peter Drucker has noted that "meetings are by definition a concession to deficient organization. For one either meets or one works. One cannot do both at the same time."[32] This may be something of an overstatement, but there is little dispute that too frequent meetings cannot only consume time but can also lead to a preoccupation with details that only exaggerates their significance.

Generally, the larger the organizational unit involved, the fewer the meetings. Thus, a field office staff may meet once a week while the head of the field office may attend regional meetings once a month.

Another problem that frequently arises in connection with meetings is that of who should be invited. A general staff meeting should, of course, include almost everybody. Even file clerks and typists can benefit from learning what the organization's problems are and what efforts are under discussion to resolve them. They also may have something to contribute to decision making. Furthermore, their sense of affinity to the organization is likely to increase if they are invited to its conferences.

But many meetings do not even require all members of the professional staff, and inviting everyone to attend not only lengthens the meeting but keeps other work from going forward. The problem is that failure to invite some employees to the meeting can badly hurt their feelings as well as damage their position in the organization.

Sometimes this is consciously done. It was noted in the previous chapter that one technique some administrators use to get rid of an unwanted employee is to drop his or her name from the meeting list. This technique can also be used simply to indicate that the subordinate is in disfavor.

When Hubert Humphrey as vice-president voiced objections to bombing North Vietnam in 1965, he soon found himself omitted from all White House conferences. The vice-president soon became an object of pity or scorn in official Washington as he sent his small staff scurrying around the city desperately trying to find out what was going on. Humphrey found that many journalists knew more about what was happening in the executive branch than he did. Within a year, he had changed his mind and climbed aboard the bombing bandwagon.[33]

Usually, however, omitting people from meetings is not intended to show disfavor or disdain, and this confronts the administrator with the need to see to it that the omission scars no egos and injures no feelings. Drucker suggests an approach such as the following: The executive issues a notice saying he or she has invited certain members of the organization to meet at a certain time to discuss a particular matter. Any staff member who felt he or she had something to contribute or who wanted the information could then be told to "feel free to drop in."[34]

This discussion of the problems of staff meetings should not obscure their potentialities. Essentially, they remain an excellent device for exchanging information, building morale, and making better and better-executed decisions. As such, they are, when properly used, an important part of every public manager's means for accomplishing his mission.

Up, Down, and Across

Information moves in three basic directions, upward from subordinate to superior, downward from superior to subordinate, and horizontally from one organizational unit to another. No matter which way it flows, however, it runs into problems.

Perhaps the most difficult route is upward. As information wends its way up the organizational ladder it becomes increasingly stale. Just how severe the problem becomes is a question of the particular situation involved. It may take a fire fighter inside a blazing building only a few minutes to convey information to his immediate superior, but in that few minutes his information may have become tragically outdated. Most matters, fortunately, are not quite so urgent, but even so, the information needed to act on them may come too late. The situation may have already changed or at least developed nuances that make the information less satisfactory as a basis for action.

This problem affects all communication flow, no matter what its direction. Communicating consumes time, and nearly all delays involve some disadvantage. Of course, delays often turn out to be helpful to an organization in that they permit a reappraisal of the situation or the introduction of new elements into the decision. However, in this case, the information itself has changed. If it is a question of communicating a specific piece of valid information, then usually the quicker it reaches its destination, the more effective it is.

A much greater problem with upward-moving information is that it tends to change as it advances. This too, is a problem of all communication flows. If A relates a message to B and B, in turn, relates it to C, then the information that C has received is likely to be a little bit different from the message that B received. However, when B is A's superior and when C is B's superior, some special factors often magnify the problem.

Consciously or unconsciously, subordinates frequently distort information as they pass it to those above them. They may do this for a variety of reasons. First and probably foremost is their simple reluctance to serve as bearers of ill tidings. All too often in human history the bearer of ill tidings has become identified as the producer of such tidings, and as such has incurred the wrath of the recipients. Even when the bearer has no such fears for his or her fate, he or she may still try to soften and shade unwelcome news out of a simple desire to protect the harassed superior from unpleasantness. As former New York City Mayor John Lindsay once wrote, "I think nothing is more dangerous to an executive than isolation from the people and reliance on advisors who, however competent, may tend to tell the executive what they think he wants to hear. It's not very likely that an aide will say 'Mr. Mayor, they think you're a nigger lover in my neighborhood and they hate you for it.' But it is likely that in some neighborhoods that is precisely what I will hear."[35]

Sometimes subordinates are merely trying to spare their superiors from simple fatigue. George E. Reedy, who served for a while as Lyndon Johnson's press secretary, tells of being called in by one of the president's most trusted assistants and finding him furious over the fact that two separate staff members had submitted memos offering contrary advice on a particular matter. Said the presidential aide indignantly, "That man is exhausted enough and has enough problems on his mind without assistants coming at him from every direction. I think I should send both memos back and tell them to get together before I allow anything to go in."[36]

Subordinates sometimes have more selfish reasons for withholding or manipulating information. They may fear that the action such information would produce would prove disadvantageous to their interests. Or, if others stand a chance of being adversely affected, they may be fearful of being cast in the role of the informer.

This particular problem in upward communication, it should be noted, reflects problems inherent in hierarchy itself. As the French writer Albert Camus once noted, "There is nothing in common, in effect, between a master and a slave. One cannot speak or communicate with a subjugated human being. In place of that natural and free dialogue by which we acknowledge our resemblance and consecrate our destiny, servitude causes to reign the most terrible of silences."[37] Of course, bureaucratic relationships are rarely those of a master and slave, but wherever hierarchy is introduced, it will tend to act in this fashion. Chester Barnard once noted that information received from a low-status person will often receive scant attention, while information received from a high-status person may set off a reaction well beyond what was ever intended.[38] Katz and Kahn point out that a superior is supposed to give orders and a subordinate is supposed to receive them. This means that upward communication goes against the organizational grain, for the subordinate is not used to telling things to the superior and the superior is not used to listening to things from the subordinate.[39]

History supplies numerous examples of leaders who succumbed to this weakness and suffered severe setbacks as a result. Among them were such presidents as Woodrow Wilson, Lyndon Johnson, and Richard Nixon. Dictators, however, seem particularly prone to such behavior. When the reign of the last shah of Iran was rapidly crumbling, it became nearly a crime to mention any bad news in the shah's presence. Reports of widespread unrest in the country were watered down to minor incidents so as not to incur his displeasure.[40]

The Vietnam war provides the administrative analyst with a virtual treasure trove of illustrations as to how the upward flow of communication can become distorted out of all proportion. Vietnamese peasants, being interviewed by U.S. officials in the field, would give the answers that they thought the Americans wanted to hear. The translators would usually touch up the answers still more before rendering them in English. When the information reached Saigon, its negative aspects would be pruned again. This process would continue right into the White House, where aides would cull those items that they thought Walt Rostow, who was Johnson's chief conduit, would most want to receive. Rostow, in turn, would package it into as agreeable a form as possible and pass it on to the president.[41] Rostow performed a similar tailoring operation on information coming in from other sources as well. As a result, Lyndon Johnson, in some respects, knew less of what was going on in Vietnam than did the average American newspaper reader and television viewer.

Within the military itself, there were numerous instances where the upward flow of communication took an erratic and erroneous course. According to one writer, Morris J. Blackman, the ineffectiveness of the bombing of the North was consistently distorted, because those who were carrying out the missions did not want to tell those who ordered them the truth. As Blackman puts it, "It would have taken a certain amount of courage for a colonel to tell a general that the air strike the general had ordered—and for whose success the colonel felt he would be held responsible—was a failure."[42]

Then there were the infamous massacres at My Lai and Song My. On

March 27, 1970, the *New York Times* published a story under the headline "Panel Finds Songmy Data Diluted at Each Echelon." The news story recounted how the field investigators of the massacre estimated the number of innocent Vietnamese killed at 175 to 200. This, in itself, represented a scaling down of other estimates, which had put the reported number of dead at closer to 400. However, as the lower figures were forwarded "from echelon to echelon up the military chain of command, the reported number of Vietnamese killed became smaller and smaller," said the *Times*. "By the time these reports reached the headquarters of the American Division, where they stopped, the number of Vietnamese killed had been reduced to an estimate of 20 to 28."

Unplugging the Upward Flow

Perhaps the most important step that an administrator can take in resolving or at least reducing these impediments to the upward passage of information lies in his or her own conduct. If he or she genuinely believes and acts on the belief that all information should move swiftly and surely upward, then the information is much more likely to do so. If he or she shows subordinates that the bad news should be told along with the good, and in as fresh and pure a form as possible, they will not only be more inclined to do so but will also be more likely to deal with their own subordinates in the same way.

However, in an organization of any size and complexity, this will not be enough. Fortunately, there are other ways and means of seeing to it that those above are kept adequately informed by those below.

One such device is the trade union. As we saw in chapter 5, informing those on top of what is happening beneath them is one of the major contributions that unions can make to the administrative process. Many an executive who has been shielded by middle management from much of what is going on at the rank-and-file level finds the unions a valuable supplier of needed information. And he or she usually can be assured that the union's representatives will not omit any unpleasant news.

Other means for improving the upward information flow are formal devices for hearing complaints. These may include grievance committees, appeals boards, and various clientele service units. For example, a mayor who sets up little city halls throughout the city in order to receive and process complaints may find that these complaints will give some excellent clues as to where problems may exist in his or her administration.

Investigatory units can also prove helpful in this regard. Many large police departments have a special unit to investigate police officers. The heads of the "shoefly squad," as it is usually called, can often provide the police commissioner with information that he might not hear from other subordinates.

Sometimes executives make their own field inspections, talking directly with rank-and-file personnel. This does not always have to take the form of a formal inspection. When Jerome Kretchmer was environmental-protection commissioner of New York City, he made it his practice to leave home once a week at 6:00 A.M. in order to stop off at a car barn and talk to the sanitation workers as they were assembling for work. He would then listen to their complaints and suggestions, usually, of course, receiving more of the former than the latter.[43]

An executive can also disregard the chain of command on occasion and call someone several levels below to his or her office for some direct conversation. He or she may stipulate a period each week or month when the office door would be open to anyone within the organization who had a matter to discuss.

Suggestion boxes can also play a helpful role in getting information from the bottom to the top. Not only will the suggestions sometimes be useful in themselves but they may well illuminate problems that the manager may not know about. Surveys and polls of the organization's members and of its clients may also provide valuable information as well as indications as to how the upward communications process is working.

There are, in short, many means available to ensure a relatively swift and smooth flow of upward communication. Any public manager who truly wants an undistorted picture of what is going on in the organization should experience no great trouble in obtaining it.

Communicating Downward

While information may run downward a bit more smoothly than upward, it also encounters numerous obstacles and impediments. When it is oral, downward communication is subject to almost all the alterations that can creep in when it moves the other way. The captain tells the lieutenant to have the men ready at 0800. The lieutenant, to protect himself, tells the sergeant to have the men ready at 0700. And the sergeant, in a further manifestation of the same fear, makes sure the men are ready at 0600. Thus, the captain then finds the men sleepy and disgruntled when he orders them into action.

When communication moves down in written form, it can also develop difficulties. It may be misinterpreted either because it is not complete or because the recipient is simply not willing to accept its message. The biggest problem, however, is probably the inability or the refusal of the recipient to absorb all the information that seems to be cascading onto him or her. As we have already seen, memoranda senders encounter persistent problems in this respect.

Organizations have tried to get around this in many ways. In some organizations, important messages are sent to the recipient's home, occasionally by special messenger, as an insurance that he or she will read it. And at least one school system makes a practice of following up the written messages that it distributes to its teachers in the school by broadcasting the same message through a loudspeaker.

There are other and usually better ways of surmounting this difficulty. People will often read material on bulletin boards that they might ignore if placed in their agency mail slots. This is particularly true if the bulletin board also carries other information besides that which emanates from the "front office." Consequently, a notice placed on a bulletin board can score a greater impact than if it is sent individually to each organization member.

Another useful device is the organization publication or house organ. Such publications usually depend for their appeal on the reporting of a wide range of personal items within the organization. However, the adroit administrator will seek to sandwich in useful information regarding company policy, et cetera. Some private organizations have begun using in-house TV. They broadcast interviews with employees, both managerial and nonmanagerial, along with news of what the company is doing. Some of them also televise the company's annual stockholders' meeting.

Whatever the means used, the wise public manager will develop some techniques for checking up to see that the information he or she has sent has truly gotten through to those for whom it is intended. And the manager will check for feedback as to how they have responded. Not infrequently, the way in which a decision has been communicated will have a greater effect on agency operations than the substance of the decision itself.

Cross-Communication

A generation or so ago, lateral communication received relatively little attention from administrative thinkers. Now, it is becoming as important, and in some cases more important, than communication up and down. The growth of specialization and interdependency is making it increasingly vital for information to flow *through* the organization as well as to move up and down its ranks.

Staff meetings can be particularly helpful in stimulating cross-communication. This assumes, of course, that they are genuine interchanges of ideas and data and not just monologues by the person who presides. Within a broader context, interdepartmental committees may also aid the lateral communications process. And house organs, bulletin boards, and many of the other devices already cited can and usually do aid in spreading information from one section of the organization to another.

Physical arrangements can also play an important role in either helping or hampering cross-communication. Organizational units put in one building will tend to communicate more than when they are housed separately. Spreading them along the same corridor will usually encourage more communication than placing them on separate floors. And removing partitions that divide offices and work places from one another may greatly assist the cross-communication flow.

Organizational practices designed to resolve other problems may foster cross-communication as well. In-service training, for example, may bring people from various parts of the organization together and result in a good deal of cross-communication taking place. Organization-wide activities, such as bowling teams or hobby clubs, and an organizationally run cafeteria or dining room will also bring employees together and thus may lead to an interchange of information. Many of the tough problems that arise on Israeli kibbutzes are solved over the dining-room tables in the evening.

Rotation of employees is also useful in improving cross-communication. The rotated employee can give new co-workers a better understanding of how things operate "over there." More importantly, former relationships can be used to maintain some communication flow with his or her former work unit. In any case, he or she is likely to meet his ex-colleagues, from time to time and fill them in on what is happening at the new assignment.

As the technological society advances, and as organizations become more complex, cross-communication will become increasingly important. It is a subject that administrators will have to devote much more attention to in the future than they have in the past.

CASE STUDY

Action This Day[44]

Words always came easily to Winston Churchill. As a young man, he engaged in many daring exploits while serving as a lieutenant with the British forces in India and later in South Africa. But it was not so much the exploits themselves but his skill in writing about them that gained him the prominence that was to win him a seat in Parliament and launch his political career.

His bitter denunciations of Britain's appeasement policies during the 1930s acquired sharpness and thrust through the pungent language he so often employed. "These are the years when the locust has eaten" was one of the phrases he used to describe that sorry period. And when he served as prime minister during the war that ensued, he managed to warm the hearts and rally the spirits of his countrymen with the stirring speeches he delivered in what he called "England's darkest hour."

Churchill's abilities as a communicator also characterized his administration, and they offer an interesting illustration of how a particular administrator sought to handle his many communication problems at a crucial time.

From the outset of his administration, Churchill placed a heavy emphasis on the written word. "Let it be very clearly understood," he informed his war cabinet, "that all directions emanating from me are made in writing, or should be immediately afterwards confirmed in writing, and that I do not accept any responsibility for matters relating to national defense on which I am alleged to have given decisions unless they are recorded in writing."

The message itself indicates one of the main reasons he adopted such a policy. War administration is crisis administration, and as such can lead to considerable confusion. Orders given in a hurry and quickly passed down can easily be misunderstood, with dire results. Other orders that are vital may go unheeded or become lost in the far-flung and fast-moving governmental machinery. Churchill wanted none of that, and since he had no problem in handling the written word, he used this facility to keep intermediaries at a minimum and to stay in direct touch with a vast number of people.

Through the timesaving device of formal communication Churchill was thus able to direct personally much of Britain's governmental activity. He retained for himself the cabinet post of minister of defense, and there is no indication that wearing two hats in the cabinet impeded Britain's effort in any way. Indeed, most accounts of Britain's history during this time indicate that the country was better off with the prime minister playing such a dual role.

His extended use of personal memoranda, all of which carried the imprint of his personal style and bore his signature or initials, also had an invigorating impact on the whole government. An official several ranks below him might find on his desk a message from the prime minister himself directing him to do such and such. In the words of Cabinet Secretary Lord Normanbrook, such messages often had a "startling effect."

There was yet another reason for Churchill's heavy reliance on written communication. This was the discipline it imposed on him. He was less likely to get carried away by some whim of the moment if he made it a point never to give orders that were not confirmed in writing afterward.

Although the profuse stream of memoranda that issued from his office bore his distinct personal style, usually opening with the phrase "Pray tell me . . . ," they were by no means literary extravaganzas. He could be remarkably concise, as when he once ordered the mass production of a controversial new weapon. His memo read, "Sticky bombs—make one million—WSC." As he once noted, "It is sheer laziness not compressing information in a reasonable space."

Churchill also insisted that subordinates follow the same policy in dealing with him. He spent little time in interviewing people; instead, they were to address him in writing. All such correspondence was put into a box, and he would work on it at the beginning or the end of the day or at odd moments through the day. When any crisis erupted, he never had to cancel a lot of personal appointments.

He demanded that those who addressed him adhere to the rules of brevity as closely as he did himself. In 1941 he sent the following memo to the first lord of the admiralty: "Pray state this day, *on one side of a sheet of paper,* how the Royal Navy is being adapted to meet the conditions of modern warfare." (Emphasis added.) He was particularly hard on the needless use of banalities and truisms. He once replied to an official's memo by pointing out to the hapless fellow that his memo had employed every cliché in the English language except the British men's room admonition "Please adjust your dress before leaving."

None of this is meant to imply that Churchill disdained the use of the spoken word, rather that he reserved it for those times and occasions when it could be used most effectively. When Eisenhower was in London, Churchill made it a part of his regular schedule to lunch with him every Tuesday. As he said later, nothing but shop was ever discussed on these occasions. He encouraged spirited discussion in meetings, at least at the beginning of his administration, and urged anyone having a dissenting viewpoint to "Fight your corner." When one attendee once remarked, "I have tried to present my case fairly," Churchill growled at him, "That's a very dangerous thing to do."

Churchill made sure that he did not spend all his time talking to higher-ups. He kept his lines of communication continually open to those down below. As Robin Maugham writes, "Throughout the war, Churchill was always more interested in talking to junior officers than to the top brass—partly from pure kindness, partly from his knowledge that it was from the men in the field that he could discover what was really going on." Maugham, who served as a lieutenant in the tank corps during the war, mentions how Churchill asked him after the fall of France if he and his fellows were ready to repel a German invasion. When Maugham replied that many of their tanks could not move for want of a spring in their trackpins, Churchill exploded in fury and immediately set the whole British government into action. By nightfall, the springs had been delivered and were in place.

Despite the personal manner in which he conducted his administration, Churchill did not neglect the use of that traditional British device, the committee. As we saw in the preceding chapter, he would frequently set up one group to give him information on a subject and then establish another group to supply him with advice on what to do with the information. On a more informal level, he would often set up dinner parties or after-dinner gatherings with some of the best minds both within and without the government for stimulating, if sometimes rambling, conversation. This institution, which became known as the "Midnight Follies" because of Churchill's predilection for staying up into the wee hours of the morning, was the source of many of the ideas that enlivened his administration.

However, his communications style did present drawbacks. He would frequently try to handle too much and consequently many matters would go neglected. Things that did not interest him would tend to pile up, and the stack of paper in his box would remorselessly rise until his secretaries could cajole him into spending more time trying to whittle it down. His personality was such that it too easily dominated any meeting at which he presided, and toward the end of the war, when fatigue and possibly age were setting in, he showed himself less and less receptive to ideas from others within the coalition cabinet. The Labour party ministers began protesting that his cabinet meetings were becoming monologues.

Although he continued to remain more open to advice on the scientific and technical level, even here he became somewhat more remote as war weariness set in and, perhaps, as he became too infatuated with his own way of doing things. He listened too exclusively to his own science adviser, F. A. Lindeman (later Lord Cherwell), and failed to consult other scientists. As a result, he ordered, on the basis of Lindeman's faulty statistics, the rather fruitless and possibly even counterproductive saturation bombing raids on Germany.

Churchill's communications policy reflected his leadership policy and both reflected the man himself. As such, the question becomes one of judging whether his communications style suited the role he had to play at the time and in the circumstances in which he had to play it. On balance, the judgment of history seems to be that it did.

The Question of Secrecy

The practice of government always requires some degree of secrecy. Negotiations with another government would often prove difficult and even dangerous if conducted in the open glare of publicity. There is little doubt that the sensitive talks that finally brought the Vietnam war to a close would have soon collapsed had newsmen been invited to sit in on the negotiating sessions. Indeed, so important is secrecy to the conduct of foreign affairs that Alexis de Tocqueville claimed that no democracy would ever succeed in carrying out a foreign policy, because democracy, he reasoned, by its very nature must continually lay itself open to public view. While democracies have learned to conduct foreign relations, they have managed to do so only because they have learned to keep some things secret.

Sometimes it is necessary for a government not only to hide the truth from other governments but even from its own people. When Franklin Roosevelt sought to cover up the extent of the damage that the Japanese had inflicted in their raid on Pearl Harbor, he did so not just to mislead the Japanese but also the U.S. citizenry. If the country had realized how badly the Japanese had crippled our Pacific fleet, public morale would have fallen to a dangerous ebb.

Secrecy is also essential in many less spectacular functions of government. Few people would want to have their income tax records available for anyone to inspect. Few welfare clients would want to have their status easily ascertainable by any neighbor who might choose to check on them. Adoption agencies require a great deal of personal data from a couple seeking to adopt; making these data available to all would doubtless deter many couples from making such a move. And a police department that allowed complete access to its files would not only imperil many of its investigations but would also jeopardize the rights and damage the reputations of many innocent people.

The need for secrecy also makes itself felt in the university. A committee on academic standing would probably need to have a student's psychiatric history and other personal data before it could make an intelligent and humane judgment on whether to suspend him. If, for example, he had a bad record but was currently undergoing psychotherapy, this would undoubtedly temper their action. However, to allow such information to become general knowledge on the campus would obviously be unjust to the student. In a possibly parallel problem, New Jersey teachers fought for two years to prevent the state from releasing the results of statewide reading tests. The teachers, along with other opponents, argued that making such data public would put counterproductive pressures on teachers and damage the self-image and possibly the future achievements of pupils in the schools whose students performed less well. Many also claimed that the tests were culturally biased. However, others contended that the public is entitled to know how well the schools are performing and that the reading tests provide a measure of accountability.[45]

Thus, no government and few organizations, no matter how democratic they may be, can hope to dispense completely with secrecy. Some covert elements find their way into most agencies and most administrations. Few administrators may wish to go as far as Frederick the Great when he said that if his coat knew of his plans, he would burn it. But most administrators at one time or another have felt compelled not to reveal all they know.

Yet, secrecy imposes a heavy price and presents an obvious peril to the practice of administration. "Everything secret degenerates," observed Lord Acton, and he added, "Nothing is safe that does not show it can bear discrimination and publicity."[46] His more recent countryman C. P. Snow put it even more forcibly. "The results of closed politics can run precisely contrary to the results of open politics," he said.[47]

What are some of the dangers and difficulties that secrecy presents? To quote C. P. Snow again, "The most obvious fact which hits you in the eye is that personalities and personal relations carry a weight of responsibility which is out of proportion greater than any they carry in open politics. Despite appearances, we are much nearer in ordinary government to personal power and personal choice."[48] Secret government therefore tends to become government by whim and caprice. Accountability withers away and objectivity also shrinks. Favoritism, discrimination, and arbitrariness flourish in an environment of secrecy.

Secrecy creates inequalities that did not previously exist and exacerbates those that did. Those who are "in the know" tend to develop an arrogance and contempt for those who are not. Even when they manage to avoid such feelings, they still become sealed off from those who are excluded from the charmed circle of insiders. Secrecy obviously reduces communication and leaves decision makers, even when they possess the best will in the world, with diminished capacity to make the best decisions.

Richard Neustadt has pointed out how the secrecy that World War II imposed on much of Franklin Roosevelt's activity severely curbed its effectiveness. He could no longer assign the same projects to more than one person or group of people and thereby obtain more than one point of view before making a decision. He could no longer dispatch troubleshooters, observers, and assistants wherever and whenever he wanted. And he could not utilize the knowledge and the opinions of outsiders in the way he liked to, for now such outsiders simply would not know enough to be of maximum helpfulness.[49]

In limiting decision making to a relatively few insiders, secrecy tends to limit discussion and debate. Frequently, the decision is made by those who are too personally involved and have too much at stake. Morton H. Halperin of the Brookings Institute and Jeremy J. Stone of the American Federation of Scientists found this to be true in a study they undertook of the Central Intelligence Agency. The supersecret atmosphere tends to limit participation in covert decisions to those who support them and earn their living from them, they said. "The lack of vigorous dissent, so common in other proposals of a controversial nature, tends to lead to routine approval."[50]

The effect of secret knowledge can also prove injurious to those who possess it, even to the point of disturbing their mental balance. "It takes a very strong head to keep secrets for years and not go slightly mad," says Snow. And he adds, "it isn't wise to be advised by anyone who is slightly mad."[51]

Finally, trying to keep a matter hidden may only result in its becoming better known. Secrecy sows suspicion; the more secret any activity is, the more interest the press and the public will show in trying to find out about it. It then becomes too easy and too tempting for a disgruntled participant or employee not to reveal covertly what the covert operation is all about. Some do not have to be disgruntled to leak out the knowledge. They may just want to enjoy the sense of power that revealing important information can provide.

History affords no shortage of examples to illustrate all the many problems and pitfalls that secrecy engenders. The Watergate affair, in all its many ramifications, provides a graphic illustration of most of them. However, the same difficulties posed by secrecy can also be seen in previous presidential administrations, although usually in considerably diminished form. The abortive invasion of Cuba during the early months of President Kennedy's administration owes its failure, at least in part, to the veil of secrecy in which the venture was enshrouded. The *New York Times* and the *New Republic* both learned of the event beforehand, but both publications decided out of a misguided sense of patriotism not to disclose their information. Afterward, President Kennedy told them that they would have done both him and the country a tremendous service if they had.

Secrecy and U.S. Administration

U.S. administrators can take comfort in the fact that secrecy clamps far fewer restraints on them than it does on their colleagues abroad. In Britain, for example, a postal clerk who once wrote a letter to his local newspaper complaining of the postal service's shortage of help ran afoul of his country's strict and strictly enforced Official Secrets Act. And in West Germany the police once roused the editor of one of the country's leading magazines, *Der Spiegel*, out of bed at three in the morning and placed him under arrest for having published a report unfavorable to the German army. (The report showed that in some recent NATO maneuvers, the West German forces had received NATO's worst performance rating).

But if Americans can feel themselves fortunate in enjoying a much freer flow of information than their European counterparts, this should not blind them to the fact that secrecy still poses problems here as elsewhere. This became painfully apparent in the early 1970s, when the controversy over the Pentagon Papers and other information concerning the Vietnam war cast the whole problem of secrecy into bold relief.

Among the many incidents indicating abuse of administrative secrecy that came to light in this period were the following:

• The General Services Administration had refused to allow public disclosure of the rent it was paying to lease office space in a privately owned building.

• The Justice Department had withheld a report on expense-paid trips to shooting matches by border-patrol inspectors.

• The State Department refused to allow news reporters to see gifts that foreign governments had given certain federal officials on grounds that the gifts were stored in a "classified building."

• The Forest Service refused to release the names of persons who had been granted permits to graze cattle in a national forest.

• The Civil Service Commission declined to divulge the results of an investigation it had conducted into alleged irregularities of an examination for rural mail carriers.

• The Department of Health, Education and Welfare had clamped a tight lid of secrecy on a report that listed studies of human-reproduction problems.[52]

It was the Defense Department, however, that became the greatest target for those attacking alleged abuses of administrative secrecy. The air force was accused of having put the stamp of secrecy on pictures of the interiors of transport planes because it did not want the public to see the plush lounges that had been installed for the comfort of traveling military officials. The navy still had a secrecy stamp on a report of attacks made by sharks on seamen in New York Harbor in 1916. The navy also had classified as secret a series of published newspaper articles until a red-faced official issued an order saying that newspaper clippings should no longer be considered secret. When one of the joint chiefs wrote a note to the others suggesting less use of the secrecy stamp, his note was stamped TOP SECRET. According to William G. Florence, who retired in 1971 as a security-classification expert, only .5 percent of the Pentagon's twenty million classified documents truly merited being shielded from public inspection.

In many cases, the use of secrecy was found not only to be excessive but inconsistent. Thus, while the Washington Zoo in 1960 was proudly exhibiting a monkey that had a sign on its cage saying that the animal had flown in space, the State Department was withholding all news that a monkey had ever been sent up in a space capsule.[53] In 1965 Dean Rusk gave a talk before a group of high school students outlining his views of the Vietnam conflict. The next day, he sent a memo on the same subject to the president. Although he labeled his memo EYES ONLY, meaning that it was strictly to be read by the president himself and no one else, the message, according to reporter David Halberstam, contained "word for word" the exact presentation he had made the previous day to the high school students.

Faced with a rising clamor of concern over secrecy excesses in the federal bureaucracy, President Nixon moved in 1972 to ease access to public documents. In an executive order that went into effect on June 1 of that year, the president stipulated that papers labeled CONFIDENTIAL must be opened to the public after six years; papers bearing the imprint SECRET must be released after eight years, and documents carrying the TOP SECRET stamp could not be kept secret more than ten years.[54]

His order provided for some exemptions but permitted anyone to challenge them. The burden of proof for keeping any document secret would then fall on the government. This marked a reversal of previous policy, which had left to the applicant the task of showing why it should be made public. Furthermore, the number of federal officials allowed to wield secrecy stamps was reduced by more than two-thirds, from fifty-five thousand to eighteen thousand, with only a little over one thousand having the power to assign the top-secret rating.

The enactment of the Privacy Act in 1974, along with the passage of some amendments to the Freedom of Information Act that same year, opened the gates still wider. Long-bottled-up information concerning such controversial cases as those of Alger Hiss and the Rosenbergs came pouring out. Internal staff memoranda and other materials were now readily obtainable if they had been used as a basis for an agency's decisions.

Like so many reforms, the Freedom of Information Act has proved a mixed blessing. It has certainly helped clarify many critical issues and has shed light on the workings of the federal government. In some cases this light has illuminated important imperfections, as when the data released on the John F. Kennedy and Martin Luther King assassinations showed much sloppy investigative work. In other cases it has helped vindicate government agencies. Many people, for example, long believed that the FBI framed Julius and Ethel Rosenberg, a couple who were convicted and executed in 1952 for allegedly giving atomic secrets to the Russians. The release of their dossiers showed that Julius, at least, was almost certainly guilty.

But most requests for information under the F.O.I.A. do not come from crusaders or scholars. Nearly three out of four requests originate from business or law firms. Convicted or accused criminals constitute another large source for requests, and one imprisoned felon has admitted using the information thus obtained to have an informant killed.

Opening up the informational floodgates has proven costly as well. In 1974 the FBI had only 8 people working on such requests; by the end of the decade the number has grown to 305. By 1980 the total costs to the federal government of processing requests for information under the act were approaching $50 million.[55]

Beyond and above the inconveniences, costs and possible abuses stem-
ming from the F.O.I.A.'s liberalized provisions, there remains the tough
problems of individual privacy and public security. As an example of the
first problems, take the case of Edward Michaels, a retired caretaker from
Northlake, Illinois. He arose from the dinner table in the spring of 1968
and announced to his family that he was going for a walk. He was never
heard from again.

Seven years later his wife asked a court to declare him dead so that she
could collect his back Social Security payments. The court moved to do
so but the Social Security Administration proved less obliging. They said
that Mr. Michaels was still alive. However, they refused to disclose the
whereabouts of the runaway husband, citing an HEW rule forbidding
anyone from looking into anyone else's personal file. Mrs. Michaels thus
could neither obtain the Social Security payments nor the information she
needed to secure separate support.

To take another and quite different example, early in 1977 the *Washington Post* revealed that the CIA had been making yearly payments of $1
million or more to Jordan's King Hussein. The disclosure aroused a good
deal of acrimony and even alarm. Some noted that Hussein had been a
moderating and somewhat pro-Western force in Mideast politics. Divulging these payments would weaken his position, they claimed, and increase general tensions in that already highly tense area. Others, however, maintained that the CIA had no right to spend the money of the
American people for such purposes without informing them about it.

Columnist Tom Wicker defended the *Post*'s disclosure, saying that "a
newspaper's obligation under the First Amendment is not to the success of
a diplomatic mission but to the knowledge of the American people."[56] But
Harvard Law School Professor Donald F. Turner took issue with this assertion. Said Turner, "The interests of the 'people' and the 'Government'
are not wholly antagonistic in these matters. The 'people' have a strong
interest in their government's ability to conduct successful diplomacy and

intelligence gathering, and *some* secrecy, in *some* particulars, for *some* period of time is often essential to those tasks."[57]

Soon after taking office, President Reagan moved to tighten up the act's operational procedures. By means of an executive order the president set up three new categories under which information could be classified as secret. Even some information now available to the public could be restored to secrecy if it had not actually become public. Historians and other scholars promptly complained that the new restrictions would greatly limit their access to government documents and thereby hamper their research.

The problem is scarcely new. De Tocqueville felt that a democracy would find it impossible to carry on a successful foreign policy because it could not conduct its affairs in secret. Since his time, democracies have managed to keep some foreign and domestic matters under wraps. But the price for doing so has been an ongoing and at times onerous dispute over the public's right to know, and its government's right to say no.

Notes

1. Chester I. Barnard, *The Functions of the Executive* (Cambridge, Mass.: Harvard University Press, 1968), 89.

2. Herbert A. Simon, *Administrative Behavior* (New York: Free Press, 1957), 154.

3. Charles Redfield, *Communication in Management* (Chicago: University of Chicago Press, 1953), 7.

4. William L. Shirer, *The Collapse of the Third Republic* (New York: Simon & Schuster, 1969), chaps. 27, 28, and 29.

5. Ludwig C. Moyzisch, *Operation Cicero* (New York: Coward-McCann, 1950).

6. Edward Crankshaw, ed., *Khrushchev Remembers* (Boston: Little, Brown, 1970).

7. Joseph M. Jordan, *Theory Y: An Urgent Need* (unpublished paper, Department of Political Science, Northeastern University, 1972).

8. William J. Lederer and Don D. Jackson, *The Mirages of Marriage* (New York: W. W. Norton, 1968), chap. 42.

9. Harold Nicolson, *Peacemaking 1919* (New York: Harcourt, Brace, 1939).

10. James MacGregor Burns, *Roosevelt: Soldier of Freedom* (New York: Harcourt Brace Jovanovich, 1970).

11. *New York Times*, 20 February 1973.

12. David Halberstam, *The Best and the Brightest* (New York: Random House, 1969), 215.

13. Frederick V. Malek, "Executive in Washington," *Harvard Business Review* (September–October 1972).

14. *Boston Record-American,* 19 November 1972.

15. *Newsweek,* 10 May 1971, 30.

16. *Public Administration Times,* 15 January 1981.

17. Harold Macmillan, *The Blast of War 1939–1945* (New York: Harper & Row, 1968).

18. Halberstam, *Best and Brightest,* 432.

19. J. C. Masterman, *The Double Cross Game* (New York: Avon Books, 1972), 55.

20. *Detroit Free Press,* 28 September 1967.

21. *Time,* 18 June 1973, p. 67.

22. *Boston Herald-American,* 9 May 1972.

23. Marvin H. Swift, "Clear Writing Means Clear Thinking Means . . . ," *Harvard Business Review* (January–February 1973).

24. *Atlantic* (December 1967), 40.

25. *New York Times,* 6 February 1968.

26. Robert Townsend, "Up the Organization," *Harper's Magazine* (March 1970).

27. C. Northcote Parkinson, *The Law and the Profits* (New York: Ballantine Books, 1971), 181.

28. *Time,* 7 February 1972, 57.

29. Martin R. Smith, *I Hate to See a Manager Cry* (Reading, Mass.: Addison-Wesley, 1973), 26.

30. Don E. Jones, "The Employee Handbook," *Personnel* (February 1973).

31. Burke Davis, *Gray Fox* (New York: Rinehart, 1956), 80–81.

32. Peter F. Drucker, *The Effective Executive* (New York: Harper & Row, 1967), 44.

33. Halberstam, *Best and Brightest,* 534.

34. Drucker, *Effective Executive,* 39.

35. John Lindsay, *The City* (New York: W. W. Norton, 1969), 89.

36. George E. Reedy, "What the White House Does to Presidents," *Boston Sunday Globe Magazine,* 4 April 1970.

37. Albert Camus, *L'homme révolté* (Paris: Editions Gallimard, 1951), 340.

38. Chester I. Barnard, *Organization and Management* (Cambridge, Mass.: Harvard University Press, 1948), chap. 9, especially footnote on p. 231.

39. Daniel Katz and Robert L. Kahn, *The Social Psychology of Organizations* (New York: John Wiley, 1966), 245–246.

40. *Time,* 13 December 1979.

41. Townsend Hoopes, *The Limits of Intervention* (New York: David McKay, 1969), 218.

42. Morris J. Blackman, "The Stupidity of Intelligence," in Charles Peters and Timothy J. Adams, eds., *Inside the System* (New York: Praeger Publishers, 1970).

43. Fred Powledge, "Can Kretchmer Make a Clean Sweep?" *New York Times,* 22 March 1971.

44. Material for this case was largely drawn from Sir John Wheeler-Bennett, ed., *Action This Day: Working with Churchill, Memoirs of Lord Normanbrook and Others,* (New York: St. Martin's Press, 1969). The quotation of Robin Maugham is from his *Escape from the Shadows* (New York: McGraw-Hill, 1973), 108–109.

45. *New York Times*, 7 April 1974.

46. Quoted in George E. Berkley, *The Democratic Policeman* (Boston: Beacon Press, 1969), 159.

47. C. P. Snow, *Science and Government* (New York: New American Library, 1962), 37.

48. Ibid., 53.

49. Richard E. Neustadt, "Approaches to Staffing the Presidency: Notes on FDR and JFK," *American Political Science Review* 57 (December 1963).

50. *New York Times*, 20 May 1971.

51. Snow, *Science and Government*, 65.

52. *Time*, 5 July 1971, 14.

53. *New York Times*, 9 April 1973 (speech by Edmund C. Muskie).

54. Richard Halloran, "The Word Now Is: 'Easier on the Stamp,'" *New York Times*, 12 March 1972 News in Review section. Also see editorial "Crack in the Secrecy Wall" in the same edition.

55. Allen Weinstein, "Open Season on Open Government," *New York Times Magazine*, 10 June 1979. Also see a symposium on the subject in *Public Administration Review* (July–August 1979).

56. *New York Times*, 27 February 1977.

57. *New York Times*, 12 March 1972, Letters to the Editor section.

8

Budgeting

Many students of public administration shudder when the course turns to the subject of budgeting. They tend to regard the budget as merely a ponderous tome of dreary figures and to view the process of budgeting as simply a tedious and humdrum chore that lacks all the human interaction that makes things like personnel and leadership so much more palatable. In responding in such a way, they could not be more wrong.

Most, although certainly not all, of the issues and conflicts that spring from the administrative process take the form of contests over monetary allocations. If politics is sometimes defined as the process of deciding who gets what, administrative politics often becomes the process of deciding who gets what amount of money. Consequently, whether one department or individual is to be favored over another or whether one program or policy is to be supported over another usually becomes translated into a budgetary decision. In this way, budgets are not just political documents *in addition* to being other things as well; budgets are political documents *before* they are other things as well.

This does not mean that deciphering budgets is an easy task. If budgets are essentially political documents, the politics is often veiled. To the untrained eye, a budget often conceals much more than it reveals. Expertise in cloaking some of the political aspects in a budget has advanced more than one administrator's career, while skill in figuring out what was being

done has helped more than one politician's status. The late Senator Richard Russell of Georgia became one of the most influential men in the
United States Senate—he was the senator to whom Lyndon Johnson most
listened and deferred when Johnson was Senate majority leader—in part
because of his ability to read a budget. As one Johnson aide once said,
Russell "could glance at a Defense Department budget request that is
sixty pages long and in 30 seconds could pick up the tricks."[1]

It is not enough, however, to call attention to the political aspects of
budgeting in order to define just what budgeting is. Budgets are also instruments of coordination, control, and planning. They thus govern nearly
all aspects of administration and confer a great deal of power on those
who prepare them. In New York City, the post of budget director is considered the most influential nonelective position in the city government.
In Washington, President Nixon transformed the Bureau of the Budget
into the Office of Management and Budget, thus giving the budget agency
extensive formal power over the entire federal bureaucracy.[2] And in Great
Britain and Canada, the Treasury Department, which makes up the budgets in these countries, has traditionally exercised many managerial functions as well. Indeed, the prime minister of Great Britain was long known
as the first lord of the treasury.

The fiscal crisis currently confronting nearly all governments both in
the United States and abroad has only magnified the role of the budget
along with the roles of those who shape it. Worries and wrangles over the
federal budget dominated the headlines during the Reagan administration's first two years in office, while a survey conducted by the Council of
State Governments as 1982 approached showed state leaders placing the
budget at the top of their list of priorities for the coming year.[3] And in
North Carolina a survey of that state's Human Services Managers released
at about the same time found them spending as much time on "Budget
Management" as on "Staff Supervision and Development."[4]

As for the fledgling administrator, he or she will frequently find that a
term of service in an organization's budgetary branch will furnish knowledge and insights that can be obtained from few of the organization's
other subunits. And if an administrator does start out in a line department
or on another staff unit, he will usually discover that budget preparation
constitutes one of the unit's most important survival activities, sometimes
overriding in care and concern the unit's main focus of operation. As long
as resources continue to be relatively scarce in terms of what any organizational unit wishes to do, the budgetary process will continue to cast a
long shadow over administrative activity.

The first director of the federal government's Bureau of the Budget described his bureau's work as merely shoveling coal in the stokehouse of
the ship of state. Today, it is apparent that those who draw up the budget
have their hands to the tiller as well.

Traditional Budgeting

As might be expected, traditional budgeting is a lengthy process. It usually begins with comparatively small subunits figuring out what they need or feel they need for the coming year and submitting these figures as requests to higher levels. At each stage, the figures are customarily reviewed and frequently reduced. Eventually, all the requests will converge in the organization's budgetary office or in the office of its chief executive or both.

From the organization, the figures travel to the government's overall budgetary department, which in the federal bureaucracy is the Office of Management and Budget. There they are once again reviewed and often reshaped. The tendency here, as at previous review stages, is to cut down rather than to expand the requested amounts. Often, the agency heads and the budgeting office officials find themselves in adversary positions. The former stoutly maintain that they need all the money they are requesting and even more, while the latter keep insisting that they are overstating their organization's needs and inflating its role.

After fashioning an overall spending blueprint, the budgetary office and the chief executive submit it to the legislative body. Here it will almost always be initially assigned to one or more committees before being adopted by the body as a whole. And here, as previously, the tendency will be to pare down the proposed sums. If the legislative body consists of two chambers, as does the Congress of the United States and all but one of the country's state legislatures, the process may have to be repeated a second time before a final budget becomes enacted.

With some exceptions, budgets in this country cover only one year, which makes the budgeting process an annual one. However, preparation for the budget may begin, as it does in the federal government, well over two years prior to the period that it is designed to cover. Thus, a president inaugurated in January will find that the spending policies of his administration are already committed for the most part for the forthcoming eighteen months. (The federal government's budget, it should be pointed out, does not coincide with the calendar year; rather, it runs from October 1 to September 30, which forms the fiscal year. Many states and municipalities use the same system.)

Capital Budgets

Most of America's approximately eighty-thousand governments divide their budgets into two sections, one for capital projects, the other for expenses. Often they are considered as two separate budgets.

The rationale for segregating capital expenditures in a separate budget is that such projects usually entail a considerable expenditure that may occur only once in a generation or even once in several generations. Trying to cover the expenditure involved in one year would be troublesome and often impossible. A small community faced with building a new high school could bankrupt many of its citizens if it sought to pay for the cost through one year's collection of taxes. Capital budgeting enables the community to break out of the one-year budget cycle and spread the cost over many years. Since such projects are usually financed from the sale of bonds that are to be paid over twenty, thirty, or even forty years, placing such expenditures outside the annual expense budget makes a good deal of sense.

Another aspect of capital improvements also warrants spreading out their costs. Capital projects confer benefits for extended periods of time. Modern-day Rome, for example, is still using some of the sewers built in the time of the Caesars. Consequently, it is only equitable that those who will subsequently benefit from the expenditures should shoulder part of the burden. A capital budget permits them to do so.

Because capital projects do not involve immediate expenditures—usually they do not get launched until a year or two after they are authorized—there is a tendency to utilize them in political ways. Some state legislatures have been known to pass bloated capital budgets as a way of appeasing their constituencies without imposing any new immediate tax burdens. Legislators can return to their district boasting about how they have wangled a new road, dredging project, et cetera, for their constituents while escaping the onus of having voted for new taxes. Of course, eventually new funds will be required to pay off the debts incurred for the approved capital expenditure. But for the present at least, the lawmakers are "home free."

A more flagrant abuse of the capital budget occurs when political leaders cram into it items that properly belong in the expense budget. In doing so they manage to avoid cutting expenditures or raising taxes. However, in taking such a step they are paying for current expenses with borrowed money, money that must eventually be paid back with interest. Consequently such an expedient only defers and compounds the problem. New York City was using nearly a quarter of its capital budget to pay such operating expenses as policemen's salaries when it went broke in 1975. A few years later, Cleveland, also confronted with collapse, was starting to do the same.[5]

But if capital budgeting can lead to political abuses, its absence may produce even worse consequences. The federal government does not make use of capital budgets, and in some respects there seems to be no compelling reason why it should. Unlike states, municipalities, and other governments, federal agencies are rarely faced with one-shot expenditures that would completely disrupt their budget cycles. They are so large that capital projects of one kind or another are a continual activity. Furthermore, the federal government, because it controls the money supply, is not compelled to float bonds to finance its projects.

Nevertheless, the failure of the federal bureaucracy to use capital budgeting has drawn the fire of many critics in recent years. They claim that the lack of a capital budget has promulgated or aggravated an assortment of ills.

For one thing, the absence of a capital budget at the federal level means an absence of systematic review procedures to establish the economic desirability of capital projects. To put it more simply, capital projects are made too haphazardly. Many accounting practices do not properly consider the total and unit costs. Useful and accurate estimates of the cost savings that a capital expenditure may produce are difficult to come by.

Furthermore, despite the fact that the federal government is constantly making capital expenditures, the refusal to segregate them in a separate account may, and often does, make any particular agency head, division chief, or branch manager more reluctant to initiate such expenditures. Such outlays will simply bulk too large in a current all-in-one budget and thus make the administrator look like a heavy spender. If those who review the budget approve a substantial capital project, they may cut back in other areas as partial compensation. Furthermore, in terms of his or her own career, the administrator may not be around to take credit for the economies that such capital expenditures may eventually yield. As a result, an administrator will often feel inclined to let his or her successor set up the new computer system or purchase the new maintenance equipment.

According to Senator William Proxmire, the lack of a capital budget at the federal level has induced government agencies to resort to various stratagems. These include hidden subsidies to sponsor various programs, many of which are, in themselves, quite deserving of public support. He cites as an example several of the federal government's housing programs. Backers of such programs, says Proxmire, devised an array of tax, credit, and other subsidies to escape the fiscal and political impact of putting such items in a one-year budget. "As a consequence, the ultimate costs of the program skyrocketed in order to preserve a small annual cost. In this way costs rose while control over the program was lost."[6]

To sum up, capital budgeting, as a device to be used within the framework of traditional budgeting, makes a good deal of sense for most state and local governments. It might also prove useful for the federal government as well. It does, however, lend itself to certain manipulations and machinations that have proved costly to some states and municipalities. But then the expense budget is even more prone to the playing of political games, as we shall see.

Expense Budgets

The basic document in traditional budgeting is the expense budget. This details the operational expenditures for the coming year. Like the capital budget, it is an array of items to be purchased and the prices to be paid. The items include manpower as well as heat, electricity, and less tangible purchases. Nearly all the basic objects of expenditure are customarily covered and set down clearly in page after page of neat rows.

Usually, some attempt is made at categorizing the various objects of expenditure. There may be one account for permanent personnel, another for temporary personnel, a third for consultants, and so forth. And within each of these categories there will most likely be subcategories. Thus, there may be one or more rows in the permanent personnel account listing the number of employees needed for each job classification and the total amount of expenditure they represent.

The traditional line-item budget is often highly detailed. It frequently provides the viewer with precise data on where every dollar is being spent. Yet, at the same time, such budgets tend to reflect and reinforce the organizational pathologies that we noted in chapter 3.

The basic problem of traditional line-item budgets is that they fail to show what the money is being used for in terms of *programs*. The Public Works Department budget may specify the amount of machinery on hand and what will be needed to keep it in repair, as well as any new machines that may be purchased. It may tell us how many employees will be used to operate the machinery and how much they will be paid. And it may indicate how many temporary employees may be hired and how much private equipment may be rented to cover specialized tasks or emergencies. But it will not tell us, for instance, just how many miles of streets all this expenditure is designed to tar or pave and whether tarring a street is cheaper than paving it and, if so, how much cheaper.

Because of this lack of program information, the line-item budget lends itself to stagnation. Possessing little information as to the costs and effectiveness of its various activities, the organization tends to base its budget requests on simply what it has used in the past. Last year's appropriation becomes the basis for this year's requests. Outmoded programs are not phased out and new programs are not eagerly embraced. By failing to provide program information, line-item budgeting tends to perpetuate the status quo.

The Defense Department budget during the 1950s offers a vivid illustration of how the stagnation factor enters into traditional budgeting. Dur-

ing the eight years of the Eisenhower administration, the proportion of
defense funds going to the three military services remained almost constant. The air force received around 47 percent of the department's appropriation, the navy received about 29 percent, and the army approximately
22 percent. Slight changes occurred from year to year, but essentially the
proportions at the end of the decade did not appreciably differ from those
at the beginning. Yet, during this time, great changes took place in defense technology, changes that, so it would seem, should have forced
some substantial reallocations of the department's budget.

The status-quo-reinforcing effect of traditional line-item budgeting—
often referred to as *incremental budgeting*, because it concerns itself with
increments of change rather than program change—can influence whole
governments. Ira Sharkansky attributes to incremental budgeting the fact
that the relative spending positions of the American states have remained
basically the same since the turn of the century. Despite the fact that
many states have experienced startling growth and change while others
have suffered relative decline, those that were the big spenders in 1903
are still at the top of the spending list today. Incremental budgeting,
claims Sharkansky, tends to lead to static governmental expenditure
policies.[7]

The term *incremental*, however, does imply some change—change that
will occur in terms of spending more or less rather than in terms of spending money for different purposes and programs. Nevertheless, it should
be noted that incremental changes tend to go in just one direction. They
almost invariably take the form of more rather than less.

There are many reasons for this, some of them perfectly legitimate as
far as administration is concerned. Population tends to grow, hence requiring more expenditures to serve more people. Furthermore, price levels have also shown a pronounced predilection for going up, particularly
in the inflation that has characterized most societies since World War II.
Then, people seem to expect more and more from government. And increasing prosperity itself takes its toll. The more cars we have, the more
highways, parking lots, traffic police, et cetera, we will need.

However, there are other factors inherent in the incremental budgeting
process that tend to push expenditures to ever-higher plateaus. For one
thing, there is little inducement to the administrator to save money. On
the contrary, traditional line-item budgeting tends to punish the parsimonious public manager. If he or she cuts costs and comes up with a surplus at the end of the fiscal year, then his or her overseers, such as hierarchical superiors and particularly members of the legislative committee
that approves the budget, will decide that he or she did not need all that
money in the first place. Instead of receiving a medal, the public manager
will most likely be given a cut in appropriations the following year.

Matthew Dumont, a psychiatrist who once served in the Department of

Health, Education and Welfare, provides a pertinent and rather pointed analogy to describe how stupid it would be for an agency head to return unspent money that Congress had appropriated for his agency. "It would be like a bum asking for a handout for a cup of coffee. A passerby offers a quarter and the bum returns 15 cents, saying 'coffee is only a dime, schmuck.' "[8]

In the days when the federal fiscal year ended on June 30, Washington bureaucrats used to speak of the "spring spending spree." This term denoted the desperate haste with which federal agencies went about spending or committing whatever funds remained in their accounts as the fiscal year drew to a close. One chief of naval operations even dispatched telegrams to his commanders urging them to proceed with full speed ahead in meeting their "outlay targets" for the current fiscal year in order to avoid "reluctant adverse effects" on next year's appropriations.[9]

Changing the federal fiscal year to October 1 to September 30 only transformed the spring spending spree into a late-summer one. And efforts to curb this practice by requiring all agencies to report their unexpended balances every three months proved unsuccessful. During one summer, for example, a conservation camp operated by the U.S. Fish and Wildlife Service purchased over one thousand pairs of protective leg coverings and nearly thirty-eight hundred pairs of gloves for its 136 enrollees. As one budget watcher once remarked, "the political process abhors a surplus."

Incremental budgeting not only provides an administrator with few inducements to cut costs, it actually adds to the pressures to increase costs (i.e., to ask for money). Thomas J. Anton points out that an administrator must try to appease three separate "audiences."[10] One of these is his or her own employees, who look to the administrator to preserve and, if possible, enhance their working conditions and their status. Such considerations can be met by increasing the organization's appropriation. Then, there is the agency's clientele group. They also desire increased funds for the agency, since they are usually the most direct beneficiaries of the agency's expenditures. These two pressures for budgeting increases would probably exist under any form of budgeting. Then there is the third audience. These are the review officials, including hierarchical superiors, budget bureau officials, and legislators. All of these, but particularly the latter, have an interest in being able to cut the budget. In making cuts they achieve a sense of fulfillment and importance.

All these factors translate into a simple process that characterizes budgeting throughout the U.S. political system. Agency heads greatly inflate their appropriations requests; review officials continually pare them down. The agency is more often than not allowed some additional funding, however.

Many administrators have become quite adroit in procuring increased allocations. They will usually ask for money for one of their more popular activities regardless of whether or not all or even part of the new funds will actually be targeted for that purpose. They may latch on to a popular cause or concept and say they need the money to do something more or something new in response to it. Or they may ask to undertake a new activity and seek only limited funds to get started. This is known as the "foot in the door" approach. However, once launched, the new enterprise tends to cost more and more.

The Department of Defense has made frequent use of the "foot in the door" approach. It will set down a low initial cost to get a program started, and Congress will often grant the money without fully realizing what the final bill will be. Another related device employed by the Defense Department has been the creation of shortages. The department will overextend its commitments and then urgently plead for more money. Thus, the army will set up a goal of so many divisions and then bemoan the fact that it lacks the funds to maintain them. "The worst thing you can do to a service," one observer once noted, "is to take away its shortages."[11]

Similar stratagems are employed by other organizations as well. Universities are by no means exempt. As Katz and Kahn have pointed out, an academic department may ask to teach new courses, claiming it can do so with existing personnel. It may be perfectly sincere, but as its work volume expands, it finds itself asking for additional funds.[12]

All these pressures and policies converge to force the level of spending to ever-higher levels. In his study of budgeting in the state government of Illinois, Anton compares the budget document "to a huge mountain which is constantly being pushed higher and higher by geologic convulsions." He describes the governor as a blindfolded man "seeking to reduce the height of the mountain by dislodging pebbles with a teaspoon."[13]

Of course, elective officials are not completely powerless in this situation. Except for "earmarked" funds that have to be allocated and spent because of constitutional restrictions, prior commitments, et cetera, they can wield the scalpel as deeply as they wish. However, in addition to various outside political pressures—such as the agency's clientele group—many other considerations may stay their hand, for budget cutting can be a hazardous game.

The problem once again is related to the lack of program direction and content in the traditional line-item budget. As a result, a budget cut can be translated into various forms. And sometimes it can end up actually increasing costs.

A line-item budget will generally include categories for personnel, equipment, and maintenance, among others. An administrator confronted with a general slash in funds will often cut maintenance costs first and personnel costs last. The reasons are fairly obvious. In the short run, reductions in maintenance disrupt an agency's operations the least. Reductions in personnel are apt to disrupt operations the most, particularly when the morale of those remaining on the job is taken into account. Unfortunately, equipment and buildings not properly maintained eventually increase an agency's costs over what would otherwise be the case.

A startling and a saddening event in the summer of 1980 finally stirred up some public awareness of this pernicious practice. A desperate effort by President Carter to free some fifty American hostages came to grief on the sands of Iran when three of the eight helicopters assigned to the task force broke down. Although many other factors figured into the mission's failure, the inability of nearly half of its helicopters to function showed that the military had been concentrating too much money and attention on buying new weaponry and too little on maintaining what it already had.

To be sure, administrators will sometimes respond to a budget cut by actually phasing out whole programs or dismissing personnel. All too often this is done for the express purpose of generating pressure for their restoration. For example, when a new administration in one major U.S. city attempted, as part of a needed austerity program, to cut the budget of its main library, the library's director announced that he would be forced to close the library building two evenings a week and on Saturdays. As it so happens, Saturdays and evening hours were the most popular periods of library use. (During the morning hours, the library actually had more staff than readers on its premises.) The public outcry that ensued from the library director's announcement forced the mayor to temper this proposed cutback in funds.[14]

As budget constraints began to beleaguer most U.S. cities in the early 1980s, some of them responded by first making often unnecessarily deep cuts in their police and fire departments. These, of course, are among the most essential of city services, and such cuts were apparently made with the hope of generating support for increased funding from an alarmed public.

In addition to promoting static though swollen administration, incremental budgeting has also been criticized for many other ills. Although its numerous details or expenditures would seem to make it a good vehicle for public scrutiny, the reverse may be the case. Indeed, the more detailed the data on objects of expenditure are, the more they may obscure. Large, bulky documents filled with page after page containing row after row of expenditure items may reveal very little of what an agency is doing and how well it is doing it. Appropriations for any one activity may be scattered throughout the budget and be almost impossible to piece together. Foreign military assistance was thought to be costing the United

States about one-half billion dollars a year at the beginning of the current decade. It took an exhaustive study by Senator Proxmire's Subcommittee on Economy and Government to bring out the fact that such assistance was actually amounting to three or four billion a year.[15]

The stratagems administrators often have to employ in working with incremental budgets do little to enhance their own integrity or that of the budget process itself. Incremental budgeting has been accused with some justification of making liars out of honest people. Requesting more money than one needs or expects simply to satisfy the rules of the game would scarcely seem a way to promote rationality and honesty in administration.

Such considerations as these have spurred efforts to find newer and better ways of dealing with the budgetary process in modern administration. It is to some of these efforts that we will now turn.

The Coming of PPBS

As government grew in size and complexity, dissatisfaction with traditional budgeting grew apace. The failure of line-item budgets to reveal the impact of expenditures on programs, to show future costs and effects, to analyze the relationships between capital and operating costs and to propose alternatives—all these and other problems came to rankle more and more of those who were dedicated to improving administrative performance. Surely, they reasoned, there must be a better way of budgeting than simply drawing up a list of expenditures every year, a list that, based as it is on last year's list, tends to change in only being larger. A better way of budgeting, one more conducive to change and evaluation, was felt to be needed.

By the early 1950s, the Hoover Commission was proposing a new type of federal budget. It would be a budget "based upon functions, activities and projects." Such a budget would be a "performance budget" and it would include, along with the mass of itemized objects of expenditure, some additional information as to what all this expenditure was to provide in the way of public services. If the Public Works Department was to spend so much for personnel, equipment, et cetera, then how many miles of streets would be paved as a result? Early performance budgeters attempted to provide this information by adding an additional column in the traditional budget and setting down within it the actual work to be performed.

Some, however, were still not satisfied. They felt that simply tacking an additional column onto the existing line-item budget did not go far enough. What was needed was a whole new budget geared to actual programs, that is, to what the agency is really doing. C. Northcote Parkinson

CITY OF BOSTON AND COUNTY OF SUFFOLK 1973 PROGRAM BUDGET	FORM NO. 1 DEPARTMENT SUMMARY

DEPARTMENT	FUND	ACCOUNT NO.
Public Works	General Revenue	1 03-11

BUDGET COMMENTS

The Public Works Department was created in 1911 under the provision of Chapter 486, Acts of 1909, through the consolidation of the existing street, water and engineering departments. The department is in the charge of a Commissioner who is required by ordinance to be a Civil Engineer. The department now operates through its Central Office - Engineering and four major divisions. These divisions carry out the major programs of the department; namely, the maintenance and construction of highways, street lighting, snow removal, sewerage construction and maintenance, water construction and maintenance, street cleaning, and removal of garbage and rubbish.

EXPLANATION OF DECREASE

1972 Collective Bargaining	235,576
1973 Collective Bargaining	140,146
Step Rates	49,477
Decrease in Rubbish Contracts	(554,144)
Increase in Supplies and Materials	71,128
Decrease in Equipment	(87,765)
Total Decrease:	(145,582)

COST SUMMARY BY PROGRAM ELEMENT

PROGRAM ELEMENT	1971 EXPENDITURE	1972 APPROPRIATION	1973 BUDGET REQUESTED BY DEPARTMENT	1973 BUDGET RECOMMENDED BY MAYOR	INCREASE OR (DECREASE)
Adm. Support and Direction	1,371,783	1,742,639	1,985,476	1,726,032	(16,607)
Transportation	7,722,760	9,066,738	10,979,774	9,351,574	284,836
Sanitary-Solid Waste Control	8,442,970	9,697,936	10,541,669	9,431,328	(266,608)
DEPARTMENT TOTAL					

COST SUMMARY BY CLASS

DESCRIPTION	1970 EXPENDITURE	1971 EXPENDITURE	1972 APPROPRIATION	1973 BUDGET REQUESTED BY DEPARTMENT	1973 BUDGET RECOMMENDED BY MAYOR	INCREASE OR (DECREASE)
Personal Services	6,722,370	6,860,852	7,506,206	8,069,593	9,879,543	563,387
Contractual Services	7,770,632	9,579,328	10,904,702	10,355,358	11,108,393	(549,344)
Supplies and Materials	634,880	692,021	876,405	947,533	947,533	71,128
Current Charges and Obligations	11,790	36,585	30,000	49,215	39,215	9,215
Equipment	80,032	51,297	500,000	412,235	412,235	(87,765)
Structures and Improvements	451,026	317,430	690,000	685,000	1,110,000	(5,000)
Land and Nonstructural Improvements						
Special Appropriation						
DEPARTMENT TOTAL	15,670,730	17,537,513	20,507,313	20,508,934	23,506,919	1,621

This is the summary page of the city of Boston's Public Works Department budget for 1973. It is primarily a line-item budget and subsequent pages itemize the various expenditures in each of the main categories listed at the bottom of the page. Note, however, that some attempt has been made to group expenditures by program element as well. (Source: Boston Finance Commission.)

had once noted that the budget for the British army was broken down into a series of accounts. Account number one covered pay, account number seven comprised supplies, and so forth. The navy's budget was similarly classified. "But," objected Parkinson, "neither the Navy nor the Army is organized like that. The Navy is organized into units afloat and ashore. The Army is organized into battalions, batteries, depots and schools for which individually no cost is shown."[16]

The problem that Parkinson noted was as prevalent in America as it was in Britain. And, in some quarters at least, it was causing even more concern. Finally, with the inauguration of John F. Kennedy in 1961, steps began to be taken to respond to Parkinson's complaint.

Kennedy's secretary of defense, Robert McNamara, found his department's budget organized into the following broad categories:

1 Military personnel
2 Operations and maintenance
3 Construction
4 Research and development

Although he had probably never read Parkinson, this method of budgeting bothered McNamara. By the time he left the Defense Department seven years later, the department's basic budget categories read as follows:

1 Strategic forces:
   a. Offensive forces
   b. Defensive forces
   c. Civil defense
2 General purpose forces
3 Specialized activities (intelligence)
4 Airlift and sealift

Note well the difference between the two sets of categories. The first simply lists expenditures grouped according to the *type of expenditure.* The second groups expenditures according to the *purpose these expenditures are to achieve.* The first grouping would not tell us just how much the country is spending for, say, offensive forces as compared to other defense activities. The second grouping bases itself on providing just such information.

However, grouping expenditures on the basis of program rather than on merely type of expenditure was only part of McNamara's new system. The rationale for putting expenditures into program categories was to find out whether the Defense Department was spending its money wisely. To

TABLE 1

PLAN	COST OF PROJECT	AVERAGE DAMAGE	BENEFIT (REDUCTION OF DAMAGE)
No protection	0	$38,000	0
Levees	$ 3,000	$32,000	$ 6,000
Small reservoir	$10,000	$22,000	$16,000
Medium reservoir	$18,000	$13,000	$25,000
Large reservoir	$30,000	$ 6,000	$32,000

Source: Adapted from Otto Eckstein, *Public Finance* (Englewood Cliffs, N.J.: Prentice-Hall, 1945), reprinted in Virginia Held, "PPBS Comes to Washington," *The Public Interest* (Summer 1966).

make such a determination, a further tool was needed. This was cost-benefit analysis.

The use of cost-benefit analysis actually predated McNamara's arrival in the federal government. Many years before, economists had been weighing the costs versus the benefits of certain water-resource projects in an attempt to find out just what projects would be most effective in terms of dollars spent. Otto Eckstein in his book *Public Finance* gives an example of using such an approach to determine the most effective way of dealing with a flood-control problem (table 1).

Which of these projects is the most desirable method of dealing with the flood damage in question? On a percentage basis, the best project appears to be levees, since their construction would return double the amount of benefit in relation to outlay. On an absolute basis, the best approach might be found in constructing a large reservoir, for it provides the greatest dollar amount of benefits. However, Eckstein says the estimates show that the medium reservoir is the productive project because it provides the *greatest amount of dollar benefit in relation to cost.* The net savings that a medium reservoir would produce amount to seven thousand dollars a year as compared to three thousand a year from levees and only two thousand a year from a large reservoir.

Note that the savings and cost are figured on an annual basis. However, most of the money involved in such projects is spent at the outset in constructing the levees of the reservoir. Maintenance and operation costs during the time the facility is in use are usually minimal. However, to arrive at an annual cost figure, the amount of the initial outlay is spread over the life of the project.

This would mean that a project costing $10 million to build and lasting ten years would be figured as costing $1 million a year in addition to any operational, maintenance, and other costs that may be involved in operating the project. But cost-benefit analysis does not stop with simply dividing up the initial outlay over the project's projected life. It also uses what is called the *discount rate* or *interest rate* to arrive at a more accurate picture of both costs and benefits.

To understand the use of a discount rate, imagine that you have the chance to receive one thousand dollars right away or one thousand dollars a year hence. Which would you accept? Obviously, the one thousand dollars right away. Even if you do not wish to spend it, you can put it in the bank and earn, say, 5 percent interest on it during the coming year. This means that one thousand dollars now is worth at least one thousand and fifty dollars next year.

Or take the reverse situation. Suppose you have the alternative of paying a one-thousand-dollar bill this year or next. Obviously, even if you have the money, you will prefer to pay it next year, for in the meantime you can use the money for another purpose or, at a minimum, let it accumulate interest in a bank. Thus, a bill for one thousand dollars actually will cost you less next year than if paid right away.

These two simple illustrations indicate that the value of money must be calculated in relationship to the time it is spent or received. Cost-benefit analysis incorporates this concept through what it calls the discount rate. If a project involves an initial cost of $10 million and will provide benefits of $11 or $12 million at the end of ten years, then the project will be considered a losing proposition. Why? Because even if one figured that money was worth only 2 percent a year, this would still make $10 million worth more than $12 million at the end of ten years. (We are, of course, compounding the interest.) Similarly, if a project provides an initial savings of $10 million but a cost of $12 million after ten years, then it would more than pay for itself.

The discount rate used by the federal government when PPBS was in its heyday was 5.75 percent, which many feel is too low. The lower the discount rate, the easier it usually becomes to justify an expenditure. A little thinking on this subject will show why.

McNamara joined cost-benefit analysis to his new budget classifications. Not only would expenditures be grouped according to programs, but cost-benefit analysis would be used to decide whether such programs were actually effective, or, if they were effective, whether they were the most effective approaches available in terms of the expenditure involved. This amalgamation of budget classification according to program, with cost-benefit analysis for deciding program effectiveness, produced a new method of budgeting called the planned-program budgeting system, better known as PPBS.

Yet the path of progress for PPBS proved to be far from facile. The new budgetary concept soon confronted a rising tide of resistance and rancor from both academic specialists and working administrators.

The academic opponents pointed, first, to the very real problems presented by the move to measure costs and benefits. How does one put a proper price tag on a social commodity? How do we calculate the happiness produced by a recreation program and then weigh it against the joy generated by using the same funds for better street cleaning? Indeed, how can budget makers arrive at an acceptable discount- or interest-rate figure? Raising or lowering the rate 2 or 1 or even .5 percent can transform an undesirable program into a desirable one and vice versa. Despite its goal of making the budget process objective and rational, PPBS, so its critics claimed, lends itself to all kinds of machinations and manipulations.

TO RENT OR TO BUY

The discount rate can be applied to a variety of situations, often with unexpected results. For example, suppose that an agency needs a new truck and finds that it can buy one for nine thousand dollars that will last for four years. If it wishes to lease a truck instead, it will have to pay twenty-five hundred dollars a year. Which should it do?

Offhand, purchasing the truck would seem the obvious choice, since leasing one over a four year period would total ten thousand dollars. But if we assume a discount rate of 10 percent—not an unreasonable figure given the inflation of recent years—then we find the following:

YEAR	DISCOUNTED COST
Year 1	$2,500.00
Year 2	$2,250.00
Year 3	$2,025.00
Year 4	$1,822.50
	$8,597.50

Thus, the cost of leasing, if we assume a discount rate of 10 percent, would be less than the cost of outright purchase.

But even when such objective and rational measures can be found, how desirable is it to use them? Political costs and benefits must also be taken into account. A program or policy may show great cost effectiveness, but its pursuit may engulf the political system and even the entire social system in all kinds of stresses and strains. For example, cost-benefit analysis might reveal that remarkable economic efficiencies could result from dispensing with individually owned farms and replacing them with larger, corporately owned farms. But would such a goal be actually worthwhile to pursue? Might it not produce severe political and social costs that would offset any economic gains it might generate?

Similarly, an existing program or policy might fail to meet the cost-benefit criteria of PPBS but still might represent a political value well worth retaining and even, perhaps, reinforcing. Aaron Wildavsky cites federalism itself as a possible example of this.[17]

Finally, PPBS is very complicated. It requires a lot of skilled manpower to amass the needed data and make all the necessary calculations. This alone can represent a considerable cost in time as well as money. And even with all the care in the world, erroneous decisions can result. An HEW study once showed a public-relations campaign designed to encourage motorcyclists to wear helmets as yielding a benefit-to-cost ratio of 55 to 1. But the data used to arrive at this result were so speculative and shaky that it evoked a good deal of well-deserved critical scorn.[18]

At the practical level, hostility toward PPBS proved much more troublesome. Many federal managers experienced difficulty in understanding it and even more difficulty in accepting it. To the extent that it did not work, more to the extent that it did work, PPBS for them proved to be problem-producing rather than problem-solving. Pet programs might fail to meet the cost-benefit criteria, while new and nettlesome programs might arise to take their place. Even the task of grouping an agency's activities on a program basis could prove not only difficult but dangerous, because it might show too much money being spent on the wrong things.

Congressional oversight committees also showed themselves to be far from friendly to the new budget system. Not only was programmed budgeting difficult to get used to, but, carried to its logical conclusion, might well require changes in the jurisdictions of some of the committees. Furthermore, grouping an agency's activities according to programs and their using cost-benefit analysis to evaluate these programs threatened many enterprises and endeavors favored by influential congressmen.

By the end of the 1960s, PPBS, like so many of the promising ideas that arose during that stormy decade, seemed to be fading from the scene.

In 1970, Montgomery County, Maryland, adopted a program budget. This figure shows the program groupings for Category I, Protection of Person, Rights, and Property of the Individual. (Other categories were Promotion of the Individual's Physical and Mental Well-Being, Intellectual Development, etc.) On the right-hand side are the governmental units that will be involved in each program of Category I. Some of these units appear more than once, which means that portions of their budgets will be allocated or charged off against various programs. (Source: *The Six-Year Public Services Program*, Montgomery County, Maryland, p. 31.)

CATEGORY I. PROTECTION OF PERSON, RIGHTS, AND PROPERTY OF THE INDIVIDUAL

A. Crime Prevention and Control
   1. Crime Prevention — Patrol Div., Dept. of Police (PS)
      Canine Div., Dept. of Police (PS)
   2. Crime Investigation — County Medical Examiner (PS)
      Invest. Div., Dept. of Police (PS)
      Juvenile Court Committee
   3. Supporting Services — Headquarters, Dept. of Police (PS)
      Services Division, Dept. of Police (PS)

B. Adjudication of Criminal Offenses
   1. Adjudication of Adult Offenses — Circuit Court (GG)
      People's Court (GG)
      Off. of State's Attorney (GG)
      Off. of Public Defender (GG)
   2. Adjudication of Juvenile Offenses — People's Court for Juvenile Causes (GG)
   3. Supporting Services — Circuit Court (GG)
      Judicial and Adm. Sec., People's Court (GG)
      People's Court for Juvenile Causes (GG)
      Off. of Co. Sheriff (PS)

C. Rehabilitation of Criminals
   1. Rehabilitation While Not Confined — People's Court (GG)
   2. Rehabilitation While Confined — Detention Div., Dept. of Gen. Serv. (PS)
      Correction Advisory Committee

D. Adjudication of Civil Cases
   1. Investigation of Civil Suit — Circuit Court (GG)
   2. Judgment of Civil Suit — People's Court (GG)
   3. Protection of Minors — People's Court for Juvenile Causes (GG)
   4. Domestic Relations — Circuit Court (GG)

E. Safe and Efficient Movement of Traffic
   1. Traffic Movement and Control — Bur. of Traf. Eng., Dept. of Pub. Wks. (PW)
      Div. of Traf. Ops., Dept. of Pub. Wks. (PW)
      Maryland State Roads Commission
   2. Enforcement of Traffic Regulations — People's Court (GG)
      Traffic Division, Dept. of Police (PS)
      Parking Meter Enf. Sec., Dept. of Pub. Wks. (PW)
   3. Traffic Accident Prevention — Sign. Review Board (PS)
   4. Supporting Services — Div. of Traf. Plan. & Surv., Dept. of Pub. Wks. (PW)

F. Fire Prevention and Control
   1. Fire Prevention — Div. of Fire Prev., Dept. of Gen. Serv. (PS)
      Div. of Bldg. Elec. & Plbg. Insp., Dept. of Insp. & Lic. (PS)
   2. Fire Fighting — St. Dept. of Forest & Parks
   3. Supporting Services — Div. of Comm., Dept. of Gen. Serv. (GG)
      County Fire Board

G. Protection from Animals — Animal Shelter, Dept. of Insp. & Lic. (PS)
      County Resident Veterinarian

H. Protection from Natural and Man-Made Disasters
   1. Civil Defense and Protection from Disasters — Div. of Civil Defense, Dept. of Gen. Serv. (PS)
      Civil Defense Advisory Board
   2. Emergency Rescue Squads — Vol. Fire Departments Rescue Squads

I. Prevention of Food and Drug Hazards, Non-traffic Accidents, and Occupational Hazards — Div. of Bldg. Elec. & Plbg. Insp. (PS)
      Div. of Envir. Hlth. Serv., Dept. of Health (PH)
      Range Approval Committee

J. Research and Planning — Services Division, Dept. of Police (PS)
      Law Enforcement and Crim. Justice Committee

K. Supporting Services — Services Division, Dept. of Police (PS)
      Police and Fire Training Review Committee

Most federal agencies had begun to phase out their PPBS programs, and schools of public administration were putting less stress on its inculcation. Yet PPBS's defenders were not ready to surrender.

They could, on the practical level, point to some states, such as California and Wisconsin, and to a few counties and municipalities that were making increasing use of PPBS or at least aspects of it. As a matter of fact, some federal agencies were still utilizing some of its elements.

PPBS supporters did concede the validity of much of the criticism it had provoked. As one of them noted, PPBS bears some resemblance to Wagner's music, in that "it sounds better than it is." Yet, they continued to insist that it had much to offer modern administrators.

Allen Shick boils down its potential benefits to three. First, it will usually spotlight the worst programs even if it cannot always delineate the best ones. This in itself is no small blessing. Second, it will usually provide some improvements in existing programs. Third, it encourages administrators, politicians, and even the public at large to start thinking along different and more constructive lines.[19]

This last-cited benefit is considered the most important. It is the process, not the product, that counts the most. As one federal official observed, "The numbers are lousy and always will be in the civilian area. But the need to produce them pushes people in the right direction."[20]

Since the heyday of PPBS, progress in this direction has proceeded apace. However, the pathways selected have varied. In some cases they have taken the form of various versions of PPBS. In other cases, different but nonetheless related budget systems have been adopted. Other non-

---

COSTLY CUTBACKS

Many projects and programs that seem so economically desirable seem a lot less so when subjected to the harsh light of cost-benefit analysis. This may be especially true for undertakings designed to save money, as a study of cutback management strikingly indicates.

Two researchers compared two alternative ways of reducing a public agency's work force: by immediate layoffs or by attrition over a one-year period. Attrition won, hands down.

Layoffs, to be sure, provided payroll savings right away. But they also generated numerous costs, such as

• increased administrative expense, including the expense of processing grievances;
• lowered productivity because of poor morale, increased alcohol abuse, and increased fear and resistance to change ("insecure workers tend to cling to whatever stability they have");

> • the need to replace those whose abilities are needed but who may quit voluntarily due to the atmosphere of job insecurity, which the layoffs produce;
> • the cost of increased workmen's compensation claims along with the loss in income taxes.
>
> Although the study was a theoretical one, a story appearing in the *Wall Street Journal* a year later indicates it was pretty much on target. In describing how the Reagan administration's cutbacks were affecting federal employees in Denver, the newspaper used three headlines: AS THE BUDGET AX FALLS, SO DOES PRODUCTIVITY OF GRIM U.S. WORKERS. GLOOM AT AGENCIES IN DENVER IS SO DEEP SOME STAFFERS JUST GO THROUGH MOTIONS, and THE BRIGHT GUYS QUIT FIRST.
>
> Leonard Greenhalgh and Robert B. McKersie, "Cost-Effectiveness of Alternative Strategies for Cut-Back Management," Public Administration Review (November–December 1980). Wall Street Journal, 17 August 1981.

budgetary devices, such as productivity measures, program evaluation, and management by objectives, have emerged. While they are certainly not PPBS, they do exhibit some of the same methodology and approach that characterize PPBS. As Harry S. Havens, who heads the Office of Program Analysis of the U.S. Accounting Office, has noted, "PPBS really consisted of two distinct parts. One was a formal structure through which passed volumes of paper. The other was an analytical concept—a way of thinking about problems. The formal structure of PPBS is now dead; the analytical concept is very much alive."[21]

ZBB: Starting from Scratch

That the analytical approach that PPBS represents continues to be alive and (fairly) well can be seen in the developing popularity of a new form of budgeting—zero-based budgeting. The process represents a somewhat simpler and possibly more successful attempt to alleviate some of the problems presented by incremental, line-item budgeting.

Like so many other new developments being adopted in government, ZBB owes its origins to private industry. Texas Instruments started the new system when it ordered its departments and divisions to formulate their budgets anew each year. When Peter Pyhrr, treasurer of Texas Instruments and creator of ZBB, wrote an article about it for the *Harvard Business Review*, it came to the attention of the newly inaugurated governor of Georgia, Jimmy Carter. Impressed with what he read and dismayed at the problems he was confronting as governor, Carter brought

Pyhrr to Atlanta to help implement the system in Georgia's state government.

Carter was soon claiming great success with ZBB, and upon his assumption of the presidency eagerly sought to implement the new budgeting technique throughout the federal bureaucracy. Peter Pyhrr's book soon became a Washington best seller. As one seasoned bureaucrat was heard to remark, "never has a management fad more completely taken over this town."

Carter's departure from Washington in 1981 pretty much ended its brief reign in the federal bureaucracy. Nevertheless, ZBB seems to be more than a management fad, for the new budgeting system has found considerable favor at the grass roots. Nearly half the states and a growing number of municipalities now employ some form of it in at least some of their agencies. Whether ZBB really represents the budgeting wave of the future remains to be seen. But it is showing some signs of staying power.

The ZBB Process

One of the attractive aspects about ZBB, and one which suggests that it will enjoy a longer and more expansive existence than PPBS, lies in its greater ease of execution. It does, however, require its practitioners to learn two new terms and three new basic budgeting steps.

The two terms are *decision units* and *decision packages.* A decision unit has been defined as a "meaningful element," that is, any activity, large, isolated, or "meaningful" enough to require its own budget. A decision unit does not have to be big enough to constitute a whole program; often a subprogram or even less will suffice. But whatever its scope, a decision unit does need to possess enough discretion and dimension to warrant its own budget.

The second term, *decision package,* is slightly more complex and may not become completely clear until we have examined an example of ZBB in action. The term stands for any particular level of effort by any designated decision unit. For example, if an agency's microfilm unit was considered to have sufficient size and scope to be a decision unit, then a decision package would be written up for each possible volume of activity that the agency might want to consider for this microfilm unit.

Let us now see how we can utilize decision units and decision packages to provide a new way of budgeting.

The Three Steps of ZBB

The first step an agency must take to implement ZBB is the *identification of its decision units.* This is not a strictly scientific process, for the agency can and should exercise a certain degree of discretion in deciding which of its activities should constitute separate decision units and which should not. (Activities not considered a decision unit will still be part of another decision unit as long as they require any funding at all.) If an agency makes its decision units too small, it will then have made them too numerous and will be swamped by paper work as a result (always a problem with ZBB). If it makes them too large, it will impair the ability of ZBB to provide useful analysis.

Once the decision units have been designated, the agency is ready for step two, *the formation of the decision packages.* Here is where the levels of effort come in.

Almost all an agency's programs and subprograms can operate at various degrees of intensity and scope, depending, among other things, on how fully they are funded. Under ZBB, the heads of these decision units must single out several possible gradations of activity and then show what resources each will require, what outputs it will generate, et cetera. This information becomes a decision package, and there must be a separate package for each designated level of effort.

How many levels of effort should be considered? The answer to this question will vary depending upon the proficiency of the ZBB practitioner, the zealousness of the superiors, et cetera. The first level, as the name suggests could be zero. The decision package written up for this level would simply show the consequences of its being completely unfunded, that is, the work of this decision unit would not be performed at all.

The next level might be the minimum level. This would be the lowest possible practical level of funding for a decision unit. Below this level, one might as well discontinue it altogether. For our microfilm unit, for example, this might reflect the cost of renting the cheapest possible machine and using one part-time employee, or one regular employee part time, to operate it. Any sum insufficient to cover these expenses would make it impossible to have any microfilm unit at all.

Above the minimum level we might have decision packages representing one or more reduced levels. These would show the costs and consequences of trimming the unit's budget various degrees below its current level of operation, but still leaving it above the irreducible minimum. Then there would be a package for the current level and, finally, packages for one or more improvement levels. The latter will show what we can expect if we increase the unit's budget by, say, 20 percent, 40 percent, or more.

How many levels of effort should be considered? In theory, up to ten can be used; in practice, usually no more than five, and often no more than three, are employed. When five are used they customarily represent the minimum level, a reduced level, the current level, and two improvement levels. When only three are used, then it usually becomes a case of

DECISION PACKAGE RANKING AND CONSOLIDATION PROCESS ILLUSTRATED

EXHIBIT 1
BULLETIN NO. 77-9

Managers A, B, and C each rank packages for their units and send to Manager X

Manager X receives packages and evaluates and ranks them within each unit

Manager X ranks packages for units A, B, and C against each other, and sends to Manager R

Manager R evaluates packages from Managers X and Y, and then ranks them against each other

Manager R prepares some consolidated decision packages before submitting budget request to next higher level

Decision Unit A

Package #	Funding increment	Funding Total
A1	100	100
A2	15	115
A3	5	120
A4	30	150

Revised

Package #	Funding increment	Funding Total
A1	100	100
A2	5	105
A3	30	135
A4	15	150

Decision Unit B

B1, B2, B3, B4, B5

Decision Unit C

C1, C2, C3, C4, C5, C6

MANAGER X

X1	A1
X2	B1
X3	A2
X4	C1
X5	B2
X6	A3
X7	B3
X8	C2
X9	C3
X10	A4
X11	B4
X12	C4
X13	B5
X14	C5

MANAGER Y

Y1	A1
Y2	B1
Y3	B2
Y4	B3
Y5	A2
Y6	A3
Y7	A4
Y8	B4
Y9	C1

1	X1
2	X2
3	Y1
4	Y2
5	Y3
6	Y4
7	Y5
8	Y6
9	Y7
10	X3
11	X4
12	X5
13	X6
14	X7
15	X8
16	X9
17	Y8
18	Y9
19	X10
20	X11
21	X12
22	X13
23	X14

R1	X1-X2 Y1-Y2
R2	Y3-Y7
R3	X3-X9
R4	Y8-Y9
R5	X10
R6	X11-X14

1 Higher level manager readers the proposed priorities of the subordinate decision unit managers. The packages may be revised by either the initial decision unit manager or the higher level manager.

2 Higher level manager accepts proposed priorities of the subordinate manager.

3 Higher level manager accepts proposed priorities of the subordinate manager, but chooses not to propose funding of lowest priority package.

This chart, prepared by the Office of Management and Budget, depicts an example of the ZBB ranking process. Note that Manager X slightly rejuggles the rankings of subordinate Manager A while leaving those of Managers B and C intact. Manager X then combines all three groups into one larger group and submits it to Manager R. Manager R has also received the rankings of the other subordinate manager Y; he or she first combines them all into a new set of ranked decision packages and then consolidates them into six superpackages.

278

considering a reduced level, the current level, and one improvement level. Remember that each level considered requires a separate decision package.

Once the agency has formulated its decision packages, it must then rank them. *Ranking the decision packages* makes up the third and most controversial step in the ZBB process.

The controversy does not customarily come at the level of the decision unit itself. It will generally rank its minimum, or lowest, level first, the next lowest second, and so on, for obviously its most important requirement is to get enough funds to keep functioning. This basic fact gives us what one ZBB authority, Peter Sarant, calls "Ranking Rule I." This rule, says Sarant, stipulates that "the minimum level for a decision unit is always higher than any increment for the same unit."[22]

Once they are ranked, the decision unit's packages go up to the next administrative level above it. Now they must compete with packages from one or more other decision units at the administrative level, and those in charge at this higher level must make up a new set of packages. This set of packages will consist of combinations of the packages of the decision units beneath them, but combining these lower unit packages puts ZBB to the test.

The most obvious way of doing it is simply to take the lowest level package from each of the subordinate decision units and combine them into a new minimum level package for the overall unit, but this may not be the best way. Suppose the microfilm unit and the computer center have both submitted twenty-five-thousand-dollar packages for their minimum levels of effort and fifty-thousand-dollar packages as their second level of effort. It is possible that the staff services manager may find that funding the computer center at the fifty-thousand-dollar level is more important than funding both the center and the microfilm section at the minimum level. Therefore his or her combined packages may show, at the minimum level, a fifty-thousand-dollar-a-year computer center and no microfilm unit at all. This is the type of decision making that ZBB's backers hope to encourage, for their system, let us not forget, represents another attempt to replace routine with rationality in government budgeting.

ZBB at Work

A description alone will never show anyone how ZBB is done and what it can and cannot do, so let us take an example, simplified and hypothetical, yet by no means unrealistic.[23]

Suppose you are in charge of air-pollution control in one of the new state-level environmental protection agencies that have sprung up in recent years, and your state has decided to switch to ZBB. How do you go about it?

You must first identify your decision units. Let us assume there are only two: an air quality monitoring laboratory and an on-site inspection program. In a large state each of these might be too large for a single decision unit, but in a smaller state they might well be the right size for such categorization.

Now we come to step number two—drawing up the decision packages. Let us suppose that your state has decided to use only three levels— reduced, current, and improved. You therefore instruct the head of your monitoring laboratory and the head of your inspection program to formulate packages representing each of the three levels. In practice, of course, they might carefully consult with some or all of their own subordinates in executing this assignment. They might even turn the entire task over to a committee from within their ranks, but if one person bears overall responsibility for the unit, then he or she will obviously bear final responsibility for that unit's decision packages.

The packages from the air-monitoring lab show a minimum level of $150,000, a current level of $200,000, and an improvement level set at $300,000. At the reduced level, the laboratory will test the air in the five urban areas having the worst pollution. Some 70 percent of the state's population will be covered. At the current level the laboratory will continue to test the air in the same five urban areas and also in eight other areas that show signs of having some pollution problems. Let us assume that the air breathed by 80 percent of the population is being monitored at this level.

At the third, or improvement, level the laboratory would test the air breathed by 90 percent of the state's people. At this level the unit will now start covering some sparsely populated areas, and so the additional 10-percent increase in population covered requires a 50-percent increase in funding (from $200,000 at the current level to $300,000 at this level).

Turning to the other decision unit, the on-site inspection program, let us suppose that this unit finds it can operate at the current level for $100,000, at a reduced level for $50,000, and at an improved level for $200,000. It draws up decision packages showing what it can deliver at each level. (The main output measure used could be the number of inspections to be performed at each level of funding.)

Now we are ready for step three: ranking. For the two units in question, ranking raises no serious difficulties. They will rank their reduced levels first, current levels second, and improved levels last. But as head of the air-pollution-control division, you must rank the packages of one versus the other, for you must make up what are sometimes called "superpackages," which will show how you would want to divide the money between the units, at various levels of funding, for the entire air-pollution-control division.

For example, suppose you decide that the first two levels of operation

TABLE 2

ACTIVITY	INCREMENTAL COST	CUMULATIVE COST
1. Air Monitoring (minimum)	$150,000	$150,000
2. Air Monitoring (current)	$ 50,000	$200,000
3. Inspections (minimum)	$ 50,000	$250,000
4. Inspections (current)	$ 50,000	$300,000
5. Inspections (improved)	$100,000	$400,000
6. Air monitoring (improved)	$100,000	$500,000

for the laboratory represent the most important activities for your division. However, the improved level for this unit requires greatly increased funding with little benefit, for at this level, it will be recalled, it is testing the air in sparsely populated areas, which, presumably present few pollution problems. Consequently, you may want to rank last in priority the improved level for the laboratory. With this in mind, you may end up with a table similar to table 2.

This table shows just what your division would hope to accomplish at various levels of funding. The problem now moves up to the next higher level—the state's commission on environmental affairs, which takes your rankings into account, along with those of the commission's other divisions, say, those of water pollution and noise pollution. The commission will then combine decision packages to create still bigger and broader ones. For example, a reduced-level package might consist of simply the minimum level from each of the commission's divisions, or it might eliminate one or more divisions completely in order to fund a higher level of output with one or more others. As Sarant's "Ranking Rule II" states, "a minimum level package for a given decision unit *does not* need to be ranked higher than any other decision package of other decision units."[24]

ZBB: Summing Up

Zero-based budgeting bears an obvious resemblance to planned-program budgeting, which to some degree it has replaced. Like PPBS, ZBB sets out to show not just what government is spending its money on, but what it is spending its money for. Its goal is to get government agencies, and those who make up their budgets, to abandon the sacrosanct "base" and to set their sights on more significant, if sometimes more speculative, targets. It seeks to provide a clear and close interlocking between money spent and services provided. In so doing, ZBB enables public administrators to get the most for the least.

ZBB does differ with PPBS in less obvious ways. Although it can require a lot of work, it remains a somewhat less complex procedure than

PPBS. It even contains some characteristics of line-item budgeting, for like the traditional budgeting technique, ZBB also makes use of incrementalism. Its comparative crudeness, however, has made ZBB easier to implement than PPBS and, so its advocates hope, will give it greater staying power as well.

Like PPBS, ZBB has not lacked for critics. Many prestigious and perceptive observers have been quick to point a finger at its many alleged deficiencies and drawbacks. Political scientists Jack Knott and Aaron Wildavsky claim that in a study of the use of ZBB in Georgia's state government, Carter and his people devoted their time and talents to making increases and decreases in the budget or examining a few problem areas. In other words, they ended up making largely incremental adjustments just as their predecessors had done under line-item budgeting. Knott and Wildavsky say their interview with ZBB participants in Georgia revealed that 85 percent of them thought no shifts in spending had been made, while the 15 percent who did feel such shifts had occurred could not recall any.

Knott and Wildavsky call attention to another problem they say ZBB produces:

> Everything at every period is subject to searching scrutiny. As a result, calculations become unmanageable. Figuring out how everything relates to everything else, or, worse still, how other things would look if most things were changed, defeats every best effort. Consequently, attempts to apply intelligence to programs about which something can and needs to be done are defeated by endless mounds of paper. The trivial drowns out the important because, if everything must be examined, nothing can receive special attention. At last report, the state of Georgia was trying somehow to survey some ten-thousand decision elements in its zero-base budget.[25]

Even ZBB's biggest backers admit the applicability of this last allegation. Peter Pyhrr, for instance, calls the "volume problem" one of the most serious impediments to implementing such a system in a large-scale organization. And skeptics in Washington point out that HUD more than tripled its budgeting staff the first year it sought to use ZBB, while the Consumer Product Safety Commission saw its amount of budget material increase 3,000 percent.

As public administration advanced into the 1980s, reports on how the system was doing at the grass roots began trickling in. These reports did lend some credence to the system's critics. In most instances ZBB had failed to produce sweeping or even substantial changes in program operations and costs. At the same time it had made the budgeting process itself more expensive and exhausting.

But despite some disappointments and doubts, most of these studies still managed to report quite a few good things about ZBB. It had apparently brought the budgeting process out of the financial office and made it into a managerial task. In many instances it had helped identify program initiatives and improvements, and in some instances it had helped to control spending as well. In a very few instances it had produced rather spectacular savings. In Oregon, for example, a modified form of ZBB was credited with enabling one agency alone to save *$80 million* without a single statutory change in its makeup or functions. No wonder, then, that the state's governor, Victor Atiyeh, had become one of the system's biggest boosters, saying flatly "I believe in analysis, and zero-based budgeting promotes analysis."[26]

Support had also emerged from those who had to do the actual work. A survey of thirty-five municipal budget directors using ZBB found them giving it moderately high grades as an instrument for reallocating resources from lower to higher areas, for providing a basis for more rational budget cuts or at least restricting increases, and for informing managers more fully about the activities and problems of their agencies. One budget director claimed his mayor learned more about what his departments were doing in the first year of ZBB than he had in his eight previous years in office. As for the 35 budget directors themselves, while most of them would have liked to have seen the system become more simplified, only one of them wanted to see it discontinued.[27]

In summary, then, zero-based budgeting provides no magic elixir, no all-pervasive panacea to guarantee administrative effectiveness and cost efficiency. Yet it does furnish the public manager with another potentially useful tool for tackling the troublesome administrative tasks of today's and tomorrow's world. Even its detractors concede that it tends to open up the budgetary process and that it pushes people to think more about what they want to accomplish and how they want to accomplish it. As with PPBS, the process may be more important than the product.

CASE STUDY

Putting ZBB to Work in Wilmington[28]

With a mere eighty thousand residents, Wilmington, Delaware, scarcely rates as a major metropolis. Yet by 1975 it was suffering many of the same maladies that were afflicting its big-city cousins. These included a shrinking and increasingly impoverished population, a growing crime rate, and a weakening fiscal base.

Fortunately, it also possessed some potential strengths in the form of a home-rule charter, a strong mayoral form of government, and an incumbent mayor willing to seek out and try new remedies for his ailing city.

While Mayor Thomas Maloney had managed to keep the city's expenditure growth below the inflation level, he knew he faced ever-worsening fiscal problems ahead. Such factors as locked-in-wage-increase settlements; a high proportion of fixed expenses, such as debt service, insurance, et cetera; inflation; a continuing clamor for new or expanded services; and little or no foreseeable growth in revenue made the city's financial future look bleak indeed.

Maloney viewed the city's traditional, line-item budget as exacerbating his problem. The faults he found with it were the familiar ones. It assumed the existing levels of service, made no provision for trade-offs, and provided little useful information as to what the city was getting and achieving for its money. Surely, he reasoned, there must be a better way.

The mayor and his staff had been hearing about ZBB and decided to check it out. After reading up on the new budget system and making a trip to Garland, Texas, to examine it in operation, they decided to bring ZBB to Wilmington.

With less than five months to go before their next budget was due for submission to the city council, they set to work with determination and dispatch. Right away they exempted the schools and fixed costs, because there was little they could do about them anyway, but they included virtually all other city operations, even those that were financed by user fees, such as water service.

In taking step one—identifying decision units—the budgeters for the most part took the easy and speedy way out. Instead of carving out new organizational entities, they simply took existing organizational subunits and made them the decision units. Each of the Public Works Department's divisions became a decision unit, as did each of the four divisions of the Planning and Development Department. Smaller agencies such as the Treasury and Auditing departments, which lacked subunits, became single decision units. However, in a few departments with exceptionally large divisions, such as fire and police, some existing divisions were divided into two or more decision units.

For step two, the drawing up of decision packages, the ZBB team designed seven different forms plus a manual. Each team member was then assigned to a department to see that the manual was read and the forms filled out. Workshops for managers at all levels were also held. Some resistance from certain managers did develop, but generally cooperation was good if not excellent.

In most decision packages four service levels were used. They comprised two reduced levels, with the first being 40 to 60 percent of the existing level, then the current level, and then one improvement level. However, there were some exceptions.

One of these was the Sanitation Division of Public Works, which drew up packages for only three levels:

1 Once weekly; pickup at the curb.
2 Twice weekly; pickup at the curb.
3 Twice weekly; pickup from the rear or side yard, along with some special services and school pickup.

Level three was the current level, and no improvement level was submitted, because that would entail thrice-weekly pickups, which were considered completely unnecessary. In other words there was no real room for improvement, at least as far as sheer output was concerned.

Another exception to the four-level rule was the Patrol Division of the Police Department. This decision unit ended up using six levels:

1 Basic patrol along with preliminary investigation of major crimes.
2 Preliminary investigation of all criminal complaints plus response to priority noncriminal calls.
3 Follow-up on all criminal and noncriminal calls, enforcement of parking laws on a selective basis, and operation of the jail.
4 Increased parking enforcement and full-service response to noncriminal calls.
5 Additional patrols and school crossing guards. (This level represented the current level.)
6 Expansion of patrol, parking enforcement, and school-crossing functions.

As might be expected, output measures posed a major problem. Each decision unit could use up to seven. The problem lay in getting them to fashion and fulfill them. Department heads were unaccustomed to such instruments and lacked the information to produce them. But with the help of the workshop training, the manual, the seven forms, and the training team members, reasonably suitable measures for each decision unit were created and applied. Once these performance measures were in place, the paper work involved in formulating the decision packages did not turn out to be especially difficult. It was, however, quite time consuming.

Step three began when the 196 packages that resulted from step two landed on the desk of Mayor Maloney. To simplify the job of ranking them, the mayor and his staff decided to accept without discussion the 34 packages representing the basic service levels of such essential services as fire, police, and sanitation. Funding them would cost $10 million, leaving the city with $7.8 million for the remaining 162 which, if accepted in their entirety, would cost $9 million. Some obviously would have to be discarded.

Instead of trying to numerically rank each of the remaining 162 packages, the budget makers once again simplified and speeded up their task by dividing these packages into high-, medium- and low priority categories. Since revenues sufficed to fund all high- and medium-priority packages, they accepted them carte blanche. With enough funds left over to finance about half of the 56 packages that still remained, the budget team now ranked them in order of desirability and accepted them on a one-by-one basis until the money ran out.

After they had finished they found that the new system had resulted in some distinct, if not deep, program changes. Twenty-one current levels of services had failed to make it to the cutoff point, while two new or expanded service levels had managed to do so.

After some modifications to ease the pain of discharging employees in those units that were not to be funded at the current level, the budget, complete with packages and reams of supplementary data, was submitted to the council. The councillors were all part-timers and lacked the time and inclination to delve into the new budget in detail. But on skimming through the packages, many councillors expressed the wish to include four units that had failed to make it. The mayor agreed to accept the four, funding them by shifting a federal grant and by reducing funds for all the other service levels by .1 percent. This miniscule, across-the-board reduction was to be realized by slightly increasing the time for filling vacancies as they occurred in city agencies over the course of the year.

Both the mayor and the council were generally pleased with the ZBB experiment. The councillors felt they now had a better idea of just what they were voting for. The mayor felt that he now had something resembling a systematic grasp on city operations. And his department heads, so it seemed, had become more aware of what they were doing, what they should be accomplishing, and what it all should cost.

Of course there were some caveats and cavils. The amount of time and paperwork, the question of a suitable first level—some felt 40 to 60 percent to be too high—and the lack of emphasis on actual productivity improvement figured among the criticisms. But all in all there seemed to be a consensus that ZBB had worked quite well in Wilmington.

The Great Debate

Budgeting casts into bold relief two basic kinds of bureaucratic behavior—rational and incremental. And while these two can be and have been used to categorize decision making in virtually all fields of human endeavor, public administration has made the most use of them, for they denote and describe two fundamental and fundamentally different approaches to administrative decision making. And of all administrative activities, budgeting appears to be the area where they are most easily and clearly applied.

The rational approach was first articulated by the American philosopher John Dewey in the early part of this century. According to Dewey, intelligent problem solving involves the posing and answering of three basic questions: What is the problem? What are the alternatives? Which alternative is best?[29]

In more recent years administrative theorists have greatly enlarged and embellished Dewey's somewhat skeletal model. They have, for example, frequently added a fourth question concerning how one implements the alternative chosen. They have also broken down the basic ones into two or more parts, sometimes couched as commands. Thus, What are the alternatives? may end up as "assemble all the alternatives" and then "evaluate these alternatives." But Dewey's essentials remain essentially intact. Today as in 1910, when Dewey's first promulgated them, they furnish the framework for rational decision making.

At first glance the rational approach to decision making will hardly strike anyone as unusual or unacceptable. It seems the most obvious and common-sense way to make decisions. Why, then, all the fuss?

The problem, according to antagonists, is that what might seem to make good common sense may not make good political or administrative sense. In a real-life setting, particularly of the kind that public administration presents, what may work well on paper may fare poorly in practice.

Rational decision making requires the problem solver to assemble all the information necessary about the alternatives, in order to make a proper determination as to their respective merits and demerits. But in real life we almost always lack the time, money, and other resources to do this. What's more, even if we could gather all this information, we would still need a gargantuan amount of talent and time to analyze it fully. The rational approach may represent the best of all possible worlds, but it may well require the best of all possible worlds to realize it.

This brings us to another flaw that the foes of rational decision making find. Supposing one could, say, discover or develop all the possible alternatives, and suppose one could evaluate them all judiciously so as to select the best: the problem of implementing it yet remains. If public administration were carried on in a vacuum, then this might pose few problems. But such is not the case. Public decision makers constantly confront all kinds of pressures and cross-pressures arising both from within and without their organizations. These pressures almost invariably limit, and limit greatly, their field of vision, to say nothing of their terrain of action.

To illustrate this argument, let us assume that a police department of a coastal city has been maintaining a boat staffed with police officers to patrol its harbor. Then because of a decline in harbor use or the opening of a new Coast Guard base or some other development, this harbor patrol is no longer necessary. In the meantime a serious problem with juvenile gangs has arisen in the city's southeastern sector.

For the rational decision maker the solution is simple. Phase out the harbor patrol and utilize the manpower and other resources that will thereby become available to set up a special squad to deal with the juvenile gangs. Nothing, so it seems, could be simpler.

However, it is likely that the police chief will find himself contending with a multitude of conflicting interests if he seeks to implement such a plan. Harbor interests, such as boat owners and dockside businesses, may protest vigorously the harbor patrol's end. The harbor patrol officers themselves might do the same, possibly getting their union to go to bat for them. Even one or two news editors or reporters, especially if they are also boat owners, may lament the loss of the colorful, if by now unneeded, harbor patrol. At the same time, the police department's juvenile officers may be opposing the establishment of a new unit, staffed with many new officers, to deal with the juvenile-gang problem. Finally, the chief himself may not be all that sure that a new squad will provide the best solution.

Constrained by all these contending currents, the police chief may opt to retain the harbor-patrol boat and to refrain from setting up a new juvenile squad. He may reduce the patrol's size by simply not filling one or two vacancies as they occur and by using the slots to beef up his juvenile division. He may slightly reduce the amount of money customarily allocated for the boat's operation and upkeep. But this will be all.

If he pursues this more modest course, the chief will have used the incrementalist approach. He will have seen and accepted the limitations that circumscribe his choices and will have adjusted his decision making accordingly.

To its champions, incremental decision making is not only usually necessary but often deeply desirable. We rarely know enough in advance, they maintain, to initiate the wholesale changes that rationalism tends to inspire. Moreover, launching the initiatives it so often requires may, and often does, ignite hostility and inflame conflict. Consequently, the rational approach, even on those rare occasions when it might be easily implemented, could well create troublesome difficulties not just for the public decision maker but for democracy itself.

The public decision maker's task, then, becomes one of adjusting to change by trimming a little here and adding a little there, while avoiding, for the most part, major or abrupt shifts in either policy or practice. Engulfed by political, technical, and personal constraints, the public manager responds, and probably should respond, in the words of one of incrementalism's foremost exponents, by simply seeking to "muddle through."[30] In the process, he or she does not attempt to satisfy all the claimants who are clamoring for a share of the public purse, because a full assuagement of their appetites is usually impossible. Instead, he or she will seek to "satisfice," i.e., accommodate them enough so that none or almost none will feel completely disregarded.[31] Public decision making becomes, therefore, something of a balancing act aimed at keeping the ship of state on an even keel in the usually choppy waters that swirl around it.

The seductiveness of the incrementalist point of view stems from its apparent hardheaded realism. But we should not forget what it forces us to forgo. While it may keep the ship of state upright it may not promote its progress. Steadiness may be obtained at the price of stagnation. And although it appears to adapt administration to the force of circumstance, it often does so by virtually denying such circumstance. Thus the police chief in the above-mentioned example adjusts to the problem of an unnecessary harbor patrol and a growth in juvenile gangs by largely ignoring it. Needless to add, questions of administrative efficiency and effectiveness often must take a backseat when incrementalism comes into play.

Appalled by the drawbacks that pure incrementalism presents, yet appreciative of the difficulties that pure rationality produces, some have attempted to carve out a middle way or best-of-both approach. One of these efforts, *contingency theory*, will be examined in the concluding chapter. In the meantime, suffice it to point out what, from the standpoint of budgeting, should be fairly obvious. Traditional budgeting represents incrementalism, so much so in fact that the traditional line-item budget is often called an incremental budget. PPBS and, to a somewhat lesser extent, ZBB represent attempts to introduce the rational approach into the budgetary process.

The growing emphasis on rationality springs from a growing concern with administrative effectiveness. The cost-conscious climate now clouding the public sector is spurring on efforts to seek out better ways to budget public expenditures. And such efforts seem likely to increase and intensify in the difficult days that lie ahead.

Notes

1. David Halberstam, *The Best and the Brightest* (New York: Random House, 1969), 146.

2. Presidential message in the *New York Times,* 13 March 1970.

3. *Public Administration Times,* 15 December 1981.

4. Laurel A. Files, "The Human Services Management Task: A Time Allocation Study" *Public Administration Review.*

5. *New York Times,* 8 July 1973.

6. William Proxmire, *Uncle Sam: The Last of the Bigtime Spenders* (New York: Simon and Schuster, 1972), 35.

7. Ira Sharkansky, *Spending in the American State* (Chicago: Rand McNally, 1968).

8. Matthew Dumont, "Down the Bureaucracy!" *Trans-action* (October 1970).

9. *New York Times,* 29 March 1972. For Admiral Zumwalt's reply, see his letter to the editor on April 28 and for Senator William Proxmire's counter-reply, see his letter to the editor on May 8.

10. Thomas J. Anton, "Roles and Symbols in the Determination of State Expenditures," *Midwest Journal of Political Science* (November 1967).

11. Alain C. Enthoven and K. Wayne Smith, *How Much Is Enough?* (New York: Harper & Row, 1971), 17–18.

12. Daniel Katz and Robert L. Kahn, *The Social Psychology of Organizations* (New York: John Wiley, 1966), 103.

13. Anton, "Roles and Symbols," 146.

14. The incident is based on the author's experience as an aide to Mayor John F. Collins of Boston in 1960.

15. Proxmire, *Uncle Sam*, 94–103.

16. C. Northcote Parkinson, *The Law and the Profits* (New York: Ballantine Books, 1971), 11.

17. Aaron Wildavsky, "The Political Economy of Efficiency: Cost-Benefit Analysis, Systems Analysis and Program Budgeting," *Public Administration Review* (Spring 1966). This article is one of the most complete and one of the best critiques of PPBS.

18. The study was outlined by Graeme Taylor of The Brookings Institution in a seminar on PPBS for Boston city officials in May 1970.

19. In remarks made to a seminar on PPBS for Boston city officials, May 1970.

20. "Putting a Dollar Sign on Everything," *Business Week*, 16 July 1966. Reprinted in James W. Davis, Jr., ed., *Politics, Programs and Budgets*, (Englewood Cliffs, N.J.: Prentice-Hall, 1969).

21. Harry S. Havens, "MBO and Program Evaluation, or Whatever Happened to PPBS," *Public Administration Review* (January–February 1976).

22. Peter S. Sarant, *Zero-Base Budgeting in the Public Sector* (Reading, Mass.: Addison-Wesley, 1978), 104.

23. The example is adapted from one presented by Peter Pyhrr in "The Zero Based Approach to Government Budgeting," *Public Administration Review* (January–February 1977).

24. Sarant, *Zero-Base Budgeting*, 106.

25. Jack Knott and Aaron Wildavsky, "Jimmy Carter's Theory of Governing," *Woodrow Wilson Quarterly* (Winter 1977).

26. Jerry McCaffery, "The Transformation of Zero-Based Budgeting: Program Level Budgeting in Oregon," *Public Budgeting and Finance* (Winter 1981).

27. Perry Moore, "Zero-Based Budgeting in American Cities," *Public Administration Review* (May–June 1980). For other studes of ZBB see Frank D. Draper and Bernard T. Pitsvada, "ZBB—Looking Back After Ten Years," *Public Administration Review* (January–February 1981) and Allen Schick, *Zero Base '80* (Washington, D.C.: *Urban Institute*, 1980).

28. This case study is based on material presented in David W. Singleton, Bruce A. Smith, and James R. Cleveland, "Zero-Based Budgeting in Wilmington," *Governmental Finance* (August 1976). *Governmental Finance* is the official publication of the Municipal Finance Officers Association. The article has been widely reprinted.

29. John Dewey, *How We Think* (New York: D.C. Heath, 1918), chap. 8.

30. The term *muddle through* comes from Charles E. Lindblom, whose article "The Science of Muddling Through" constitutes something of a landmark in the development of public administration theory. It appeared in the Spring 1959 issue of *Public Administration Review*. One of the best contemporary expositors of incrementalism, especially as it applies to budgeting, is Aaron Wildavsky. In addi-

tion to the article of his cited earlier in this chapter, see anything else he has written, including his book *The Politics of the Budgetary Process* (Boston: Little, Brown, 1964).

31. The term *satisfice* comes from Herbert Simon, whose book *Administration Behavior* is considered by some to be the most important single book ever written in public administration theory.

9

The Productivity Problem

As noted in chapter 1, public administration entered the 1980s under heavy attack for its presumed lack of productivity. The newer forms of budgeting discussed in the previous chapter represent attempts to come to grips with this problem. In this chapter we will examine three other budget-related efforts all aimed at bolstering bureaucratic output. They are *Productivity Measurement, Program Evaluation,* and *Management by Objectives.*

Productivity Measurement

Measuring productivity has long been an accepted, almost routine practice in business. This, however, has not been the case in government. With some exceptions, up to recent times governments generally showed little interest in the subject. Now more government agencies, some reluctantly, some eagerly, are exploring ways and means of measuring their output. For various reasons, most of them are finding it a difficult task.

Measuring Public Productivity: The Pitfalls

The public sector usually deals in services, which, because they are intangible and often widely variable, almost always present problems in productivity measurement. How does one compare the productivity of heart surgeon A versus heart surgeon B? Surgeon A may perform more operations per week and her patients may show a greater recovery rate, but how do we know that they are suffering from roughly the same heart problems as surgeon B's cases? And what if surgeon A's patients are richer and can afford more follow-up care or are more educated and thus are perhaps more likely to adhere to recommended diets and other advice than are the patients of surgeon B?

Even if one analyzes what might seem to be a fairly routine operation in health care, the administration of chest X rays for instance, one can encounter measurement difficulties. X-ray unit A may consistently outperform X-ray unit B in number of chests examined each week. But perhaps unit B operates in poorer areas where people can't afford X rays. Or perhaps B's unit handles more children than A's, and children, it turns out, are harder to X-ray. Measuring productivity of services is a troublesome and touchy task.

Many government experts concede that some public-sector operations are simply not measurable with the tools currently at hand. Posing particular difficulties are numerous staff operations, such as personnel work, as. well as much case work. As for the latter, one has only to think of the complexities involved in trying to measure the productivity of a caseworker in a public welfare office. Should the caseworker be rated on how many cases he or she clears from the welfare rolls or on how many people he or she adds to the welfare rolls? Using either standard can produce all kinds of distortions.

Related to these problems is the central one of distinguishing between efficiency and effectiveness. Efficiency means doing things well, while effectiveness means doing the *right* things well. As one commentator once noted, a man might be efficient in driving nails into a table. Effectiveness enters the picture when we question whether he should be driving nails into a table at all.

Questions regarding quality make the public productivity measurer's task still more of a hazard as well as a hassle. A fiddler isn't necessarily producing more by fiddling faster. Nor can a pianist be hailed as especially productive for playing Chopin's *Minute Waltz* in fifty seconds. On a more mundane and realistic level, a narcotics squad that makes a lot of arrests may be performing poorly if those arrested are merely small-time, street-corner peddlers. Some city police departments that had established arrest quotas for their narcotic divisions had to change them when they realized that such productivity measures were not producing "quality" arrests, i.e., arrests of major dealers.[1]

Measurement of productivity of poverty programs is also susceptible to distortions. In order to show impressive rehabilitation rates, for example, many programs have practiced what is called "creaming." This means that they take only the most easily rehabilitated cases and leave the harder cases untouched. In some instances, they may take a case that they know will fail in the long run but will show good results in the short run. Thus, in one such case, a man on welfare who had good work motivation and some basic skills was trained as an auto mechanic and put to work in a garage. The agency then credited itself with a success. However, the man was unemployed to begin with because of a bad back, and soon this same problem forced him to give up his new trade and go back on welfare.

This brings us to a further dimension of the problem of productivity measurement. It may produce behavior that is actually antithetical to good results. Correction officials may release inmates before they are rehabilitated and then send them out of the state to hold down their recidivism rates. Hospitals, if placed under carelessly drawn productivity measures, could end up turning away the hopelessly ill because they would not show up well on the balance sheets. Deceptive practices may also find favor. Some drug shelters established to house and cure addicts have reported "cure" rates of 50 percent or higher. In some cases, however, they were counting only those who had stayed in the program until completion. Since about 75 percent of those who were entering such programs in the early 1970s dropped out before completion, the "cure" rate represented only 50 percent of the one-fourth who finished the program.

Productivity measures can produce counterproductive behavior in employees even when the organization itself is attempting to use such measures for perfectly legitimate ends. Peter Blau has described a public employment agency where interviewers were evaluated on the number of applicants they interviewed each month. This led the interviewers to dismiss clients who would require too much of their time. The agency then changed its system to judge interviewers on the number of jobs they actually filled. This caused the interviewers to try to outdo each other in getting hold of the slips that reported job openings, even to the point of hiding the slips from each other.[2]

Sometimes, an agency may know which measurement device to use but not how to scale it. The Division of Social Security one summer placed college students in offices of the Internal Revenue Service to check Schedule C forms of tax returns. It is a very simple exercise that can be executed at a speedy pace. Social Security officials set a work norm of forty-five hundred a day per student. However, it was found that in an office when no norm had been set, the students were checking nine to twelve thousand per day!

Accounting problems also add to the administrator's travail in setting productivity measures. Shall man-hours or cost-per-output be used? Cost-per-output is sometimes almost impossible to measure, while man-hour tabulations may not reflect the cost of new equipment. Another item that is often hard to figure is overhead costs. Then there is the problem of a changing and usually rising price level. Shall the costs be figured in current dollars, which do not adjust for price-level changes, or shall they be calculated in terms of constant dollars, which do? Both approaches create difficulties. And there is the problem of side costs, which the private sector can often ignore but which the public sector cannot. A new street-cleaning program may show measurable improvements in productivity but may also require more police costs. Or it may require residents to bring their trash cans to the curb. In this latter case, whose productivity has been increased, the sanitation crew's or the residents'?

Legal problems can also impede and impair the use of productivity measures. Civil service rules and regulations are examples of these. New York City's former Deputy Mayor Edward K. Hamilton has claimed that "parts of state civil service laws sometimes appear to have been written precisely to frustrate a productivity effort."[3] Even laws not specially related to public employment can bog down a productivity drive. One New York State law requires all medical admissions into hospitals to be in handwriting. With admission to some hospital emergency wards having risen 400 percent and more during the past decade, one can see why hospitals are having admission problems.

Labor unions may often resist productivity measurements. Many work contracts are written in such a way as to nullify the use of nearly all such criteria. Fortunately, unions, if properly handled, can help as well as hinder the implementation of productivity measures.

Finally, there are the political problems involved. Like PPBS, to which they are obviously related, productivity measures can collide with the interests of many elements in the politico-administrative process. These include administrative officeholders who find such measures threatening to their own pet ways of doing things, legislators who react negatively to measures which may show their favorite programs misfiring, and public interest groups whose preferred projects fail to measure up under the new criteria.

Productivity measures can even prove upsetting to whole sectors of the public who otherwise may be clamoring for increased public-sector productivity. For example, conservatives are often in the forefront in demanding more efficient government. But productivity measures may show that incarceration of criminal offenders is much less productive in terms of crime control than parole and probation. Other measures may show that much of the nation's extensive military hardware, such as aircraft carriers, produces little in the way of added security. Since incarceration and defense are programs that conservatives tend to favor, they may react with outrage.

Liberals, too, are not immune from the dangers that productivity measures can pose to programs that they ideologically support. Liberals have responded angrily when the use of productivity measures showed that many initial programs designed to help the poor, such as Head Start or Job Corps camps, yielded little or nothing in the way of measurable benefits.

All these factors make the introduction and implementation of productivity measures an exacting and often excruciating undertaking. Yet, there are numerous indications to suggest that the problems are far from insurmountable, that the task is far from hopeless.

Productivity: Progress Report

Despite all the difficulties and dilemmas that they engender, productivity measures have started to assume increasing importance in public administration. Progress has been neither smooth nor swift but it has occurred. In some instances remarkable successes have been achieved.

One of the first federal agencies to use efficiency measurements was the Division of Social Security. In the mid-1950s, it began its work-sampling program. Under this program, an employee in every office periodically measures the amount of work being done by various employees. These samples are not taken in an attempt to judge the employees' efficiency but to determine how long it takes to handle the various operations that the office is performing. This information from all Social Security offices is then compiled into averages, and each office is subsequently rated as to how it performs in respect to the overall averages for its region and for the nation as a whole.

The averages provide a useful yardstick to measure how any one office is operating. Of course, numerous factors may make any particular office rate above or below its regional or national average. An office may be so small, for example, that maintenance functions, as opposed to line operations, consume too large a proportion of its man-hours. Nevertheless, the averages, once all such factors have been taken into account, do provide a tool that indicates which regions, which offices, are even which individuals are performing well and which are not.

In the early 1960s the then Bureau of the Budget decided to see if other federal functions could not use productivity measures. It attempted to develop such measures for five federal agencies and two years later announced that it had succeeded in doing so. In 1971 the bureau—now called the Office of Management and Budget—teamed up with the General Accounting Office and the Civil Service Commission to launch a more all-encompassing attack on the productivity problem. This joint effort soon produced productivity measures covering 56 percent of the federal civil work force. Pleased with this success, OMB issued formal instructions to each federal agency with two hundred or more employees to report annually on what progress it was making to promote productivity.

As public discontent with public-sector performance mounted during the 1970s, many states and municipalities began following the federal government's lead. One of the more noteworthy efforts occurred in New Jersey, which in 1978 appointed a productivity coordinator for each department of the state government. Using a combined carrot-and-stick approach, New Jersey ordered all its departments to file quarterly reports on what they were doing to improve productivity, while at the same time they offered them the opportunity to tap a newly established Productivity Investment Fund to finance such initiatives.

The program soon began bearing fruit. By early 1980 the fund had financed sixteen proposals among the one hundred submitted. Many involved such simple steps as installing food freezers at a mental hospital, thereby enabling the institution to serve prepackaged frozen foods and save seventy thousand dollars by reducing personnel costs. More ambitious endeavors included new equipment in the Division of Motor Vehicles, which produced annual savings of a quarter million dollars; revised motor license procedures, which allowed an earlier deposit of receipts; recycling program for obsolete paper records, which turned an expense into a financial benefit; and conversion of the state's Vital Statistics and Registration program to microfilm, which cut retrieval time by 50 percent.[4]

It is generally felt that productivity measures lend themselves most easily to certain types of operations. In other words, particular functions rather than whole programs may provide the measurer with the most fruitful terrain in which to launch his or her labors. Gordon T. Yamada, chief of management systems information for OMB, offers an example of how productivity measures could be employed in processing various applications, urban renewal projects, grazing permits, university admissions, et cetera. The use of four different criteria used to determine productivity in such an operation is shown in table 3.

It is also possible, at least in many cases, to determine the productivity of a particular facility. Harry P. Hatry and Diana R. Dunn, in their study *Measuring the Effectiveness of Local Government Services: Recreation* published by the Urban Institute, offer some ways of measuring the effectiveness of a recreation facility.

First, one can measure the number of people within so many miles or so many minutes of the facility in order to determine its *accessibility*. If it is a specialized facility, such as a playground, then the measure could be limited to the number of children in the appropriate age group. Census maps, police listings, and other data can be used to discover whether the facility is conveniently located. The proximity to public transportation can also be taken into account.

TABLE 3   APPLICATIONS PROCESSING

	FISCAL YEAR 1	FISCAL YEAR 2
Productivity		
Applications processed per man-year	7,600	8,300
Service		
Total processing time per application in minutes	12	10
Quality		
Percentage of applications requiring reprocessing	7.5	7.2
Cost		
Unit cost per application in dollars	$1.00	$0.98

Source: Adapted from Gordon T. Yamada, "Improving Management Effectiveness in the Federal Government," *Public Administration Review* (November–December 1972).

From there we can go on to measure *usage*, taking into account how many persons actually use the facility, how often they use it, and for how long. This can be estimated by visiting the facility at representative times and taking random samples of the participants, asking them how often they come, what services they use, how long they stay, et cetera. Some estimate of crowdedness can also be made by examining sign-up sheets or by observation of waiting times. The evaluator can also ask users if they feel crowded.

Safety is another factor that should enter into the evaluation. What is the rate of drownings or injuries? What about crime? These data can be supplemented by asking users if they felt the facility was dangerous. The accidents and the crime that may occur in the facility must be balanced, however, with the accidents and crime that it may have averted else-where. Unsupervised swimming and playing on public streets also leads to accidents. while lack of recreational outlets can also stimulate in-creased crime. Has the facility had any impact on crime and accidents in the neighborhoods it serves?

Attractiveness is another, although perhaps lesser, criterion that can be utilized in weighing the productivity of a recreational facility. Does it contribute to the neighborhood's physical design? Does it upgrade the neighborhood? Here, in addition to the opinion of residents, one can check the effect, if any, on property valuations and possibly on the amount of business done by nearby commercial establishments.

Then there is the final and determining factor of *overall satisfaction*. People in the area served by the facility can be asked such questions as

"Would you say that the recreational opportunities in this community are excellent, good, fair, or poor?" Doing this on a yearly basis will provide some idea of trends.

It will be noted that much of the evaluation will be achieved through polling. This, however, need not be extensive or expensive, for only a reasonably representative sample is required. The results can be matched against other data. If, for example, the community served by the facility had a population of one hundred thousand and attendance at the facility came to fifty thousand, and if a random sample of one hundred users showed that they used the facility 2.5 times a year, it can be estimated that about twenty thousand people, or one-fifth of the community, are being served.

Hatry and Dunn claim that evaluations of recreational programs can be done at a cost of no more than 1 or 2 percent of the recreation budget. It would seem to be an expenditure that might be well worth making.

It is also possible to develop productivity measures for entire programs. The Institute of Traffic Management at Northwestern University, for example, has worked out what it calls a law enforcement index for evaluating the effectiveness of a police department in enforcing traffic laws. It is based on a simple equation in long division, the number of citations divided by the number of fatal and personal injury accidents:

$$\text{Enforcement Index} = \frac{\text{citations with penalty}}{\text{number of fatal and personal-injury accidents}}$$

The institute says that the Enforcement Index, or EI, should equal twenty. In other words, a police department should give out penalty citations equal to twenty times the number of fatalities and personal-injury accidents caused by motorists.

It should be noted that the approach differs considerably from the more simplistic quota system used by many police departments. Under the latter system, traffic officers are instructed to hand out a fixed number of citations every day or week. The Enforcement Index established a *relationship* between enforcement and accidents, and, since evidence indicates that accident rates do respond positively to traffic enforcement, the number of citations is allowed to fall as the number of accidents declines. Thus, if a department could reduce its number of such accidents to one a year, it would need to give out only twenty citations in order to meet the standard set by the index.

Crime control, however, remains much more illusive when it comes to establishing productivity measures. It is possible, for example, that improved police work can bring about an *increase* in the *reported* crime rate. Why is this? Simply because most crimes do not get reported. If a

police department starts improving its operations, including the strengthening of its relationships with the community, this could cause more
crimes to be reported. For this, as well as other reasons, crime rates by
themselves do not provide a basic reliable measure of police effectiveness.

Yet, crime rates often do tell us something, and when used in conjunction with other measures they may offer valuable clues in assessing the
quality of law enforcement. What are some of these other measures? They
include such things as attitude surveys (i.e., do people feel they are better
protected?); pedestrian flows, particularly at night; merchants keeping
open after dark; the number of arrests and the number of cases won in
court (the latter element is often omitted in reports of cases cleared by the
police); the number of complaints against the police; the number of police officers and civilians killed or injured in police-civilian encounters.
The task of evaluating police effectiveness in fighting crime is by no
means easy but by no means impossible.

One city that has attempted not only to measure police productivity but
to tie it into police pay is Orange, California. In 1973 this middle-class
city of eighty-nine thousand put into effect a plan to raise police salaries
1 percent for each 3-percent drop in the rate of robbery, rape, auto theft,
and burglary. Some sixteen months later the rate in those categories of
crime had gone down by 19 percent, and the city officers were looking
forward to a pay raise of $119 a month.

Not all observers were impressed with the results. Concern was expressed that the figures might have been juggled in one way or another to
make a better showing. However, the Urban Institute, in an evaluation
study of the experiment, said, "The incentive agreement . . . appears to
have been successful in achieving its immediate goal of reducing the total
number of reported rapes, robberies, burglaries and auto thefts."[5]

Productivity and Its Payoffs

Assuming that productivity measures can be developed and implemented, the benefits to public administration and the public in general
would seem to be immense. First and foremost, of course, is an increase
in output both in terms of efficiency and effectiveness. Katz and Kahn
claim that "knowledge of results in itself motivates people toward improving their performance. Level of aspiration studies," they say, "indicate that individuals tend to raise their sights when they see the outcome
of their efforts. If there is continuous feedback on the basis of some objective criterion of behavior, people will be motivated to improve their
scores."[6]

It must not be assumed that this reaction leads to exhausted and eventually exasperated employees. On the contrary, such goal raising is likely to increase employee satisfaction. Marshall Edward and Gladys Ogden Dimock cite research indicating that employee work satisfaction goes up when standards are raised.[7] Productivity measures, therefore, despite the fears and frustrations that they may initially arouse, should lead to increased employee morale and increased work satisfaction.

Evidence of this has already been seen in New York City. Former Deputy Mayor Hamilton describes how under a productivity improvement program, the city Parks and Recreation Department abolished their policy of assigning one or more employees on a permanent basis to take care of a particular park. Instead, the workers were grouped into three crews of three and sent from park to park as a team. According to Hamilton, not only did the output of the crews double that achieved by persons working alone with permanent assignments, but "the morale of the work force increased noticeably because, as they said, they could see the results of their work and they took the new system as evidence that someone was taking an interest in their jobs."[8]

Productivity measures tend to work for, rather than against, the public employee in other ways as well. In the absence of productivity measures and ratings, the bad often tends to show up more than the good. Attention is more easily aroused when things go wrong than when things go right. Productivity measures make it easier to bring to light superior as well as substandard performance.

In doing this, productivity measurement offers a better method for determining promotions of one kind or another. Use of such measures may obviate the need for traditional efficiency ratings and all the problems that they present. They also may permit a reduced emphasis on seniority. A good set of productivity measures can provide administrators with an impartial method of determining and rewarding merit.

Measuring productivity may also provide a basis for deemphasizing rules, regulations, and even supervision itself. Working with a good set of productivity measures, the employee can often become his or her own boss, at least to a substantial extent. Objective criteria, rather than a supervisor, guide an employee's labors and determine his or her achievements.

All of these factors can foster innovation, for once specific goals have been set they should tend to become more important than the procedures for achieving them. The increased flexibility that results, along with the spur to use it, can widen and enrich the employee's scope of work. To cite one example, Wisconsin Correction Department officials, responding to a productivity effort, abolished the rule limiting female probation officers to counseling only women offenders. By doing away with this rule, the department was able to equalize work loads and reduce the overall number of probationary employees needed. At the same time, it broadened the work experience of one group of probation officers.[9]

Productivity measures may also strengthen the good features of the small group while modifying its less advantageous aspects. The genial alcoholic whose failings were previously covered up by his associates may now find himself forced to confront his problem as his comrades balk at his failure to contribute his share to their measurable output. A member of the group, on the other hand, who may have been ostracized for reading poetry rather than joining in the lunchtime card game, may win a greater measure of acceptance by making a worthwhile contribution to the group's performance.

Management's attitude may also change for a more beneficent effect. The U.S. National Commission on Productivity in a 1972 study of British experiences in productivity bargaining found that it "induced management to abandon its defensive posture toward work rules and practices and to take the initiative in improving both the health of the enterprise and the welfare of the workers."[10]

In summary, then, productivity measures, despite the problems they present and the limitations under which they must work, may have much to offer present-day public administration. At a session of the New York City conference on productivity, former Ford Foundation President McGeorge Bundy called such initiatives "the beginning of the kind of human endeavor in which nearly everybody wins."[11]

Program Evaluation

When PPBS began to diminish in the federal bureaucracy, many found a replacement in another analytical device, program evaluation. In 1970 over one thousand program evaluations were carried out in federal agencies, and countless others have been conducted since then. Some state and municipal governments have also warmly welcomed this new technique and have even set up offices to evaluate their program performance.

Legislative backing and buttressing have played a major role in the flourishing of program evaluation at all government levels. Conservatives looked to the technique to bring out all sorts of failures in the numerous social service programs of the 1960s. Liberals hoped to use it to show the efficacy of such endeavors. And underlying all these partisan or ideological concerns was growing citizen dissatisfaction over rising taxes and what seemed to many a decreasing quality of public services.

Today, program evaluation seems quite firmly entrenched in U.S. government. Congress now has two federal agencies—the Congressional Research Service and the General Accounting Office—spending over a quarter-billion dollars a year in making such appraisals. Over two-thirds of the states also engage in some form of systematic evaluation along with a rising number of cities. However, disputes continue to rage over the role and impact of such activity assessments.

The overall goals of program evaluation, or PE as it is sometimes called, can be simply stated. PE should increase our understanding of government activities. It should lead to governmental improvements. And it should produce some financial savings. The tools it uses also seem fairly familiar. For the most part, they greatly resemble the types of analytical devices developed for PPBS, ZBB, MBO, productivity measures, and other techniques. Like these other techniques, program evaluation can also, through ignorance or intrigue, be manipulated and abused.

The first task of the program evaluator is to know and state just what he or she is to evaluate. This may sound like a monstrous platitude, yet it frequently presents perplexing problems. The program evaluators may have one thing in mind, the agency for whom they work may have another, those operating the program being evaluated may have another, and so on. Some clear-cut consensus should prevail on the specific purpose(s) of the evaluation before those making it start to work.

The desirability of clarifying the specific goals of the evaluation should not cause the evaluators to overlook incidental pieces of information that result from their efforts. Sometimes these incidental results yield more important information than the main thrust of the study itself.

To take one example, the Indianapolis Police Department in the mid-1960s decided to let their police officers take their patrol cars home and use them as their regular, off-duty means of transportation. It was hoped that this would create more police visibility and therefore lower the crime rate. An evaluation conducted by the Urban Institute one year after the launching of the program failed to show any significant drop in the rate of crime. However, it did reveal a rather remarkable reduction in the number of fatal auto accidents. The number of such fatalities declined from fifty-nine to forty, a decrease of almost one-third. Since auto accidents take far more lives than homicides, this "side effect" of the program may have been more important than the program's stipulated goal.

EVALUATIONS VS. EXPECTATIONS

If program evaluation has failed to achieve the deep impact its supporters have sought for it, the problem probably lies less in the technical difficulties it presents than in the emotional reactions it evokes. For analytical appraisals of public activities will frequently yield not only unexpected but unwanted results.

For example, systematic studies in law enforcement reveal no appreciable relationship between the amount and intensity of visible police patrol and a neighborhood's crime rate. An analysis of the Food Stamp Program has shown that it has nutritionally *lowered* the diet of its presumed "beneficiaries" by encouraging them to consume highly processed and highly sugared foods. And a study on what happens to people's health when doctors go on strike show that such cutbacks in medical care lead to dramatic *declines* in death rates. (The death rates promptly rise again to their former levels when the doctors go back to full-time work.)

Despite such findings, however, most people continue to demand more police visibility, few have ever challenged the Food Stamp Program on nutritional grounds, and nearly all of us look to our doctors to help us stay healthy. Such responses, it would seem, might cast some doubt on Socrates' stipulation that man is a rational animal.

In another example, those patients receiving emergency-room treatment in a hospital who needed follow-up care were divided into two groups. One was assigned to a follow-up clerk, who telephoned them to remind them of their appointments. The other group received the simple appointment slip that constituted the hospital's standard procedure. Assignment to either group was on a random basis.

The follow-up telephone call seemed quite successful. Those who received the phone call showed up with much greater regularity for their subsequent appointments. As a result, they received substantially more medical care than the others. Thus, the program, in terms of its stated goals, was a success. But the program evaluators went a step further and measured the two groups in terms of basic health criteria. In doing so, they found no difference between them. In other words, *the increased health care had failed to produce increased health.* This would seem to be a much more significant finding than the fact that the program succeeded in getting more patients to show up for appointments.

The studies above were based on statistical correlations. This is a method frequently used in making program evaluations. One must, however, proceed cautiously in drawing conclusions from such correlations. For one thing, the fact that two consequences go hand in hand does not necessarily mean that one directly influences the other. As one skeptic observed when the statistical relationship between cigarettes and lung cancer came to light, a similar correlation could be found between the rise in lung cancer and the rise in the use of nylon stockings. (As it so happens, the cancer-cigarette researchers used highly refined statistical techniques to establish a distinct and direct relationship between cigarette smoking and lung cancer. But cruder correlations might have made the whole study suspect.)

In comparing two groups to determine a program's efficacy, the evaluator should strive to secure as much randomness as possible in the selection of these groups. If it can be shown that the members of the experimental group and the members of the control group were both chosen at random from the same basic population, then it is more likely that any differences that may occur to the experimental group would stem from the program and not from other factors. But if the experimental group consists of those who volunteered for the program while the control group comprises those who did not, then any differences in the behavior of the two groups could merely reflect differences in their composition and not differences in the program impact.

For example, during the late 1960s the federal government sponsored some experiments in giving children from poor families a specially enriched educational program prior to their entering kindergarten. Those receiving this educational enrichment were subsequently compared to another and seemingly similar group of poor children. It was found that both groups performed at about the same level when they reached first grade. Thus, Head Start, as the program was called, was deemed a failure.

Some, however, have rejected the reported results of this evaluation. Why? Because the control group, that is, the group who did not undergo the program, was comprised of children whose parents had not enrolled them in Head Start. Consequently, they may have differed from the Head Start youngsters. This problem would not have occurred had the program managers taken both groups from those children enrolled in Head Start. In other words, only some of the children who were signed up for the program would then have received it while the other children would have served as "controls."

The program evaluator must also watch for the "Hawthorne Effect." You will recall that in chapter 3 we saw how a group of young women performed better in a variety of test situations simply because they knew that others were observing them. This happens frequently in PE. People's behavior often changes when they learn that such behavior is being studied. And if they know that they are participating in an experiment that will eventually end, their behavior may vary greatly from what it would be if the new experimental conditions were to be permanent. For example, the federal government once ran a test with a group of working poor families in New Jersey to see what they would do if they received income supplements. Eventually, the results had to be discarded, however, when it became known that most of them had adjusted their behavior to the fact that the experiment would soon end.

Time factors can distort and disrupt an evaluation effort in many ways. A social service agency may lay claim to a remarkable record in placing poor people into jobs. But if most of them soon leave these jobs, then how

successful can the agency's endeavors and efforts be judged? A correction
system may claim a low rate of recidivism, but to evaluate its results we
must know what time span they are using. It is one thing to find that a
low number of prison inmates have ended up back in prison ten years
after being discharged. It is another thing to find that the number of re-
cidivists is low after only six months.

A program may create costs other than those that seem directly related
to it. It may take up more of the agency head's time, it may damage the
morale of those working on other programs in the agency, and/or it may
lead to dissension within the agency or to disruption of its relations with
other agencies. On the other hand, it may create indirect benefits, such as
freeing the agency head to give more attention to other matters, improving the morale of the agency, and facilitating better relations both within
and without the agency. All of these matters should be taken into account,
though such costs and benefits may not only be hard to figure out but also
may be only temporary in nature.

Who should do the evaluations? Agencies often like to do their own. But
this obviously presents problems. Some degree of insulation is probably
necessary for the program evaluators if they are to do their job properly.
On the other hand, insulating them too fully from those who are running
the program may make it too difficult for them to discover what is going
on. As it is they are likely to encounter resistence, for "the lower level
program administrator and his/her staff literally see their bread and butter
at risk when the program evaluator arrives on the scene."[12]

But low-level administrators are not the only ones who tend to turn skit-
tish when the evaluators come into view. Higher-level administrators and
politicians frequently find evaluations disquieting. Large portions of the
public itself with a deep financial or ideological or simply emotional involvement in a particular program may disown or disregard an evaluation
that fails to confirm their commitment. Finally, evaluators themselves
often come to their job encumbered with predilections and prejudices
that can contaminate their conclusions.

The difficulties that program evaluation entails have brought dismay to
many, including some of its initial boosters. But while thoroughly complete and careful evaluations may remain rare, reasonably sound appraisals of ongoing and proposed programs have been made and put to effective use. In the early 1970s, conservative Republicans relied on such
evaluations to end some of the least productive—they may have even
been counterproductive—poverty programs. In the early 1980s, a negative
evaluation of the MX missile system helped liberal Democrats in Congress garner enough votes to block the program, at least temporarily.
Meanwhile, back at the grass roots many public managers are using pro-

gram evaluations, albeit often in an abridged form, to help them bring their activities more into step with the demands and desires of a changing and increasingly cost-conscious society.

Management by Objectives

Perhaps the most popular device yet developed for promoting productivity, and one that incorporates many of the tools and techniques of productivity measurement and program evaluation, is management by objectives (MBO). It expands the basic elements of productivity measurement and program evaluation into a system for operating the entire organization.

MBO owes its origination to Peter Drucker and did much to establish him as the presiding "guru" of modern management theory. Drucker has long insisted that all one *can* measure is performance and that all one *should* measure is performance. He evolved MBO as a method of putting this principle into practice.[13]

MBO's inherent idea certainly provides few perplexities. It simply stipulates that organizations and their leaders should be judged strictly by their results. Personnel practices, communication flows, administrative structure, and all the other ingredients of organizational life become important only to the extent that they contribute to or detract from organizational achievement. Results alone count.

To many, this seemingly single-minded focus on results may seem to smack of fanaticism and folly. It also calls to mind the philosophically dubious premise that the end always justifies the means. However, the priority of ends over means has been recognized since Aristotle.[14] And if in some areas of human activity the intensive implementation of this principle may lead to morally reprehensible deeds, in management, claims Drucker and his growing band of believers, the results of emphasizing results will be far, far different.

The MBO Process

MBO starts out with some organizational soul-searching to define its *mission*. The organization must attempt to answer the question "For what purpose does our organization exist?" ("What are we here for?")

The missions of most organizations are essentially ongoing and open-ended; they do not have a fixed, terminated point. But this isn't true for all. Some organizations exist to accomplish a particular purpose, and once they accomplish it, they dissolve. The differences will, of course, be reflected in their stated missions. However, most organizations will adopt broad and inclusive mission statements listing no specific and measurably achievable ends.

Earlier in the book we saw that nearly every organization is a part of another, larger organization. This obviously will influence its mission statement. Normally, an organization's mission will be narrower and less inclusive than its parent organization while broader and more inclusive than those of its own subunits. Thus a state department of conservation may take as its mission the maintenance of a healthy and attractive environment; its division of air quality may make its mission the maintenance of air that is safe and healthful to breathe; and the air monitoring laboratory within this division may limit its mission to simply the testing of air to see if it meets air quality-control standards.

After determining its mission, the organization must then give itself a goal. The goal has been defined as "a statement of intended output in the broadest terms. It is normally not related to a specific time period."[15]

This makes the goal sound identical to the mission, but an important difference does exist. It is found in the words "intended output." The mission statement generally deals only with the outcome of an agency's activity. The goal statement gives us the output. One way of distinguishing between the two is by noting that the laws setting up an agency usually provide the basis for its mission; its goals will usually be formulated by itself. In drawing up and divulging its goals, top management communicates its decisions regarding the organizations aims and relative priorities and provides general guidance to its employer, clients, political overseers, et cetera, or the organization's proposed strategy.

Once it has defined its mission and designed one or more long-range goals, including the general means to achieve that mission, the organization now proceeds to hammer out its objectives. Objectives, that is the results to be accomplished within a certain period of time, should exhibit four essential features—concreteness, attainability, desirability, measurability.

Objectives can be major or minor; if major, they will relate much more directly and impact more sharply on the organization's basic goals. They may also be long-term, requiring more than a year for their fulfillment, or short-term, being achievable within the budget year.

Finally, the organization and its subunits will normally establish *milestones*. As the name implies, these are checkpoints placed along the way toward the objectives. Thus, if the long-range objective of a school is to reduce its truancy by 30 percent, and if its short-range objective is to accomplish a 15-percent drop in truancy during the current school year, it might well want to check periodically to see how well it is doing. Each of these monitoring events will constitute a milestone in its MBO operation.

MBO: A Balance Sheet

The relationship of MBO to productivity measurement and program evaluation should be reasonably apparent. In the course of monitoring the attainment (or nonattainment) of those objectives, it is conducting something very akin to program evaluations. MBO makes use of the same approach and very nearly the same tools of these other techniques but seeks to incorporate them into a more inclusive, wide-ranging system.

MBO's kinship with PPBS and ZBB is also easy to see. Although it is not a budgeting system per se, it has obvious budgetary implications. It seems to have an especially close relationship with ZBB; as a matter of fact, many of those governments and agencies that first adopted ZBB were those already using MBO.

Like PPBS and ZBB, MBO has not lacked critics and detractors. These critics have raised some valuable issues and revealed some valid weaknesses.

Managerial work, it has been pointed out, is highly interconnected and interdependent. What any particular manager may do often depends heavily on the actions of many others. This makes it difficult to hold the manager and his or her unit responsible for any particular shopping list of objectives.

Another aspect of this problem is that a manager may have a good deal of impact on the extent to which certain other managers and their units attain their objectives. Yet this impact, be it positive or negative, will not normally be taken into account. An MBO system will tend to reward the manager who attains many of his or her own objectives even though he or she may impede others from reaching theirs; it will, on the other hand, tend to penalize the manager who fails to meet many objectives of his or her own but who in various ways helps others reach theirs.

Critics also charge that MBO leads an organization to emphasize the quantifiable aspects of its actions. This is certainly understandable, but the consequence will be a neglect of the nonquantifiable. As we have seen, many of these new schemes designed to put more rationality into administrative operations have difficulty coping with the problem of quality and sometimes it is omitted altogether.

Many find the whole business of setting and sticking to objectives dehumanizing. They claim it ignores people's personal needs and intensifies the organizational rat race as the struggle to meet goals and objectives sweeps away all other considerations. According to a prominent industrial psychologist, Harry Levinson, "the typical MBO effort perpetuates and intensifies hostility, resentment, and distrust between managers and subordinates." It is, he says, "industrial engineering with a new name."[16]

These kinds of problems may become more persistent and pernicious when top management flatly imposes objectives on its subordinates and when headquarters does the same on its field offices. Yet, if subunits and those responsible for them are allowed to set their own, they may set objectives that are too vague, too easy, or that are inconsistent with the organization's overall mission.

Then there are the more technical problems, such as finding the right measurement criteria and keeping the amount of paperwork and preparation effort under control. These difficulties are as much a part of MBO as they are of other efforts aimed at introducing more rationality into public administration.

The peculiarities of the public sector often compound these problems. As has been seen, government work is often vague and uncertain, which makes the task of defining and measuring objectives even more difficult. Thus, when President Nixon directed the federal bureaucracy to start making use of MBO, the National Aeronautics and Space Administration set "exploring the universe" as one of its key objectives—certainly an ambitious aim but one whose attainment might be a bit hard to measure with any precision.[17]

The oft-lamented inflexibility of government obviously does not make MBO's adoption any easier. Civil-service systems, detailed budgets, and other characteristics of modern bureaucratic operations hinder the setting of objectives, let alone their attainment.

Political factors may also bedevil MBO's progress through the bureaucracy. An agency may have more than one mission, and these various missions may be essentially contradictory. Sometimes they almost have to be in order to satisfy contending sides. Conservatives and liberals, for instance, view most social welfare agencies from quite different perspectives and will frequently express vastly different ideas on what these agencies' missions should be. Conflicting views may also characterize an agency's mission and objectives as seen by its clientele and by the public at large. Most Americans probably consider the primary task of the Department of Agriculture to promote agricultural production. The nation's farmers, however, think the department's main function is to help them. Helping the individual farmer in some instances could impair rather than increase farm output.

All these dilemmas might seem to make it impossible for MBO to work successfully in the public sector. Yet, a large and growing number of agencies have adopted MBO, and most seem pleased with its results. As with the other productivity-improving processes we have looked at, MBO has not lived up to the promises of its enthusiasts. Yet, it has enabled many organizations to deliver public services more effectively. Moreover, it has made their operations more, rather than less, humanistic.

Regarding this latter point, MBO does not work well when it is done

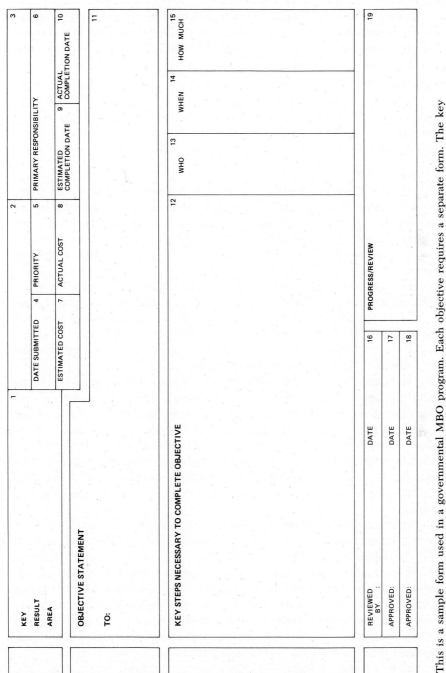

1			2		3
KEY RESULT AREA	DATE SUBMITTED	4	PRIORITY	5	PRIMARY RESPONSIBILITY	6
	ESTIMATED COST	7	ACTUAL COST	8	ESTIMATED COMPLETION DATE	9	ACTUAL COMPLETION DATE	10

OBJECTIVE STATEMENT

TO: 11

KEY STEPS NECESSARY TO COMPLETE OBJECTIVE   12

WHO	13	WHEN	14	HOW MUCH	15

PROGRESS/REVIEW   19

REVIEWED BY :	DATE	16
APPROVED:	DATE	17
APPROVED:	DATE	18

This is a sample form used in a governmental MBO program. Each objective requires a separate form. The key result area of each objective must also be identified. The form does not specify milestones but does make some provision for keeping track of progress toward the stated objective.

strictly from the top down. On the contrary, it requires a great deal of input from those below and a good deal of interaction between hierarchical
levels. For example, one device often used in MBO systems is the manager's letter to his or her superior. This includes

- objectives of the superior's job as well as the manager's own job;
- performance standards for the manager;
- things he or she must do to meet the goals;
- obstacles to achieving these objectives and the things the superior

and the organization can do to help overcome them.

The letter will probably include additional details, such as distinctions
between long-range and short-range objectives, suggested milestones, et
cetera. If the superior agrees with the latter, fine. If not, the two must
work out a mutually acceptable alternative. Such a letter then becomes in
effect the manager's charter providing him or her with a fair degree of
discretion.

This points up the fact that MBO, with its stress on results, only increases a subordinate's latitude as to methods and means. Indeed, it
opens the door more widely to individual initiative and actually requires
a high degree of self-management and self-control. As Robert Golembiewski puts it, "MBO seeks to increase the degree of internal motivation
and to decrease the reliance on external motivation."[18]

MBO also makes other demands on organizations that would seek to
put it to use. They would integrate their goals as much as possible and
circumscribe their boundaries as clearly as they can. MBO works best for
organizations with clear-cut, well-demarcated boundaries, for such an organization can exercise more control over its product. Police departments,
for example, will normally have a harder time than fire departments in implementing MBO, because the police department can usually exercise
less influence over the crime rate than the fire department can over the
rate of fire.

Finally, the MBO organization must place priority on such things as
good communication and feedback processes, positive attitudes toward
change, and leadership support. MBO, properly planned and properly
practiced, customarily enhances an organization's humane qualities. As
Richard Cornuelle points out in his interesting little book *De-Managing
America,* "Management which manages by specifying *behavior* is dehumanizing and inefficient. Management which manages by specifying *results* is emancipating. It opens to all the possibility of inventiveness and
resourcefulness. . . ."[19]

CASE STUDY

Putting MBO to Work in Pennsylvania[20]

During the 1970s, prodded by a variety of pressures from the federal government—from public interest groups and from rising public concern—
many states created new departments of conservation. One of the first
states to do so was Pennsylvania, which in 1971 set up a Department of
Environmental Resources.

Like most of these new agencies, Pennsylvania's conservation department was not a wholly new creation, but the merger of several existing
state agencies. The most important of the now-merged units was the Department of Forests and Waters, and that agency's chief of staff, Edward
M. Seladones, became the new department's secretary of administration.

Seladones had instituted a rather crude form of MBO at his former
agency and hoped to do the same at DER, as the new Department of Environmental Resources was called. DER's new personnel director, Den-
nis Butler, shared Seladones' enthusiasm and they soon had such a system in operation in DER's personnel division.

It wasn't too long, however, before they realized that their MBO
scheme was not working well. Their MBO operation was plagued by

• too many objectives (about thirty or forty per manager).
• too much top-down decision making with little input from or consideration for subordinate managers. The objectives were handed out like
assignments, with little give-and-take discussion.
• too little effort expended on developing methods for achieving objectives. Also, milestones were frequently inconsistent with each other and
were often overlooked until the final deadline, when, of course, it was too
late.
   no real tie-in between accomplishment of objectives, performance appraisal, and the reward system generally.

Confronted with such problems, they decided to call in a consultant. The
person they picked was George Morrissey, a well-known expert in instituting public-sector MBO systems.

Morrissey soon saw where the difficulties lay and drew up a list of recommendations. His three principal recommendations were for them to
take more care and time to

• define clearly and concisely roles and missions;
• single out Key Result Areas from their division's welter of activities;
• develop workable operational strategies.

With Morrissey's findings in front of them, Seladones and Butler went to work. They combed through the personnel division's two hundred activities and pinpointed twenty as Key Result Areas (KRAs). They also carefully refined their division's mission statement. In its final form it read "through consultation and some regulation to effectively and efficiently acquire, develop, maintain, and utilize an optimally productive and satisfied workforce."

All of this took nearly a year to accomplish. The reason it consumed so much time was that the pair made sure to discuss the project at length and get feedback from everyone in the division.

Their new MBO plan led to some structured changes in the division. Previously the personnel unit had been divided into subunits on the basis of functions or process; now it was grouped according to Key Result Areas. For example, formerly all the typists handling payroll documents had been grouped together; now they became separated into two groups, with one responsible for putting names and other information on the payroll and the other responsible for removing them. The fact that both performed the same function, typing, was no longer sufficient grounds for grouping them together. The *purposes* of their work differed, and this now provided the basis for arranging them.

The MBO-dictated reorganization reduced the amount of hierarchy in the bureau and flattened its organizational chart. Whereas its subunits were once arranged in four horizontal rows, they were now aligned in only three. And the bureau's name was changed from the Bureau of Personnel Service to the Bureau of Human Resource Management to reflect its new mission statement.

The reduction in structured hierarchy has been accompanied by an increase in top-to-bottom communication. A representative from each work group is selected to attend a yearly, week-long conference at an off-site center. On this occasion, they review the last year's performance and plan for the coming year. The participants also hold a smilar conference mid-year in order to review what progress is being made and what problems have developed in meeting the current year's objectives.

In addition, each work group prepares quarterly reports. These will list milestones and other pertinent information, such as new services performed, improvements in existing services made, cost savings achieved, et cetera. Even personal accomplishments and commendations received should be set down.

Although such quarterly reports give each group a chance to toot its own horn, many groups would refuse to take the task seriously. Some would even pad reports with token and rather worthless material. But Seladones and Butler used a variety of techniques, including sensitivity training to break down the mistrust that lay behind these barriers.

One very helpful stratagem was to have representatives from less forthcoming groups sit in when the more productive groups made their reports. This usually stimulated the observers to return to their own groups with the aim of stimulating their co-workers to try to do more.

The new MBO system soon began producing payoffs. Although typists, for example, were now divided into two groups, they were able to work more efficiently and with less typing errors. As a result, one typist position was dropped from the payroll.

Problems continued to persist, many of them the result of factors over which the bureau and its managers had little control. One was the lack of a real reward system for those who performed exceptionally well in attaining objectives. Another was the apathy and often-times resistance of many government managers and legislators to the idea of pinpointing responsibility and results. Then there was the seemingly perpetual fuzziness about funding. Politicians in our system simply make too many promises, and this makes it difficult for them or their governmental managers to draw up precise policies and to implement clear-cut priorities.

Yet given these and all the other problems inherent in the public sector use of MBO, at the DER's Bureau of Human Resource Management in Harrisburg, the MBO system is alive and well.

MBO and the Decentralization Dilemma

In chapter 2 we examined and discussed the question of decentralization, taking note of its many drawbacks along with its numerous delights. There is probably no perfect way out of this quandary, no path the public administrator can pursue that will enable him or her to reap all the advantages each has to offer while avoiding all the disadvantages that each may impose. Yet some public managers view MBO as offering an opportunity to achieve the optimum mix between centralization and decentralization.

The best balance between the two approaches has sometimes been summarized in the following statement: *centralize policy making, decentralize decision making.* Let headquarters, top management, or both assume responsibility for, and therefore final authority over, the organization's basic policies and purposes; let its subordinate subunits and/or field offices determine how they will go about realizing them. There are other ways of saying the same thing, e.g., centralize ends, decentralize means, or centralize politically, decentralize administratively.

Of course, the distinction between policy making and decision making, between means and ends, are not always clear-cut. One area frequently blurs into the other. Still, the prescription provides the public manager with an approach to the whole decentralization dilemma. And should such an approach be adopted, then MBO may provide the most convenient way of putting it into practice.

For example, if a school system wanted to decentralize then it could have its principals or district superintendents work out, with the help of subordinates and parents' advisory groups, a mission-and-goals statement along with a list of long-term and short-term objectives and milestones. Once approved by headquarters, the school or district could then proceed with a fair degree of discretion to try to meet its objectives. There undoubtedly would be periodic consultations with headquarters or field supervisors during the year to see how each school or district was coming along, but most of top management's attentions would be directed toward helping the subunits meet objectives. Each would have a vested interest in working cooperatively for a victory, for one would be a victory for the other.

In actual practice such a system would not work so simply or smoothly. Yet the possibilities for using MBO to achieve a reasonable balance between centralization and decentralization do exist, and more and more agencies are making use of this system as they struggle to solve the decentralization dilemma.

Policy Analysis

That productivity measurement, program evaluation, and MBO share a common bond, in fact several common bonds, should be quite apparent. From one perspective each successive technique may be viewed as an enlargement of the previous one. Thus, program evaluation incorporates many of the tools and techniques of productivity measurement and makes use of them to analyze and appraise complete programs. MBO draws on the devices of both to establish a systematic way of structuring the work of an organization. Looked at in this way, one can, if one wishes, visualize them as three concentric circles with productivity management representing the smallest, program evaluation the next, and MBO the largest.

If we wish to maintain this perspective, and it is certainly not the only one and possibly not even the best one for examining the productivity problem, we can think of policy analysis as representing a still larger circle, one that stretches the strategies comprised in the smaller ones into an expanded dimension. In effect, policy analysis utilizes their basic approaches not just to implement policy but to initiate and institute it as well.

According to Duncan MacRae, Jr., one of the new discipline's more perceptive theoreticians, policy analysis deals with "government actions"— the conditions under which they should be undertaken, conditions for their efficiency, conditions for their implementation, and the possible establishment of structures that will facilitate the proper choice and implementation of policies.[21] In a more operational sense, policy analysis calls for the use of logic and evidence, the two basic tools of both scholarship and science, to formulate or select a public policy.

Professor MacRae breaks down policy analysis into three basic steps. The first involves defining or determining the problem. This is seldom as easy a task as it may at first glance appear, for it requires the public policy maker or analyst to weigh questions of political as well as technical feasibility. Regarding the former, the analyst must not just research the policy itself but also those whom it involves. Are they open to change or at least modification in the operations that will be affected? If so, to what extent and on what aspects? Is the political environment itself conducive or constraining? Sometimes the policy maker can and must modify the problem definition to exclude those parts of the problem that do not meet the political-feasibility criterion.

To drive home his point MacRae draws upon a formula suggested by another writer on the subject, James Vaupel. The formula is Pd>C where

> P = Probability that analysis will make a difference
> d = the difference it will make
> C = the cost of doing the analysis

The formula can be easily illustrated. If an analysis can produce savings worth, say, twice what it costs to make, then as long as the probability that it will be successfully complimented is greater than 50 percent, it should be done. If the probabilities in this instance are less than 50 percent, then the effort should be abandoned.

MacRae's second step calls for formulating criteria. Here too, strictly technical considerations will not suffice, for "measurement cannot be separated from the more basic question as to whether the things measured are really the values we wish to achieve." The policy analyst may have to develop "subjective social indicators" such as the satisfaction or happiness of those who will be affected. (However, in this instance one can arrive at the subjective indicator by objective means by simply polling the affected individuals or at least a sample of them.)

In proceeding to step three the policy analyst sets down the various alternatives that his or her analysis has yielded along with their respective costs and benefits. In doing so the analyst may make use of models, implicitly if not explicitly. One model of special significance, says MacRae, "is the economic model of the free, competitive market, including possible departures from this model and means of coping with them." But he also warns that the use of this private-sector model for public policy analysis is tricky, because (1) public policy usually involves many more influences and impacts than private policy, and it is hard to be aware of, let alone cover, all the bases; and (2) it is also hard to predict what human beings will do in any specific situation.

If MacRae's three basic steps sound familiar, they should, because they relate rather remarkably to John Dewey's three steps for problem solving that were cited in the previous chapter. As we saw then, Dewey's three-step procedure provided the basis for rational, as opposed to incremental, decision making. Policy analysis, along with productivity measurement, program evaluation, MBO, and other such implementation strategies that it more or less subsumes, represents another effort to introduce more rational decision making into public administration. But it also recognizes the political and emotional factors that can frustrate its realization. As James R. Schlesinger, an economics professor who held cabinet posts in both the Ford and Carter administrations, has put it, "[Policy] analysis cannot achieve wonders; it cannot transmute the dross of politics into the fine gold of platonic decision-making . . . political decisions in a democratic society can hardly be more 'rational' than the public, the ultimate sovereign, is willing to tolerate."[22]

Notes

1. *New York Times*, 20 April 1971.

2. Peter Blau, *Bureaucracy in Modern Society* (New York: Random House, 1956), 58–59.

3. Edward K. Hamilton, "Productivity: The New York Approach," *Public Administration Review* (November–December 1972).

4. Richard F. Keevey, "State Productivity Improvements: Building on Existing Strengths," *Public Administration Review* (September–October 1980).

5. *New York Times* 10 November 1974.

6. Daniel Katz and Robert L. Kahn, *The Social Psychology of Organizations* (New York: John Wiley, 1966), 421.

7. Marshall E. Dimock and Gladys O. Dimock, *Public Administration*, 4th ed. (New York: Holt, Rinehart and Winston, 1969), 377.

8. Hamilton, "Productivity."

9. Patrick J. Lucey, *Wisconsin's Productivity Policy* (November–December 1972).

10. U.S. Civil Service Commission, General Accounting Office, and Office of Management and Budget, *Measuring and enhancing productivity in the federal sector*, mimeograph edition (Washington, D.C.: June 1972).

11. *New York Times*, 20 March 1973.

12. Thomas V. Greer and Joanne G. Greer, "Problems in Evaluating Costs and Benefits of Social Programs," *Public Administration Review* (March April 1982).

13. Peter Drucker, *The Practice of Management* (New York: Harper & Row, 1954). This was his first book to describe MBO. See especially chapter 11.

14. The opening paragraphs of Aristotle's *Nicomachean Ethics* not only underscore this point but actually provide some of the underlying premises for MBO.

15. George S. Odiorne, *Management by Objectives: A System of Managerial Leadership* (New York: Pitman, 1965), 18.

16. Harry Levinson, "Management by Whose Objectives?" *Harvard Business Review* (July–August 1970). Reprinted in Robert T. Golembiewski and Jack Rabin, *Public Budgeting and Finance* (Itasca, Ill.: F. E. Peacock, 1975).

17. Rodney H. Brady, "MBO Goes to Work in the Public Sector," *Harvard Business Review* (March–April 1973). For an interesting assessment on how MBO fared in the federal government during Nixon's first term.

18. Golembiewski and Rabin, *Public Budgeting*, 241.

19. Richard Cornuelle, *De-Managing America* (New York: Random House, 1975), 100.

20. The following case study is based upon material presented in George L. Morrisey *Management by Objectives and Results in the Public Sector* (Reading, Mass.: Addison-Wesley, 1970), 249–261.

21. Duncan MacRae, Jr., "Concepts and Methods of Policy Analysis," *Current Issues in Public Administration*, Frederick S. Lane, ed. (New York: St. Martin's Press, 1982).

22. James R. Schlesinger, "System Analysis and the Political Process." *Current Issues in Public Administration*, Frederick S. Lane, ed. (New York: St. Martin's Press, 1982).

10

The Challenges of Change

To many, the most distinctive feature of the modern age, the one that demarcates it most clearly from previous times, is its rapid pace of change. Ours is an age where alteration and amendment, mutation and permutation have become the natural order of events. Innovation seems to follow innovation at an accelerating rate, and the individual who fails to adjust to successive shifts in the pattern of his or her existence may soon be outmoded.

What holds true for the individual holds equally true for the organization. It, too, finds itself caught up in the currents of change, and it can hope to shield itself from its onslaught only at the risk of atrophy and decay. Today's organization must do a good degree of running simply to stand in the same place; to move forward requires still greater exertion.

Unfortunately, as we noted in chapter 3, such flexibility rarely comes easily to an organization. Katz and Kahn have pointed out that an organization naturally tends to proceed on the principle that it is easier for the world to adjust to it than for it to adjust to the world. When change in the external environment causes the organization to malfunction, it tends to assign the blame to the external forces rather than undertake internal alterations to correct the problem.

The natural reluctance to change becomes especially noticeable in the administrative sphere. Although technical changes may be welcome, because they are more easily demonstrable and provable and may not involve emotional and personal values, administrative changes strike much deeper and may affect those things that the organization holds most dear.

As Katz and Kahn note, this tendency parallels the response of an individual.[1] A person may easily discard an icebox for a refrigerator and give up an old car for a better one. However, he or she will not so lightly yield political and religious beliefs. The same holds true for organizations. They also possess ideologies, attitudes, and patterns of behavior that they do not lightly surrender.

This aversion to administrative change is particularly marked in public organizations. With private companies, change is often a *sine qua non* of survival. In an age of automobiles, a buggy-whip manufacturer who insists on turning out the same product will find it hard to meet his payroll. A public organization is not usually confronted with the same bracing pressures. On the contrary, public organizations may actually come under pressures to retain the status quo. These pressures are not just internal, such as resistance by their employees to alter their patterns of performance, but external as well. An organization's clientele or its political overseers or both may want things to stay the way they are.

Consequently, public organizations have often found the task of transforming themselves to accommodate the winds of change to be difficult indeed. Many have avoided the task almost completely. However, an increasing number of public agencies are becoming cognizant of the fact that they do so at their peril. In the face of the growing hostility to public organizations, and in the face of their inability to meet the challenges that confront them, they are starting to stir themselves out of the ruts and routines into which they so easily become enmeshed. They are increasingly feeling the need to make innovation a part of their way of life.

PPBS, MBO, productivity measures, and many of the other emerging developments in public administration help to stimulate and support the forces of change. In this chapter, we will examine other mechanisms that are more specifically oriented toward this end. These devices are disparate, and their examination will take us into varying aspects of administrative activity. Yet they all are part of the freshening currents now coursing through the corridors of contemporary organizational life.

Agents of Change: Planning

The last quarter century has witnessed a great growth in government planning. Such nations as France, Sweden, and Japan have developed highly articulated techniques for anticipating future economic and social problems. These nations have generally been rewarded with high rates of economic growth and increasing prosperity. Many business firms have also learned how to plan, and the ones that have planned the best have often fared the best. IBM is only one of the more notable examples.

Planning also has much to offer public administration. Here, as elsewhere, planning permits the organization not only to anticipate and prepare for change but to some extent select and shape such change. Planning offers a way of institutionalizing vision and stabilizing innovation. It permits the future to shape the past rather than the opposite. An organization that plans is an organization that, at least theoretically, has accepted the value and necessity of change.

The role of planning, it should be stressed, is not just to encourage change but to encourage constructive change. When new equipment for learning languages came on the market, many schools rushed to buy it. They often set up "language labs" with a full-fledged array of audiovisual apparatus without weighing carefully the merits of the various devices and, more importantly, without defining, or redefining, their long-term goals in language instruction. As a result, these expensive language labs failed to yield results commensurate with their costs. Proper planning could have prevented this, for not only can it facilitate change but forestall change that is too rapid or too little considered.

Planning can also be a way of sparing the organization the abrupt changes that may occur because of any number of events, such as a change in leadership. It can smooth out a transitional process and allow it to take place in a way that will not shatter or shake the organization in a traumatic manner.

In helping to deal with the problems of change, planning can also help the organization in other ways. It should stimulate the minds of its members, jogging their brains and leading them to innovations. Planning, like all change, can create tensions, to be sure. But in many instances these will be tensions that were festering long before the change was contemplated. Planning may only bring them to the surface where they can be dealt with. At the same time, planning can also reduce various strains and stresses within the organization, for it may modify annoying conditions and alleviate monotony. "The quest for a change of pace by people caught in routinized jobs, the introduction of elements of risk or uncertainty in situations, providing only a boring regularity," writes Wilbert E. Moore, "offer testimony to the need for change as a way of alleviating strain as well as a source of further tension."[2]

Planning, properly conceived and executed, also provides two further benefits for the employees of the organization. One of these is increased participation, the role of which we will be examining shortly. The second is predictability. The employees now have a better idea of what to expect and can make their personal plans accordingly. As Herbert Simon has noted, "A major purpose of the planning and organizing that precedes any administrative activity is not merely to put each participant in the job he can best fill, but to permit each to form accurate expectations as to what others are going to do."[3] Simon was speaking only of the casual planning required in all administrative operations. More developed planning enables an employee to decide more intelligently just what the role he or she may want to play in the organization in the future or whether he or she wants to play any role at all.

Planning also affords management an additional tool for evaluating the employee. Innovation, so it seems, is one way of helping to sift the wheat from the chaff for, generally speaking, it will be the better employees who will be the ones to respond most positively to the challenges of change. In a federal agency studied by Peter Blau, most of the less competent half of the employees resisted changes in the agency's rules and regulations. The more competent employees welcomed such changes. Ironically, then, those agents who were the most adept at working with the existing procedures were the ones who were the most willing to see those procedures altered or eliminated. Change appeals to the more capable, and an organization that accepts the need for change by making planning an integral part of its operations is one that is more likely to recruit and retain capable employees.

The Planning Process

Planning in the public sector encounters many obstacles. In addition to the problems of administrative conservatism noted earlier, there is the problem of administrative personality. "Administrators," C. P. Snow has written, "are by temperament active men. Their tendency, which is strengthened by the nature of their job, is to live in the short term, to become masters of the short-term solution."[4] Ron A. Webber, in his book *Time and Management*, echoes the same belief and develops it more fully. Managers, he says, believe in keeping busy and actually acquire guilt feelings when they are not bustling with activity. Planning, on the other hand requires thought and contemplation. It also requires an expenditure of resources for results that will not be immediately realizable. Furthermore, the future is always uncertain and ambiguous, and formulating plans for it can be not only difficult but even threatening.

Why threatening? According to Webber:

> The threat is two-fold: first, because managers tend to fear the kind of time necessary, for such thought; it must be unstructured, open and seemingly ill-directed—all attributes which run counter to time-haunted, efficiency-minded men. Wide open time like space can be frightening. Second, incorporating concern about the future into the present necessitates clarifying what we really want, and this means defining fundamental values of management, organizations and society.[5]

These problems may loom particularly large in U.S. administration. "Our difficulty," writes Townsend Hoopes, "is that, as a nation of short-term pragmatists accustomed to dealing with the future only when it has become the present, we find it hard to regard future trends as serious realities. We have not achieved the capacity to experience as real and urgent—as demanding action today—problems which appear in critical dimension only at some future date."[6] Hoopes believes that our lack of planning greatly helped to entrap us in the Vietnam quagmire.

The U.S. administrator who hopes to plan ahead faces still other problems beyond those of his or her own and others' temperaments. The U.S. political system with its deep fragmentation of authority makes administrative planning difficult and even dangerous. No matter how large the agency and no matter how sweeping its mandate of authority, it rarely can carry out meaningful planning without concurrences and clearances from numerous other sources. Annual budgets tend to crimp administrative planning further, for an agency can seldom be sure of what its financial resources will be from one year to the next. Political appointments complicate the planning process still more, for they can lead to abrupt changes in agency leadership and agency policy. Finally, planning, if not handled with political astuteness, can put an agency on a collision course with its legislative overseers. A legislator, concerned with power and prerogatives, may regard the planning function as a threat to his or her right to exercise continual supervision and influence over agency actions.

Despite all these and other constraints, administrative planning, even in a system such as ours, can take place. The first planning task is the most obvious but often the most difficult one—that of deciding what the goals of the organization really are and what they should be. What are the purposes of our organization? What should it be doing? What does the public really want us to do? These are only some of the questions that must be answered before planning can begin.

Successful planning next requires information, a great deal of information. To begin with, planners have to find out all they can about their own organization, its purposes and policies, its culture and characteristics, its strengths and weaknesses. Then they must find out what other organizations like their own are doing and what successes or setbacks these organizations are experiencing and why. At the same time they must keep tabs on the doings and designs of organizations that can affect their organization's activities in many ways. Finally, the planners have to know the total environment in which their organization functions. They must acquire an awareness of what is going on in society and an appreciation of how the changes occurring in society may influence their organization's future. Before anything else, planning is an information-gathering function.

To meet this information need, planning requires large-scale participation. All the organization's members, from those at the very bottom to those at the very top, will usually have something to contribute to the planning process. At the operating levels, the front lines, so to speak, people see the specific problems much more clearly. Even if it is assumed that they lack the education and development to make proper evaluations, an often incorrect assumption, they still have a kind of knowledge that those higher up will almost never be able to attain. The lowly porter who pushes a mop through the corridors will have perspectives and insights into the organization's physical plant that even the supervisor of maintenance will lack.

In its quest for information, the planning process must reach up as well as down, for top management also has a role to play in this initial phase. People at the top often have a better view of the broader picture. They can more easily grasp the interconnections between components of the organization. They should be able to see much more fully the relationship of the organization to its environment. Successful planning thus requires that all elements of the organization be brought into the process.

There is yet another reason why successful planning requires large-scale participation. Good plans are nothing in themselves: to acquire significance, they must be implemented. This, in turn, requires a measure of acceptance from all levels of the organization. Employees who have had a chance to share in the formulation of plans will generally be more willing to implement them, even when the ideas finally adopted are contrary to their wishes, for at least their own ideas will have been heard, and in most cases some accommodation will have been made to their concerns. Here, too, the participation of those at the upper levels as well as those at the bottom is important, for if those at the top have not been actively involved in the planning process, they may evince little enthusiasm for the results of that process. "Real and lasting change requires the sustained involvement of top management," writes Argyris, and he notes that an executive who has helped design the new system is more likely to make an "internal commitment" to its realization.[7]

The requirement of wide-scale participation in order to meet these information and implementation needs obviously becomes a determining factor in setting up the organizational arrangements and apparatus for planning. An organization may create an office staffed with full-time employees expressly for the purpose of planning. Or it may set up one or more committees of employees whose full-time assignments lie elsewhere in the organizational nexus. Or it may use any combination or variation of these two approaches. In any case, those who do the planning must seek to involve as large a proportion of the organization's membership as fully as possible in the planning process.

One device developed by Floyd Mann and his colleagues at the University of Michigan's Survey Research Center calls for setting up what are called organizational "families." Each such family consists of a supervisor and those reporting to him or her. This means that each supervisor actually belongs to two families, the one consisting of him- or herself and subordinates and another consisting of colleagues and his or her own superior. Such a system establishes linkages up, down, and, to some extent, across the organization and provides feedback to guide the planning process. Each organizational family enjoys discretion to consider and work out the implications of matters at its own level, although the designation of the basic problem areas may come from above. This device has been used successfully in many instances.[8]

The "family" system satisfies another requisite for good planning besides the participation necessary to meet its information and implementation needs. This is the opportunity it creates for those who do the planning to execute it. This carries the implementation problem one step forward. Just as it is important for those who are to execute the plans to have some say in their formulation, so it is important for those who formulate the plans to participate in their execution. A planning committee should not go out of existence once the plans have been made but should continue on, assisting in the implementation of the plans and continually checking on their status. As Henry Taylor noted over a century ago, "There are few things more important in the business of the state than that the results of inquiry and research should be realized by those who have had the conduct of it."[9] In other words, the planning function cannot be strictly demarcated from the operating function. Those who execute must plan and those who plan must execute. A planning group not actively involved in the fulfillment of its plans will soon fail to function properly.

The reasons for this stipulation are many. In being allowed and even required to play a role in the implementation of their plans, the planners acquire a more realistic awareness of the problems involved. This should in itself result in better-formulated plans. Furthermore, it will spare the planners the agony of seeing their efforts dissipated by the errors of those who lack the knowledge of or the commitment to those efforts. If the policies adopted strike a sudden snag, then those who were most instrumental in drafting the policies should be best prepared to adapt them to a new situation. Successful planning is not an isolated exercise.

Although actively involving the planners in the implementation of their plans should place some realistic constraints on their activities, in general the planners should enjoy a great deal of discretion. The best planning takes place under conditions of maximum freedom. Planning groups should work within the confines of prescribed goals and guidelines, but these should be kept as broad as possible. Restricting the lines of inquiry will tend to restrict the results.

In utilizing their discretion, planners should take into account two important but often neglected aspects of the planning process. The first is the need for alternative plans in the event that one or more basic elements of the initial plan become outmoded or are otherwise unsuccessful. Given the uncertain environment within which the planning process takes place and the variety of variables that may influence its outcome, plans should be kept flexible.

A good example of this failure to have contingency plans occurred when Congress in 1971 killed the long-worked-on plans for the supersonic transport plane. Following the SST's congressional defeat, it soon became appallingly apparent that the plane's backers both within and without the government had devised no arrangements to deal with such a setback. They were completely unprepared for such tasks as finding jobs for the fourteen thousand workers who had been employed on the project, disposing of $850 million worth of hardware, patents, and blueprints, and liquidating the numerous obligations and contracts that the project had created. "At every level of government," wrote the *New York Times*, "the new questions were being discussed in a mood of general confusion and incredulity that the long SST fight was over. One federal official commented, 'I can't comprehend that there was never a Plan B, but it's obvious now that nobody ever considered the chance of an SST defeat.' "[10] A good planning group will always have a plan B ready, and possibly a plan C as well.

Another aspect of planning often neglected is the decision of what *not* to do. This involves not simply rejecting ideas for future action but also eliminating things that the organization is already doing. According to Robert Townsend, "It's about eleven times as easy to start something as it is to stop something," and he urges all organizations to "make it a practice to wipe out their worst product, service or activity every so often."[11] We have, in earlier chapters, called attention to such bureaucratic pathologies as the tendency to resist elimination or even modification of any function and to such leadership failures as the reluctance to "slough off yesterday." Good planning is designed to reduce these and other perversities in organizational life.

The Tools and Techniques of Planning

If planning, to paraphrase Thomas Hobbes, is characterized by a perpetual and restless desire for information, a quest that ceases only with the death of the planning group or its parent organization, then how is this information to be obtained?

The starting place in most instances is the organization's own records. What are its expenditures for various activities and how are these related to results? This is an obvious key question. It shows the relationship that fruitful planning has to proper budgeting, whether it is programmed budgeting or some other system. Well-developed and well-utilized accounting practices are also mandatory. In short, the planners must have a good grasp of what the organization is currently doing and how it is doing it if they are to map a path for the future.

However, many other sources of information exist besides those linked to the organization's budgetary and accounting process. Complaints, for example, form a valuable planning resource; so do requests for service. A police department planning unit will want to keep a careful check on the quantity and variety of police calls, and it will also go over the various reports submitted by patrolmen and -women, detectives, and so on. An urban-renewal agency will want to study the number and kinds of applications it receives, along with their eventual disposition. And both agencies will want to carefully tabulate and evaluate the complaints they receive.

In making such studies, the planners will usually want more than just a picture of what is happening at one moment in time. In cataloging and classifying police calls, for example, they will want to compare one year with the previous year and possibly with other still more previous years. In this way, they may be able to detect possible trends. For example, if the number of calls involving family disputes is rising every year, this could indicate a need for providing officers with special training to cope with such problems. (Of course, straight-line projections of current trends can be hazardous and should always be subjected to close evaluation of all the factors involved.)

Surveys can also help meet the information needs of planning and help satisfy its participation requirement as well. Organizational planners will want to obtain inputs from as many members of the organization as they can, and often a survey is the only means for doing so. In making such surveys, employees may be interviewed individually or may simply be asked to fill out a form. At some stage of the planning process, however, it is usually advisable to have all those who will be affected by the plans participate in a dialogue regarding them. This is more apt to bring out information hitherto undisclosed and to ease the task of subsequent implementation.

Such surveys should not be confined to people within the organization. It is important and often imperative to involve the agency's clientele in the information process as well, for it obviously has aspects and angles worth considering. Furthermore, its cooperation may be as crucial to making the plans work as the cooperation of the organization's own employees.

This relentless quest for information will not stop at the organization's boundaries. As was noted earlier, the planners will normally reach out into the organization's total environment. They should examine what other organizations are doing by writing letters, paying on-site visits, going over the reports of these organizations, and reading about their activities in journals. They will also want to know what plans these organizations are making for their own future. Finally, the planners will show some interest in finding out current and future events in society that could in some way influence their course.

Once they have amassed all this information, they then face the formidable task of digesting it. Here, they will find it necessary to establish some sort of system for classifying all these inputs. This should assist them in arriving at certain quantitative assumptions regarding what it has to reveal. This, in turn, will enable the planners to utilize it more effectively. Some information can even be fed into a computer, which can be programmed to calculate a wide range of consequences and consider a wide range of alternatives. The final decisions, however, will always have to be made by the individuals concerned.

Even if all the safeguards regarding information gathering and assessment along with participation are zealously and minutely followed, planning will still remain a risky business. Future events can seldom be foretold with complete accuracy, and the effects of planned developments can often be quite different from what was anticipated. This state of affairs frequently leads a planning group to undertake one or more experiments before finalizing their planning efforts.

One great advocate of the need for experimentation was Franklin Roosevelt. "It is common sense," he once said, "to take a method and try it; if it fails, admit it frankly and try another. But above all, try something."[12] Experimentation, at least on occasion, is indispensable to productive planning.

Experimentation often takes the form of a demonstration project. The organization will try out an idea in one of its subunits or on one sector of its clientele to see how it works. Then it assesses the results and determines whether the new concept is essentially workable, and, if it is, what further modifications or amplifications may be necessary to put it into practice. Demonstrations may also serve a further purpose, one that may be more important than that of providing information as to a new idea's workability. This is the persuasive function. The demonstration may help to convince the organization's employees, clientele, or political overseers that the new way of doing things is sound and helpful. In this way, the demonstration may help break down resistance to, and generate support for, the planned change. (It goes without saying that the demonstration project can also serve a contrary purpose. It may be used to demonstrate to one or more employees, clientele, or political groups that an idea that they are urging upon the organization is unsound and unworkable.)

Demonstration projects are not without problems of their own. It is difficult, for one thing, to find a "pure" situation. The laboratory scientist can carry out an experiment free of any external conditions that could influence the experiment's outcome. The social scientist rarely enjoys such a happy state of affairs. For example, a new idea may be tried out in field office A and may be found to have worked successfully. But field office A may be different in one or more respects from field office B. Its employees may be more eager for change, its clientele may be less organized to resist change, its geographic location may lend itself to the proposed change. Consequently, the demonstration that goes well in field office A does not necessarily signal its success as an organization-wide policy.

This problem is further compounded by what has come to be known as the "Hawthorne Effect." The reader will recall from chapter 3 how the group of working women who were put in the test room during the experiments conducted at Western Electric's Hawthorne plant responded positively to nearly every change that was made in their working conditions. Similarly, field office A, if asked to try out a planned change, may make the change work more effectively than it otherwise would simply because the office knows it is being watched. The fact that it is engaged in an experiment makes the field office function differently than it would if it were simply adjusting to a change that was being implemented throughout the organization.

These difficulties encumber experimentation in other fields besides administrative planning. In medicine they have prompted experimenters to create what is sometimes called the "double-blind" study. Under the double-blind approach, one group of test subjects receives the medicine while the other receives placebos, and neither the test subjects nor those conducting the test know which are which. Such a method was used at the Universities of Toronto and Strathclyde in 1972 to test the efficacy of vitamin C in preventing colds. Only after they had made up their lists of those student volunteers who had gotten colds and those who had not and had tabulated how long and how severe the colds were did the researchers as well as the students learn which students had received the vitamin C.

Demonstration projects in administrative planning usually require safeguards such as these if they are to yield valid results. The California State Insurance Compensation Fund for example, proposed changes that were first tried out at a field office. Two other field offices were established as "controls." One of these field offices was told that it was serving as a basis of comparison; the other was not. In this way, the experimenters were able to allow for the influences of the Hawthorne Effect.[13]

Even when such steps are taken, however, result evaluation in administrative demonstration projects can be troublesome. One basic difficulty is finding definitive ways of measuring results. We have already covered these snags and snarls in our discussions of PPBS, productivity measures, and MBO. It goes almost without saying that demonstration projects and, indeed, virtually all administrative planning require a systematic and sound method for evaluating results, and an organization will have a hard time planning successfully unless it confronts and conquers this particular problem. But assuming that an organization has done so, it still has to deal with another difficulty. It takes time to run a demonstration project and to calculate costs and benefits. Sometimes, by the time the final report is ready, the situation has changed to the point where the contemplated plan would no longer be applicable. And so the planners have to start all over again, hoping that this time they will not be overtaken by events.

One final problem remains for the evaluators. This is the need to distinguish between short-term and long-term results. Sometimes they can be quite different. For example, an organization might try out a system of tighter supervision, which in the short run might produce substantial benefits in terms of reduced waste and increased output. Yet, the long-term effects could prove disastrous as the better workers, chafing under such constraints, leave the organization while others turn hostile and begin sabotaging it. It is sometimes necessary to show short-term results in order to convince the organization, its clients, or its political overseers that something is being accomplished. But it is also necessary to exercise caution and care lest such considerations weaken or even wipe out long-term achievement.

Putting the Plan to Work

As was noted earlier, planning does not stop when the proposed change or changes are finally drawn up, packaged, and handed out for implementation. The planning process must include the implementing process as well. And not only should the planners help execute their plans, they should even draw up plans for such execution.

One tool that has evolved to assist in this task is PERT, an acronym for "program evaluation and review technique." PERT was developed by the navy's Special Projects Office to implement the service's newly authorized ballistic-missile program. According to Professor Harvey Sapolsky, it is characterized by four main features. The first is "a network that geographically describes the interrelationship of the steps [called events] involved in developing a specific end item." The second consists of "three time estimates for reaching each event in the network." These estimates are categorized as the most optimistic, the most likely, and the most pessimistic. Then, a formula is arrived at "for calculating the probability distribution of the 'expected' time for completing the expected activity." Finally, the implementers identify "the longest expected time sequence through the network, which is labeled 'the critical path.'" It is understood that the total project will not be realized until this critical path has been completed.[14]

This new technique seemed to have worked well for the navy during the 1950s and gradually became adopted by other agencies. NASA has made use of it in the development and construction of its space vehicles as well as in its moon-shot program. Even private industry has perked up its ears and borrowed at least some of the techniques. For example, Dupont now sets up a critical path for various projects and then calculates the variances along the "path" to determine the probability of finishing on schedule. However, the company uses only one time estimate per task along the way, not the three that are utilized by the navy.

Sapolsky, who has written a scholarly study on the navy's use of PERT, claims it was largely a public-relations stunt and "had little to do with the effectiveness of the effort to develop the Polaris" submarine. He presents strong evidence to support his claim and, in fact, the loud hosannas that were originally sung to the new system have begun to die down. It does tend to encourage more systematic thinking, however, and its basic approach can lead to improved results.

As an example of how the PERT approach can work, New York City found in 1966 that its capital construction program was floundering. It was taking the city government ten years or more to build a school, hospital, or other major capital facility. The site-selection and planning phase alone

NETWORK DIAGRAM

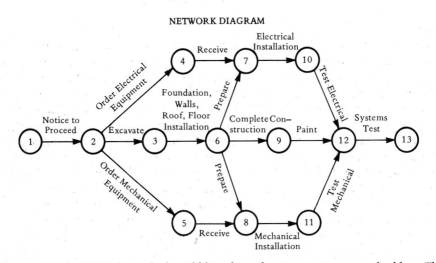

This is a sample PERT chart, which could have been drawn up to construct a building. The numbers stand for events and the arrows signify the activities necessary for reaching the events. Note that after event 2, three arrows branch out simultaneously to events 3, 4, and 5. This means that these activities can be undertaken at the same time. (In PERT parlance, this is called a "burst point.") The "merge point" occurs at 12. The "critical path" is the longest path through the network, yet it represents the shortest time possible for completing the program. Can you think of why? (See the diagram on the next page for the answer.) (Source: U.S. Civil Service Commission.)

frequently consumed more than five years. A study of the problem showed that such construction would often involve twelve or more different agencies, most of them operating under strict state regulations. As a result, the process of building a new school required some four thousand separate steps. By the time the process was completed, population changes, technological innovations, or political realignments may have made the completed facility somewhat outmoded.

The following year the city set up its Capital Construction Information System to provide monthly reports on progress and completion projections for two thousand three hundred projects. Milestones for each project were established and monthly progress reviews were prepared for the officials bearing responsibility for them. The mayor also named a single director of construction for projects under control of city hall. Planning and construction time for capital projects was cut almost in half as a result.[15]

The New York City system lacks some of the main features of PERT and may seem in some respects more closely related to MBO, discussed before. Actually, it is related to both and as such serves to show how deeply interrelated so many elements in the administrative process are. A clear understanding and an ability to cope with these manifold interrelationships can help administrations and administrators meet the challenges of change.

CRITICAL PATH DETERMINATION

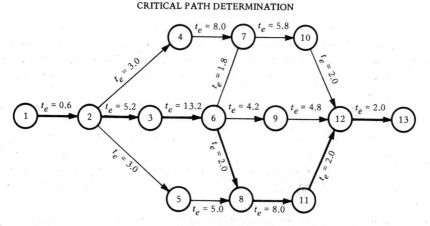

The symbol t_e simply represents the estimated time necessary to reach an event, while the figures stand for units of time, which can be days, weeks, months, or even years. The critical path consists of 1, 2, 3, 6, 8, 11, 12, and 13. If any other route is used, it would not provide enough time for all the events to be realized. (If we proceed from 6 to 9 to 12, we would reach event 13, or completion, more rapidly, but we would not leave enough time to complete events 8 through 11, although we would be able to achieve events 7 and 10.) The chart shows us, among other things, that it would be unwise to pay overtime to complete events 7 and 10 earlier since they are not on the critical path. Can PERT be used in other activities, such as planning a dinner party? (Source: U.S. Civil Service Commission.)

CASE STUDY

Human Resources Finds a New Resource[16]

Daniel R. Jensen has developed a six-step planning process, which he describes as "easy to learn, simple to manage, and applicable in a wide variety of situations." Jensen, who is chief of the Office of Productivity and Development for the Washington State Department of Social and Health Services, offers as an example the use of his process by the Human Resources Division of a large (fifteen thousand employees) state agency.

The first step in Jensen's planning mechanism calls for each agency unit to identify and state its core mission. This must be done carefully, he stresses, since all the other steps follow from it. The manager in charge bears responsibility for doing this but others can, and normally should, contribute.

The Human Resources Division he cites was made up of five offices: personnel operations, personnel management, labor relations, equal opportunity, and productivity and development. Their initial attempts at this task yielded statements that were too vague and open-ended. With guidance, however, they managed to produce simpler and more specific statements. Thus "to facilitate the development of agency employees" became "to provide trained supervisors and managers," and "to improve labor relations" became "to assure uniform administration of collective bargaining contracts."

Step 2 requires the units to analyze and describe their current conditions, including their resources and outputs together with their successes and problems. This procedure apparently raised no real difficulties. However, step 3, which can be viewed as an extension of step 2, proved more complex. This step requires the unit to analyze its environment, including the community, clientele groups, other agencies, and all other institutions and forces that have an impact upon it. At the same time it must not neglect its internal environment, including such factors as organizational structure, staffing levels, morale, et cetera.

For the division in question this meant assessing the effects of continuing inflation, reduced federal support, growing pressure to cut back administrative personnel, more stringent personnel regulations imposed by the central state personnel agency on all state agencies, et cetera.

The task of ferreting out and figuring in all these factors and forces proved trying and troublesome but, says Jensen, it also by itself generated some benefits. Gathering all this data and sifting through it for trends not only made the units more hard-nosed and realistic but also gave them a feeling of being on top of things. In the past they, like so many government agencies, had tended to be reactive. Now they felt they could to some extent fashion their own future.

This made them ready for step 4, namely to describe the "improved condition," which on the basis of the information they have compiled and the core mission statement they have adopted, they should seek to achieve. This "improved condition" could be couched first as a general statement but then should be broken down into tangible terms.

The Employee Development Unit offers an example of how this was done. This was the unit that had framed the core mission statement "to provide trained supervisors and managers." Based on the analysis and assessments it had made under steps 2 and 3, the unit decided that its mission could be best realized by reducing its scope and sharpening its focus. In the future it would do fewer things but do them better. To bring about this "improved condition" the unit decided to hold ten one-week supervisory workshops and four executive core workshops a year aimed at serving twenty-four participants a session. These participants should achieve average evaluation ratings of 85 percent. All workshops should be scheduled at least six months in advance, and their high quality should produce waiting lists of employees wanting to attend.

The last two steps of Jensen's planning framework involve identifying "key accomplishments" and "key decisions." For the Employee Development Unit the key decisions involved answering such questions as

- Is a core training program needed for mid-level managers?
- Which applied-skills workshops should be taught?
- What services and training programs should be discontinued?

The key accomplishments for this unit included such things as

- producing a core-training program for mid-level managers;
- completing a needs assessment;
- delivering applied skills workshop;
- discontinuing services not related to the core mission.

By and large, says Jensen, these goals were fulfilled. Other accomplishments achieved by other offices of the division included the combination of the personnel and payroll sections into one unit, the development and implementation of a management information system to monitor affirmative-action complaints and their resolution, implementation of a "charge-back" system for staff training activities, development of a "unit cost" system for a variety of procedures, et cetera.

All in all, says Jensen, the planning process worked and worked well in this state agency, and his data seems to support his claim. What is of special interest is that the agency and its offices not only undertook new functions or enlarged and improved some existing ones, but they also phased down or out others that no longer seemed worthwhile. For example, the Employee Development Unit curtailed some of its less crucial services, such as audio-visual loans, and disbanded two staff development centers. Planning had served as a true agent of change.

The process utilized more of the techniques mentioned earlier than this condensed account makes apparent. There was, for instance, a good deal of participation at all or most levels of the organization. Office chiefs and their principal aides met jointly with a special coordinator appointed by the division director prior to each of the six steps. This was followed by further meetings within each office. Morale improved and many employees, especially middle managers, who had disdained or distrusted the whole idea of planning, gradually became accepting and even enthusiastic. As even one of its diehard opponents grudgingly conceded, "I used to detest planning; now I only dislike it."

Agents of Change: Management Information Systems

The Baltimore Orioles ended the regular 1979 baseball season with the best winning percentage in the major leagues. They then went on to win the divisional playoffs in five games (out of a possible seven) and to come within a run or two of winning the World Series. What made their achievement so intriguing was the fact that the Orioles operated on a shoestring budget, one of the lowest in major league baseball. They had almost no superstars on their playing squad, and even their better pitchers were in many cases earning only about half the money being paid to their colleagues on other teams.

The Orioles' startling success was largely credited to their manager, Earl Weaver. Just what did Weaver do to earn such laurels for himself and his team?

For one thing, he became the first baseball manager to make the computer part of his operation. He used computers to assemble and assess the batting record of every one of his fielders against every pitcher in the American League. This information enabled him to change his batters to suit whatever pitchers the opposing team might bring to the mound.

What Weaver had done was to install and operate the first true management information system in professional baseball. But if such systems were still unique in the sports world at the end of the 1970s, they had become a fixture in many business concerns and in a growing number of government agencies as well. Francis Bacon's seventeenth century pronouncement, "Knowledge is power" has taken on a steadily increasing significance in the information-hungry twentieth century. Successful administration today requires adequate and timely knowledge, and those who would administer successfully must take advantage of the tools and techniques that have evolved to supply it.

A management information system serves primarily to provide managers with the knowledge they need for day-to-day, week-to-week, or month-to-month operations. Such a system will also generally furnish a great deal of useful information for planning and other forms of change. For example, an MIS installed in a fire department could probably develop data on the number and kinds of fires in the city during the course of a year. The department could use that information in assigning and scheduling its apparatus and personnel. This information should also spotlight longstanding problems and bring to light any changes in the city's general fire pattern. It thus would greatly assist the department in anticipating the future and in adapting itself to meet it.

The Essential Question

The most important decision to make when it comes to MIS is determining what information to collect. The possibilities for most organizations seem also limitless. A school department will want to know certain basic kinds of data, such as reading scores, truancy rates, and per pupil expenditure costs. Many other less obvious kinds of information can be collected and put to use, however. These might include vandalism costs, teacher absenteeism patterns, attendance at and frequency of parent-teacher meetings, et cetera. All such data can assist school administrators in planning the future as well as in managing the present.

How much detail should such data provide? Frequently more will be better than less. It may not be enough to know current vandalism costs compared to last year; the superintendent and his or her associates will want to know what kinds of schools experience the most vandalism, when it seems worst, et cetera.

This brings us to another consideration. The MIS user must also decide the extent to which the information should be kept current. The answers will vary depending on the subject. The school administrator may want daily reports on pupil absenteeism rates, but may need only weekly or monthly reports on teacher absenteeism or vandalism rates.

Who should collect all this information? Having those who will use it collect the information offers some rather obvious advantages. They will know what they need and therefore will avoid unnecessary data. The very fact that they are gathering the information themselves means that they are more likely to act upon it. They may also know best where the information may be found and how to extract it.

However, having outsiders install and operate the management information system has some advantages that are nearly as apparent, Outsiders are more apt to possess the expertise to design and operate such a system most efficiently. They are also in a better position to deal more objectively with the data. Their efforts would also free the other members of the administrative staff to spend more time assessing the data and then implementing the consequent decisions.

The actual technology of management information systems is heavily dependent on data processing. Indeed, it is the computer that has made the modern MIS possible, for it not only gathers and interprets but also stores vast bodies of material. Management information systems represent one form of organizational response to the computer.

But MIS is not solely a computer product. Some of the more imaginative and intrepid managers in history instituted systematic ways of collecting and compiling information long before the computer's advent. Napoleon had prepared for each regiment in the Austrian army a card that contained as much information as his intelligence services could supply about the regiment. This information system helped him to stage his series of successful battles against the Austrian forces.

Today many managers, especially those with more limited responsibilities and resources, can make use of MIS techniques without using computers. A school principal, for instance, may simply wish to prepare a chart showing which teachers have reported sick on which days of the week and during which weeks and months of the year. Such a simple chart may be very revealing. Similarly, the head of a field office for, say, the Department of Housing and Urban Development may wish to prepare a form for field agents to report periodic progress in housing and other projects under their supervision. Here again, unless the numbers involved are substantial, computers may not be needed to assemble and assess such information. And the information itself can provide the manager with material useful not only for dealing with the present but with the future as well.

Dangers and Disappointments

The acquisition of increased information in a systematic manner would seem to be an innocuous activity that could only benefit those involved. But such is not the case. MIS also can do harm if not properly handled.

One common mistake made by MIS enthusiasts is its understandable overuse. Too much information is churned out for the organization and its administrators to absorb, let alone apply. We saw in chapter 7 the difficulties and dangers that communication overload can produce. An overelaborate and overworked management information system can seriously aggravate the overload problem.

Another problem is overextending any particular system so that it reaches into too many areas of the organization. As Gilbert W. Fairholm, a seasoned administrator who has held several high-level positions with the New York State government has observed, "a fully-integrated, agency-wide system can completely diffuse responsibility in the organization. An error or failure at one point can jam the gears all over the organization."[17]

Most important of all, perhaps, is the danger of overreliance on such systems. To quote Fairholm again, "the basic ingredients of managerial decisions—and of managerial success—are judgment, initiative, intuition, and common-sense. It is a rare MIS which has these characteristics."[18]

Business school professor H. Edward Wrapp goes even further, claiming MIS has become a "highly visible miscarriage of modern management." As Wrapp sees it, "the 'professional' general manager presses for total systems where every shred of data is collected and analyzed and printed on forms that engulf everyone's desk. The mountains of paper provide him a kind of assurance that everything is under control."[19]

These criticisms notwithstanding, improved means for acquiring more information on a systematic basis are virtually mandatory for most modern-day public managers. Instinct, "common sense," or even experience is no longer sufficient for coping with the complex conditions now confronting administrators. The new productivity and budgeting techniques discussed in the two previous chapters require improved techniques for gathering information. In one form or another, MIS has a vital role to play in modern-day administration.

MIS COMES TO THE CAMPUS

Reeling under the whiplash of rising costs and tightening revenues, many academic institutions have begun installing information systems to help them get a better handle on what they are doing. For example, each time a book is borrowed from the libraries of New York University, the departmental affiliation of the borrower, whether student or faculty member, is registered. This allows the university to apportion, in an accounting sense, the costs of the library's operations among the various departments.

Perhaps no university, however, has made more extensive use of MIS than has Brown. With its tuition and room and board charges approaching twelve thousand dollars a year for the 1982–1983 academic year, the Rhode Island institution had even begun making systematic tabulations on what food its students liked and how much of these foods they consumed. Such data had enabled the university to set up a computerized meal-planning system that had cut food waste and saved over one hundred thousand dollars in two years.

MIS was also helping the university raise revenues as well. Thanks in part to a computerized system for keeping alumni records up-to-date, Brown's capital-fund drive had raised $134 million by the spring of 1982.

Agents of Change: Interdepartmental Committees

Let us assume that a city manager suddenly finds that a particular neighborhood is suffering from an outbreak of teenage crime and general juvenile misbehavior. Something must be done. What should he or she do?

Several suggestions come to mind: consult the neighborhood institutions, the parents, and even the teenagers themselves. But in order for their ideas to be sifted, refined, and, most important, implemented, the city government must come into play. Which agency of the government should this be? Although the police would seem to be the most directly concerned, they have neither the resources nor the capacity to deal with the problem in a deep and comprehensive manner. What now?

One solution would be to set up an interdepartmental committee. Such a committee could include representatives from the police, the school department, the parks and/or recreation department, the health department, the welfare department, and any other agency that might have some input to make in diagnosing the problem and some contribution to make in alleviating it. Working with neighborhood groups and citizens, they could jointly undertake a program of what might be termed "meaningful change."

In ways such as this, an interdepartmental committee can serve as an agent of change. It is a device that frequently serves other functions, of course, primarily those of coordination and adjudication. It is particularly useful in dealing with disputes involving jurisdiction (i.e., determining which agency has authority in which area). It can also serve, as we shall shortly see, as a means of preventing or forestalling change. But despite sometimes contradictory functions, interdepartmental committees have been used for adapting organizations to new problems and new processes.

In a sense, the interdepartmental committee has a long history in U.S. administration, for its origins go back to the beginnings of the republic. The president's cabinet is, at least to some extent, such a committee, and George Washington, who took his cabinet fairly seriously, used it for this purpose. However, the really great growth of interdepartmental committees occurred during World War II, when U.S. officials had to work closely with various agencies of the British government. They found that the British were making extensive use of this device to good effect.

One particularly outstanding British example of such a committee was the famed "Twenty Committee," which met weekly from January 1941 to May 1945. This committee was set up to decide what information to give the string of German agents that the British had managed to convert to double-agent status. In order to build up their credibility with their Nazi superiors, the agents had to be supplied with bona fide information and even had to be allowed to carry out some successful sabotage. Handling the double agents in this way required intensive cooperation from many government agencies and the "Twenty" managed to obtain it."[20]

While few if any Americans learned much about the "Twenty Committee" at the time, they did acquire a knowledge and appreciation of how skillfully the British seemed to be able to use such an administrative tool in less secret situations to improve communication, encourage cooperation, and respond to vicissitudes of war. By the end of the war, the interdepartmental committee had become firmly entrenched in our own federal bureaucracy.

After the war, many interdepartmental committees disappeared, though many continued and still others came into existence. The most notable of the latter—it is today the most important such committee in the nation— is the National Security Council, formed in 1947. It consists of the president and essentially whomever the president wants to have on it. The other members usually include the vice president; the secretaries of state, defense, and the treasury; the directors of the Office of Management and Budget and the Central Intelligence Agency; the chairman of the Joint Chiefs; and others. Some, such as the secretary of state and the chairman of the Joint Chiefs, participate in nearly all committee deliberations. Others may only attend on occasion. The council has a small staff but no operational responsibilities.[21]

The National Security Council became fairly active under Eisenhower, but according to James W. Davis, Jr., it seemed to decline in importance under Presidents Kennedy and Johnson.[22] Both presidents also made little use of cabinet meetings, preferring to handle matters pertaining to security with ad hoc groups whose membership might even include persons holding no official government position. The council seemed to experience a revived role under President Nixon. When Nixon issued a low-keyed alert to the armed forces during the 1973 Arab-Israeli war, it was suggested by some that he was doing so only to divert attention from the exploding Watergate scandal. Secretary of State Henry Kissinger sought to squelch such speculation by pointing out that the president's action was taken only in response to a unanimous National Security Council decision.

Many other less lustrous interdepartmental committees have also thrived within the federal bureaucracy. One little known but quite successful one was the Federal Committee on Pest Control set up in 1964 to combat a rather serious agricultural problem. Its membership consisted of representatives from the Departments of Defense, Interior, and HEW, as well as Agriculture. The departments cooperated well, bringing about productive and reasonably prompt results.[23]

The interdepartmental committee has also secured a measure of acceptance and usage at the state and local government level. Many mayors during the 1960s, such as John Lindsay of New York and Kevin White of Boston, began holding weekly meetings of their department heads to encourage greater interdepartmental cooperation and a more unified and comprehensive approach to problem solving. Lindsay also set up an interdepartmental committee on industrial development, comprising representatives from the city's Department of Housing and Redevelopment, the City Planning Commission, the Department of Marine and Aviation, the Department of Real Estate, and the mayor's office. It was considered something of a revolutionary concept in the history of New York City's fragmented administration.[24]

The interdepartmental committee, however, cannot be given a clean bill of health. Although such committees are designed to smooth out and speed up interagency action, they sometimes do the reverse. They add still more units to the administrative network and thus increase its complexity and possibly its confusion as well. This is particularly true when such committees start creating a staff of their own. They then become more and more like operational agencies, and in so doing they can make for less rather than more unified action.

Depriving the committee of any separate staff, facilities, and so on, may ease this problem but may, at the same time, aggravate another one. If committee decisions are to be effective, they must be implemented, and without a staff to at least check up and follow through, such implementation may not take place. What further hampers implementation is that top officials tend to be overburdened with demands made on their time and start assigning lesser officials to serve on the committees. The lesser officials may have the time to serve on the committee or committees and may do so faithfully and intelligently. When it comes to putting the committee's decisions into practice within their own agency, however, they frequently find that they lack the power to do so. An agency will normally feel less obliged to abide by an interagency decision when the decision is brought back by someone of lesser stature. Of course, if the agency representative can persuade his or her superiors to push forward with the decision, this may substantially solve the problem. Higher officials will feel much less committed to implementing a decision, however, if they did not participate directly in making it.

The problem of getting participant agencies to abide by the decisions that these committees make is a constant one but is often superseded by another problem—arriving at a decision in the first place. While interdepartmental committees can serve as agents for change, they can, as was noted above, also serve as a bulwark for the status quo. Agency representatives may attend the meetings not so much to create change as to protect their own agency's powers, prerogatives, and position. In an effort to appease its various members, the committee either ends up as a talking shop or arrives at decisions that are so watered down as to be virtually meaningless. As Dean Acheson once noted, "One can always get an agreed paper by increasing the vagueness and generality of its statements. The staff of any inter-departmental committee has a fatal weakness for this kind of agreement by exhaustion."[25]

Finally, such committees become prone to many of the bureaucratic pathologies that were cited in chapter 3, particularly the one of persistence. Even when formed to deal with only a single, transient problem, the committee may linger on, especially if it has established a staff. The Hoover Commission, while finding that such committees could prove worthwhile, expressed concern over their tendency to survive long after they had outlived their usefulness. It recommended a reappraisal of all such committees every year with the termination of those whose work was no longer necessary. This recommendation failed to take hold, and as new committees arose, the number of such groups increased to approximately 850 by 1970. The State Department alone chaired 62 such committees and sat on many others.

Dean Don K. Price of the John F. Kennedy Institute of Politics at Harvard University has sought to come to grips with both the problems and potentialities of interdepartmental committees, drawing upon a lifetime of service in and out of government. According to Price, such committees can be useful if not too much is expected of them. The most important issue, says Price, is "whether the departmental representatives are sent to the meeting to come to an agreement or with instruction to prevent anything from happening." Another criterion he puts forth concerns their formal status. "If . . . such a committee acquires legal status, *esprit de corps* and jurisdictional interests of its own, and is looked to by Congress and the public as the source of policy, the only outcome can be a muddle."[26] Thus, he argues that interdepartmental committees should not be given any formal authority but rather should be used as auxiliaries in a responsible system of executive organization.

In the meantime, an approach has evolved to ease some of the problems of translating committee decisions into departmental policy. This allows the head of an agency to send a representative to committees involving that agency rather than attending him- or herself. However, all the representatives attending are permitted to make decisions that will be binding on their respective agencies if no agency head objects to the decision within a stated period of time. For example, the governors of New England meet four times a year as the New England Regional Commission. Their representatives, called alternates, meet every six weeks. The alternates hammer out decisions on various matters, and if no governor casts a veto within ten days following their meeting, the decisions become final.

It is hoped that these and other ways of improving the operations of interdepartmental committees will become more widespread as time goes on. Certainly, such committees will continue to be needed, for in a society in which problems are becoming increasingly multidimensional, the need for interdepartmental decision making will doubtlessly grow apace.

Agents of Change: Study Commissions and Task Forces

During his second term, President George Washington confronted a crisis that threatened not only the authority of the president but that of the federal government itself. A band of irate Pennsylvania distillers, angry over a federal tax on their products, had refused to pay it. The governor of Pennsylvania was no help, since he was fearful of losing his own popularity in the state and, in any case, had a Jeffersonian outlook, which made him reluctant to take harsh governmental action. It was up to Washington and his administration to meet this initial test of federal sovereignty.

Washington eventually summoned a force of fifteen thousand militiamen from four states and stamped out the Whiskey Rebellion, as it was called. But before taking this step, he appointed a commission to study the problem. The commission authorized his hitherto-unprecedented action. The authority of the federal government had weathered its first major test.

Since that time, presidents, along with lesser chief executives and administrators, have set up commissions and task forces to help them resolve pressing problems. As was the case with Washington's commission, these bodies are by no means exclusively agents of change. They serve a variety of purposes, including, on occasion, the prevention of change. Yet they are usually intended to bring about some form of change and hence warrant our consideration.

The use of commissions at the presidential level has become particularly pronounced in the last forty years. Franklin Roosevelt made fairly extensive use of this device, as did his successor, Harry Truman. Both presidents established commissions to study the executive branch of the federal government and to suggest ways of improving its operations. President Eisenhower appointed a commission to seek ways of shifting some of the federal government's activities back to the states. And John F. Kennedy appointed a variety of task forces to help him man policy before he even took office.

The presidential commission, however, reached its flowering under Lyndon Johnson. This hyperactivist president had a variety of study commissions at work during his tenure in the White House. Many of these became well known, such as those concerned with law enforcement, riots, and violence. Others remained more obscure, such as the Commission on Crime in the District of Columbia. The popularity of the device diminished during President Nixon's first term but did not die out completely. Nixon named commissions to study such matters as nutrition, heart disease, and federal statistics.

As has been noted, a commission, be it presidential or otherwise, may serve a multitude of purposes, only some of which may foster change. Elizabeth Drew, who is perhaps the country's outstanding reporter on administrative matters, has listed in somewhat cynical, if nevertheless perceptive fashion, eight such purposes.[27]

The first, according to Drew, is "to obtain the blessing of distinguished men for something you want to do anyway." This is probably the oldest rationale for establishing a commission and was most likely the main motivation behind George Washington's appointment of commissioners to study the Whiskey Rebellion. It certainly played a role in the appointment by Presidents Roosevelt and Truman of commissions to study the executive branch. Both men, Roosevelt in particular, wanted to strengthen the hand of the president in running the bureaucracy. To have suggested this themselves would have brought a storm of controversy on their heads. But an impartial commission of distinguished men—Truman's commission was headed by former Republican President Herbert Hoover—could make such a move seem quite legitimate.

Governors, mayors, city managers, and even department heads and bureau chiefs sometimes use the commission device for this purpose. This does not mean that they always "stack" the commission with people who will do their bidding or that they try to manipulate it for this covert purpose. Rather it may indicate that what they want to do is what any group of intelligent people who have studied the situation would recommend, and so they appoint a commission knowing full well that it will come up with suggestions along the lines of what they already have in mind.

In serving such a function, the study commission is still serving as an agent of change. According to Drew, however, another frequent purpose of such a commission is to postpone action while giving the impression that work on the problem is proceeding. Tied to this purpose as well as to the first purpose is a third: "to act as a lightning rod, drawing political heat away from the White House."

Some would see this latter motive at work in the first concrete step that President Nixon suggested in response to the Watergate affair. In the spring of 1973, as the scandal was starting to unfold, the president called on Congress to set up a seventeen-member bipartisan commission to study the electoral process. The reaction from Congress and the press was decidedly negative. The *New York Times* pointed out that the study commission was a "traditional temporizing device."

Howard E. Schuman, who served as executive director of the Commission on the Problems of the American City, agrees that study commissions can often be used in this way. "A presidential commission," he has written, "is generally established to buy time on an immediate and politically tender issue—or, as someone else has said, to treat the politics of a situation rather than the situation itself. Commission members are expected to go into seclusion and not rock the boat. They usually report many months later—after public clamor has died down—and their work gets filed with the great unread literature of the World."[28] Schuman does say that commissions can aid the process of change. The work of his own commission, he claims, did have some impact in the shaping of policy, although probably much less than the commission and staff members had hoped.

Drew also admits that commissions can prove a positive force in policy making. In addition to helping secure public acceptance for doing something that needs to be done, they educate their own members in the problems they are confronting. They may also lay to rest rumors and "convince the public of the validity of one particular set of facts." She cites the Warren Commission, which probed and reported on the assassination of President Kennedy, as an example of the latter type (although the rumors of a widespread conspiracy being responsible for the president's death still continue to circulate). Finally, she concedes that a commission can uncover facts that the administrator has not uncovered and can suggest programs and policies that he or she and the staff have not devised. With all their shortcomings and their susceptibility to political manipulation, study commissions can serve as agents of change.

The Study Commission at Work

Setting up a study commission is a delicate task. Obviously it must contain people with some acknowledged expertise in the problem or problems to be investigated. A committee on nutrition with no physicians or nutritionists among its members would scarcely command any public support. At the same time, however, the commission must be representative of the groups most directly concerned. Thus, while a commission on urban problems should contain some recognized urbanologists, it should also include representatives of those sectors of the population, such as minority groups, that may have the most at stake in the resolution of urban problems. Finally, the commission must number among its members some distinguished representatives of the general public. A commission composed solely of experts and clientele representatives will often lack the perspective as well as the political clout for drawing up proposals that are both essentially sound and administratively feasible.

The selection of the chairperson demands particular care. He or she should almost always be a public member, or at least someone with no direct and personal interest in the commission's outcome. He or she also should be someone who can command the respect of the public and, hopefully, the support of the political figures whose cooperation will be needed to implement the findings. Harry Truman's selection of Herbert Hoover to head his commission on reorganization of the federal bureaucracy was probably a masterstroke in this respect. Hoover, as an ex-president, could be considered well qualified for the task. At the same time, he had long since retired from politics and consequently had no personal involvement in what the commission was studying. Finally, Hoover was a Republican, and any Republican congressperson who might choose to contest the commission's recommendations would thereby have to repudiate the former leader of his or her own party.

If the commission is authorized and funded to have a staff, then appointment of this staff constitutes one of its first and probably its most important task. What makes the staff so important is that if the commission is representative, and if it consists of distinguished people, then it will be composed of people who lack both the expertise and the time to delve fully into the designated problem areas. Thus, the role of the staff looms large. Frequently, the commission will become a captive of its staff, ratifying with only minor changes proposals that the staff members devise.

ROYAL COMMISSION

If you're pestered by critics and hounded by faction,
to take some precipitate, positive action,
the proper procedure, to take my advice, is
appoint a commission and stave off the crisis.
By shelving the matter you daunt opposition
and blunt its impatience by months of attrition,
Replying meanwhile, with a shrug and a smile,
"The matter's referred to a Royal Commission."

　　　—from, "Royal Commission," Geoffrey Parsons, *Punch*, 24 August 1955

Given the prominence of the staff in shaping the commission's output, great care should be exercised in selecting it. Unfortunately this cannot always be done. The commission is usually under instructions to get going as soon as possible. More important, it can only offer temporary employment. Since many able people are not immediately available for what is essentially a one-shot opportunity, staffing commissions presents problems. On the positive side, though, is the fact that the prominence and often dominance of the staff in deciding what the commission shall eventually recommend makes service on such commissions appealing to many who would otherwise not be interested.

The commission may have to confront other issues as it winds its way toward its final report. Should it issue interim reports along the way or should it wait until it has its final report ready? There are advantages in both procedures. Interim reports may come at a time closer to the events that prompted the commission's formation and therefore may score a greater impact. They may also allow speedier action to be taken by presenting proposals for action sooner than would be the case if the commission waited until it had completed all its work. And the interim report may whet the public interest for the commission's subsequent findings. On the other hand, interim reports may be premature and lack completeness, even if they are confined to certain aspects of the problem area. They may lead to fragmented action and may hinder the public from obtaining a broad view of the entire situation. They may also weaken the impact of the final report.

The commission will usually face a more vexing problem in getting agreement within itself on just what is to be said in its report or reports. There will often be a clash of viewpoints. The danger then arises that, far from swallowing the staff's reports whole, the commission waters them down to the point where they become almost meaningless. It will be recalled, this is the same danger that Dean Acheson warned about concerning interdepartmental committees. Many members as well as the staff personnel of Lyndon Johnson's Commission on Law Enforcement and the Administration of Justice wanted to discuss in detail the problem of police corruption. However, the law-enforcement members on the commission managed to block any in-depth treatment of this subject.

If the conflicting viewpoints on the commission result in a report that is less specific and hard-hitting than many might wish, they will help produce a report that will stand a better chance of acceptance. As Harold Wolman has pointed out, "The benefits derived from a 'representative' outside task force are several. Most important, if the task force report is unanimous, a supporting coalition representing most of the major elements in American society will already have been built. Issues dividing builders, labor, financiers, cities, civil rights groups and others will have been bargained out and settled prior to the Congressional battle."[29] Wolman was speaking in particular reference to commissions on housing, but the same factors apply to commissions on other matters as well. It might be just as well to deal with the political problems involved before the report as after it.

How effective are outside study commissions? Few if any of them have seen all their recommendations translated into firm operational policy.

Perhaps the most successful in this respect were the two Hoover commissions. Their proposals brought about the unification of the armed services into a single Department of Defense, a modernization of the federal government's budgetary procedures, and several other changes. Others have not fared so well, but most have seen at least some of their suggestions acted upon. Furthermore, their proposals, along with the data upon which they are based, become published and often constitute a valuable source of information for those who are interested in the problems they have tackled. Used in college courses, for example, such material may influence the next generation of leadership.

Finally, there is the role they play in educating some influential people (i.e., their own members) in some of the crucial issues of the day. As a member of Johnson's staff noted how appointing conservative members to a commission on housing can create change, "We ... in effect, co-opt them. We rub their noses in the problem and bring them along with the solutions. Hell, some of them have never seen slums and ghettos before. We bring them into the slums and they are amazed that such things can exist. It's surprising how radical some of them become."[30]

Agents of Change: Consultants

In an attempt to keep abreast of the currents of change and their impact on their own operations, organizations have begun to make increasing use of consultants. The practice of calling in such outside experts for aid and assistance is already far advanced in the private sector and is gradually becoming more common in the public sector as well. By the early 1980s it was estimated that nonprofit institutions of one kind or another were generating a quarter billion dollars worth of business for managerial consultants every year.

This growing trend has not failed to incite a drumfire of criticism. A consultant, in Robert Townsend's definition, is a person who borrows your watch to tell you what time it is and then walks off with it. Ida Hoos is somewhat less sarcastic but more specific in her reservations. "When outside information experts descend on inhouse staff, with the blessing of oversold executives, they make demands for 'cooperation'—the gathering of data, records, etc., that often interrupts necessary tasks and interferes with normal activity. Free from the cost/benefit sword of Damocles that hangs over the in-house planners and programs, they generate and perpetuate systems that are cumbersome, often unworkable and even an impediment to the achievement of goals."[31]

If consultants, in addition to being expensive, tend to interfere with the normal operations of an organization and to make recommendations that, because of their limited knowledge of the organization, tend to be dysfunctional, why are they so often used? According to critics, consultants are used to serve three purposes.

First, consultants can be a way of getting around civil-service laws. An agency can hire the people it wants, when it wants, and for how long it wants without having to put up with civil-service restrictions if it can classify and fund them as consultants. This practice can easily lead to a second abuse—the use of consultantships as a means of patronage. Contracts for professional services are rarely put out to bid, for the members of the profession usually have strict rules regarding such competitive practices. Thus, the contract can be awarded on grounds other than that of the lowest price. Ostensibly, the grounds should be those of quality of performance, but since this cannot be predetermined with any exactitude, those who award the contract have a fair degree of discretion in deciding who is going to get it. As a result, consultants who contribute to the campaigns of winning mayoral candidates, for example, frequently find themselves favored when city hall needs some consulting services.

Although local and state government may be the most flagrant abuse of the "consultant connection," the federal bureaucracy can hardly claim complete innocence of such practices. A confidential audit of the Nuclear Regulatory Commission in 1978 disclosed a large number of heretofore unreported and unnoticed consultants. The agency had concealed their presence by manipulating personnel and payroll records. Among these nearly invisible consultants were two former congressmen, each of whom the agency was paying $465 a day. This was more than three times the maximum that the law then allowed.[32]

COSTLY CONSULTING

The Department of Agriculture once hired a consultant to find ways of cutting the cost of inspecting meat. The consultant came up with what at first seemed a feasible proposal, but both consumer groups and meat packers immediately challenged it, forcing the department to hire another consultant to study the first consultant's report. Nearly a half million dollars was spent in this cost-cutting effort.

Perhaps the greatest and most widespread criticism leveled against the use of consultants is that often they are engaged to tell the employers what they want to hear. In other words, they are hired not so much to present the contractee with new ideas but to legitimize the ideas the contractee already has.

Lewis A. Dexter has sketched some of the dimensions of this aspect of consulting.[33] The first consultant he ever met, said Dexter, told him that he always wrote two reports after he had completed an assignment with an organization. The first report represented the situation as the head of the organization wanted to see it; the second report presented the situation as it really was. Apparently, this consultant and any others who follow the same or similar practices do well to do so, for Dexter goes on to quote a highly placed government official as expressing little regard for a consultant whom his department frequently engaged. Why, then, did he contract for the consultant's services so often? "We have to use him," said the official. "He always tells us what we want to hear."

Of course, many times an organization or even its leadership is not unified as to what it wants to hear. There may be splits over various policy matters. These can pose quite a problem for the consultant. He or she may become, says Dexter, allied with one group and opposed to another. "Consultants," says Dexter, "are not neutral. People who advise on anything one can think of may be inclined to one interest or another in a way of which they are unaware until they get to work." Consequently, even if a consultant is determined to "tell it like it is," his or her work may yield little in terms of positive results. The fundamental rule, according to Dexter, is that "advice and advisors are likely to be accepted, esteemed, hired and rejected in terms of the internal politics of the commissioning organization, as viewed by the members of the organization."[34]

But while consultants can be expensive, meddlesome, irresponsible, and encumbered with all manner of political considerations and constraints, they nevertheless have their uses.

Marvin Bower, a director of the international consulting firm of McKinsey and Company and a former president of the Institute of Management Consultants, has stressed two advantages that outside consultants can bring to an organization.[35] One is the diversity of their backgrounds. They have worked with a variety of organizations, including many which have similar functions or problems and thus can draw from a broader range of knowledge. They have probably seen other organizations wrestle with the same or similar dilemmas, and how they succeeded or failed in resolving them provides valuable knowledge, which they can offer to the organization.

The second advantage the consultant possesses is independence. This may sound strange in view of what was noted earlier about the consultant's proclivity to play politics with the organization to gain its favor. If an organization is really determined to utilize what the consultant has to offer, however, it may find that the most valuable thing he or she has to offer is a detached perspective.

The consultant is not wedded to the everyday operation and is not enmeshed in the organization's habits, customs, and culture. He or she can see things that the organization's own members do not see. Furthermore, given the right conditions, the consultant may speak up more candidly than an insider, since he or she has not the same ties of everyday association that may constrain the organization's own members. Along the same lines, many of the organization's members may speak more candidly to him or her than they would to their own colleagues and superiors. Similarly, his or her recommendations may secure greater acceptance from them since the consultant's relationship is relatively uncolored by the experiences and emotions, the attachments and animosities, that can influence reaction to suggestions made by superiors, subordinates, or colleagues. Thus, a good consultant will almost invariably come up with information about the organization that the organization's top management would find hard to obtain and/or accept.

The fact that he or she is not an integral part of the organization and has no day-in, day-out duties benefits the consultant and the organization in still other ways. It was pointed out previously how important it is to treat problems, not symptoms. The consultant does not have to treat symptoms since he or she has no connection with the daily business and routine of the organization, but can concentrate his or her full efforts on more substantial areas of concern.

One final advantage involved in consultant usage is worthy of note for its particular applicability to the public sector. Consultants, unlike most public employees, are easily disposed of. Although the public manager cannot fire or phase out an unwanted or unnecessary employee without undergoing a great deal of trouble, he or she usually has no such problem in handling consultants. The utilization of outside experts brings a note of flexibility into what are often overly rigid personnel structures. It can thus be argued that the employment of consultants to circumvent civil-service laws is not an abuse so long as the consultants only consult and do not administer.

Consultants, in short, can aid and abet the processes of change. C. Northcote Parkinson writes:

> If there is a feature of the medieval court which the modern office needs to reproduce, it is the ancient office of fool or jester. It was the fool's privilege and duty to put forward another point of view, neither that of the establishment nor that of the group currently out of favor. If the traditions of the office mean anything, the official jester would seem to have been at least as clever as any other official. There was no need to take his advice seriously, but neither was there much excuse for taking offense at anything he said. After all, to talk out of turn was what he was paid to do. There is reason to think that he served a useful purpose and there is even some reason to suspect that he might be useful now.[36]

The properly utilized modern-day consultant may be or could be what Parkinson had in mind.

Dos and Don'ts in the Use of Consultants

Consultants rarely come cheap, so those who hire them should take care to see that they obtain their money's worth. A few pointers gleaned from those who employ them as well as from consultants themselves may prove helpful in this regard.

At the outset, the commissioning organization should make sure that it knows just why it is hiring a consultant and just what it wants him to do. "The clearer the notion we had on what we wanted, the better the results we got out of consultants," says former New York City Budget Director Frederick Hayes.[37] No public agency should sign on a consultant in order for the consultant to tell the agency what it wants the consultant to do. If the agency wants the best return on its expenditure, it should take care to sort out its wishes and wants and define them so that they will be clear to whatever consultant it may hire. Of course, the agency may err by going too far in this direction and thereby constrict the consultant's scope of work. A consultant needs a certain amount of freedom in order to come up with the best range of ideas. Yet, when forced to choose between giving the consultant freedom or focus, it is usually better to stress the latter than the former. Consultants do have to know what is expected of them if they are to help the organization in a significant way.

Then those hiring the consultant should make sure they hire the consultant or consultants with the right expertise. A psychiatrist is not an industrial sociologist, and a certified public accountant is not necessarily imbued with a good grasp of government budgeting. It is particularly important to acquire consultants who have skills, background, and even viewpoints that are *not* too similar to those found within the organization. There is no point in paying outsiders to tell you what people whom you are already paying can tell you anyway.

It goes without saying that once the consultant starts work he or she should be given any assistance he or she needs. He or she should have access to those who will ratify and implement his or her recommendations. This usually includes top management and thus constitutes another burden on their time. Nevertheless, a consultant worth hiring is worth keeping in touch with. Confining his or her contacts to those who will not have the final say on the product will result in a weaker product.

But if successful consulting requires input from the implementers, then successful implementation demands input from the consultants. Too often, the consultant is hired for a certain study, does it, and is then sent away. The agency should instead make sure that he or she plays a role in putting the proposals into effect. As a matter of fact, many consultants as well as those who hire them stress the undesirability of using consultants on a one-shot basis. It is better to engage a consultant intermittently over a longer period of time than on a continuous basis for one long and terminal stretch. The consultant's assignment should not end with his or her final report.

Last and most important, organizations and those who manage them should not overuse consultants. Most organizations have more capability in house than they realize, and they should seek to utilize it to the utmost. In so doing, not only will they save consultant fees but they will also boost the spirits and develop the capacities of their own members. Consultants themselves will often admit that many organizations resort to their services to handle matters that they, the organizations, could deal with internally. Consultants do have a role to play as agents of change and have often played it well. (Much of the dramatic turnaround in productivity that New York City finally began to achieve in the late 1970s was stimulated and guided by experts from the famous Rand Corporation.) Yet, any government or government agency that relies too much on their services may fail to develop its own capacities for coping with the challenges of change.

The Limits of Change

As we stressed at the outset, change comes hard for public organizations, and this condition itself must change if they are to keep in step with the societies they serve. Much of the current disfavor public bureaucracies are now experiencing can be laid at the door of their static patterns of behavior. Change itself must become a built-in feature of the public agency if it hopes to meet its increasing and evolving responsibilities.

Yet, no administrative admonition can be set down without at the same time issuing some caveats. Like nearly every other principle, precept, and prescription we have examined, change is fine *up to a point*. When that point is reached, it becomes costly and counterproductive. While the process of change can be an exciting and energizing experience, it can also be an exhausting and enervating ordeal.

Seymour Berlin and his associates point out some of the negative aspects of change. "The organization can't work while it knows it's going to be changed, it can't work while it's being changed, and it takes a long time for it to start working following a change."[38] Those who so sharply condemn the old and so eagerly grasp the new would do well to remember the price that will have to be paid. The Environmental Protection Agency went through a series of reorganizations early in its existence, and the cumulative effect nearly crippled the agency.

Viewing the problem from a broader perspective, we should bear in mind that sometimes the completed change represents a step backward rather than forward. There is scarcely any public organization that is doing such a bad job that it could not be altered in such a way as to make it do a still worse one. In other words, not all change is change for the better. Hitler, Mussolini, and many of the other tyrants of history, so Frank Marini reminds us, were agents of change.[39] Transformation is not an end in itself, and the impetuous and impatient would do well to keep this in mind as they and their organizations struggle to respond to the challenges of change.

Notes

1. Daniel Katz and Robert L. Kahn, *The Social Psychology of Organizations* (New York: John Wiley, 1966), 92.

2. Wilbert E. Moore, *The Conduct of the Corporation* (New York: Random House, 1962), 191.

3. Herbert A. Simon, *Administrative Behavior* (New York: Free Press, 1957), 71–72.

4. C. P. Snow, *Science and Government* (New York: New American Library, 1962), 73.

5. Ron A. Webber, *Time and Management* (New York: Van Nostrand Reinhold, 1972), 160–161.

6. Townsend Hoopes, *The Limits of Intervention* (New York: David McKay, 1969), 1.

7. Chris Argyris, "The CEO's Behavior: Key to Organizational Development," *Harvard Business Review* (March–April 1973).

8. Katz and Kahn, *Social Psychology of Organizations*, 418.

9. Henry Taylor, *The Statesman* (New York: New American Library, 1958), 123.

10. *New York Times*, 26 March 1971.

11. Robert Townsend, "Up the Organization," *Harper's Magazine* (March 1970).

12. Frances Perkins, *The Roosevelt I Knew* (New York: Harper & Row, 1964).

13. George E. Berkley, *The Administrative Revolution: Notes on the Passing of Organization Man* (Englewood Cliffs, N.J.: Prentice-Hall, 1971), 29.

14. Harvey M. Sapolsky, *The Polaris System Development: Bureaucratic and Programmatic Success in Government* (Cambridge, Mass.: Harvard University Press, 1972), chap. 4.

15. Edward K. Hamilton, "Productivity: The New York City Approach," *Public Administration Review* (November–December 1972).

16. This case study is drawn from Daniel R. Jensen "Unifying Planning and Management in Public Organizations," *Public Administration Review* (March–April 1982).

17. Gilbert W. Fairholm, "A Reality Basis for Management Information System Decisions," *Public Administration Review* (March–April 1979).

18. Ibid.

19. H. Edward Wrapp, "A Plague of Professional Managers," *New York Times,* 8 April 1979, Business and Financial section.

20. J. C. Masterman, *The Double Cross Game* (New York: Avon Books, 1972), 36–37.

21. James W. Davis, Jr., *The National Executive Branch* (New York: Free Press, 1970), 25–26.

22. Ibid., 26.

23. *The Federal Committee on Pest Control. What It Is, What It Does* (Washington, D.C.: Government Printing Office, 1967).

24. Nat Hentoff, *A Political Life: The Education of John V. Lindsay* (New York: Alfred A. Knopf, 1969), 119.

25. Dean Acheson, *Present at the Creation* (New York: W. W. Norton, 1969), 242.

26. Don K. Price, *The Secretary of State* (Englewood Cliffs, N.J.: Prentice-Hall, 1960).

27. Elizabeth B. Drew, "On Giving Oneself a Hotfoot: Government by Commission," *The Atlantic Monthly* (May 1968).

28. Howard E. Schuman, "Behind the Scenes and Under the Rug: One Man's Presidential Commission," in Charles Peters and Timothy J. Adams, eds., *Inside the System* (New York: Praeger Publishers, 1970).

29. Harold Wolman, *Politics of Federal Housing* (New York: Dodd, Mead, 1971), 90.

30. Ibid., 88.

31. Ida R. Hoos, "Systems Techniques for Managing Society: A Critique," *Public Administration Review* (March–April 1973).

32. *New York Times,* 12 March 1978.

33. Lewis A. Dexter, "The Internal Politics of Organizations and the Role of Consultant." (Paper presented at the annual meeting of the American Political Science Association, 1972.

34. Ibid.

35. In a letter published in the *New York Times,* 4 March 1973, Business and Finance section.

36. C. Northcote Parkinson, *The Law of Delay* (New York: Ballantine Books, 1970), 48–49.

37. Frederick O'R. Hayes, "Things Are Picking Up in the Sanitation Department," *New York Times,* 9 July 1973.

38. Seymour S. Berlin et al., "A Guide for Political Appointees: Entering the System," *Good Government* (Winter 1972).

39. Unwritten remarks made during a panel session at the annual convention of the American Society of Public Administration, Los Angeles, 1974.

11

Administrative Law and Control

During the first hundred years of U.S. history, several factors conspired to keep the administrative sector of our many governments comparatively small and weak. These factors relate to the characteristics of our political system examined in chapter 1. Fragmentation and personalism, for example, deterred the growth of large and formalized bureaucracies like those starting to emerge in Europe. The antigovernmental attitudes of the American people probably acted as an even greater deterrent. But our legalistic approach to governmental problems may have served as the greatest deterrent of all.

Just how U.S. legalism imposed limits on, and even substituted for, administrative power was noticed by Lord James Bryce, that perceptive British observer who began visiting our shores late in the nineteenth century. In his 1888 book *The American Commonwealth*, Bryce wrote

> It is a great merit of American government that it relies very little on officials [administrators] and arms them with little power of arbitrary interference.... [The government] has taken the direction of acting through the law rather than through the officials. That is to say, when it prescribes to the citizen a particular course of action it has relied upon the ordinary legal sanctions, instead of investing the administrative officers with inquisitional duties or powers that might prove oppressive.[1]

As the quotation suggests, Bryce wholly approved of this approach. Had he been more legalistically trained or oriented himself, he might have pointed to a particular legalistic feature of our system that served as the main roadblock to a greater assumption of power and responsibility by U.S. administrators. This feature is our constitutionally enshrined principle of separation of powers.

The Constitution stipulates that the legislative branch shall enact the laws and the executive branch shall execute and enforce them. Through the first century of our existence, the courts—the third, judicial branch—took a particularly rigorous attitude toward this demarcation of authority. They ruled that Congress could not give away its power even if it wanted to. Consequently, all efforts to bestow substantial discretion on any administrator or administrative agency drew the Supreme Court's prompt disapproval. Congress, said the Court, could not delegate its powers. Rules and regulations that would have the force of law would have to be passed by the body charged with passing laws.

Yet as Bryce was writing his book the Court was getting ready to alter the whole course of U.S. administrative history. Congress, confronted with the pressing need to regulate the country's sprawling railroad industry, realized that it could not possibly devote the continuous time and effort that such a task demanded and passed the Interstate Commerce Act of 1887. This act set up a new agency, the Interstate Commerce Commission, to carry out this function. In a landmark decision that signaled a major change in policy, the Supreme Court ruled the act, along with the agency it established, to be constitutional.

It should be pointed out that the newly created ICC was scarcely given carte blanche discretion. Congress set down specific standards regarding its jurisdiction and prescribed rather detailed criteria for use of its discretionary power in policing the railroads. Congress even spelled out the various forms of misbehavior that the ICC was to police, such as rebating, rate discrimination, and pooling. The new regulatory commission was, in the words of Theodore Lowi, "relatively well shackled by clear standards of public policy, as stated in the statute and as understood in common law."[2]

From this time on, Congress, along with most state legislatures, began delegating more and more legislative power to administrative agencies, and the Supreme Court became increasingly cooperative in permitting them to do so. Thus, when Congress amplified the ICC's powers by passing the Transportation Act of 1920, the Court let the act stand even though the increased powers were accompanied by far fewer specific criteria to guide and control their application.

But though the Court had backtracked considerably over its once hard-line stand on delegation, it was still not ready to capitulate completely. The Court, for example, played havoc with the Federal Trade Commis-

sion during the first twenty years of its life, invalidating order after order
of the agency on the ground that the congressionally imposed standard of
"unfair method of competition," which the agency was charged with enforcing, was too vague. Such vagueness, said the Court, gave the agency
too much discretionary power.[3]

The New Deal brought the issue to its head when President Roosevelt,
trying to wield broad executive power to pull the country out of the
depression, found himself on a collision course with the nation's highest
tribunal. While Roosevelt managed to obtain from Congress wide-scale
discretionary authority for his New Deal agencies, the conservative Court
frequently balked at approving such sweeping delegations of power. This
led to a series of hostile Court decisions, culminating in the famous
Schechter case of 1934.[4] In this case, a majority of the justices struck
down the National Recovery Act and with it the elaborate planning machinery and the wide blanket of administrative power that the act had
promulgated.

But the Schechter case marked the beginning of the end. Although the
Court continued for the next two years to hand down similar decisions,
and although Roosevelt's subsequent attempt to change the composition
of the Court failed, an alteration in the Court's attitude soon occurred.
One justice died, another retired, and a third changed his mind. Roosevelt
replaced the first two with judges more to his liking, and in 1937 the
Court's approach to delegation underwent a 180-degree turn. Since then,
the justices have allowed Congress steadily increasing leeway in delegating power to administrative agencies. And although the Court continues
to insist on some sort of standard to govern the application of such authority, since the late 1930s it has never found any standard so vague as
to warrant the outlawing of an act on the grounds of an improper delegation of power.

A good example of the Court's new thinking was its upholding of the
Economic Stabilization Act of 1970. This act authorized the president "to
issue such orders and regulations as he may deem appropriate to stabilize
prices, wages and salaries at levels not less than those prevailing on May
25, 1970," together with such adjustment as might be necessary "to prevent gross inequities." As the language of the act clearly indicates, it constitutes what in former times would have seemed an awesome grant of
power, particularly when one remembers that the act left it up to the president to decide when and where he would choose to exercise such power.
Yet, when the Amalgamated Meat Cutters Union contested the constitutionality of the act in 1971, the Court rejected the suit, claiming that the
criterion of a legislatively prescribed standard had been met. In reviewing the Court's decision, the *Duke* (University) *Law Journal* noted that

"the case leaves the impression that Congress would be hard put to contrive a delegation that would *not* be judicially sustained."[5] (Emphasis added.)

During the past forty years, the administrative sector has surged forward, spurred on by what might be called the permissive attitude that the Court has taken toward the delegation issue. Administrative agencies have acquired increasing functions along with more powers to carry them out. They may prescribe rules and issue orders that have the force of law and may impose penalties on those who disobey. Some agencies have even acquired the subpoena power and/or the contempt power. What were once the closely guarded prerogatives of elected officials increasingly have been placed into the hands of nonelected functionaries. United States government has entered the era of the administrative state.

The actions that administrative agencies may take under their new grants of authority often have distinct policy implications. For example, when the Postal Service decided in 1968 to require all shipments of firearms through the mail to be clearly labeled as such, and when it announced that it was planning to report all deliveries of such shipments to local law-enforcement authorities, it was clearly playing a role in the policy-making arena. Similarly, when the Internal Revenue Service announced on April 10, 1973, that it would henceforth allow abortions, vasectomies, and birth-control pills to be deductible items, it was making policy as well as executing it. Sometimes administrative power has been used to get at problems that lie beyond the immediate scope of the agency involved. Mayor John Lindsay, for example, used New York City's rent-control agency to prod landlords to observe the building and sanitation codes. Exasperated over the failure of the courts to crack down on delinquent real estate owners, Lindsay ordered the board to lower the rents of those buildings that were persistently found to be in violation of the codes.

The penalties administrative agencies can impose are sometimes more severe than those usually levied by courts. Thus, an alien can be deported, a stock brokerage firm can be put out of business, and a motorist can lose his or her license, all through administrative action. As for the last-cited action, some states empower their automobile registration agency to lift a driver's license only *after* he or she has failed to pay overdue parking tickets. In this instance, the administrative agency actually functions as a higher court and imposes the final penalty.

Many have viewed the increasing discretion being vested in administrative agencies with anger and alarm. Others have claimed that it is inevitable, because no legislative body can hope to prescribe all the detailed rules and regulations needed by government to cope with the problems of a complex and rapidly changing society. Congress or a state legislature, for example, may pass an air-pollution-control act, but can such a legislative body really specify all the various steps that should or should not be taken to resolve all the situations that may arise within the air-pollution-control agency's jurisdiction? The flexibility and expertise required to handle such problems, it is contended, demand loose grants of authority.

In any case, whether or not Congress and the courts have gone too far in bestowing increasing influence on the administrative sector, they have accompanied such bestowals with certain restrictions. The growth of administrative authority has ushered in a parallel growth in administrative law.

The New Limits on Administrative Discretion

Although administrators today find themselves blessed with powers their predecessors little dreamed of possessing, they also find themselves subjected to new restraints as well. The legislative and judicial branches of government have not been content to stand aside and let administrators run the country, subject only to broad policy prescriptions and rather vague standards regarding the public interest. And one way the other two branches have acted to limit administrative discretion is by imposing increasingly strict standards on *how* administrators may use their new prerogatives.

Congress first took action in 1946 through passage of the Administrative Procedures Act. This detailed piece of legislation set down fairly specific rules on the ways in which administrative agencies were to proceed. The courts have since taken up the task, and basing themselves on broadened interpretations of the "due process" clauses in the Fifth and Fourteenth Amendments to the Constitution as well as on the Administrative Procedures Act itself, they have subjected administrative actions to stricter and stricter review.

It is important to note that judicial review since the Schechter case has focused not so much on matters of substance as on matters of procedure. In other words, the courts have concerned themselves less and less with *what the* administrative sector is doing and more and more on *how* it is doing it. The judges have, in effect, admitted that they do not have the expertise to determine whether a drug is safe, a welfare payment is adequate, or a highway route is well designed. As long as the administrative agency can show that its decisions in such matters are not arbitrary but are based on some legitimate rationale, the judges will not be inclined to interfere. They have become increasingly disposed to speak out, however, when they find that the agency is proceeding in a manner contrary to administrative due process.

What is administrative due process? Practically speaking, writes Lewis Mainzer, "Administrative due process is that procedure which will normally be accepted by the courts as reasonable under the circumstances, whether or not the judge thinks the substantive decision was correct."[6] Kenneth Culp Davis puts it this way: "The dominant tendency in both state courts and federal courts is toward the middle position known as the substantial-evidence rule . . . the court decides questions of law but limits itself to the test of reasonableness in reviewing findings of fact."[7]

Due process, however, is not fully encapsulated by the criterion of "reasonableness" alone. It also implies what the Supreme Court has referred to as the criterion of "fundamental fairness." In attempting to set up standards for administrative due process, the courts, basing themselves on the federal government's Administrative Procedures Acts and similar state acts, as well as on their new interpretations of the Constitution, have worked out a fairly strict set of rules that administrators must follow to meet due process requirements.

Adequate Notice

Before administrators or agencies can take any action that would directly affect one or more persons or institutions, they must generally give such affected parties adequate notice. How much notice is adequate? This depends on the circumstances and often becomes a matter of litigation before the courts. Rarely is a period of less than thirty days deemed to be adequate, and frequently a much longer interval is required.

In some situations, however, administrative agencies are empowered to act with scarcely any notice at all. Thus, if a building inspector finds a structure so unsafe as to be in danger of collapse at any moment, or a health inspector finds a restaurant serving contaminated food, they can usually order the situation remedied immediately. Unless it can be shown that the public safety demands precipitate action, however, the rule of adequate notice must govern.

Disclosure of Reasons

In addition to giving adequate notice, administrative agencies are usually required to state their reasons for taking their intended action. In most instances the affected party may demand that the agency put these reasons in writing. This tends to deter agencies from acting in an arbitrary and capricious manner, and at least gives the affected party written evidence to use in seeking subsequent redress in the courts. (See, in this connection, the advantages of formal communication in chapter 7.)

The Right to a Hearing

Beginning in the late 1960s, the courts began to broaden dramatically the right of aggrieved parties to have a hearing. Motorists deprived of their licenses, welfare clients deprived of their benefits, public-housing tenants faced with eviction, and prisoners sentenced to solitary confinement all sued for the right to be heard and were sustained by the courts.[8] Even the private sector found itself coming under the dictum as students faced with expulsion were also granted such a right.

The expansion that has taken place in requiring hearings has also affected rule making. Today, agencies that seek to promulgate new rules must usually schedule hearings and allow those who think differently to state their case. Even those who may not be directly affected by the new rule can have their voices heard.

At one time courts were not prone to require a hearing when benefits were at stake. Starting in 1970, however, the Supreme Court began insisting that such benefits as welfare payments, passports, unemployment insurance, driving licenses, and public housing accommodations could not be denied or removed without an evidentiary hearing, even though these were customarily termed privileges and not rights. Essentially, the Court held that when the government has issued a benefit to an individual, it cannot rescind it on mere administrative and fiscal considerations without a prior hearing.[9]

Hearings, of course, are not court trials, but they are increasingly coming to resemble them. An aggrieved party now can often demand not only the right to appear in his or her own behalf but to be represented by counsel. In many instances, he or she or the counsel can cross-examine witnesses who may be testifying in behalf of the agency. The affected party can further ask that the hearing be made public. Here, however, the courts may allow the agency some discretion in denying such a request. In two cases involving students protesting their expulsion, the courts allowed their respective universities to hold closed hearings. In one case the grounds were that a public hearing might endanger the public safety; in the other, that the reputations of innocent students might be injured.[10]

The Right to Further Appeal

If, after a hearing, the protesting party is still not satisfied, he or she may appeal to a higher echelon within the agency and, as a last step, to the courts. Available figures suggest that increasing numbers of citizens are taking this final step. One estimate made during the 1960s indicated that 20 percent of all Supreme Court decisions dealt with administrative matters.[11] And according to the *Statistical Abstract* of 1970, approximately 28 percent of all the civil cases begun in federal district courts in 1969 involved the federal government as either plaintiff or defendant.

The aggrieved party may seek judicial redress on grounds that he or she was not given adequate notice, that the agency's procedures are not clear, that the agency is not abiding by administrative due process or even its own procedures, that it has behaved in an arbitrary or discriminatory manner, or that the agency lacks jurisdiction in doing what it did or plans to do. As Mainzer points out, "Despite the Administrative Procedures Act and mountains of court opinion, the standards of administrative due process are extraordinarily indefinite."[12] Thus, numerous possibilities exist for carrying administrative issues into the courtroom.

However, there are at the same time numerous limitations on utilizing the courts to reverse or mitigate administrative actions. First. the courts will not entertain the case until the petitioner has exhausted all recourse within the administrative agency itself. Furthermore, the courts will not intervene in cases where there is no remedy. Finally, as was previously noted, the courts nowadays balk at deciding questions of fact or weighing the validity of one expert opinion against another. They prefer to confine themselves to questions of law and procedure.

To see how this works, let us assume that a citizen wishes to contest a decision on a new highway route that will require the taking of her house. She protests the decision to the highway commission, is turned down, and so takes her case to court. She may argue in court that an alternative route would have been a better one and may offer evidence and expert witnesses to support her view. But, if the highway commission can show any evidence and bring forth any expert testimony of its own to indicate that it had a valid reason for choosing the route that it did, the court will generally turn a deaf ear to the citizen's plea. However, if the irate homeowner can show that the highway commission's selection flies in the face of nearly all logic and expert opinion, and if she can further show that the commission may have a reason for being prejudiced against her and consequently would have a motive in picking a route that would take her home, then she will stand a chance of getting the commission's action struck down.

This, of course, is a hypothetical case. Let us now turn to some actual cases that will shed further light on the nuances and ramifications of present-day administrative law.

Administrative Law at Work

In February 1968, the Federal Aviation Administration fired a thirty-six-year-old traffic controller on grounds that he had engaged in "sexual relations with a woman other than his wife." To make matters more complicated, the other woman was a former employee of the agency. The FAA further alleged that the dismissed controller had been involved in a car accident while under the influence of alcohol.

The controller, a father of five, was understandably upset. He pointed out that he was separated from his wife during a large portion of the alleged affair and that he had actually reconciled with his wife prior to his discharge. More important, he contended that his sex life had nothing to do with his efficiency as an air-traffic controller. He took his case to the FAA's Board of Appeals and lost. He then asked for a review by the Civil Service Commission and lost again. He thereupon went to court.

In February 1970, the U.S. Federal District Court in Washington, D.C., found that the government had failed to show any correlation between the air controller's private life and his efficiency as an air-traffic controller. Because a hearing examiner who had studied the controller's work record had rated it "satisfactory in all respects," the court ordered the FAA to reinstate the man in his former position.[13]

Three years after this case, a discharged local government employee won a somewhat similar vindication from a U.S. district court. In January 1973, the Federal District Court in Portland, Oregon, ruled that a local school board had no right to fire a schoolteacher on grounds of "immorality" simply because she was a lesbian. The school board was ordered to give the woman one and a half years back pay and expunge from her records all references to "immorality," since lesbianism by itself did not constitute proper grounds for such a charge.[14]

Then, there is the case of John F. Shaw, an FBI agent who in 1971 wrote a letter that was critical, in part, of the FBI and of its director, J. Edgar Hoover. Shaw's letter was designed to be read only by the person for whom it was intended. This was a professor who had made some derogatory remarks about the agency in a college course that Shaw was taking while stationed in the FBI's New York City office. Shaw's letter to the professor was actually a defense of the FBI, but in certain passages he did make reference to some of the agency's failings. When the letter was discovered by his superiors, Shaw was given a transfer to Butte, Montana, the FBI's "Siberia" office. Aware that the transfer meant a limited future in the FBI and unwilling to leave the East in any case, Shaw resigned. Hoover accepted his resignation "with prejudice."

Shaw then filed a suit in federal court claiming that he had been the victim of a "capricious and vindictive act of personal retribution" by the FBI director. The FBI, sensing, perhaps, the new spirit now animating court decisions on administrative discretion, settled with Shaw out of court. The agency agreed to remove the phrase "with prejudice" from his resignation record and, in addition, to pay him thirteen thousand dollars, partly as the salary he would have received during the previous nine months.[15]

These incidents illustrate the new approach courts are taking toward the problem of administrative discretion, and they show how this approach is starting to affect even such formerly autocratic agencies as the FBI. This is not to imply that all the questions that may arise over employee dismissals have been settled. Many issues still remain. For example, can an agency dismiss an employee when he or she invokes the Fifth Amendment privilege and refuses to answer superiors' questions? Generally, the courts have held that a public agency may discharge an employee who refuses to answer questions directly related to the job. At the same time, the Supreme Court has emphasized that the invocation of a constitutional privilege cannot, in and of itself, constitute grounds for the imposition of a penalty. Thus, no simple rule governing all "Fifth Amendment dismissals" has been or can be set down.[16]

The new protectiveness that the courts have begun to evince toward people affected by administrative actions is by no means limited to administrative employees. Members of the public who find themselves similarly affected have also been scoring victories before the bench.

During the Vietnam war, many college students burned their draft cards or returned them to the Selective Service System as a way of protesting the United States involvement in the conflict. Many of them also sought to interfere with the work of the Selective Service System or with that of military recruiters. Insofar as their activities violated the law, the students became subject to criminal prosecution. However, when the Selective Service System itself began to penalize them for such behavior, the courts intervened.

One landmark case was that of *Oestereich* v. *Selective Service System Local Board No. 11, Cheyenne, Wyoming, et al.*, which was decided in 1968. Oestereich was a theology student and consequently had been classified as IV-D and exempted from the draft. However, the preceding year he had returned his draft registration certificate "for the sole purpose of expressing dissent from the participation of the United States in the war in Vietnam." His board then declared him delinquent for failing to have his registration certificate in his possession and for failing to notify the board of his change in classification and his new status. After turning down his appeal, the Selective Service ordered him to report for induction.

Oestereich then brought his case to the Supreme Court. In its decision, the Court struck down the board's action on the grounds that it had exceeded its powers. The Selective Service System has no authorization, said the Court, to devise regulations governing delinquency and then use them to deprive registrants of their statutory exemptions. "There is no suggestion in the legislative history that, when Congress has granted an exemption and a registrant meets its terms and conditions, a Board can nonetheless withhold it from him for activities or conduct *not material to the grant or withdrawal of the exemption.* So to hold would make the Boards free-wheeling agencies meting out their brand of justice in a vindictive manner."[17] (Emphasis added.)

Increasingly, those injured by the acts of government agencies are finding it easier not only to win judicial vindication but also financial compensation. The Federal Tort Claims Act of 1946 allowed the federal government to be sued "in the same manner and to the same extent as a private individual," subject to a limited number of exceptions. In subsequent decisions, the Supreme Court has expanded and strengthened this right. For example, it has held that federal law-enforcement agents can be sued for engaging in an illegal search of a person's home.

In the early 1980s the Supreme Court, in several noteworthy rulings, drastically tightened up its control of state as well as local government officials, holding them strictly and severely liable for constitutional violations even when acting in good faith. In doing so it stripped them of much of the immunity that they inherited from the old Anglo-Saxon concept that the king—the sovereign—can do no wrong.

The court's new crackdown began in April 1980 when, in deciding a case involving the city of Independence, Missouri, the justices held municipalities liable for any actions by their officials that violate an individual's constitutional rights. Two months later, in deciding the case of a welfare recipient who was suing the state of Maine, the court gave individuals the right on constitutional grounds to challenge the methods by which a state administers a host of federal programs.

The following year the Supreme Court heard the case of a music promoter who had sued the city of Newport, Rhode Island, for canceling his permit to put on a show. The city had rescinded its permit only when the promoter had substituted a rock group (Blood, Sweat and Tears) for the jazz performer (Sarah Vaughan) that he had originally stipulated for his program. Yet a district court awarded him seventy-five thousand dollars in compensatory damages and two hundred thousand dollars in punitive damages from the city, plus another eighty thousand dollars in damages from the mayor and city council in their personal capacities. The Supreme Court struck down the punitive damages but let the compensatory damages stand, along with an allowance for "reasonable" attorney fees.[18]

As 1982 began, the nation's highest tribunal had more bad news for the nation's grass-roots governments. In a case involving Boulder, Colorado, and a cable television company, the justices opened the door to legal action against local authorities on grounds of antitrust violations. Only if the government activity being challenged carried out a specific state statute could it be considered immune from such a suit. Without such a direct linkage, any action by any local government could become challengeable on antitrust grounds. The court's ruling triggered a snowballing series of lawsuits against local jurisdictions. By the start of 1983, Tuscon, Arizona; Ventura County, California; and several other local authorities had been hit by suits involving cable television; Richmond, Virginia, was under antitrust attack for refusing to allow construction of a new Hilton Hotel, which conflicted with its urban redevelopment plan; Akron, Ohio, was defending itself against a suit in conjunction with its "flow controls" on municipal trash, while the Dallas–Fort Worth airport was fighting a legal challenge to its taxicab arrangements.[19]

All this activity does not mean that the courts have declared an open season on bureaucrats. They have, for example, allowed state and local governments to remove children from foster homes without holding hearings, and they have even allowed them to suspend the licenses of drivers who refuse to take breathalyzer tests. And the federal government may still refuse to give security clearances to homosexuals on grounds they may become vulnerable to blackmail. Nevertheless, the trend generally appears to have been in the other direction, namely toward subjecting governmental actions to increased scrutiny and supervision to see that they conform to the court's concept of the constitution and its requirements.

As we saw in chapter 1, Federal Appeals Judge David Bazelon had prophesied in 1975 that "As the constitutional right to due process expands, more and more administrators will find themselves locked into involuntary partnerships with the courts."[20] Developments since that time would seem to have proven him conspicuously correct.

Issues in Administrative Law

As the preceding section has indicated, the field of administrative law, after a century of intense litigation and adjudication, remains alive with simmering issues. Administration being what it is, and the law being what *it* is, it seems unlikely that many of these issues will shrivel up and fade away. Legal complications and complexities appear destined to provide a fertile field of litigation for lawyers and a Pandora's box of perplexities for administrators for many years to come.

One issue yet to be fully resolved is the question of hearsay evidence. Hearsay is a report of a statement made by someone who is not present for cross-examination. It is therefore considered secondhand evidence and, as such, is excluded from U.S. courtrooms. Should it be barred from administrative proceedings as well?

The Administrative Procedures Act of 1946 ruled out any evidence that would be "irrelevant, immaterial or unduly repetitious," but did not go so far as to outlaw hearsay evidence as such. In a 1971 case the Supreme Court held that uncorroborated hearsay evidence can constitute "substantial evidence" sufficient to support an administrative ruling.[21] This did not mean that all such evidence was to be indiscriminately accepted. It would have to be relevant, reliable, and supportive of the point for which it was being used. Material "without a basis in evidence having rationality and probative force" would not meet the Court's standard.

Such a ruling as this one, of course, does not close the door on the issue but only opens it wider. Wrangles can erupt at any time on whether a particular piece of hearsay evidence meets the criteria for relevance and probative value. Many, meanwhile, still question whether any hearsay evidence should be allowed to influence administrative action. Since the consequences of administrative decision making can frequently exceed those of a court trial, it is only right and proper, so the argument goes, that those who would have to bear these consequences should benefit from the safeguards enjoyed by those who are subject to a court trial. Others contend, however, that there is nothing inherently evil about hearsay evidence. Such evidence, as a matter of fact, is admissible in even criminal trials in most countries in the world, including most democratic countries. To bar it from the hearing room, they contend, would only hinder administrative tribunals from making informed and judicious decisions.

A still more lively controversy regarding the administrative process arises over whether an agency should be allowed to play the double role of judge and prosecutor. When an agency discharges or demotes an employee or deprives an individual or a group of some benefit or right, the agency first brings the charges and then, during the hearing, sits in judgment on these charges. In effect, it seems to be sitting in judgment on itself. To many lawyers this is inherently unfair and contrary to both the spirit and intent of due process. They claim the affected party should possess the right to have the charges decided by a completely external body.

While most administrative agencies adjudicate their own charges and complaints, they usually utilize special employees to do so. These officials are customarily called hearing examiners in most local and some state bureaucracies, but in a few states as well as at the federal level they bear the more prestigious title of administrative law judges. The federal government's corps of 1,153 such judges consists of highly qualified lawyers—they currently include a former chief justice of a state supreme court—who in 1982 were earning fifty-seven thousand dollars a year. Sometimes referred to as "Washington's hybrids" or "the hidden judiciary" they adjudicate cases for twenty-nine federal agencies. Although most of them work for the Social Security Administration, others make their presence felt in a variety of other agencies, where they decide such matters as whether two railroads can merge or who is to receive a lucrative television license. A decision by an ALP, as they are called, in the late 1970s broke up American Telephone & Telegraph's near monopoly of the public telephone and opened up the entire communications industry to greater competition.[22]

Although federal ALPs are employees of the agency whose cases they adjudicate, their qualifications and civil-service status have given them virtual immunity from normal agency pressures. They have frequently counteracted and contradicted the expressed wishes of their agencies. When the Social Security Administration attempted to use the Reagan administration's stricter guidelines to pare nearly a quarter million from the rolls of its recipients, it found itself on a collision course with its seven hundred ALPs. The ALPs, using the looser and more liberal standards of the Supreme Court, reinstated approximately three-fifths of those who appealed their loss of benefits. Their actions infuriated the heads of Social Security, who overruled many of the reinstatements. This, in turn, riled the ALPs, who felt they had acted as they should, i.e., as independent judicial officers and not as "mere bureaucrats."

Despite the independence and integrity that ALPs have generally shown, some observers continue to express doubts as to whether an agency employee should preside over a case in which the agency itself is a party of interest. To obviate this objection as well as to make better use of ALP manpower, eight states have formed their administrative law judges in an agency of their own, assigning them to other agencies to handle cases on a random basis. At least one of these states, New Jersey, says it has also saved money in doing so. Some would like to see the federal government take a similar step.

Another suggestion would have ALPs hand down decisions, not just recommendations. While agency higher-ups could still overrule their findings, presumably they would feel more compunction about doing so if such findings were couched in the form of decisions instead of recommendations.

Suggestions have been made to divorce them completely from any particular agency, setting up, in effect, a new administrative unit in the federal bureaucracy that would assign them to different agencies as cases arose. This would give them still more independence but would reduce their expertise in the matters under dispute, for they would no longer be specialized in the work of one agency. Others suggest that the administrative law judges hand down not just recommendations but decisions. The agency head or heads could still overrule them but in doing so would have to overturn a decision rather than simply disregard a recommendation. Presumably, this would in practice prove more difficult to do.

Underlying these and many other issues that plague the process of administrative law is this: To what extent should the administrative process be subject to all the safeguards found in the judicial process? Spearheading the drive toward ever-increasing judicialization of the administrative process has been the American Bar Association. It has sought, with considerable success, to make administrative hearings more and more like court trials. It has fought to give affected parties a greater right to representation by counsel and a greater right to cross-examine witnesses, as well as increased access to judicial review. It has been frequently aided in this drive by civil liberties groups, who look with understandable horror at the expanding scope of administrative power.

The idea has obvious attractions for all those who are worried about the nature of governmental power in a democratic society. Certainly, if administrative agencies legislate and even adjudicate and punish, then those who bear the effects of their actions must be supplied with ample weapons to protect themselves. The United States has evolved an elaborate set of procedures to protect the individual who runs afoul of the criminal justice system. Should not an equal set of safeguards protect the person who runs afoul of the increasingly powerful bureaucracy?

The problem is that such protection imposes a heavy price. To the extent that administrative activities have already become highly judicialized, they have become costly and complicated to all concerned. Further judicialization, its opponents argue, would only hamper them all the more. If the demotion of an errant employee or the widening of a street is always going to involve the detailed and difficult process of a full-fledged court proceeding, then agencies simply will not be able to function properly. They will refuse to undertake many actions simply because of the time and expense involved. Furthermore, many of the activities they do undertake will fail to yield commensurate benefits, because they will too often be subjected to months and even years of delay while the full judicial process is gone through. Innovation, flexibility, and responsiveness will all suffer.

In this connection, it is interesting to note that civil libertarians are not the only ones who have shown an interest in curbing administrative discretion. Many major corporations and their representatives have shown an even greater zeal for expanding and extending judicial safeguards in the administrative process. Shortly after the enactment of the Administrative Procedures Act, the *New York Times* reported that "utility, rail and numerous other industries" were "celebrating" the law's enactment.[23] Since that time, these interests and their lawyers have eagerly taken advantage of the numerous opportunities the act provides for striking down or at least delaying administrative actions. According to Winton B. Rankin, former deputy commissioner of the Food and Drug Administration,

There is endless repetition of testimony, witnesses saying the same thing over and over. When several industry lawyers are involved, they won't get together and let one of them do the cross-examining. Everyone has to speak. They'll ask for a recess of weeks to study documents that are put into evidence, even though the documents were available in advance. . . . And appeals to the courts at every stage; you set a hearing date, they ask for a postponement, you deny it, they go to court. They seldom win but everything stops while it is argued.[24]

OUGHT THERE TO BE A LAW?

"Increasingly there oughtn't," says Roger C. Cramton, dean of the Cornell University Law School. According to Dean Cramton, too many laws are being passed and too many issues are being brought into court. The consequence is a form of "legal pollution," which may undermine the basic structure of our society. Judges are deciding more and more issues that should be left to the people themselves or their representatives, he says.

Thinking along the same lines is Archibald Cox, Harvard Law School professor and, until Nixon fired him, special Watergate prosecutor. Cox also warns against allowing courts to play such a dominating role in the nation's political, economic, and social life.

These tactics pay off handsomely for many of Washington's fifteen thousand lawyers as well as for the corporations they represent. Joseph C. Goulden has chronicled what happened when the FDA wanted to establish a rule that any product marketed as a peanut butter had to contain 95 percent peanuts. The commission first proposed the rule on July 2, 1959. However, it was not until March 3, 1971, some twelve years later, that it was finally able to promulgate it, and even then it had been forced to lower the required percentage of peanuts to 90 percent. In the interim, lawyers for the Peanut Butter Manufacturers Association had argued and fought the case all the way to the Supreme Court.[25]

Judicialization also converts administrative hearings into adversary proceedings, and this raises additional problems. Lawyers for the affected party or parties treat those testifying for the government as "hostile witnesses" and seek relentlessly to discredit their testimony, their qualifications, and even their integrity. This tends to make many witnesses, particularly professional experts, reluctant to testify. Many scientists turn down FDA work for this reason. Also open to question is whether attacking expert witnesses in this way constitutes the best procedure for ferreting out the facts necessary for making sound administrative decisions.

Judicialization of the administrative process is thus no magic cure-all for making the bureaucracy behave in a responsible manner. It can frequently have the reverse effect. Even when it comes to protecting the rights of the affected party, it can sometimes cut both ways, as the following case study will show.

CASE STUDY

The Trial of J. Robert Oppenheimer[26]

On the Monday afternoon of December 21, 1953, J. Robert Oppenheimer showed up by invitation at the office of the chairman of the Atomic Energy Commission, Lewis Strauss. There was certainly nothing unusual in Strauss having invited the distinguished scientist to pay him a call. Although now heading an institute at Princeton University, Oppenheimer still held a consultant's contract with the AEC. It allowed the Atomic Energy Commission to call upon him for advice and assistance from time to time, and presumably this was one of those times.

It was, however, nothing of the sort. While the meeting got under way casually enough with some joint lament over the recent death of a mutual friend, it changed abruptly when Strauss handed Oppenheimer a three thousand four hundred-word letter. The letter informed Oppenheimer that the AEC was stripping him of his security clearance and detailed its reasons for doing so.

The action came as a surprise and a shock, not only to Oppenheimer but to most of the world. The renowned physicist had eight years earlier built the atomic bomb, and in so doing had carried around with him more secrets than almost any person in the United States outside of the president. Indeed, just a year previous to his meeting with Strauss, Oppenheimer had received from outgoing President Truman a warm letter praising him for his "lasting and immensely valuable contribution to the national security and to atomic energy progress in the nation." Now the scientist had been found unfit and untrustworthy for even the most meager of all clearances, one that had been extended to thousands of typists and clerks as well as scientists and officials in numerous government agencies.

What was the basis for the AEC's startling action? The essence of its charges against Oppenheimer, as spelled out in its letter, was that he had shown himself indiscreet, at the least, in associating with Communists and Communist causes and had also on occasion shown himself deceptive in answering questions about such incidents in his past. More specifically, he was accused of having had numerous contacts with Communists, with having given money to what were called Communist-front causes, and with having at one time subscribed to a Communist newspaper, *The People's World*. He had also lied about one incident involving his association with a suspected Communist agent.

What was unique about these charges was, in effect, that they were not

unique at all. All of them dated back to the 1930s and early 1940s, and all
of them had been presented to Oppenheimer before he was asked to assume the leadership of Los Alamos. At that time, Oppenheimer had satisfied the government's security officers by pointing out his political
naïveté in associating with Communists and Communist-linked organizations, and by claiming that in the incident in which he had lied, or at
least not quite told the truth, he was prompted by a desire to shield a
friend. The government had accepted his explanations at that time and he
had gone on to prove himself most worthy of the nation's trust. Why,
then, resurrect all these ancient charges at this late date in a move to
deny him security clearance?

Philip Stern's detailed and thorough account of the case, entitled "In
The Matter of J. Robert Oppenheimer," offers three reasons for the sudden about-face in the government's attitude toward the physicist. For one
thing, Oppenheimer, the builder of the atomic bomb, had become somewhat remorseful over the weapon he had done so much for to give the
world, and for this and other reasons he had opposed the development of
its successor, the hydrogen bomb. Given his reputation and influence,
Oppenheimer's opposition had hampered the government in generating
support for the project, particularly in the scientific community. This had
scarcely endeared him to the atomic establishment in Washington and
had caused many to question once again his degree of devotion to the
country's best interests.

Another reason was much more picayune, but, as any student of politics
and administration soon learns, often the most innocuous of incidents can
lead to dire developments. Although Oppenheimer had maintained a cor-
dial relationship with Strauss, he had, somewhat inadvertently, made a
joke at Strauss's expense while testifying before a congressional committee. A proud man, Strauss was not one to take such matters lightly.

The third and perhaps most important reason for the AEC's move was
the climate of the times. Senator Joseph McCarthy was then at the height
of his powers, and his virulent anticommunism was causing government
agencies and officials, not excluding the president of the United States,
to cringe. All of official Washington was on the defensive concerning potential charges of harboring Communists or Communist sympathizers. By
purging itself of its connection with Oppenheimer, the government was
removing a potential source of trouble and exhibiting a get-tough policy
toward possible traitors, a policy that could curry public favor.

One ironical aspect of the affair is that the AEC's action, justified or
not, was completely unnecessary. If the commission really considered
Oppenheimer a security risk, it could simply have refrained from using
his services for the next six months, at which time his contract would
have elapsed. Yet the commission decided to undertake the formal and
publicized procedure of declaring the builder of the A-bomb to be a risk
to the nation's security.

For his part, Oppenheimer could have easily accepted the AEC's decision. His position at Princeton was quite secure, and even if he were to

prevent the commission's action, they would almost certainly never call on his services again. Nevertheless, after meeting with Strauss and then conferring with his lawyers, the scientist decided to fight. To accept termination of his contract, as he expressed it in a letter to Strauss, "would mean that I accept and concur in the view that I am not fit to serve the government that I have served for 12 years. This I cannot do."

The stage was thus set for a hearing. Since this proceeding has become the subject of a lengthy book and even the basis of a Broadway play, it may duly be deemed the most famous administrative hearing in U.S. history. One writer has called it "the century's most famous treason trial." As such, it illuminates a rather inglorious chapter of our national past and points to some weaknesses in our political culture. At the same time it illustrates some interesting and important issues in administrative law.

The AEC felt Oppenheimer's stature made it mandatory that it set up a special hearing board of eminent men whose position was roughly comparable to that of the defendant. Only such a board, reasoned the commission, could secure public acceptance of its verdict. To head the panel, the AEC picked Gordon Grey, a former assistant secretary of the army who had gone on to become president of the University of North Carolina. Grey was a Democrat, but a conservative one who came from a southern aristocratic background. He was also a lawyer.

Selected to serve with Grey were Thomas A. Morgan, a self-made businessman who had risen from the job of salesman to president of Sperry Rand, Incorporated, and Ward V. Evans, the chairman of the Chemistry Department at Northwestern University. Known as a "character" because of his idiosyncrasies of dress and manner, Evans was nevertheless an archconservative who prided himself on a near-perfect Republican voting record.

As its "prosecutor" to present the commission's charges to the board, the AEC chose Roger Robb, a former assistant U.S. attorney who had won esteem for having obtained a high percentage of convictions in the numerous murder cases he had prosecuted during his government service. Robb was also considered a man of strong right-wing convictions.

To defend him, Oppenheimer and his friends settled on Lloyd K. Garrison, a former president of the National Urban League and a leading civil libertarian. Garrison was a brilliant lawyer and was certainly devoted to Oppenheimer and his cause. However, as Stern describes him, he was "mild-mannered, almost saintly, at home in the world of intellect and compassion," with little experience in, or apparent taste for, the rough-and-tumble world of an adversary, courtroom-type proceeding.

The hearing got under way at ten o'clock on the morning of April 12, 1954, and ran for three weeks. Oppenheimer was the first witness and spent a grueling twenty hours on the stand. He was followed by a parade of witnesses who testified in his behalf. Among them were two former chairmen of the AEC and three former commissioners. Then the commission presented its own and much shorter list of witnesses. The most distinguished of them was Edward Teller, the noted physicist who later went on to develop the reputation of having been the "father of the H-bomb."

Summations were delivered by the attorneys of both sides, with Oppenheimer's Lloyd Garrison making the passionate plea that "America must not devour her own children . . . we must not devour the best and most gifted of our citizens." The hearing panel then voted two-to-one to uphold the commission's charges. The dissenting vote was cast by Evans, who summarized his opinion in a little over a page. Grey and Morgan used fifteen thousand words in stating the majority view. They affirmed Oppenheimer's essential loyalty to the United States but through a convoluted process of legalistic reasoning found him a security risk.

The case then went to the Atomic Energy Commission itself for final action, and the commission predictably voted four to one to accept the majority report and to strip Oppenheimer of his security clearance. The lone physicist on the commission cast the single dissenting vote. Despite this adverse action or perhaps because of it, Oppenheimer went back to Princeton more like a returning hero than a man in disgrace. His colleagues and the scientific community generally rallied to his support, and the elderly Albert Einstein personally came to call on him.

Teller, however, remained stricken with remorse over his part in the proceeding, and in 1963 he personally nominated Oppenheimer for the Enrico Fermi award, a citation given annually by the AEC. With Joseph McCarthy and the era he created now dead, and with a new, liberal administration in power, the commission voted unanimously to confer its highest distinction on a man it had previously decreed unworthy of the most rudimentary trust. (Of course, the membership of the commission had also changed in the interim.) President John F. Kennedy said he would personally bestow the award at a White House ceremony, and when an assassin's bullet kept him from doing so, President Lyndon Johnson gladly took on the task.

Three years later, J. Robert Oppenheimer lay dead of cancer at the age of sixty-four. In the eulogy delivered at his funeral, George Kennan said, "The truth is that the United States Government never had a servant more devoted at heart than this one, in the sense of wanting to make a constructive contribution." No discernible public voice arose to dispute his finding.

While the Oppenheimer affair has obvious ramifications that transcend the boundaries of administrative law, it nevertheless sheds a good deal of light on some of the issues we have been examining. To assess some of these implications, let us return to the hearing that found Oppenheimer "guilty."

At the outset of the hearing, Chairman Grey pointed out that the proceeding would not be subject to the strict rules and procedures that govern courtroom trials. He implied that such relative informality would prove helpful to the "defendant" in allowing him more flexibility. "Yet," writes Stern, "Oppenheimer, like other security-risk 'defendants,' would come to wish that his 'hearing' were governed by certain of the rules and procedures of a trial."

It is easy to see what Stern means. For example, the problem of the administrative agency playing the double role of prosecutor and judge colored the train of events from beginning to end. This first occurred when AEC lawyer Harold P. Green was drafting the statement of charges against Oppenheimer. The commission's general manager, Kenneth D. Nichols, called Green frequently with various ideas and bits of data to help strengthen his case. Comments Stern, "It was as if during a prosecuting attorney's preparation of a criminal case, the prospective trial judge had sought to whet the lawyer's appetite for the impending prosecution." Stern's characterization is not completely accurate, because Nichols did not formally serve on the panel that would adjudicate the case and Green was not really serving as the prosecutor, but it does have certain validity. A more obvious instance was the AEC's hiring of Roger Robb to present the charges at the hearing. Since the AEC was to be the final arbiter—the hearing board was only to make a recommendation—the commission would eventually be deciding the validity of a case developed by its own appointee. A further instance of overlapping roles occurred in the appearance of Edward Teller as a prosecution witness. Teller, it was later learned, did not want to testify and only did so under pressure from Nichols. Thus, Nichols, who was associated with the body that was to sit in judgment, worked to strengthen the prosecution's case.

Other aspects of the hearing that failed to conform to courtroom procedure also hampered Oppenheimer and his counsel. Prior to the hearing, he had to hand over all AEC documents in his possession. This helped the government's prosecutor but hindered his own attorneys in preparing his defense.

The right to examine many of the pertinent documents in the case required security clearance. It took the AEC only eight days to give Robb an emergency clearance. It took eight weeks to do the same for Garrison, and since Garrison was late in applying for the clearance to begin with, he did not receive it until the hearing was almost over. As a result, not only was he unable to examine much of the evidence against his client, but he and his associate attorneys had to leave the hearing room on four occasions, leaving his client undefended, when the questioning centered on matters affecting national security.

One persistent and powerful aspect of the hearing that hurt Oppenheimer was the absence of the "blank pad rule," which did not at that time govern security-risk hearings. This meant that Oppenheimer's fate was being decided by "judges" who had already read the investigative file, virtually all of which was negative. Indeed, the members of the tribunal spent a full week going over the file with the prosecuting attorney before the hearing began. Such a practice would have been unthinkable in a court of law. When the hearing got under way, each "judge" had a thick black notebook in front of him full of information about the case, information that Oppenheimer and his attorneys had not seen. No wonder that by the second day of the hearing, before Oppenheimer had begun to testify, Grey was already giving hints that he suspected Oppenheimer of deviousness.

Hearsay played a major role in the case. Statements made by persons who were not only absent but who were not even named were introduced into evidence. One such anonymous informant was later found to be mentally deranged.

In the light of the foregoing, a case can easily be made that the lack of full-scale courtroom procedures proved damaging to Oppenheimer and his case. However, viewed from another perspective, a case could be made that Oppenheimer suffered because the proceeding was too much like a trial.

First, there were the courtroom tactics that Robb skillfully employed. He badgered and bullied Oppenheimer and Oppenheimer's witnesses almost mercilessly, seeking to score a trial lawyer's points. He would persistently try to catch the defendant and those appearing in his behalf in errors. None of the witnesses, with one exception, had any experience in being exposed to such tactics, and most of them proved vulnerable to their use. Oppenheimer in particular showed up badly, at one time even blurting out "I was an idiot." He might have been better served by a procedure that smacked less of the adversary proceeding of a courtroom.

An adversary, courtroom-type proceeding, so the rationale goes, is the best means for discovering the truth. Too often, however, it becomes instead a method for discovering which side has the best lawyer. Certainly, it places a heavy emphasis on the respective legal skills employed by the two contending parties, and in this case the defense was at a distinct disadvantage. Garrison was simply no match for a man who had prosecuted twenty-seven accused murderers. And so thanks to the triallike nature of the proceeding, Oppenheimer lost again.

A full-blown, triallike administrative hearing also tends to run up the same costs as a full-scale courtroom trial. The hearing cost Oppenheimer approximately twenty-five thousand dollars in direct, out-of-pocket expenses. At today's prices, it would cost much more. But even adjusting for inflation would grossly understate the real expense, for Garrison and his associates did not charge him for the six months of work that they put into the case. He only had to pay their travel expenses between New York and Washington. Furthermore, all of Oppenheimer's witnesses paid their own expenses and none of them took a witness fee. If these fortuitous circumstances had not prevailed, then Oppenheimer's defense, adjusted for today's price level, could have cost him close to a quarter of a million dollars.

The Oppenheimer case provides ammunition for both sides of the argument when it comes to deciding the extent to which the administrative process should be judicialized. While Stern notes that Oppenheimer would have fared better in certain respects if the hearing had been more like a courtroom trial, he nevertheless notes that an ordinary hearing would have been "less formal and combative" and this might have helped rather than hurt the scientist. He quotes Green, the AEC lawyer who drafted the original charges, as saying that some matters injurious to Oppenheimer would not have been raised "if the case had been handled normally before a regular experienced AEC hearing board; as an inquiry, not a trial; and without a full-fledged prosecution." Under such a less judicialized procedure, the panel would call most of the witnesses and do most of the questioning with the government and defense attorneys playing only supplementary roles.

The Oppenheimer case, then, shows the perils of both too much and too little judicialization. It thus can furnish support for each side as the controversy over judicialization of the administrative process continues to rage.

Administrative Control

In the fifty-first of their famous Federalist Papers, James Madison and Alexander Hamilton pointed out,

> If men were angels no government would be necessary. If angels were to govern men, neither external nor internal controls on government would be necessary. In framing a government which is to be administered by men over men, the great difficulty lies in this: you must first enable the government to control the governed; and in the next place oblige it to control itself. A dependence on the people is, no doubt, the primary control of the government; but experience has taught mankind the necessity of auxiliary precautions.[27]

The judicial safeguards so far examined in this chapter constitute an important part of the "auxiliary precautions" that Hamilton and Madison referred to, but they by no means embrace them all. As administration has grown in size and scope, as it has become increasingly comprehensive and complex, a welter of "auxiliary precautions" have evolved in a continuing effort to keep it within controllable bounds.

As the writers of *The Federalist* perceptively noted, there are really two aspects to the subject of administrative control. One is the control that agencies must exercise over their own constituent elements, be they subunits or individuals; the other is the control that must be imposed on the agency itself. These two forms of control overlap and even duplicate in many areas. In other respects, however, they diverge and even conflict. An agency may show itself quite zealous in *exercising* internal control but equally zealous in *contesting* external control. Thus, the question of administrative control has two quite distinct aspects that, though they often make use of the same techniques and devices, warrant separate consideration.

Internal Control

In chapter 3 we noted that staff units and their personnel frequently perform a controlling function even when they have no authority or mandate to do so. This is what frequently makes them disliked by people on the line. The school social worker has no right to tell the teacher what to do. However, dealing with one or more of the teacher's pupils means contact with the teacher and usually leads, at a minimum, to some joint consultation. And while the social worker has no authority to give the teacher orders, he or she will most likely appeal to the teacher's department head or principal if the suggestions are rejected. Furthermore, in talking with pupils, the social worker is, to some extent, checking up and may disclose what he or she finds to the teacher's colleagues if not the superior. Thus, although teachers do not commonly regard social workers as enemies and instead often welcome their assistance, an element of control is nearly always present in their relationships.

What holds true for the teacher's relationship with the social worker also characterizes the teacher's relationship with the guidance counselor, the school secretary, the custodian, and other nonline personnel. As they carry out their duties they are likely to come into contact with the teacher and are thus likely to become aware of what he or she may or may not be doing. If the teacher is not doing anything untoward, then he or she may not feel any pressure at all from these contacts. But if he or she were to "step out of line," word would get around, causing reverberations that he or she would subsequently experience as disquieting. All of these staff personnel may also make demands upon the teacher, and though he or she has the option, in most instances, of refusing them, each refusal is likely to have negative connotations, even if it is only an attenuation of relations that makes the organizational environment a little less pleasant.

In this manner, then, staff services tend to provide internal control even when they are not expressly designed to do so. However, many staff services are expressly designed with a control function at least partly in mind.

One of these is the personnel department. If it enjoys a fair degree of authority, as many such departments do, it can wield a considerable influence in determining how line departments and line officials deal with their personnel problems. But even when a personnel unit has no power other than to recommend, it still does not lack influence. There is always a price to be paid for saying no. Thus, personnel departments are inevitably units that perform a controlling function.

When it comes to staff services involving financial matters, the control function becomes still more apparent. The budget bureau or budgeting office of any agency or any government obviously exercises a high degree of control, for it plays a crucial role in deciding who gets what amount of money for what purpose. Since this function has already been the subject of an entire previous chapter, it requires no further elaboration here.

Another staff department that plays a very direct role in exercising financial control is the purchasing office. Generally, line departments as well as staff bureaus must apply to the purchasing agent when they want to buy anything other than small, petty-cash-type items. The purchasing agent, in turn, must usually adhere to certain prescribed rules in filling requests. One of the most important of these rules requires putting out for bids contracts to purchase an item or service and accepting the lowest qualified bidder. This stipulation is often waived in whole or in part when the contract is quite small or when it calls for an exceptional type of equipment or service that can only be supplied by one firm. Even in this latter instance the purchasing agent will normally exercise some care to see to it that the exceptions are justified.

Perhaps the most important financial control unit is the auditing branch. Certainly it is the one expressly charged with control and with little else. For obvious reasons, auditing is best performed by a unit that is as separate as possible from the activities that it is auditing. As such, it more often falls into the category of external control. Yet, some organizations, particularly large ones, have their own auditing units, and an organization the size of the Defense Department actually has specialized auditing offices. For example, in 1964 the department set up its Defense Contract Audit Agency to centralize the auditing of defense contracts.

There have been some important changes in the auditing function in recent years. First, there has been a shift of emphasis from preaudit to postaudit activities. Auditing offices have begun exercising less and less control over expenditures before they are made and instead have begun centering efforts on checking up afterward. To some this seems like locking the barn door after the horse is stolen. Others point out that this is really just as effective, since awareness that the books will be examined will generally provide the proper deterrent to financial abuses. It also makes for less work by the auditors and is less aggravating to those they are auditing since they now do not have to clear every expenditure ahead of time.

Another change following along these lines has been to replace complete audits of all expenditures with selected audits of only some expenditures. The selection is usually done by means of a carefully worked out sampling procedure. Congress in 1964 gave all federal agencies permission to use such a procedure in checking vouchers amounting to one hundred dollars or less. This saves the auditing forces a lot of time and effort, and if the sampling technique is statistically well prepared, it results in no significant loss in financial control. The use of sampling techniques, it should be pointed out, is not confined to simple financial disbursements. Some welfare systems, for example, use such a procedure to check whether their clients are eligible, and the Internal Revenue Service uses a complex and highly secret statistical sampling technique for determining which tax returns it will review.

While the internal audit office, when it exists, is usually the only *financial* staff function that has control as its primary purpose, other staff units may also exist expressly to perform such a function in other control areas. Some sizable organizations maintain special units that do nothing but keep watch on the activities of the rest of the organization. Big-city police departments, for example, usually have an internal inspection division, or "shoefly squad," to maintain surveillance over possibly erring organization members. In 1978 Congress established the Office of Inspector General in fifteen federal departments and agencies to investigate allegations of waste and fraud and to institute better procedures for preventing such abuses. President Reagan sought to tie in the Office of Management and Budget with the work of the IGs to make sure that agencies follow up on their IG's findings and recommendations.[28]

Most organizations of any size also utilize a form of control called the *field inspection*. Sometimes these inspections are done by internal investigation units, but more often they are performed by simple field inspectors and sometimes by regular line officials. In any case, it has become customary to try to eliminate some of the aura of "snooping" from these field checkups. Instead, the emphasis is being placed upon the positive aspects of such inspections. The inspectors profess a goal of only seeking to assist the branch or field office they are inspecting. While their protestations of good intent are often greeted with cynicism by those being inspected, still a change in emphasis is taking place.

The goal of trying to make field inspections into a positive rather than a negative phenomenon is best achieved when field inspections are made on an announced and scheduled basis. Unannounced inspections do permit the inspectors to catch the unit unawares, and thus unable to put on a deceptive camouflage for the inspection visit. Its costs may outweigh its benefits, however. First, the local officials may be away or busy on the day the inspectors have chosen to pounce on them and thus may not be able to supply records, answer questions, and so on. Then the unit itself may be undergoing an unusually critical or unusually slack period. Consequently, just because the inspectors have arrived unannounced does not mean that they have caught the unit on a typical day and can fairly judge its overall performance.

The fact that the possibilities of deception are supposedly increased when inspections are announced beforehand should present no great problem. Experienced and alert inspectors, equipped with the proper tools and techniques and oriented toward inspecting for substantive rather than superficial problems, should have no great difficulty in seeing through any deceptive strategy they may encounter.

Most important of all is that the announced inspection does not create fear, distrust, and hostility, but tends to encourage the positive and cooperative attitude that an organization needs to perform in an optimally effective manner.

The Forest Service offers an example of the possibilities inherent in announced inspections. The service places a great emphasis on its field inspections and tries to use them to strengthen the ranger's affinity to the organization and to develop his or her skills. In *The Forest Ranger* Kaufman writes,

> There are no surprise visits, for the objectives of inspection are not so much to catch personnel in the wrong as to find out what is happening in the woods to train forest officers in the organizationally approved methods of resource management. Besides, unless advance notice is given to the units to be visited, there is a chance that the entire staff will be out working when the inspectors arrive, and the inspectors will lose valuable time (and be thrown off their own schedules) while they wait for the return of those they came to see.[29]

After detailing some of the matters that are likely to be covered in such an inspection, Kaufman goes on to point out that

> the atmosphere of inspection is not one of a trial or even a competitive examination. In the evenings, when the work is done and the notes written up, the inspectors and the inspected gather socially to discuss personal and organizational affairs. . . . Men in the field, rather than fearing inspections, tend to welcome the opportunities it affords them to keep abreast of developments in the organization, to learn the latest rumors and gossip, and to give their own ideas to their superiors at first hand.[30]

External Control

Along with the courts, whose role in providing external control we have already examined, numerous other agents and agencies exist to curb administrative power. Since many of these forces constitute sources of support for administrators, a more detailed analysis of their relationship with administration must await the next chapter. At this juncture, we will limit ourselves to a brief review of their function as agents of restraint and regulation.

The instrumentality that is most expressly charged with controlling administration is the legislative branch of government. Legislatures exercise this function in many different ways. The first is by the customary control over expenditures. Even the least powerful of city councils can usually cut a mayor's or city manager's budget, while many city councils, to say nothing of state legislatures and the Congress, can add, cut, and shift around appropriations pretty much as they see fit (subject in most cases to a chief executive's veto). Joseph Harris, in his authoritative work *Congressional Control of Administration,* says that Congress's power over expenditures is "perhaps the most important single control over the departments."[31]

This power is largely, although not exclusively, exercised during budget hearings. And it is a power than can strike terror into the hearts of administrators. Richard F. Fenno, Jr., in his book *The Power of the Purse,* quotes a Washington bureaucrat as saying, "There is not a bureau head here whose blood pressure doesn't go up before the appropriations hearing. It's an ordeal. You don't know what questions they might ask or what case they might bring up."[32] Budget hearings, which are annual affairs in most legislative bodies, provide legislative committees excellent opportunities not only to make or to pass on key decisions regarding future agency operations but also to review the agency's activities. Such hearings thus can become probing and quite painful proceedings whose outcomes can prove decisive for an agency's continued well-being or even survival.

Another way in which legislative bodies can exercise control over administration is through confirmation of appointments. The United States Senate must advise and consent on most presidential appointments to agencies situated outside what is called the Executive Office of the President. Since only a small portion of the federal bureaucracy is situated within the Executive Office—they include the Office of Management and Budget, the National Security Council, the Office of Science and Technology, and some others—this gives the nation's upper house a fair degree of at least residual power over the administrative branch. In practice the Senate usually goes along with the president's nominee. Presidents will also make at least some appointments at the behest of certain key senators. Furthermore, at times the Senate has succeeded in exacting policy commitments from presidential appointees before confirming them and on occasion has turned down appointees. Many state legislatures and not a few city councils also possess the power to pass on certain gubernatorial or mayoral appointments, and they often exhibit a greater interest in influencing such appointments than does the U.S. Senate.

The most well-known power legislative bodies exercise over administrative ones is the power to investigate and expose. Congress, state legislatures, and city councils can generally summon administrative officials to appear before them to answer questions. Legislatures and their staffs may also examine administrative records and documents. Most investigations are conducted by the legislative committee concerned, though at the municipal level it is not unusual for the entire town or city council to become engaged in the probe. Congress, all state legislatures, and some city councils also possess the subpoena power that enables them to command the appearances of witnesses and the production of documents outside the government proper.

One limitation on this power at the federal level involves executive privilege. Presidents have often claimed that their personal staffs are not subject to congressional demands to testify and that many of the in-house documents they generate are similarly off-bounds to congressional scrutinizers. This power has never been adequately demarcated or defined. In the Watergate investigation, President Nixon allowed his aides to testify at the Senate committee's public hearings but refused to surrender the tapes of his White House conferences and telephone calls until forced to do so. In 1983 the issue once again came before the court, as the Reagan administration refused to allow the administrator of the Environmental Protection Agency to give Congress certain records that the legislators were seeking. However, the president relented and agreed to Congress's request before the court reached a decision.

How effective is the legislative investigation as a tool for controlling administration? Dean Acheson answered the question in the negative. "The most publicized weapon of Congress—and one which as often as not proves frustrating to those who employ it—is the investigation," he once noted.[33] He then went on to quote with approval Woodrow Wilson's opinion on this subject: "Congress stands almost helplessly outside the departments. Even the special, irksome, ungracious investigations which it from time to time institutes . . . do not afford it more than a glimpse of the inside of a small province of federal administration. . . ."[34]

Legislative investigations do lack continuity, often becoming one-shot affairs that, although they may result in some sensational public hearings, do not provide for following through on recommendations. They have often been launched and executed with publicity factors in mind, and this, needless to say, limits their depth and, in some cases, desirability. Finally, they tend to focus on negative aspects alone, and this curbs their ability to provide a rounded picture of what is taking place and limits their capacity for offering ideas.

But despite these drawbacks, there are reasons for viewing such investigations in a more favorable light. There is first of all the "lighthouse theory." No one ever knows how many ships a lighthouse may save, and similarly no one knows just how many abuses the investigatory weapon may prevent. Since administrators seldom welcome such probes, the fear of prompting one may well deter much error and wrongdoing in government agencies. The threat of an investigation probably accomplishes more in terms of controlling administration than the actual use of the device.

Then, other factors are improving the possibilities for continuity and follow-up. Legislative committees have begun showing more long-term responsibility in overseeing the work of the department entrusted to their care. The Legislative Reorganization Act of 1946 formally mandated to the standing committees of Congress "continuous watchfulness of the execution by the administrative agencies concerned of any new law the subject matter of which falls within the jurisdiction of such committee."[35] Committee staffing, at the state as well as at the new congressional level, has improved markedly in recent years, providing the basis for more diligent overseeing of administrative agencies.

Finally, civil liberties lawyer Charles Rembar has noted a rather sharp change in the focus of congressional investigative committees during the past two decades. They are, he says, becoming more responsible and more useful. "The Senate tries to pry information out of an unwilling Executive and present it to the public. Instead of stifling free expression, the committees, by and large, promote it. And the target of investigations at the present time is fact rather than opinion."[36]

Another means by which Congress and some state and local legislative bodies exercise surveillance over their respective bureaucracies is auditing. Many state legislatures and city councils appoint an auditor to examine the books of the executive department. Congress maintains for this purpose a department of its own, the General Accounting Office. Staffed by five thousand six hundred men and women with headquarters in Washington but with field offices in the various regions and even at federal installations overseas, the GAO acts as the watchdog of the legislative branch. At its head is the comptroller-general, who, though appointed by the president, holds the post for fifteen years, is not eligible for reappointment, and can be fired only by Congress and not by the president. Consequently, there is little dispute over where his or her loyalty lies and whose interests are served.

The GAO has seldom been accused of lack of vigor when it comes to monitoring the activities of the executive branch. Indeed, it has often been accused of being too meddlesome. The auditing office has, however, somewhat shifted its emphasis in recent years. In line with the current trends in auditing, it has taken to concentrating on postauditing rather than requiring agencies to clear expenditures in advance. It has also begun to use sampling techniques rather than make complete examinations of expenditure accounts. At the same time, under a congressional mandate to expand its scope beyond the strictly financial sphere, it has begun using the services of economists, engineers, management consultants, and other specialists. With such added resources, it now is able to undertake what are called "management audits." As Comptroller-General Elmer Staats has put it, the GAO has begun shifting its focus away from examinations of "individual mismanagement and waste to some of the broader implications of Government operations."[37]

Congress has begun relying more and more heavily on the GAO. If senators or congressmen or women find evidence of something going amiss in the federal bureaucracy, they are likely to ask the comptroller-general and his or her staff to investigate and give them a report. In 1972, Congress established a new Office of Federal Elections within the auditing office. The GAO, however, still lacks the subpoena power and this curtails some of its activities. It cannot examine income tax records unless the Internal Revenue Service chooses to let it do so, for example.

One last means through which legislatures oversee administration is through "casework." Members of Congress, state legislators, and city councillors frequently receive complaints against administrative agencies, and checking them out provides opportunities to find out what these agencies are doing and how they are doing it. The performance of casework frequently leads to many other forms of legislative oversight. Thus, if a legislator, in looking into a matter brought to his or her attention by a disgruntled constituent, finds an indication of some greater wrong, then he or she may call for an investigation or ask the auditors to look into the agency or subject the agency's officials to some tough questioning at the next round of budget hearings.

In some countries and in certain jurisdictions in the United States, the processing of complaints is done by an official expressly charged with this task. Such an official is called the *ombudsman*. The term is a Swedish word meaning "representative," and in the Scandinavian countries, where the office originated, the ombudsman functions as the people's representative against the bureaucracy. He or she is always a highly esteemed individual, often a distinguished former judge, who has been appointed for a long term. Equipped with a sizable staff and a sizable scope of power, he or she can conduct searching investigations and even prosecute mal- or nonfeasant administrators. Although in most cases he or she acts in response to a complaint, the ombudsman can initiate action when he or she has reason to believe that an administrative agency is not performing its job properly.

The office of ombudsman has a long and successful record in Scandinavia, and during the 1960s other countries began adopting it. Great Britain and many of the Commonwealth nations, such as New Zealand, Australia, and Canada, have set up ombudsmen, as have at least ten of the United States and several U.S. cities. The U.S. governmental units that have adopted the ombudsman concept usually give the office a different title and rarely confer on its holder the sweeping and formal powers that Scandinavian counterparts enjoy. Nevertheless, the concept has made headway and does seem to be bearing fruit. Dayton, Ohio, established its Joint Office of Citizen Complaints in March 1971 and named the former chief editorial writer of a local newspaper as its head. With a staff of twenty, including eight volunteers, the office handles two to three thousand complaints a year.

Citizens are not the only ones who lodge complaints against public agencies. Sometimes the agency's own employees find grounds for rebellion and resistance, and this too results in a form of administrative control. Thus, the development of public employee unionism can be viewed as a manifestation of control, as can the emergence of "underground newspapers," which are published and circulated through some agencies by dissident employees. Such publications flourished at HEW's Washington headquarters during the 1960s. However, a more striking, although not necessarily more important, form of employee control has been the rise of the "whistle blower."

The term *whistle blower* was originated by Ralph Nader to categorize those public employees who, in effect, blow the whistle on acts by their own agencies when they deem such acts to be improper.[38] Some of the more famous whistle blowers during the early 1970s were Gordon Rule, the navy's director of procurement, who challenged extravagant cost overruns and claims for extra compensation by navy suppliers; A. Ernest Fitzgerald, the Pentagon cost analyst who called attention to some similar cost overruns in conjunction with the air force's C-5A transport jet; and Frank Serpico, the New York City patrolman whose reports on corruption in his department touched off a wide-ranging investigation that culminated in numerous indictments as well as shake-ups in the city's constabulary.

Many factors account for the growing prominence of whistle blowers as agents of administrative control. One of them is the development of administrative law and the safeguards it extends to public employees. When the Nixon administration attempted to discharge Fitzgerald, for example, by eliminating his job, he fought back through the courts and won.[39] A midwestern high school teacher who was fired after he sent a letter to a local newspaper criticizing his school board won similar reinstatement. In general, the courts have become increasingly protective of whistle-blowing employees.

WHISTLING IN THE DARK?

Early in 1979 the federal government decided to allow anyone to become a whistle blower. It installed a special hot line, which any citizen could use to report instances of abuse, especially fraud, involving federal agencies or programs.

By mid-June 1981 the hot line had logged twenty-nine thousand calls. Only about one-third of these were deemed worthy of submission to the inspector general's office, and of these, almost half were soon found to be without merit. Those that survived the screening involved mostly "nickel-and-dime stuff" such as a perfectly well employee taking sick leave. The end result—a few suspensions and reprimands but not one criminal prosecution in two and a half years of operation.

Another factor that has encouraged whistle blowing has been the development of the news media. In this connection it is important to note that the press, in and by itself, has long played an active and aggressive role in controlling administrative actions. "I fear three newspapers more than I fear 3,000 bayonettes," Napoleon once remarked, while an English contemporary, philosopher Jeremy Bentham, observed that "Without publicity, all checks are inefficient; in comparison to publicity, all checks are of small account."[40]

The development of broadcast journalism, particularly television news, and the growth of public awareness of and interest in government generally have made the news media today a form of control that rivals if it does not exceed that of legislative bodies. This is particularly true in the United States, which does not have a government-owned television and radio network and which has a long muckraking tradition. The media is not only important for what it does on its own but for the help it provides other forms of control. It has encouraged and strengthened whistle blowing by providing considerable publicity to the whistle blowers. It also has stimulated legislative control by providing headlines and coverage for legislative exposés. Furthermore, many newspapers and radio and TV stations even act as ombudsmen, soliciting citizen complaints against the bureaucracy and then checking them out.

Another instrumentality of control over an administrative agency is its clientele. For reasons that will be more fully discussed in the next chapter, administrators, particularly U.S. ones, usually need considerable cooperation from their clientele, and the clientele often seize upon this to exercise some countervailing influence over administrators. Sometimes this takes dramatic and violent forms, such as the client takeovers of welfare offices, the student rebellions of the 1960s, and the prison riots of the early 1970s. More often, however, clients exercise control by simply refusing to comply with policies they do not like.

One final form of control that often receives little attention but that plays an important role in constraining many administrative agencies is the control exercised by competing agencies. As we saw in chapter 3, agencies are frequently locked in combat in fights over jurisdiction, funding, and so on. In their continual jousting for power and position, agencies tend to control each other. James Madison actually saw this as one of the most effective forms of control. In a well-known passage in *The Federalist* he noted, "Ambition must be made to counteract ambition . . . the constant aim is to divide and arrange the several offices in such a manner that each may be a check on the other—that the private interest of every individual may be a sentinel over the public rights."[41]

In summary, then, the substantial grants of powers that have been increasingly conferred on administrative agencies have been accompanied with increasing means and methods of control. This leads us to the question that forms the concluding section of this chapter.

Law and Control: How Much Is Enough?

Democratic government rests on such principles as accountability and responsibility, and the realization of such principles requires a comprehensive system of administrative control. The public has a right to demand and administrators have a need to accept a widespread network of restraints and restrictions on administrative activity. Democratic government is controlled government.

Of course, administrators often find such controls irksome and irritating. They are by nature active men and women who wish to "get on with the job." It would be strange if they did not frequently chafe at curbs placed upon their actions. In the long run, however, they, too, benefit from a suitable system of control. Such a system will point out their errors before they go too far and will also reassure the public that they are not behaving capriciously or coercively. Many administrators in countries that have ombudsmen, for example, have found that their presence is beneficial. By giving timely warnings when needed, constructively pointing out errors, and investigating complaints, the ombudsman may assist the administrator in carrying out his or her mission.

The idea of bureaucracy as a dominant and power-hungry force in modern life is not the only negative image that administrators have to struggle against. They must also contend with an equally pervasive picture of bureaucracy as an institution mired in sloth and sluggishness. If bureaucratic agencies are frequently accused of becoming too meddlesome and interfering, they are also constantly being flayed for laziness and laxity.

While administrative controls can help allay the first type of criticism, they can aggravate the second. Controls, although they impede administrative abuse, may also inhibit administrative innovation and enterprise. Administrative agencies are continually being rebuked for the "red tape" that seems to engulf so many of their activities. Yet this "red tape" is in many instances the direct result of a desire to monitor and control their decisions, and to maintain standards of accountability and responsibility. "Too often in American public administration we assure legality and propriety in hiring, purchasing, building and the like, but prevent not only corruption but action prompt and vigorous enough to be effective," writes Lewis Mainzer. And he goes on to add, "Harmless government is not good enough."[42]

Another writer on administration, Peter Woll, expresses the same concern. "Guaranteeing that agencies will follow certain procedures in no way assures that they will take any action at all," he writes. The issue is an important one, he claims, because, owing to the limitations of the courts and the chief executive in directing and implementing policy, "the bureaucracy inevitably becomes the primary instrument of positive government to maintain the public interest." As a result, "the central problem today is not how to curb its [the bureaucracy's] power, but how to guarantee that it will take the necessary action to deal with critical public needs."[43]

Looked at in this light, control, or at least extensive control, can be counterproductive. Carried too far, it can render government ineffectual and even inert, leaving the way clear for less savory and less responsible forces to operate. As we saw in our examination of administrative law, the judicialization of the administrative process has proved to be a bonanza to various business interests that use the safeguards imposed on administrative agents to perpetuate or prolong questionable activities.

Too much control also breeds a climate of conflict and distrust, which can result in a great deal of dysfunctional behavior. If it refuses to resign itself to relative immobility, an agency straitjacketed with a strict system of controls may dissipate so much of its energies in trying to overcome obstacles to action that it may have little energy left to serve the public. Furthermore, it may respond to the distrust that extensive control indicates by meriting such distrust. The American statesman Henry L. Stimson, who served in many high government positions before and during World War II, once observed that one way to make a man trustworthy is to trust him.[44] The reverse may also be true. Certainly, the distrust that pervasive control fosters does little to encourage candor and cooperation.

It is interesting to note in this connection that while control plays an essential role in the workings of democratic government, it may play an even greater role in the operation of totalitarian regimes. One reason why Russian factories have such a low level of per capita output is that they have a much higher proportion of administrative employees to production workers. The main reason for this disparity is to fulfill the Soviet system of extensive control.

The Nazi regime offers an even better example of this phenomenon. Albert Speer claimed that his success in dramatically increasing war production despite the allied bombing raids and the absence of so many workers at the front during World War II resulted from his successful attempt to dismantle, at least in part, the elaborate control apparatus that the Nazi state had established. Speer said he was able to encourage initiative and speed as well as free six hundred to eight hundred thousand workers for the war effort "merely by substituting trust for mistrust within the administrative system."[45]

As the Soviet and Nazi cases suggest, the costs of control are not only felt in the effect it has on the agencies being controlled but also in the costs of maintaining the controllers. Sometimes such costs can reach ludicrous proportions. In 1887 Lord Randolph Churchill, in conducting a campaign against waste in the British armed services, pointed out that one branch of the armed services spent £5,000 a year to supervise another branch whose expenses amounted to only £250 a year.[46] To take an example closer to home, the United States, according to Robert Presthus, spent $350 million in 1955 to protect the federal government against supposedly subversive elements. This program resulted in the firing of between one-twentieth and one-thirtieth of 1 percent of all the employees subject to the program's control.[47] Given the nature of those rather hysterical times, it is questionable how many of those caught in the elaborate net of the government's security program were really culpable.

One final fact concerning the cost of control should be taken into account. As Peter Drucker has pointed out, control of the last 10 percent of a program or project is nearly always more expensive than control of the preceding 90 percent. Consequently, the cost of control increases significantly as control itself increases. "If control tries to account for everything, it becomes prohibitively expensive," says Drucker.[48]

In conclusion, then, control, whether exercised through legalistic or other means, has its limits if the ends of democratic society are to be served. Fortunately some of the changes now buffeting administration may help alleviate some of the problems it poses. Programmed budgeting, productivity measures, management by objectives, and some of the other new techniques coming to the fore may increase responsibility and accountability while replacing or reducing the role of negative controls, that is, control for its own sake. In addition, the growing professionalism that is also starting to characterize public administration may make extensive and elaborate control systems somewhat less necessary. Nevertheless, some systems of control will continue to be needed and the problems they present will doubtless persist.

Notes

1. James Bryce, *The American Commonwealth* (1888), quoted in Theodore J. Lowi, *The End of Liberalism* (New York: W. W. Norton, 1969), 128–129.

2. Lowi, *End of Liberalism*, 131.

3. Ibid., 132.

4. *A.L.A. Schechter Poultry Corporation v. United States*, 295 U.S. 495 (1935).

5. "Administrative Law Developments—1971," *Duke Law Journal*, 1972, no. 1.

6. Lewis C. Mainzer, *Political Bureaucracy* (Glenview, Ill.: Scott, Foresman, 1973), 62.

7. Kenneth Culp Davis, *Administrative Law and Government* (St. Paul, Minn.: West Publishing, 1960), 463. Quoted in Mainzer, *Political Bureaucracy*, 50.

8. For an interesting though scarcely disinterested account of a leading decision regarding prisoners' rights, see Editorial, Tom Wicker, "Due Process for Prisoners," *New York Times*, 18 June 1970.

9. "Administrative Law Developments—1971," sec. 3.

10. Ibid. For a more readable but less profound account of the expansion of this right, see "Toward Greater Fairness for All," *Time*, 26 February 1973, 95.

11. Martin Shapiro, *The Supreme Court and Administrative Agencies* (New York: Free Press, 1968), 13.

12. Mainzer, *Political Bureaucracy*, 37.

13. *Parade*, March 15, 1970, 4. I have omitted the name of the individual concerned to spare needless embarrassment to him and his family. The same policy is followed in certain other cases mentioned subsequently.

14. *The Boston Sunday Globe*, 4 February 1973.

15. "The Heresy of John F. Shaw," *New York Times*, 18 June 1971.

16. *Garrity v. New Jersey*, 385 U.S. 493 87 S.Ct. 616 17 L.Ed. 2nd 562 (1967).

17. For an account of the Supreme Court's disposition of some other cases involving the attempt by General Lewis B. Hershey, former director, to use the authority of his office to punish draft protestors, see the *New York Times*, 27 January 1970.

18. *Fact Concerts, Inc. v. Newport* (1981). The earlier two cases referred to were *Owen v. City of Independence* (1980) and *State of Maine v. Thiboutot* (1980).

19. The Boulder, Colorado, suit referred to was *Community Communications Company, Inc. v. City of Boulder* (1982). For a summary of the other suits together with a review of the entire situation, see *Public Administration Times*, 1 December 1982.

20. David Bazelon, "The Impact of the Courts on Public Administration", *Indiana Law Journal* (Fall 1976).

21. *Richardson* v. *Perales*, 402 U.S. 389 (1971).

22. "The 'Hidden Judiciary' and What It Does," *U.S. News and World Report*, 1 November 1982.

23. Quoted in Joseph C. Goulden, *The Superlawyers* (New York: Dell Publishing, 1973), 186.

24. Ibid., 194.

25. Ibid., 191–194.

26. The material, including quotations, for this case study was taken almost exclusively from Philip M. Stern and Harold P. Green, *The Oppenheimer Case; Security on Trial* (New York: Harper & Row, 1969).

27. Alexander Hamilton, John Jay, and James Madison, *The Federalist* (New York: Modern Library, n.d.), 337.

28. *Public Administration Times*, 15 October 1981.

29. Herbert Kaufman, *The Forest Ranger* (Baltimore, Md.: Johns Hopkins Press, 1960), 142–143.

30. Ibid., 145.

31. Joseph P. Harris, *Congressional Control of Administration* (Garden City, N.Y.: Anchor Books, 1965), 8.

32. Richard F. Fenno, Jr., *The Power of the Purse* (Boston: Little, Brown, 1966), 283.

33. Dean Acheson, *Present at the Creation* (New York: W. W. Norton, 1969), 146.

34. W. Woodrow Wilson, *Congressional Government* (Boston: Houghton Mifflin, 1885), 271. Quoted in Acheson, *Present at the Creation*, 146.

35. Quoted in Mainzer, *Political Bureaucracy*, 76.

36. Charles Rembar, "The First Amendment on Trial: The Government, the Press and the Public," *The Atlantic* (April 1973).

37. Quoted by Philip Shabecoff, "Watching the Money," *New York Times*, 25 February 1972, Business and Finance section.

38. Ralph Nader, Peter Petkas, and Kate Blackwell, eds., *Whistle Blowing* (New York: Bantam Books, 1972).

39. Ibid., 39–55.

40. Quoted in George E. Berkley, *The Democratic Policeman* (Boston: Beacon Press, 1969), 159–160.

41. Hamilton, Jay, and Madison, *Federalist*, 337.

42. Mainzer, *Political Bureaucracy*, 89.

43. Peter Woll, "Administrative Law in the Seventies," *Public Administration Review* (September–October 1972).

44. McGeorge Bundy, *The Strength of Government* (Cambridge, Mass.: Harvard University Press, 1968), 56.

45. Albert Speer, *Inside the Third Reich* (New York: Macmillan, 1970), 635.

46. C. Northcote Parkinson, *The Law and the Profits* (New York: Ballantine Books, 1971), 140.

47. Robert Presthus, *The Organizational Society* (New York: Random House, 1962), 304.

48. Peter F. Drucker, *The Effective Executive* (New York: Harper & Row, 1967), 84.

12

The Search for Support

Perhaps nothing differentiates U.S. administrators so much from their European counterparts as the Americans' unending quest to secure support for their agencies and programs. The reasons for this relate very directly to the distinguishing features of the country's political culture, as discussed in chapter 1. The fragmentation and personalism of our political system in particular tend to make the typical administrative agency something of an isolated entity, which must continually develop and maintain its own sources of support.

In his highly regarded and oft-cited essay "The Federal System," the late Morton Grodzins maintained that "the administrator must play politics for the same reason that the politician is able to play in administration: the parties are without program and without discipline. In response to the unprotected position in which the party situation places him, the administrator is forced to seek support where he can find it."[1] Francis Rourke has sounded a similar note. "The political neutralization of bureaucracy is impossible in a country in which the political parties are incapable of performing the functions expected of them in the governmental structure of which they are a part. When the parties do not provide for program developments and the mobilization of political support, executive agencies must perform these tasks for themselves."[2]

While these two writers stress the role played by the fragmented nature of our political parties in producing the U.S. administrator's difficult and slippery situation, other factors also enter in. The variability and vigor of the various levels of government, the separation of powers in the various governments found at so many of these levels, the hostility or at least ambivalence with which the American people tend to regard activist government—all play a part. The upshot is that the U.S. administrator must indeed cultivate and exercise the skills of the politician if he or she is to achieve success, and must develop and maintain support.

Where is one to look for such support? As noted in chapter 11, those elements that control administration also support it. The courts, for example, in clamping procedural restrictions on administrative behavior also give it sanction, for once the administrator has abided by the prescriptions of procedural due process, he or she can then look to the courts for legal vindication of his actions. Similarly, the ombudsman, when he or she investigates a complaint and finds it invalid, tends to bolster the position of the agency in question. Indeed, many administrators in those countries that have ombudsmen have found such investigatory officials to be helpful in deflecting public irritation and encouraging public approval of their actions.

For the most part, however, administrators must assume a more activist role in developing support. This leads them to take affirmative steps to strengthen and promote their relationship with other components in their control networks. For example, when the navy set up its Special Projects Office to handle the service's ballistic missile program, the new office wisely saw that it would need the cooperation or at least passive compliance of other navy units in order to succeed. So the Special Projects Office farmed out parts of the program to other navy units in order to gain, if not their active support, at least their acceptance of the new program.[3]

However, although developing support from other administrative agencies is often useful and even necessary, most public managers tend to concentrate efforts in support development in three basic areas—clientele, the public, and political leaders, particularly legislators. While all three sectors obviously overlap and interrelate, developing and improving relationships will each bring into play somewhat different strategies and skills.

Clientele Relations

United States administrators often work hard at developing what Rourke calls "fervent and substantial constituencies." In many cases, such constituencies are as important to the bureaucrat as they are to the elected politician. They not only help the agency to successfully formulate and implement its programs but, more important perhaps, may help generate the support necessary to gain political approval and funding for these programs. A fervent and substantial constituency can produce an outcry that will make any elected political leader think twice before cutting back an agency's scope or reducing its funding. The fact that the Department of Defense has had large and influential clientele groups while the State Department has lacked them explains, at least in part, the ascendancy of the former over the latter during the 1950s and 1960s.

What makes a clientele effective? One rather obvious factor is size. Other things being equal, an agency with a larger clientele will benefit from more support than an agency with a smaller one. Another factor is *dispersion*. An agency with a large clientele that is concentrated in only a few states will seldom gain as much influence and power as another agency with an equal number of clients that are more widely dispersed.

A third and quite vital element in assessing clientele support is the clientele's *degree of organization*. The gun lobby, which generally supports the Department of Defense, is quite well organized. Welfare clients, on the other hand, lack the strong organization that could make them an effective source of support for the Department of Health and Human Services as well as for state and local welfare departments. The fact that programs benefiting the poor suffer from this lack of organized clientele support has often prompted administrators to organize and build up clientele groups on their own initiative. Sometimes this has worked successfully and sometimes not. In the poverty programs of the 1960s, for example, a number of the organizations purporting to speak for the poor, which arose as a result of such initiative, struck many politicians and members of the public as being too demanding and too controlled by a self-seeking minority of the poor. As a result, such clientele support in many instances proved detrimental to building the programs' overall support base.

A fourth factor that must be taken into account is the *degree of ardor* that the clientele may manifest in rendering support. The State Department, for instance, does have what might be called clientele groups of a sort. These are World Affairs Councils and similar organizations, which, although not organized expressly to support the State Department, do speak for policies and programs that often accrue to the department's benefit. The members of such organizations, however, while sincere and intelligent, lack the intensity of commitment that may characterize some of the support groups of the Defense Department. Among the latter might be found the defense industries and their unions, whose very existence to a great extent depends on the department's well-being.

Usually, the degree of devotion that a clientele group manifests in supporting an agency roughly correlates with its degree of dependence on the agency. This may not always be the case, however. Many liberal and humanitarian organizations support programs for the poor even though the membership of most of these organizations is primarily middle or upper class. The fact that these people do not necessarily have an economic interest in the programs they espouse does not ipso facto dampen their degree of dedication. In general, such organizations have rendered more effective support for poverty programs than have the presumed beneficiaries of these programs.

How do administrators take advantage of the potential support that a clientele has to offer? It must first strive to secure the clientele's cooperation. To this end, it may appoint members of the clientele group to positions, sometimes the highest ones, in the agency. When Franklin D. Roosevelt named financier Joseph P. Kennedy to head the newly created Securities and Exchange Commission, he was motivated in part by the desire to win over the securities industry to cooperate with the new regulatory commission. For the same reason, presidents today usually appoint a business person to head the Department of Commerce, a labor leader or someone with close ties to the labor movement to serve as secretary of labor, and in recent years a Native American to preside over the Bureau of Indian Affairs. Similar tendencies are also becoming more widespread at state and local levels; for instance, the greater concern of minority groups with housing problems has led to frequent appointments of blacks to head municipal housing commissions.

Such efforts at clientele involvement are not confined to the upper level of administration. At lower echelons, the use of what are sometimes called "paraprofessionals" has become increasingly popular in many areas of U.S. public administration. School departments are using parents as "teacher's aides," police departments are setting up auxiliaries, correction departments have even begun using rehabilitated offenders to rehabilitate other offenders. Chester Barnard maintained that the customers of an organization should be considered as part of the organization. Modern administration has shown an increasing tendency to carry out this dictum and in so doing has often increased clientele support.

A related method of securing clientele support is through the awarding of contracts. This, of course, has played a key role in the powerful support the Defense Department has managed to build up through the years. Other departments, however, have also not shown themselves lax in this regard. HEW and, to a lesser extent, HUD have also parceled out work to individuals and institutions outside of the government. This does not mean that the sole or even primary purpose of such contracts is to build clientele support. Often such arrangements are not only useful but necessary for an agency. The alternative for the Defense Department in contracting with war suppliers would be to set up its own armaments industry, a move that would require a major and controversial reversal of a deeply rooted American attitude regarding the relationship of government to the economy. Yet, such contracts and grants do foster clientele support.

Important as such activities have become, few agencies can hope to "buy" all the support they need in this manner. They must also learn to gain the backing of their clientele through other means. While space does not permit a full-scale analysis of all the means and methods that administrators have utilized to achieve this end, we can briefly examine three of them before going on to appraise some of the dangers that the task of developing clientele support presents to the administrator and to the society he or she serves.

Strategies of Support: Advisory Committees

If administrators are to elicit the favor and not the fury of their clients, then they must set up effective ways of listening to what their clients have to say. One tool for doing this is the advisory committee.

Ideally, the advisory committee can assist an agency in a variety of ways. It can act as a weather vane, pointing out to the agency what ideological and emotional currents are blowing among its various clientele groups. It can also serve as a sifter for new ideas that the agency may wish to implement. It can further help by serving as a lightning rod, deflecting many of the criticisms and complaints flung at the agency. Finally, it can provide a resource to help the agency carry out its programs.

In order for it to be able to perform all these roles, the advisory committee must be as fully representative as possible of all the segments of the agency's clientele. If it is an advisory committee for a police precinct station in a mixed neighborhood, then it should include residents and businesspeople, blacks and whites, poor and nonpoor, young and old. Often it will be necessary to include divergent interests among its membership. An advisory committee for a housing agency should, for example, include both tenants and landlords. Such a breadth of membership may make committee meetings more tumultuous but also more productive.

The Federal Water Pollution Control Act of 1972 charged the Environmental Protection Agency with making maximum use of public participation. To develop guidelines for such participation, the agency set up a committee that included representatives of conservation groups as well as of mining and industrial interests that would have to bear much of the brunt of antipollution enforcement. The first meeting, in the words of one EPA official, "blew up" as the conservation members expressed outrage at the presence of the business interests on the committee. They claimed it was equivalent to letting the fox watch the chicken coop. EPA Administrator William Ruckelshaus replied that since in this case the fox had no teeth, the chickens need have no anxieties. Subsequent meetings proved more harmonious, and on February 23, 1973, the EPA was able to publish a proposed set of rules for securing the public participation that the act demanded.[4]

Another administrator who made wide use of the advisory committee technique was Chester Bowles. As head of the Office of Price Administration during World War II, Bowles wisely set up an advisory committee for each industry and directed that no significant change could be made in any price, rent, or rationing regulation until the appropriate committee had been consulted. The more than one thousand committees established under this mandate contributed much to OPA's generally esteemed efficency in keeping a lid on inflation during the war years.[5]

Both these examples illustrate the validity of Rourke's observation that at best "the public dialogue as well as the bureaucratic dialogue may be greatly improved by having outsiders participate in the internal deliberations of executive agencies. The bureaucratic dialogue may immediately become more spirited, and the public dialogue may eventually become more informed."[6]

Advisory committees can do more than simply provide useful inputs for policy formulation. They can, like unions, serve as a two-way transmission system for communication, bringing to the agency clients' concerns and bringing to the clients the agency's problems. They can explain the agency's problems and help win acceptance for its proposed solutions. In some cases, they can even help implement the solutions.

Using advisory committees in this expanded role requires giving them expanded powers. While many agencies and their administrators have been reluctant to take such a step, others have not. One area where clientele advisory committees are assuming more and more authority and responsibility is in public housing. The State Housing Board of Massachusetts promulgated a regulation in 1973 giving representative tenant groups in all the state's housing projects the right to approve all employee hiring. In some cities, tenants have actually won the right to operate the entire project. Meanwhile, the Bureau of Indian Affairs, faced with rising ferment on the nation's reservations, has been moving to shift more responsibilities into the hands of Native Americans themselves.[7]

Such attempts at clientele involvement are by no means uniformly successful. Frequently, they only produce added stresses. The poverty programs offer an example, in some instances at least, of the wrong kind of clientele involvement, since the "grass roots" leadership that developed did not always represent the interests of the clientele. However, although the trend toward clientele participation in policy making presents problems and will require caution and care, it seems likely to be a trend that will continue and grow.

Strategies of Support: Complaint Handling

Although involving clients or their representatives in agency operations should do much to allay the fears and appease the demands of the agency's clientele, it can hardly hope to ensure complete and continuous contentment. Any agency, no matter how well run, will always stir up some dissatisfaction on the part of clients. Furthermore, this dissatisfaction will often have a basis in fact, for even the best of agencies creates occasional injustices. Therefore, any agency of significant size would usually do well to establish a formal and expeditious way of receiving and processing complaints.

A good complaint-handling system can benefit an agency in many ways. It can provide discontented clients with a means of registering their grievances and, if found justified, of having them redressed. Even when the grievance has not been found sufficiently valid for corrective action, the client will often experience some satisfaction in knowing that at least the complaint was heard and examined.

Another and sometimes more important contribution of good complaint handling is providing the agency with valuable information. If complaints appear to cluster around one particular segment of the agency's operations or seem to be directed against individuals, the agency may want to take a closer look at the operation or the individuals in question. Complaints can aid in the process of internal control and can also assist the agency in evaluating present operations, while helping it in planning future ones.

To make maximum use of complaint handling for purposes of building clientele support, exercising internal control, and evaluating current and planning future operations, administrators may find the following guidelines useful:

1 Adopt an attitude of welcoming complaints and see to it that your agency's clients understand this. Set up a regular procedure and, if possible, a regular branch for receiving and processing complaints, and publicize its operation. If possible, have forms printed up to help complainants record their grievances. Above all, try to avoid giving the complainant the impression that he or she is being given the runaround.

2 Make sure that your complaint-handling procedure provides for following through on the complaint. Too often complaints are accepted but then disappear. Every complainant should be informed of the disposition of the complaint, along with the reasons why no action is to be taken, if that is the case.

3 To make sure that the complaint-handling function is taken seriously by all members of the agency, invest those in charge with some prestige and power. They will need the cooperation of the rest of the agency in checking out the complaint and may experience difficulty in obtaining it unless they can speak with some authority. Furthermore, complainants themselves are more apt to feel that they are being given adequate treatment when their grievances are heard by someone who holds a position of some authority. U.S. customs officers, for example, usually refer complainants to their supervisors. At one time, the Customs Service ran short of supervisor badges and so aggrieved parties had to be directed to officials who, while supervisors, were wearing ordinary badges. This only compounded the complainants' annoyance and made many of them outspokenly irate. When the new supervisor badges finally arrived things quieted down considerably.

4 Make sure that you explain the value and need for a complaint-handling procedure to all agency employees and stress the fact that it should not threaten them in any way. Good employees will actually benefit by receiving a low number of valid complaints. Should such employees receive a high number of complaints, then the problem most likely will come from outside their jurisdiction and investigative action will usually uncover and correct it with benefits to them as well as to the complainants.

5 Make sure you have a system for cataloging complaints. Often an agency may want to multiindex them. Thus, a police department may wish to file its complaints according to the area of the city from which they come, according to the type of police work they involve, such as criminal investigation or handling of family disputes, and according to the individuals involved. Only by maintaining a good filing system can an agency make full use of the information that complaint processing can provide.

In recent years, many administrative agencies have begun to institute ombudsmen to handle clientele complaints. These are not ombudsmen in the strict sense, since they are employees of the same agency against whom the complaint is being lodged. However, they often enjoy a measure of independence and discretion in seeing that the grievances brought to their attention are heard and, if valid, acted upon. The U.S. Immigration Service has set up an ombudsman in its New York City office to process both complaints and appeals for help. "One of my primary functions," says Cono Trubiano, who first held the position, "is to cut through red tape and to zoom in on officials who could attend to a case swiftly."[8] The U.S. Department of Commerce has also set up an "Ombudsman for Business," who, working directly under the department's secretary, gives aid and advice to businesspersons in their dealings with the department. Several large business corporations have attempted to do the same, often giving their complaint-handling official vice-presidential status.[9]

Probably no organization in the country, public or private, creates as much clientele disfavor as the Internal Revenue Service. The very nature of its work brings it into an adversary relationship with vast numbers of the country's population every year. However, it gives serious attention to complaints and maintains suggestion boxes in its field offices where such complaints can be submitted. In handling complaints, it also maintains a useful sense of humor. Thus, when an irate taxpayer sent in a turnip with his tax return, saying the government was welcome to all the blood they could get out of it, an IRS official cut a slice out of the turnip and mailed it back to the taxpayer with a letter saying "Enclosed please find refund. Affectionately, U.S. Treasury."[10]

Strategies of Support: Public Hearings

In recounting his adventures as head of OPA during World War II, Chester Bowles relates how a Louisiana senator once frantically called him and asked if he would see "an army of muskrat hunters" who were besieging the senator's office in angry protest over the price ceiling on muskrat hides. Bowles agreed and shortly thereafter a group of angry men clad in hunting shirts and heavy boots trooped into his office. Bowles began by saying that he had trapped muskrats in New England as a boy and was curious as to how it was done in Louisiana. This prompted a forty-minute discussion, whereupon one of Bowles's aides appeared by prearrangement and informed him in urgent tones, "The president wants to see you at the White House immediately." Bowles excused himself and fled to a "sanctuary" elsewhere in the building. "I never heard from the muskrat hunters again."[11]

The story illustrates not only the imagination and enterprise that administrators are frequently called upon to muster but of the efficacy of letting people talk. In more recent years, this stratagem has crystallized in the form of the public hearing.

As we saw in chapter 11, the public hearing has in many instances become part of administrative due process. Administrative agencies are generally required to hold them before they can change their rules, discharge a tenured employee, and so on. Even when they are not required by law to hold such hearings, agencies have increasingly done so, for such hearings may offer opportunities to win support or defuse antagonism. New York City's Board of Education, for example, holds a hearing one evening every month, allowing any citizen to speak for four minutes on any topic of his or her choosing, provided that it is related to the city schools.

As a method of improving clientele relations, the hearing is most useful in "clearing the air" rather than in mobilizing support. It brings hostilities, complaints, and rumors out into the open and thereby enables administrators to deal with them on a more informed basis. Frequently it provides new information that can be used to modify and occasionally reverse an agency's course of action. At a minimum it offers an outlet for resentment which, if kept bottled up, could eventually explode and cause serious damage to the agency and its goals.

Hearings should be adequately advertised and publicized in advance and should be held at convenient times and places. Some sort of record should be kept that should be available for inspection afterward. The agency holding the hearing should also take care to see that both sides are represented and that no one faction dominates the proceedings. To this end, the agency may alternate limited time periods to proponents and opponents. Those parties that stand to be the most deeply affected by the issue involved may be given first priority in having their views heard. Thus, an urban-renewal agency holding a hearing on a proposed project may allow residents and businesspeople in the project area to speak first.

Though sometimes useful, hearings do have their liabilities and limitations. They delay action, consume time (particularly in preparation), and add to expense. The rules that the Environmental Protection Agency eventually promulgated under the Federal Water Pollution Control Act of 1972 required hearings on almost every action the agency could undertake.[12] Frequently, the EPA's field offices found themselves expending a great deal of time and money in locating hearing rooms in areas where the agency was planning to undertake some enforcement action only to find one or two people showing up to be heard.

More important, perhaps, is the fact that despite all the safeguards an agency may take to see that both sides are adequately heard, the negative side often tends to predominate. Those who are opposed to an action are usually the most vocal and vociferous and so an agency contemplating a proposed move will often find itself confronted with a preponderance of outspoken antagonists when it holds hearings, even though majority sentiment may be in its favor. News reports based on the hearing may thus give the impression that the opposition is much more widespread than it really is. Furthermore, although hearings can clear the air, they can sometimes do the reverse, embittering already rocky relationships and strengthening entrenched positions.

The pitfalls that public hearings sometimes present have prompted many administrators to become somewhat wary about using them to secure citizen input into administrative activity. While required in many instances to meet standards of administrative due process, and while in some instances useful in improving clientele relations, they nevertheless may sometimes prove more harmful than helpful. As a result, many administrators and their organizations have begun to look to other devices.

One interesting and possibly significant development occurred in Seattle in 1972. In 1968 and 1970 the Puget Sound Governmental Conference had presented plans for a badly needed mass transit system to the voters. On both occasions, the voters said no. After the second defeat of its referendum proposals, the conference abandoned public hearings as a technique for soliciting citizen views and instead set up work groups consisting of representative citizens and technicians. These work groups gradually fashioned a new set of proposals with citizens participating in nearly all elements of the design process, including selection of routes, schedules, and shelters. In the 1972 election, Seattle voters again found a proposed mass transit plan on their ballots. And although this plan was more expensive than the previous ones and would require a 3-percent additional sales tax, the voters this time said yes.[13]

Clientele Support: How Much Is Too Much?

One of the first major federal agencies to undertake a major program of clientele involvement was the Tennessee Valley Authority. It is not difficult to understand why. Censured and condemned from the beginning as a "socialist" and thereby "un-American" enterprise, this New Deal venture faced a compelling need to win local support. To this end, the TVA appointed representatives of influential local institutions to its policy-making body and deferred generally to local customs and sentiments. By assiduously cultivating clientele support, the public power facility was able to prosper and grow.

The authority paid a heavy price for such grass-roots support, however. It ended up discriminating against blacks, retrenching on conservation measures in order to protect local real estate interests, and hindering programs of other New Deal agencies, such as the Soil Conservation Service, which it sought to exclude from operating in the valley area. What started out as a highly progressive undertaking became, in large part, a conservative institution as a result of its responsiveness to its presumed clientele.[14]

The TVA case is by no means unique. As Rourke points out, the relationship between a public agency and its clientele is nearly always a two-way street. An agency may achieve great success in marshaling clientele support only to find that it has surrendered its independence and, in so doing, has impaired its commitment to the public as a whole. The clientele may manipulate the agency to serve their own limited interests with consequential detriment to general public policy.

Examples of clientele capture abound in the federal bureaucracy. The regulatory commissions, for example, have often been accused of actually being regulated by those they are supposed to regulate. The Veterans Administration has become heavily dependent on and influenced by veterans' organizations, which hold a near veto on much of its policy making. Even cabinet departments are not immune. Agriculture, Commerce, and Labor are often regarded as particularly susceptible to clientele dictation, and many presidents have wanted to merge the latter two departments, partly to release them from this bondage.

Agencies that serve only one highly demarcated group are particularly vulnerable to this problem. And when the agency lacks broad support and when its operations tend to attract insufficient public interest, the problem deepens.

Two current trends in public administration may only serve to increase the amount of clientele capture in U.S. public administration. One of these is the trend toward the clientele basis of organization, noted in chapter 2. Structuring and orienting public agencies on the basis of clientele, while it often offers many advantages in terms of effectiveness and humaneness, will also open up more possibilities for clientele influence to get out of hand.

A second trend that could create increasing difficulties is the drive toward decentralization. "Where considerable authority is devolved upon field officials," David Truman once wrote, "there is always the danger . . . that policy will be unduly influenced by those private individuals and groups who are in closer and more intimate contact with the field than are the superior officers." Such a situation, says Truman, "if carried to any great lengths, is likely to beget such differences of policy between field officers that national policy will be a fiction."[15] We saw some of the ramifications of this when we examined the problems of centralization in chapter 9.

Fortunately, some corrective forces are also at work to counter these trends and possibly redress the whole situation. One is the move toward integration of activities. The interdependence between agencies and programs that characterizes today's bureaucratic milieu may make clientele capture of any particular agency increasingly difficult. Programs intermesh, and sometimes clientele do as well. The sight of a highly differentiated clientele clustered around a highly independent agency may become increasingly rare.

In addition, many of the new developments in public administration, such as programmed budgeting and management by objectives, should make it difficult for a clientele group to induce or coerce an agency to depart from publicly sanctioned policies. Finally, the increased visibility accorded public agencies and their activities, while it will hopefully increase their responsiveness to those they serve, will also increase their responsibility to policies espoused by the entire community. For example, federal regulatory commissions became much less dominated by clientele groups during the past decade, thanks in part to the increased attention they received from the news media and the public. Such countervailing developments as these may well succeed in offsetting the dangers that increased decentralization and increased clientele orientation may present.

Public Relations

James Forrestal, who became the country's first secretary of defense when the combined department was created after World War II, wrote in his diaries that "the difficulty of government work is that not only has it to be done well, but the public has to be convinced that it is being done well. In other words, there is a necessity both for competence and exposition, and I hold it extremely difficult to combine the two in the same person."[16]

Forrestal, a brooding sort of man who eventually committed suicide, may have overstated the problem, but his words do have a ring of truth. Good public administrators would rather do things than talk about doing things, and they often experience the need to explain and expound on what they are doing as a hindrance to action. They frequently begrudge the time and effort that public relations activities take, and even when they do not, they still often find such work distracting and even distasteful.

Compounding the problem is that those who oversee public administration often tend to take a still more critical attitude toward such public-relations activity. One might say that the task of image building has itself acquired a bad image. Congress passed legislation as far back as 1913 barring the use of public funds to pay "any publicity expert unless explicitly appropriated for that purpose."[17] Although no poll has ever been taken on this question, such legislation probably reflects widespread sentiment within the public itself, not only then but today. To many it does not seem quite proper for a public agency to spend public funds to promote itself in the public eye.

Yet, public relations is an integral part of successful public administration. An agency that eschews the public spotlight, that prefers to transact its business in obscurity, may not only fail to generate support for or acceptance of its programs but may encourage public distrust and suspicion. Furthermore, in shielding itself from the public view, it is only creating a climate that makes such distrust and suspicion justifiable. The late Supreme Court Justice Felix Frankfurter once defined democratic government as "the government which accepts in the fullest sense the responsibility to explain itself." A public agency that refuses to do so is seldom worthy of the public trust.

On a less lofty level, good public relations may enable an agency to do more and to do it more effectively and expeditiously. It may even enable it to save money. When Chester Bowles asked for $5 million to launch a public-relations program for the Office of Price Administration, he claimed that without such a program, he would need $15 million for inspectors to investigate and prosecute minor offenders. Only by intensively disseminating the OPA's rules and regulations as widely as possible, he said, could the new agency keep broad sectors of the public from unwittingly committing illegal acts. His argument persuaded Congress not to slash the OPA's budget request for this purpose.[18]

Congress has generally come to accept the idea that public administration requires public-relations efforts. Although the 1913 legislation remains on the statute books, federal agencies have easily learned how to circumvent it. For example, they may hire public-relations personnel but simply call them public-information or even public-education employees. It is interesting to note that no one has been prosecuted under the act since it was passed. The same general state of affairs holds true for many state and municipal governments as well. Both public managers and those who oversee their activities have come to realize the desirability for public relations activities as a way of making public administration more effective.

PR: HOW MUCH IS TOO MUCH?

Although few any longer dispute the need of public agencies to spend money to inform the public on their actions, some fear the practice has gotten out of hand. In 1978 the federal bureaucracy utilized twenty thousand employees and spent over $1 billion on public relations. The Defense Department alone employed over fifteen hundred people for this purpose, while the Department of Agriculture maintained a public-relations staff of more than one thousand. The most controversial activity carried on by these agencies was film making. According to Presidential Media Adviser Barry Jogoda, $500 million a year was being spent producing films whose main purpose was to glorify the agencies making them.

Working with the News Media

Normally, the most important means by which administrators reach the broad public (i.e., the public that exists beyond their own clientele) is through the news media. Where once such media consisted largely of newspapers, it now encompasses television, radio, and a growing number of periodicals. Traditionally news reporters have tended to slight administrative activity, preferring to concentrate their attention on elective officials. But thanks to the rapid expansion of administrative activity in recent years, their interest is starting slowly to shift. It may be expected that the news media will subject administrative agencies to increasing scrutiny as the realization of their growing influence becomes still more widespread.

How does a public administrator work with the news media to create support for projects and programs? First of all, he or she should be as frank and open with them and their representatives as possible. Attempts to deceive the news media nearly always backfire. Presidents Johnson and Nixon both experienced a great deal of difficulty through their failure to deal candidly with the White House press corps. Of course, at times the administrator cannot divulge all that the press may want to know. In such cases, it is better to state so frankly than to resort to stratagems in an attempt to cover up and conceal pertinent information. The administrator may be able to ease the tensions that failure to make full disclosure can produce by offering to go "off the record" or by setting a time when further facts will be disclosed. In any case, the press-conscious public manager will try to supply all the information he or she can as soon as possible, because refusal to reveal information may not only make reporters suspicious but may induce them to seek it elsewhere, often from sources that will provide it in a less complete and less objective form.

The administrator who wishes to maintain a "good press" will not, however, simply wait for the press to come to him or her, but will see to it that his or her agency provides a good bit of news on its own initiative. In selecting and shaping such news, he or she will be wise to keep certain things in mind.

For one thing, he should focus on those aspects that *directly* rather than indirectly affect the public. For example, an internal reorganization of an agency is not in itself very newsworthy. However, a change in the delivery of a service to the public can be singled out and publicized. If the reorganization is going to save some money, this also can be highlighted, assuming that the sum, at least in percentages, represents an appreciable saving. In any case, good public relations at all times requires the ability to see and judge things from the *public's* point of view.

In disseminating news about his or her agency, the administrator should also remember that the specific often scores a greater impact than the general. Thus, a story about one person helped by an agency may ignite more public interest than a general story about all the people helped by the agency. This does not mean that the latter should be neglected; it simply means that the former should also be kept in mind. Those concerned with agency public relations should be on the alert for good "human interest" stories that can be distributed to the news media.

Another means for creating legitimate news is to scan agency records and reports for interesting patterns or news trends. Year-to-year or even month-to-month changes in requests and demands for services may make newsworthy material, and their publication may inform the public about agency activities.

Timing often plays an important role in working with the news media. The administrator should remember that reporters usually work on tight deadlines and also that they pride themselves on getting a story as soon as possible. Consequently, he should cooperate in getting the news to them in an expeditious manner. This does not mean that he or she must distribute all the news as soon as it is ready but may send it out for release at a designated time. This will not only enable the newspeople to study it more carefully before printing or broadcasting it but will enable the administrator to choose the time he or she wants it to appear. Some administrators and their public-relations assistants, for example, like to "embargo" news stories for Sunday night and Monday morning release. This is because the news is usually light on the weekend, and thus their story may not have to compete with too many other newsworthy activities for space and attention. On the other hand, if they have some news to release that they do *not* want highly publicized, such as the closing out of a facility or the phasing out of a popular program, they may release it on late Friday afternoon, knowing that people read fewer newspapers and hear fewer newscasts on Saturday mornings.

The problem of proper timing may involve more than simply choosing appropriate days of the week for releasing material. An organization devoted to traffic safety will find that a news story with a safety message may be more effective if released before a holiday weekend than afterward. A news story that points up the dangers and costs of forest fires will probably fail to score its greatest impact if released in mid-winter. The Internal Revenue Service often seems to time its most newsworthy indictments and prosecutions for tax evasion to coincide with the period when taxpayers are filing out their returns.

What about news that places the agency in an unfavorable light? Here, again, a policy of candor and openness usually pays off. When Harry Hopkins took over the newly created Works Progress Administration during the New Deal, he realized that the hastily launched and sprawling organization would encounter numerous problems with corruption. He decided to deal with the situation by aggressively finding out about such corruption before the newspapers did and by announcing it himself.[19] Hopkins exposed more corruption in his own organization than all the

newspapers combined, and although it provided some unpleasant headlines for the WPA, most would agree that the agency benefited from his
approach. The air force adopted a similar policy in Vietnam, taking the
initiative to announce some of its more grievous errors, such as the bombing of friendly villages by mistake. While the announcements hurt the air
force, they undoubtedly did less damage than would have occurred had
the war correspondents found out about these mistakes themselves. (Unfortunately for the army, it adopted no such policy in regard to the My Lai
and Song My massacres, with the result that these grim episodes, once
they leaked out, created a tremendous furor.)

Another problem that frequently plagues administrators is determining
who gives out the news. Ideally, it should be the public manager or his or
her public-relations office. The press, however, often wants to talk to
those directly involved, who may be several echelons down or far removed from headquarters. Obviously, the administrator and the public-
relations officer should know what information other members of the organization are giving out to the press, but they should be wary of trying
to establish too firm a control over such interchanges. Carl Friedrich tells
the story of how "at one time a federal department head ruled that no official in his organization was to give any more interviews, because one of
them had annoyed him. Thereupon," says Friedrich, "six reporters proceeded to that department and got six different stories, all of which were
printed and sent to the administrative head to show him that his rule had
been foolish and could not really be enforced."[20]

While cracking down on employees who talk to the press on their own
is often a hazardous undertaking, trying to crack down on the press itself
is usually even riskier. Politicians generally subscribe to the saying that
"you can't win a battle with a newspaper," and administrators would do
well to heed the same axiom. Newspeople tend to be critical and somewhat suspicious—when they are not, they are probably not very good
newspeople—and they also usually work under great pressure, which
sometimes makes them slipshod on details. Thus, every administrator will
sooner or later find reason to become exasperated over what he or she
feels are misstatements and misquotes or, more seriously, over a failure to
understand his or her problems and point of view. But trying to correct
newspeople usually makes the problem worse, and trying to fight them
can often prove fatal.

When it comes to misstating facts or misquoting statements, the administrator can avoid much trouble by issuing as much of his or her material
as possible in written form, usually as a press release, and allowing the
media sufficient time to peruse it before a news deadline. When misquotes and misstatements still appear, the administrator would be wise to

adopt the attitude that *he* or *she* was at fault by not being clear and resolve to try harder next time. This approach will usually yield better public relations than calling up the offending journalists and berating them.

When it comes to critical or even hostile reporting on the administrator personally, the agency, or its programs, the administrator should still try to restrain his or her rancor. Franklin Roosevelt's postmaster general and patronage chief, James Farley, had a unique and useful way of dealing with this problem. Every time a Washington reporter or columnist wrote unfavorably about him, he would call the writer and in a good-natured, jocular tone congratulate him on his good work. At no time would he indicate in the slightest that he thought the journalist had written anything he regarded as wrong.

All public administrators should accept that no matter how high-principled they may feel, and no matter how well they may think they are handling their job, they will, if they have any continuing contact with the press, sooner or later read or hear unfavorable reports. They should be prepared to shrug them off with good grace and may experience less pain if they keep in mind that only a few people will read or hear the unfavorable story, and most of those who do will soon forget it.

On occasion, critical and even caustic comments in the press can help an administrator and an agency. Such comments may uncover weaknesses that he or she had not been aware of, or it may provide a bargaining point in fending off political demands (look what the press is already doing to me, he or she can say) or it may, on the other hand, provide a bargaining point for making some demands of his or her own. For instance, he or she may cite unfavorable reports to buttress the case for increased funding or to make changes in the agency's operations. Furthermore, attacks on the agency from any source may help rally the agency's defenders and strengthen the cohesion of its employees. Kaufman found that attacks on the Forest Service often gave its rangers a heightened sense of identification with the service.[21]

Just as critical press comment may not be all bad, so favorable comment may not be all good. Although every administrator will usually find it advantageous to maintain generally good press relations, too much favorable publicity can, in the long run, prove injurious to his or her cause. This is particularly true when it comes to winning political support. While elected politicians will often be kinder to an agency that is well regarded by the media, they may become hostile to one that is enjoying too much beneficial attention. "Legislators are capable of being very sensitive to what they regard as improper administrative propagandizing," writes J. Leiper Freeman, "especially when it encroaches on their domain. It does not help administrative leaders and the agencies they represent to become branded as propagandist."[22]

Not only may too much favorable press comment backfire in terms of the agency's relationship with legislators, but it may do the same in its relationships with the press itself. The more favorable the media treatment of an agency or its leaders, the more disillusioned and acrimonious reporters are likely to become when they find that things are not quite as rosy as they have described them. The administrator who previously could do no wrong now becomes transformed into one who can do no right. And the fact that the administrator or the agency has risen so high in public esteem only makes their fall from grace all the more newsworthy.

In brief, while good relationships with the news media are worth any administrator's time and attention, he or she should be careful not to exaggerate this aspect of the job. In the final analysis, one may do oneself and one's agency as much harm from doing too much as from doing too little.

Other Public Relations Activities

While cultivating and utilizing good relationships with the news media form an important part of an administrator's public-relations work, it should not comprise it all. There are many other avenues for reaching the public that managers can use, often with quite good results. Furthermore, public-relations considerations may properly be integrated into other aspects of agency policy and programs.

One of the more basic ways in which such concerns may be felt is in the choice of a name for a new subunit or for the organization itself. The Internal Revenue Service was once known as the Internal Revenue Bureau; it changed the last word of its title in an attempt to foster a more positive image of its activities. Suggestions have often been made that police departments should refer to themselves as a police service rather than a police force in order to promote a more positive tone. Researchers as well as police officers themselves have often pointed out that over three-fourths of a department's calls are service calls, and consequently such a change in appellation would be more descriptive of what police departments actually do. Correction departments were once called penal departments but changed titles as the idea of rehabilitation gained favor. And the Social Security Administration's unit for handling requests from congressmen and -women changed its name from Political Inquiries Group to Political Inquiries Branch. The cause of change here was the undesirability of the acronym that the first name gives rise to.

While such concern for titles and names may seem trivial, they often matter. John F. Kennedy encountered much resistance when he sought to transform the Housing and Home Finance Agency into the Department of

Urban Affairs because of the name he had chosen for it. Many members of Congress feared the department would be too oriented toward the larger cities and therefore would neglect smaller municipalities.

The most startling impact ever achieved by a change of name occurred when someone—no one knows precisely who—began referring to the nation's network of doctors, drug companies, hospitals, et cetera as the "health-care system" instead of as the "medical-care system." The health-care system has continued to function essentially as the previous medical-care system with nearly all its resources concentrated on curative rather than preventive approaches. Yet thanks in great part to its change of name it has managed to secure for itself 10 percent of the nation's gross national product. Public opinion polls repeatedly show a majority of Americans willing to go along with heavy expenditures for health care.

Public-relations factors should not just influence such seemingly superficial matters as name and title but also some of the most basic features of the organization's structure and style. An organization that is able to infuse its employees with zeal for what it is doing and that can demonstrate to its clients that it is achieving its goals can count on having two groups within the community that will speak out on its behalf. Satisfied clients and devoted employees make some of the best public-relations people that an organization can hope to have.

LADY OF MANY LAMPS

Public relations is often considered one of the new administrative arts, yet the record shows it has a long, if not necessarily proud, history. Shakespeare himself realized the importance of public relations; his Richard III assiduously works at building up his image while the proud Coriolanus comes to grief for disdaining to pursue such practices.

One of the most successful public relations practitioners in administrative history was the founder of modern nursing and, in many respects, modern medical care—Florence Nightingale (1820–1910). Once, when she wanted to gain maximum impact for an important report she was releasing, she had it illustrated with colored circles, squares, and wedges—the first time such techniques had ever been employed. Then she sent out over a thousand copies, almost all with an accompanying personal letter to everyone of influence she could think of, starting with Queen Victoria. Finally, she drew up a list of suitable contributors to every important magazine. She then suggested to each of the contributors the kind of article she wished them to write. The final result: all but one editor and contributor went along with her scheme.

At the same time, there are many more specific activities that an organization may undertake to generate public support. It may encourage its employees to participate in community affairs and join various community organizations, and may, as an organization, take part itself in such community endeavors as United Fund campaigns and blood bank drives. It may also encourage employee sports groups, such as bowling and softball teams, that play teams from other groups in the community.

A public agency can also maintain a speaker's bureau, sending out employees to describe its programs and policies to fraternal groups, schools, universities, et cetera. It may operate an intern program that allows high school and/or college students to work for the agency part time or during the summer. It may hold a periodic open house or give regular tours through its more interesting facilities, or it may send out displays and exhibits.

But these forms of public relations can often be overdone. The Department of Defense has frequently come under fire for spending tens of millions of dollars annually to sponsor special aerial performing teams, military bands, all kinds of films, et cetera. More recently other departments have come in for similar criticism. Congress, for example, cut the Department of Transportation public-relations budget by 10 percent in 1980 when it found the agency issuing scores of pamphlets such as one entitled "When Lobsters Travel They Go by Air."

High-powered public-relations efforts pose still greater dangers to an organization than from the possibility of creating, in themselves, adverse reactions from those they are designed to influence. They may also undermine the agency's fundamental role and goals. An agency may become so worried about its image that it actually starts to do less rather than more. It begins to fear new programs and other innovations, because they may take it into uncharted and dangerous waters in which it might lose face. It seeks to cover up rather than correct its mistakes and consequently only adds to its problems. In other words, it sacrifices substance for superficiality with results that, in the long term, can prove even more disastrous for itself than for the public it serves. In the following case study we will see examples of both the good and the evil that can come from the active pursuit of public relations.

CASE STUDY

Two Police Forces in Search of an Image[23]

When a young government lawyer named J. Edgar Hoover took over the leadership of the Justice Department's Bureau of Investigation in 1926, he displayed little initiative or interest in public relations. On the contrary, he seemed to prefer keeping the bureau out of the limelight as much as possible. Consequently, during his first years as its head, little was written or said about the FBI's activities. Most Americans did not even know of its existence.

During the early 1930s the bureau's relative obscurity changed as it sought to catch what is regarded as notoriously dangerous criminals in raids that produced considerable gunfire and bloodshed. The first effects of this new and essentially unwanted publicity were adverse. The public showed a tendency to identify more with the pursued than the pursuers, and the FBI, in making its captures, seemed to be ganging up in cowardly fashion on brave and desperate men.

This turn of events aggravated and alarmed the still-young Mr. Hoover. It prompted him to revise his previous policy of avoiding all unnecessary contacts with the press and, instead, to undertake what a later critic was to call "the most successful job of salesmanship in the history of Western Bureaucracy."

He started by launching a volley of verbal puffery that was to continue up to his death nearly forty years later. Soon books, articles, news stories, letters began to appear, extolling the FBI, its men, and its exploits. One magazine published sixteen articles on the agency in less than two years while four books on the FBI, each with an introduction by its director, showed up in bookstores in an even shorter span of time.

Hoover not only encouraged others to write about his agency but did considerable writing himself (or at least had considerable writing published under his name). By his death in 1972, he had published several books and more than one hundred articles in major magazines alone, along with probably an equal number of articles in magazines not indexed by *Reader's Guide*. His letterwriting campaign was even more remarkable. An editor of an obscure small-town weekly newspaper who might see fit to publish an editorial praising the FBI would soon find a letter on his desk from the agency's director, thanking and commending him for his noble efforts in behalf of the forces of justice. Sometimes letters under Hoover's name were written with the purpose of getting them before the public. When a former Kentucky governor publicly punched a "hippie" in the nose, Hoover sent him a letter of congratulations. The letter itself soon appeared in print and became news.

Hoover's intense utilization of the written word did not lead him to neglect the spoken one. The bureau chief made numerous speeches and encouraged his agents to do the same. Such speeches were designed to glorify the agency and its work before civic groups, school audiences, and others. The FBI also stood ready to "assist" others, including congressmen, in preparing speeches that would praise the bureau and its leader.

Radio, meanwhile, was coming into its own as a powerful weapon for influencing public opinion, and Hoover eagerly cultivated its potential. "The FBI in Peace and War" became a popular weekly program and recruited its younger listeners into a club that the FBI sponsored called the Junior G-Men. When motion picture producers indicated an interest in the agency, Hoover gladly obliged by opening FBI files for story ideas and by supplying "consultants" for the filming. On occasion, FBI agents served as actors in certain scenes.

Hoover also moved resolutely, though carefully, to take advantage of television. After eight years of deliberation and negotiation, a program on the FBI made its debut in 1957. Soon some 45 million Americans were watching the show every week. Although the program's producers claimed that the scripts were "inspired" by real FBI cases, the plots were usually dreamed up by scriptwriters out of thin air.

In his all-out drive to curry public favor, Hoover also transformed the FBI's Washington headquarters into a major tourist attraction. Visitors frequently were given guided tours through the agency, tours that included exhibitions and other demonstrations of the organization's proficiency. So successful were these tours that a visit to the FBI became almost as much a part of the typical Washington tourist's itinerary as a visit to the Washington Monument or the Lincoln Memorial.

For a while these efforts paid off handsomely. The agency became synonymous with everything good in the minds of a majority of its public, and its director became, in the words of a British journalist, "the most powerful police chief in the World." Even Congress often acted as if the FBI could do no wrong. Both branches gave Hoover nearly everything he asked for and seldom disconcerted him during budget hearings by posing an unfriendly or critical question.[24] But Hoover's single-minded pursuit of a glorified image for himself and his bureau led to some dire consequences for the country and eventually for the FBI itself, including its director.

Although Hoover liked to celebrate the FBI as an agency engaged in all sorts of difficult and dangerous missions, in actuality he centered much of the bureau's efforts on minor matters. One of these was the recovery of stolen cars. Agents would spend long hours going through airport parking lots in the hope of finding a stolen out-of-state vehicle. If they found one, the FBI could, in effect, give itself a double credit, one for the recovered vehicle, the other for its recovery value, which was put into a separate category. Furthermore, prosecution of such crimes was usually quite easy and therefore increased the bureau's conviction rate.

The FBI also focused a good deal of effort on picking up fugitives from justice and eagerly publicized its accomplishments in this area. For example, it claimed to have arrested 30,318 such fugitives in fiscal year 1970. However, more than half of these fugitives were military deserters, not seasoned criminals. Furthermore, most of these fugitives were actually caught by local officials. When it came to pursuing and catching those criminals who appeared on its highly touted "public enemy" list, the FBI also managed to score seemingly impressive records. However, Washington reporters began to discover that often a criminal's name would appear on the list shortly before he was captured, and speculation grew that a good lead on a miscreant's whereabouts may have been an important factor in securing him a place on the list.

Of course, the FBI did not confine itself solely to picking up stolen cars or fugitives from justice, or even its much touted "public enemies." It also entered into other and much more important investigations. Even here the bureau and its leader liked to pick cases that were not only congenial to their own personal ideologies but also were likely to win headlines and elicit public approval. Thus, the bureau participated vigorously in the wave of anticommunism that swept the country after World War II, catching alleged Russian spies and often prosecuting them with questionable evidence. At the same time, the FBI showed little zeal for cracking down on domestic Fascists or enforcing civil rights.

One area where the FBI's lack of interest became increasingly conspicuous was organized crime. For years, indeed, decades, Hoover sought to maintain that there was no real syndicated crime in the United States, and his agents did little to prove him wrong, although records now indicate that Mafia leaders were holding nationwide meetings at least as far back as 1928. It was not until the Mafia began engaging in drug traffic during the 1950s and thereby stirred the Treasury Department's T-men into investigating its activities that the true ramifications of the underworld began to become known. In the early 1960s Attorney General Robert Kennedy tried to push the FBI into fighting organized crime but met with only partial success. The bureau was even reluctant to open its files to the Treasury Department's narcotics agents, who by then had plunged into the fight.

Hoover's strange reluctance even to acknowledge the existence of organized crime has given rise to much speculation. Some claim that he did not want to alienate those members of Congress, few in number, perhaps, but sometimes powerful in position, who were in any way beholden to Mafia elements. Others have wondered if he was personally friendly with some of the underworld. The FBI chief was an enthusiastic fan of horse racing, and at least one ex-agent mentions taking Hoover to the track and seeing him exchange warm salutations with a local underworld figure. Most observers believe, however, that Hoover's abstemiousness where organized crime was concerned resulted from a fear of what combatting it could do to its bureau's image. His agents might become corrupted or, worse still, might show themselves ineffective in wrestling with such a serious and powerful enemy.

In general, Hoover was obsessed with avoiding any involvement that could tarnish the bureau's image. This obsession was noted by agent John Shaw, who, as we saw in chapter 11, wrote a letter that brought about his separation from the agency. In his letter, Shaw claimed that the FBI was so concerned with public approval that "punishment is usually meted out in direct proportion to the amount of bad publicity generated by the particular mistake or incident."[25] Shaw then went on to assess some of the effects of this excessive concern with publicity.

> One effect of the Bureau's promoting its image so vociferously through publicity is the acquired characteristic of "overcaution." I believe it is possible for an organization to become so conscious of its public image—its unsullied reputation—that it is

actually reduced in its effectiveness. At a time when the entire governmental "establishment" is under assault, the Bureau of course is even more sensitive to criticism from any quarter. I suggest that if avoidance of criticism becomes the chief consideration of an agency, there is little likelihood that its members will be distinguishable for their imagination, initiative and aggressive action. There is a haunting phrase that echoes throughout the Bureau. "Do not embarrass the Director." This has been so widely interpreted and liberally applied that there is some question today what action or conduct cannot be considered "embarrassing," "indiscreet," "imprudent" or "ill-timed."[26]

Shaw's observations are readily confirmed by many other ex-agents. One of them, Bernard F. Connors, wrote a novel about the FBI entitled *Don't Embarrass the Bureau.*

The problem with image building is that it can only be carried for so long. When it rests upon weak foundations, the façade eventually buckles. This proved to be the case with the Federal Bureau of Investigation. As its mania for good publicity caused increasing dysfunction in its operations, its public-relations efforts began to backfire. The news media and increasing numbers of the informed public began to question why it was failing to meet the challenges of the time. As disgruntled former agents began to speak out, this sentiment grew. Nothing collapses so completely as an overswollen balloon, and the FBI's bloated image began to suffer the same effects. Magazines and newspapers that had once lavished fulsome praise on the agency began to voice increasingly critical and caustic comments.

The tide particularly started to turn with regard to Hoover himself. Having built himself up as a symbol of his agency, he now began to find himself a frequent subject of attack. Even members of Congress started to turn hostile. The very stature that he had acquired seemed only to make him a better target. Although he clung to a residue of support, his image was crumbling badly when death finally removed him from the scene and ended a whole era in federal law enforcement.

Another Police Force, Another Approach

Like the FBI in the early thirties, the West German police in the late forties found themselves confronting an unfriendly public. Only in their case, the problem was much more severe. During the latter stages of World War II, the German police had begun showing ordinary citizens some of the same brutality and corruption that they had heretofore reserved for Jews, foreigners, and other selected state enemies. As a result, the postwar German government had to deal with a populace that was distinctly hostile to any sort of constabulary. In addition, West Germans had now become attracted to the idea of democracy and had an exaggerated idea as to what it meant. Often, when a policeman would seek to stop a citizen for, say, a traffic offense, the citizen would reply, in effect, "Why are you bothering me? Don't you know that we now have a democracy in Germany?"

To counteract this sentiment, the new postwar police forces launched a sweeping and thorough public-relations drive that was unprecedented in the history of law enforcement. To begin with, the police organizations throughout the country adopted the slogan "The Police: Your Friend and Helper" and set out in determined fashion to put it into effect. They centered much of their attention on children, realizing that this was the best way to start fostering long-term good relations with the public. For the youngest children, police departments organized three-man squads of theatrically inclined police officers to give puppet shows at kindergartens and play centers. These puppet shows were designed to teach traffic safety and to warn the youngsters about accepting rides from unknown adults. (Child molestation was and still is a severe problem in Germany.) After each such presentation, the police-puppeteers would come out and talk with the children. They would always be in uniform because, as one put it, "It is important for the children to know that policemen are staging these things. We want them to develop a positive feeling toward the police so that they would not hesitate to come to a policeman on the street if they were lost or were being bothered by a child molester."

When the children became a little older they would receive invitations to come to their local police station on designated occasions and play in the "traffic kindergarten." These were large rooms equipped with model vehicles, which the youngsters could peddle along designated street patterns painted on the floor. A policeman would give traffic signals and instruct children on how to respond to them. For still older children, the police would hold training classes in how to ride a bicycle. These classes were also held in the local police stations. Once a youngster had satisfactorily completed such a course, he or she would receive a police certificate. Such a certificate was not required to ride a bicycle, but parents soon began to require their children to obtain one before buying them a bicycle.

Adults were by no means neglected by the police in their all-out attempt to overcome negative attitudes and mobilize public support. Police departments would give bus tours to elderly citizens, pointing out pedestrian traffic hazards; sponsor crime clinics for businessmen and -women as well as ordinary citizens to instruct them on ways to prevent crime; maintain lists of doctors available to the public for weekend emergencies; and perform a host of other "positive" functions.

Traffic, meanwhile, became a very bothersome problem as car ownership started to rise; it also proved particularly damaging to police-citizen relations because it frequently brought the police into adversary contact with otherwise honest and upright citizens. To meet this challenge, police departments sent out brochures, made TV and radio broadcasts, and undertook other efforts to instruct the populace in the safety laws and the need for obeying them. One police force even printed apologetic messages on its parking tickets in an attempt to allay motorist hostility. Another police force began giving annual parties for all younger motorists who had been served traffic summonses during the year. The parties would get under way with a film on traffic safety but would then be followed by a dance with a police band providing the music and policemen and policewomen providing dancing partners for the former offenders.

Each police station began holding an "open house" one day a year, inviting all members of its district to see its facilities and talk with its personnel, and nearly every police force held an annual police show at which men, women, and children could, for only a slight charge, see police officers demonstrating various aspects of their jobs and performing somewhat spectacular stunts. The latter might include twelve police officers delicately balanced on three moving motorcycles or dogs jumping through hoops of fire. Police bands would also give concerts at old people's homes, while exhibits and speakers would be sent to schools, businesses, clubs.

The new German police forces also adopted a healthy attitude toward complaints and frequently encouraged irate citizens to file them. Often, a police force would set up a booth at a nonpolice function or event not only to publicize their work but to solicit complaints against themselves. Some police training schools began using certain illustrative complaints that had been found valid as part of their instructional material for recruits. At the same time, many police forces took positive steps to foster better behavior by their members. For example, several would periodically hold a "friendliest policeman of the month" contest in which citizens would submit the name or badge number of a police officer who had proven particularly helpful to them.

The West German police also took several steps to improve their relationship with the news media. Police officers were instructed to cooperate with news reporters as much as possible. News clippings about the police, favorable or not, were frequently posted on the bulletin boards of police stations and particularly in recruit training schools. Recruits were actually given some instruction in press relations and were cautioned about becoming too irate when the press criticized the police. One basic text used in police training schools reminds recruits that if the press often criticizes the police, it also frequently praises them, and, in any event, a newspaper is only printed for one day, and that there is no need to become unduly alarmed.

Nearly all West German police officers soon became union members, and these union organizations also sought to improve police-community relations. To children, for example, the unions would distribute calendars showing school holidays as well as balloons emblazoned with the message "The Trade Union of Police: Good Friends." The unions also printed articles in their own publications emphasizing the importance of good public-relations programs and detailing ways to carry them out.

Every so often, the major police union would hold what it called a "floating press conference." It would invite a representative group of union officials and members along with a group of news reporters for a three-day cruise on the Rhine, during which the passengers would engage in lively and productive interchanges regarding police-press relations.

All this zealous activity scored an impact on police work, and in almost every respect it was a favorable one. Traffic deaths of children, for example, immediately started to drop when the puppet programs and traffic kindergartens were introduced. Citizen cooperation with the police went up, and seldom did a police department have to pay informers to gain needed information. Police behavior on the beat changed, and soon the German police officer, in his or her nonmilitaristic uniform with club and gun carefully kept out of sight, became one of the friendliest and most helpful police officers in Europe.

The West German police, in their way, took public relations as seriously as did the FBI. They used at least some of the same basic techniques, but with a different emphasis and a different attitude. They adopted a positive image and then changed or modified their basic operations to bolster this image. Thus they made the image into a goal, which they then strove to meet. In so doing, they provide an example of what good public relations is all about.

Relations with Politicians

Public administration obviously functions within a political setting, and it is probably no exaggeration to say that the relationship of politics to administration is that of sex to life; one engenders the other. Without politics there would be no government and without government there would, of course, be no public administration.

Yet despite this close relationship, administrators rarely look upon politicians as colleagues or cohorts. All too often the reverse is true. A study of federal bureaucrats in the 1950s showed that the majority of them were fairly hostile to congressmen and -women, feeling that the members of our country's highest legislative body tended to be selfish or stupid or both. One Agriculture Department official who had formerly worked in the State Department was quoted as saying, "I've attended lots of these meetings within the department where budget questions and the like were decided, and I've never heard a respectful word spoken about Congress at one of them."[27]

Robert Spadaro of Temple University found that the same attitudes prevail in state bureaucracies as well. He studied the perceptions politicians and public administrators had of each other in three states, and in every state he discovered that each group had a low opinion of the other. Over 90 percent of the administrators, he reports, felt that they represented the public interest best. They were willing to concede politicians jurisdiction only on the broadest matters of policy. (The percentage of the politicians who had a low opinion of the administrators also topped 90 percent.)[28]

It is no troublesome task to dig out and designate the sources of this tension. Administrators are subject to the control of politicians, and no one likes to be controlled. This situation is particularly true of U.S. administrators, for reasons indicated in our discussion of the U.S. political system in chapter 1. As we saw then, the fragmentation and personalism in our political system tend to make U.S. administration more publicized than is usually the case in other industrial nations. The U.S. administrator must consequently exert extra efforts to win the favor and backing of political leaders.

This constant and compelling need to placate and persuade politicians is probably a major reason why business people often fare poorly when they attempt to put their skills to work in the public sector. Frederick V. Malek, who served as a special assistant to President Nixon had the job of getting businesspersons involved in government work, and took note of this particular difficulty. "Most corporate executives are accustomed to giving orders and having them carried out without question," he wrote. "The unaccustomed necessity of cajoling and persuading a large number of strong-willed and diverse men can prove to be a time-consuming, frustrating and humbling exercise."[29]

True, administrators have acquired more and more power in recent decades. This power, however, has been granted to them by politicians who are still prone to assert themselves in ways that administrators often find disturbing and even humiliating. For example, former Representative Daniel Flood of Pennsylvania once chaired the House appropriations subcommittee that oversees HEW's budget. Elizabeth Drew quotes an HEW official as saying, "The budget always reflects political realities. We say, 'That's Dan Flood's favorite program. It's lousy. Let's keep it.' "[30]

The critical and often contemptuous attitude that administrators frequently manifest toward their political overseers is easily understood, for politicians often seem to emphasize matters administrators find picayune or nonsensical. Early in 1964 the motion-picture actor Richard Burton applied for and was granted a visa to enter the United States to appear in a Broadway production of *Hamlet*. Burton at that time had separated from his wife and had become the paramour of Elizabeth Taylor, the American film star whom he subsequently married. At this point, however, Miss Taylor was still legally married to someone else.

The fact that Burton had obtained a visa to come to the United States where he presumably would also see Miss Taylor again rankled certain members of the House of Representatives Subcommittee Number 1 of the Committee of the Judiciary, which deals with immigration matters. The subcommittee convened a closed hearing to investigate the matter. Abba Schwartz, who at the time was assistant secretary of state in charge of immigration, refugee, and travel-control policies, was summoned as the main witness. In his book *The Open Society,* Schwartz reports the following interchange with Representative Arch Moore of West Virginia.

> Congressman Moore: . . . I want to know, is Richard Burton guilty of adultery?
>
> Mr. Schwartz: I have no knowledge.
>
> Congressman Moore: I assume, having seen the affectionate embraces spread across the newspapers of America, it is reasonable to conclude that at some time or other, this indiscretion has occurred, but I am talking about legally and technically. Richard Burton is a divorced man?
>
> Mr. Schwartz: I raised the question. I have no answer to it.
>
> Congressman Moore: I would like an answer to it. In our statute it is the United States citizen who has another mate legally.
>
> Mr. Schwartz: . . . I do not have an answer whether or not the divorced person is guilty of adultery. There is no question that the married person is.
>
> Congressman Moore: . . . There is not any question of the fact that his coming to the United States is to deal in an immoral act; whether the term "adultery" or "immoral act" is interchangeable . . . I do not know, but certainly he is going to come in here to fornicate, at least, which is the very, very minimum. But I question whether or not if you are going to exclude him on the fact that he is coming here to commit adultery, legally he is guilty of adultery?
>
> Mr. Schwartz: . . . He is coming in here principally . . . as far as I know . . . to appear in the play *Hamlet* in New York.[31]

Needless to add, this same divergence of viewpoints on what is important and what is not, and what should be done and what should not, often characterizes politico-administrative relations on drawing up a comprehensive traffic plan only to find the city council deeply involved and irritated over a crackdown on illegal parking on one or two particular streets. And the school superintendent may eagerly come to the school committee meeting with a new plan to rejuggle the school system only to find the committee members in an uproar over an inadvertent remark dropped by a teacher in a sex-education class.

It is not difficult to see, then, why administrators so often view politicians with annoyance and even alarm. Furthermore, this uneasy relationship between the two groups, while perhaps more aggravated in the United States, nevertheless has parallels abroad. Anthony Sampson in his book *The New Anatomy of Britain* mentions how civil servants talk about "politics as a yachtsman might talk of the wind—a wild irrational force, always liable to upset the navigators' calculations, yet having to be calculated for by systems of tacking, reefing or battening down."[32] The French president François Mitterand has used a somewhat different metaphor to state the problem. "Administration looks upon politics," he says, "as a loose woman who runs around the streets while she, administration, wise virgin that she is, guards the house."[33]

Administrators and Politicians: Another Approach

In a study done during the mid-1960s, Robert S. Friedman and his associates found that the personnel of government agencies could fall into three basic categories, "politicos," "professionals," and "administrators." The researchers found the politicos to be most sensitive to outside pressures and interests and most apt to take the broadest view of the constituencies involved in administrative decision making. Administrators were seen as taking the *narrowest* view of the various interests affected by the agency's activities.[34]

This study substantiates and supports what many politicians and perceptive public managers have learned from experience. Some even feel that U.S. administration, or at least some parts of it, could benefit from more political influence than it now has to contend with. Former North Carolina Governor Terry Sanford, for example, claims that one reason why the health departments of most states are inadequate is that they are overprofessionalized and, in a sense, underpoliticized. Sanford also feels that many state departments of welfare and education suffer the same problem.[35] Paul Appleby, who served as assistant to the secretary of agriculture during much of the New Deal, felt there was too little rather than too much politics in the federal bureaucracy. He claimed that the Washington bureaucrats operated too far from the party in power and resisted it too much. Another college professor who went to Washington learned a similar lesson. Said George Schultz after four years as secretary of the treasury in the first Nixon administration, "I have more respect for politicians after four years in Washington. They have an instinct for what's troubling people and why."[36]

What all these people are suggesting is that no strict line of demarcation separates administration and politics. The two are and perhaps should be inextricably intertwined. They are also saying that such a forced marriage is desirable and necessary. "I remember trying to convince a mayor, who was smarter than I, that I would make the administrative decisions and he and the council would make the political decisions," writes William V. Donaldson, the city manager of Tacoma, Washington. "This was a classy way, I thought, of telling him not to bug around with administration but confine himself to the dirty area of politics. I never tried this argument again, when he said, 'Oh! You mean you will handle the easy problems and the council and I will solve the hard ones.' "[37]

Working with Politicians: I

As the foregoing section has made clear, administrators must learn to work with politicians. They must do so not just to ensure political support for their programs but to make sure that they have the right programs. So often what has seemed like an expertly worked out project has ended in disaster, not just because it failed to elicit the backing of politicians but because it failed to take into account all the problems and pressures that such a project might encounter from various quarters. Administrators may fume and rage at politicians, but all too often objections political leaders raise and the concerns they cite are those that administrators need to have called to their attention. Politicians are usually much more knowledgeable about what is going on in society generally than are administrators, and hence they can contribute many valuable insights to the administrative process. In any case, their support is ultimately indispensable.

The first step toward achieving a good working relationship with politicians is to understand their problems. Any administrator who has ever held elective office or even run for elective office will usually acquire an understanding and tolerance for political leaders that will help him or her work effectively with them. Of course, the opportunity to acquire such experience is not open to most administrators, but they can obtain some good knowledge about politicians and their problems by assisting in a political campaign. City Manager Donaldson heartily urges all administrators to get involved in such activity provided that it lies outside their own area of responsibility. (The Hatch Act, it should be recalled, does not prohibit political activity in nonpartisan contests.) "Politics," he writes, "is like lovemaking in that you have to do it to improve. No amount of study of the *Kama Sutra* will be of much value to your love life unless you have someone to practice with. . . ." Donaldson recommends that administrators not just help a person get elected but try to understand the incumbent's problems. "The problems of dealing with the bureaucracy and constituents will seem quite different when you see them from this point of view, and that insight will improve your ability to respond intelligently to the demands of your elected masters," he says.[38]

Meanwhile, the demands of one's own "elected masters" continue to pour in, and administrators must make sure to maintain good lines of communication with them in order to develop and deepen mutual understanding and trust. Often administrative agencies maintain special employees and even special subunits to establish and strengthen their rapport with politicians, particularly legislators. Federal legislation was enacted in 1919 to expressly prohibit federal agencies from expending any funds to "influence in any manner a member of Congress, to favor or oppose, by vote or otherwise, any legislation or appropriation by Congress."[39] Nevertheless, the law has, in many respects, been honored more in the breach than in the observance. Data compiled in 1963 showed that federal agencies were spending nearly $5.5 million a year and employing some five hundred people for liaison activities with Congress.[40] Indeed, the Hoover Commission itself recommended that the State Department create a post of assistant secretary for congressional relations, a recommendation that was subsequently put into effect.

Occasionally, members of congress have complained about such practices, particularly when they seem to have gone too far. But generally, Congress has responded affirmatively to such measures. "Legislators at all levels of government, despite their defensiveness toward bureaucracy, like to hear from the bureaucrats most intimately concerned when making up their minds about proposed legislation, and the bureaucrats oblige them energetically," writes J. Leiper Freeman.[41] He quotes Representative Frank Buchanan, who chaired a House of Representatives committee that investigated bureaucratic lobbying during the 1950s, as saying, "It is equally necessary for the executive branch of government to be able to make its views known to Congress on all matters in which it has responsibilities, duties and opinions. The executive agencies have a definite requirement to express views to Congress, to make suggestions, to request needed legislation, to draft proposed bills or amendments."[42]

In their quest for good relationships with legislators and other political figures, however, administrators must often be prepared to do more than this. They must be prepared to help them with their more crassly political problems as well. Politicians have to get elected, and once elected must appease their constituents. Given the nature of our political system, they must usually succeed on their own with little help from their parties. Administrators should accept this fact and try to work with it. They must therefore often be prepared to give politicians the credit for the good that happens in government while they themselves shoulder the blame.

This takes many forms in actual practice. One typical device is to allow the politician to announce any good news, such as a new park, school, or other facility for his or her district. When it is a question of closing down a popular facility or refusing to go ahead with a desired program, the administrator will offer to make the announcement personally.

James Hagerty, President Eisenhower's dexterous press secretary, began a policy of having all good news concerning major developments in the federal bureaucracy announced by the White House; the departments

and agencies, however, were left to announce the bad news. This policy
has more or less continued to the present day. At one time during the
Vietnam war, President Johnson announced the suspension of the bombing of North Vietnam, a gesture designed ostensibly to encourage peace
talks. The bombing suspension had lasted a few days when reporters
queried him whether it was leading to anything and whether it would be
continued. Johnson replied by saying that Secretary of State Rusk would
hold a news conference on this the next day. Experienced Washington observers were able to guess right away that the administration was going to
end the suspension and resume bombing. Otherwise, they reasoned,
Johnson would have made the announcement himself. Predictably, Rush
called the short-lived bombing halt a failure and disclosed that the bombing of the North would resume.

Many a would-be administrator rebels at pursuing a policy that requires
him or her to be the bearer of ill tidings while the politician is allowed to
reveal the news that people want to hear. It does seem unfair and even
unethical. But a case can be made for its fairness as well as for its practi-
cality in securing political support. A New York City councilman, Matthew J. Troy, Jr., once publicly called upon all city agencies to announce
local projects through the district councilmembers. He explained his demand by pointing out that a councilmember would often fight hard to get
a traffic light or a sewer project in the budget only to have it announced
a year later by a mayoral appointee. Constituents would then say, "Well,
what do we need a councilman for?"[43]

Politicians not only pressure administrators with demands for favorable
publicity but also like to pass on to them constituent complaints with a
request for action. The wise administrator will do well to respond expeditiously and thoroughly. The Social Security Administration set up its
Political Inquiries Branch specifically to handle such complaints. The
PIB seeks to acknowledge such complaints within forty-eight hours and
to answer them within a week. This does not mean that it always finds the
complaint justified or that it renders the complainant special service simply because the grievance was routed to them by a member of Congress.
However, it does try to check out each such complaint as quickly as possible and inform the particular congressperson of its status.

Politicians do, of course, like to see the administrator act positively to
correct whatever the constituent has complained about. But most politicians do not expect administrators to do so unless the complaint is really
justified. "Most legislators support constituent cases irrespective of their
merit," writes Lewis Mainzer, "but will not press for more than an explanation or prompt action. Speeding up a decision is probably the most frequent consequence."[44] The politician is usually satisfied if he or she can
just show the constituent a willingness to get the constituent's case heard,

and most administrators usually support the politician to this extent. Former Internal Revenue Commissioner Mortimer Caplin says, "I never turned down a request [from] a congressman to see someone, but sometimes I'd reply, 'Sure, I'll see him but why?' What they do a lot of times is pass on a constituent just to get them out of their hair. They know I can't—or wouldn't—do anything for them, but the constituent is satisfied he had a hearing. Part of the job of being commissioner, I suppose."[45]

In disposing of complaints, the administrator may follow the same policy that is followed in publicizing positive and negative developments. That is, when he or she finds a complaint justified and sets about correcting it, he or she may let the politician disclose this fact to the constituent. When the complaint has no basis, he or she may offer to inform the constituent of this personally. The complainant will then feel that the politician at least took some action and did what he or she could, and if the complainant remains disgruntled then he or she will more likely focus dissatisfaction on the administrator and not the politician.

Politicians, however, may importune administrators for more than just favorable publicity or for an expeditious and fair disposal of complaints. All too often they make demands for actual patronage. To what extent is an administrator justified in meeting such demands?

Paul Appleby relates how in staffing the Department of Agriculture's Civilian Conservation Corps program during the New Deal he called in the head of the Forest Service and asked him to find one hundred jobs that could be filled by political appointments. Appleby said that he told the chief forester that he, the chief forester, could determine just what jobs were to be earmarked for the "politicos." He could also set the requirements for those jobs, and could even do all the actual selecting of the people to fill them. If he could not find enough qualified people on the list of politically sponsored nominees to fill the jobs, he could then ask for more names until he was able to do so. But he would have to choose from a list consisting of names submitted by politicians.

The chief forester, according to Appleby, was at first horrified at the prospect of allowing patronage to intrude into one of his agency's programs, but eventually he agreed to go along. The proposal, Appleby later claimed, worked well. It satisfied the demands of numerous members of Congress and other political figures while it did no injury to the new CCC.[46]

The same technique has been adopted by other administrators in dealing with patronage demands. One such administrator was Joseph Lohman, a criminologist who, during one of the reform waves that intermittently sweep Chicago, won election as sheriff of Cook County. Lohman knew he had to achieve some measure of cooperation with the Windy City's numerous and powerful precinct captains, and so he proposed to them the following plan: The precinct captains could send him their nominees for appointment, and if these nominees were suitable, he would appoint them. If they were not, he would ask for new nominees. "In some instances," said Lohman, "a precinct captain would send me applicant after applicant and I would continually reject them. But always I asked him to send a new applicant and eventually I would get what I was looking for."[47]

Charles Goodwin Sauers used this technique extensively as superintendent of parks in Philadelphia during the 1950s. Sauers felt that the majority of jobs in a park department were nontechnical and could be filled by political appointees. He therefore let the proper political leaders know that he would be willing to try almost anybody in these positions provided the probationary period was short and the dismissal fast and firm should the applicant not work out. He describes some of the responses he gave their sponsors when such appointees failed to perform satisfactorily.

- The fellow you sent me only shows up three days a week—please replace him.
- He reports late, skips out early and wants an hour and a half for lunch. Send me another.
- He is a good workman but shows up drunk and useless. We will pay him only for the days he is able to work well.
- He is not physically well but is willing—we will try him another month and see if his health improves.[48]

Handling patronage demands in the ways in which Appleby, Lohman, and Sauers dealt with them can produce many benefits for the administrator and his or her agency. As was noted earlier, political appointees can open up an agency and bring in broader and fresher points of view. Even those political appointees who qualify only for the more menial jobs usually have something to offer in this regard. The fact that they have a political connection usually means that they or their families have engaged in some political activity and have acquired some knowledge of what is going on in the community.

In terms of building political support, this system can also work well. It actually allows the politician to submit many names without incurring the blame for those who fail to make the grade. The administrator is still able to pretty much pick and choose the types of people he or she wants to work in the agency.

Finally, while many regard patronage as an unmitigated evil that, while it must sometimes be endured, should never be embraced, it does have benefits for the entire system. Appleby claimed that patronage helps to bring the legislative and executive branches together. It thus may provide a thread of unity to our fragmented political and administrative system.

Working with Politicians: II

Although there are ways in which administrators can work congenially and cooperatively with politicians, they cannot always expect to do so. Sometimes politicians will make demands an administrator cannot ethically or practically fulfill. Sometimes politicians will find an administrator's operational practices and policies objectionable. And sometimes politicians will find fault with an administrator on personal grounds. It is not all that unusual for a politician who has a grudge against a member of an administrator's family to take some of his or her acrimony out on the administrator. For these and other reasons, administrators cannot usually hope to achieve uniformly smooth relations with politicians, and on occasion they must prepare themselves to oppose them.

Fighting with politicians is always dangerous. Even when administrators win the battle, they sometimes lose the war, for defeated politicians only become more hostile toward administrators and seek with added zeal another opportunity to denigrate or destroy them. Yet, administrators must at times be prepared to fight back.

In opposing a politician, the administrator can make use of some of the techniques pointed out in chapter 5, such as choosing his battles and fighting only one front at a time. There are, however, some additional ways in which the administrator can cope with the animosity and opposition of political leaders.

One of these is to try to get someone else to fight the battles. Often this can take the form of a friendly politician who can be asked or encouraged to stand up to the opponent. "There is, in fact, no better lobbyist for any administrative agency than a legislator," writes Francis Rourke,[49] and the same principle holds true when it comes to defending the agency against onslaughts from its political foes. The administrator can also seek to take advantage of whatever support he or she can muster among his clientele groups or from the media to put pressure on antagonistic politicians. This must be done carefully, however, for sometimes it will only strengthen the politician's resolution and make him or her more openly antagonistic than ever.

President Woodrow Wilson and his Secretary of State, Robert Lansing, adroitly used the press to put pressure on Congress in the case of the famous "Zimmerman Telegram." This was a telegram that revealed Germany's hostile intentions toward the United States at a period during World War I when we were ostensibly neutral. The telegram had been intercepted by the British, decoded, translated, and made available to the United States. Wilson and Lansing were alarmed over its contents and wanted desperately to bring it to the attention of Congress. However, many congressmen and -women were belligerently anti-British and also anti-Wilson and would react negatively to anything that smacked of direct presidential pressure.

It was decided that Lansing would call a reporter from the Associated Press to his home, and, without disclosing the actual phrasing of the telegram, would give the reporter a paraphrase of its text and a briefing on its background, at the same time pledging him to the strictest secrecy as to how he had obtained it. The story broke the next morning and, in the words of historian Barbara Tuchman, "The House erupted in patriotic oratory" and hurriedly passed the Wilson administration's armed neutrality bill, giving the United States increased military might to deal with the coming holocaust.[50]

While working indirectly in this fashion is usually more effective, there are times when more direct methods may be called for. Chester Bowles tells of how a senator threatened to hold up the Office of Price Administration's budget appropriation unless the OPA dropped some charges that it had lodged against one of the senator's relatives. Bowles decided to fight back. He was scheduled to give a radio address and prepared for it by writing two speeches. One of them was a general account of how price control was working; the other was a detailed step-by-step account of his problems with the senator and his relative. He showed both speeches to the senator and asked him which one he should give. "The appropriation sailed through without a hitch," says Bowles.[51]

While Bowles' strategy seems to have worked successfully, the incident should be taken as illustrating the exception rather than the rule. Any administrator who attempts to play the role of a noble knight, ready and eager to slay the dragons of petty politics, will usually only succeed in destroying his or her own effectiveness. Not only will political opponents scrutinize every move, waiting for the inevitable misstep in order to pounce, but political supporters, to say nothing of his or her superiors, will soon grow tired of defending him or her. The administrator may soon find himself being given less and less responsibility.

But if administrators must be wary of proceeding too antagonistically toward politicians, they should also be mindful of going too far in the opposite direction. Conciliation does not mean capitulation. An administrator who falls at the feet of his political overseers, who stands ready to carry out their every whim and wish, may purchase support at far too high a price. Administrators and agencies that have pursued such a course may have often achieved great growth but they have paid for it not only in terms of ethical responsibility but also in terms of true effectiveness. Furthermore, such a fawning attitude sooner or later breeds suspicion and hostility in other quarters, which may eventually bring discredit and disavowal.

Examples of such excessive deference are all too prevalent in the federal bureaucracy, to say nothing of numerous state and local government bureaucracies. The Department of Agriculture, for example, in its efforts to placate its "permanent undersecretary," Representative James Whitten, once expressed a willingness to help underwrite a $265,000 loan for a golf course in Whitten's home district.[52] And for another example, the Army Corps of Engineers has managed to achieve its remarkable degree of independence from the Pentagon only by becoming a near-errand boy for influential members of Congress. Both agencies have incurred much bad publicity and public hostility through their overcompliance with congressional directives.

Perhaps the agency that has become most infamous for its currying of congressional favor is the Department of Defense. In their 1968 book *The Case Against Congress*, Drew Pearson and Jack Anderson detailed some of the many ways in which the defense establishment seeks to obtain and maintain congressional support. These include placing military facilities and awarding contracts in the districts of influential congressmen, handing out reserve commissions and medals, and providing a host of other favors. "For a worthy Congressional group, the Air Force will provide a plane from Special Air Mission—complete with escort officers, pretty stewardesses, baggage handlers and sometimes even a doctor with a first-aid kit of bicarbonate of soda. The military escorts, boon companions all, pick up the tab for everything."[53]

When it comes to reserve commissions, Pearson and Anderson reported how one congressman who entered the House holding a second lieutenant's commission in the army reserves found himself a major in four years and a major general in seventeen years. Another congressman who had had no previous military service managed to finish his first two-year term as a colonel in the air force reserves. Senator Henry "Scoop" Jackson, who never rose above the rank of an enlisted man during World War II, became a major in the army reserves during his very first year in the Senate. As for medals, the navy once awarded a Silver Star for gallantry to a young congressman who took a short flight as an observer on a navy plane in the South Pacific during World War II. The heroic congressman was Lyndon B. Johnson.

The problems entailed in soliciting political support, as well as those involved in generating clientele and public support, often raise grave issues of administrative responsibility, a very sensitive area.

Responsibility

The question of administrative responsibility not only encompasses the question of accountability but surpasses it. Proper and desirable behavior requires something more than accountability, for no set of standards, no matter how clearly set down or how vigorously enforced can cover the full range of administrative actions. Those who toil at even the lowest levels of the organization will still retain a remarkable degree of discretion. How does one make sure that they, as well as their superiors, exercise this discretion responsibly?

To gain some idea of the complexity that the issues involve, let us take the case of what may be the lowest-ranking employee in an administrative office, the receptionist. Let us further assume that she has been instructed to treat all those who come in with fairness and courtesy. Ostensibly, she may do so. However, undoubtedly there will be some clients to whom she will respond more positively than to others, and certain subtleties in her demeanor may reflect her preferences and prejudices. She may say the same things and do the same things in her relationships with all those who enter her office, but her manner will convey more warmth in some situations than in others. Some clients may find themselves put off and discouraged by how she treats them, and yet they may find that they have no basis for a valid complaint. Nor will investigation by the office manager produce any evidence that she has failed to conform to the standards set down for her. As Carl Friedrich has observed, "Responsible conduct of administrative functions is not so much enforced as elicited."[54]

Unfortunately, this is only part of the problem of responsibility and quite possibly not the most important part. Let us assume that the receptionist has definitely decided to suppress any personal feelings she may have toward any clients that come into the office and has firmly resolved to carry out the office policy of fairness and courtesy to the utmost. She may then find difficult decisions waiting for her at every turn. She may decide, for example, that living up to such a code means that she should be as helpful as she can to every client that comes in. However, the more helpful she becomes to client A, the more she keeps clients B, C, et cetera, waiting. And rendering the same amount of service to clients B and C only makes clients D and E wait still longer.

Of course, she may set a maximum of service beyond which she will not go. However, some clients do require more attention than others. They may have special problems or they may be less able to cope with even routine problems than others. For example, a client who is blind or who comes from another part of the country may simply not be able to obtain his or her rightful share of the office's services without some special attention. Thus, treating them in exactly the same manner as everyone else would seem to fall short of achieving the maximum in administrative responsibility.

This means that the responsible receptionist must make what are often difficult decisions. She must decide to which clients she will render extra service and, more troublesome to determine, how much extra service to provide them. Every bit of additional service, we must remember, lengthens the time that other clients must wait for their turn. Often this means keeping them from their jobs or families.

Let us take another example. Suppose that a public utility is seeking to increase its rates. The examiner hearing its case looks at the record and finds that the company's profits are at an all-time high. Furthermore, the company's stock is largely in the hands of people who are quite well off. The responsible course of conduct for the hearing examiner therefore seems quite obvious: recommend rejection of the rate rise.

However, some other factors may complicate the situation. The company's profits may be at an all-time high in terms of current dollars but not constant dollars. After adjusting for inflation, its profits may actually have declined or at least stood still. Then, the company may want the rate increase to generate additional funds for expansion. The area it serves may have a good deal of unemployment, and increased electrical power might help it attract more industry. Finally, while much of the company's stock may be owned by wealthy people, some of it is in the hands of widows, orphans, and others who need its dividends badly. Since the company has not increased its dividends in line with inflation, the real incomes of these particular stockholders are going down. Such considerations do not mean that the responsible decision for the examiner is simply to approve the requested rate increase. They do indicate, however, that with all the best will in the world, the responsible decision is not always easy to determine.

Although the examples above are hypothetical, they are by no means unrepresentative of the types of dilemmas that administrators must constantly wrestle with as they seek to plot out responsible courses of action. Shall the personnel officer favor a local resident or a minority-group member for a job when he or she could secure the services of an out-of-state resident or a non-minority-group member who may be somewhat more qualified? Shall the environmental inspector shut down the factory that does not quite meet the air pollution standards but whose closing will throw many people out of work and perhaps even bankrupt some small businesses in the bargain? Shall the office manager allow a faithful employee to continue working when the employee has suffered a debilitating illness and can no longer perform an adequate job? Many might seek to answer these questions by saying that it depends on the degree of debilitation, or pollution, or difference in skill. But how is the administrator involved to determine the point at which he or she will take one action and not another?

One problem bureaucrats confront on occasion is the need to back a superior's policy before a legislative committee when they really disagree with it. For example, an administrator may be in charge of the federal government's urban renewal program at a time when the administration in power has decided to cut back on urban renewal. The administrator appears before the committee to argue for his budget. A liberal Democrat on the committee notes that the sum of money being requested is less than that of the previous year. She asks questions, seeking to put the administrator on record as personally favoring a much larger appropriation. The administrator knows that the congresswoman will use any testimony he may give to such effect as a weapon with which to attack the current administration, including his own cabinet secretary. How shall he respond to the congresswoman's questions?

This brings us to perhaps the most significant decision that any administrator may make regarding responsibility, and that is under what circumstances should he or she resign? Philosophy professor Charles Frankel felt that an administrator should not take such a step lightly.

> Assuming that the government for which he works is a constitutional one, a permanent official's conscience must not bleed when he is asked to carry out a policy that doesn't fit his own ideas. Indeed, he requires a conscience which tells him, except in extreme circumstances, to pipe down after he has had his say, and to get to work even in support of what he thinks is wrong. For the electorate hasn't bet on his political opinions or conscience. The only bet it has made, and for which it has paid its taxes, is on his professional integrity and competence.[55]

Seymour Berlin and his associates seem to take a slightly more positive but essentially similar attitude toward the resignation issue, at least as far as the politically appointed administrator is concerned.

> Perhaps the most fundamental advice to the political appointee who wants to serve his country well is this: never want the job too much. If you can be clear about your own values, and distinguish between your closely held convictions and your vanity, you will know when you are free to compromise and when you must take a stand. Always be willing to use the power you can acquire when you are ready to resign, but use it only if the cause is vital.[56]

The question of when to resign proved particularly vexing to at least some top-level administrators in the Department of Defense during the latter days of the Johnson administration. They had become increasingly disenchanted with the president's policy in conducting the Vietnam war and thus had begun to give serious thought to the possibility of quitting in protest. They did not have to fear for their livelihood, because they could easily have made more money working in the private sector than they were earning in government. But most of them refrained from taking such a step. Their primary rationale for not resigning was that they could work more effectively to change the country's policy if they were inside the government than out of it. Other considerations stayed their hand.

Townsend Hoopes, who as former undersecretary of the air force was one of those who struggled with this problem, recounts how a blend of such considerations may have kept his chief, Defense Secretary Robert McNamara, from stepping down. According to Hoopes, "McNamara gave evidence that he had ruled out resignation because he believed the situation would grow worse if he left the field to Rusk, Rostow, and the joint chiefs, but also because the idea ran strongly against the grain of his temperament, and his considered philosophy of organizational effectiveness."[57] Thus, if Hoopes is correct, McNamara's perseverance in office, until he was transferred by Johnson to the World Bank, was dictated by considerations of responsibility but only as they were filtered through the prism of his own personality and ideology. This offers further support for the contention that even when administrators are determined to behave as responsibly as possible, they cannot always be sure they are doing so.

Responsibility: The Search for Solutions

In casting about for answers to the question of responsibility, we are at the outset likely to come across the phrase "the public interest." Many see the entire solution to the question neatly encapsulated in this phrase. An administrator need only resolve to serve the public interest and his or her problems concerning responsibility will vanish.

Yet this solution, like so many other easy solutions to difficult problems, only raises more questions than it answers. The most basic one is this: Just what is the public interest? Walter Lippman once claimed that "The public interest may be what men would choose if they saw clearly, thought rationally, and acted disinterestedly and benevolently."[58] This leaves us with the task of defining clear vision and rational thought, concepts that, in practice, seem quite susceptible to varying interpretations. Even deciding what course of action is truly benevolent and disinterested may produce more controversy than it settles.

Political scientist Glendon Shubert sought to grapple with the concept of public interest in a book bearing that title. After exhaustively examining the subject, he says, "It may be somewhat difficult for some readers to accept the conclusion that there is no public interest theory worthy of the name."[59]

Another solution that often presents itself is the maxim of "following one's conscience." This, too, fails to furnish a usable guideline. The enforcers of the Inquisition who burned hundreds of thousands of heretics at the stake felt they were following the most lofty appeals to conscience. The same can be said for so many other appalling actions that men have so often taken against their fellows. As Carl Friedrich has noted, "Autocratic and arbitrary abuse of power has characterized the officialdom of a government bound only by the dictates of conscience."[60]

But while Friedrich rules out the use of conscience as a means of ensuring responsibility, he does have some positive ideas to offer in its place. "We have a right to call such a policy irresponsible if it can be shown that it was adopted without proper regard to the existing sum of human knowledge concerning the technical issues involved; we have also a right to call it irresponsible if it can be shown that it was adopted without proper regard for existing preference in the community and more particularly its prevailing majority."[61]

In keeping with this admonition Friedrich sees the solution to the question of administrative responsibility lying in two areas: professionalism and participation. Professionals generally have been conditioned to uphold certain standards. Furthermore, they usually subscribe to a code of ethics that governs the practice of their profession. As Friedrich sees it, professionalism constitutes something of an "inner check" on administrative irresponsibility. Participation, meanwhile, means that administrators must consult more and more interests and listen to more and more points of view. Allowing divergent parties to share in decision making should make that process less arbitrary and subjective and more responsive and responsible.

To Friedrich's twin safeguards of professionalism and participation can be added a third protective device, publicity. Directing the public spotlight onto administrative decision making should make such a decision making more responsible. Secrecy or even mere obscurity have rarely led to improved administrative decisions or better administrative behavior.

Professionalism, participation, and *publicity* do not in themselves guarantee responsible administration. Professionals can act irresponsibly, and shared decision making can produce irresponsible decisions. Publicity can on occasion distort an administrator's perspective, because what is immediate "good press" is not always most beneficial to the public.

These caveats notwithstanding, the three "Ps" presented above provide a basis for better public management. If they become more and more a part of bureaucratic behavior, then such behavior may move closer toward meeting the desires and demands of the American people.

Notes

1. Morton Grodzins, "The Federal System," in *Goals for Americans: The Report of the President's Commission on National Goals* (Englewood Cliffs, N.J.: Prentice-Hall, 1965).

2. Francis E. Rourke, *Bureaucracy, Politics, and Public Policy* (Boston: Little, Brown, 1969), 12.

3. Harvey M. Sapolsky, *The Polaris System Development: Bureaucratic and Programmatic Success in Government* (Cambridge, Mass.: Harvard University Press, 1972), chap. 2.

4. Lackland F. Blair in a short talk at the annual convention, American Society for Public Administration, Los Angeles, 1973.

5. Chester Bowles, *Promises to Keep* (New York: Harper & Row, 1971), chap. 5.

6. Rourke, *Bureaucracy, Politics, and Public Policy*, 103.

7. *New York Times*, 3 December 1970.

8. *New York Times*, 4 March 1972.

9. Leonard Sloane, "Corporate Ombudsmen Respond to Consumers," *New York Times*, 21 March 1971, Business and Finance section.

10. Diogenes [pseud.], *The April Game* (Chicago: Playboy Press, 1973), 6–7.

11. Bowles, *Promises to Keep*, 122–123.

12. *Federal Register*, 23 February 1973, vol. 38, no. 36, p. II.

13. *National Civic Review* (February 1973), 100.

14. Philip Selznick, *TVA and the Grass Roots* (Berkeley, Cal.: University of California Press, 1949).

15. David Truman, *Administrative Decentralization; A study of the United States Department of Agriculture* (Chicago: University of Chicago Press, 1940).

16. Quoted in John J. Corson, "Distinguishing Characteristics of Public Administration," *Public Administration Review* (Spring 1952).

17. 38 Stat.L.212.

18. Bowles, *Promises to Keep*, 93.

19. Robert Sherwood, *Roosevelt and Hopkins* (New York: Harper, 1948), chap. 3.

20. Carl Friedrich, "Public Policy and the Nature of Administrative Responsibility," in *The Politics of the Federal Bureaucracy* (New York: Dodd, Mead, 1968).

21. Herbert Kaufman, *The Forest Ranger* (Baltimore, Md.: Johns Hopkins Press, 1960).

22. J. Leiper Freeman, "The Bureaucracy in Pressure Politics," *Annals of the American Academy of Political Science* 319 (September 1958).

23. Material on the FBI in the following case study is taken principally from Pat Walters and Stephen Gillers, eds., *Investigating the FBI* (Garden City, N.Y.: Doubleday, 1973). Other sources included Sanford J. Ungar, "The Undoing of the Justice Department," *The Atlantic* (December 1973); "The Heresy of John F. Shaw," *The Nation*, 8 February 1971; "The FBI in Politics," *Time*, 26 March 1973. Material on the German police is from George E. Berkley, *The Democratic Policeman* (Boston: Beacon Press, 1969).

24. There were other reasons besides his public acclaim which made members of Congress so hesitant to exercise any genuine oversight over Hoover. Some of these will be touched on in the next section.

25. "Heresy of John F. Shaw."

26. Ibid.

27. James Burnham, "Some Administrators Unkindly View Congress," in *Public Administration*, Robert T. Golembiewski, Frank Gibson, and Geoffrey Y. Cornog, eds. (Chicago: Rand McNally, 1966).

28. Robert Spadaro, "Role Perception of Politicians vis-à-vis Public Administrators." (Paper presented at the annual convention, American Society of Public Administration, Los Angeles, 1973).

29. "When Businessmen Turn Their Talents to Government," *U.S. News and World Report*, 2 October 1927.

30. *The Atlantic* (April 1973), 12.

31. Abba P. Schwartz, *The Open Society* (New York: Simon & Schuster, 1969), 59.

32. Anthony Sampson, *The New Anatomy of Britain* (New York: Stein and Day, 1971), 242.

33. Quoted in Charles Debbasch, *L'Administration au pouvoir* (Paris: Calmann-Lévy, 1969), 31.

34. Robert S. Friedman et al., "Administrative Agencies and the Publics They Serve," *Public Administration Review* (September 1966).

35. Terry Sanford, *Storm over the States* (New York: McGraw-Hill, 1967), 199.

36. *Time*, 26 February 1973, 80.

37. William V. Donaldson, "Continuing Education for City Managers," *Public Administration Review* (November–December 1973).

38. Ibid.

39. 41 Stat.L.68.

40. G. Russell Pipe, "Congressional Liaison: The Executive Branch Consolidates Its Relations with Congress," *Public Administration Review* (Spring 1966).

41. Freeman, "The Bureaucracy in Pressure Politics."

42. Ibid.

43. *New York Times*, 19 February 1973.

44. Lewis C. Mainzer, *Political Bureaucracy* (Glenview, Ill.: Scott, Foresman, 1973), 82.

45. Quoted in Joseph C. Goulden, *The Superlawyers* (New York: Dell Publishing, 1973), 220.

46. Paul H. Appleby, *Big Democracy* (New York: Alfred A. Knopf, 1949), chap. 15.

47. In an interview with the author at Berkeley, California, April 1967.

48. Charles Goodwin Sauers, Sr., "Parks and Politics," *Parks and Recreation* (April 1959).

49. Rourke, *Bureaucracy, Politics, and Public Policy*, 28.

50. Barbara W. Tuchman, *The Zimmerman Telegram* (New York: Bantam Books, 1971), 171.

51. Bowles, *Promises to Keep*, 144.

52. Martin Tolchin and Susan Tolchin, *To the Victor . . .* (New York: Random House, 1971), 191–192.

53. Drew Pearson and Jack Anderson, *The Case Against Congress* (New York: Simon & Schuster, 1968), 336–339.

54. Friedrich, "Public Policy and the Nature of Administrative Responsibility."

55. Charles Frankel, *High on Foggy Bottom* (New York: Harper & Row, 1968), 109.

56. Seymour S. Berlin et al., "A Guide for Political Appointees: Entering the System," *Good Government* (Winter 1972).

57. Townsend Hoopes, *The Limits of Intervention* (New York: David McKay, 1969), 53.

58. Walter Lippman, *The Public Philosophy* (Boston: Little, Brown, 1955), 42.

59. Glendon A. Shubert, Jr., *The Public Interest* (New York: Free Press, 1952), 223.

60. Friedrich, "Public Policy and the Nature of Administrative Responsibility."

61. Ibid.

13

Doing More with Less

The title for this concluding chapter may strike the reader as more insipid than inspired, but it does denote the theme that appears to be animating, and often aggravating, the craft of public administration today. In fact, two independently authored books bearing this very same title were published in 1982 alone. Doing more with less, so it seemed, had become nearly every public manager's professed, if not always practiced, goal.[1]

Of course, public administration, like most other phenomena of modern life, frequently falls prey to fleeting fancies and fads. Perhaps the current emphasis on greater effectiveness could be only another instance of this. But such an eventuality, while certainly possible, does not seem probable. On the contrary, many factors and forces afoot or arising seem likely to subject tomorrow's public manager to greater pressures and problems than those that assail the administrator of today.

One potential cause of future concern and constraint is the wearing out of the nation's public facilities. From 1965 to 1979, America's public-works investment, as measured in constant dollars, drastically declined. The overall drop was 28 percent; the per capita drop was 36 percent. As a result, the country's infrastructure was crumbling. By 1982 one out of every five bridges in the land needed major rehabilitation, if not total reconstruction, and nearly one out of every four miles of interstate highway required replacement. Half of the nation's communities could not accommodate new plant locations or even major expansions of existing ones because of inadequate water and waste-water-treatment facilities. One-third of the sewers of Albuquerque, New Mexico, had decayed so badly that trucks rolling down the street would crush them. Houston was losing 30 percent of its water every day through leaky mains; Boston was losing 50 percent.[2] In the words of social scientist Amitai Etzioni, the U.S. had become "an underdeveloping country."[3]

In the waning hours of 1982 Congress approved a five-cent increase in the gasoline tax to provide funds for road and bridge reconstruction. But the rotting away of other components of the country's public capital stock remains as yet unremedied. It places, in effect, a heavy lien on future public budgets.

Another developing crisis may clamp an even greater lien on public-sector resources. This concerns the unfunded and increasing pension liabilities, which most U.S. governments including the federal government have as yet declined to deal with. Only a handful of governments have been setting aside sufficient funds to meet their future public-employee pension payments. The others simply use up all or most of their current pension payments plus any other cash they can find to meet their current costs, leaving the future to take care of itself. The situation has been likened to a time bomb steadily ticking away.

The graying of the American population generally will also put an increasing strain on the public purse. While a presidential commission early in 1983 finally came up with a plan to rescue social security and medicare from impending bankruptcy, its plan was at best a stopgap solution. Further and greater problems loom down the road. Moreover, any increase in longevity would greatly add to them. An indication of the effect such an otherwise welcome development of this nature would have can be seen in a cost-benefit analysis done in Great Britain. This analysis showed that if every British cigarette smoker stopped smoking, the country's economy would collapse. For while the event would yield substantial savings in reduced medical costs and even in reduced fire costs, the enormous escalation in retirement costs created by the resulting increase in the average life-span would vastly outweigh them.

Finally the growing legalization of America poses a growing threat to public revenues. As noted in chapter 11, the Supreme Court has stripped away much of the sovereign immunity that state and local governments have hitherto enjoyed. As a consequence these governments already find themselves embroiled in constant and costly litigation. By the fall of 1982 South Tucson, Arizona (population 6,500), was faced with having to pay $3.6 million to a man mistakenly shot by one of its policemen, while tiny

Cashion, Oklahoma (population 550), was under a court order to pay
$157,000 to members of a family injured in a sewer-gas explosion. All
told, federal court claims pending against local governments alone
amounted to a benumbing $7 *billion* by the start of 1983, and more and
more lawsuits were being filed all the time.[4]

These mounting fiscal pressures, coupled with the public's developing
dissatisfaction with the way its governments are performing, present an
enormous challenge to today's, and more especially, tomorrow's public
managers. The public sector, it would seem, will simply have to become
more efficient and effective. It will have to learn how to do more with
less.

How will it accomplish such an ambitious aim? Obviously no clear-cut
and concise formulas exist to effect its easy and speedy realization. (Or if
they do exist, no one seems to have discovered them.) But recent research
in public administration, viewed against a background of broader, ongoing trends in society, suggest at least four basic areas where progress toward such a goal might possibly be achieved.

Flexibility

In chapter 10 we saw how a rapid rate of change has become a major feature of modern society. In this chapter we have seen how the pressure for
increased performance at reduced cost seems likely to intensify. The two
phenomena join in making increased flexibility vital to the health, if not
the very survivability, of public organizations and those who operate
them.

It is obvious that without more flexibility the traditionally (and inherently) conservative public organization cannot stay in step with the society it seeks to serve. It should be almost as obvious that without more
flexibility it will fail to achieve anything approaching maximum effectiveness.

Public organizations need such flexibility in order to manipulate and
maneuver their increasingly scarce resources to cope with increasingly
changing problems. In the past they could often respond to new pressures
and undertake new pursuits by simply securing bigger budgets. They
could then hope to make some accommodation with the new while leaving the old and outmoded pretty much undisturbed. That option, however, is fast disappearing. The squeeze is on while the pressure for performance grows apace.

The drive for greater flexibility faces some formidable opposing forces.
They include constricting civil-service laws and constricting budget for-
mats. They also include unions, clientele groups, and constituency-ori-

ented elected officials. And then there is the traditional and inherently conservative character of public organizations.

There is yet a further aspect to this problem to be considered. The transformation of government from guardian state to welfare state, while it has opened many new opportunities for public managers, has at the same time placed new constraints upon them. As two European social scientists, Ann Robinson and Bengt-Christer Ysander, point out, under the guardian-state concept, the impact of government expenditure was limited. Therefore changes and choices could be made without causing too much commotion. The welfare state has fundamentally altered this situation. "When the government's commitments directly touch on the individual's private welfare," they write, "it is only natural that these commitments are perceived as social contracts, the obligations of which must be honored. No one is likely to sue the government for damage because it is postponing a weapons acquisition, a new courthouse, or a national road project. Any short-term tampering with the conditions for pensions or any other social-insurance benefit is, on the other hand, likely to cause a public outcry about infringement of rights and contractual obligations."[5]

To make matters worse, argue these two authors, the buildup of the welfare state, while it has tended to reduce the flexibility of public budgeting, has actually made increased flexibility more and more necessary. The modern, welfare-state government now finds itself spread all over the social landscape and consequently must adjust to the continually changing topography of that landscape. Thus the need for flexibility has grown while the possibilities for flexibility seem to have shrunk.

While such difficulties as these would appear to place public administration in a no-win situation, some steps for improvement do suggest themselves. They may never really resolve the problem, but they may help make public organization more supple and therefore better able to act effectively.

To begin with, public agencies will have to become less bureaucratic. This means flatter, less hierarchical, organizational structures with wider spans of discretion and shorter chains of command. It also means less detailed rules and regulations. Broad and basic principles will increasingly have to replace tight, detailed procedures in governing the operation of public organizations if such organizations are to respond effectively to the demands of the future.

In terms of personnel practices, such modifications will necessitate less concise job classifications and, in some cases, less precise job specifications. "Broad-banding," that is, the widening out of job classifications, may and indeed should become more and more common. This will permit public agencies to reassign and regroup personnel more easily.

In line with this, there may well have to be less centralized control over personnel practices. Agencies will have to be given more discretion in hiring and possibly even firing their employees. Doing so may open the door to such abuses as favoritism and patronage, but not doing so may only lead to the abuses of ineffectiveness and inertia. Furthermore, other changes now taking place, changes that will be discussed shortly, should limit in many if not most instances, the problems that might otherwise arise by giving public agencies more leeway in personnel matters.

In like manner, public organizations will require more discretion over their budgets. If their funds are to be limited, then public managers should at least have more say over how to use them. As we have seen, some of the newer forms of budgeting, such as ZBB, do provide for greater middle-management input into the budgeting process. But even with traditional line-item budgets, more agency involvement in determining how to make the best use of allocated funds can be granted. For example, the relatively narrow categories of accounts that most line-item budgets utilize can be enlarged, and the restrictions usually imposed on shifting money from one account to another can be reduced. Rigorous post audits, along with other devices, are available to cut down on any misuse of such budgetary freedom.

What about multiyear budgets and, in a broader sense, the stepped-up emphasis on planning that they reflect? Won't planning and multiyear budgets work at cross purposes to the growing demand for flexibility?

Obviously, to some extent, they will. The longer and tighter its plan, the less ground an agency has to maneuver. Yet planning can survive and even go forward providing certain adjustments are made. The plans themselves should be fashioned in a flexible manner, leaving several options available, especially over the longer terms. A flexible planning system can coexist with and even aid and abet a flexible administration, for planning, let us not forget, is predicated on the need for change.

In its pursuit of pliability the public agency may find itself making, or wanting to make, greater use of outside contractors and possibly volunteer labor as well. Such steps may enable it not just to cut costs but to initiate changes in programs and procedures more easily, because outside contractors and volunteers will usually offer less resistance to such changes than will an agency's own work force.

This brings us to another point in the drive to bring more flexibility to public administration. Employee enthusiasm for the alterations it requires can by no means be assumed. Nor can the support of clientele groups and constituency-oriented politicians be taken for granted. On the contrary, such groups may all too effectively oppose such efforts. Winning their support will provide the public manager of the future with challenges galore. But for most there will be no escaping them, for, as one observer has noted, "managing change is the changing role of the manager."[6]

THE DAWN OF SUNSET

The spread of sunset laws both reflects and stimulates the stepped-up concern with administrative flexibility. Now on the books of almost two-thirds of the states, these laws require the agencies they cover to obtain new legislative mandates at periodic intervals. Any agency that fails to convince its legislative overseers of its continued usefulness finds itself faced with automatic extinction. In effect, sunset laws seek to apply the age-old principle of "adapt or die" to public administration.

A survey undertaken by Common Cause in the spring of 1981 found twenty-three of the thirty-five states that have sunset laws reporting increased governmental efficiency and public accountability as a result. And although only ten of these states had laws covering all or most of their agencies, a majority of the other states were attempting to broaden their own to include more components of their administrative apparatus.

The state that had gone furthest in this respect was Washington, which even required sunset review of individual positions. Such reviews in the three and a half years they had been used had already led to the elimination of 115 positions for a total saving of $1.8 million. Another 95 positions had been rescaled downward. According to former Governor Dixy Lee Ray, the elimination of nonproductive jobs had actually increased the morale of the other workers.

Participation

In the fall of 1982, the Work in America Institute issued a new study entitled *Productivity Through Work Innovation*. A lengthy and detailed report, it focused essentially on one basic trend, which it claimed was boosting productivity in firms throughout the country. That trend was worker participation.

What had long been a dream and, to numerous critics, a delusion as well, was now becoming a hard-nosed reality. Hundreds of employers, faced with the rigors of coping with a recession-plagued economy, had begun "harnessing workers' brainpower." As institute president Jerome R. Rostow commented, "work innovations, based on grass-roots employee involvement in decision-making, are not a gimmick or a passing fad. They are, in fact, 'a new look' in management, offering profitability through a different approach to the work force."[7]

Worker participation as a productivity-promoting device is scarcely new. In 1899, for example, two Boston merchants, Edward A. and A. Lin-

coln Filene, began allowing and encouraging their employees to help
shape store policies. Within the next thirteen years their enterprise developed into the world's largest specialty store. Today certain trends are
making such employee involvement not only desirable but necessary.

For one thing the mood and values of the U.S. population have
changed. As noted in chapter 2, people have become more demanding of
their rights and more desirous of expressing their ideas. At the 1981 meeting of the Association for Humanistic Psychology, a speaker cited the results of a recent Louis Harris poll to confirm this fact. It showed 72 percent of the respondents wanting to become involved in cooperative
efforts, 63 percent believing that it is more important to appreciate human
values over material values, and 84 percent welcoming challenges to their
own creative ability. Commented psychologist Carl Rogers, "There is
much reason to believe that we are . . . involved in the birth process of a
new human being . . ." And, he added, "to empower the person is to create an enormous new source of energy for decision-making, for action."[8]

Several forces currently at work should only foster and further this
trend. The work force, including, especially perhaps, the public work
force, is becoming more educated and professionalized. Educated professionals more than most others do not function effectively as mere execu-
tors of their superiors' wishes and whims. They have normally acquired
their skills at considerable effort and expense and usually insist on a substantial degree of latitude in order to utilize them. They also tend to feel
they can and should contribute to most of the decisions that play a direct
role in their working lives.

Compounding this problem, if it is in fact a problem and not simply an
opportunity, is another development. The headlines of a front-page story
in the *Wall Street Journal* of October 22, 1981 well sums it up: PROMO-
TIONS GROW FEW AS 'BABY BOOM' GROUP EYES MANAGERS' JOBS. DEMOG-
RAPHERS SEE A DECADE OF FRUSTRATED EMPLOYEES WITH THWARTED
GOALS. NEW DEFINITIONS OF SUCCESS.

The first class of the baby-boom generation, which began in 1948, had
turned thirty-five, and this is the age when one normally expects to move
into a management-level position. The trouble lay in an insufficiency of
such positions to accommodate this large bulge in the nation's work force.
The baby boom was producing a bottleneck. And since the boom did not
end until 1962, and since also more and more older workers were delaying retirement, the demographers were foreseeing a decade of "frustrated
employees with thwarted goals." According to one gloomy expert, "The
aging of the baby-boom generation promises to create personnel problems
in the 1980s such as U.S. Industry has never faced before."

Since it most likely will be impossible to make all competent baby-
boomers into managers, it may become mandatory to give them at least as

big a slice of authority as possible. The use of worker-participation techniques obviously dovetails with such a development.

Fortunately it also dovetails with the need, noted earlier, to reduce bureaucratization and hierarchy so as to promote flexibility. What Likert calls "System 4" and what McGregor called "Theory Y" and what still others call "matrix management" will start to become more of a practical, everyday reality in organizational life. This is not to say that System 4, Theory Y, and matrix management are all identical. But they all base themselves on Maslow's hierarchy of needs theory (see chapter 3) in calling for looser and more open organizational structures oriented toward increasing employee self-actualization. Yesterday's dreams may yet become tomorrow's realities.

CRUMBLING CITADEL

That last bastion of rigid authoritarianism, team sports, is starting to respond to the participation syndrome.

In 1978 manager Bob Lemon led the New York Yankees to the World Series championship by giving his players a fairly free hand. Lemon explained his success, shrugging, "I just fill out the lineup card and watch 'em play."

The following fall Fred Shero, in taking over as coach of the New York Rangers, abolished most of the hockey team's club rules and set up a six-man players committee to enforce the rest. He also allowed the players to pick their own goalee for the play-offs. The Rangers had not been expected even to make the play-offs, but they managed to play their way to the final round.

In the 1981–1982 season, coach Pat Riley of the Los Angeles Lakers produced a championship team by allowing his players to make most of their own decisions during each game. His eschewing of the traditional paternal role of head coach prompted one sportswriter to observe that "Future generations of sports historians will pinpoint the 1980s as a time when the hallowed institutions of professional head coaching changed forever."

But it's not only professional sports that is feeling the impact of the new trend. In 1982 the coach of the Groton Academy football team allowed the team members to pick by ballot the starting lineup for each game. The result? The Massachusetts prep school team doubled its number of wins over the previous season.

It is highly unlikely, however, that this new trend will proceed as far and as fast as its backers believe it should. Political as well as functional realities will necessarily limit it. But that such a trend is underway seems clear. It also seems clear that it represents not just a frivolous fad of the moment but the beginnings of a basic shift in organizational philosophy and practice.

This new participatory administration will require managers equipped with some very sizable skills. The ability to handle human-relations problems, a skill sometimes referred to as interpersonal competence, has always been important for managerial success. It will become even more so as the new manager finds himself or herself forced to rely more on negotiation and less on formal authority to induce people to do what he or she wants them to do. "The traditional image of an effective manager who makes decisions is not compatible with effective matrix management," write C. E. Teasley and R. K. Ready. "Influence management is a new ball game, and managers have a slim chance of succeeding unless they know the new rules and are given a chance to practice the skills necessary for success."[9]

As another commentator, J. R. Morton, points out, "Good managers manage the work, not the people," because "creative people want to manage themselves."[10]

Measurement

Measurement bears a rather obvious relationship to effectiveness, for in order to do more with less, one must have ways of measuring the "more" along with the "less." No public agency can become results oriented without relatively simple and reliable methods for determining and assessing its results.

But measurement also bears a distinct if somewhat less direct relationship to the other elements of effectiveness we have examined. Public administration in a democratic society can not hope to secure the flexibility it needs unless and until it can demonstrate that it is using this new freedom responsibly. It must provide its overseers in politics, as well as the press and public, with ways to hold its activities to account. The loosening of restrictions over what it is doing must, therefore, be accompanied by a tighter scrutiny over what it is accomplishing.

For much the same reason, participation and other self-actualization techniques also make measurement more mandatory. Giving employees a freer rein and more authority can scarcely be counted on to increase effectiveness if the employees, to say nothing of their employers, lack the means to evaluate the fruits of their efforts. So here again we find that less control over the process must be balanced by more control over the product.

The public sector is in fact becoming much more conscious of the need for measurement and somewhat more conscientious in responding to it. Productivity measurements, program evaluations, management information systems, and MBO concepts are all coming increasingly into play. A sample survey of the nation's cities in which two-thirds of them responded found almost two-thirds of these respondents using performance measures of some kind. Although less than half of this group actually attempted to measure effectiveness and efficiency—the others were simply trying to gauge effort—most of the larger cities fell in this category.[11]

At the federal level, where a good deal of activity along these lines has been going on for some time, the U. S. Navy launched a five-year demonstration project in 1980 to see if such performance measures could be integrated into the personnel process. The experiment, which illustrates among other things how measurement ties in with flexibility and self-actualization approaches, aims to relate pay directly to performance. Its main features, as reported in the January 15, 1981 issue of *Public Administration Times*, include:

• a more flexible, manageable, and understandable classification system.
• a performance appraisal system that links performance objectives, compensation, and organizational effectiveness.
• an expanded application of the merit-pay concept.
• recognition of demonstrated individual performance when it comes to carrying out RIF (Reduction-in-Force) directives.
• the use of suspended penalties in certain adverse-action situations.

Of course nearly all efforts to measure effectiveness must be tied in with the budget. In many cases they may originate in or spring from the budget, as is the case with PPBS and ZBB. But performance measures can be grafted onto, and used effectively with, line-item budgets, provided such budgets are not made overly constrictive. (See the earlier discussion of this under "Flexibility.")

THE UNMEASUREABLE ALSO MATTERS

There is more to productivity than may meet the manager's eye, warns John Nalbandian. Writing in the May–June 1981 issue of *Public Administration Review*, Nalbandian calls attention to some important but often overlooked aspects of assessing individual output.

A worker who outproduces others but who at the same time annoys and disturbs them with loud talk, interruption, tobacco smoke, et cetera, may well be a drag on overall output. On the other hand, he points out, an employee with only modest output to his credit may give a ride to a fellow worker, console another over a loss, and generally bolster the morale of those in his unit.

"By attempting to remove *all* criteria which are not related to an individual's *production*," writes Nalbandian, "we also define away some activities which establish and maintain the productivity, cohesion and sociability of a work group."

As 1983 got underway it became evident that the Reagan administration was attempting to move in this direction. A new initiative called "Reform '88" has emerged from the White House drawing boards, its title reflecting the five-year span that its implementation would require. It would establish a central policy-planning process to draw up key programmatic goals and translate these goals into the budget. Federal agencies would report quarterly on what progress they were making toward achieving these goals. Undergirding the whole reform would be a network of integrated information systems to provide the executive office with such down-to-earth data as the amount of U.S. government property in the hands of contractors, the amount and age of money owed the federal government, the government's cash balances, the market value of federal real estate, the amount the federal government had committed to state and local governments, et cetera. Such relevant information had hitherto been unavailable.

The Office of Management and Budget would serve as the key agency in the new system. Indeed the plan was described as putting the M into the OMB. But according to OMB'S Deputy Director Joseph Wright, the office would function as something of a "holding company," centralizing policy and coordination but leaving responsibility for execution in the hands of the various operating agencies. No one was calling it MBO or any of the other names that the new goal-oriented and measurement-centered trend has spawned, but it represents still another effort to bring measurement and management into accord.

On a more theoretical level one can view these mushrooming efforts at performance measurement as representing neither pure rationality nor pure incrementalism. A new theory may offer the best approach to explaining them. This is contingency theory, which calls for the context and circumstances to shape whatever approach seems best for the particular situation. Contingency theory, according to two of its theoreticians, is a matter of "identifying and developing functional relationships between environmental, management, and performance variables," and then adopting an approach that best fits these relationships and variables.[12] As such it allows the decision maker or decision makers to use a largely incremental approach in one instance, a largely rational approach in another, and a blend of both in a third.

Today's public managers are faced with certain pressures, such as the demand to do more with less, that prod them toward rationality. At the same time they are still beleaguered by other forces, such as political and clientele pressures along with limited time, expertise, and information, which incline them toward incrementalism. Consequently, many of them, whether or not they know what contingency theory actually means, may find themselves using its supple, situational approach as they strive to fulfill the seemingly impossible dream of doing more with less.

CASE STUDY

Success at Sanitation[13]

If one wanted to see an example of the problems crippling New York City's government in the 1970s, one had only to look at the Bureau of Motor Equipment in the city's sanitation department. This bureau is responsible for maintaining nearly five thousand vehicles plus all the equipment associated with them. In 1978, three years after the metropolis had begun to fight its way back from the brink of bankruptcy, the bureau was still floundering. Nearly half the vehicles it was supposed to service were down at any one time, while its shortfall in maintaining the equipment needed stood at 30 percent. This state of affairs was creating a lot of expensive overtime work. It was also forcing the department to assign those trucks that were in service to double-shift duty, a practice that only caused further breakdowns.

But 1978 also marked the year when things started to change. All the top-level managers submitted their resignations, and in December the city appointed Robert Contino as the bureau's new director. It was an unusual appointment, for not only did Contino lack an extensive background in motor vehicle maintenance but he also had no experience to speak of in New York City government. His previous positions had been in private industry and with the federal government as well as with the County of San Diego, California. In the latter post he had headed the Office of Program Evaluation.

Contino's first step was to identify the fundamental components of the entire repair and maintenance system. Finding them to be six in number, he named a manager for each one. He also set up a bureauwide labor-management committee complemented by separate committees at the shop level. Their first task was to take surveys to develop some basic data regarding the most frequent problems, et cetera. From this data an MBO system with specific performance targets was evolved. It was supported by a carefully and extensively developed management-information system.

The results were not long in coming. Typically the sanitation department had started out each snow season with over 20 percent of its salt spreaders already out of service. At the start of the 1980 snow season, however, less than 10 percent of these vehicles were nonfunctioning. Preventive maintenance on trucks had previously been done only once every twenty-one weeks. Soon Contino's men were performing major preventive maintenance work on each truck every nine weeks and minor work every four or five weeks.

By the end of 1981, less than three years after the director was appointed and the turnaround began, the average number of trucks down at any one time had dropped from near 50 percent to less than 20 percent, while the equipment shortfall had declined from 30 percent to 17 percent. Costs had sharply gone down as well. With inflation factored in at a fairly conservative 10 percent a year for the years in question—in one of these years the cost of living index actually rose over 12 percent—the total savings in the first two years of Contino's reign were figured at $13.7 million, a truly remarkable figure when one keeps in mind that the bureau's annual budget in these years came to just over $30 million.

The size and speed of the savings plus the fact that those who would take credit for them were the ones who computed them might well make any intelligent observer skeptical. Yet substantial savings were apparently achieved. For example the bureau not only began making many of its own replacement parts cheaper than it had previously purchased them but it began generating income by doing work for other city agencies and even billing vendors for warranty work performed by its own personnel.

Contino claims that any manager can utilize the lessons his bureau learned in its successful turnaround. According to him, those lessons include strong support from top management, clear channels of communication between managers and all levels of the work force, an organizationwide climate of cooperation and trust, and encouragement of an open-minded attitude by employees. Others might wish to point to the desirability of well-designed performance measures supported by a carefully crafted information system as well. The benefits, in Contino's view, will come not only in the form of better service and reduced costs but in a greatly increased feeling of satisfaction on the part of all concerned. Such, he says, was certainly the case at BME.

Ethics

Although a few cynics may think otherwise, nearly all those who have studied the subject believe, and believe strongly, that administrative effectiveness requires and rests upon a firm ethical basis. Corruption of any kind greatly detracts from, when it does not actually destroy, organizational capability. As Chester Barnard, a successful organizational executive who became an even more successful organizational theoretician, once pointed out, "Organizations endure . . . in proportion to the breadth of morality by which they are governed."

Many of the links in this management-morality relationship are fairly easy to establish. Employees are not encouraged to give their best to an organization or a manager whom they perceive as acting in a dishonest and/or discriminatory manner. On the contrary, such patterns of conduct will only incline them to behave in the same way. The manager who appropriates organizational resources for his own gain will find his employees doing the same. The manager who lies to his superior will find his subordinates lying to him.

Much of the apparatus of government is aimed at curbing such misfeasance and malfeasance. The budget itself, for example, has, among its other primary functions, the task of making sure that public funds are not illegally or improperly spent. Civil-service laws and systems are designed, among other things, to prevent favoritism, let alone the selling of offices.

Conflict-of-interest laws have been promulgated to deter still more subtle kinds of misdeeds. Such laws make it a crime for a public official to do such things as award a government contract to a firm in which the official or his or her immediate family have an interest or to purchase land in an area where a hitherto unannounced government development will increase land values. Today the federal government and all fifty states have such laws, although fairly substantial differences exist between them as to how far these laws extend and how rigorously they are enforced.

The federal government's conflict-of-interest legislation dates back to the Civil War. This legislation was updated and codified in 1962. But the Watergate affair and some lesser scandals prompted Congress to enact the Ethics in Government Act of 1978. This act requires elected officials and key employees of all three branches of the federal government to disclose all their financial interests. It also places restrictions on their activities while in office and, for executive-branch employees, after they leave office as well. For example, a federal employee is prohibited for one year after leaving the federal government from any attempt to influence his or her former agency on behalf of any private party and is barred for life from representing anyone on a particular matter that he or she "personally and substantially handled" as a federal employee.

The act also set up the Office of Government Ethics to obtain financial disclosure reports from all officeholders subject to the act. While the office performs little else in the way of prescribed duties, it does supplement its monitoring activities with occasional conferences and similar events.

Despite these and other efforts, such as the establishment of the Office of Inspector General in fifteen cabinet departments and large agencies, the multifaceted problem of corruption has continued to haunt the federal establishment. In 1981, the General Accounting Office reported on a two-and-a-half-year investigation of twenty-one agencies. It found that "Fraud against government programs is widespread. . . ." Most of it went undetected, and those instances that did come to light often went unprosecuted. Concluded the GAO, "the sad truth is that crime against the government does pay."[14]

As if this wasn't a sufficient indictment, the U.S. Merit Systems Protection Board released at about the same time the results of a survey it had taken of a randomly selected sample of federal employees in fifteen departments and agencies. Nearly half of the sampled employees admitted having personally observed or obtained direct evidence of fraud, waste, or mismanagement within the past year alone. Almost one in every ten claimed knowledge of an activity involving more than one hundred thousand dollars.[15]

Some quotations from the respondents themselves portray the far from pleasant picture that underlay these figures.

> By placing the administration of this program under [local governments], fraud, waste and total mismanagement is the result. I have personally observed embezzlement of federal funds in excess of $200,000.

> The . . . hospital spends thousands of dollars each year for new and replacement carpeting. The carpets are ripped up and replaced as often as every six months. . . . There seems to be an endless supply of money for hospital maintenance while money for patient care is scarce.

> I was instructed on several occasions to find contractors who would bill the agency for work that had not been started or even planned. This was done so large sums of excess budget monies could be spent rather than returned at the end of the fiscal year.

At this juncture one might start to wonder why more of these employees had not blown the whistle on such acts of impropriety. A few of them had done so but despite the increased support such whistle blowing has begun to attract, their disclosures had often caused more harm to themselves than to those responsible for the offenses they had observed.

Dr. Kurt Luedtke, for example, had established a spotless record as chief of neuropsychiatry at the Memphis Naval Station. But when he protested that his superiors were filling their recruitment quotas by signing up men with a history of mental instability and violent behavior, he found himself abruptly hustled off to Bethesda Naval Hospital for mental tests. Though pronounced thoroughly safe and sane, he resigned from the navy in disillusionment.

Richard Floyd of the National Security Agency had a similar experience. When he complained of numerous conflicts and irregularities in the agency's contracting methods, his superiors gave him an adverse performance appraisal and told him to see a psychiatrist. He also ended up resigning.[16]

Virtually all such administrative abuses as have been mentioned have, in one form or another and to one degree or another, been a part of most state and many local governments as well. In fact some of the worst offenses involving federal funds have taken place when these funds came into local hands. Very few public agencies of any size or scope can claim to be totally free of such malpractices.

At the same time, however, efforts to curb them continue to mount. In 1981 Congress passed and the president signed a bill authorizing the payment of bonuses to whistle blowers whose disclosures result in saving the federal government money. And in 1982 legislation was filed in Congress providing specific safeguards to protect those who report incidents of waste and misuse of federal funds. Meanwhile the executive branch has begun to take more seriously the task of policing itself. The Reagan administration transferred responsibility for fifteen Offices of Inspector General from the Justice Department to the OMB. The announced object of the shift was to have them center more effort on developing ways to prevent such practices from taking place.[17] It was also hoped that better budgeting procedures, backed up by better information systems, might also reduce these impediments to effective administration.

Ethics: A Different and Deeper Dimension

There are other aspects to the problem of public-service morality, and these aspects are much more pervasive and possibly much more pernicious than instances of outright fraud and theft, as outrageous as the latter may appear. These are the deceitful practices engaged in by men and women who in all other respects we would consider, and who would consider themselves, to be upstanding public citizens and committed public servants.

What are these practices? Some have already been described in the earlier chapters on personnel and budgeting. In fact they are so common that most public managers, including at one time the writer of this book, has engaged in at least some of them. They are customarily considered to be part of the rules of the game and therefore fair game for all who play it.

Public budgeting, for example, has been described as a process that almost inevitably "makes liars out of honest men." Through such routine rituals as overstating their real needs in order to maximize their allocations, and understating future costs in order to get a program approved, public managers become proficient practitioners of deceit, often on a grand scale. They are doing so, they may claim, only in order to enable their agency to perform its functions. But this doesn't alter the fact that they are lying.

Furthermore, the excuse that effectiveness in government regimes requires such practices seems weak indeed when applied to many of the deceptive devices so commonly employed. Does allowing and even assisting an employee to expand the specifications of his or her position in order to get an upgraded, higher-paying job classification really promote the public's betterment? What about keeping a nonfunctioning alcoholic on the payroll because it would be too brutal (or, more likely, too bothersome) to get rid of him? And what about the frequently used stratagem of giving an ineffective or troublesome employee a laudatory reference in order to facilitate his or her transfer to another agency? Can this be considered ethical behavior? Does it serve the public's well-being?

Viewed from one perspective the problem can be described as one of divided and even divergent loyalty. The public manager may profess a quite sincere devotion to serving the public. But he or she also feels a great loyalty to subordinates and co-workers as well. These two sets of loyalties do not always coincide, and when they do not, the latter often predominates.

Adding a further disturbing note to this situation is the fact that devotion to one's agency and its employees frequently dovetails all too nicely with devotion to one's own welfare. Public managers who secure increased funding, expanded promotional opportunities for employees, et cetera, while dodging the difficult tasks of disciplining or dismissing unproductive workers and phasing out unproductive functions, often end up enhancing their own interests as well. For public managers gain, or retain, prestige, power, and "perks" through enlarging, or conserving, the resources at their disposal. And using these resources to please or at least placate their subordinates only makes their own job more pleasant still. Consequently, as Marjorie Boyd has pointed out, "Every person in the Civil Service System has a powerful financial interest in seeing the government get bigger."[18] The real danger is that the loyalties involved tend to blend together so that the public servant loses the ability to accurately distinguish where one leaves off and the other begins. As Murray Lincoln, founder of CARE and a leader of the American Cooperative Movement has put it, "It seems to be inevitable that people start out working with all their hearts for a great cause. Then the cause becomes an institution and they work for that. Next they wind up working for their own place in that institution."[19]

Antidotes and Answers

This less overt and more insidious dimension of the problem of public-service ethics may well prove the hardest of all to rectify. Complicating its correction is the fact that two of the remedies so often recommended, while they may improve some parts of the problem, may only make other parts of it worse. These two remedies are increased idealism and increased professionalism.

Most assuredly, some measure of idealism is desirable and even necessary for effective and ethical public service. But too much idealism expressed in the form of a too great attachment to one's own agency along with its activities and purposes can produce a cure worse than the disease. We find examples of this on every hand. The Pentagon's vast appetite for more weapons systems can by no means be written off as simply a power grab. On the contrary it is prompted and powered to a great extent by the military's deep commitment to defend the country from its enemies. Even the most questionable, from an effectiveness standpoint, of these weapon systems is supported by men whose motivations, in the main, spring from a sincere desire to serve their country's best interests.

The same holds true for the Pentagon's controversial and virtually independent subunit, the Army Corps of Engineers. When the corps was dragged into court in 1979 on a charge of exceeding its authority in expanding the Tennessee-Tombigbee Waterway, the lieutenant general who commanded the corps at the time seemed, in the words of the *New York Times*, "puzzled." He could not understand how anyone could accuse his engineers of deception just because they wanted to build the best and biggest waterway possible through Mississippi and Alabama. Moreover, internal memorandums disclosed in the case, said the *Times*, "indicate that the Corps feels something like a religious need to move earth and pour concrete on a grand scale."[20]

As with weapons systems and waterways, so with most of the other activities that public agencies pursue. Even some of the most praiseworthy and pure efforts can yield unproductive and counterproductive results when an excess of zeal clouds critical judgement. For example, making a liberal arts education available to all will strike many as a valuable if not vital goal for any democracy that takes its professed virtues seriously. But, as political scientist Lewis A. Dexter points out, making such education free reduces the number of people who would otherwise go into the skilled trades. This in turn reduces the availability of services while increasing their costs.[21] One might also add that many of the young people encouraged by its ready availability to pursue a liberal arts education may also suffer, for they may well end up earning less money and enjoying less independence than if they had become electricians, plumbers, refrigeration mechanics and the like. Finally we might note that creating a large surplus of broadly educated but unskilled liberal arts graduates can produce a threat to social stability, as it did in Germany in the early 1930s and as it is doing in India and some other countries today.

Another example of excessive zeal is supplied by urbanologist Melville C. Branch. Professor Branch claims that city planners, acting on the most laudable of impulses, have often greatly injured the public they so desperately desired to serve. In their zeal for community improvement they have produced visionary and inflexible master plans, requiring a rash of regulations and red tape and, for developers, continual reviews and delays. As a consequence, he says, they have driven up the cost and choked off the supply of badly needed housing and development.[22]

The problems that Branch discerns and decries among city planners derive from a broader movement called *advocacy administration,* which gripped larger sections of the public sector during the 1960s. The movement stemmed from the essentially correct perception that administration could no longer be completely divorced from policy making. The complexities of modern life had simply made it impossible for elected officials to decide everything of importance. Therefore increased discretion must necessarily devolve into the hands of those whose function had hitherto been deemed as limited merely to carrying out policies.

Animated by this awareness, and also by a new atmosphere and attitude that viewed government as an activist force with nearly unlimited potential for creating a new and better society, advocacy administration came into its own.

There is little question that public administrators must make decisions that bear upon policy. Moreover, their expertise and their closeness to the scene require them on occasion to assume an advocacy role in the sense of recommending some policies while arguing against others. But such a role must continually be balanced by other considerations. For one thing their very commitment as well as closeness to the area of their concern can limit their perspective. For another thing, as unelected officeholders in a democratic society they should hesitate to thwart the public will, even when they believe the public to be wrong. Finally they should remember that too much activism on their part, no matter how well intentioned, can produce a reaction that can greatly injure not only their programs but even themselves. Advocacy administration may have helped bring on the rising tide of resentment that currently buffets much of the public sector.

To sum up then, while public servants must strive to serve the public conscientiously and aggressively, they must also accept and respect the boundaries that of necessity must circumscribe their actions. The line between policy and administration, says Don Devine, director of the U.S.

Office of Personnel Management, "will always be blurred in the real world." But, he adds, "the distinction is absolutely critical in the theoretical world. This distinction between policy and administration rests upon the broader distinction between the policy-making elected public official and the responsive civil servant, upon which democracy rests."[23]

As an appointee and supporter of president Reagan, Devine might be considered as merely voicing the rigid conservative philosophy of his boss. But his position on this particular point apparently concurs with the stand taken by his more liberal predecessor, Alan Campbell. For under Campbell, the office issued a publication affirming that "the dominant theme in public personnel reform is to improve the responsiveness of Civil Service personnel to management and hence to the general public to which management is ultimately responsible."[24]

MR. FOSS'S FOLLY

In 1939 an enterprising Republican congressman named Everett Dirkson got wind of a rash of promotions at the Rural Electrification Agency (REA). Since he had always opposed this New Deal public-power agency he immediately inquired. The REA's director of personnel, a former newspaper reporter named Kendell Foss, foreseeing the bad publicity that might result, omitted a large number of the promotions on the dubious ground that they were only advancements within grade.

Unfortunately for Mr. Foss the total list leaked out, a congressional hearing was held, and his questionable conduct was revealed. Both Foss and the agency he sought so zealously to protect suffered as a result. Foss's folly was not motivated by self-interest. "I submit," he told the congressional panel, "there is to the best of my knowledge no personal gain for me in my attempt to read as painless a report as I could out of what on the face of it appears to have been an orgy of promotions." Foss merely wanted to protect his agency from what he saw as the predatory private-power interests, represented by Dirksen, who opposed it. Like Shakespeare's Othello, Foss loved not wisely but too well.

But there is a further irony in the situation. Many of the areas that the REA was eagerly seeking to electrify were those that the Department of Agriculture was trying to withdraw from farming. The nation at the time suffered from an enormous surplus of farmers and farmland, and the agency for which Foss so unselfishly sacrificed his career was actually frustrating the government's own efforts to resolve the problem.

Excessive professionalism can pose some of the same problems to administrative ethics as excessive zeal. It can lead to what philosopher Kenneth Burke calls "that state of affairs where one's very abilities can function as blindness"[25] and thereby lead to erroneous decisions and counterproductive behavior. Professionals tend to become involved, sometimes to the point of a near-obsession, in things that they find interesting and that they hope their fellow professionals will find impressive. Unfortunately, such things are not always what the public needs, wants, or expects. And the more professional they become, the more single-minded they can become in pursuing their specialized concerns to the exclusion of other considerations.

Financial factors may add further aggravations. All too often professional gain not only increased esteem but also increased income through a more exhaustive, and thereby expensive, utilization of their skills. When architects design bigger-than-necessary buildings, when doctors disdain simpler therapies for more complex ones, when lawyers carry litigation to greater lengths and more numerous levels, they usually earn more money in the process. The reward systems of most professions, like the reward systems of government agencies themselves, can easily conflict with the will and well-being of those they serve.

Similar perils may plague an overprofessionalized public administration as well. For while there is no gainsaying the need for better educated and better skilled personnel in the public service, such professionalization, while undoubtedly helping to resolve certain ethical problems, may well exacerbate other ones. The American Society for Public Administration has shown some awareness of this issue, although it tilts, as it should, toward the side of greater professionalism. In a workbook on the subject, the society notes that "Administrators in the public sector are confronted with two primary imperatives—satisfying their individual standards of professional performance, conduct and ethics and adhering to those imposed upon them by their agencies, public policies and a critical public." This duality, it says, often generates "thorny conflicts."[26]

One of the society's senior members, in also calling attention to this problem, indicates at the same time a possible solution. "Professionalization and democracy," writes Barry D. Karl, "exist on a collision course which requires some kind of political mediation by a leadership not closely identified with either side of the debate."[27]

But to professors Richard F. Mayer and Michael M. Harmon, the entire quandary, viewed from a still broader perspective, contains at the least the seeds of its solution. Public administrators feel the push and pull of three different pressures or, as they characterize them, responsibilities. There is the responsibility to professional codes and standards, the responsibility to the public and its elected representatives, and the responsibilities to their own personal interests. But these three distinct responsibilities are "neither additive nor exclusive notions." Rather they complement each other with each acting as a check and balance on the others.[28]

"Political responsibility, for example, rescues both professionalism from being a narrow instrumentalism and personal responsibility from being either ethical narcissism or moral dogmatism," they write. "Professional responsibility, in turn, checks both the tendency of the political to degenerate into opportunism and the personal to lapse into naïve impracticality." And responsibility to one's own interests "helps clarify the difference between political responsibility and unquestioning obedience as well as between professionalism and mindless technicism."

As a result of such a three-way division of responsibility, a new administrative ethos emerges. It is one that "accommodates and calls for the constant negotiation of the tensions between these three categories of responsible action."

A career requiring the constant negotiation of inherent, and probably irradicable, tensions may strike many as most unappealing. But others who are equipped with the requisite abilities and attitude might feel differently. For them, the craft of public administration should offer unparalleled opportunities for advancement and accomplishment in the difficult days and decades that lie ahead.

REWARDS IN REVERSE

According to some reports, over one hundred thousand of the country's foster children could be placed in permanent homes, where they would receive loving and, from the government's standpoint, cost-free care. These are youngsters who are eligible for adoption and for whom potential parents exist. So why are they not put up for adoption? One reason is that many foster-care agencies lack the incentive to do so. Taking the youngsters out of foster care would reduce their own agency's work load, thereby threatening their growth and possibly reducing their payrolls as well.

Many public agencies labor under similar inverted, if not perverted, reward systems. A fire department that prevents fires may only suffer at budget time as a result. (As one fireman told his public administration professor, "we always get uneasy when a month goes by without a major alarm.") Reduced crime might reduce the need for police officers as well as for court and correction personnel. And if the health care system actually made everybody healthy, most of its institutions and practitioners would go bankrupt.

Performance measurement may at least help create more awareness of this problem, for such measures, along with the systems that incorporate them, only work well when missions and goals have been accurately defined and fully accepted. And defining missions and goals frequently forces an agency to confront some manifestations of this problem, if not the problem itself.

Notes

1. The two books mentioned were by Jacob B. Ukeles and John Careley. The former was published by the American Management Association, the latter by the Columbia University Press, both of New York.

2. Susan Walters and Pat Choate, *America in Ruins: Beyond Public Works Barrel* (Washington, D.C.: Council of State Planning Agencies, 1981).

3. Quoted in "The Repairing of America," *Time*, 10 January 1983.

4. "Dragging Cities into Court," *Time*, 13 September 1982.

5. Ann Robinson and Bengt-Christer Ysander, "Re-establishing Budgetary Flexibility," *Public Budgeting and Finance* (Autumn 1982).

6. L. A. Morton, *Organizing for Innovation* (New York: McGraw-Hill, 1971), 165.

7. *Public Administration Times*, 1 December 1982.

8. Quoted in Dori Smith, "The New Psychologies," *Whole Life Times* (March 1982).

9. C. E. Teasley and R. K. Ready, "Human Services Matrix: Managerial Problems and Prospects," *Public Administration Review* (March–April 1981).

10. Morton, *Organizing for Innovation*, 5.

11. Charles L. Usher and Gary C. Cornia, "Goal Setting and Performance Assessment in Municipal Budgeting," *Public Administration Review* (March–April 1981).

12. Fred Luthans and Todd Steward, "A General Contingency Theory of Management." *Academy of Management Review*, vol. 2, 1977.

13. The material for this case study was taken from Robert Contino and Robert Lorusso, "The Theory Z Turnaround of a Public Agency," *Public Administration Review* (January–February 1982).

14. *Boston Herald-American*, 12 August 1981.

15. "Blowing the Whistle on Waste: A Thankless Job," *U.S. News and World Report*, 29 June 1981.

16. These and other cases are described by columnist Jack Anderson in "Dear Mr. President . . . ," *Parade*, 26 April 1971.

17. *Public Administration Times*, 15 October 1981.

18. Marjorie Boyd, "Inflated Grades," *Washington Monthly* (April 1977).

19. Quoted by Warren Brooks in "Is the Federal Bureaucracy Our Modern Tower of Babel?" *Boston Herald-American*, 13 January 1981.

20. *New York Times*, 4 February 1979, News in Review section.

21. Professor Dexter's remarks are contained in an unpublished manuscript, *Leaning Against the Wind*, which he has kindly allowed the writer to read.

22. Melville C. Branch, "Sins of City Planners," *Public Administration Review* (January–February 1982).

23. *Public Administration Times*, 1 May 1981.

24. U.S. Office of Personnel Management, "Common Themes in Public Personnel Reform" (Washington, D.C.: Government Printing Office, 1979). For further discussion on this point see Richard A. Loverd, "Taming Techniques for Public Purposes: A Personnel Management Challenge for the Eighties," *Public Administration Review* (July–August 1981).

25. Kenneth Burke, *Permanence and Change,* 2nd ed., rev. (Indianapolis: Bobbs-Merrill, 1965) 81.

26. *Applying Professional Standards and Ethics in the Eighties: A Workbook and Study Guide for Public Administrators* (Washington, D.C.: American Society for Public Administration, 1982).

27. Barry D. Karl, "Louis Brownlow," *Public Administration Review* (November–December 1979).

28. Richard T. Mayer and Michael M. Harmon, "Teaching Moral Education in Public Administration," *Southern Review of Public Administration* (Summer 1982).

STATEMENT OF PRINCIPLES OF THE
AMERICAN SOCIETY OF PUBLIC ADMINISTRATION
Adopted December 6, 1981

The American Society for Public Administration exists to advance the science, processes, and art of public administration. The Society affirms its responsibility to develop the spirit of professionalism within its membership, and to increase public awareness of moral standards in public service by its example. To this end we, the members of the Society, commit ourselves to the following principles:

1 Service to the public is beyond service to oneself.
2 The people are sovereign and those in public service are ultimately responsible to them.
3 Laws govern all actions of the public service. Where laws or regulations are ambiguous, leave discretion, or require change, we will seek to serve the best interests of the public.
4 Efficient and effective management is basic to public administration. Subversion through misuse of influence, fraud, waste, or abuse is intolerable. Employees who responsibly call attention to wrongdoing will be encouraged.
5 The merit system, equal opportunity, and affirmative action principles will be supported, implemented, and promoted.
6 Safeguarding the public trust is paramount. Conflicts of interest, bribes, gifts, or favors which subordinate public positions to private gain are unacceptable.
7 Service to the public creates demands for special sensitivity to the qualities of justice, courage, honesty, equity, competence and compassion. We esteem these qualities, and we will actively promote them.

8 Conscience performs a critical role in choosing among courses of action. It takes into account the moral ambiguities of life, and the necessity to examine value priorities: good ends never justify immoral means.

9 Public administrators are not engaged merely in preventing wrong, but in pursuing right through timely and energetic execution of their responsibilities.

APPENDIX 2

A PUBLIC ADMINISTRATION BIBLIOGRAPHY

Prepared by John E. Rouse, Jr.
ASSOCIATE PROFESSOR
BALL STATE UNIVERSITY

Public administration is an emerging superdiscipline with roots in political science, business administration, history, economics, psychology, and sociology. The literature is diverse and everchanging. This necessarily limited bibliographic account is designed to be useful to the student in some practical sense and helpful for a comprehensive coverage of the literature.

The brief descriptions of each entry is limited to two items: (1) a description of the text or journal; and (2) why the listing is of value to the reader. The literature is divided into nine categories: (1) "Classics of Public Administration"; (2) "Reference Works and Bibliographies"; (3) "Administrative Organization, Federalism"; (4) "Systemic and Bureaucratic Dynamics"; (5) "Personnel Administration, Including Administrative Law"; (6) "Communication and Leadership"; (7) "Productivity, Performance Appraisal, and Evaluation"; (8) Budgetary Politics and Financial Administration; and (9) Journals of Public-Sector Significance.

The materials discussed by Professor Rouse are listed in full at the end of his essay, along with leading journals in the field.

1. Classics of Public Administration

Barnard (1938) provides a comprehensive theory of cooperative behavior in formal organizations. The student will find useful Barnard's analysis of the individual and organization, his theoretical breakdown of the structure of formal organizations, his functional analysis of organizations in cooperative systems, and his dissection of the nature of executive responsibility.

Gulick and Urwick (1937) offer a classic that examines the development and growth of public administration during the New Deal years. The authors of these essays were instrumental in shaping American impressions of the "birth" of bureaucracy.

McGregor (1960) delineates administrative behavior into the categories of Theories X and Y. Theory X is the traditional view of direction and control, while Theory Y includes the integration of individual and organizational goals. The author's extremes state that the average human being has an inherent dislike for work and will avoid it if he or she can (Theory X) or that the expenditure of physical and mental efforts in work is as natural as play or rest (Theory Y).

Simon's test (1945) is known for its development of a theory of human choice or decision making. The author distinguishes between fact and value, end and means, and discusses rationality in administrative decision making. In 1978, the author was awarded a Nobel Peace Prize for this classic.

Taylor's essay (1911) has served as a primer for administrators and for students of managerial techniques for nearly three generations. The author focuses upon the fusion of resources and manpower to promote predetermined goals in the most efficient manner. Taylor is considered the founder of scientific management. This concept implies repetitive tasks requiring no decision making or problem solving.

Waldo (1948) discusses the public administration movement from the viewpoint of political theory and the history of ideas. He seeks to review and analyze the theoretical element in administrative writings and to present the development of the public administration movement as a chapter in the history of American political thought.

2. Reference Works and Bibliographies

Chandler and Plano (1982) offer a valuable handbook of public administration definitions for the introductory student of this superdiscipline. The authors include definitions of public administration terms of the discipline's fundamentals, public policy, public management, administration organization, personnel, financial administration, public law, and regulation.

Cutchin's volume (1981) is significant for its definitions and explanations of public administration concepts, theories, and facts, and for its annotated bibliography of research sources, including journals and abstracts.

The Gawthrops (1979) compile a complete history of every entry in *Public Administration Review*, the official journal of the American Society for Public Administration, inclusive of volumes 1 through 39. Entries include letters to the editor, reports, panel discussions, book review essays, and ASPA constitutions and constitutional amendments.

Rouse (1980) offers a comprehensive annotated bibliography of nearly seventeen hundred selections from the diverse literature of public administration. This reference text comprises literature concerning federalism and administrative structure, governmental divisions and administrative processes, the discipline of public administration, discrimination and equal employment, productivity, political economy and finance, centralization and decentralization, and comparative and developmental administration.

3. Administrative Organization, Federalism

Gawthrop (1969) examines the manner in which the executive branch of the federal government resolves internal conflict, makes decisions, develops a sense of loyalty within its ranks, and responds to the internal and external forces of changes. He presents a concise analytical model, which can be used in explaining the functioning of bureaucratic systems.

Katz and Kahn (1966, 1978) champion the cause of the open-systems approach to the study of organizations. The authors emphasize that social psychological principles may be applied to all forms of collective organized effort. In contrast to classical organization theories, this book proposes that the means of open-system theory constitute resolution of more traditional theoretical difficulties.

Pfiffner and Sherwood (1960) write one of the "near-classic" volumes of administration organization studies. In analyzing societal organizations, organization structures; modifying systems of culture, status, communication, power, politics, and leadership; two models of organization; and future perspectives, the authors provide introductory students with an outstanding basic review of organizational dynamics.

Seidman (1975), a practitioner of public administration gives the views of executive branch organization from the White House and Congress. The author's text on politics, position, and power affords students of public administration a valuable discourse concerning the dynamics of federal organization. Seidman describes with expertise the politics of government organization.

Thompson (1967) is concerned with organizational rationality. In this focus, he explores strategies for studying organizations, domains of organized action, organizational design, technology, and structure. The author's second concern is with the exercise of discretion by organizational members. In this focus, he examines human contributions, control of complex organizations, and the administrative process. Thompson's insights on organizational rationality will be of particular value to introductory public administration students.

Waldo's second contribution (1980) to this bibliographic essay is an excellent complement to his first (1948). In this second volume, Waldo explores the richness, controversy, creativeness, power, weakness, contribution, and future of public administration and its literature. As Waldo's first volume focuses upon the administrative state's relevance to society, this text provides students a philosophical view of modern bureaucracy in a democracy, from the New Deal era to the present.

4. Systemic and Bureaucratic Dynamics

Caiden (1969) defines administrative reform as "the artificial inducement of administrative transformation, against resistance." His book entails approaches, processes, and obstacles to reform. Because administrative reform and change are constants, this book is of particular value to introductory public administration students.

Downs's (1967) central hypotheses are that bureaucratic officials seek to attain their goals rationally, that such officials have a complex set of goals, and that the social functions of every organization strongly influence its internal structure and behavior. This text is of importance to students because of Downs's research on the life cycle of bureaus, internal characteristics, bureau communications, control processes, territories, change, and ideologies. The author concludes with a listing of twenty-one hypotheses of bureaucratic behaviors.

Drucker (1980) indicates that the immediate future of business, society, and economy are entering a new economic era with new trends, new markets, and new institutions. In concentrating upon management fundamentals, new population structure and dynamics, and turbulent environments, the author offers both a comparative and developmental analysis of organizational dynamics. This volume is both futuristic and international in systemic emphases.

In one of the most provocative examinations of public administration literature, Ostrom (1974) delineates the crisis of confidence in the super-discipline, reviews the intellectual mainstream in American public administration (Wilson, Weber, Gulick, Simon), notes the contributions of contemporary political economists, presents theories of bureaucratic and democratic administrations, and probes the choice of alternative futures.

5. Personnel Administration, Including Administrative Law

Cayer (1975) researches public personnel administration (PPA) in context of the political environment in which PPA functions. Conscious that personnel administration for some students is a dull, technical field of examinations, the author focuses upon the political dynamics of the personnel process. He reviews the evolution of the personnel system, operation of the merit system, rights and duties of public employees, and international and comparative variations of personnel administration.

Gellhorn (1972) outlines the delegation doctrine of judicial control, the political process of nonjudicial control; discusses judicial review; examines agency jurisdiction; describes information and investigation aspects; notes the informal administrative process; states the rules and related rulemaking, orders and adjudications of formal processes; describes requirements of a hearing; and details the aspects of the hearing process. When the *Code of Federal Regulations* and *Federal Register* are daily contributions of regulatory life of bureaucracies, the student is well served by this text.

Imundo (1980) pens everything students need to know about selecting, orienting, and training employees; improving communication; understanding leadership styles; promoting effective employee discipline; managing employee absenteeism; resolving employee complaints; establishing standards and assessing employee performance; counseling employees; and developing a system of time management. This handbook serves as a practical guide for students visualizing supervisor responsibilities.

Januz and Jones (1981) concentrate their research upon effective time management for executives. Recognizing that time is one of life's great equalizers, the authors offer a practical, useful handbook for a variety of personnel concerns. Emphases include goals and planning, personal organization, telephoning, face-to-face conversations, meetings, delegation, office interaction, paper work, filing, dictation, reading and speed reading, traveling, interruptions, stress and crisis, home and family, and time-saving resources.

MacNeilage and Adams (1982) relate frankly the complexities of personal and professional dilemmas confronting students considering public service careers. The authors offer the promise of enhancing personal power and professional skills in the workplace. Basic concepts include the fundamentals of assertiveness and keeping your perspective; practical applications entail handling requests, clarity, change, and anger; personal transitions comprise job hunting and interviewing, upward mobility and creative leadership, identity and life-style.

Maslow (1968) writes of a psychology of health, defense, and growth; peak experiences; creativity; self-actualizing people; values; and cognition in a volume that could be categorized as a "near classic." The author's basic propositions of a growth and self-actualization psychology are of particular value to students concerned with probing the relations of one's emotional health and compatible organizational health.

McConkey (1974) offers students a practical guide to no-nonsense delegation. The author examines the delegation concept in relation to symptoms, causes, foundation, truths, role, requirements, levels, controls, authority, association with decision-making, accountability and participation, and evaluation. Introductory public administration students will find the author's checklist and action plan useful in determining how much to delegate.

The focus of the Mosher (1968, 1982) volume is upon public service and its relation to democracy as an idea and as a manner of governing. Of particular interest to students of public administration will be Mosher's development of education and the public service, changing concepts of the civil service, the importance of the Brownlow Report, the delineation of merit systems, the public-sector labor explosion, the impacts of professional elites, and the role of morality in the public service.

The Office of Personnel Management (1982) offers a useful handbook for federal government managers. Most of the material is based on law, regulation, and administrative procedures, which provide the framework for personnel management in the federal service. Emphases include personnel management resources; hiring, staffing, reduction-in-force; job classification; performance appraisals; training; compensation; incentive awards; and health safety in the workplace; attendance and leave considerations; benefits programs; affirmative employment; labor-management relations; appeals and grievances; ethics in public service; productivity improvement; and executive development. A bibliography and glossary of terms for the above concerns are included.

Stahl (1936, 1983) is the classic source for all students of public personnel administration. This volume constitutes the author's eighth edition of cataloging various aspects of the milieu of the public service. Foci include staffing, structure, performance, rewards, employment conditions, accountability, conduct, collective relations, and perspective for the future. The text is unique in its comprehensiveness and its foundation on the preponderance of prevailing experience in the field. Since 1936, Stahl's editions have proved to be the bibliographic source to consult for developments and changes in public personnel administration.

6. Communication and Leadership

Jennings (1960) concludes that all outstanding persons who mold the character and direction of their organizations possess a rare and delicate mixture of the power-directed prince, the purpose-directed hero, and the self-directed superman. He uses a cross-cultural approach to examine a growing loss of faith in leadership and to emphasize the need to revive individual powers of innovation and courage to assume and sustain great risks. The value of this book to students is its delineation between mediocrity in human behavior and the outstanding qualities of a great leader.

Kaufman (1973) studies administrative feedback from subordinates to leaders in nine federal bureaus. He describes the processes by which upward communication reaches leaders at headquarters and examines communications in order to determine if leaders utilize feedback effectively. Since knowledge is power for administrators, this brief essay is of special worth to students for administrative feedback's potential for redistributing power in bureaucracies.

McGregor and Robinson (1981) point out aspects of the communication matrix. They organize the matrix along lines of staff/professionals, front-line managers, middle managers, and top managers. It is also organized according to tasks and tools for communicating with oneself, one or a few others, and medium to large groups. The significance of this text for students is its emphasis upon communication according to level of responsibility and number of persons with whom administrators communicate. This is a practical book that aids students and prospective administrators to consider their strengths and shortcomings.

Meltzer (1981) believes that information is a commodity that should be managed, relates how information affects the manager's role, recognizes that information is not free, probes the effects of information upon organizational structure and vice versa, and includes a selected list of data bases, a selected bibliography, and federal information resources. Because knowledge management is crucial to the young administrator, this book is of particular value to students.

Snell (1979) teaches readers how to accomplish their goals during meetings. He underscores the point that meetings are places of decision making with force and persuasion. The author stresses both talents and techniques for success in winning the meeting agenda. This book is a practical guide for students lacking experience in such decision-making sessions.

Vroom and Yetton (1973) offer a normative model of managerial styles that favors participation where possible. Students will find particular insight to the dilemmas of leadership and decision making by differentiating the authors' four elemental leadership processes—autocratic, consultative, group, and delegated—used to solve organizational problems. This normative approach treats what a leader should do in a set of hypothetical situations. In training young administrators in decision making, this model shows students how to examine their leadership styles.

Zand (1981) analyzes the interaction between managerial behavior and the organization's increasing dependence upon knowledge. He estimates the effects of knowledge on organizations and their decision processes. The author explores the characteristics of organizations in a knowledge society, considers several crucial aspects of management in context of a knowledge society, reflects upon the demand in every organization to manage stability and change, and explores the role of the individual—the industrial citizen—in a knowledge society. This text is a good primer for students considering employment in the service economy.

7. Productivity, Performance Appraisal, and Evaluation

In this very useful book on productivity in the public sector, Balk (1975) provides an overview of productivity programs in the public sector, describes motivation within public agencies for productivity, discusses measurement and information systems, examines agency environments and processes of influence, and states some basic assumptions concerning program implementation.

The editors of *Fortune* (1982) compile a series of essays concerning the prospects for productivity, the quality of working life, and the impacts of industrial change, corporate culture, bureaucratic obstacles, union/employee participation, and the compensation/productivity formula for government workers in an effort to encourage Americans to put more brainpower into their working lives. This volume posits a cross-cultural review of ways to work smarter.

The General Accounting Office (1978) assesses the most effective ways in which the federal government can promote state and local government productivity improvement. The GAO suggests that the federal government may help state and local governments improve their productivity by developing a general management improvement program in executing innovative improvement projects, sponsoring needed research and development of national interest, altering the grants system to remove negative barriers and promote positive incentives, and establishing a strong federal focal point for monitoring productivity efforts.

Hayes (1977) catalogues productivity programs from Dallas, Detroit, Milwaukee, New York's Nassau County, Palo Alto, Phoenix, and Tacoma. This discussion of municipal/county results provides a basis for developing a better understanding of managerial change and innovation in local government. The text serves as an excellent introduction to local government productivity programs.

Latham and Wexley (1981) emphasize practical applications of the theoretical principles of goal setting, reinforcement, role clarity, and team building. The authors explore laws prohibiting employment discrimination, different ways of defining and developing measures of an individual's productivity, six sources of a performance appraisal, motivational procedures, a formal appraisal interview, and a case study that illustrates their concerns. Appendixes include behavioral-observation scales for appraising employee performances. This practical book combines literature with on-the-job dilemmas.

MacDonald (1982) presents and describes a methodology for making management by objectives work in the operating environment. This text concerns managerial productivity and ways of improving it. The value of this text is its practical applicability. MacDonald includes a series of self-appraisal checklists for implementing MBO.

The Research and Policy Committee of the Committee for Economic Development (1976) identifies four areas of opportunity for improving productivity: strengthening management, motivating the work force, improving technology and increasing capital investment, and measuring results and the full impact of government programs. This report is of value for its summary analysis and suggestions for productivity concerns in the mid-1970s.

Wholey (1983) illustrates how evaluators may assist government managers and policy makers improve efficiency, effectiveness, and responsiveness of public programs. The author points out how evaluability assessment, rapid-feedback evaluation, service-delivery assessment, and outcome monitoring promote evaluation and effective public management.

8. Budgetary Politics and Financial Administration

Austin and Cheek (1979) introduce basic concepts of zero-base budgeting, provide detailed step-by-step discussions on how to develop and rank decision packages, include a postinstallation ZBB performance audit, and present sample decision packages and ranking sheets from private and public organizations. The value of this manual is its practical applicability.

The *Congressional Quarterly* (1982) provides an excellent summary analysis of the politics and process of federal spending. This edition reviews the responsibilities of President Reagan, Congress, and the budget; outlines United States economic history from 1929 to 1980; focuses upon control of the purse strings; probes the struggle for spending control; examines the impacts of the 1974 budget law; and critiques the issues of Social Security and "Reaganomics."

The General Accounting Office (1981) catalogues terms used in the Federal budget process. The emphasis is upon budget terms, but the text includes relevant accounting, economic, and taxation terms. This useful text includes an overview of the federal budget process. This is a valuable source for those students concerned with studying the federal budget.

Levine (1980) edits a series of in-depth analyses on the causes and consequences of financial stress. The authors discuss situational factors that cause or contribute to fiscal stress; suggest directions for managerial action (decision making, revenue generation, productivity improvement, and cutbacks and terminations); and deal with problems and alternatives confronting state and local governments. This volume is the source to consult for exploring these issues.

Lyden and Miller (1968, 1978) include essays on the historical evolution of budgeting in the United States up to and including the advent of planning, programming, budgeting systems (PPBS); the role and potential of budgeting in the political process; the program planning and evaluation base of budgeting, program structure, and information systems; the problem of relating goals to systems; problems and experiences faced in the implementation of program budgeting and program evaluation; and future potentialities of PPBS. This is an excellent source for its summary analysis.

The Office of Management and Budget (1983) outlines on an annual basis the budget of the United States. This brief version of the federal budget includes the budget message of the president, economic assumptions and budget outlook, federal programs by function, describes the budget process, and lists budget receipts and outlays from 1789 until the current year (1984). This publication is of immense value to the introductory student of public administration.

Ott and Ott (1977) help the nontechnical reader understand the budget and how budget decisions are made. The authors trace the history of federal expenditures, taxes, and the national debt; describe the budget process and explain concepts used in the budget; analyze the effect of fiscal policy on economic activity; and discuss methods of determining the appropriate level of federal expenditures.

Wildavsky (1964, 1979) offers the definitive source on the politics of the federal budgetary process. The author concludes that objectives are not rational, that calculations are not comprehensive, that power and history are relevant. This book is the source to consult for understanding the volatility of fiscal and budgetary processes in the United States. This incisive work may tell students more about political economy in the United States than any written source yet scribed.

Sources

1. Classics of Public Administration

Barnard, Chester I. *The Functions of the Executive.* Cambridge, Mass.: Harvard University Press, 1938.

Gulick, Luther, and Urwick, L. eds. *Papers on the Science of Administration.* New York: Institute of Public Administration, 1937.

McGregor, Douglas. *The Human Side of Enterprise.* New York: McGraw-Hill, 1960.

Simon, Herbert A. *Administrative Behavior.* New York: Macmillan, 1945.

Taylor, Frederick W. *The Principles of Scientific Management.* New York: Harper & Row, [1911] 1947.
Waldo, Dwight. *The Administrative State.* New York: Ronald Press, 1948.

2. Reference Works and Bibliographies

Chandler, Ralph C., and Plano, Jack C. *The Public Administration Dictionary.* New York: John Wiley, 1982.
Cutchin, D.A. *Guide to Public Administration.* (Itasca, Ill: F. E. Peacock, 1981.
Gawthrop, Louis C., and Gawthrop, Virginia L., eds. *PAR: Public Administration Review Cumulative Index, 1940–1979.* Washington, D.C.: American Society for Public Administration, 1979.
Rouse, John E., Jr., ed. *Public Administration in American Society.* Detroit: Gale Research, 1980. Also see his "Boundaries of an Emerging Superdiscipline: A Review of Recent and Selected Older Bibliographic Materials in Public Administration," *Public Administration Review* 42, no. 4 (July–August 1982): 390–398.

3. Administrative Organization, Federalism

Gawthrop, Louis C. *Bureaucratic Behavior in the Executive Branch: An Analysis of Organizational Change.* New York: Free Press, 1969.
Katz, Daniel, and Kahn, Robert L. *The Social Psychology of Organizations.* New York: John Wiley, [1966] 1978.
Pfiffner, John M., and Sherwood, Frank P. *Administrative Organization.* Englewood Cliffs, N.J.: Prentice-Hall, 1960.
Seidman, Harold. *Politics, Position, and Power: The Dynamics of Federal Organization.* New York: Oxford University Press, 1975.
Thompson, James D. *Organizations in Action.* New York: McGraw-Hill, 1967.
Waldo, Dwight. *The Enterprise of Public Administration: A Summary View.* (Novato, Cal.: Chandler & Sharp 1980.

4. Systemic and Bureaucratic Dynamics

Caiden, Gerald E. *Administrative Reform.* Chicago: Aldine Publishing, 1969).
Downs, Anthony. *Inside Bureaucracy.* Boston: Little, Brown, 1966.
Drucker, Peter F. *Managing in Turbulent Times.* New York: Harper & Row, 1980.
Ostrom, Vincent. *The Intellectual Crisis in American Public Administration.* (University, Ala.: University of Alabama Press, 1974.

5. Personnel Administration, Including Administrative Law

Cayer, N. Joseph. *Public Personnel Administration in the United States.* New York: St. Martin's Press, 1975.
Gellhorn, Ernest. *Administrative Law and Process in a Nutshell.* St. Paul, Minn.: West Publishing, 1972.
Imundo, Louis V. *The Supervisor's Handbook.* New York: AMACOM, 1980.
Januz, Lauren Robert, and Jones, Susan K. *Time-Management for Executives.* New York: Charles Scribner's Sons, 1981.
MacNeilage, Linda A., and Adams, Kathleen A. *Assertiveness at Work: How to Increase Your Personal Power on the Job.* Englewood Cliffs, N.J.: Prentice-Hall, 1982.

Maslow, Abraham H. *Toward A Psychology of Being*. New York: Van Nostrand Reinhold, 1968.

McConkey, Dale D. *No-Nonsense Delegation*. New York: AMACOM, 1974.

Mosher, Frederick C. *Democracy and the Public Service*. New York: Oxford University Press, [1968] 1982.

U.S. Office of Personnel Management. *Manager's Handbook*. Washington, D.C.: Government Printing Office, 1982.

Stahl, O. Glenn. *Public Personnel Administration*, 8th ed. New York: Harper & Row, [1936] 1983.

6. Communication and Leadership

Jennings, Eugene E. *An Anatomy of Leadership: Princes, Heroes, and Supermen*. New York: McGraw-Hill, 1960.

Kaufman, Herbert. *Administrative Feedback*. Washington, D.C.: Brookings Institution, 1973.

McGregor, Georgette F., and Robinson, Joseph A. *The Communication Matrix: Ways of Winning with Words*. New York: AMACOM, 1981.

Meltzer, Morton F. *Information: The Ultimate Management Resource*. New York: AMACOM, 1981.

Snell, Frank. *How to Win the Meeting*. New York: Hawthorn Books, 1979.

Vroom, Victor H. and Yetton, Phillip W. *Leadership and Decision-Making*. Pittsburgh, Pa.: University of Pittsburgh Press, 1973.

Zand, Dale E. *Information, Organization, and Power: Effective Management in the Knowledge Society*. New York: McGraw-Hill, 1981.

7. Productivity, Performance Appraisal, and Evaluation

Balk, Walter L. *Improving Government Productivity: Some Policy Perspectives*. Beverly Hills, Cal.: Sage Publications, 1975.

Editors of *Fortune*. *Working Smarter*. New York: Viking Press, 1982.

U.S. General Accounting Office. *State and Local Government Productivity Improvement: What Is The Federal Role?* Washington, D.C.: Government Printing Office, 1978.

Hayes, Frederick O'R. *Productivity in Local Government*. Lexington, Mass.: Lexington Books, 1977.

Latham, Gary P., and Wexley, Kenneth N. *Increasing Productivity Through Performance Appraisal*. Reading, Mass.: Addison-Wesley, 1981.

MacDonald, Charles R. *MBO Can Work! How To Manage by Contract*. New York: McGraw-Hill, 1982.

Research and Policy Committee. *Improving Productivity in State and Local Government*. New York: Committee for Economic Development, 1976.

Wholey, Joseph S. *Evaluation and Effective Public Management*. Boston: Little, Brown, 1983.

8. Budgetary Politics and Financial Administration

Austin, L. Allan, and Cheek, Logan M. *Zero Base Budgeting: A Decision Package Manual*. New York: AMACOM, 1979.

Congressional Quarterly. *Budgeting for America: The Politics and Process of Federal Spending*. Washington, D.C.: Congressional Quarterly, 1982.

U.S. General Accounting Office. *A Glossary of Terms Used in the Federal Budget Process: and Related Accounting, Economic, and Tax Terms.* Washington, D.C.: Government Printing Office, 1981.

Levine, Charles H., ed. *Managing Fiscal Stress: The Crisis in the Public Sector.* Chatham, N.J.: Chatham House, 1980.

Lyden, Fremont J., and Miller, Ernest G., eds. *Public Budgeting: Program Planning and Evaluation.* Chicago: Rand McNally, 1978. *Revision of Planning Programming Budgeting: A Systems Approach to Management.* Chicago: Rand McNally, [1968] 1972.

Office of Management and Budget. *The United States Budget in Brief: Fiscal Year 1983.* Washington, D.C.: Government Printing Office, 1983.

Ott, David J., and Ott, Attiat, F. *Federal Budget Policy.* Washington, D.C.: Brookings Institution, 1977.

Wildavsky, Aaron. *The Politics of the Budgetary Process.* Boston: Little, Brown, [1964] 1979.

9. Journals of Public-Sector Significance

The format of these journal entries includes title, address, original date of publication, and frequency of publication.

Administration and Society
Sage Publications
275 South Beverly Drive
Beverly Hills, CA 90212
Published initially as *Journal of Comparative Administration* in 1969; changed to
    Administration and Society in 1974
Quarterly

Administrative Science Quarterly
Graduate School of Business and Public Administration
Cornell University
Malott Hall
Ithaca, NY 14853
Published initially in 1956
Quarterly

American Review of Public Administration
Park College
Kansas City, MO 64152
Published initially as *Midwest Review of Public Administration* in 1967; changed
    to *American Review of Public Administration* in 1981
Quarterly

The Bureaucrat
Department of Public Administration
Florida International University
North Miami, FL 33181
Published initially in 1972
Quarterly

Governmental Finance
Municipal Finance Officers Association of the United States and Canada
180 North Michigan Avenue
Chicago, IL 60601
Published since 1926, formerly *Municipal Finance*
Quarterly

Intergovernmental Perspective
Advisory Commission on Intergovernmental Relations
Washington, DC 20575
Published initially in 1975
Quarterly

National Journal
Government Research Corporation
1730 M Street, N.W.
Washington, DC 20036
Published initially in 1969
Weekly

Public Administration Quarterly
Department of Government
Auburn University at Montgomery
Montgomery, AL 36193
Published initially as *Southern Review of Public Administration* in 1977; changed
    to *Public Administration Quarterly* in 1983
Quarterly

Public Administration Review
American Society for Public Administration
1120 G Street, N.W.
Washington, DC 20005
Published initially in 1940
Bimonthly

Public Management
International City Management Association
1120 G Street, N.W.
Washington, DC 20005
Published initially as *City Manager Bulletin* in 1919
Monthly

Public Personnel Management
International Personnel Management Association—United States
1850 K Street, N.W., Suite 870
Washington, DC 20006
Published initially as *Public Personnel Management* in 1972; current publication
    combined efforts of *Public Personnel Review* and *Personnel Administration*
    (two related journals that ceased publication).
Quarterly

Public Productivity Review
National Center for Public Productivity
John Jay College of Criminal Justice
City University of New York
445 West 59th Street
New York, NY 10019
Published initially in 1975
Quarterly

Sage Public Administration Abstracts
Sage Publications
275 South Beverly Drive
Beverly Hills, CA 90212
Published initially in 1974
Quarterly

Index